The SAGE
Handbook of
Criminological
Theory

The International Editorial Board

The SAGE
Handbook of
Criminological
Theory

Edited by

Eugene McLaughlin and Tim Newburn

Los Angeles | London | New Delhi
Singapore | Washington DC

SAGE Publications Ltd
1 Oliver's Yard
55 City Road
London EC1Y 1SP

SAGE Publications Inc.
2455 Teller Road
Thousand Oaks, California 91320

SAGE Publications India Pvt Ltd
B 1/I 1 Mohan Cooperative Industrial Area
Mathura Road
New Delhi 110 044

SAGE Publications Asia-Pacific Pvt Ltd
33 Pekin Street #02-01
Far East Square
Singapore 048763

Library of Congress Control Number Available

British Library Cataloguing in Publication data

A catalogue record for this book is available from the British Library

ISBN 978-1-4129-2038-4

Typeset by Glyph International
Printed by MPG Books Group, Bodmin, Cornwall
Printed on paper from sustainable resources

Mixed Sources

Product group from well-managed
forests and other controlled sources
www.fsc.org Cert no. SA-COC-1565
© 1996 Forest Stewardship Council

FSC

CONTENTS

ACKNOWLEDGEMENTS

Putting this Handbook together has been much more complicated and drawn out than we originally anticipated. Consequently, we would like to thank our contributors not only for taking part in this project, and for their support, but also for their commitment and their patience. In addition, we owe a number of people a debt of gratitude for their contribution to the eventual shape of the Handbook. When we were working up a structure and rationale, and at other key moments, we were given advice, constructive criticism and feedback from John Braithwaite, Lynn Chancer, Ron Clarke, Kathy Daly, Richard Ericson, David Farrington, Marcus Felson, Jeff Ferrell, Mark Finnane, Roger Matthews, David Nelken, Pat O'Malley, Jonathan Simon, Richard Sparks, and Charles Tittle. We were shocked and saddened to learn of the untimely death of Richard Ericson who was in the process of completing a chapter on risk and insurance for the Handbook. Richard's unique contribution to advancing theoretical criminology will be missed. Finally, but very importantly, we would like to express our gratitude to Miranda Nunhofer and Caroline Porter at Sage who have been incredibly supportive throughout and to the whole Sage production team who have handled the process in an exemplary manner.

NOTES ON CONTRIBUTORS

Katja Franko Aas is Professor of Criminology at the Department of Criminology and Sociology of Law, University of Oslo. She has written extensively on issues of globalization, surveillance and uses of information and communication technologies in contemporary penal systems. Her recent publications include *Cosmopolitan Justice and its Discontents* (with C. Baillet, forthcoming), *Technologies of Insecurity: the Surveillance of Everyday Life* (with H.M. Lomell and H.O. Gundhus, Routledge-Cavendish, 2009), *Globalization and Crime* (Sage, 2007) and *Sentencing in the Age of Information: From Faust to Macintosh* (Routledge-Cavendish, 2005).

Robert Agnew is Samuel Candler Dobbs Professor of Sociology at Emory University. His research focuses on the causes of crime and delinquency, particularly his general strain theory of delinquency. He is currently working on a book dealing with the underlying assumptions of crime theory, including assumptions regarding free will and the nature of human nature. His most recent works include *Juvenile Delinquency: Causes and Control* (Oxford, 2009); *Pressured Into Crime: An Overview of General Strain Theory* (Oxford, 2006); and *Why Do Criminals Offend: A General Theory of Crime and Delinquency* (Oxford, 2005).

Ronald L. Akers is a Professor of Criminology and Sociology at the University of Florida. He is recipient of the Edwin H. Sutherland Award and a Fellow of the American Society of Criminology. Dr Akers has authored over 100 journal articles and book chapters on theory, research and policy in criminology, criminal justice, corrections, law, and deviance. He is best known for his development and testing of social learning theory, and the social structure social learning model, as a general theory of crime and deviant behavior. He is author of *Criminological Theories: Introduction, Evaluation, and Application* (now in its 5th edition, with Christine Sellers, Oxford University Press, 2008); *Law and Control in Society* (with Richard Hawkins, Prentice Hall, 1975); *Drugs, Alcohol and Society* (Wadsworth, 1992); *Deviant Behavior: A Social Learning Approach* (Wadsworth, 1973, 1977, and 1985), *and Social Learning and Social Structure: A General Theory of Crime and Deviance* (Northeastern University Press, 1998 and Transaction Publishers, 2009).

Ronet Bachman worked as a statistician and research analyst at the Bureau of Justice Statistics before going back to teaching at the University of Delaware, where she is now a Professor and Chair of the Department of Sociology and Criminal Justice.

She has written several books on research methods and statistics, along with books on issues related to violence and victimization. She is currently the PI of a National Institute of Justice funded project exploring the differential trajectories of desistance for male and female drug involved offenders over a 20 year time period. She lives with her husband and co-author (Ray), their son, John, and their dog, Mickey II, in Newark, Delaware.

Laura A. Baker is currently a Professor of Psychology at the University of Southern California in Los Angeles. Her research interests include the development, refinement, and application of quantitative genetic models in the study of individual differences in human psychological traits, including both social and cognitive domains. Of particular interest are genetic models of delinquency, human aggression, psychopathic traits and criminal behavior. The application of biometrical growth curve models to the study of stability and change in behavior and psychological traits throughout the lifespan is also of special interest. Baker is Director of the Southern California Twin Project, in which she coordinates a comprehensive longitudinal twin study of risk factors for aggressive and antisocial behavior. In addition to mentoring graduating students and postdoctoral associates, she teaches courses in Behavioral Genetics and Multivariate Statistics in Psychology. Recent journal articles can be found in *Journal of Child Abnormal Psychology*, *Journal of Adolescence*, *Psychophysiology*, *Development and Psychopathology*, *British Journal of Developmental Psychology*, and *Behavior Genetics*.

Gregg Barak is a Professor of Criminology and Criminal Justice at Eastern Michigan University and former Visiting Distinguished Professor in the College of Justice and Safety at Eastern Kentucky University. He is the author and/or editor of 16 books, including *Criminology: An Integrated Approach* (Rowman and Littlefield, 2009). Dr Barak is a Fellow of the Academy of Criminal Justice Sciences and the recipient of the Lifetime Achievement Award from Critical Division of the American Society of Criminology.

Timothy Brezina is Associate Professor of Criminal Justice at Georgia State University. His research and teaching interests include criminological theory and youth violence. Currently, he is conducting multi-methods research, combining quantitative data analyses with findings obtained from in-depth interviews with active street offenders. This research focuses on the attitudes, perceptions, beliefs and experiences that contribute to serious persistent offending among young people, such as the anticipation of an early death, or the belief that one is 'successful' at crime. Recent publications appear in the journals *Criminology*, *Justice Quarterly*, *Journal of Drug Issues*, and *Deviant Behavior*.

Michael Cavadino is Professor of Law at the University of Central Lancashire. He has researched and written widely on penology and mental health law. He is author of *The Penal System: An Introduction* (with James Dignan, 4th edn, Sage Publications, 2007), Penal Systems: A Comparative Approach (with James Dignan, Sage, 2006), *Criminal Justice 2000: Strategies for a New Century* (with Iain Crow and James Dignan, Waterside Press, 1999), *The Law of Gravity: Offence Seriousness* *and Criminal Justice* (Joint Unit for Social Services Research, 1997) and *Mental Health Law in Context: Doctors' Orders?* (Dartmouth, 1989)

Sharon Chamard is an Associate Professor with the Justice Center at the University of Alaska Anchorage. She is interested in the spatial distribution of crime, and along these lines has conducted research on geographic patterns of sexual assault and youth violence. Currently she is focusing on the displacement movements of chronic public inebriates. She has written two Problem-Oriented Guides for Police for the Office of Community Oriented Policing Services, one on partnering with businesses to address public safety problems, and the other on homeless encampments. She is the co-editor, with Rashi Shukla, of the February 2010 special issue of *Security Journal* containing papers given at the July 2008 Environmental Criminology and Crime Analysis (ECCA) symposium. She is the research consultant to the Community Action Policing Team (a problem-oriented policing unit) of the Anchorage Police Department, and frequently works with community groups in Anchorage to develop, implement, and evaluate solutions to crime and disorder problems.

Ronald Clarke is University Professor at Rutgers and Visiting Professor at the Jill Dando Institute, University College London. He worked for 15 years in the British Home Office and was head of the Research and Planning Unit from 1982–84. While at the Home Office he helped to develop situational crime prevention and to launch the British Crime Survey. He is author or joint author of more than 220 publications including *Designing out Crime* (HMSO, 1980), *The Reasoning Criminal* (Springer-Verlag, 1986), *Superhighway Robbery: Preventing E-commerce Crime* (Willan Publishing, 2003), *Crime Analysis for Problem Solvers* (US Department of Justice, 2005) and *Outsmarting the Terrorists* (Praeger, 2006). His current research interest is wildlife crime.

Kathleen Daly is Professor of Criminology and Criminal Justice, Griffith University (Brisbane). She writes on gender, race, crime, and justice; and on restorative, Indigenous, and international criminal justice. Her book, *Gender, Crime, and Punishment* (1994, Yale University Press) received the Michael Hindelang award from the American Society of Criminology. With Lisa Maher, she co-edited *Criminology at the Crossroads: Feminist Readings in Crime and Justice* (Oxford University Press, 1998); and with Andrew Goldsmith and Mark Israel, *Crime and Justice: A Guide to Criminology* (Lawbook Company, 2006). First based in the United States, she travelled to Australia in 1995 as a Senior Fulbright Scholar to study restorative justice. From 1998 to 2006, she received three Australian Research Council (ARC) grants to research restorative justice and the race/gender politics of new justice practices. In 2008, she began an international project on innovative responses to sexual violence; and in 2009, as co-PI with Elena Marchetti and Jackie Huggins, a project on sentencing Indigenous partner violence in Australia, both funded by the ARC. In addition to books and edited volumes, she has published over 70 articles in journals, law reviews, and books. She is a Fellow of the Academy of the Social Sciences in Australia, and immediate past President of the Australian and New Zealand Society of Criminology.

David P. Farrington, O.B.E., is Professor of Psychological Criminology at the Institute of Criminology, Cambridge University. He is a Fellow of the British Academy, of the Academy of Medical Sciences, of the British Psychological Society and of the American Society of Criminology. He is a Chartered Forensic Psychologist, co-chair of the US National Institute of Justice Study Group on Transitions from Juvenile Delinquency to Adult Crime and co-chair of the US Centre for Disease Control's Expert Panel on Promotive and Protective Factors for Youth Violence. He has been President of the American Society of Criminology (the first person from outside North America to be elected to this office), President of the European Association of Psychology and Law, President of the British Society of Criminology, President of the Academy of Experimental Criminology and Chair of the Division of Forensic Psychology of the British Psychological Society. His major research interest is in developmental criminology, and he is Director of the Cambridge Study in Delinquent Development, which is a prospective longitudinal survey of over 400 London males from age 8 to age 48. In addition to 500 published journal articles and book chapters on criminological and psychological topics, he has published 75 books, monographs and government publications.

Jeff Ferrell is Professor of Sociology at Texas Christian University, USA, and Visiting Professor of Criminology at the University of Kent, UK. He is the author of the books *Crimes of Style* (Garland, 1993; Northeastern University Press, 1996), *Tearing Down the Streets* (Palgrave/Macmillan/St. Martin's, 2001/2002), *Empire of Scrounge* (New York University Press, 2006) and, with Keith Hayward and Jock Young, *Cultural Criminology: An Invitation* (Sage, 2008), winner of the 2009 Distinguished Book Award from the Division of International Criminology, American Society of Criminology. He is also the co-editor of the books *Cultural Criminology* (Northeastern University Press, 1995), *Ethnography at the Edge* (Northeastern University Press, 1998), *Making Trouble* (Aldine de Gruyter, 1999), *Cultural Criminology Unleashed* (Routledge/Cavendish/Glasshouse, 2004), and *Cultural Criminology: Theories of Crime* (Ashgate, 2010, forthcoming). He is the founding and current editor of the New York University Press book series Alternative Criminology, and one of the founding editors of the journal *Crime, Media, Culture: An International Journal* (Sage), winner of the Association of Learned and Professional Society Publishers' 2006 Charlesworth Award for Best New Journal. In 1998 Ferrell received the Critical Criminologist of the Year Award from the Division of Critical Criminology, American Society of Criminology.

Chris Greer is Senior Lecturer in the Department of Sociology at City University London. His primary research interests lie at the intersections between crime, media and culture and he has written extensively in this area. In addition to authoring numerous journal articles, chapters and official reports, Chris's books include *Sex Crime and the Media: Sex Offending and the Press in a Divided Society* (Willan, 2003), *Victims, Crime and Society* (edited with Pam Davies and Peter Francis, Sage, 2007) and *Crime and Media: A Reader* (Routledge, 2009). Chris is currently working on a monograph called *Crime News* (Routledge, forthcoming), which expands on a number of the themes discussed in the chapter in this collection. Chris is also founder and co-editor of the award-winning *Crime, Media, Culture: An International Journal* (Sage).

Simon Hallsworth is Professor of Social Research at London Metropolitan University where he is also Director of the Centre for Social and Evaluation Research. He has written extensively on urban street violence and is an acknowledged expert on street organisations such as gangs. He has also written on contemporary penal change and development. Publications in these two substantive areas of his research include *Street Crime* (Willan, 2005) and *The New Punitiveness: Issues, Themes and Perspectives* (with Pratt, Brown, Brown and Morrison, Willan, 2005). He is currently exploring (with John Lea) the emerging contours of what they term the 'Security State'.

Tony Jefferson has been a Professor of Criminology at Keele University and at Sheffield University. He has also held Visiting Professorships in Sweden, Denmark, Australia and the USA, where he has recently completed a year (2007–08) as a Visiting Presidential Scholar at John Jay College of Criminal Justice, City University of New York. He has researched and published widely on questions to do with youth subcultures, the media, policing, race and crime, masculinity, fear of crime and, most recently, racial violence. His published works include *Psychosocial Criminology* (with Dave Gadd, Sage, 2007), *Doing Qualitative Research Differently* (with Wendy Hollway, Sage, 2000), *The Case Against Paramilitary Policing* (Oxford University Press, 1990), *Interpreting Policework* (with Roger Grimshaw, 1987) and *Controlling the Constable* (with Roger Grimshaw, HarperCollins, 1984), *Policing the Crisis* (with Stuart Hall et al., Palgrave MacMillan, 1978) and *Resistance through Rituals*, 1976/2006 (edited with Stuart Hall, Routledge, 1976 and 2006). Between 1999 and 2002 he was the British Editor for the journal *Theoretical Criminology*.

Gary F. Jensen is Professor of Sociology and Religious Studies at Vanderbilt University. He is a Fellow of the American Society of Criminology and has published 66 articles and eight books. Most of his work involves the quantitative analysis of data on crime and delinquency. He is best known for research on delinquency and juvenile justice, social learning theory, and issues involving the social ecology of guns, gender issues in delinquency research, and religion and crime. Outside of criminology, he is an expert on societal responses to epidemic disease, witch hunts, and new forms of religious identity. He has been a consultant on survey methods in the study of crime and regularly advises colleagues in the use of time series analysis in criminology.

Darrick Jolliffe is a Senior Lecturer in Criminology at the University of Leicester. Dr Jolliffe's main research interest is individual differences and offending, particularly the relationship between empathy and offending. Dr Jolliffe has published many systematic reviews and meta-analyses and he has also conducted a number of evaluations of various interventions including community justice initiatives, interventions for female offenders or 'at risk' females and interventions for young offenders. Dr Jolliffe's recent publications can be found in the *Journal of Adolescence*, *Violence and Victims* and *Legal and Criminological Psychology*.

Susanne Karstedt is Professor of Criminology and Criminal Justice at the Centre for Criminal Justice Studies, University of Leeds. She is currently one of the editors of the *British Journal of Criminology*. She was recipient of the Sellin-Glueck-Award of the American Society of Criminology in 2007. Her research interests lie in comparative and international criminology, including violence and mass atrocities, white collar and middle class crime, and punishment. Her current research primarily focuses on democracy, crime and justice, and she has edited (with Gary LaFree) a special issue of the *Annals of the American Academy of Political and Social Sciences* on the topic (2006). She has researched and published widely on transitional justice, and her most recent publication is an edited collection on *Legal Institutions and Collective Memories* (Hart, 2009).

Eugene McLaughlin is Professor of Criminology in the Department of Sociology, City University London. He is currently co-director of the *Law, Justice and Journalism Research Centre*. He has written extensively on police governance and reform, police–community relations, the managerialisation of criminal justice and contemporary criminological theory. His current research concentrates on the theory and practice of policing in multi-pluralist societies, the news-media and crime, and the contemporary knowledge practices of critical criminology. His most recent book is *The New Policing* (Sage, 2007). He is also the co-editor of *Public Criminologies* (Special Issue of *Theoretical Criminology*, edited with Lynn Chancer, 2007) and *The SAGE Dictionary of Criminology* (Sage, 2005, edited with John Muncie). He is a member of the editorial boards of the *British Journal of Criminology, Crime, Media, Culture* and *Theoretical Criminology*.

Roger Matthews is Professor of Criminology at London South Bank University. He is author of a number of publications on realist criminology including *Issues in Realist Criminology* (edited with Jock Young, Sage, 1992) and *Rethinking Criminology: The Realist Debate* (edited with Jock Young, Sage, 1992). More recently he has published *Prostitution, Politics and Policy* (Routledge-Cavendish, 2008) and *Doing Time: An Introduction to the Sociology of Imprisonment,* 2nd edn (Palgrave/Macmillan, 2009).

John Muncie is Professor of Criminology and Director of the International Centre for Comparative Criminological Research (ICCCR) at the Open University, UK. He is the author of the best selling text *Youth and Crime* (Sage, 3rd edition, 2009). His most recent research is on the impact of globalisation and neo-liberal penality on the formulation of law and penal policy for young people. He has published widely on issues in comparative youth justice and children's rights, including the co-edited companion volumes *Youth Crime and Justice* and *Comparative Youth Justice* (Sage, 2006). His other recent books are the edited works: *Crime: Local and Global* (Willan/Open University, 2010), *Criminal Justice: Local and Global* (Willan/Open University, 2010), *The SAGE Library of Criminology: Youth Crime and Juvenile Justice* (3 volumes, Sage, 2009), *The SAGE Library of Criminology: Criminal Justice and Crime Control* (3 volumes, Sage, 2007), *The SAGE Library of Criminology: Criminology* (3 volumes, Sage, 2006), *The SAGE Dictionary of Criminology* (Sage, 2nd edition, 2006) and *Criminological Perspectives: Essential Readings* (Sage/Open University, 2nd edition, 2003). He is editor (with Barry Goldson) of the Sage journal *Youth Justice: An International Journal*.

Pat O'Malley is Professorial Research Fellow in Law at the University of Sydney, Australia. His work over the past 20 years has focused on risk in government and especially criminal justice, and more recently on how money, risk and telemetry have been brought together to create new forms of justice. Recent publications include *Crime and Risk* (Sage, 2010), *The Currency of Justice: Fines Risks and Damages in Consumer Societies* (Routledge, 2009) and, with Kelly Hannah-Moffat, *Gendered Risks* (Cavendish, 2006). Currently he is working on a monograph – *Crime, Risk and Excitement* – that explores the nexus between excitement, risk-taking and consumer culture.

Tim Newburn is Professor of Criminology and Social Policy at the London School of Economics and a past President of the British Society of Criminology. He was a founding editor of the journal *Criminology and Criminal Justice* and is the author or editor of over 30 books, the most recent of which are: *Criminology* (Willan, 2007); *Policy Transfer and Criminal Justice* (with Jones, Open University Press, 2007); *Handbook of Policing* (Willan, 2008); *Key Readings in Criminology* (Willan, 2009); and *Policing Developing Democracies* (edited with Hinton, Routledge, 2009). He is currently working (with David Downes and Paul Rock) on an official history of post-war criminal justice.

Ray Paternoster is Professor in the Department of Criminology and Criminal Justice at the University of Maryland, and research affiliate at the Maryland Population Research Center. His research interests include rational choice theory, the interface between criminology and behavioral economics, the transition between adolescence and adulthood, quantitative methods, and issues related to capital punishment. He received his Ph.D in 1978 from Florida State University and has been on the faculty at the University of Maryland since 1982.

Adrian Raine is University Professor and the Richard Perry Professor of Criminology, Psychiatry, and Psychology at the University of Pennsylvania. He has published five books and 257 journal articles and book chapters, been the principal investigator on 17 extramural research grants and main mentor on 9 NIH pre- and post-doctoral awards, and given 228 invited presentations in 25 countries. For the past 33 years, Dr Raine's research has focused on the biosocial bases of antisocial and violent behavior in both children and adults. His research interests include the neurobiology of violence, psychopathic, and antisocial behavior; nutritional interventions to prevent child behavior problems; positive psychology; schizotypal personality; alcoholism; brain imaging; psychophysiology; neurochemistry; neuropsychology; environmental toxins, and behavioral and molecular genetics. His awards include a Research Scientist Development Award and an Independent Scientist Award from NIMH, the Joseph Zubin Memorial Award, the Robert G. Wright Professorship of Psychology at USC, and a University Professorship from the University of Pennsylvania.

Paul Rock is Emeritus Professor of Sociology at the LSE and Visiting Professor of Criminology at the University of Pennsylvania. He has been a Visiting Professor at the University of California, San Diego; Simon Fraser University; the University of British Columbia and Princeton University; a Visiting Scholar at the Ministry of the Solicitor General of Canada; a Fellow of the Center for the Advanced Study of the Behavioral Sciences in Stanford, California; a resident at the Rockefeller Foundation Center at the Villa Serbelloni, Bellagio; and a Visiting Fellow at the Australian National University in Canberra. His books include *The Social World of an English Crown Court* (1993, Clarendon Press), *Reconstructing a Women's Prison* (1996, Clarendon Press), *After Homicide: Practical and Political Responses to Bereavement* (1998, Clarendon Press), *Understanding Deviance* (with David Downes, 6th edn, Oxford University Press, 2007; Canadian edition 2009) and *Constructing Victims' Rights* (September 2004, Clarendon Press). In collaboration with David Downes and Tim Newburn, he is currently working on the official history of criminal justice.

Lee E. Ross is Associate Professor of Criminal Justice at the University of Central Florida. A graduate of Rutgers University, his research interests span a variety of areas, from his seminal work on religion and social control theory to more recent explorations into unintended consequences of mandatory arrest policies and the dynamics of domestic violence among African-Americans. As editor of *The War Against Domestic Violence* (CRC Press, 2010), his scholarship can be found in a variety of academic journals, including *Justice Quarterly*, *Journal of Criminal Justice*, *Journal of Crime and Justice*, *Journal of Criminal Justice Education*, *The Encyclopedia of Race, Crime, and Justice*, *The Justice Professional*, *Sociological Spectrum*, *Sociological Focus*, and *Corrections Today*. Professor Ross also spent several years as a group facilitator to the Milwaukee Domestic Abuse Intervention Program. Currently, he teaches graduate and undergraduate level courses in the area of domestic violence, race, crime, and justice, and cultural diversity in the criminal justice system.

Lawrence Sherman is Wolfson Professor of Criminology at the Cambridge University Institute of Criminology, and Director of the Jerry Lee Center of Criminology at the University of Pennsylvania. He is the author of 'Defiance, deterrence and irrelevance: a theory of the criminal sanction' (*Journal of Research in Crime and Delinquency*, 1993) and has a continuing interest in the moral basis of criminal offending. The architect of over 30 randomized field experiments in the US, UK and Australia, he is author of a series of reports on experiments in restorative justice with Heather Strang, with whom he directs the Cambridge Police Executive Programme.

Catherine Tuvblad currently holds a research associate position at the University of Southern California, Department of Psychology. Catherine has a long-standing interest in individual differences and deviant behavior, particularly the causes behind the development of such behaviors. Her main research focus is on the development of antisocial, delinquent and criminal behavior. More specifically: the interplay of genetic and environmental influences on the development of antisocial and criminal behavior; identifying cognitive, psychophysiological, and biological endophenotypes for criminal behavior; personality, including normal and psychopathic personality traits in relationship to criminal behavior; social development, e.g., peer relationships, social interaction; psychiatric illnesses and disorders in relation to criminal behavior; the interplay with social risk factors on the development of antisocial and criminal behavior, e.g., peers, parents, school, media, neighborhood, socioeconomic status. Her recent publications can be found in *Journal of Abnormal Child Psychology*, *Psychophysiology*, *Development and Psychopathology*, *Aggressive Behavior*, *Behavior Genetics*, and *Child Development*.

Rob White is Professor of Criminology at the University of Tasmania, Australia. He has written extensively in the areas of juvenile justice, youth studies, crime prevention and eco-global criminology. Among his recent books are *Controversies in Environmental Sociology* (Cambridge University Press, 2004), *Crimes Against Nature: Environmental Criminology and Ecological Justice* (Willan, 2008), *Environmental Crime: A Reader* (Willan, 2009), and *Global Environmental Harm: Criminological Perspectives* (Willan, 2010).

Tara Young is Senior Research Fellow at the Centre for Social and Evaluation Research at London Metropolitan University. She has expertise in qualitative and evaluation research and is currently teaching MSc Criminological Research Methods at London Metropolitan University. Tara has worked on a number of research projects focusing on group delinquency and gang membership. Her work on gangs in the UK, (with Professor Simon Hallsworth) has influenced policy at local and national levels. She has co-authored several journal articles on street-based youth groups. Her most recent publications can be found in the journals *Youth Justice*, *Theoretical Criminology*, *Crime,* and the books *Practical Interventions for Young People at Risk* (edited by Kathryn Geldard, Sage, 2009) and *Children Behaving Badly?* (edited by Christine Barker, Wiley, 2010).

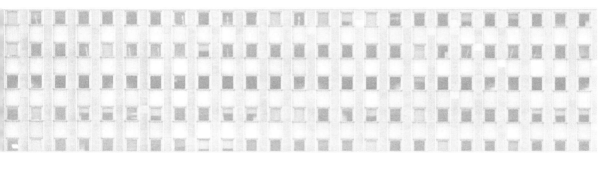

Introduction

Eugene McLaughlin and Tim Newburn

THINKING ABOUT CRIMINOLOGY

A volume such as this must inevitably begin with a few explanatory words. We will come to what we take the term 'theory' to cover shortly. First, however, we must say something about what counts as a *criminological* theory or, at least, what has informed the choices lying behind the selection of chapters in this volume. At heart, the focus here – criminology – is nothing more or less than a 'specific genre of discourse and inquiry about crime' (Garland, 2002: 8); it is a peculiarly modern form of talking and thinking about those activities commonly thought of as criminal. Though an incomplete definition, many of us still turn regularly to Edwin Sutherland and Donald Cressey's (1960) classic summary of the subject as the study of the making of laws, the breaking of laws, and of society's reaction to the breaking of laws.

> Criminology is the body of knowledge regarding crime as a social phenomenon. It includes within its scope the process of making laws, of breaking laws and reacting to the breaking of laws. ... The objective of criminology is the development of a body of general and verifiable principles and of other types of knowledge regarding the process of law, crime and treatment.
>
> (1960: 3)

In outlining 'defiance theory' Lawrence Sherman argues that, additionally, criminology must also attempt to explain why people 'create, enforce or nullify laws'. As the quote indicates, Sutherland and Cressey (1960) went on to argue that the objective of criminology was the development of '*a body of general and verified principles and of other types of knowledge regarding the process of law, crime, and treatment or prevention*'. The 'other types of knowledge' were social scientific in nature and in this sense criminological knowledge would be distinguishable from common sense, opinion, theology and mythology. Of course, the problematic term in all this is 'crime'. The majority of readers of this volume will not need repetition of arguments about the problematic ontological status of 'crime'. Suffice to say, Sutherland and Cressey presume that criminology has a distinct and self-evident subject matter. However, a connecting theme for several chapters in this Handbook, is that much that appears theoretically solid about 'crime' can very easily melt into air.

What is the status of criminology? Is it a discipline, sub-discipline, an intellectual orientation, a subject, a policy site? Neither of us is especially preoccupied by such arguments. What we recognise as being immensely important is that criminology, as David Downes once expressed it, is a 'rendezvous subject'. It is a field of inquiry where people from a variety of intellectual and scholarly backgrounds come together to engage in research and deliberation. This inter-disciplinarity remains one of the great strengths of criminology. The fact that it has the potential to draw on a broad range of disciplinary resources gives it vibrancy and a reflexivity that allows it to adapt to rapidly changing circumstances (of which more below). The range and diversity of theoretical approaches and substantive issues contained in this volume is a testament to the richness of criminology's history – despite its relatively short existence. Moreover, this range of theories in such close proximity gives the lie, we think, to any notion that there is a single explanatory framework or approach, no matter how integrative in aspiration, that trumps all others. As Sherman puts it in relation to his restatement of defiance theory, 'Its ambition is not to answer every question in criminology, but rather to reveal the theoretical connections that may advance the development of other theories as well'. This does not mean that at any given moment criminology is not subject to the settlement claims of particular disciplines. A significant number of the major criminology reference books are in agreement with Sumner's (2002) insistence that sociology is the predominant intellectual orientation because crime and deviance are essential 'social facts'. In turn, sociological criminology has been most comfortable with Mertonian middle range theorising that is applicable to a limited range of data.

WHAT IS BEING THEORISED?

Karstedt makes the important point that criminology has been a seedbed for a set of *perspectives* rather than fully-fledged theories: approaches which offer a framework or concepts rather than, necessarily, a set of hypotheses or a general theoretical account (see also McLaughlin *et al.*, 2001). That said, she acknowledges – in some detail – the broader claims made by, *inter alia*, Messner and Rosenfeld's Institutional Anomie Theory and what might be thought of as LaFree's Institutional Legitimacy Theory. All three of Sutherland and Cressey's streams of inquiry – the making of laws, the breaking of laws and social reactions to the breaking of laws – as well as somewhat broader concerns about the nature and impact of other forms of 'social harm' and 'social sanctioning' are the focus of the theoretical perspectives outlined here. This reminds us that the core of criminological knowledge has been generated from and in turn is applied to: definitions of crime; the measurement of crime; the prevalence of crime; the causes of crime; criminal motivation and intention; criminal innovation; crime trends and patterns; victimisation; crime control and criminal justice rationales and practices.

In their discussion of the state of contemporary social theory, Ritzer and Smart (2001) argue that theoretical renewal and recalibration comes about through seven processes. We think that this typological construct is also applicable to under-standing criminology's knowledge production process.

1 *Innovation*: which happens when there are Kuhnian epistemological paradigm shifts. Intellectual revolutions in the social sciences are, of course, few in nature.
2 *Retrieval*: which occurs through the generational rediscovery of older or voided theories.
3 *Translation*: with the discovery of new works of classical theorists or the publication of neglected works that have not been available before.
4 *Reinterpretation*: in the light of new intellectual concerns.
5 *Changing intellectual priorities*: that either validates or censures a theoretical perspective, irrespective of empirical evidence.
6 *Changing social conditions*: new 'social facts' associated with broader socio-economic and cultural transformations cannot be ignored.
7 *Developments in cognate fields of inquiry*: findings and analysis which would not imme-diately be recognised as criminological come to have a significant impact on the discipline.

However, arguably criminology operates within a somewhat different impure context. Unlike social theory it does not have the possibility of existing in a self-referential vacuum. Criminology's theoretical positions and research findings inevitably co-exist uncomfortably with, and are tested by, the everyday knowledges that constitute 'common sense' and strong public opinion, in a multi-mediated envi-ronment, about the causes of crime and how best to control it. Indeed, in certain respects, we have popular entertainment to thank for disseminating an authoritative criminological imaginary. This reminds us of the *cultural* centrality of our subject matter and the fact that the *public* status of applied criminological knowledge is contested.

PUTTING THEORY TO WORK: NORMATIVE ENGAGEMENT, PUBLIC DISCOURSE AND POLICY MATTERS

Stan Cohen (1988: 31) has noted that perhaps more than any other social science field 'the student of crime and its control suffers from the pressures and delusions of relevance, impact, the wish to be listened to by the powerful'. And David Nelken (1994: 25) has posed the 'knowing and acting' problem as follows:

> How does and should criminological theorising relate to the practical consideration of those who make policy or play roles in the criminal process – or to the political projects of those who seek to challenge this process?

This anxiety about criminology's capacity for action, was revisited in 2007 when the journal *Theoretical Criminology* ran a special issue on 'Public Criminologies'. This was also in the context of broader high profile debates about the emergence of a competitive market place of 'ideas' inhabited by think tanks, pressure groups, professional lobbyists, networks of special advisors, spin doctors, opinion formers, journalists and commentators (for overviews see, for example, Etzioni, 2006; Fuller, 2006; Furedi, 2005; Michael, 2002; Pearce, 2005; Posner, 2003). Chancer and McLaughlin (2007) identified the different positions criminologists had taken on the question of their contemporary role and relevance. This survey is the basis for the next part of our discussion in which we highlight and develop key points of their argument.

David Garland and Richard Sparks (2000) have taken a predominantly socio-cultural approach to making sense of the question of the contemporary relationship between criminological knowledge and public debate and policy making. They were themselves stimulated to confront the challenges facing late modern criminology by reading Margaret Zahn's (1999) American Society of Criminology (ASC) presidential address in which she reflected on the future of criminology as an academic discipline from the perspective of a public policy actor and as a contributor to the building of 'just communities'. It is worth noting that Zahn's and Garland and Sparks's deliberations predated Michael Burawoy's (2004, 2005) clarion call for the development of a 'public sociology' that contributes to 'a triple dialogue – a dialogue among sociologists, between sociologists and publics and most importantly within public themselves'. For Burawoy, the responsibilities and reach of 'public sociology' distinguish it, in the academic division of labour, from 'professional', 'policy' and 'critical' sociologies (Burawoy, 2004, 2005; see also Clawson et al., 2007).

The primary historical reference point for Garland and Sparks was British criminology as it was constituted in the immediate post-war period. This, for them, was a high point when criminological knowledge was 'an integral part of policy making and criminal justice practice' and exercised an identifiable progressive influence on public understanding and debate. A tightly knit group of what might be defined as Mandarin academics, policy makers, senior practitioners and opinion formers synthesised criminological scholarship and policy to promote enlightened practices (see also Loader and Sparks, 2004; Radzinowicz, 1999; Reiner, 1988). It also helped that this institutional epistemology was in tune with the broader governmental rationalities of post-war social democratic welfare state. And relatively low crime rates and perceived high levels of public safety meant that criminal justice policy making was, at least by today's standards, relatively insulated from the realm of electoral politics and public opinion.

Over the last several decades, though, Garland and Sparks posit that contemporary Anglo-American criminology has come to be marked by a stark contradiction. As many have noted, on the one hand, it is in vigorous professional and institutional health having established itself as a distinctive professional field in the academy. There has been a dramatic growth in university degree programmes, the number of faculty posts, the establishment of specialist research centres, a proliferation of professional associations and national and international conferences, the publication of specialist journals and books by prestigious academic presses and the expanding professional fields of criminal justice, police, correctional and security studies. This rapid expansion stands in sharp contrast to the fading popularity of traditional 'social' science disciplines. It might be thought that the growing popularity and visibility of criminology within the university sector would be paralleled by the increasing importance of the role that criminological knowledge would play in informing policy development and setting the agenda for public debate.

In fact, with the rise of neo-liberalism from the 1980s onwards, Garland and Sparks cautioned criminologists against making overly confident assumptions about the future. For what has gradually happened, in terms of public authority and credibility, is a noticeable decline in public understanding of and engagement with academic criminological knowledge and policy expertise. With notable exceptions, criminologists have apparently had 'limited success in shaping the public discussion of 'its' uses and its faltering influence on public policy and decision-making' (2000: 190). Indeed, an acute observer of the scene, John Braithwaite (2000) has argued that the boom in criminology has less to do with its intellectual accomplishments, and is much more a reflection of the dramatic expansion of criminal justice occupations in the public and private sectors. This also reminds us that in any general discussion about the state of criminology, the criminal justice and penal system remain the proverbial elephant in the room!

Though the declining influence of criminological expertise in government policy-making seems undeniable, it is important not to exaggerate the centrality of criminological or indeed social science research in the past. It is always worth keeping in mind Keynes classic quote 'There is nothing a government hates more than to be well-informed; for it makes the process of arriving at decisions much more complicated and difficult (Keynes, 1982; vol. 21, 409). And writing in the early 1970s and reflecting on the recent experience of UK crime policy advisory bodies, Roger Hood (1974: 417) concluded that 'the belief that expert advice based on criminological and penological research is the foundation of penal change, is only a screen behind which ideological and political factors, perhaps inevitably, shape those attitudes which imbue legislation'.

Late modernity has thrown up a range of new crime problems that have significant implications for 'the intellectual dispositions, strategic aims and political constraints that criminology inevitably entails' (Garland and Sparks, 2000: 189). Specifically:

- high levels of crime consciousness are embedded in the routines of everyday life and across risk categories
- 'crime talk' is institutionalised in the media and popular culture
- the collective experience of having to adjust to the risks and threats posed by living in an environment disordered by crime and delinquency has generated a punitive public mood
- the categorisations that a generation of postwar criminologists had taken for granted has been undermined by the emotionalization and politicization of crime and criminal justice policy and the re-emergence of private sector interest in crime control.

For Garland and Sparks, criminologists have had to confront the embarrassing fact that in a society saturated with 'crime talk' they had utmost difficulty in communicating in a meaningful manner with politicians, policy makers, professionals and a fearful public. Criminological reasoning, like all academic reasoning, is now mediated and contested by a range of vociferous interest groups, activists and a multitude of institutional actors and public opinions.

Criminologists, it is argued, are alienated from late modern political culture because crime, policing and punishment are now key electoral issues: crime policy has been changed into crime politics. Garland and Sparks also cautioned that in the academy, criminology's traditional explanatory propositions were also being contested, most obviously by common sense discourses of routine activity and rational choice perspectives but also by other academic disciplines who were addressing the problem of crime through very different frameworks some of which could be deemed to be more relevant to government concerns. They concluded by laying out the strategic choices confronting criminology. Although only briefly touching on the subject, Garland and Sparks did begin to examine the differences between the tasks of policy-oriented criminology, critical criminology and their preferred 'public criminology'. It could turn inwards, with practitioners insisting that their key role as policy experts is to refine their methodologies in order to produce the research findings that will generate evidence-led recommendations for policy makers. One danger in this is that criminologists will continue to respond to the state's crime control priorities rather than articulating a broader criminological agenda and they would have little to no control over how their data would be used (Hillyard *et al.*, 2004; Morgan, 2000). Hence, there may be inherent tensions within, and serious political limits to, the expert role of policy criminologists. For Garland and Sparks the cultural centrality of crime was 'an opportunity for criminology to embrace a more critical, more public, more wide-ranging role' (p. 201). For them criminologists cannot side step their responsibility as citizens to participate in the broader public conversation and civic practice. This was a general call for criminologists to engage with a public audience. To do so criminologists would have to sharpen their reflexive understanding of 'the way that crime is experienced, represented and regulated' and how the broader political culture works.

They sense that dominant criminological conceptualisations are out of step with rapid societal developments. At this point we wish to quote from Nico Stehr (2002) who sums up the developments that Garland and Sparks are referring to:

> The old rules, certainties and trajectories no longer apply. Of course there are few opportunities for fresh starts in history. None the less, the future of modern society no longer mimics the past to the extent to which this has been the case ... the future is made from fewer fragments of the past. As a result, sentiments with respect to history that are becoming more pervasive are those of fragility and dislocation. History will be full of unanticipated incertitudes, peculiar reversals, proliferating surprises, and we will have to cope with ever-greater speed of significantly compressed events. The changing agendas of social, political and economic life as the result of our growing capacity to make history will also place inordinate demands on our mental capacities. The fit or lack of fit between our knowledgability and what society, the economy and culture mentally demands is one of the major challenges of knowledge societies.
>
> (Stehr, 2002: 503–4)

From this perspective, the discipline must replenish itself as an intellectual field of study. For Garland and Sparks criminologists need to engage with the cross-cutting explanatory frameworks of contemporary social theorists such as Zygmunt Bauman, Anthony Giddens, Nikolas Rose and others who are asking new questions and making 'connections between apparently unconnected phenomena in ways that allow substantive research to grasp more perspicuously the peculiarities of its current environment' (p. 203; see also Nelken, 1996). However, they also argued for responsible engagement with new theoretical developments, cautioning against indulging in faddish anti-modernist 'theoretical theory' that mystifies rather than clarifies (see also, Holdaway and Rock, 1998; Cullen *et al.*, 2008).

Jock Young (2002, 2003) was one of the few criminologists that responded to Garland and Sparks. Young also took a broader approach to understanding criminology's relationship to public policy, albeit stressing quite different developments. He cautioned against intellectual histories that constructed a 'golden age' of

criminological influence. For him the emergence in the 1970s of a radical criminology committed to 'a full social theory of deviance' was a response to the limitations
of the post-war correctionalist ethos propagated by an intellectual-adminstrative
elite. And of course the broader intention was to also re-align the analysis of crime
and social control within post-positivist sociology. The result had been the creation
of an international school of critical scholarship that redefined the field of study and
many of its key ideas had been assimilated into public debate (see also, Cohen,
1988). These fundamental differences between the two criminological sensibilities
cannot be massaged away or 'consensualised'.

   Young noted that late modern criminology was characterised by a healthy plurality of perspectives and the collapsing of boundaries over who is authorised to speak
about crime and on what terms and had impacted on policy and politics. He observed
how in the 1980s right realist and administrative criminologists managed to construct
an institutional base by working within the logics and rationales of the criminal
system. Populist soundbites enabled them also to enjoy a productive relationship with
the news media and public commentators that also allowed them to redefine the terms
of the debate about criminal justice policy and social policy (see, for example, Wilson
and Kelling, 1982; Murray, 1989). Young also noted that feminist criminologists,
working on sexual and domestic violence, as well as criminologists who called attention to issues of racial discrimination, had been influencing policy debates in the same
decades that Garland and Sparks characterised as ones of declining criminological
relevance. And in the most hostile of political and ideological circumstances, critical
criminology had acted a strategic counter-voice to free market and neo-conservative
anti-crime ideologies 'and the minimalist, theoretical 'noise' constantly arising from
out of the crime control complex' (2002: 260).

   However, Young does have his own concerns. Dramatic rises in crime and disorder
had produced an 'aetiological crisis' for sociologically-based criminology. Like
Garland and Sparks, for him the manifest failures of the contemporary criminological imagination are associated with a discernible turning away from the concerns of
classical sociological theory and a noticeable lack of interest in new developments
in philosophy, political science and cultural studies. This is compounded by what
might be described as a quantitative 'methodolatry'. Furthermore, he has argued that
there is an urgent need for reflexive criminological thinking about the complex of
private troubles and public ills that defined late modernity (Young, 2003: 29).

   But, even if some criminologists have managed to call public and policy attention
to important issues overall, questions of marginality remain. In both the UK and the
US, explicitly policy-oriented criminologists have presented explanations that point
to the structural weakness of the knowledge base rather than consideration of
broader cultural transformations. Tending to presume agreed-on definitions of social
science data, these criminologists argue that conventional knowledge is not capable
of generating convincing research data.

   For example, Elliott Currie (1999) has argued for a more unified, engaged
criminology – one which seeks to change public consciousness around crime and its
control. In the UK, Paul Wiles (2002) argues that for criminology to contribute to the
'public good' it is obligated to produce expert knowledge that has credibility with
policy makers. He argued that the defining characteristics and motivations of contemporary (British) criminology meant that it had not generated the evidence-based
knowledge on offences, offenders, victims and their interconnections that would

allow it to guide policy-making. Pervasive theoretical and methodological limitations, he suggests, helps to explain the poor state of public knowledge on key policy issues such as criminal victimization, offender characteristics and risk factors. The rapid institutionalisation of the discipline within universities had resulted in the privatisation of criminological knowledge production. In order to establish their academic credentials and professional careers, criminologists were specialising in increasingly narrow research areas, addressing their work to a primary audience of their peers and students, were building disciplinary boundaries and pursuing theoretical disputes. Disciplinary closure meant that they were sheltered from 'the wider blasts of criticism on which all good social science depends' and an 'inability to express their ideas in everyday language and summarise complex evidence in straightforward points' (Wiles, 2002: 248). This explains why criminology was a 'missing voice' in public debate about crime and criminal justice. Criminology needed to re-skill and reorient itself in preparation for engagement with a dramatically changed policy environment. Contributing to the twenty-first century 'public good', meant that criminology 'can no longer be a domestic criminology. Indeed, the "public good" also needs to be thought of in a broader context'. If crime was globalising then a more global understanding of crime problems was needed (2002: 250).

Similar arguments have appeared in the US context with regular exchanges of views about whether a 'tipping point' (Gladwell, 2002) has been reached regarding the relevance of criminological research. Among US policy oriented criminologists, widespread agreement seems to exist that criminology has a credibility problem with its authority claims – and, interestingly enough, that an important reason has to do with 'irrelevant' research. For instance, James Austin (2003) attempted to stimulate debate with his provocative views about criminology's 'impotence' in 'shaping and improving criminal justice policy'. Criminology's reputation, according to Austin, has been compromised because the majority of published studies 'are so deeply flawed that they are essentially useless. Conceptual imprecision, methodological deficiencies and unacknowledged and unexamined bias have resulted in the dissemination of 'irresponsible and highly misleading conclusions'. This has damaged criminal justice policy and practice and communities and wasted scarce public resources. Criminology has also been impaired by over-dependence on a narrow range of funding sources that have used 'a small but highly influential circles of criminologists' to 'exert a disproportionate influence on what is funded and who gets funded' (p. 569). For Charles Tittle (2004), there is not a single criminological issue about which 'even a modestly demanding critic could be convinced' (2004: 1641). This is because 'research is limited, and our data are always incomplete, error prone, and accepted as supporting an argument if it simply shows something 'better than chance'. This echoes some of Lawrence Sherman's (2005) concerns that much that passes for criminological knowledge is either impressionist description or misleading in terms of its analysis and conclusions.

In a recent overview, Cullen *et al.* (2008) argue that (US) criminology has experienced 'unprecedented theoretical diversity' for three reasons. First, there is increasing recognition that 'crime' is a more complicated, multi-dimensional, mutating phenomenon than even criminologists thought. Second, criminology is undergoing the latest wave of inter-disciplinization with scholars from a variety of backgrounds researching different aspects of the problem of crime. Finally, value defined positions, whether liberal, conservative or radical in nature ensure that 'a comfortable theoretical consensus does not emerge' (Cullen *et al.*, 2008, p. 1). Consequently criminology remains a fiercely contested discipline. However, for them, a vibrant criminological imagination, while welcome, is generating serious problems. It is, for example, becoming increasingly difficult to keep up with the sheer volume of what may loosely defined as 'criminological' publications. Fragmentation and specialisation has resulted in the rapid proliferation of peer reviewed criminology journals as well as those representing numerous sub-fields of study. What is very evident is that the quality thresholds are variable. Perhaps more significantly, for Cullen *et al.*, is the difficulty for the professional criminologist of being truly knowledgeable about the scientific robustness of different theoretical perspectives that are currently on offer. How should we judge? It is of course much easier to remain an advocate of a seemingly tried and tested traditional theory than to engage in critical analysis of assumptions through rigorous empirical testing. They argue that there is also a pressing need to jettison or at least steam clean criminological perspectives that have 'scant empirical support' (2008, p. 2). This will indicate whether empirically dependable time-tested theories of perennial questions require re-furbished and allow genuine intellectual innovation to take place and emergent issues of primary importance to be identified. Presumably this house-keeping exercise will also allow for clarification of what is really intellectually distinctive about *criminological* theorising

> As a discipline we need to have a clear sense of where we are and where we should be heading. If not then criminology risks being a field of study in which many ideas are developed and all are chosen – in which all theories have equal claim to legitimacy and in which only the most specialised scholars can separate out the theoretical chaff from the wheat
>
> (Cullen *et al.*, 2008, p. 2).

The Cullen *et al.* collection also evidenced just how difficult it is for criminologists to be reflective about their preferred perspectives and professional practices.

What might be done to remedy this seemingly ruinous state of affairs? A notable response has been to argue the case for scientific modernization. This can be achieved, according to Austin (2003) by the utilization of experimental designs, the rigorous re-analysis of research data and conduct of replication studies, diversification of funding streams, and enhanced regulation and oversight of professional practice and standards. Sherman (2005) argues for a fully-fledged 'experimental criminology' which would improve research designs and this would provide 'unbiased empirical guidance' to inform key policy choices in crime and criminal justice. He acknowledges that even methodologically meticulous criminologists face an uphill battle influencing the contemporary policy environment. Usefulness 'does not guarantee that the information will be *used*' (Sherman, 2005: 130). And of course 'the extent to which evidence guides practice may depend heavily on whether the consumers of evidence trust the social scientists who produce it and the methods they use' (Sherman, 2003: 8). Experimental criminology has the advantage that it relates directly to the world of practitioners, providing them with 'what works' choices and has the potential to excite the public imagination regarding 'discoveries' about criminal behaviour and crime prevention (for critical reviews see Hope, 2009; Tilley, 2009). There is the obvious implication that some domains of criminological inquiry

are more amenable to experimental methods than others but this has yet to be specified. On this point it is worth noting the deliberations of the Campbell Crime and
Justice Group on the prospects for an 'evidence-based criminology' (http://www.
campbellcollaboration.org/).

Clarke (2004) moves this agenda one step further arguing that criminology must
become an applied crime (control) science whose core task is to explain crime (rather
than criminality) and how crime is committed (rather than why it is committed). To
do so it will have to disconnect itself from a dominant sociological orientation and
become genuinely interdisciplinary, linking up with disciplines such as economics,
biology, demography, geography, architecture, and engineering (see also Walsh and
Ellis, 2007). It will have to work with industry and business rather than the criminal
justice system in order to comprehend how crime is being transformed by new technologies and globalisation. This would, of course, make most of criminology's
preferred perspectives and methodologies redundant. If criminologists do not think
through the policy lens, Clarke warns that they will be replaced by the new discipline
of 'Crime Science' (see also Laycock, 2003).

Other criminologists have cautioned against the temptation to prioritise and over-
sell the policy relevance of the discipline. Tittle (2004), for example, warns
practitioners against the desire to proselytise: Criminologists 'are as likely to be
wrong as right and in the process they can easily cause damage. Here we are not
talking about innocuous outcomes but instead about matters of human life, safety
and freedom. Being wrong can be very costly' (2004: 1641). The advocacy and bias
that inevitably flows from and constructs public engagement endangers the 'precious
little' public legitimacy that is currently accorded to social scientists. Criminologists
do not have 'that body of reliable knowledge and the public pretence that we do
actually undermines any hope of influencing society or of obtaining the support
necessary for developing such a knowledge'. The public 'know we have weak
knowledge and in response they accord us little credibility. We, in turn continually
undermine the little respect we might otherwise have by trying to promote our ideas
(a form of ideology) in the guise of superior knowledge. Most of the time we actually do not know as much as we pretend and even when there is a chance we might
provide or compile useful information, people do not trust us (Tittle, 2004: 1642).

For Laub (2004: 20) the discipline's intellectual history tells criminologists
that they must produce sound research that will allow for the testing of durable
theory and seek to engage in meaningful dialogue across a range of domains. But he
also cautions: 'the reality is most policy issues are moral questions that cannot be
answered by theory or for that matter by research. ... Moreover the idea that scholarly knowledge and this knowledge alone should determine policy outcomes is
naïve' (2004: 18). Cullen's (2005) examination of the efforts of a small group of
criminologists to save what is left of the 'rehabilitative ideal' is that there is a need
to develop an understanding of when and why criminology has mattered to policy
and practice (see also Clear and Frost, 2001).

Certain critical criminologists have addressed the down-side of criminology's
desire to be relevant. In the early 1990s, Ericson and Carriere asked criminologists
to reflect on whether their practices were contributing to 'an increasingly destruc-
tured, fragmented, and reflexive existence in risk society' (1994: 105). Hillyard *et al.*
(2004) have located what they view to be the impoverished state of criminological
scholarship with the commodification and 'statisation' of the research process. For

them, uncritical acceptance of the strictures of state commissioned criminological research has strip-mined the discipline's broader intellectual credibility, integrity and autonomy. Entrepreneurial criminologists have profited directly from their willingness to accept the research agenda of criminal justice agencies and through competing for contracts in an evaluative research market place, the state's surveillance, criminalisation and punishment capacities go unchallenged and may even be strengthened. Tighter political control of the commissioning process across a range of policy sites also means that critical criminologists are finding it difficult to access funding 'to conduct rigorous, challenging and socially relevant research that will alleviate rather than exacerbate problems caused by conventional crime, while simultaneously confronting the social harms generated by the powerful' (Hillyard *et al.*, 2004: 385). Hence, for Hillyard *et al.* the critical question is how is criminology being re-shaped by the policy-making process.

Before we leave this matter it is important, we think, to make one observation about policy-making that should always be at the forefront of scholars' minds when discussing the practical relevance and impact of their discipline. That is that it is vital not to over-estimate the degree of coherence of the policy-making process. The idea of 'evidence-led' policy-making can be associated with a highly rational model of public policy formulation in which policy emerges from a distinct set of problem-solving processes: problem definition, formulation of alternative solutions, weighing up the implications of alternatives and experimentation with the preferred choice. Although having some analytical value, this view is overly mechanistic and simplified as a model of how policy-making actually works in practice. The content of policies is negotiated continuously in the problem definition, legislation, regulation and court decisions, and again in the decisions made by street-level bureaucrats (Lipsky, 1980). Moreover, policy outcomes are frequently an unintended by-product, or simply emerge very gradually. Understanding the frequently serendipitous and unpredictable nature of policy-making should make those who seek to influence think carefully about how such objectives might be achieved (see also Clear, 2010).

We have, thus far, discussed a number of issues affecting contemporary criminology and criminological thinking. In doing so, we have, for convenience, skimmed over national, comparative differences in criminological theory and practice. Indeed, the approach taken in this volume has largely been to assume that the theoretical ideas and perspectives outlined here have common currency and that there is a broad, international interpretive community. And, of course, historically there has been much sharing of theoretical ideas – particularly between the US, the UK and other key nodes in the English-speaking nations. But, just as we increasingly do in relation to our analyses of criminal justice developments, so in connection with theory it is vital that we analyse both the global flow and dissemination of concepts and ideas whilst simultaneously testing their applicability in particular national, local, cultural sites. As with other criminological commodities (Jones and Newburn, 2006; Newburn and Sparks, 2004) we must ask why particular ideas developed in one context gain popularity and appear to resonate elsewhere? Why do some criminological ideas, rather than others, take root? Second, what knowledge actors (individual and institutional) are involved in the process of the transfer of ideas for, as Rogers (1995: 7) notes, 'innovations do not sell themselves'.

The lesson of comparative criminology is that we should also examine critically how well criminological ideas play in different jurisdictions. One of the more salutary conclusions from comparative research is that ideas and terms that appear superficially similar turn out on closer examination to be distinct in interesting and meaningful ways (the term 'gang' would be one obvious example; others would be 'community' and 'neighbourhood', see Cain, 2000; Lacey and Zedner, 1998). A crucial question therefore is how different are the ways in which ostensibly similar vocabularies are taken up and applied in the distinct settings they encounter? As Melossi (2000: 144) correctly observes, 'generally speaking any term, even the simplest, is embedded within a cultural context, or milieu, that gives it its meaning'. Such considerations are important to bear in mind when framing or operationalising theoretical perspectives.

WHAT THE VOLUME COVERS

The volume is divided in two. We have distinguished, in broad terms, between 'contemporary criminological theories' and 'new directions'. Needless to say, this is in some respects a somewhat artificial distinction. In general terms, the first tranche of chapters cover what might be thought of as well-established criminological perspectives – many of long-standing. These range from strain theory and labelling perspectives to routine activities/rational choice and social disorganisation.

Early chapters focus on those factors that may predispose some individuals rather than others toward offending – what Jolliffe and Farrington refer to as 'criminal potential'. Early positivistic studies focused on physical/biological and, later, psychological characteristics. Modern criminology has moved some distance from such approaches. Contemporary studies are now exploring the relationship between, for example, genetic make-up and environment, with some showing apparently high levels (around the 40–50 per cent mark) of heritability in relation to various forms of criminal or antisocial behaviour. Similarly, those studies which focus on risk factors such as high impulsiveness, low intelligence and low empathy and offending also present these as explanatory variables rather than 'explanations'. In their very different ways, such work shares a concern with social learning theory – one which seeks to understand individual-level features and yet link these to macro-level processes. As Akers and Jensen put it, 'social learning theory has evolved … from a perspective emphasising the social-behavioural mechanisms operating to explain individual variations in behaviour … to also addressing the structural and cultural circumstances that shape schedules of reinforcement and punishment. In parallel, as Chamard describes it, Routine Activities Theory is both a micro-level approach (identifying likely offenders, suitable targets and capable guardians) as well as a macro-level theory that relates broad social changes, via changes in opportunity, to shifts in levels of crime.

A similar tension can be seen in relation to control theories. The plural here is important for Paternoster and Bachman are not discussing a single *theory*, but rather a body of work that works at different levels (they distinguish between community or neighbourhood control theory and individual level control theory). One distinguishing feature, and potential strength, of control theories is their avoidance of the knotty problem of criminal motivation. Rather than a concern with motivations, control theorists assume the matter to be explained is restraint or inhibition – how we control ourselves and/or we are controlled. The very attractiveness of such a formulation helps explain why aspects of control theory are to be found embedded within other criminological perspectives.

The 1960s witnessed a critical turn in theorising around crime and control. Interactionism led scholars to question the basis upon which particular forms of conduct are subject to intervention and sanction. Distinctively, as Muncie puts it, labelling perspectives argued that no act is intrinsically criminal and he quotes Willem de Haan's observation that 'what we need is not a better theory of crime, but a more powerful critique of crime'. In McLaughlin's chapter we see how scholars from a variety of radical perspectives – much influenced by Marxism – turned their attention to processes of criminalisation, crimes of the powerful, including the state itself, and to trenchant critiques of the traditional criminological project. Ironically this anti-criminological tradition is now very much part of the orthodox history of criminology!

In turn, however, a critique of radical perspectives emerged – largely from previous adherents – which advocated the embracing of greater 'realism' and, in particular, greater attention, as Matthews puts it, to the 'lived realities of its subjects'. He argues that contemporary criminology suffers from a number of problems, not least its increasing division into a number of reasonably distinct groupings. There are indeed dangers in fragmentation and, as we will come on to below, certain schisms have already led to scholars from a number of perspectives arguing against the use of the term criminology at all. As a counter to this, there are those – represented most obviously by Gregg Barak in this volume – that actively seek and promote what they call an 'integrative criminology'. This, he is quick to point out, is sometimes wrongly reduced to the idea of theoretical integration – which is necessarily part of such a project – but, in practice, it is a broader project involving a multi-disciplinary approach to the broad range of criminological problems.

Arguably, feminist perspectives represent one classic form of 'doing' integrative criminology. There is, as Daly argues, an 'extraordinary range and sophistication in feminist work'. As she then notes, this is in large part a consequence of the fact that scholars working in this tradition, encompass both specialist and generalist orientations, and represent great disciplinary breadth. Moreover, the feminist critique has led to a reconsideration – in some circles at least – of male conduct and, more particularly, of the problematic process of 'doing masculinity'.

The second tranche of contributions to this volume are loosely arranged under the heading 'new directions'. In short, we take them to represent, in differing ways, streams of activity in current criminological theorising together with ideas about how work in this field may, or is hoped might, develop in coming years. Again, work varies considerably in its substantive focus: some being preoccupied with offending, some with the operation and consequences of criminal justice interventions, and others with issues as varied as victimization and comparative political economy. A highly influential perspective, a relatively recent development, and one that has brought the study of the individual firmly back into the mainstream, concerns life course or developmental perspectives. Such theoretical work is distinctive, in part, because it is closely linked with a particular research methodology: prospective longitudinal studies. Here, again, the label (developmental and life course) masks a considerable variety of approaches, some more psychological orientation, others of a more sociological flavour. Each seeks to explain how events in the life course shape and affect the development of criminal or antisocial behaviour. Summarising such work, one of David Farrington's conclusions is that greater effort needs to be put into comparing and contrasting the differing developmental approaches.

As was noted above, a recent fundamental challenge to criminological thinking – or at least to certain styles of sociologically based criminological thinking – has come from a group of scholars locating themselves under the banner of 'crime science'. As Ron Clarke argues crime science seeks to occupy different territory from traditional criminological concerns. In short, where criminology is concerned with offenders and dispositions, crime science is concerned with (criminal) events and situations. Whilst acknowledging the apparently substantial differences in outlook and concern between what are sometimes portrayed as different disciplines, Clarke concedes that these dissimilarities may be no more than exist within other academic disciplines in universities. Readers will have their own views on whether it is better to attempt to proceed as if we – 'criminologists' and 'crime scientists' – are involved in a common endeavour, but coming at it from different, possibly radically different, angles, or whether it is the case that these approaches to crime are truly paradigmatically distinctive.

In some cases, or respects, 'new directions' are predictably attempts to recover and build upon long-standing attempts to understand offending. Thus, as Tony Jefferson argues, criminology has always been psychosocial and, yet, for much of its history the psyche and the social have been kept largely separate. In reviewing the history of the field he argues for the importance of an understanding of subjectivity as the basis for going beyond the identification of risk factors and their like and producing an account which offers some hope of theorising the mechanisms at work in specific cases rather than average 'social types'. Some cognate concerns underpin the emergence of 'cultural criminology'; in particular, a worry, as Jeff Ferrell puts it, that criminology is increasingly unwilling or unable to engage 'with the experiential reality of crime and victimisation'. He outlines a criminology which at the very least seeks to balance what he sees as its current preoccupation with large-scale survey research with a renewed commitment to ethnography and a willingness to embrace narrative and visual styles.

There follow a series of contributions which, in differing ways, deal with questions of power. In the first, Pat O'Malley outlines the main features of 'governmental criminology' – a body of work particularly influenced by Michel Foucault's work on discipline and punishment and, more particularly, to his observations on the nature of power and knowledge. O'Malley analyses the new 'vocabulary' offered in Foucault's vision; indeed, arguably, offering a vocabulary with which to attempt to analyse and understand the (post-social) world is precisely theory's primary role. Governmental analyses have become increasingly prominent, not least through studies of risk and actuarialism. Foucault's work is also deeply inscribed in recent developments in that body of work within criminology that is concerned with study of punishment. From Cohen's 'dispersal of discipline' thesis, to Garland's 'culture of control' thesis, one can identify the considerable influence of ideas derived from governmentality theory. As Dignan outlines, contemporary work in the field of penology is increasingly turning its attention to matters of comparative political economy and its relationship to the nature and scale of punishment. The big question facing scholars working in this field has concerned the *nature* of the relationship between political economy and punishment. What are the mechanisms at work? This, as Susanne Karstedt points out, has led a number of writers to focus on the centrality of political and civil institutions and, more particularly, on the idea of 'comparative institutional advantage'. She argues the case for the development of a new institutional criminology – one which sees 'crime and justice as outcomes of specific arrangements and clusters of institutions' and, importantly, where sometimes subtle differences in these arrangements can lead to substantially different outcomes.

Power also appears centrally in Lawrence Sherman's reworking of 'defiance theory'. In his terms, where conflict theories view the criminal law as a struggle for material power of policing and punishment, defiance theory 'recognises the material force of that power, but also predicts the long-term control of that power in terms of the moral intuitive power of the contestants'. He illustrates the potential of defiance theory by reference to the criminology of race in the United States between the early seventeenth and twenty-first centuries. More particularly, he suggests that the moral obligation which leads to defiance of the status quo can be seen in the law-making, law-enforcing and law-breaking in connection with race in America in this period.

Lee E. Ross discusses 'critical race theory', a perspective originating in critical legal studies, and one which puts issues of race and oppression at the heart of its considerations. Sharing critical criminology's concerns with inequality and injustice, critical race theory focuses less on questions of material disparity and places at the centre of attention the variety of forms of racism that can be identified within justice systems. By contrast, but with similar critical criminological underpinnings, 'green criminology' is focused on issues of environmental harm, ecology and animal rights. Rob White outlines three methods of studying and analysing environmental harms: the socio-legal, regulatory and social action approaches. Each has parallels in the study of more traditional criminological concerns and yet the field nevertheless constitutes a departure from mainstream concerns.

Much of the stimulus for an emergent green criminology has come from what is perceived to be the destructive anti-social nature of global capitalism. It is this, broadly drawn, that is the focus of Katja Franco Aas's concern in her discussion of 'global criminology'. For understandable reasons criminology, as traditionally practised, has been dominated by a concern with the state, its institutions and capacities. However, globalising shifts have begun to challenge us to think beyond the state. This encompasses such matters and the cross-jurisdictional flow of criminal commodities, crime control institutions and criminological ideas. In particular, she argues, global transformations have prompted a shift in focus from state security toward 'human security' and to develop a new vocabulary which is able to conceive of security as a 'global public good'. One danger in connection with the apparently globalised nature of much in the criminal justice and penal spheres is that we focus overly on the commonalities within and between jurisdictions rather than, equally, seeking to understand divergence and differences (and how these are to be understood and explained). The field of penology, as Michael Cavadino discusses, is now perhaps the foremost site in which comparative scholarship seeks to address such questions. New languages and ideas are just emerging and one has the sense that this will be one of the most productive and exciting areas of criminological scholarship in coming years.

The two concluding chapters focus on victimisation and the role of the media. In relation to the former, Paul Rock begins by observing that 'it would be difficult to argue that there is a fully coherent victimological theory'. This is, at least in part, understandable he suggests, and derives, inter alia, from a broader ignorance about the nature of victimisation, from theoretical and empirical preoccupations with other matters and, in some quarters, from an ideological preference for siding with those labelled as 'offenders' rather than 'victims'. In fact, recent decades have seen something of an explosion of work in this field, in part stimulated by feminist scholarship, but also as a result of the centrality of victims to other perspectives such as routine activities and reintegrative shaming. As Rock concludes, this particular field may still be 'somewhat ragged and incoherent', but it has demanded that 'we are now obliged to look much cautiously at our stock of academic, moral and political ideas about the world of crime, deviance and control'. Another area that, traditionally, has received relatively little criminological attention but where, again, that is now changing, concerns the news media. For Greer, key ideas in this field include 'newsworthiness', 'moral panics' and 'fear of crime' and, as with so many of the matters considered in this section of the book, the key challenge is perhaps understanding and theorising the significant and swift changes that have taken place in relation to local, national and global news media. Criminology is currently ill-equipped to deal with these changes Greer argues. In part, this is a practical empirical failing – criminologists, he suggests, simply no longer engage with journalists in the way they once did – but is also theoretical, for new analytical tools are required.

Finally, one aspect of criminological theory that we had hoped to devote greater attention to in this volume than has proved to be the case is its intellectual history. Our original plan was to commission a series of essays at the beginning of the volume that would examine the intellectual origins of criminology in North America, in Europe/UK and in Australia. In the event this proved particularly difficult to achieve. In part, we think, this reflects the relatively small number of scholars working on the intellectual history of criminology and who, potentially, one might reasonably therefore approach to make such a contribution. Many of those we did speak with were either already over-committed or, for a variety of reasons, did not feel they wished to take on such a task. After much trying we were eventually forced to concede defeat to abandon this particular aspect of the volume. We mention this here for two reasons. First, to acknowledge the 'absent presence' – reviewers may well point to it themselves and we wanted to admit to our failure in this regard. Second, we have not given up on the idea. We anticipate that there will be a second edition of this Handbook and we would very much like to add these vitally important framing chapters at that stage.

REFERENCES

Austin, J. (2003) Why criminology is irrelevant?, *Criminology and Public Policy* 2: 557–564.
Braithwaite, J. (2005) For public social science, *British Journal of Sociology* 56(3): 345–353.
Burawoy, M. (2004) Public sociology: contradictions, dilemmas and possibilities, *Social Forces* 82(4): 1603–1618.
Burawoy, M. (2005) For public sociology, *American Sociological Review* 70(1): 4–28.
Cain, M. (2000) Orientalism, occidentalism and the sociology of crime, *British Journal of Criminology* 40: 2.
Chancer, L. and McLaughlin, E. (2007) Public criminologies: diverse perspectives on academia and policy, *Theoretical Criminology*, 11(2): 155–173.

Clarke, R. V. (2004) Technology, criminology and crime science, *European Journal on Criminal Policy and Research* 10: 55–63.

Clawson, D., Zussman, R., Misra, J., Gerstel, N. and Stokes, R. (eds) (2008) *Public Sociology*. Berkely: University of California Press.

Clear, T. R. (2010) Policy and evidence: the challenge to the American Society of Criminology, *Criminology* 4(1): 1–25.

Clear, T. and Frost, N. (1999) Informing public policy, *Criminology and Public Policy* 6(4): 633–40.

Cohen, S. (1988) Footprints on the sand: a further report on criminology and the sociology of deviance in Britain. In: Fitzgerald, M., McLennan, G. and Pawson, J. (eds), *Crime and Society: Readings in History and Theory*. London: Routledge and Kegan Paul.

Cullen, F. (2005) The twelve people who saved rehabilitation: how the science of criminology made a difference, *Criminology* 43(1): 1–42.

Cullen, F.T., Wright, J. P. and Blevins, K. R. (eds) (2008) *Taking Stock: the Status of Criminological Theory*. New Brunswick: Transaction Publishers.

Currie, E. (1999) Reflections on crime and criminology at the millenium, *Western Criminology Review* 2(1).

Ericson, R. (2005) Publicising sociology, *British Journal of Sociology* 56(3): 365–372.

Ericson, R. and Carriere, K. (1994) The fragmentation of criminology. In: D. Nelken (ed.) (1996) *The Futures of Criminology*. London: Sage.

Etzioni, A. (2006) *Public Intellectuals: An Endangered Species*. New York: Rowan and Littlefield.

Fuller, S. (2006) *The Intellectual*. London: Icon Books.

Furedi, F. (2005) *Where Have all the Intellectuals Gone?* London: Continuum Books.

Garland, D. (2002) Of crime and criminals: The development of criminology in Britain. In: Maguire, M., Morgan, R. and Reiner, R. (eds) *Oxford Handbook of Criminology*. Oxford: OUP (third edition).

Garland, D. and Sparks, R. (2000) Criminology, social theory and the challenge of our times, *British Journal of Criminology* 40: 189–204.

Gladwell, M. (2002) *The Tipping Point*. London/New York: Abacus.

Hillyard, P., Sim, J., Tombs, S. and Whyte, D. (2004) Leaving a 'stain upon the silence': contemporary criminology and the politics of dissent, *British Journal of Criminology* 44: 369–390.

Holdaway, S. and Rock, P. (eds) (1998) *Thinking about Criminology*. London: UCL Press.

Hood, R. (1974) Criminology and penal change: A case study of the nature and impact of some recent advice to governments. In: Hood, R. (ed.), *Crime, Criminology and Public Policy: Essays in Honour of Sir Leon Radzinowicz*. London: Heinemann.

Hope, T. (2009) The illusion of control: A response to Professor Sherman, *Criminology and Criminal Justice* 9(2): 125–134.

Jones, T. and Newburn, T. (2006) *Policy Transfer and Criminal Justice*. Buckingham: Open University Press.

Keynes, M. (1982) *Collected Writings*, Vol. 21. Activities 1931–1939, World crises and policies in Britain and America, Basingstoke: Macmillan.

Lacey, N. and Zedner, L. (1998) Community in German criminal justice: a significant absence? *Social and Legal Studies* 7: 7–25.

Laycock, G. (2003) *Launching Crime Science*, London: UCL website.

Laub, J. H. (2004) The life-course of criminology in the United States, *Criminology* 42(1): 126.

Lipsky, M. (1980) *Street-Level Bureaucracy: Dilemmas of the Individual in Public Services*. New York: Russell Sage Foundation.

Loader, I. and Sparks, R. (2004) For an historical sociology of crime policy in England and Wales since 1968, *Critical Review of International Social and Political Philosophy* 7(2): 5–32.

McLaughlin, E., Muncie, J. and Hughes, G. (2001) *Criminological Perspectives: Essential Readings*, 2nd edition. London: Sage.

Melossi, D. (2000) Translating social control: reflections on the comparison of Italian and North American cultures concerning social control, with a few consequences for 'critical' criminology. In: S. Karstedt and K.-D. Bussmann (eds) *Social Dynamics of Crime and Control*. Oxford: Hart.

Michael, J. (2002) *Anxious Intellects*. Durham NC: Duke University Press.

Morgan, R. (2000) The politics of criminological research. In: R. King and E. Wincup (eds), *Doing Research on Crime and Justice*. Oxford: Oxford University Press.

Murray, C. (1989) *The Underclass: Sunday Times.* London: IEA/Sunday Times.

Nelken, D. (ed.) (1994) *The Futures of Criminology.* London: Sage.

Newburn, T. and Sparks, R. (2004) Criminal justice and political cultures. In: T. Newburn and R. Sparks (eds), *Criminal Justice and Political Cultures: National and International Dimensions of Crime Control.* Cullompton: Willan.

Pearce, N. (2005) Mix in with mandrins, *Times Higher Educational Supplement,* 15 April.

Posner, R. A. (2003) *Public Intellectuals; A Study of Decline.* Cambridge MA: Harvard University Press.

Radzinowicz, Sir L. (1999) *Adventures in Criminology.* London: Routledge.

Reiner, R. (1988) British criminology and the state. *British Journal of Criminology* 28: 138–158.

Ritzer, G. and Smart, B. (2001) *The Sage Handbook of Social Theory.* London: Sage.

Rogers, E. M. (1995) *The Diffusion of Innovations,* fourth edition New York: The Free Press.

Sherman, L. W. (2003) Misleading evidence and evidence-led policy: making social science more experimental, *ANNALS, AAPS* 589: 6–19.

Sherman, L. W. (2005) The use and usefulness of criminology, 1751–2005: enlightened justice and its failures, *ANNALS, AAPSS* 6000: 115–135.

Stehr, N. (2002) Modern societies as knowledge societies. In: G. Ritzer and B. Smart (eds) (2001) *The Sage Handbook of Social Theory.* London: Sage.

Sumner, C. (2002) *Blackwell Companion to Criminology.* Oxford: Blackwell.

Sutherland, E. and Cressey, D. (1960) *Principles of Criminology,* sixth edition. Philadelphia: J.B. Lippincott.

Tilley, N. (2009) Sherman vs Sherman: Realism vs rhetoric, *Criminology and Criminal Justice* 9(2): 135–144.

Tittle, C. (2004) The arrogance of public criminology, *Social Forces* 82(4): 1639–1643.

Walsh, A. and Ellis, L. (2007) *Criminology: An Interdisciplinary Approach.* London: Sage.

Wiles, P. (2002) Criminology in the twenty-first century: public good or private interest? *Australian and New Zealand Journal of Criminology* 35(22): 238–52.

Wilson, J. Q. and Kelling, G. (1982) Broken windows: the police and neighbourhood safety, *Atlantic Monthly* 249: 29–38.

Young, J. (2002) Critical criminology in the twenty-first century: critique, irony and the always unfinished. In: K. Carrington and R. Hogg (eds), *Critical Criminology: Issues, Debates and Challenges.* Cullompton: Willan.

Young, J. (2003) Mayhem and measurement in late modernity. In: K. Aroma and S. Nevala (eds), *Crime and Crime Control in an Integrated Europe,* Helsinki: HEUNI.

Zahn, M. (1999) Thoughts on the future of criminology – the American Society of Criminology, 1998 Presidential Address, *Criminology* 37(1): 1–15.

PART I

Contemporary Criminological Theory

1

Genetics and Crime

Laura A. Baker, Catherine Tuvblad
and Adrian Raine

The idea that inherited genetic predispositions may underlie the risk for engaging in criminal behavior is not exactly new. Perhaps most convincingly, several adoption studies in the 1970s and 1980s provided powerful evidence that having an incarcerated birth parent raised one's own risk of earning a criminal conviction as an adult, even if reared by pro-social, law-abiding – but genetically unrelated – foster parents. This remarkable finding was replicated in adoptive cohorts across cultures, including two Scandinavian studies (Cloninger *et al.*, 1982; Mednick *et al.*, 1984) as well as in the United States (Cadoret *et al.*, 1983). Based on these adoption studies, the genetic effect on criminal outcomes appears important for both sexes, although individual genetic risk is typically more extreme for female than male offenders (Baker *et al.*, 1989). Heritable influences also differ in these studies according to the type of crimes committed, with petty, non-violent offending showing larger genetic influence than violent offenses (Mednick *et al.*, 1984).

Most importantly, however, these early adoption studies shared one other remarkable and profound result, which is that the genetic risk for criminal behavior could be exacerbated by adverse environmental circumstances, such as coming from a low socioeconomic background (Van Dusen, 1983), or being raised in a family with at least one criminal adoptive parent (Cloninger *et al.*, 1982; Mednick *et al.*, 1984). Such effects fall under the realm of genotype by environment (GxE) interactions, and highlight the complexity of the genetic and environmental effects in criminal outcomes.

The provocative findings from these early adoption studies have since sparked numerous lines of research attempting to replicate and further refine our understanding of both genetic and environmental causes of crime and violence. A plethora of twin and adoption studies subsequently confirmed the genetic effect on criminal outcomes, and on the wider constructs of antisocial behavior (see Rhee and Waldman, 2002) and externalizing behavior disorders. Although dozens of studies have replicated the genetic effect in antisocial behavior across a variety of cultures, the genetic influences have been almost entirely unspecified, with little understanding about how many genes, their location in the human genome, or the specific environments or experiences that lead to gene expression.

So what is new in research on genetics of crime? Current genetic research on antisocial behavior – including criminal offending – aims to specify the nature of both genetic and environmental influences, and how they may interact with one another to lead to criminal outcomes. This is being done in a variety of ways, including molecular genetic studies attempting to identify specific genes which increase risk for criminal behavior or its correlates such as impulsivity, risky decision making, and aggression, as well as investigations of biological and social risk factors and how their relations to crime may be mediated by genes and environment. Our goal in this chapter is to review the ways in which we have begun to unpack the black boxes of genetic and environmental influences in antisocial behavior, with a focus on studies that include criminal offending. We first briefly review the evidence for (anonymous) genetic influences and gene–environment interactions in antisocial behavior, including the various ways in which these effects have been shown to vary – across type of crime, gender, and development. This is followed by a review of recent studies attempting to identify specific genes and the factors that may potentially modify their expression.

UNSPECIFIED GENETIC AND ENVIRONMENTAL EFFECTS ON CRIMINAL BEHAVIOR

The strongest evidence for a genetic effect on criminality comes from the early twin and adoption studies conducted in several countries, including the United States (Cadoret *et al.*, 1995), Sweden (Sigvardsson *et al.*, 1982), Denmark (Mednick *et al.*, 1984), and Norway (Torgersen *et al.*, 1993). These effects are especially strong for crimes against property, including theft, vandalism, and property damage. Twin concordance for convictions is consistently greater for genetically identical (monozygotic) than for non-identical/fraternal (dizygotic) twin pairs for property crimes such as vandalism and theft (Cloninger and Gottesman, 1987). For adopted individuals, there is increased risk for property crime convictions when his or her birth parent evidenced a similar conviction, further suggesting the importance of genetic influences on property offending. In the absence of birth parent convictions, however, there is little or no increase in risk when raised by adoptive parents with property crime convictions (Mednick *et al.*, 1984), indicating little importance of shared family environment, at least when genetic risk is low. Environmental influences on non-violent criminality thus appear largely non-familial and specific to the individual rather than shared by relatives living together.

Further, it is well documented that males are much more likely than females to engage in most forms of criminal behavior (Junger-Tas *et al.*, 1994; Moffitt *et al.*, 2001; Rutter *et al.*, 2003). This sex difference is widest for violent offending (Rutter *et al.*, 1998; Smith and Visher, 1980), and narrowest for drug and alcohol related crimes (Moffitt *et al.*, 2001). Although males are arrested and convicted far more often than females the heritability of non-violent criminality is comparable for the two sexes (Baker *et al.*, 1989; Rhee and Waldman, 2002). Twin studies have shown greater identical (monozygotic) than fraternal (dizygotic) concordance for non-violent criminal convictions in both male and female same-sex pairs. Nonetheless, there is some evidence for sex-limited genetic effects, whereby different genetic or environmental factors may be important in males and females, in that opposite-sex fraternal (dizygotic) twins are often less similar than same-sex fraternal twin pairs (Cloninger and Gottesman, 1987).

The broader construct of antisocial behavior – which includes criminal offending, as well as aggression – also shows substantial genetic influence. In a meta-analysis combining effect sizes in 51 twin and adoption studies, Rhee and Waldman (2002) reported a heritability estimate of 41 per cent, with the remaining 59 per cent of variance being due to environmental factors. Interestingly, when comparing results for various definitions of antisocial behavior, only criminal offending appeared to be influenced by both additive genetic effects and non-additive genetic effects – possibly due to genetic dominance and epistatic interactions between genes – based on a pattern of results whereby, on average, identical (monozygotic) twin correlations are more than twice the value of fraternal (dizygotic) twin correlations, and also that biological parent–offspring correlations are less than fraternal twin correlations. Such non-additive genetic effects could arise if one or more high risk alleles act in a recessive fashion, or if certain alleles at one locus affect gene expression at other loci (epistasis).

One intriguing aspect of the literature on genetics and crime is that the strong and consistent genetic influence seen for property offending does not hold true for violent criminal convictions. None of the major adoption studies in Scandinavia or the United States found any elevated risk for violent convictions as a function of either biological or adoptive parent criminal offending, although one early twin study did find greater identical (monozygotic) than fraternal (dizygotic) concordance for violent convictions (see Cloninger and Gottesman, 1987). This pattern of twin, but not parent-offspring, similarity for violent criminal behavior suggests the possibility of non-additive genetic effects due to dominance or epistasis, which would result in increased resemblance for siblings (and twins), but not for parents and offspring. Thus, there may be genetic risk for violent crimes such as murder and rape, which may stem from rare recessive genes, or specific combinations of alleles that do not appear in studies of vertical transmission across generations.

Developmental effects

How early in life do genetic influences for criminal offending appear? Limited access to official court records for crimes committed prior to age 18 have made it difficult to investigate the etiology of law-breaking behaviors in youth in the same manner as in the large twin and adoption studies. Nonetheless, a large literature exists for studies using parent and teacher ratings of children and adolescents and youth self-report methods, which aim to understand early rule-breaking and other behavior problems in childhood and adolescence that may give way eventually to law-breaking behaviors in adulthood.

In the aforementioned meta-analysis review of twin and adoption studies of the wider construct of antisocial behavior (Rhee and Waldman, 2002) genetic influences appear to be at least as important (if not more so) in children and adolescents compared to adults. In fact, their meta-analysis suggested a significant decrease in genetic influences across age, although sample differences in age across studies are confounded with the definition and method of assessment of antisocial behavior. Studies of younger children tend to rely more often on parent and teacher ratings of children's aggressive and rule-breaking behaviors, while studies of adults are more apt to use self-report or official records of convictions. Thus, it is difficult to know exactly whether and how genetic influences on criminal offending might emerge across development. This highlights the importance of using multi-method assessments in longitudinal studies, in which narrow age bands are studied. A few such longitudinal studies of antisocial behavior have begun to shed more light on the developmental course of genetic etiologies.

In our own longitudinal twin study of antisocial behavior we have found a high heritability (over 90 per cent) of a common view obtained by ratings of childhood antisocial behavior from both the parents and teachers, as well as through self-reports from the children themselves (Baker *et al.*, 2007). In addition to the genetic effects common to all three reporters of the child's antisocial behavior, there appear to be additional genetic influences specific to a given reporter (Baker *et al.*, 2007; Baker *et al.*, 2008). The genetic influences also appear to be quite stable from childhood to adolescence both for a general antisocial behavior factor (Baker *et al.*, 2009) as well as narrower measures of proactive and reactive aggression (Tuvblad *et al.*, 2009).

Age of onset is often considered as a moderator of genetic effects in criminal behavior. Official statistics and victim surveys consistently show that adolescents account for a large proportion (approximately one fourth to one third) of all crimes. From self-report studies we also know that between 50 and 80 per cent of all juveniles participate in antisocial behavior at some time during childhood or adolescence. However, a small proportion of all antisocial individuals (5–7 per cent) accounts for approximately half of all antisocial acts (Loeber and Farrington, 1998; Rutter *et al.*, 1998; Vermeiren, 2003). Most of the antisocial acts committed are theft-related, and only a small proportion is aggressive and violent (Farrington and Loeber, 2000). There are also some well-established developmental patterns in antisocial behavior. For example, individuals with an early age of onset are more likely to persist in antisocial behavior (Loeber and Farrington, 2000; Robins, 1978; Simonoff *et al.*, 2004; Stouthamer-Loeber and Loeber, 2002; Tremblay *et al.*, 1994). Finally, antisocial behavior has been found to increase in early adolescence, to peak in mid-adolescence, and then to drop sharply in young adulthood (Moffitt, 1993). The fact that antisocial behavior peaks in adolescence and that age of onset is related to persistence is the starting point for a developmental taxonomy of antisocial behavior that differentiates the most deviant over the life course from those likely to show temporary difficulties during adolescence. The theory proposes that 'life-course persistent' and 'adolescent-limited' antisocial behavior differs in terms of etiology, developmental course, prognosis, and classification of behavior as pathological versus normative. Life-course persistent antisocial behavior is thought to have a neuro-developmental origin, and to begin at a very young age and continue from adolescence into adulthood. In contrast, adolescence-limited antisocial behavior is thought to be limited to adolescent years and to be more influenced by social peer pressure (Moffitt, 1993). DiLalla and Gottesman (1989) had previously suggested a similar theory, but they referred to life-course persistent as continuous antisocials, and 'adolescent-limited' antisocial behavior as transitory delinquents. They further suggested a third group called 'late bloomers', who are thought to begin their offending in adulthood (DiLalla and Gottesman, 1989). Genetic influences are generally thought to contribute more to persistent antisocial behavior, than to adolescent onset or transitory antisocial behavior (Moffitt, 2005a). Only a few behavioral genetic studies have reported findings that can be interpreted in support of these developmental theories, or at least in support of different aspects of these theories. A recent study showed that a common genetic factor was influencing antisocial behavior in males beginning at age ten and through young adulthood, hence, reflecting persistent antisocial behavior. Whereas a common shared environmental factor was found for adolescent and adult antisocial behavior, this was interpreted by the authors to reflect adolescent onset or transitory antisocial behavior (Silberg *et al.*, 2007).

Genetics of violent vs. non-violent behavior in children

Although the distinction between violent and non-violent *criminal offending* is more difficult to make in children and adolescents compared to adults, a number of studies have compared the genetic etiologies for different forms of aggressive and antisocial behavior in younger subjects. Researchers often delineate between overt, physical and possibly violent behaviors (referred to as 'aggression') and covert antisocial behavior which includes property damage and theft (referred to as 'delinquency') (Achenbach, 1991; Frick *et al.*, 1993; Loeber and Hay, 1997). Longitudinal studies have shown differences in violent and non-violent behavior, with violent and aggressive behavior generally being more stable across time, compared with non-violent and delinquent behaviors (Stanger *et al.*, 1997; Tolan and Gorman-Smith, 1998). Further support for this distinction is provided by twin studies, in that aggressive and violent behavior has been found to be highly heritable (Edelbrock *et al.*, 1995; Eley *et al.*, 1999; Ghodesian-Carpey and Baker, 1987; Hudziak *et al.*, 2003), whereas non-violent behavior shows a roughly equal influence of genes and shared environment (Bartels *et al.*, 2003; Edelbrock *et al.*, 1995; Eley *et al.*, 2003). Twin studies have also demonstrated that aggressive and violent behavior and non-violent behavior share common genetic factors and environmental influence, but there are also genetic and environmental factors unique to each type of behavior (Button *et al.*, 2004; Gelhorn *et al.*, 2006).

Peer and sibling influences: partners in crime?

Numerous studies have shown that to have antisocial peers or siblings is a strong risk factor for antisocial behavior (Farrington and Loeber, 2000; Hawkins *et al.*, 1998). In other words, antisocial individuals tend to have antisocial friends. This could be due to a selection process, but it could also be explained by an influence process. Regardless of the causal direction involved, most antisocial activities are not perpetuated by individuals acting alone, but rather are undertaken together with others. Differential association theorists argue that antisocial behavior is largely learned through personal interactions in the peer group (Sutherland and Cressey, 1978). Through interaction with others, individuals learn the values, attitudes, techniques, and motives for criminal and antisocial behavior. Peer influences have a large impact during adolescence (Lipsey and Derzon, 1998), and this is also when the nature of the peer group changes and an individual tends to spend more time with his/her peers, compared with a younger child (Rutter *et al.*, 1998). Related to this is the fact that antisocial behavior is most prevalent in adolescence. It increases in early adolescence, reaches its peak in mid-adolescence, and then largely disappears by young adulthood (Moffitt, 1993).

Regardless, peers and siblings may influence one another and the effect of such phenotypic reciprocal interaction can be investigated using a twin sample. Siblings may either imitate each other's behavior, that is, the behavior in one twin leads to the behavior in the other twin. Or they may take on opposite or competing behaviors. In other words, the behavior of one twin has an inhibitory effect on the behavior of the other twin (Carey, 1986, 1992). This type of competing or contrast interaction effect has been repeatedly found in studies investigating symptoms of attention-deficit hyperactivity disorder (ADHD) (van Beijsterveldt *et al.*, 2004; Vierikko *et al.*, 2004). However, many of these studies used parent reported data, which make it difficult to determine if the observed interaction effect is a true contrast effect or if it is due to rater bias. An imitation effect is confounded in the shared environment, and a contrast effect is confounded within dominant non-additive genetic effects (Rietveld *et al.*, 2003). However, if there is sibling interaction, variance differences between monozygotic and dizygotic twins are expected.

Several studies investigating antisocial behavior have found a positive interaction between twins, indicating that siblings sometimes co-operate and 'become partners in crime' (Carey, 1992; Rowe, 1983; Rowe *et al.*, 1992). An early study by Rowe (1983) found that genetic, as well as shared environmental influences were important in the development of adolescent antisocial and delinquent behavior. Further analyses showed however, that monozygotic twins were more likely to commit delinquent acts together, compared to dizygotic twins. It was therefore concluded that since twins may influence one another, this may partly explain the shared environmental influences. In another study, Carey (1992) investigated sibling interaction effects for antisocial behavior in a large set of Danish twins. The twins were followed through official police and court records. A modest heritability and positive sibling interaction effect was found, indicating that the combination of heritability and sibling imitation processes contribute to liability toward antisocial and criminal behavior.

GxE INTERACTIONS IN CRIMINAL BEHAVIOR

The complex interplay between genes and environment must also be considered, in addition to their main effects in criminal behavior. Genetic influences, for example, can be exacerbated through certain experiences or exposure to specific circumstances. Likewise, individuals with different genotypes may respond differently to the same environmental exposure. Conversely, some environments may serve as protective factors, such that the genetic effects on criminal outcomes are reduced or eliminated for some individuals. The dependence of genetic effects on different environments or vice versa is referred to as gene–environment interaction. Although gene–environment interactions have become of particular interest in recent research on psychopathology (Moffitt *et al.*, 2005; Rutter *et al.*, 2006), these complex effects have long been known to occur for criminal behavior.

There are a number of ways in which gene–environment interactions may be tested in genetically informative studies. The classic approach is based on analysis of variance (ANOVA) in adoption studies in which mean levels of criminal outcomes (e.g., conviction rates) are examined as a function of genetic risk (i.e., criminal background in biological parents) and environmental risk (i.e., criminal background in adoptive parents). Some of the strongest evidence for gene–environment interaction in criminal behavior comes from the early adoption studies using this approach. It has been repeatedly found that genetic predisposition for crime (e.g., crime or psychopathology in biological parents) combined with a high risk environment (i.e., adoptive home environment) leads to greater risk for criminal offending the offspring than what would be expected from the (additive) main effects of genes and environment. This synergistic effect (illustrated in Figure 1.1) has been replicated for property offending in each of the major adoption studies of criminal behavior (Bohman *et al.*, 1982; Cadoret *et al.*, 1983, 1995; Cloninger *et al.*, 1982; Crowe, 1974; Mednick *et al.*, 1984).

A similar gene–environment interaction has been reported for childhood conduct problems, using a measured environmental risk factor approach in twins. Jaffee *et al.* (2005) found that measured environmental risk (childhood maltreatment) exacerbated the genetic risk for conduct problems (based on the co-twin's conduct problems). That is, the (environmental) effect of maltreatment on the risk for conduct problems was greater among those children who had higher genetic liability for conduct disorder, compared to those who had a low genetic liability. This finding parallels the gene–environment interaction consistently reported in the early adoption studies of criminal offending, in which genetic effects were more severe in adverse environments. This gene–environment interaction can also be framed in a more positive manner, such that favorable genotypes may provide the greatest protection against problem behaviors in adverse circumstances such as maltreatment during childhood (Jaffee *et al.*, 2005).

Another major approach for studying gene–environment interactions is through the estimation of genetic *variance* (and its relative importance, i.e., heritability)

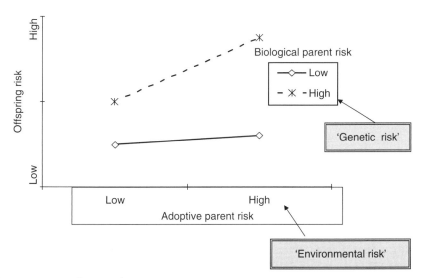

Figure 1.1   GxE interaction.

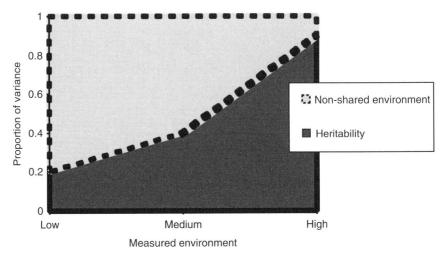

Figure 1.2   GxE Interaction: differential heritability across measured environments.

across a range of different environments. For example, genetic influences on the propensity toward criminal offending could be of lesser or greater importance for individuals raised in favorable versus impoverished surroundings, such as neighborhood or schools. Figure 1.2 illustrates this type of gene–environment interaction, whereby heritability increases across the favorability of the environment. This approach to studying gene–environment interactions does not require adoption designs, but can be made in twin studies as well.

One recent twin study using this differential heritability across environments approach found that relative importance of genetic influences on antisocial behavior in 16 to 17-year-old boys to be *larger* for more advantaged ($h^2 = 0.37$) than less advantaged ($h^2 = 0.01$) neighborhoods in Sweden (Tuvblad *et al.*, 2004). Family environmental effects, on the other hand, were of greater importance in less advantaged neighborhoods ($c^2 = 0.69$) than in more advantaged ones ($c^2 = 0.13$). Although the differences across environments were less marked for girls, the same pattern was found with greater heritability ($h^2 = 0.69$) and smaller shared environment ($c^2 = 0.06$) for more advantaged environments compared to relative effects in less advantaged neighborhoods ($h^2 = 0.61$, $c^2 = 0.16$), see Figure 1.3.

At a glance, the nature of this gene–environment interaction – with larger genetic variance in favorable environments – may seem at odds with the well-replicated finding using the ANOVA approach in adoption studies, in which larger genetic effects are evident in more adverse environments. Certainly the studies using the different approaches to study gene–environment interactions differ in the measures of antisocial behavior (i.e., criminal offending vs. the broader construct of aggression and delinquency), which might explain some of the discrepancy. More importantly, however, the two approaches for studying gene–environment interaction differ in that the differential heritability approach (e.g., Tuvblad *et al.*) focuses on *variance* of antisocial outcomes, while mean levels of deviant behavior are the focus of the ANOVAs in the adoption studies (e.g., Mednick *et al.*, 1984). What the adoption studies demonstrate is that the greatest overall *incidence* of criminal offending

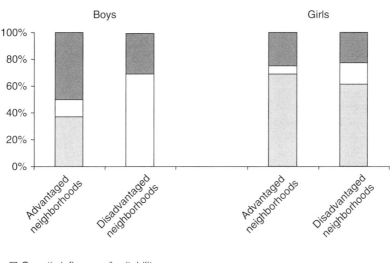

Antisocial behavior in 16–17-year-old twins

☐ Genetic influences/heritability

☐ Shared environmental influences i.e., contribute to similarity within pairs of twins

■ Non-shared environmental influences i.e., influences that make siblings dissimilar

Figure 1.3 The heritability of antisocial behavior differs with socioeconomic status. (From Tuvblad *et al.* (2006) *Journal of Child Psychology and Psychiatry*.)

occurs when both genetic and environmental adversity occur together, while the twin study findings such as those of Tuvblad *et al.* suggest that individual differences in deviant behavior are explained by genetic factors differently according to the environmental circumstances. The latter findings are consistent with Raine's (2002a) 'social push hypothesis', in which biological risk factors (which includes genetic predisposition) appear less influential (i.e., explain less variance) in individuals from adverse environments, since environmental risks *push* him or her toward antisocial behavior and biological risk factors are masked in these disadvantaged individuals. Conversely, individuals from favorable environments lack the social push, and effectively have less environmental variation, so that biological risk factors are more likely to be revealed and thus explain individual differences in deviant outcomes (see Raine, 2002b; Tuvblad *et al.*, 2004).

In spite of the well-replicated findings of both main effects for genetics and gene–environment interaction in criminal behavior, for many years both the genetic and environmental risk factors have remained anonymous. That is, the nature of the genetic influences are unspecified in the classic approach, with no information being provided about the number of genes involved, their location in the genome, or the specific alleles which contribute to the highest risk for criminal offending. Similarly, environmental risk factors as defined by adoptive parent criminal background in no way specifies the child's experiences or how these may lead to criminal offending. With advances in molecular genetics and gene identification methods, however, research is beginning to give identity to both genetic and environmental risk factors for criminal and other antisocial behavior, as discussed next.

UNPACKING THE BLACK BOXES OF GENES AND ENVIRONMENT

The holy grail in genetic research on pathological behavior in general is twofold: (1) to identify specific allelic variations that explain observable phenotypic variation or an increase in the risk for deviant outcomes, and (2) to understand the conditions under which such high risk alleles have the greatest or least effect. With the rapid technological developments in molecular genetics and methods for genotyping large groups of individuals using hundreds of DNA markers, researchers in the social sciences are becoming immersed in the search for the holy grail in both normal and abnormal trait variation in a wide array of behaviors. Although to date there are no genome wide studies of criminal behavior *per se*, there are a handful of studies that have specifically focused on antisocial behavior (including criminal offending) and several others studying many correlates of criminal outcomes. In spite of the surge of interest in 'gene identification' studies of human behavior, this research is still in its infancy, particularly with regard to studies of antisocial behavior and especially criminal offending. The few studies to date are reviewed here.

Other attempts to unpack both the genetic and environmental black boxes in antisocial behavior involve the study of measured risk factors, which may include both biological and social variables which predict antisocial outcomes. The extent to which these risk factor–antisocial behavior outcomes may be genetically and environmentally mediated can be understood in the context of genetically informative designs, such as twin and adoption studies, even when DNA markers are not studied. The risk factor approach is tantamount to studying endophenotypes, which are other measurable variables with significant genetic covariation with antisocial outcomes. An endophenotype is a type of biomarker, but with more strict criteria. An endophenotype has to be associated with the outcome in the population, it has to be heritable, and to be found in an individual regardless of the outcome it manifested. Also, an endophenotype is expected to be found in non-affected family members at a higher rate than in the general population (Gottesman and Gould, 2003). Genetically informative studies of risk factors for criminal offending are thus also reviewed following the review of gene identification studies.

Gene identification

In spite of the overwhelming evidence for genetic influences in criminal and other antisocial behaviors, research attempting to identify specific genes that increase risk for criminal offending and the biochemical pathways between genes and behavior is still relatively rare. The first study to demonstrate a link between a specific genotype and antisocial behavior (Brunner *et al.*, 1993) investigated a large, multigeneration Dutch family that had several members (particularly males) who were prone to violent, aggressive, and impulsive behavior, with histories of fighting, arson, attempted rape, and exhibitionism. Through analyses of DNA samples in this large pedigree, it was shown that the aggressive males shared a mutant form of the gene that codes for the enzyme MAO-A (monoamine oxidase A). MAO-A breaks down neurotransmitters (including serotonin, noradrenaline, and dopamine) which are known to be important in impulsive behaviors and reward dependence. The mutant alleles inherited by the aggressive and antisocial males, however, resulted in deficient production of the MAO-A enzyme, which in turn led to large quantities in the blood and ineffective functioning of the neurotransmitters necessary for proper impulse control and reward pathways in the brain (Brunner *et al.*, 1993). This finding of increased aggression being associated with MAO deficiency produced by a genetic mutation in the MAO-A allele coincides with animal research using knockout strains of mice (Shih, 2004), where the same finding has been well-replicated. Moreover, associations between aggression with neurotransmitters serotonin, dopamine, and noradrenaline have been found in both humans and animals (Arce and Santisteban, 2006). Although the main effects of the MAO-A mutation have not replicated yet in any other large human pedigrees, this genetic defect remains the first such link to aggressive behavior in humans.

It has also been suggested that environmental factors may moderate the effects of the MAO-A mutations on aggression, which one could easily predict given the well-replicated finding of gene–environment interactions in criminal behavior in adults and conduct problems and antisocial behavior in youth. One highly cited finding illustrates such a gene–environment interaction in antisocial behavior using a meas- ured gene/measured environment approach (Caspi *et al.*, 2002). A functional polymorphism in the MAO-A gene was found to increase the risk for conduct prob- lems (including violence) in adolescent males, but only in conjunction with early childhood maltreatment. More specifically, maltreated boys (i.e., with adverse envi- ronmental) who had the adverse genotype conferring MAO deficiency (due to inheritance of the mutant allele) were more likely to develop conduct disorder as a youth, and antisocial personality disorder and violent criminal behavior as adults (see Figure 1.4). The fact that the main effect of the MAO-A mutation as found in Brunner *et al.* (1993) was not found in the Caspi *et al.* (2002) study underscores the

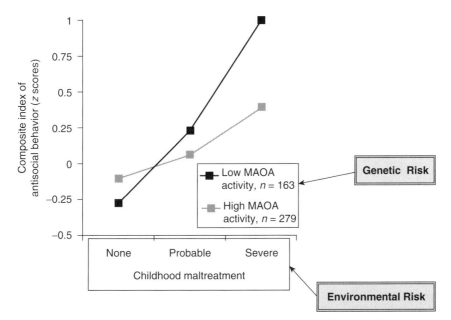

Figure 1.4   Genotype (MAO-A) x environment (maltreatment) interaction in antisocial behavior. (From Caspi *et al.* (2002) *Science.*)

importance of investigating specific genetic effects under a variety of environmental circumstances in order to fully understand the risk for criminal offending and other antisocial behavior. The Caspi *et al.* (2002) finding is particularly intriguing since it was one of the first studies to illustrate the well-replicated GxE interaction in criminal behavior using a measured gene/measured environment approach. To date, there has only been a few replications of this interesting finding (Foley *et al.*, 2004; Kim-Cohen *et al.*, 2006; Nilsson *et al.*, 2006) and one published failure to replicate (Haberstick *et al.*, 2005). For instance, Kim-Cohen and colleagues (2006) found that the MAOA polymorphism moderated the development of psychopathology after exposure to physical abuse in a sample of 975 seven-year-old boys. This finding was extended to the maltreatment experience closer in time compared with previous work by Caspi *et al.* (2002), and therefore the possibility of a spurious finding by accounting for passive and evocative gene–environment correlation could be ruled out. It should be mentioned that passive gene–environment correlation refers to the association between the genotype a child inherits from her parents and the environment in which the child is raised, and evocative gene–environment correlation occurs when an individual's (heritable) behavior evokes an environmental response. Moreover, the authors also conducted a meta-analysis. Across five included studies (Caspi *et al.*, 2002; Foley *et al.*, 2004; Haberstick *et al.*, 2005; Kim-Cohen *et al.*, 2006; Nilsson *et al.*, 2006) the adverse mental health problems were greatest for maltreated boys with the genotype conferring low MAOA activity. It was concluded that these findings provide strong evidence suggesting that the MAOA gene influences vulnerability to environmental stress, and that this biological process can be initiated early in life. However, these findings need to be replicated in samples including females.

A gene–environment interaction has also been identified for variation in the *age of onset* for criminal offending using a measured gene/measured environment approach. Based on data from the National Longitudinal Study of Adolescent Health (AdHealth), DeLisi *et al.* (2008) found that polymorphisms in genes related to the neurotransmitter dopamine were associated with age of first police contact and arrests, but only for youth from *low risk* family environments. More specifically, among those adolescents with a history of criminal offending, those at greatest risk for later onset were those with the A1 allelic form of the DRD2 gene, in combination with favorable home environments as defined by maternal attachment, involvement, and engagement (DeLisi *et al.*, 2008). It is important to emphasize that the DeLisi *et al.* (2008) finding involves the age of onset of first police contact, and not the overall risk for offending vs. not offending. However, different forms of the DRD2 allele have demonstrated associations with criminal victimization (Beaver *et al.*, 2007) and age of first sexual intercourse (Miller *et al.*, 1999), as well as normal personality variation (Munafò *et al.*, 2003). Other studies have also found gene–gene interactions between DRD2 and DRD4 in predicting conduct disorder in childhood and criminal offending in adults (Beaver *et al.*, 2007). Still, the finding of enhanced risk for later onset criminal offending as a function of high genetic risk combined with low environmental risk is contrary to predictions from other developmental models of antisocial behavior. Both Moffitt (2005) and Lahey *et al.* (1999) have suggested that early-onset forms should be more pervasive over time and more influenced by genetic factors than late-onset, transient forms of delinquency, yet the converse pattern was found by DeLisi *et al.* (2008). Nonetheless, the DeLisi *et al.* (2008) findings are particularly interesting in that they also demonstrate a GxE interaction in criminal offending using specific genetic markers and well-defined measures of the environment.

Further, several behaviors and disorders are associated with antisocial and criminal behavior; these include, for example, attention deficit hyperactivity disorder (ADHD) and drug and alcohol abuse. A few genes related to some of these associated behaviors and disorders have been identified. Hence, some of these genes could either be considered as candidate genes for antisocial and criminal behavior or as predictors. A recent study found evidence of linkage to a region of chromosome 7, which appears to contain genes conferring risk to externalizing behaviors, including alcohol, drug dependence, conduct disorder, antisocial personality disorder, novelty and sensation seeking (Dick *et al.*, 2008). It may be that a broader spectrum of externalizing behaviors and disorders should be studied in order to identify susceptibility genes. As previously mentioned, ADHD often co-occurs with antisocial and criminal behavior (Hechtman, 1999) and longitudinal studies show that ADHD leads to antisocial behavior not the other way around (Kutcher *et al.*, 2004). Using our longitudinal sample we were able to show that the covariation between antisocial behavior and ADHD is in part explained by common genes (Tuvblad *et al.*, 2009). Related to this, a recent study by Caspi and colleagues found evidence that the COMT valine/methionine polymorphism at codon 158 (COMT Val158Met) was associated with phenotypic variation among children with ADHD. Valine/valine homozygotes also had more symptoms of conduct disorder, were more aggressive, and were more likely to be convicted of criminal offenses. However, COMT was not a susceptibility gene for aggression and antisocial behavior, rather COMT influenced the phenotypic variation in ADHD and predicted which children would engage in antisocial behavior (Caspi *et al.*, 2008).

Risk factors (endophenotypes) for criminal behavior

Empirical research has established a number of risk factors that are associated with the risk for engaging in criminal behavior. These factors include broad biological and social risk factors (e.g., low resting heart rate) (Ortiz and Raine, 2004); prenatal factors (e.g., fetal exposure to alcohol, smoking and/or malnutrition) (Raine, 2002a); personality factors (e.g., impulsivity, callous and unemotional traits, stimulation-seeking, fearlessness) (Lahey *et al.*, 2003; Raine, 2002a; Viding *et al.*, 2005); family factors (e.g., parental criminality, poor child rearing practices, parental substance use, low socioeconomic status, maltreatment) (Caspi *et al.*, 2002; Farrington *et al.*, 1996; Lipsey and Derzon, 1998; Loeber and Dishion, 1983); school related factors (e.g., poor academic performance, weak bonding to school) (Hawkins *et al.*, 1998; Loeber and Farrington, 2000); peer factors (e.g., delinquent peers and siblings, gang membership, peer rejection) (Farrington and Loeber, 2000); and contextual factors (e.g., neighborhood poverty, availability of weapons) (Beyers *et al.*, 2001; Brooks-Gunn *et al.*, 1993; Sampson *et al.*, 1997).

Even though it is well-known which risk factors are related to criminal behavior, less is known about the underlying mechanisms of how these factors are related to the development of criminal behavior. This has led several researchers to conclude that the study of criminal behavior is 'stuck in the risk factor stage' (Hinshaw, 2002; Moffitt, 2005b; Rutter, 2003). One way to further examine how some of these factors are associated with antisocial behavior is to use a genetic informative design. For example, the family concentration of criminal behavior (Putkonen *et al.*, 2007) may be explained by common genetic influences across generations, but it may also be due to an environmental mediation, or a combination of both. Behavior genetic studies may be helpful here; by using twin and family studies it is possible to disentangle such effects. Another important area where behavior genetic research can be useful is in the field of endophenotypes (Moffitt, 2005a). Research examining the relationship between endophenotypes and criminal behavior may increase the understanding of the underlying genetic mechanism in antisocial behavior. In our own longitudinal twin study of antisocial behavior we examined a particularly robust endophenotype for antisocial behavior: resting heart rate. The results showed that the association between low resting heart rate and antisocial behavior was significantly and entirely explained by common genetic factors, although the heritable component of heart rate explained only a small portion (1–4 per cent) of the substantial genetic variance in antisocial behavior. Despite the effect size being small, children with low resting heart rate appear to be genetically predisposed towards externalizing behavior problems as early as age 9 years old (Baker *et al.*, 2009).

SUMMARY AND FUTURE DIRECTIONS

There is no question that genetic influences are important to criminal and other forms of antisocial behavior, with twin and adoption studies convincingly showing strong heritability for both law breaking offenses and various forms of aggression. It appears, however, that the magnitude and nature of genetic effects may well vary across types of criminal offending in adults, with crimes against property showing greater heritability compared to violent crimes against persons. Conversely, aggressive behaviors (which generally involve actions against others) in children and adolescents tend to show stronger genetic effects than delinquent behaviors (which involve actions against property). The relative importance of genes and environment do thus clearly vary across both age as well as the type of antisocial behavior. Moreover, the exact nature of these genetic influences is largely unspecified in twin and adoption studies, as is the specific ways in which environmental factors influence criminal and other antisocial outcomes.

Two avenues of research show promise for elucidating these specific genes and their pathways leading to crime and aggression. First, molecular genetic studies have the potential to identify specific gene variants that increase risk for criminal offending, aggressive behavior, and externalizing behavior disorders. Some polymorphisms, such as mutations in the MAO-A gene, have already shown relationships to antisocial behavior, including violence, across several studies. Second, risk factor research enables identification of measurable biological variables that may have genetic overlap with criminal behavior. However, even well-known and highly heritable risk factors such as resting heart rate, for example, are being shown to explain only very small portions of the large genetic effects in antisocial behavior. Future studies may require comprehensive investigations of many measured risk factors and specific genetic markers in order to explain these genetic effects more extensively.

One of the most important findings to emerge in genetic research on criminal behavior is the fact that the magnitude of genetic effects depends on social circumstances and other environmental factors. All major adoption studies of criminal behavior have shown that genetic risk is amplified in the presence of adverse environmental factors – e.g., defined as measurable, specific social variables such as childhood maltreatment, or as something as general as the presence of a convicted adoptive parent in the home. Viewed differently, the substantial genetic risk for criminal offending may be ameliorated in low risk environments. The nature of these environmentally based protective factors need greater attention in future genetic research on crime and aggression.

The fact that genetic predispositions exist for criminal offending does in no way imply that environmental factors are unimportant, nor that effective treatment and prevention programs cannot be developed and implemented to reduce the chances that an individual will engage in law-breaking or other antisocial behaviors. Heritability estimates for criminal behavior are only moderate at best, according to the Rhee and Waldman (2002) meta-analysis, with that of environmental influences for criminal outcomes being equally strong. Yet, even for disorders completely determined by genetic mutations, such as PKU, environmental interventions such as dietary modifications can ameliorate the adverse effects on cognitive and behavioral outcomes. It is reasonable to assume that detailed understanding of the genetically-based mechanisms underlying risk for criminal behavior could lead to effective social interventions and prevention programs. Given the well-replicated GxE interaction found in behavior genetic studies of criminal behavior, it is important to consider the possibility that certain treatments and interventions may have varying effects for different individuals based on their genetic inheritance.

REFERENCES

Achenbach, T. M. (1991). *Manual for the Child Behavior Checklist/4-18 and 1991 Profile*. Burlington, VT: University of Vermont Department of Psychiatry.

Arce, E. and Santisteban, C. (2006). Impulsivity: a review. *Psicothema* 18(2): 213–220.

Baker, L. A., Mack, W., Moffitt, T. E. and Medncik, S. A. (1989). Sex differences in property crime in a Danish adoption cohort. *Behavior Genetics* 19: 355–370.

Baker, L. A., Jacobson, K. C., Raine, A., Lozano, D. I. and Bezdjian, S. (2007). Genetic and environmental bases of childhood antisocial behavior: A multi-informant twin study. *Journal of Abnormal Psychology* 116(2): 219–235.

Baker, L. A., Raine, A., Liu, J.-H., and Jacobson, K. C. (2008). Genetic and environmental influences in reactive and proactive aggression in children. *Journal of Child Abnormal Psychology* 36: 1265–1278.

Baker, L. A., Tuvblad, C., Reynolds, C., Zheng, M. and Raine, A. (2009). Resting heart rate and the development of antisocial behavior from age 9–14: Genetic and environmental influences. *Development and Psychopathology* 21: 939–960.

Bartels, M., Hudziak, J. J., van den Oord, E. J. C. G., van Beijsterveldt, C. E. M., Rietveld, M. J. H. and Boomsma, D. (2003). Co-occurence of aggressive behavior and rule-breaking behavior at age 12: multi-rater analyses. *Behavior Genetics* 33: 607–621.

Beaver, K. M., Wright, J. P., Delisi, M., Daigle, L. E., Swatt, M. L. and Gibson, C. L. (2007). Evidence of a gene x environment interaction in the creation of victimization: results from a longitudinal sample of adolescents. *International Journal of Offender Therapy and Comparitive Criminology* 51(6): 620–645.

Beyers, J. M., Loeber, R., Wikström, P.-O. H. and Stouthamer-Loeber, M. (2001). What predicts adolescent violence in better-off neighbourhoods? *Journal of Abnormal Child Psychology* 29(5): 379–381.

Bohman, M., Cloninger, C. R., Sigvardsson, S. and von Knorring, A.-L. (1982). Predisposition to petty criminality in Swedish adoptees. *Archives of General Psychiatry* 39: 1233–1241.

Brooks-Gunn, J., Duncan, G., Klebanov, P. K. and Sealand, N. (1993). Do neighbourhoods influence child and adolescent development? *American Journal of Sociology* 99: 353–395.

Brunner, H. G., Nelen, M., Breakefield, X. O., Ropers, H. H. and van Oost, B. A. (1993). Abnormal behavior associated with a point mutation in the structural gene for monoamine oxidase A. *Science* 262(5133): 578–580.

Button, T. M. M., Scourfield, J., Martin, N. and McGuffin, P. (2004). Do aggressive and non-aggressive antisocial behaviors in adolescents result from the same genetic and environmental effects? *American Journal of Medical Genetics Part B (Neuropsychiatric Genetics)* 129 B: 59–63.

Cadoret, R. J., Cain, C. A. and Crowe, R. R. (1983). Evidence for gene–environment interaction in the development of adolescent antisocial behavior. *Behavior Genetics* 13: 301–310.

Cadoret, R. J., Yates, W. R., Troughton, E., Woodworth, G. and Stewart, M. A. (1995). Genetic–environmental interaction in the genesis of aggressivity and conduct disorders. *Archives of General Psychiatry* 52(11): 916–924.

Carey, G. (1986). Sibling imitation and contrast effects. *Behavior Genetics* 16: 319–341.

Carey, G. (1992). Twin imitation for antisocial behavior: implications for genetic and family environment research. *Journal of Abnormal Psychology* 101(1): 18–25.

Caspi, A., McClay, J., Moffitt, T. E., Mill, J., Martin, J., Craig, I. W., Taylor, A. and Poulton, R. (2002). Role of genotype in the cycle of violence in maltreated children. *Science* 297(5582): 851–854.

Caspi, A., Langley, K., Milne, B., Moffitt, T. E., O'Donovan, M., Owen, M. J., Polo Tomas, M., Poulton, R., Rutter, M., Taylor, A., Williams, B. and Thapar, A. (2008). A replicated molecular genetic basis for subtyping antisocial behavior in children with attention-deficit/hyperactivity disorder. *Archives of General Psychiatry* 65(2): 203–210.

Cloninger, C. R. and Gottesman, I. I. (1987). Genetic and environmental factors in antisocial behavior disorders. *The Causes of Crime: New Biological Approaches* (pp. 96–100).

Cloninger, C. R., Sigvardsson, S., Bohman, M. and von Knorring, A. L. (1982). Predisposition to petty criminality in Swedish adoptees. II. Cross-fostering analysis of gene–environment interaction. *Archives of General Psychiatry* 39: 1242–1247.

Crowe, R. R. (1974). An adoption study of antisocial personality. *Archives of General Psychiatry* 31: 785–791.

DeLisi, M., Beaver, K. M., Wright, J. P. and Vaughn, M. G. (2008). The etiology of criminal onset: the enduring salience of nature and nurture. *Journal of Criminal Justice* 36: 217–223.

Dick, D. M., Aliev, F., Wang, J. C., Grucza, R. A., Schuckit, M., Kuperman, S., Kramer, J., Hinrichs, A., Bertelsen, S., Budde, J. P., Hesselbrock, V., Porjesz, B., Edenberg, H. J., Bierut, L. J. and Goate, A. (2008). Using dimensional models of externalizing psychopathology to aid in gene identification. *Archives of General Psychiatry* 65(3): 310–318.

DiLalla, L. F. and Gottesman, I. (1989). Heterogeneity of causes for delinquency and criminality: Lifespan perspectives. *Development and Psychopathology* 1: 339–349.

Edelbrock, C., Rende, R., Plomin, R. and Thompson, L. A. (1995). A twin study of competence and problem behavior in childhood and early adolescence. *Journal of Child Psychology and Psychiatry* 36(5): 775–785.

Eley, T. C., Lichtenstein, P. and Stevenson, J. (1999). Sex differences in the etiology of aggressive and nonaggressive antisocial behavior: results from two twin studies. *Child Development* 70(1): 155–168.

Eley, T. C., Lichtenstein, P. and Moffitt, T. E. (2003). A longitudinal behavioral genetic analysis of the etiology of aggressive and non-aggressive antisocial behavior. *Development and Psychopathology* 15(2): 383–402.

Farrington, D. P. and Loeber, R. (2000). Epidemiology of juvenile violence. *Child and Adolescent Psychiatric Clinics of North America* 9(4): 733–748.

Farrington, D. P., Barnes, G. C. and Lambert, S. (1996). The concentration of offending in families. *Legal and Criminological Psychology* 1: 47–63.

Foley, D. L., Eaves, L., Wormley, B., Silberg, J., Maes, H., Kuhn, J. and Riley, B. (2004). Childhood adversity, monoamine oxidase a genotype, and risk for conduct disorder. *Archives of General Psychiatry* 61: 738–744.

Frick, P. J., Lahey, B. B., Loeber, R., Tannenbaum, L., Van Horn, Y., Christ, M. A. G., Hart, E. A. and Hanson, K. (1993). Oppositional defiant disorder and conduct disorder: A meta-analytic review of factor analyses and cross-validation in a clinic sample. *Clinical Psychology Review* 13(4): 319–340.

Gelhorn, H. L., Stallings, M. C., Young, S. E., Corely, R. P., Rhee, S. H., Hopfer, C. and Hewitt, J. K. (2006). Common and specific genetic influences on agressive and nonaggressive conduct disorder domains. *Journal of American Academy of Child and Adolescent Psychiatry* 45(5): 570–577.

Ghodesian-Carpey, J. and Baker, L. A. (1987). Genetic and environmental influences on aggression in 4- to 7-year-old twins. *Aggressive Behavior* 13: 173–186.

Gottesman, I. I. and Gould, T. D. (2003). The endophenotype concept in psychiatry: etymology and strategic intentions. *American Journal of Psychiatry* 1160: 636–645.

Haberstick, B. C., Lessem, J. M., Hopfer, C. J., Smolen, A., Ehringer, M. A., Timberlake, D. and Hewitt, J. K. (2005). Monoamine oxidase A (MAOA) and antisocial behaviors in the presence of childhood and adolescent maltreatment. *American Journal of Medical Genetics Part B (Neuropsychiatric Genetics)* 135B(1): 59–64.

Hawkins, J. D., Herrenkohl, T., Farrington, D. P., Brewer, D., Catalano, R. F. and Harachi, T. W. (1998). A review of predictors of youth violence. In Loeber, R. and Farrington, D.P. (eds), *Serious and Violent Juvenile Offenders: Risk Factors and Successful Interventions* (pp. 106–146). Sage CA: Thousands Oaks.

Hechtman, L. (1999). Predictors of long-term outcome in children with attention-deficit/hyperactivity disorder. *Pediatric Clinics of North America* 46(5): 1039–1052.

Hinshaw, S. P. (2002). Intervention research, theoretical mechanisms, and causal processes related to externalizing behavior patterns. *Development and Psychopathology* 14: 789–818.

Hudziak, J. J., van Beijsterveldt, C. E. M., Bartels, M., Rietveld, M. J. H., Rettew, D. C., Derks, E. M. and Boomsma, D. (2003). Individual differences in aggression: Genetic analyses by age, gender, and informant in 3-, 7-, and 10-year-old Dutch twins. *Behavior Genetics* 33(5): 575–589.

Jaffee, S. R., Caspi, A., Moffitt, T. E., Dodge, K. A., Rutter, M., Taylor, A. and Tully, L. A. (2005). Nature X nurture: genetic vulnerabilities interact with physical maltreatment to promote conduct problems. *Development and Psychopathology* 17(1): 67–84.

Junger-Tas, J., Terlouw, G.-J. and Klein, M. W. (1994). *Delinquent Behavior Among Young People in the Western World.* Amsterdam: Kugler Publications.

Kim-Cohen, J., Caspi, A., Taylor, A., Williams, B., Newcombe, R., Craig, I. W. and Moffitt, T. E. (2006). MAOA, maltreatment, and gene–environment interaction predicting children's mental health: new evidence and a meta-analysis. *Molecular Psychiatry*, 1–11.

Kutcher, S., Aman, M., Brooks, S. J., Buitelaar, J., van Daalen, E., Fegert, J., Findling, R. L., Fisman, S., Greenhill, L. L., Huss, M., Kusumakar, V., Pine, D., Taylor, E. and Tyano, S. (2004). International consensus statement on attention-deficit/hyperactivity disorder (ADHD) and disruptive behaviour disorders (DBDs): clinical implications and treatment practice suggestions. *European Neuropsychopharmacology* 14(1): 11–28.

Lahey, B. B., Waldman, I. D., and McBurnett, K. (1999). The development of antisocial behavior: An integrative causal model. *Journal of Child Psychology and Psychiatry*, 40(5): 669–682.

Lahey, B. B., Moffitt, T. E. and Caspi, A. (eds), (2003). *Causes of Conduct Disorder and Juvenile Delinquency.* New York: Guilford Press.

Lipsey, M. W. and Derzon, J. H. (1998). Predictors of violence or serious delinquency in adolescence and early adulthood. In Loeber, R. and Farrington, D. P. (eds), *Serious and Violent Juvenile Offenders* (pp. 86–105). Sage CA: Thousand Oaks.

Loeber, R. and Dishion, T. J. (1983). Early predictors of male adolescent delinquency: A review. *Psychological Bulletin* 94: 68–99.

Loeber, R. and Farrington, D. P. (1998). *Serious and Vilolent Juvenile Offenders. Risk Factors and Successful Interventions.* Thousands Oaks, California: SAGE Publications, Inc.

Loeber, R. and Farrington, D. P. (2000). Young children who commit crime: Epidemiology, development, origins, risk factors, early interventions, and policy implications. *Developmental Psychology* 12: 737–762.

Loeber, R. and Hay, D. (1997). Key issues in the development of aggression and violence from childhood to early adulthood. *Annual Review of Psychology* 48: 371–410.

Mednick, S. A., Gabrielli, W. F. and Hutchings, B. (1984). Genetic influence in criminal convictions: evidence from an adoption cohort. *Science* 224: 891–894.

Miller, W. B., Pasta, D. J., MacMurray, J., Chiu, C., Wu, H. and Comings, D. E. (1999). Dopamine receptor genes are associated with age at first sexual intercourse. *Journal of Biosocial Science* 31(1): 43–54.

Moffitt, T. E. (1993). Adolescence-limited and life-course-persistent antisocial behavior: a developmental taxonomy. *Psychological Review* 100(4): 674–701.

Moffitt, T. E. (2005a). Genetic and environmental influences on antisocial behaviors: evidence from behavioral-genetic research. *Advances in Genetics* 55: 41–99.

Moffitt, T. E. (2005b). The new look of behavioral genetics in developmental psychopathology: gene–environment interplay in antisocial behaviors. *Psychological Bulletin* 131(4): 533–554.

Moffitt, T. E., Caspi, A., Rutter, M. and Silva, P. (2001). *Sex Differnces in Antisocial Behaviour: Conduct Disorder, Delinquency and Violence in the Dunedin Longitudinal Study*. Cambridge: Cambridge University Press.

Moffitt, T. E., Caspi, A. and Rutter, M. (2005). Strategy for investigating interactions between measured genes and measured environments. *Archives of General Psychiatry* 62(5): 473–481.

Munafò, M. R., Clark, T. G., Moore, L. R., Payne, E. R. W. and Flint, J. (2003). Genetic polymorphisms and personality in healthy adults: a systematic review and meta-analysis. *Molecular Psychiatry* 8(5): 471–484.

Nilsson, K. W., Sjöberg, R. L., Damberg, M., Leppert, J., Ohrvik, J., Alm, P. O., Lindström, L. and Oreland, L. (2006). Role of monoamine oxidase A genotype and psychosocial factors in male adolescent criminal activity. *Molecular Psychiatry* 10(11): 903–913.

Ortiz, J. and Raine, A. (2004). Heart rate level and antisocial behavior in children and adolescents: A meta-analysis. *Journal of American Academy of Child and Adolescent Psychiatry* 43(2): 154–162.

Putkonen, A., Ryynänen, O. P., Eronen, M. and Tiihonen, J. (2007). Transmission of violent offending and crime across three generations. *Social Psychiatry and Psychiatric Epidemiology* 42(2): 94–99.

Raine, A. (2002a). Annotation: The role of prefrontal deficits, low autonomic arousal, and early health factors in the developmetn of antisocial and aggressive behavior in children. *Journal of Child Psychology and Psychiatry* 43(4): 417–434.

Raine, A. (2002b). Biosocial studies of antisocial and violent behavior in children and adults: a review. *Journal of Abnormal Child Psychology* 30(4): 311–326.

Rhee, S. H. and Waldman, I. D. (2002). Genetic and environmental influences on antisocial behavior: a meta-analysis of twin and adoption studies. *Psychological Bulletin* 128: 490–529.

Rietveld, M. J., Hudziak, J. J., Bartels, M., van Beijsterveldt, C. E. and Boomsma, D. I. (2003). Heritability of attention problems in children: I. cross-sectional results from a study of twins, age 3–12 years. *American Journal of Medical Genetics Part B (Neuropsychiatric Genetics)* 117(1): 102–113.

Robins, L. (1978). Sturdy childhood predictors of adult antisocial behaviour: replications from longitudinal studies. *Psychological Medicine* 8: 611–622.

Rowe, D. C. (1983). Biometrical genetic models of self-reported delinquent behavior: a twin study. *Behavior Genetics* 13(5): 473–489.

Rowe, D. C., Rodgers, J. L. and Meseck-Bushey, S. (1992). Sibling delinquency and the family environment: shared and unshared influences. *Child Development* 63(1): 59–67.

Rutter, M. (2003). Crucial paths from risk indicator to causal mechanism. In Lahey, B.B., Moffitt, T.E. and Caspi, A. (eds), *Causes of Conduct Disorder and Juvenile Delinquency*. New York: The Guilford University Press.

Rutter, M., Caspi, A. and Moffitt, T. E. (2003). Using sex differences in psychopathology to study causal mechanisms: unifying issues and research strategies. *Journal of Child Psychology and Psychiatry* 44(8): 1092–1115.

Rutter, M., Giller, H. and Hagell, A. (1998). *Antisocial Behavior by Young People.* Cambridge, UK: Cambridge University Press.

Rutter, M., Moffitt, T. E. and Caspi, A. (2006). Gene–environment interplay and psychopathology: Multiple varieties but real effects. *Journal of Child Psychology and Psychiatry* 47(3/4).

Sampson, R. J., Raudenbush, S. W. and Earls, F. (1997). Neighbourhoods and violent crime: A multilevel study of collective efficacy. *Science* 277: 918–924.

Shih, J. C. (2004). Cloning, after cloning, knock-out mice, and physiological functions of MAO A and B. *Neurotoxicology* 25(1–2): 21–30.

Sigvardsson, S., Cloninger, C. R., Bohman, M. and von Knorring, A. L. (1982). Predisposition to petty criminality in Swedish adoptees. III. Sex differences and validation of the male typology. *Archives of General Psychiatry* 39(11): 1248–1253.

Silberg, J. L., Rutter, M., Tracy, K., Maes, H. H. and Eaves, L. (2007). Etiological heterogeneity in the development of antisocial behavior: the Virginia Twin Study of Adolescent Behavioral Development and the Young Adult Follow-Up. *Psychological Medicine* 37(8): 1193–1202.

Simonoff, E., Elander, J., Homshaw, J., Pickles, A., Murray, R. and Rutter, M. (2004). Predictors of antisocial personality. *British Journal of Psychiatry* 184: 118–127.

Smith, D. A. and Visher, C. A. (1980). Sex and involvement in deviance/crime: A quantitativereview of the empirical literature. *American Sociological Review* 45: 691–701.

Stanger, C., Achenbach, T. M. and Verhulst, F. C. (1997). Accelerated longitudinal comparisons of aggressive versus delinquent syndromes. *Development and Psychopathology* 9: 43–58.

Stouthamer-Loeber, M. and Loeber, M. (2002). Lost opportunities for intervention: undetected markers for the development of serious juvenile delinquency. *Criminal Behaviour and Mental Health* 12: 69–82.

Sutherland, E. H. and Cressey, D. R. (1978). *Criminology.* Philadelphia: J. B. Lippincott.

Tolan, P. H. and Gorman-Smith, D. (1998). Development of serious and violent offending careers. In Loeber, R. and Farrington, D. P. (eds), *Serious and Violent Juvenile Offenders. Risk Factors and Successful Interventions* (pp. 68–85). SAGE Publications.

Torgersen, S., Skre, I., Onstad, S., Edvardsen, J. and Kringlen, E. (1993). The psychometric–genetic structure of *DSM–III–R* personality disorder criteria. *Journal of Personality Disorders* 7: 196–213.

Tremblay, R. E., Pihl, R. O., Vitaro, F. and Dobkin, P. L. (1994). Predicting early onset of male antisocial behavior from preschool behavior. *Archives of General Psychiatry* 51: 732–739.

Tuvblad, C., Grann, M. and Lichtenstein, P. (2004). Heritability for adolescent antisocial behavior differs with socioeconomic status: Gene–environment interaction. *Behavior Genetics* 34(6): 662.

Tuvblad, C., Raine, A., Zheng, M. and Baker, L. A. (2009). The genetic and environmental stability differs in reactive and proactive aggression. *Aggressive Behavior* 35(6): 437–452.

Tuvblad, C., Zheng, M., Raine, A. and Baker, L. A. (2009). A common genetic factor explains the covariation among ADHD ODD and CD symptoms in 9–10-year-old boys and girls. *Journal of Abnormal Child Psychology* 37: 153–167.

van Beijsterveldt, C. E. M., Verhulst, F. C., Molenaar, P. C. M. and Boomsma, D. (2004). The genetic basis of problem behavior in 5-year-old Dutch twin pairs. *Behavior Genetics* 34(3): 229–242.

Van Dusen, K. T., Mednick, S. A. and Gabrielli, W. (1983). Social class and crime in an adoption cohort. In Van Dusen, K. T. and Mednick, S. A. (eds), *Prospective Studies of Crime and Delinquency.* Hingham, Mass.: Kluwer-Nijhoff.

Vermeiren, R. (2003). Psychopathology and delinquency in adolescents: a descriptive and developmental perspective. *Clinical Psychology Review* 23(2): 277–318.

Viding, E., Blair, J. R., Moffitt, T. E. and Plomin, R. (2005). Evidence of substantial genetic risk for psychopathy in 7-year-olds. *Journal of Child Psychology and Psychiatry* 46(6): 592–597.

Vierikko, E., Pulkkinen, L., Kaprio, J. and Rose, R. J. (2004). Genetic and environmental influences on the relationship between aggression and hyperactivity-impulsivity as rated by teachers and parents. *Twin Research and Human Genetics* 7(3): 261–274.

2

Individual Differences and Offending

Darrick Jolliffe and David P. Farrington

The importance that criminologists have placed on individual differences in the explanation of criminal behaviour has varied throughout the history of the discipline. Theoretical viewpoints have evolved from placing the causes of crime wholly within the individual (e.g., early biological positivism), to viewing the individual as merely a conduit through which larger social or environmental forces exert their action (e.g., conflict theories). However, as the methodological sophistication of research examining the causes and correlates of offending has increased these two extreme views have been moderated. Presently the most influential theories of criminal behaviour acknowledge that both the individual and the environment have a role to play in understanding crime (e.g., Clarke and Cornish, 1985; Farrington, 2005). Furthermore, there may be interactions between types of individuals and types of environments.

Two key research findings which have been replicated in numerous studies make the individual aspect of this individual/environment equation essential to understanding the development of offending. First, research has clearly demonstrated that individuals differ in their potential to commit criminal and antisocial acts given a particular opportunity, situation or victim (Farrington, 2009). As crime is a socially and legally defined concept any potential to commit crime is probably part of a broader potential to commit antisocial acts, but this chapter will focus on crime.[1] Second, a great deal of criminal career research demonstrates that the relative ordering of individuals on this potential is remarkably stable over time even though the absolute level of offending and the types of offending vary with age. That is, individuals who tend to be 'worst' at one age also tend to be 'worst' at later ages (Farrington, 1998).

It is important to distinguish between descriptions of criminal potential, the results of criminal potential and the likely causes of criminal potential. Terms such as antisocial, aggressive, or hostile seem essentially to refer to people with high criminal potential, while behavioural variables such as truanting, physical fighting, and oppositional behaviour as well as delinquency and offending seem to be the outcomes or behavioural manifestations of criminal potential. Constructs such as low guilt, weak conscience, low self-control, high impulsivity, emotional coldness, callousness, low empathy, fearlessness, egocentricity (self-centredness), poor conditionability, a poor ability to delay gratification, and a poor ability to manipulate abstract concepts seem more likely to be causes of high criminal potential. Obviously, it is important to establish the key underlying constructs that are linked to individual differences in offending behavior. For ease of exposition, this section will focus on criminal potential.

Long-term between-individual differences in criminal potential (intended to explain why some people are more likely to commit offenses than other people in a particular situation) can be distinguished from short-term within-individual variations in criminal potential (intended to explain why people are more likely to commit crimes at some times and in some situations than in other times and situations). Long-term criminal potential is likely to be influenced by biological, individual, family, peer, school, community, and societal factors. Short-term criminal potential is likely to be influenced by situational events such as getting insulted or frustrated, getting drunk, or seeing a tempting criminal opportunity. While both topics are important, the focus in this chapter is on explaining long-term between-individual differences in criminal potential.

Specifically, this chapter will explore the links between offending and high impulsiveness, low intelligence, and low empathy. In isolation these (or any other) individual differences cannot fully explain offending, but the strength of the evidence suggests that any complete theory of offending would need to incorporate these factors. That is, these three factors have been identified as potential risk factors for later offending and antisocial behaviour (e.g., Farrington and Jolliffe, 2001). Risk factors are defined as factors that increase the likelihood of later offending (e.g., Kazdin *et al.*, 1997). By definition risk factors require longitudinal data in order to be identified. While there are different ways of conceptualizing a risk factor (see Farrington and Welsh, 2007) generally it refers to an extreme category of an explanatory variable. For example, the risk factor of low intelligence is an extreme category of the explanatory variable of intelligence.

It is important to try and establish which risk factors are causally related to offending. To the extent that a risk factor causes offending, interventions could be designed to reduce its impact and in turn reduce offending. However, it is extremely difficult to establish causal influences in non-experimental research. It is widely accepted that the main criteria for establishing that X causes Y is: (1) X is correlated with Y, (2) X can change or be changed within individuals, (3) X precedes Y, and (4) X predicts Y after controlling for confounding variables (Kraemer *et al.*, 2005; Murray *et al.*, 2009). Therefore, in trying to draw conclusions about whether a risk factor might have a causal influence on offending, this chapter will investigate the extent to which these conditions have been met.

IMPULSIVITY

Impulsiveness is one of many terms in the literature that refers to a general reduced ability to control one's behaviour. Other similar terms include low self-control, hyperactivity, inattention, a poor ability to delay gratification, risk-taking, sensation seeking, and not considering the consequences before acting. There are differences in the specific definitions of many of these terms, but it is safe to say that a relationship has been identified between these variables and poor life outcomes such as smoking (Burke *et al.*, 2007), gambling (Clarke, 2006), drinking (af Klinteberg *et al.*, 1993), and offending (White *et al.*, 1994).

High impulsiveness might contribute to an increased likelihood of offending either directly or indirectly. By the direct pathway, impulsiveness would have a fundamental impact on the way in which an individual would act in any given situation. With less time and cognitive energy available for contemplation of potential responses, an impulsive individual would, on balance, select the option that provides the most immediate perceived benefit. Numerous researchers and theorists have detailed how criminal offending tends to satisfy immediate urges at the risk of later, uncertain, and occasionally hypothetical consequences (e.g., Farrington and Welsh, 2007; Gottfredson and Hirschi, 1990).

This direct conceptualisation of impulsiveness comprises the backbone of two of the most influential theories in criminology. Wilson and Herrnstein (1985) developed a criminological theory that was based on the premise that individuals differ in their underlying criminal tendencies, and that whether a person chooses to commit a crime in a situation depends on whether the perceived benefits of offending are considered to outweigh the perceived costs. They focussed on how the importance of later consequences varied with the time delay for different individuals. Wilson and Herrnstein (1985) argued that those with a significant degree of impulsiveness are more likely to commit offences because their calculation of the costs and benefits of offending will be biased by their desire for immediate reinforcement. That is, an impulsive individual gives the most weight to the benefits of offending which offer instant rewards (e.g., material gain, peer approval, etc.) and will be less influenced by the later potential costs of offending (e.g., the risk of being apprehended, loss of reputation, or employment, etc.).

The General Theory of Crime proposed by Gottfredson and Hirschi (1990) is similar to the theory of Wilson and Herrnstein in the importance that it places on impulsiveness as a key explanatory factor. Gottfredson and Hirschi (1990) called this 'low self-control' which referred to the extent to which individuals were vulnerable to the temptations of the moment. People with low self-control were impulsive, took risks, had low cognitive and academic skills, were self-centred, had low empathy and had short time horizons. Hence, they found it hard to defer gratification, and their decisions to offend were insufficiently influenced by the future possible painful consequences of offending.

Other researchers have suggested that high impulsiveness may also contribute to an increased likelihood of offending indirectly through a person–environment interaction (e.g., Moffitt, 1993). For example, an impulsive child may prove a challenge to even the most conscientious parent, over time eliciting poor parenting, in itself an established risk factor for later offending (Farrington and Welsh, 2007). Similarly, impulsivity may lead to offending by reducing the likelihood of school success. Typically, formal education is delivered in a restrictive environment that might prove very difficult for those who are impulsive. Children who have low school achievement are more likely to drop out of school and are more likely to become socio-economically disadvantaged. With reduced opportunity to succeed in conventional ways, these individuals may be more likely to turn to antisocial or criminal methods to obtain rewards.

Therefore, either by directly influencing how individuals make decisions in criminal opportunities or by indirectly influencing their interactions with important individuals or institutions (or perhaps in both ways concurrently), impulsiveness can lead to an increase in the likelihood of offending.

Pratt and Cullen (2000) undertook a review and meta-analysis to empirically test the relationship between low self-control and crime. In their review low self-control was operationalised using the definition provided by Gottfredson and Hirschi (1990) in their influential General Theory of Crime; that is, someone who is 'impulsive, insensitive, physical as opposed to mental, risk taking, short sighted and non-verbal' (Gottfredson and Hirschi, 1990: 90). Pratt and Cullen (2000) analysed the results of 21 empirical studies and found that low self-control was a strong predictor of crime with a mean effect size (d) in the range of 0.47–0.58. This corresponds to a big decrease in the prevalence of reoffending (e.g., from 50 per cent to 25 per cent).

The most relevant aspect of self-control in this review was termed attitudinal self-control and this was often measured using the Grasmick self-control scale (Grasmick *et al.*, 1993), which provides an operationalisation of self-control from the perspective of Gottfredson and Hirschi (1990). However, limitations of this measure are that it does not allow for the separation of hyperactivity, impulsiveness and inattention, and it is not possible to separate these features of impulsiveness from a number of other concepts which are included in this very specific definition of self-control (e.g., lack of sympathy).

Another review was undertaken by Pratt *et al.* (2002) who examined the relationship of attention deficit hyperactivity disorder (ADHD) to crime and delinquency. Usefully, Pratt *et al.* (2002) disaggregated the ADHD construct into four sub-categories (attention deficit (AD) excluding hyperactivity, AD plus hyperactivity, hyperactivity, and an additional category for ADHD concepts such as attention problems or emotional or behavioural problems often cited as proxies of AD or ADHD) and examined their relationships to crime and delinquency. The AD excluding hyperactivity category had the strongest relationship with crime and delinquency and the ADHD concepts category had the weakest relationship. Pratt *et al.* (2002) concluded that ADHD in its various forms appeared to have a general relationship with crime and delinquency.

A major limitation of these reviews is that, because they included studies where the key construct (self-control/ADHD) was assessed retrospectively it was not possible to determine causal ordering. That is, self-control or ADHD might contribute to an increased likelihood of offending, but it is also possible that delinquent activity may cause a reduction in people's self-control or make them more impulsive and hyperactive (Moffitt, 1990). The precise form of causal ordering can only be established in prospective longitudinal studies where impulsiveness is measured before offending.

A number of prospective longitudinal surveys show that early measures of impulsiveness are related to later offending. In a study of over 4000 males in Copenhagen, hyperactivity (restlessness and poor concentration) measured at ages 11 to 13 significantly predicted arrests for violence up to age 22, especially among boys whose mothers had experienced delivery complications. More than half of those with both hyperactivity and delivery complications were arrested for violence, compared to less than 10 per cent of the remainder (Brennan *et al.*, 1993). In another prospective longitudinal study of over 7000 children followed from pregnancy in Australia,

problems of attention and restlessness at age 5 more than doubled the risk of delinquency at age 14 (Bor *et al.*, 2004).

In the Cambridge Study in Delinquent Development of 411 males followed up
from age 8 to age 48, boys identified by teachers as lacking in concentration or rest-
less, those identified by parents, peers, or teachers as the most daring or risk taking,
and those who were the most impulsive on psychomotor tests at age 8–10 all tended
to become offenders later in life. Later self-report measures of impulsiveness were
also related to offending. Daring, poor concentration, and restlessness all predicted
both official convictions and self-reported delinquency, and daring was consistently
one of the best independent predictors (Farrington, 1992).

A multi-method multi-source assessment of impulsivity was conducted using data
from over 400 males in a prospective longitudinal study of the development of antisocial behaviour in Pittsburgh (White *et al.*, 1994). The measures that were most
strongly related to self-reported delinquency at ages 10 and 13 were teacher-rated
impulsiveness (e.g., 'acts without thinking'), self-reported impulsiveness (e.g.,
scores on Eysenck impulsivity scales), self-reported undercontrol (e.g., 'unable to
delay gratification'), motor restlessness (from videotaped observations), and psychomotor impulsiveness (from the Trail Making Test). Generally, the verbal behaviour
rating tests produced stronger relationships with offending than the psychomotor
performance tasks, suggesting that cognitive impulsiveness (based on thinking processes) was more relevant to delinquency than behavioural impulsiveness (based on
psychomotor test performance). Future time perception and delay of gratification
tasks were only weakly related to self-reported offending.

Jolliffe and Farrington (2009a) undertook a systematic review and meta-analysis
of the relationship between early measures of impulsiveness and later violence using
only data from prospective longitudinal studies. The results suggested that early
measures of impulsiveness (measured as early as age 5) were quite strongly related
to later violence (measured as late as age 40). While all measures of impulsiveness
were associated with later violence, measures of daring and risk taking had a particularly strong relationship with later violence. The authors suggested that daring
and risk taking might influence offending via a direct pathway linking impulsiveness
and later offending (e.g., Gottfredson and Hirschi, 1990; Wilson and Herrnstein,
1985), whereas the other forms of impulsiveness (e.g., poor concentration) might
have a more muted effect through mediating variables (e.g., school failure).

INTELLIGENCE

Intelligence is usually measured according to the ability to manipulate abstract
concepts, and these measures often include assessments of both verbal intelligence
(e.g., producing synonyms of given words) and performance intelligence (e.g.,
replicating a picture pattern using blocks). Intelligence measures are designed to predict later success at school and they appear to do this well (Barchard, 2005). There is
strong evidence to suggest that offenders score low on measures of intelligence (e.g.,
Hirschi and Hindelang, 1977; Lynam *et al.*, 1993; Wilson and Herrnstein, 1985), and
this is especially true of verbal measures of intelligence (West and Farrington, 1973).
However, the mechanism that connects low intelligence and offending is still hotly
debated. Some researchers have asserted that the relationship between low intelligence

and offending is actually spurious, while others suggest that indirect mechanisms provide the best account of the research findings. There are also some who believe that the relationship between low intelligence and offending is direct and causal.

The argument that the relationship between low intelligence and offending is spurious is largely based on the assumption that intelligence tests are biased against persons from lower social classes or ethnic minorities. Intelligence tests are designed to measure school success, which is a very middle class value (e.g., Cohen, 1955). Individuals of lower social standing or from minority groups are more likely to be offenders, they will be less able to succeed at these tests, and further, they may also lack the motivation to complete them properly. This could create an illusory link between poor results on intelligence tests and offending. These suggestions, however, are not supported by the research. There is little evidence showing bias against social or ethnic groups on measures of intelligence (Cole, 1981; Reynolds, 1995) and, while motivation does appear to have some influence on the results of intelligence tests, the relationship between low intelligence and offending has been found after controlling for levels of motivation (Lynam et al., 1993).

Some have suggested that it is not that offenders generally are less intelligent, but only those offenders who come to the attention of the criminal justice system (and are therefore included in most studies of 'offenders'). In other words it is suggested that low intelligence leads to an increased likelihood of detection amongst offenders. Again however, there is little evidence for this so-called Differential Detection Hypothesis. For example, Farrington (1992) found that low intelligence was almost as strongly related to self-reported offending as it was to convictions. Also, Moffitt and Silva (1988) found that the average intelligence score of self-reported offenders who had or had not been detected by the police was similar, and that both of these groups had significantly lower scores than those of a comparison group who did not self-report offences. There may be a relationship between intelligence and penetration into the criminal justice system, such that those with lower levels of intelligence are more likely to be convicted and imprisoned than those with higher levels of intelligence, but this might also reflect the relationship between low intelligence and an increase in the frequency or seriousness of offending.

Another less widely explored hypothesis is that the relationship between low intelligence and offending is actually reversed (e.g., Lynam et al., 1993). Rather than low intelligence increasing the likelihood of offending, offending might actually decrease measured intelligence. Many aspects of a criminal lifestyle, such as drug/alcohol use, physical injury (especially head trauma incurred in fights), could result in impaired cognitive functioning (Moffitt, 1990). While it is plausible that offending could decrease measured intelligence this could not provide a full explanation of the link between intelligence and offending. This is because of the overwhelming evidence from prospective longitudinal studies (see below) where intelligence was measured well before offending (or offending type behaviour) had commenced (e.g., Denno, 1990; Schweinhart et al., 1993; Stattin and Klackenberg-Larson, 1993).

It has also been suggested that the low intelligence–offending relationship is actually produced by an alternative variable which results in both low intelligence and offending. Social class has most commonly been suggested as this alternative variable (e.g., Lynam et al., 1993), although other variables such as social bonding (Hirschi, 1969) and impulsivity (Felson and Staff, 2006) have also been suggested. According to this argument, it is not that low intelligence causes offending, but rather it is that an individual's low social class (or poor bonding/high impulsivity) causes both lower scores on measures of intelligence and also an increased likelihood of offending. To a great extent, however, this argument has also not been supported by the research findings. This is because studies have continued to identify a link between low intelligence and offending whilst controlling for these (and other) plausible alternative variables (e.g., Farrington and Welsh, 2007; Hirschi and Hindelang, 1977; Lynam *et al.*, 1993).

Clearly there is little, if any, evidence to support the suggestion that intelligence and offending are not really linked. In fact the results of a number of prospective longitudinal studies (where intelligence was measured early in life) clearly show that intelligence is an important predictor of later offending. For example, Stattin and Klackenberg-Larson (1993) in Sweden reported that low intelligence measured at age 3 significantly predicted officially recorded offending up to age 30. Frequent offenders (with four or more offences) were found to have particularly low intelligence. Importantly, all of these results held up after controlling for social class. Likewise, Schweinhart *et al.* (1993) found that low intelligence measured at age 4 significantly predicted the number of arrests up to age 27 and Lipsitt *et al.* (1990) also showed that low intelligence at age 4 predicted later juvenile delinquency.

Similar results have been obtained in other countries and with other samples. Denno (1990) used multiple measures of intelligence to demonstrate the link with offending. In this study, low verbal and performance intelligence, measured at ages 4 and 7, as well as low scores on the California Achievement tests at ages 13–14 (vocabulary, comprehension, math, language, spelling), all predicted arrests for violence up to age 22. In Chicago, McCord and Ensminger (1997) discovered that low intelligence at age 6 predicted arrests for violent crimes up to age 32. In Copenhagen, Hogh and Wolf (1983) found that low intelligence at age 12 significantly predicted police recorded violence between ages 15 and 22. The link between low intelligence and violence was strongest among lower class boys.

In the Cambridge Study in Delinquent Development, low intelligence and low school attainment both predicted juvenile and adult convictions (Farrington, 1992). Low intelligence at ages 8–10 was also an important independent predictor of spouse assault at age 32 (Farrington, 1994). In addition, low intelligence and attainment predicted aggression and bullying at age 14 (Farrington, 1989, 1993). Low nonverbal intelligence was especially characteristic of juvenile recidivists and those first convicted at the earliest ages (10–13). This factor was about as strong a predictor of juvenile convictions as other important early risk factors (low family income, large family size, poor parental child-rearing behaviour, poor parental supervision, and poor concentration or restlessness), but it was a weaker predictor than having a convicted parent and daring or risk-taking. Measures of intelligence and school attainment predicted measures of offending independently of other risk factors such as family income and family size (Farrington, 1990).

Because of the commonly found association between low intelligence, school failure and offending some researchers have suggested that low intelligence may have its influence on offending indirectly through increasing the probability of school failure (e.g., Hirschi and Hindelang, 1977). Low intelligence leads to failure at school and it is this failure, and the potential knock-on effects on associating with similarly situated others (e.g., peer delinquency) and later employment opportunities, that actually results in offending. Support for this hypothesis comes from the fact that measures of intelligence and school failure are strongly correlated with one another and both predict later offending (Farrington, 1992; West and Farrington, 1973). Lynam *et al.* (1993) undertook an important test of this relationship using data from the Pittsburgh Youth Study, a prospective longitudinal study of over 1500 boys. Interestingly, Lynam *et al.* (1993) drew different conclusions about the relationship between low intelligence and offending based on the ethnicity of the boys. For black boys the evidence was supportive of a relationship between low intelligence and self-reported offending mediated by school failure. For white boys school failure only marginally reduced the observed relationship between low intelligence and self-reported offending, suggesting that a direct relationship was the best explanation of the data.

A number of other variables have been suggested as potentially mediating the relationship between low intelligence and later offending. For example, low intelligence could lead to being allocated to different curriculum tracks in school. Being placed on a remedial curriculum track could have detrimental impact on self-esteem which could increase the likelihood of offending (McGloin and Pratt, 2003; Oaks, 1985). Also, low intelligence could have its influence indirectly by leading to greater impulsivity, a well-known risk factor for offending. Koolhof *et al.* (2007) investigated the role of impulsivity in the offending of 428 boys from the Pittsburgh Youth Study. The sample was divided into four groups: low IQ serious delinquents, higher IQ serious delinquents, low IQ non to moderate delinquents, and higher IQ non to moderate delinquents. The research showed that both intelligence and impulsivity were related to later offending and that those with higher IQs demonstrated lower impulsivity. Other research supports the close link between impulsivity, intelligence and offending (Felson and Staff, 2006; Lynam *et al.*, 1993; White *et al.*, 1996).

The conceptualisation of the intelligence–offending relationship as indirectly mediated by another variable tends to be viewed more favorably amongst those concerned about the deterministic implications of a direct link between low intelligence and offending. An indirect pathway offers an additional point to intervene so, regardless of the mutability or heritability of intelligence, given appropriate intervention on this indirect variable, the effect of low intelligence on offending could theoretically be reduced.

The relationship between low intelligence and offending has been viewed as direct and causal by some theorists (e.g., Wilson and Herrnstein, 1985). On this view those of lower intelligence have a limited capacity to devise non-criminal solutions to problems, which limits their ability to understand and appreciate the impact of their behaviour on others. This is linked to the suggestion that offenders possess neurological deficits, specifically in executive functioning, with intelligence as a proxy measure of this (Moffitt *et al.*, 2001). The executive functions of the brain include sustaining attention and concentration, abstract reasoning, the formation of goals, anticipating, planning and self monitoring (Farrington, 2009; Lynam *et al.*, 1993).

EMPATHY

In trying to explain offending, researchers have suggested that those who offend have less empathy than those who do not (e.g., Burke, 2001; Marcus and Gray, 1998), and there is widespread support for this belief. For example, in a recent survey of 1218 criminologists a lack of empathy was rated as the most important factor related to serious and persistent offending (Ellis *et al.*, 2008). The theoretical relationship between low empathy and offending is largely based on the definition of empathy, which commonly includes both a cognitive and affective component. Cognitive empathy refers to the ability to understand and appreciate the emotions of another person. Affective empathy involves actually experiencing another person's emotions. Therefore, those with high empathy should be less likely to offend because they are sensitized to the emotional impact of their actions on others. Those who lack empathy, however, can victimize others free from these internal cognitive and affective constraints. The theoretical relationship between low empathy and offending appears somewhat stronger for interpersonal offences such as violence and sex offences than for offences where the victim is less obvious (e.g., shoplifting, drug possession).

Support for the inverse relationship between empathy and offending also comes from the study of psychopathy. Psychopathy is a constellation of psychological and behavioural traits linked to an increased likelihood of criminal and antisocial behaviour (Harpur *et al.*, 1988). Those classified as psychopaths tend to be glib, superficial and manipulative, but, it is the lack of appropriate emotionality and empathy that is said to characterise this condition. It is well established that psychopaths are more violent and more likely to recidivate than non-psychopaths, and it is the conspicuous lack of empathy of psychopaths that is often used to explain these behavioural outcomes (e.g., Hare, 1999).

While there is clearly a strong theoretical relationship between low empathy and offending, the empirical evidence for this relationship is less impressive. For example, studies comparing the scores on measures of empathy of offenders and comparing these to scores of non-offenders have proven inconclusive. This is true amongst studies comparing general offenders to non-offenders (e.g., Goldstein and Higgins-D'Alessandro, 2001) as well as sex offenders to non-offenders (e.g., Hayashino *et al.*, 1995). These findings were contrary to expectation, especially as sex offenders have long been assumed to possess significant deficits in empathy which directly contribute to their chosen method of offending (Marshall *et al.*, 1993).

The inability to consistently identify deficits in empathy amongst sex offenders has led some to question the usefulness of global or trait-based measures of empathy with sex offenders. Instead, some researchers have suggested that the empathy deficits of sex offenders might be specific to certain victims (e.g., women or children; Finkelhor and Lewis, 1988), or even that these deficits might be specific to the victims of their own offences (Fernandez *et al.*, 1999). However, this method of conceptualizing empathy in relation to having already committed an offence means that victim empathy cannot be a risk factor. This is because 'victim' empathy cannot be measured before offending has taken place. In fact it is very difficult to determine if victim empathy is separable from the post-offence cognitive distortions (e.g., justifications and neutralisations) that have long been identified among offenders (Scully and Marolla, 1984; Sykes and Matza, 1957). Most evidence suggests that victim empathy is not associated with recidivism (Hanson and Morton-Bourgon, 2005), further calling into question the usefulness of this construct. And yet, it has been estimated that a large proportion of offender and sex offender treatment programmes address victim empathy (Freeman-Longo *et al.*, 1995).

While it appears that victim empathy is of limited use, especially when looking for risk factors for offending, trait empathy still appears to have potential as a risk factor for later offending. Jolliffe and Farrington (2004) undertook a systematic review and meta-analysis which included 35 studies comparing questionnaire measures of empathy with official records of offending. The results suggested that low cognitive empathy was strongly related to offending, but low affective empathy was only weakly related. Jolliffe and Farrington (2004) suggested that the magnitude of the relationship between cognitive empathy and offending might have been elevated by the widespread use of a weak measure of cognitive empathy.

The results of the systematic review also suggested that younger offenders and violent offenders tended to have low empathy. Most important, however, the relationship between low empathy and offending was greatly reduced after controlling for intelligence or socioeconomic status, suggesting that they might be more important risk factors or that low empathy might mediate the relationship between these risk factors and offending.

Luengo *et al.* (1995) examined the relationship between empathy and self-reported offending in a group of 103 incarcerated male adolescents and a group of 1041 adolescents in school. For both the institutionalised and non-instutitionalised adolescents they found affective empathy to be negatively related to all types of offending. Low affective empathy was particularly related to aggression, and was associated with aggression independently of cognitive empathy, impulsivity, sensation seeking and self esteem in both samples.

Jolliffe and Farrington (2006a) created the Basic Empathy Scale to measure both the cognitive and affective components of empathy. An example of a cognitive item would be '*It is hard for me to understand when my friends are sad*', and an example of an affective item would be '*After being with a friend who is sad about something, I usually feel sad*'. This scale was administered to 720 adolescents about age 15 and compared to self-reported offending (Jolliffe and Farrington, 2007). The results suggested that males who had reported any offence in the last year had lower empathy, and this was especially the case for affective empathy. Females who reported committing an offence did not have low empathy, but both males and females who reported committing violence did have low empathy. Also, males and females who were high-rate offenders also demonstrated significantly lower empathy (especially affective) compared to low-rate male and female offenders.

A similar pattern of results were evident when empathy was compared to self-reported bullying (Jolliffe and Farrington, 2006b). Both males and females who took part in frequent bullying tended to have low affective empathy. In addition, males who took part in violent bullying and females who took part in indirect bullying also had low empathy. Subsequent analyses suggested that affective empathy was related to frequent bullying by males and bullying by females independent of impulsivity, intelligence, socioeconomic status, parental supervision, alexithymia (difficulty in understanding and expressing emotions), and coming from a broken home (Jolliffe and Farrington, 2010).

These results provide support for the relationship between low empathy (especially affective empathy) and offending. However, in the absence of prospective longitudinal studies it is impossible to determine whether low empathy precedes offending or if offending, and witnessing what one believes to be minimal consequences of offending, precedes low empathy. There is also very limited evidence to suggest that low empathy is related to offending independently of other important social and individual background characteristics (e.g., intelligence, impulsivity, low SES). Hence, additional prospective longitudinal research is required to conclusively establish that low empathy is a risk factor for offending.

Despite the serious limitations in the research linking low empathy and offending, empathy training is a key component of many interventions for offenders (e.g., Mulloy et al., 1999), and sex offenders (Varker et al., 2008). For example, both the Enhanced Thinking Skills (ETS) and the Sex Offender Treatment Programme (SOTP) which are accredited and used with offenders in the UK specifically addresses deficits in empathy skills (Friendship et al., 2001).

Even if the strength of the research evidence was extended to the point that low empathy and offending had been linked conclusively and causally, these programmes may be limited in their ability to reduce reoffending. This is because these programmes are clearly designed to address deficits in cognitive empathy (understanding the emotions of others), and the bulk of research evidence has suggested that it is deficits in affective empathy that are most closely linked to offending. It is not clear to what extent role-playing or other cognitive exercises can impact affective empathy, which by its definition lies closer to a trait than a skill. Addressing non-existent deficiencies in cognitive empathy may be a waste of time and resources, but it may also be quite dangerous. It has been suggested that the glib and superficial charm that psychopaths use for manipulation derives from their ability to read the emotions of others (Hare, 1999). Furthermore, particularly sadistic offenders may enjoy witnessing the emotional suffering of others (Hanson, 2003). In these cases increasing cognitive empathy might have the unintended consequences of creating better and more efficient offenders.

DISCUSSION

It is interesting to note that all three factors of impulsivity, intelligence and empathy appear to be linked by their association with a diminished ability to reason about abstract concepts such as later consequences of actions, self-awareness and the emotions of other people. The association of these concepts with abstract reasoning suggests that the prefrontal cortex area of the brain may have an important role to play in fully understanding intelligence, impulsivity and empathy as well as their respective contribution to criminal behaviour (e.g., Farrington and Welsh, 2007; Lynam et al., 1993; Moffitt et al., 2001; Spinella, 2005).

Offenders often do better on non-verbal performance tests such as object assembly and block design, than on verbal tests (Farrington, 1989). This suggests that they find it easier to deal with concrete objects than abstract concepts, which some have suggested may be the key explanatory factor underlying the link between intelligence and delinquency (Farrington and Welsh, 2007). People who are poor at abstract reasoning tend to do badly in intelligence tests and at school, and they also tend to commit offences, probably because of their poor ability to foresee the consequences of their offending (e.g., high impulsiveness) and to appreciate the feelings of victims (e.g., low empathy). Clearly, some family backgrounds are less conducive than others to the development of abstract reasoning. For example, lower class, economically deprived parents tend to talk in terms of the concrete rather than the abstract and tend to live for the present rather than the future (Cohen, 1955).

In addition to this direct association with offending, both high impulsivity and low intelligence appear to have the potential to influence offending indirectly through a host of other variables. Future research should follow the lead of White *et al.* (1994) and Lynam *et al.* (1996) in using prospective longitudinal studies to identify and test potential mechanisms linking impulsivity, intelligence, empathy as well as other plausible variables to later offending.

In most prospective longitudinal studies, intelligence and impulsivity are treated as risk factors. That is, those with high impulsivity are compared with those of average and low levels of impulsivity on later self-reported or official measures of offending. Recently, however, researchers have started to consider how certain variables may actually be promotive as opposed to risk factors. Promotive factors are those that predict a low probability of later delinquency (e.g., Loeber *et al.*, 2008). When impulsivity is considered as a risk factor, those high on levels of impulsivity are compared to those with average and low levels of impulsivity on later offending, but when impulsivity is considered a promotive factor, those with high and average levels of impulsivity are compared to those with low levels.

In their analyses, Loeber *et al.* (2008) found that individuals who had medium levels of ADHD symptoms (the middle 50 per cent) were similar to those with high levels of ADHD symptoms (the top 25 per cent) in terms of their risk of later offending. However, those with the lowest levels of ADHD symptoms had a significantly lower probability of future offending. This finding was consistent for each of the five possible independent comparisons in their two datasets (three for the youngest cohort, two for the oldest cohort). These results suggest that ADHD acts as a promotive factor rather than a risk factor. Unfortunately, there has been little additional research in which promotive factors have been considered.

If impulsivity, intelligence and empathy are treated as risk factors but are actually promotive, prevention techniques targeted at those with high impulsiveness, low intelligence or low empathy may miss a subset of the population that might also benefit from treatment (i.e., those with moderate levels of impulsivity, intelligence and empathy). Furthermore, any intervention that reduces the impulsiveness of the most impulsive individuals may not appear to have an impact on offending unless impulsiveness is substantially reduced. Similarly, an intervention that increases intelligence may not appear to have a desirable impact on later offending unless its impact is substantial in moving those from both average and low levels up to high levels.

CONCLUSION

The evidence from prospective longitudinal studies is clear in showing that both high impulsivity and low intelligence are related to later offending. As empathy has yet to be included in such prospective longitudinal studies it is difficult to determine how, or indeed if, low empathy is related to later offending. This implies that interventions that target impulsiveness such as child skills training (Lösel and Beelman, 2006) and intelligence such as preschool enrichment programmes (Schweinhart *et al.*, 1993) should be effective in reducing later offending.

NOTE

1 The term potential is used in preference to alternative terms (e.g., propensity) that have deterministic connotations.

REFERENCES

Barchard, K. A. (2005). Does emotional intelligence assist in the prediction of academic success? *Educational and Psychological Measurement*, 63: 840–858.

Bor, W., McGee, T. R. and Fagan, A. A. (2004). Early risk factors for adolescent antisocial behaviour: An Australian longitudinal study. *Australian and New Zealand Journal of Psychiatry*, 38: 365–372.

Brennan, P. A., Mednick, B. R. and Mednick, S. A. (1993). Parental psychopathology, congenital factors, and violence. In S. Hodgins (ed.), *Mental Disorder and Crime* (pp. 244–261). Newbury Park, CA: Sage.

Burke, D. M. (2001). Empathy in sexually offending and nonoffending in adolescent males. *Journal of Interpersonal Violence*, 16: 222–233.

Burke, J. D., Loeber, R., White, H. R., Stouthamer-Loeber, M. and Pardini, D. A. (2007). Inattention as a key predictor of tobacco use in adolescence. *Journal of Abnormal Psychology*, 116: 249–259.

Clarke, D. (2006). Impulsivity as a mediator in the relationship between depression and problem gambling. *Personality and Individual Differences*, 40: 5–15.

Clarke, R. V. and Cornish, D. B. (1985). Modelling offenders' decisions: A framework for research and policy. In M. Tonry and N. Morris, *Crime and Justice* (Vol. 6. pp. 147–185). Chicago: University of Chicago Press.

Cohen, A. K. (1955). *Delinquent Boys: The Culture of the Gang*. Glencoe, Ill.: Free Press.

Cole, N. S. (1981). Bias in testing. *American Psychologist*, 36: 1067–1077.

Denno, D. W. (1990). *Biology and Violence: From Birth to Adulthood*. Cambridge: Cambridge University Press.

Ellis, L., Cooper, J. A. and Walsh, A. (2008). Criminologists' opinions about causes and theories of crime and delinquency: A follow-up. *The Criminologist*, 33: 23–26.

Farrington, D. P. (1992). Explaining the beginning, progress and ending of antisocial behavior from birth to adulthood. In J. McCord (ed.), *Facts, Framework and Forecasts: Advances in Criminological Theory* (Vol. 3, pp. 253–286). New Brunswick NJ: Transaction.

Farrington, D. P. (1989). Early predictors of adolescent aggression and adult violence. *Violence and Victims*, 4: 79–100.

Farrington, D. P. (1990). Implications of criminal career research for the prevention of offending. *Journal of Adolescence*, 13: 93–113.

Farrington, D. P. (1993). Childhood origins of teenage antisocial behaviour and adult social dysfunction. *Journal of the Royal Society of Medicine*, 86: 13–17.

Farrington, D. P. (1994). Childhood, adolescent and adult features of violent males. In R. Huesmann (ed.), *Aggressive Behavior: Current Perspectives* (pp. 215–240). New York: Plenum.

Farrington, D. P. (1998). Individual differences and offending. In M. Tonry (ed.), *The Handbook of Crime and Punishment* (pp. 241–268). New York: Oxford University Press.

Farrington, D. P. (2005). The integrated cognitive antisocial potential (ICAP) theory. In D. Farrington (ed.), *Integrated Developmental and Life-Course Theories of Offending* (pp. 1–14). New Jersey: Transaction.

Farrington, D. P. (2009). Conduct, disorder, aggression an delinquency. In R. M. Lerner and L. Sternberg (eds), *Handbook of Adolescent Psychology Third Edition*. Hoboken, NJ: Wiley (in press).

Farrington, D. P. and Jolliffe, D. (2001). Personality and crime. In N. J. Smelser and P. Baltes (eds), *International Encyclopedia of the Social and Behavioral Sciences* (Vol. 16, pp. 11260–11264). Amsterdam: Elsevier.

Farrington, D. P. and Welsh, B. C. (2007). *Saving Children From a Life of Crime*. Oxford: Oxford University Press.

Felson, R. B. and Staff, J. (2006). Explaining the academic performance–delinquency relationship. *Criminology*, 44: 299–319.

Fernandez, Y. M., Marshall, W. L., Lightbody, S. and O'Sullivan, C. (1995). The child molester empathy measure: description and examination of its reliability and validity. *Sexual Abuse: A Journal of Research and Treatment,* 11: 17–31.

Finkelhor, D. and Lewis, I. A. (1988). An epidemiologic approach to the study of child molestation. *Annals of the New York Academy of Sciences*, 528: 64–78.

Freeman-Longo, R. E., Bird, S., Stevenson, W. F. and Fiske, J. (1995). *1994 Nationwide Survey of Treatment Programmes and Models: Serving Abuse Reactive Children, Adolescent and Adult Sex Offenders*. Brandon, VT: The Safer Society Program and Press.

Friendship, C., Mann, R. and Beech, A. (2001). *The Prison-Based Sex Offender Treatment Programme – An Evaluation*, Home Office Research Findings 205. London: Home Office.

Goldstein, H. and Higgins-D'Allessandro, A. (2001). Empathy and attachment in relation to violent vs. nonviolent offense history among jail inmates. *Journal of Offender Rehabilitation*, 32: 31–53.

Gottfredson, M. and Hirschi, T. (1990). *A General Theory of Crime*. Stanford, CA: Stanford University Press.

Grasmick, H. G., Tittle, C. R., Bursik, R. J. and Arneklev, B. K. (1993). Testing the core empirical implications of Gottfredson and Hirschi's General Theory of Crime. *Journal of Research in Crime and Delinquency*, 30: 5–29.

Hanson, K. R. (2003). Empathy deficits of sexual offenders: A conceptual model. *Journal of Sexual Aggression*, 9: 13–23.

Hanson, R. K. and Morton-Bourgon, K. E. (2005). The characteristics of persistent sexual offenders: A meta-analysis of recidivism studies. *Journal of Consulting and Clinical Psychology*, 73: 1154–1163.

Hare, R. D. (1999). Psychopathy as a risk factor for violence. *Psychiatric Quarterly*, 70: 181–197.

Harpur, T. J., Hakstian, A. R. and Hare, R. D. (1988). Factor structure of the psychopathy checklist. *Journal of Consulting and Clinical Psychology*, 56: 741–747.

Hayashino, D. S., Wurtele, S. K. and Klebe, K. J. (1995). Child molesters: An examination of cognitive factors. *Journal of Interpersonal Violence*, 10: 106–116.

Hirschi, T. (1969). *Causes of Delinquency*, Berkeley, CA: University of California Press.

Hirschi, T. and Hindelang, M. J. (1977). Intelligence and delinquency: A revisionist review. *American Sociological Review*, 42: 571–587.

Hogh, E. and Wolf, P. (1983). Violent crime in a birth cohort: Copenhagen 1953–1977. In K. T. van Dusen and S. A. Mednick (eds), *Prospective Studies of Crime and Delinquency* (pp. 249–267). Boston: Kluwer, Nijhoff.

Jolliffe, D. and Farrington, D. P. (2004). Empathy and offending: a systematic review and meta-analysis. *Aggression and Violent Behavior*, 9: 441–476.

Jolliffe, D. and Farrington, D. P. (2006a). The development and validation of the basic empathy scale. *Journal of Adolescence*, 29: 589–611.

Jolliffe, D. and Farrington, D. P. (2006b). Examining the relationship between low empathy and bullying. *Aggressive Behavior*, 32: 540–550.

Jolliffe, D. and Farrington, D. P. (2007). The relationship between low empathy and self-reported offending. *Legal and Criminological Psychology*, 12: 265–286.

Jolliffe, D. and Farrington, D. P. (2009a). A systematic review of the relationship between childhood impulsiveness and later violence. In M. McMurran and R. C. Howard (eds), *Personality, Personality Disorder and Violence* (pp. 41–61). London: Wiley.

Jolliffe, D. and Farrington, D. P. (2010). Is empathy related to bullying after controlling for individual and social background variables? *Journal of Adolescence,* (in press).

Kazdin, A. E., Kraemer, H. C., Kessler, R. C., Kupfer, D. J. and Offord, D. R. (1997). Contributions of risk-factor research to the development of psychopathology. *Clinical Psychology Review*, 17: 375–406.

Klinteberg, B. A., Andersson, T., Magnusson, D. and Stattin, H. (1993). Hyperactive behavior in childhood as related to subsequent alcohol problems and violent offending: A longitudinal study of male subjects. *Personality and Individual Differences*, 15: 381–388.

Koolhof, R., Loeber, R., Wei, E. H., Pardini, D. and D'Escury, A. C. (2007). Inhibition deficits of serious delinquent boys of low intelligence. *Criminal Behaviour and Mental Health*, 17: 274–292.

Kraemer, H. C., Lowe, K. K. and Kupfer, D. J. (2005). *To Your Health?: How to Understand What Research Tells us About Risk*. Oxford: Oxford University Press.

Lipsitt, P. D., Buka, S. L. and Lipsitt, L. P. (1990). Early intelligence scores and subsequent delinquency: A prospective study. *American Journal of Family Therapy*, 18: 197–208.

Loeber, R., Farrington, D. P., Stouthamer-Loeber, M. and White, H. R. (2008). *Violence and Serious Theft: Development and Prediction from Childhood to Adulthood*. New York: Routledge.

Losel, F. and Beelman, A. (2006). Child social skills training. In B. C. Welsh and D. P. Farrington (eds), *Preventing Crime: What Works for Children, Offenders, Victims and Places* (pp. 33–71). New York, NY: Springer.

Luengo, M. A., Otero, J. M., Carrillo-De-La-Pena, M. T. and Miron, L. (1995). Dimensions of antisocial behaviour in juvenile delinquency: A study of personality variables. *Psychology, Crime and Law*, 1: 27–37.

Lynam, D., Moffitt, T. and Stouthamer-Loeber, M. (1993). Explaining the relation between IQ and delinquency: Class, race, test motivation, school failure, or self-control? *Journal of Abnormal Psychology*, 102: 187–196.

Marcus, R. F. and Gray, L. (1998). Close relationships of violent and nonviolent African American delinquents. *Violence and Victims*, 13: 31–46.

Marshall, W. L., Jones, R., Hudson, S. M. and McDonald, E. (1993). Generalized empathy in child molesters. *Journal of Child Sexual Abuse,* 2: 61–68.

McCord, J. and Ensminger, M. E. (1997). Multiple risks and comorbidity in an African American population. *Criminal Behaviour and Mental Health*, 7: 339–352.

McGloin, J. M. and Pratt, T. C. (2003). Cognitive ability and delinquent behavior among inner city youth: A life-course analysis of main, mediating, and interaction effects. *International Journal of Offender Therapy and Comparative Criminology*, 47: 253–271.

Moffitt, T. E. (1990). The neuropsychology of delinquency: A critical review of theory and research. In N. Morris and M. Tonry (eds), *Crime and Justice* (Vol. 12, pp. 99–169). Chicago: University of Chicago Press.

Moffitt, T. (1993). Adolescent-limited and life-course-persistent antisocial behavior: A developmental taxonomy. *Psychological Review*, 100: 674–701.

Moffitt, T. E., Caspi, A., Rutter, M. and Silva, P. A. (2001). *Sex Differences in Antisocial Behaviour*. Cambridge: Cambridge University Press.

Moffitt, T. E. and Silva, P. A. (1988). IQ and delinquency: A direct test of the differential detection hypothesis. *Journal of Abnormal Psychology*, 97: 330–333.

Mulloy, R., Smiley, W. C. and Mawson, D. L. (1999). The impact of empathy training on offender treatment. *Focus on Corrections Research*, 11: 15–18.

Murray, J., Farrington, D. P. and Eisner, M. P. (2009). Drawing conclusions about causes from systematic reviews of risk factors: The Cambridge Quality Checklists. *Journal of Experimental Criminology*, 5: 1–23.

Oaks, J. (1985). *Keeping Track*, New Haven, CT: Yale University Press.

Pratt, T. C. and Cullen, F. T. (2000). The empirical status of Gottfredson and Hirschi's General Theory of Crime: A meta-analysis. *Criminology*, 38: 931–960.

Pratt, T. C., Cullen, F. T., Blevins, K. R., Daigle, L. and Unnever, J. D. (2002). The relationship of attention deficit hyperactivity disorder to crime and delinquency: A meta-analysis. *International Journal of Police Science and Management*, 4: 344–360.

Reynolds, C. R. (1995). Test bias and the assessment of intelligence and personality. In D. H. Saklofske and M. Zeidner (eds), *International Handbook of Personality and Intelligence* (pp. 545–573). New York, NY: Plenum.

Schweinhart, L. J., Barnes, H. V. and Weikart, D. P. (1993). *Significant Benefits: The High/Scope Perry Preschool Study Through Age 27*. Ypsilanti, Mich: High/Scope Press.

Scully, D. and Marolla, J. (1984). Convicted rapists' vocabulary of motive: Excuses and justifications. *Social Problems*, 31: 530–544.

Spinella, M. (2005). Prefrontal substrates of empathy: Psychometric evidence in a community sample. *Biological Psychology*, 70: 175–181.

Stattin, H. and Klackenberg-Larsson, I. (1993). Early language and intelligence development and their relationship to future criminal behavior. *Journal of Abnormal Psychology*, 102: 369–378.

Sykes, G. and Matza, D. (1957). Techniques of neutralization: A theory of delinquency. *American Sociological Review,* 22: 664–670.

Varker, T., Devilly, G. J., Ward, T. and Beech, A. R. (2008). Empathy and adolescent sexual offenders: A review of the literature. *Aggression and Violent Behavior*, 13: 251–260.

West, D. J. and Farrington, D. P. (1973). *Who Becomes Delinquent?*: London: Heinemann.

White, J. L., Moffitt, T. E., Caspi, A., Bartusch, D. J., Needles, D. J. and Stouthamer-Loeberm, M. (1994). Measuring impulsivity and examining its relationship to delinquency. *Journal of Abnormal Psychology*, 103: 192–205.

Wilson, J. Q. and Herrnstein, R. J. (1985). *Crime and Human Nature*. New York: Simon and Schuster.

3

Social Learning Theory: Process and Structure in Criminal and Deviant Behavior

Ronald L. Akers and Gary F. Jensen

BRIEF OVERVIEW OF SOCIAL LEARNING THEORY OF CRIME AND DEVIANCE

Ronald L. Akers' social learning theory as a general explanation of criminal and deviant behavior was first proposed with Robert L. Burgess (Burgess and Akers, 1966) integrating Sutherland's (1947) sociological theory of differential association with principles of psychological behaviorism (Skinner, 1953).

> Burgess and Akers ... retained the concepts of differential association and definitions from Sutherland's theory, but conceptualized them in more behavioral terms and added concepts from behavioral learning theory. These concepts include differential reinforcement, whereby 'operant' behavior (the voluntary actions of the individual) is conditioned or shaped by rewards and punishments. They also contain classical or 'respondent' conditioning (the conditioning of involuntary reflex behavior); discriminative stimuli (the environmental and internal stimuli that provide cues or signals for behavior); schedules of reinforcement (the rate and ratio in which rewards and punishments follow behavioral responses); and other principles of behavior modification.
>
> (Akers and Sellers, 2004: 84)

Akers continued to develop, test, and refine the theory as a social psychological explanation of criminal and deviant behavior, and extended it to a Social Structure Social Learning (SSSL) model (Akers, 1973, 1985, 1992, 1998; Akers and Sellers, 2004).[1] The SSSL model links the sociocultural structure and context as causes of variations in rates of crime and delinquency to individual behavior through the social learning process. More recently, Gary F. Jensen, in collaboration with Akers (Akers and Jensen, 2006; Jensen and Akers, 2003), has shown how to 'take social learning global' extending and adapting micro-level social learning principles to the most macro-level of analysis, cross-national differences in crime rates (see below).

Social learning theory offers a general social psychological explanation of individual variations in criminal and deviant behavior. The social/cognitive/behavioral principles account (in probabilistic terms) not only for the novel or first time commission or initiation of a behavioral pattern, but the frequency, pattern, maintenance, increase, decrease, or desistence of behavior over time. It is capable of explaining both behavioral versatility and specialization, acts in specific situations and across situations, and both the tendency to engage in or to refrain from certain behavior. While recognizing all aspects of the learning process, the theory focuses on four major explanatory concepts that depict central features of that process relevant to criminal or conforming behavior. These are 'differential association,' 'definitions,' 'differential reinforcement,' and 'imitation' (Akers *et al.*, 1979; Akers, 1985, 1998; Akers and Sellers, 2004).

Differential association is the process in which one is in direct and indirect interaction and identification with groups and individuals – primary groups of family and friends and others as well as secondary and reference groups, including 'virtual' groups found through the internet and other media (Warr, 2002). The theory proposes that there are four principal 'modalities' by which these associations differ and the relative effect they have on one's behavior: intensity (the importance or closeness of the relationships with those with whom one associates), frequency (how often the association with others takes place), priority (associations that occur first or earliest), and duration (the period of time over which the associations occur and the relative amount of one's time spent in the associations). These associations have a normative or cultural dimension in the sense that they mutually expose one to the values, beliefs, and attitudes of others and an interactional or behavioral dimension, with effects beyond or in addition to the normative dimension, in the sense that they provide behavioral models and a context in which certain behavior is differentially encouraged or discouraged. That is, in associating with others, their behavior, support, social reactions, sanctions, and their apparent or espoused values and attitudes influence one's own attitudes and overt behavior (and of course one, in turn, has some greater or lesser influence on the others with whom he or she associates).

Differential reinforcement refers to the balance of anticipated, perceived, or actual rewards (positive, pleasurable, desirable consequences) and punishments (aversive, unpleasant, undesirable consequences) of behavior over time and in given situations. The modalities of reinforcement are amount, frequency, and probability. The greater the relative value or amount of reward over punishment, the greater the relative frequency of reward compared to punishment, and the higher the probability of reward for a given behavior (as balanced against the differential reinforcement for alternative behavior), the greater the likelihood that it will occur and be repeated. The theory focuses on social reinforcers and punishers, not only the direct reactions of others present while an act is committed, but tangible and intangible, concrete and symbolic, social and cultural outcomes valued or disvalued in society or subgroups. Even material rewards such as money and possessions are able to reinforce behavior primarily because they are associated with power, prestige, social status, approval, and other socially valued rewards. Self-reinforcement is also largely social because in exercising self-control one takes the role of others, even when no one else is present, reinforcing or punishing his or her own behavior. But social learning theory recognizes that nonsocial rewards and punishers can be involved in the shaping and sustaining of behavior. For example, the direct physical effects of drugs and alcohol (although how enjoyable or frightening these direct effects are experienced are affected by prior learned expectations and conditioning). There may also be physiological differences in the tendency of some individuals (such as those prone to sensation-seeking) more than others to find certain deviant behavior rewarding.

Definitions favorable and unfavorable to crime and deviance refer to one's own general and specific definitions of the situation, attitudes, meanings, rationalizations, definitions of the situation, view certain behavior as right or wrong, desirable or undesirable, justified or unjustified. Some of the definitions favorable to deviance are strongly held and positive toward deviant and criminal behavior, as in radical, militant, or criminal subcultures (see below). However, the theory does not confine the concept and effects of definitions favorable to crime or deviance to this type of attitudes and beliefs. In fact, it predicts that the most commonly found definitions favorable to crime and delinquency do not directly motivate action in this sense. Rather, they are more likely to be 'neutralizing definitions' that may define the behavior as wrong but excuse or justify it as all right, necessary, unavoidable or they are (consistently with Hirschi's 1969, social bonding theory) weakly held conventional beliefs or attitudes that are only slightly unfavorable to deviance whose behavioral effects are overbalanced by inducements to crime. These definitions favorable and unfavorable to criminal and delinquent behavior are themselves learned behavior that provide cognitions and internal discriminative stimuli that do not directly reinforce the behavior but shape the person's view of the situation (or situations) as an opportunity to commit an offense or one in which certain behavior is expected or appropriate.

Imitation refers to the engagement in behavior after the observation of similar behavior in others (observational learning). Whether or not the behavior modeled by others (including that portrayed or depicted in the media as well as in primary groups) will be imitated is affected by the desirable or undesirable characteristics of the models, the behavior observed, and the observed consequences (vicarious differential reinforcement) of the modeled behavior. Theoretically, imitation or modeling has greater effect on the acquisition and performance of novel behavior than in the maintenance or cessation of behavioral patterns once established, but it continues to have some effect at all phases of behavior.

Akers has offered the following concise statement of the theory encapsulating these four main concepts:

> The basic assumption in social learning theory is that the same learning process in a context of social structure, interaction, and situation, produces both conforming and deviant behavior. The difference lies in the direction ... [of] the balance of influences on behavior.
>
> The probability that persons will engage in criminal and deviant behavior is increased and the probability of their conforming to the norm is decreased when they *differentially associate* with others who commit criminal behavior and espouse definitions favorable to it, are relatively *more exposed* in-person or symbolically to *salient criminal/deviant models*,

define it as desirable or justified in a situation discriminative for the behavior, and have received in the past and anticipate in the current or future situation *relatively greater reward than punishment for the behavior*.

(Akers, 1998: 50; italics added)

RESEARCH ON SOCIAL LEARNING VARIABLES IN CRIMINAL AND DELINQUENT BEHAVIOR

There is a very large and expanding body of research conducted over a great many years, the preponderance of findings from which show that the relationships between empirical measures of the theory's four main explanatory concepts of differential association, definitions, differential reinforcement, and imitation, singly or in combination, to measures of criminal, delinquent, and deviant behavior are as hypothesized by the theory. The findings typically are strong to moderate relationships, with measures of imitation usually having weaker, but still significant, net effects than the other variables. That body of research has been extensively cited and reviewed elsewhere (see Akers, 1998; Akers and Jensen, 2006; Akers and Sellers, 2004) and will not be repeated here. Recent literature continues to report findings on delinquent, deviant, and criminal behavior that are consistent with and directly supportive of the social learning theory of delinquent, deviant, and criminal behavior. For examples, see Batton and Ogle (2003), Sellers *et al.* (2003), Brezina and Piquero (2003) and the other contributions testing social learning theory in the volume edited by Akers and Jensen (2003) as well as Triplett and Payne (2004), Durkin *et al.* (2005), Matsueda *et al.* (2006) and others. Supportive findings have also come from a growing number of studies with samples outside of the United States, indicating clearly that social learning theory applies cross-culturally, with social learning variables accounting for substantial amounts of variations in crime and deviance in quite different socio-cultural contexts (see Hwang and Akers, 2003, 2006; Junger-tas, 1992; Kim and Koto 2000; Wang and Jensen, 2003; Zhang and Messner, 1995). When measures of explanatory variables from other social psychological theories are included in the same research (in the United States or in other countries), the typical finding is that social learning variables have the strongest effects (Benda, 1994; Burton *et al.*, 1994; Hwang and Akers, 2003, 2006; Neff and Waite, 2007; Preston, 2006; Rebellon, 2002).

The effects of peer and friendship groups on delinquency as predicted by the theory's principle of differential association have been studied most frequently.

No characteristic of individuals known to criminologists is a better predictor of criminal behavior than the number of delinquent friends an individual has. ... Few, if any, empirical regularities in criminology have been documented as often or over as long a period as the association between delinquency and delinquent friends.

(Warr, 2002: 40)

Haynie (2002) found that the ratio of association with delinquent and nondelinquent friends (differential peer association) on delinquent behavior remained strong even taking into account prior delinquency, time spent with peers, attachment to peers, and other characteristics of the network of friends. Although delinquent gangs account for only a portion of all group-related delinquency, delinquent gangs and subcultures have received a great deal of attention in criminology for a long time, and gang participation has long been recognized as a special case of differential association with delinquent peers. And research continues to find the strong influence of gang membership on serious delinquency. Regardless of the frequency or seriousness of one's delinquency prior to gang involvement, participation in a gang greatly increases delinquent behavior even for marginal members, and differential association with delinquent friends, regardless of gang membership, increases frequency of delinquent behavior (Battin *et al.*, 1998; Curry *et al.*, 2002).

These findings suggest that, compared to having one or more non-gang delinquent friends, gang membership produces more frequent, intense, and enduring association with delinquent friends, exposure to delinquent models and definitions, and reinforcement for delinquent behavior. Winfree *et al.* (1994) found that the processes (definitions, social reinforcers/punishers, and differential association) specified in social learning theory are 'nearly identical to those provided by qualitative gang research. Gang members reward certain behavior in their peers and punish others, employing goals and processes that are indistinguishable from those described by Akers' (Winfree *et al.*, 1994: 149).

Research has found ample evidence for social learning processes in the effects of family on conforming or delinquent behavior including family structure, parental disciplinary practices, socialization, parental role models, family values, and differential reinforcement (Ardelt and Day, 2002; McCord, 1991; Patterson, 1995; Simons *et al.*, 2004). The 'relative rate of reinforcement for child coercion during family conflict bouts ... also predicted the child's rates of deviancy observed a week later. If we then added how frequent conflicts or training trials occurred, we could account for over 60 per cent of the variance in individual differences in deviancy' (Patterson, 2002: 12).

The cross-sectional and longitudinal tests of social learning theory and the SSSL model by Akers and his students and associates include behavior ranging from adolescent substance use and abuse to serious criminal behavior (see Akers *et al.*, 1979; Akers, 1998; Akers and Jensen, 2003, 2006). The findings from these studies strongly support empirical models derived from social learning theory incorporating family, peer, and other variables measuring differential association, differential reinforcement, imitation, and definitions.

> Indeed, it is reasonable to propose that the theory has been tested in relation to a wider range of forms of deviance, in a wider range of settings and samples ... has survived more 'crucial tests' against other theories, and is the most strongly and consistently supported by empirical data than any other social psychological explanation of crime and deviance.
>
> (Akers and Jensen, 2006: 37)

RECENT EXTENSIONS OF SOCIAL LEARNING THEORY TO TERRORIST VIOLENCE

Some of the research has supported social learning theory as an explanation of serious violent behavior such as rape (Akers, 1998; Boeringer *et al.*, 1991) as well as homicide/suicide, intimate violence, violence by juveniles, and sibling violence

(Batton and Ogle, 2003; Bellair *et al.*, 2003; Hoffman *et al.*, 2005; Sellers *et al.*, 2003). Silverman (2002) has tested a theoretical model, incorporating social learning principles, of attacks on abortion clinic property and personnel. Social learning theory has been extended to the social psychology of Islamic and other radical terrorist violence (Akers and Silverman, 2004; Akins *et al.*, 2006) but empirical tests of these models have not yet been done.

> This [learning of terrorist violence] is typically through the non-deliberative process of group and societal influence but often is through deliberate tutelage, training (including militarist training, use of weapons and explosives, suicide bombing and other terrorist techniques in collective violence), indoctrination, and socialization of children as well as current and new adult members of the group. ... [T]errorists learn an ideology that the ends justify the means; violence for political ends is accepted and rewarded. These function as definitions favorable to violence ... when, where, and how often, it is morally right or justified to engage in political violence. It is important to note that counter-balancing forces such as the dire personal, monetary, life-threatening, and life-taking consequences, both immediate and long term, of actively engaging in terrorism means that not every member who participates in or identifies with and adopts the rationalizations of such a collectivity will carry out terrorists acts themselves.
>
> (Akers and Silverman, 2004: 24, 27)

Akins *et al.* (2006) point to processes of differential association, differential definitions, social reinforcements, and imitation in becoming a suicide bomber in Gaza. Not only are they told that there will be rewards in heaven, but the bomber's family will gain honor (and often monetary reward) from such acts. In short, it is a product of normative socialization and differential reinforcement. There is considerable public and private effort to define extremely violent acts as a positive act in defense of Islamic religion. To the degree that others who have committed such acts are, in fact, depicted as martyrs, potential recruits experience vicarious reinforcement in the learning process leading to suicide bombings. In addition to these general cultural and group supports in Gaza (children's games, music, suicide bombers as cultural heroes) youths are also groomed for such roles and come to believe that they will receive rewards for their culturally acceptable defense of their religion.

The role of religious zealotry in the explanation of terrorism and suicide bombing has drawn attention to the diverse ways in which religiosity and religious beliefs can affect behavior. In general, religious institutions, beliefs, and practices have been found to discourage crime and delinquency, and a large body of research evidence makes it clear the usual impact of religiosity on individuals is to lower the probability of their committing deviant or criminal acts (for recent research and reviews Baier and Wright, 2001; Benda, 2002; Johnson *et al.*, 2000; Smith *et al.*, 2005; Welch *et al.*, 2006). Religious beliefs ordinarily are conventional beliefs that function for the individual as definitions unfavorable to lying, stealing, cheating, or doing harm to others. It is well recognized, however, that radical or fanatical adherents of any ideology or belief system, whether political, religious, economic, or cultural, can come to the point of perpetrating terrorist and criminal acts as expressions of commitment to those extreme beliefs and groups (Barlow, 2007).

Jensen (2006) hypothesizes that the dominant 'religious cosmologies' of nations are 'reproduced' at the individual level in behavior and styles of interaction that affect rates of interpersonal violence in families, among contending groups, and among individuals. Because social learning theory incorporates normative learning processes more centrally than any of the other sociological perspectives, the focus on the reproduction of systems of moral belief at meso and micro levels is particularly relevant to that theory. Jensen found that nations with 'dualistic' religious cosmologies characterized by 'dueling dieties' had significantly higher rates of homicide than nations with a 'benevolent God-only' cosmologies or with non-radical secular cosmologies. Moreover, this pattern persisted despite the incorporation of other variables stressed by other theories. Jensen proposes that 'religious and moral dualisms may coincide with other forms of dualism at the individual level,' such as found in a 'culture of violence' or 'code of the street' (Anderson, 1999) where there is little flexibility in even fairly minor disputes besides a violent response. If a youth grows up in a world where there are rigid boundaries for attaining honor, a wide range of situations in which the behavior of others are interpreted as showing disrespect, and limited cultural means for re-establishing honor, the range of situations generating violence is high. Although it may seem to be a huge step from dualist religio-cultural cosmologies to forms of interpersonal violence the broad scope of social learning theory can encompass both. This argues for more attention to moral and religious cosmologies in criminology, including their etiology and consequences as part of the social learning or other theoretical approaches, not only at the micro or individual level but also at the macro level to which we now turn.

ELABORATIONS AND EXTENSIONS OF SOCIAL LEARNING THEORY TO THE MACRO LEVEL

Rosenfeld and Messner (1995: 161–164; Messner and Rosenfeld 2001: 41–42) perceive an 'individualistic bias in contemporary criminology' and propose a shift of concentration to the macro-level study of variations in properties of nations that help explain societal variations in serious crimes. They recognize that 'Any macro-level explanation of crime will inevitably be predicated on underlying premises about individual behavior' (2001: 42) and 'it is possible ... to link these individual-level theories with macro-level explanations that share a causal logic.' But they ignore social learning theory in the discussion of their macro-level 'institutional anomie' model and their discussion of the shared logic needed to make the micro–macro link.

The omission of social learning in this discussion is puzzling because, given the robust record of empirical validity, social learning theory is the most likely candidate for successfully making the micro–macro link. This omission also ignores the fact that Akers (following the earlier conceptualization of Sutherland (1947) and Cressey (1960)) has from the beginning, with consistent statements and reiterations over many years, explicitly and clearly proposed social learning as a 'processual' or micro-level explanation compatible with and capable of linking to the major 'social structural' or macro-level causes and theories of crime rates (Akers, 1968, 1973, 1985, 1992; Burgess and Akers, 1966). Typical of these statements is that, while macro-level theories:

> [D]elineate the structural variables (class, race, anomic conditions, breakdown in social control, etc.) that yield differential rates of deviance, social learning stresses the behavioral mechanisms by which these variables produce the behavior comprising the rates. As such,

social learning is complementary to other sociological theories and could be used to integrate extant formulations to achieve more comprehensive explanations of deviance.

(Akers *et al.*, 1979: 637)

In *Social Structure and Social Learning* (1998), Akers presented a fuller and more formal conceptualization of this relationship of social learning processes to structural causes of crime (whether or not those causes had been incorporated into specific macro-level theories). He proposed a cross-level theoretical model – the SSSL or Social Structure Social Learning Model – in which the 'primary distal macro-level and meso-level causes of crime' are found in the social/cultural structure, context, and environments, 'while social learning variables reflect the primary proximate causes of criminal behavior by individuals' (Akers, 1998: 322). Under the rubric of social structure, he includes the 'general culture' of social systems and normative variables such as 'role expectations' and stresses socially structured schedules of reinforcement, values and attitudes, and models that shape the behavior of individuals. The basic proposition in the SSSL model is that cognitive/behavioral processes and variables specified in social learning theory substantially mediate the main effects of macro- or meso-level structural factors related to crime rates. Akers (1998) reviewed the evidence available at the time that could be seen as relevant to the hypothesized relationship between social structure and social learning and found it supportive of the model. A relatively small but growing body of subsequent research has produced favorable findings on SSSL hypotheses (Bellair *et al.*, 2003; Haynie and South, 2005; Holland-Davis, 2006; Jensen, 2003; Lanza-Kaduce and Capece, 2003; Lee *et al.*, 2004; Rebellon, 2002).

The main dimensions of social structure were identified in the SSSL model as: (1) differential social organization (society, community, culture); (2) differential location in the social structure (age, gender, class, race, and other); (3) theoretically defined structural variables; (4) differential social location in groups (primary, secondary, and reference groups). These structural criminogenic factors may or may not be identified as explanatory constructs in structural theories of crime under (3), but to the extent that they are, Akers proposed that social learning is 'the perspective on individual behavior that is most compatible with sociological theories and most able to explicate the process by which structural correlates of crime do or do not have an effect on criminal behavior' (Akers, 1998: 329).

While this linking is possible with any structural theory, 'the most relevant of these explanatory concepts are drawn primarily from anomie, social disorganization, and conflict theories' (Akers, 1998: 334). However, beyond this statement and the hypothesis of the mediation of structural effects by social learning processes in the SSSL model, Akers did not specify how the causal logic of social learning theory at the micro level related to or could be transformed into the causal logic at the macro level. Jensen took the lead in taking this next step of showing how those extensions could be made in 'Taking Social Learning Global' (Jensen and Akers, 2003) noting that social learning is the most relevant theory for the micro–macro link because:

the most empirically accurate macro-level theories are likely to be compatible with the causal logic of the best substantiated 'micro-level' theories ... Akers has addressed the relation of social learning to other theories ... and has been elaborating the relevance of the theory to 'macro' issues. Yet, ... the transition to a more macro-level version has not been completed.

(Jensen and Akers, 2003: 15–16)

The clearest case of macro-level analysis is one where some properties of social systems are used to explain other properties of social systems. The data used to measure such properties can come from a variety of sources, including police reports, mortality statistics, victimization, and self-report survey data collected from individuals (contrary to the position taken by Messner and Rosenfeld). The 'rates' of crime treated as a macro-level variable are simply the 'summary statements of relative amounts of individual behavior in different groups or social categories. ... The dependent variable in macro-level theories is based ultimately on the same behavior that is the dependent variable in micro-level theories' (Akers, 1998: 330).

Survey data based on self-reported behavior can be aggregated and used to measure properties of social categories, territories and time, and there is no fundamental difference between aggregated responses of people to survey questions and aggregated police decisions to code events as crimes. In short, it is the manner in which data are used that defines a macro-level analysis, not the source of the data. For example, Jensen (2004) used Monitoring the Future survey data to study variations in *rates of offense behavior* over time. The data used to compile annual rates of offending were based on individuals' self-reports of offending used to create measures of the average number of offenses in each year of the survey. Trends, surges, and valleys are characteristics of a system over time and measurement of such characteristics can use survey responses of individuals. Moreover, when those temporal variations are related to other characteristics of a social system measured over time, the analysis is a macro-level analysis, regardless of the original source of the data.

Similarly, when those survey data are used to assess variations by region, size of community, or among socio-demographic categories (e.g., gender, race, class, single-parent households, levels of education, marital status), the focus is on variation in central tendencies among differentiated categories of respondents. We may distinguish these aggregated properties from integral properties of nations or social systems, but labeling them as purely individualistic or micro-level of analysis is misleading. If they are used to test theories about structural or cultural sources of variable rates of offending in a population, the meso or macro label is appropriate whether they are aggregated from reports of individuals to survey questions or acknowledged reports of offenses to the police by individuals.

SOCIAL LEARNING THEORY AND INTERNATIONAL VARIATIONS IN CRIME

The most clearly macro level of analysis involves extensions to the explanation of variations among nations and/or variations over time within or among nations. Smaller social 'systems,' or politically and socially defined territories within systems, would qualify as well. With these observations in mind, we move beyond the cross-cultural tests of social learning theory and tests of the SSSL cited above to a variety of national settings and multivariate analyses of homicide rates among nations. We believe the evidence shows that social learning theory has more explanatory power in more different societies than any other theory (see the research cited above). On the other hand, it should be noted that tests within societies have no bearing on the ability of the theory to explain variations among nations or over time.

At the same time, the statement that the same learning mechanisms operate across cultures is a macro-level proposition.

The most ambitious steps in a macro direction are the extensions of causal logic at the micro level to the explanation of variations over time and/or variations among nations. When the characteristics of societies that have been used in prior research to explain variations in homicide rates are summarized, the variables commonly invoked parallel the logic of the social learning theory (Jensen and Akers, 2003). For example, in her analysis of global variations in homicide, Rosemary Gartner (1990: 95–96) drew on a variety of perspectives to argue that a set of five variables should be considered in the attempt to explain differences among societies: cultural heterogeneity, exposure to violence, unstable family relationships, lack of state support of social welfare, and availability of unguarded targets. A macro version of social learning principles fits at least four of her variables better than any of the theories she credits as the theoretical foundation for her hypotheses.

Gartner hypothesizes that 'cultural heterogeneity taps the potential for conflict and an absence of control among groups' and that 'exposure to violence (whether direct or indirect) generates violence either through modeling, habituation, or desensitization.' Of course, modeling, habituation, and desensitization are learning mechanisms that fit into social learning theory, and are not found in any alternative sociological theories. Furthermore, although unstable family relationships and availability can be encompassed by other theories (e.g., social bonding theory and routine activities theory), social learning is the only theory that would encompass those variables and others. Neither of the macro–micro alternatives to social learning (strain–anomie and social bond–social disorganization) include cultural heterogeneity or enduring subcultures sustained by normal social learning processes. On the other hand, only institutional anomie theory includes the strength of the social welfare network as the central causal variable in the explanation of homicide rates among nations and that variable has yielded mixed results in empirical analyses (see Jensen, 2002 and Jensen and Akers, 2003).

When the causal logic of social learning theory is extended to the macro-level and applied to violence, the resulting perspective focuses on characteristics of societies that (1) impede or undermine (a) cultural and political consensus and (b) conventional institutional relationships, but (2) enhance (a) unregulated interaction in peer groups, (b) situational opportunities to engage in, or be a victim of crime, and (c) the development of sustained tendencies for people to resolve interpersonal conflicts through violent action. The macro-learning environment structured by these characteristics includes variables stressed by social disorganization (1a, 1b) and routine activity theory (2c), but social learning is the only theory encompassing all five.

Social learning theory incorporates 'normative' or cultural variables in a unique fashion that has implications at the macro level. Both social disorganization and anomie theories assume that normative consensus and social integration produce lower rates of crime. This is the assumption also in social bonding theory. For Hirschi (1969) American society is characterized by a dominant conventional culture that is learned to varying degrees among all structurally differentiated sub-categories. Those who do not internalize that conventional culture are freer to violate laws than those who do internalize them. The only feature of the cultural system that can generate high rates of crime is weak internalization. When applied to variations among nations, the causal logic of Hirschi's social bond theory (1969) would emphasize variations in the strength of conventional institutions such as family, school, religion, and community. For institutional anomie theory, pecuniary values dominate the cultural system in American society. High ambition coupled with low opportunity generates crime and such economic dominance undermines conventional institutions. When applied to variations among nations, institutional anomie theory identifies the strength of the societal welfare safety net as the key to explaining international variations. The weaker the net, the higher the crime rate.

Social learning theory encourages a consideration of variations in cultural features of societies that can influence crime rates. However, it does not require that all forms of crime be explained by the exact same set of macro characteristics. For example, cultural homogeneity in a society tends to be associated with both low rates of homicide and a strong government safety net (Jensen, 2002). In direct conflict with institutional anomie theory, those nations with the strongest safety nets actually accord less importance to the family in their lives and have higher divorce rates (Jensen, 2003). When there are strong governmental sources of subsistence and security based on citizenship, people are less dependent on the family and other social institutions. The data actually suggest that 'decommodification' is either a product of weak institutional ties or weakens them. Institutional anomie theorists argue that decommodification lowers homicide rates by strengthening conventional institutions. Contrary to their theory, research shows that decommodification not only weakens such institutions but is not a significant correlate of crime when variables central to social learning theory are controlled (Jensen and Akers, 2003).

A unique feature of the causal logic of social learning theory is the possibility of differentials, counteraction, and balancing among learning mechanisms. Rule-breaking behavior can be learned in a variety of ways (imitation, normative socialization, reinforcement, and differential association) and every application of the theory has to address the possibility of inconsistencies, differentials, and balancing in those mechanisms. For example, parents who smoke may attempt to teach their children that it is not appropriate for the young to smoke. Yet, the fact that the parents smoke affects their children through processes of imitation and perceived vicarious reinforcement. Strong ties to such parents do not have the same inhibiting effect as strong ties to non-smoking parents. The same contingent impacts can be detected for other forms of drug use. The inhibiting impact of attempts to teach norms prohibiting youthful deviance is weakened by other learning processes that work in a contrary direction. As Akers observes 'A child reared in a ... family that professes non-violent attitudes may nonetheless come to engage in and justify violence because he has witnessed abusive behavior in the home, has been the object of abuse himself, or has otherwise learned violent behavior in spite of the nonviolent cultural norms to which he has been exposed' (1998: 103).

Extending that logic, Akers and Jensen (2006) propose that the consideration of conflicting and 'countervailing mechanisms' at the micro-level applies to the macro-level as well. Historical events or policies such as the prohibition of alcohol can have countervailing consequences operating through structurally induced shifts in reinforcement schedules. For example, prohibition should have led to a decline in alcohol consumption through its effects on price and the sanctions risked and those reductions should have had an effect on homicide rates. Yet, the murder rate went up during most of the prohibitionist era (Jensen, 2000). What might appear as an anomaly is not surprising when the countervailing mechanisms at the macro level are considered. Although prohibition did indeed reduce alcohol consumption, it also increased competition over the illicit supply of alcohol as well as limited the means available to people to resolve conflicts in drinking situations. They would be less likely to invoke formal control mechanisms to deal with such conflict. In short, prohibition structured the relative costs and rewards of the supply and situational use of alcohol in ways that both reduced overall use and increased violence through other mechanisms. Thus, the macro-level events over time had an impact through mechanisms consistent with the logic and variables of social learning theory.

CONCLUSION

Social learning theory has evolved over the years from a perspective emphasizing the social behavioral mechanisms operating to explain individual variations in behavior (whether rule-abiding or rule-violating) to also addressing the structural and cultural circumstances that shape schedules of reinforcement and punishment within societies and international and temporal variations in crime. Social learning theory applies to the distribution of crime, delinquency and other forms of deviance, including such contemporary problems as terrorist violence, among individuals, groups, territories and time. Although much work needs to be done to make the theoretical transitions from one level to the other, there is an underlying shared logic that has been partly explicated here and can be further explicated and specified. The evidence is accumulating that the theory works well at the individual, meso, and macro levels.

Social learning theory has to be viewed in terms of the full range of learning mechanisms and processes and not simply one involving the learning of normative or cultural definitions. Moreover, although the theory accords considerable importance to social learning processes involving peers, the 'differentials' emphasized in the theory allow for both inhibition and facilitation of delinquent and criminal behavior involving not only peers but parents, teachers and a variety of others comprising the individual's social milieu.

Finally, it should be reiterated that social learning theory has fared extremely well in research testing it in both absolute terms and in competition with alternative theories. Whether it will do equally well in making the transition to explaining variations over time, variations within social systems, and variations among nations remains to be seen, but the steps taken thus far in those directions have been promising.

NOTE

1 Presentations, discussion, and tests of social learning theory in the research and pedagogical literature in criminology and the sociology of deviance, most commonly have to do with Akers' sociologically oriented approach. It should be noted however that Burgess and Akers drew upon the concepts and research of behavioral theory in psychology and that Akers has always explicitly recognized in presentations, papers, and publications that his social learning theory as a cognitive/behavioral explanation of crime and deviance draws upon, has commonalities with, and is fully compatible with the social learning approaches of Albert Bandura (1977, 1986), Gerald Patterson (1975) and his associates (Patterson et al., 1992), D. A. Andrews (Andrews and Bonta, 2003), and other psychologists who have applied social learning theory to anti-social, delinquent, and criminal behavior.

REFERENCES

Akers, R. L. (1968) 'Problems in the sociology of deviance: Social definitions and behavior,' *Social Forces* 46: 455–465.

——(1973) *Deviant Behavior: A Social Learning Approach*. Belmont, CA: Wadsworth.

——(1985) *Deviant Behavior: A Social Learning Approach*. Third Edition. Belmont, CA: Wadsworth.

——(1992) *Drugs, Alcohol, and Society: Social Structure, Process and Policy*. Belmont, CA: Wadsworth.

——(1998) *Social Learning and Social Structure: A General Theory of Crime and Deviance*. Boston, MA: Northeastern University Press.

Akers, R. L. and Jensen, G. F. (2003) *Social Learning Theory and the Explanation of Crime: A Guide for the New Century*. Advances in Criminological Theory, Volume 11. New Brunswick, NJ: Transaction Publishers.

——(2006) 'The empirical status of social learning theory of crime and deviance: The past, present, and future,' pp. 37–76 in F. T. Cullen, J. P. Wright, and K. R. Blevins (eds), *Taking Stock: The Status of Criminology Theory*. Advances in Criminological Theory Volume 15. New Brunswick, NJ: Transaction Publishers.

Akers, R. L., Krohn, M. D., Kaduce, L. L. and Radosevich, M. (1979) 'Social learning and deviant behavior: A specific test of a general theory.' *American Sociological Review* 44: 635–655.

Akers, R. L. and Sellers, C. S. (2004) *Criminological Theories: Introduction, Evaluation, and Application*. Los Angeles: L Roxbury Publishing.

Akers, R. L. and Silverman, A. L. (2004) 'Toward a social learning model of violence and terrorism,' pp. 19–36 in M. A. Zahn, H. H. Brownstein, and S. L. Jackson (eds), *Violence: From Theory to Research*. Cincinnati: LexisNexis Anderson.

Akins, K., Winfree, Jr. L. T. and Sellers, C. S. (2006) 'Extending the boundaries of social learning theory: The case of the suicide bombers in Gaza.' Paper presented at the 2006 Annual Meeting of the American Society of Criminology, Toronto, Canada.

Anderson, E. (1999) *Code of the Street: Decency, Violence, and the Moral Life of the Inner City*. New York: W. W. Norton.

Andrews, D. A. and Bonta, J. (2003) *The Psychology of Criminal Conduct*. Third Edition. Cincinnati, OH: Anderson Publishing.

Ardelt, M. and Day, L. (2002) 'Parents, siblings, and peers: Close social relationships and adolescent deviance,' *Journal of Early Adolescence* 22: 310–349.

Baier, C. and Wright, B. R. E. (2001) 'If you love me, keep my commandments: A meta-analysis of the effect of religion on crime.' *Journal of Research in Crime and Delinquency* 38: 3–21.

Bandura, A. (1977) *Social Learning Theory*. Englewood Cliffs, NJ: Prentice Hall.

——(1986) *Social Foundations of Thought and Action: A Social Cognitive Theory*. Englewood Cliffs, NJ: Prentice Hall.

Barlow, H. (2007) *Dead For Good: Martyrdom and the Rise of the Suicide Bomber*. Boulder: Paradigm Publishers.

Battin, S. R., Hill, K. G., Abbott, R. D., Catalano, R. F. and Hawkins, J. D. (1998) 'The contribution of gang membership to delinquency: Beyond delinquent friends.' *Criminology* 36: 93–115.

Batton, C. and Ogle, R. S. (2003) 'Who's it gonna be – you or me?': The potential of social learning for integrated homicide–suicide theory,' pp. 85–108 in R. L. Akers and G. F. Jensen (eds), *Social Learning Theory and the Explanation of Crime: A Guide for the New Century*. Advances in Criminological Theory, Volume 11. New Brunswick, NJ: Transaction Publishers.

Bellair, P., Roscigno, V. J. and Velez, M. B. (2003) 'Occupational structure, social learning, and adolescent violence,' pp. 197–226 in Ronald L. Akers and G. F. Jensen (eds), *Social Learning Theory and the Explanation of Crime: A Guide for the New Century*. Advances in Criminological Theory, Volume 11. New Brunswick, NJ: Transaction Publishers.

Benda, B. B. (1994) 'Testing competing theoretical concepts: Adolescent alcohol consumption,' *Deviant Behavior* 15: 375–396.

Benda, B. B. (2002) 'Religion and violent offenders in boot camp: a structural equation model,' *The Journal of Research in Crime and Delinquency* 39(1): 91–123.

Boeringer, S., Shehan, C. L. and Akers, R. L. (1991) 'Social contexts and social learning in sexual coercion and aggression: Assessing the contribution of fraternity membership,' *Family Relations* 40: 558–564.

Brezina, T. and Piquero, A. R. (2003) 'Exploring the relationship between social and non-social reinforcement in the context of social learning theory,' pp. 265–288 in R. L. Akers and G. F. Jensen (eds), *Social Learning Theory and the Explanation of Crime: A Guide for the New Century.* Advances in Criminological Theory, Volume 11. New Brunswick, NJ: Transaction Publishers.

Burgess, R. L. and Akers, R. L. (1966) 'A differential association-reinforcement theory of criminal behavior,' *Social Problems* 14: 128–147.

Burton, V., Cullen, F., Evans, D. and Dunaway, R. G. (1994) 'Reconsidering strain theory: Operationalization, rival theories, and adult criminality.' *Journal of Quantitative Criminology* 10: 213–239.

Cressey, D. R. (1960) 'Epidemiology and individual conduct: A case from criminology,' *Pacific Sociological Review* 3: 47–58.

Curry, G. D., Decker, S. H. and Egley, A., Jr. (2002) 'Gang involvement and delinquency in a middle school population,' *Justice Quarterly* 19: 275–292.

Durkin, K. F., Wolfe, T. W. and Clark, G. A. (2005) 'College students and binge drinking: An evaluation of social learning theory,' *Sociological Spectrum* 25: 255–272.

Gartner, R. (1990) 'The victims of homicide: A temporal and cross-national comparison,' *American Sociological Review* 55: 92–106.

Haynie, D. L. (2002) 'Friendship networks and delinquency: The relative nature of peer delinquency,' *Journal of Quantitative Criminology* 18: 99–134.

Haynie, D. L. and South, S. J. (2005) 'Residential mobility and adolescent violence,' *Social Forces* 84: 361–374.

Hirschi, T. (1969) *Causes of Delinquency.* Berkeley, California: University of California Press.

Hoffman, K. L., Kiecolt, K. J. and Edward, J. N. (2005) 'Physical violence between siblings,' *Journal of Family Issues* 26: 1103–1130.

Holland-Davis, L. (2006) Putting Behavior in Context: A Test of the Social Structure Social Learning Model. Ph.D. Dissertation. Gainesville, FL: University of Florida.

Hwang, S. and Akers, R. L. (2003) 'Substance use by Korean adolescents: a cross-cultural test of social learning, social bonding, and self-control theories.' pp. 39–64 in *Social Learning Theory and the Explanation of Crime: A Guide for the New Century.* R. L. Akers and G. F. Jensen (eds), Advances in Criminological Theory, Volume 11. New Brunswick, NJ: Transaction Publishers.

Hwang, S. and Akers, R. L. (2006) 'Parental and peer influences on adolescent drug use in Korea.' *Asian Journal of Criminology* 1: 59–69.

Jensen, G. F. (1969) 'Crime doesn't pay: Correlates of a shared misunderstanding,' *Social Problems* 17: 189–201.

——(2000) 'Prohibition, alcohol and murder: Untangling countervailing mechanisms,' *Homicide Studies* 4: 18–36.

——(2002) 'Institutional anomie and societal variations in crime: A critical appraisal,' pp. 45–74 in C. R. Block (ed.), *Talking about Violence: Building a Foundation for Scientific Discourse through Common Definitions and Measurements.* Volume 22 of the *International Journal of Sociology and Social Policy.*

——(2003) 'Gender variation in delinquency: Self-images, beliefs, and peers as mediating mechanisms,' pp. 15–178 in R. L. Akers and G. F. Jensen (eds), *Social Learning Theory and the Explanation of Crime: A Guide for the New Century.* Advances in Criminological Theory, Volume 11. New Brunswick, NJ: Transaction Publishers.

——(2004) Self-report data on youth violence over time. In R. Block and R. Block (eds), *Public Health and Criminal Justice Approaches to Homicide Research.* Washington, DC: Federal Bureau of Investigations.

——(2006) 'Religious cosmologies and homicide rates among nations: A closer look,' *Journal of Religion and Society* 13 [http://moses.creighton.edu/JRS/2006].

Jensen, G. F. and Akers, R. L. (2003) 'Taking social learning global: Micro-macro transitions in criminological theory,' pp. 9–37 in *Social Learning and the Explanation of Crime: A Guide for the New Century*. R. L. Akers and G. F. Jensen (eds), *Advances in Criminological Theory*, Volume 11. New Brunswick, NJ: Transaction Publishers.

Johnson, B. R., Sung Joon Jang, Larson, D. B. and Spencer De Li, S. (2000) 'Does adolescent religious commitment matter?: A reexamination of the effects of religiosity in delinquency,' *Journal of Research in Crime and Delinquency* 38: 22–44.

Junger Tas, J. (1992) 'An empirical test of social control theory,' *Journal of Quantitative Criminology* 8: 9–28.

Kandel, D. B. and Adler, I. (1982) 'Socialization into marijuana use among French adolescents: a cross-cultural comparison with the United States,' *Journal of Health and Social Behavior* 23: 295–309.

Kim, T. E. and Koto, S. G. (2000) 'Peer delinquency and parental social support as predictors of Asian American adolescent delinquency.' *Deviant Behavior* 21: 331–348.

Kimball, C. (2003) *When Religion Becomes Evil*. San Francisco: HarperCollins.

Lanza Kaduce, L. and Capece, M. (2003) 'A specific test of an integrated general theory,' pp. 179–196 in R. L. Akers and G. F. Jensen (eds), *Social Learning Theory and the Explanation of Crime: A Guide for the New Century*. Advances in Criminological Theory, Volume 11. New Brunswick, NJ: Transaction Publishers.

Lee, G., Akers, R. L. and Borg, M. (2004) 'Social learning and structural factors in adolescent substance use,' *Western Criminology Review* 5: 17–34 [online] http://wcr.sonoma.edu/v5n/lee.htm

Lopez, J. M. O., Lourdes, M. R., Redondo, M. and Martin, A. L. (1989) 'Influence of family and peer group on the use of drugs by adolescents,' *The International Journal of the Addictions* 24: 1065–1082.

Luckenbill, D. F. and Doyle, D. P. (1989) 'Structural position and violence: Developing a cultural explanation.' *Criminology* 27: 419–36.

McCord, J. (1991) 'Family relationships, juvenile delinquency, and adult criminality,' *Criminology* 29: 397–418.

Matsueda, R. L., Kreager, D. A. and Huizinga, D. (2006) 'Deterring delinquents: a rational choice model of theft and violence,' *American Sociological Review* 71: 95–122.

Messner, S. F. and Rosenfeld, R. (1997) 'Political restraint of the market and levels of criminal homicide: A cross-national application of institutional anomie theory,' *Social Forces* 75: 1393–1416.

——(2001) *Crime and the American Dream*. Belmont: Wadsworth/Thomson Learning.

Neff, J. L. and Waite, D. E. (2007) 'Male versus female substance abuse patterns among incarcerated juvenile offenders: Comparing strain and social learning variables,' *Justice Quarterly* 24: 106–132.

Paul, G. S. (2005) 'Cross-national correlations of quantifiable societal health with popular religiosity and secularism in the prosperous democracies, A first look,' *Journal of Religion and Society* 7 [http://moses.creighton.edu/JRS/2005/2005–11.html].

Patterson, G. R. (1975) *Families: Applications of Social Learning to Family Life*. Champaign, IL: Research Press.

——(1995) 'Coercion as a basis for early age of onset for arrest,' pp. 81–105 in J. McCord (ed.), *Coercion and Punishment in Long Term Perspectives*. Cambridge: Cambridge University Press.

——(2002) 'A brief history of the Oregon Model,' pp. 3–24 in J. B. Reid, G. R. Patterson and J. Snyder (eds), *Antisocial Behavior in Children and Adolescents: A Developmental Analysis and Model for Intervention*. Washington, DC: American Psychological Association.

Patterson, G. R., Reid, J. B. and Dishion, T. J. (1992) *Antisocial Boys. Eugene*, OR: Castalia Publishing Co.

Preston, P. (2006) 'Marijuana use as a coping response to psychological strain: racial, ethnic, and gender differences among young adults,' *Deviant Behavior* 27: 397–422.

Rebellon, C. J. (2002) 'Reconsidering the broken homes/delinquency relationship and exploring its mediating mechanism(s),' *Criminology* 40: 103–136.

Rosenfeld, R. and Messner, S. F. (1995) 'Crime and the American dream: an institutional analysis,' *Advances in Criminological Theory* 6: 159–181.

Sellers, C. S., Cochran, J. K. and Winfree, Jr. L. T. (2003) 'Social learning theory and courtship violence: An empirical test,' pp. 109–129 in R. L. Akers and G. F. Jensen (eds), *Social Learning Theory and the Explanation of Crime: A Guide for the New Century*. Advances in Criminological Theory, Volume 11. New Brunswick, NJ: Transaction Publishers.

Silverman, A. L. (2002) *An Exploratory Analysis of an Interdisciplinary Theory of Terrorism*. Ph.D. Dissertation, University of Florida.

Simons, R. L., Simons, L. G. and Wallace, L. E. (2004) *Families, Delinquency, and Crime: Linking Society's Most Basic Institution to Antisocial Behavior*. Los Angeles: Roxbury Publishing.

Skinner, B. F. (1953) *Science and Human Behavior*. New York: Macmillan.

Smith, T. R., Rizzo, E. and Empie, K. M. (2005) 'Yielding to deviant temptation: A quasi-experimental examination of the inhibiting power of intrinsic religious motivation,' *Deviant Behavior* 26: 463–482.

Stark, R. (2003) *For the Glory of God*. Princeton: Princeton University Press.

Stark, R. and Bainbridge, W. S. (1996) *Religion, Deviance, and Social Control*. New York: Routledge.

Sutherland, E. H. (1947) *Principles of Criminology*, Fourth Edition. Philadelphia: J. B. Lippincott.

Triplett, R. and Payne, B. (2004) 'Problem solving as reinforcement in adolescent drug use: Implications for theory and policy,' *Journal of Criminal Justice* 32: 617–630.

Wang, Shu-Neu and Jensen, G. F. (2003) 'Explaining delinquency in Taiwan: A test of social learning theory,' pp. 65–84 in R. L. Akers and G. F. Jensen (eds), *Social Learning Theory and the Explanation of Crime: A Guide for the New Century*. Advances in Criminological Theory, Volume 11. New Brunswick, NJ: Transaction Publishers.

Warr, M. (2002) *Companions in Crime: The Social Aspects of Criminal Conduct*. Cambridge: Cambridge University Press.

Welch, M. R., Tittle, C. R. and Grasmick, H. G. (2006) 'Christian religiosity, self-control, and social conformity,' *Social Forces* 84: 1605–1624.

Winfree, L. T., Jr., Backstrom, T. V. and Mays, G. L. (1994) 'Social learning theory, self reported delinquency, and youth gangs: A new twist on a general theory of crime and delinquency,' *Youth and Society* 26:147–177.

Zhang, L. and Messner, S. F. (1995) 'Family deviance and delinquency in China,' *Criminology* 33: 359–388.

4

Street Collectives and Group Delinquency: Social Disorganization, Subcultures and Beyond

Simon Hallsworth and Tara Young

The sight of young people congregating in public remains a source of perennial fascination for the adult world. It is a subject that concerns the wider public, often because they are terrified by the presence of such outsiders in their midst; the mass media because their flamboyant and defiant appearance is often read as signifying the arrival of a new public enemy; and for social researchers because they are interested in understanding what these groups represent and who want to understand why they appear. In this chapter, we will examine how ongoing pre-occupation with what we genetically term 'street collectives' has resolved itself in the history of criminological thought from the early twentieth century through to the present day.

To examine the world of street collectives (a term which includes groups such as peer groups, gangs and youth subcultures more generally), we will review theoreti-cal attempts to understand the formation, structure and criminality of street collectives as this has unfolded within Anglo-American research traditions. This chapter is comprised of four sections. In the first, we profile the work of the classical American sociological traditions. We will look particularly at the theories of social disorganisation theory, strain theory and American subcultural theory. In the second section, we examine how British criminologists in the 1960s came to redevelop subcultural theory within the remit of a more critical criminology. The third section focuses on contemporary developments in criminological theory, looking specifi-cally at the rise of administrative criminology, cultural criminology and gender.

The chapter concludes by highlighting the lessons learned and suggests new lines of enquiry for research in this area.

THE CLASSICAL AMERICAN TRADITION

Our survey of the classical American tradition begins by considering the pioneering work of the Chicago School looking, in particular, at the seminal work of Frederic Thrasher (1927). Not only did these theorists reinvent the sociological study of urban delinquency, their work has contributed to, and heavily influenced, subsequent American and British criminology.

Social disorganisation theory: the Chicago School

Reasoning that human behaviour (including criminality) was heavily influenced by the environment in which people lived, scholars within the Chicago School argued that to understand crime it was necessary to take note of the structural conditions that predisposed some people towards delinquency. Early Chicago studies noticed that the juvenile delinquency rate was highest in the poor, inner city areas decreasing as one moved outwards towards affluent ones (Shaw and McKay, 1942, 1969). Furthermore, the pattern of declining rates of delinquency remained stable irrespective of the racial or ethnic composition of the population. In order to explain this phenomenon, these scholars drew upon organic analogies and envisaged the city of Chicago as a living organism with its own ecology. They found that urban areas that were physically run-down, poverty-stricken, unstable and disorganised encouraged delinquency and crime whilst stable, organised environments with settled homogenous populations tended to promote law-abiding behaviour.

By applying a '*social ecological*' framework grounded on this ontological assumption, Fredric Thrasher (1927) understood the emergence of gangs to be a response to the '*social disorganisation*' apparent in the developing industrial city that was Chicago during the 1920s. He argued that the preconditions for social disorganisation were driven by cultural conflict between ethnically diverse populations thrown together in the 'melting pot' of an industrial city expanding through mass industrialisation and inward migration. In a turbulent environment (where different cultures vied to maintain the vestiges of their own tradition) young people turned to each other and formed their own social organisations. Considered this way, the gang represented an opportunity for young men to acquire status and recognition through mobilising collectively and begin their struggle (as individuals and as members of a discernible group) for independence and economic prosperity. The gang, as such, became a *conduit* through which the young could resolve cultural conflicts, construct new identities, set their own agenda and live by their own rules. In sum, it offered the urban poor a 'substitute for what society fails to give … it fills a gap and affords an escape' (Thrasher, 1927: 33). From this frame of reference, Thrasher identified 1,313 gangs within Chicago. These he considered to be:

> … an interstitial group, originally formed spontaneously, and then integrated through conflict. It is characterised by the following types of behaviour; meeting face to face, milling,

movement through space as a unit, conflict and planning. The result of this collective behaviour is the development of tradition, unreflective internal structure, esprit de corps, solidarity, morale, group awareness, and attachment to a local territory.

(Thrasher, 1927: 46)

Thrasher did not conceive the gang as an inherently deviant or delinquent organisation but as a symptom of a society in crisis. As we will observe subsequently, this non-criminalising approach to street collectives will subsequently change.

The idea that criminality could be a response to *social environments* was, at the time, novel. It challenged the dominant view of group delinquency as biologically or genetically determined and provided the principles on which much subsequent criminological thought on youth crime was based. However progressive the urban ecology theory was in helping to forge a new way of researching and conceptualising youth delinquency it incurred criticisms that would ultimately lead to its unpopularity as an explanatory tool for understanding deviance. Despite its limits, social disorganisation theory remains an important resource upon which subsequent theories have drawn.

Anomie and strain theory

While the American criminologist Robert Merton is not recognised for having theorised the emergence of delinquent groups or subcultures, his influential attempt to rework Durkhiem's theory of anomie – into what would become strain theory – shaped the development of much subcultural theory that did. Merton sought to explain the emergence of deviant behaviour and understood it to be the product of anxiety or strain brought about by constraints inherent in modern society (Merton, 1938). For Merton, a harmonious, less deviant, society was one that balanced the acquisition of societal goals and the means by which these can be attained. Conversely, an anomic society, characterised by a state of 'normlessness' and one that encourages deviant behaviour, is one in which there is a disjuncture between the acquired goals and means. In other words, a society can be understood in terms of the social ends it induces its members to aspire towards and the availability of the institutional means by which these ends can be legitimately obtained.

Merton argued, that in America, people are socialised into a value system that celebrates status and the display of material wealth. Within this value system people are led to believe that, irrespective of culture, biology, social difference or socio-economic position, everyone has [equal] access to money and power (approved social goals) if they have the ability and work hard enough (approved social means) to achieve them (Merton, 1938). In other words, American society perpetuates the myth that everyone can live the 'American dream'.

Just as American society defines what people should aspire towards, so this value system also prescribes the legitimate means by which these goals can be socially attained. Ideally, this is supposed to be via success at school, college and university and by successful navigation through the occupational hierarchy. Crime and delinquency enter this equation because, whilst the ends to which members should aspire are available to everyone, the legitimate means by which these ends are supposed to be secured are not. In other words, not everyone is able to obtain access to the schools, colleges, and work places necessary to succeed and not everybody will excel in them. At the same time American society places a far higher premium on securing socially desirable ends than it does on obtaining them through legitimately prescribed means. What this creates is a discrepancy between means and ends, which creates the basis for 'strain' within the structure of American society. It is this profound disjunction that provokes what Merton identified as various 'delinquent adaptations' or 'solutions' (Merton, 1968).

For those who lack innate privileges and who have been bequeathed lower life chances, some may adapt to their predicament by innovating in ways that resolve themselves into delinquent solutions. This occurs as a response to the psychic shock they experience in resolving the contradiction between wanting to possess what is socially desirable but being unable to accumulate them through legitimate avenues. It is the experience of 'strain' that explains criminality. Acquisitive crimes, such as shoplifting, robbery, theft and fraud are, in Mertonian terms, forms of innovation. To cite a case of collective delinquency well known in the British context, the Kray Twins remain paradigmatic exemplars of this spirit of innovation. Born into an impoverished family in a poor neighbourhood in London's East End the Kray brothers had limited life chances. Lacking access to the legitimate means by which a good life could be bought they resolved the 'strain' of unrequited desire by 'innovating' in Merton's terms. In this case, by mobilising the one resource they did possess (which was a heightened propensity for violence) to make them, by the 1960s, millionaires and the darlings of England's tawdry celebrity circuit.

Like the Chicago School, Merton offered an explanation of delinquent behaviour that is sociological and does not reduce it to individual biology or biography. Crime and deviance is understood as a *rational* adaptation to the social situations in which people find themselves that occur independently of their will. The importance Merton placed on the influence social structure has upon individual behaviour meant that, under the certain conditions, anyone could be deviant or become a criminal. Whilst Merton's strain theory impacted significantly on the development of criminological thought its deterministic foundation that it also received much criticism. For example, strain theory does not adequately explain why some people conform whilst others 'innovate' or 'retreat' when each share a similar set of life chances. Given that large numbers of people live in poverty, one obvious criticism of Merton's approach would be to point out that it predicts higher levels of crime than actually occur (Downes and Rock, 2003). The irony is that the majority of people conform and are not criminogenic despite experiencing a considerable disjunction between the ends they have been taught to desire and the lack of available means to gratify them. Finally, this theory also fails to explain a well-recognised aspect of group delinquency which is its irrational and expressive nature. For this we need to turn to subcultural theories and eventually to phenomenology.

Subculture and the gang

Drawing upon the legacy of the Chicago school and heavily influenced by strain theory, this tradition sought to examine and explain the delinquency often associated with groups of young, poor and disadvantaged young people.

In *Delinquent Boys: the Subculture of the Gang* (1955) Albert Cohen, took issue with Mertonian strain theory. He argued that it is not the strain of being thwarted from achieving economic success that creates the delinquent adaptations that might lead to the formation of the gang; on the contrary, it was a more proximate source of frustration. Delinquency, Cohen argued derived from the experience some working class young people had when they came to realise that they are destined to lose 'status' in a social system organised around middle-class values. He believed this to be especially acute in the modern school system.

Schools, in Mertonian terms, are part of the legitimate means by which people seek to achieve material success. As institutional ensembles, however, schools are organised by middle class people, according to middle class values, which most middle class children will successfully succeed in navigating their way through precisely because they are middle class. The experience of not being able to win out in the terms schools establish as legitimate (such as obtaining high grades in exams) is experienced by some young working class men as '*status frustration*' (Cohen, 1955). Status frustration resolves itself (psychologically) in to a form of '*reaction formation*'. To resolve the anxiety provoked by the prospect of failing, some working class men respond creatively to their situation by forging a group or gang whose values consciously repudiate those of the middle class school system that has failed them. Against a dominant order that stresses the importance of forward thinking, hard work, delayed gratification, reserve and abstention from violence, the gang celebrates instead behaviours that are utilitarian, malicious, and negative, and these come to be revered in the subculture to which they belong (Cohen, 1955).

Richard Cloward and Lloyd Ohlin (1960) also found a greater proliferation of gangs in working-class communities and agreed that collective forms of delinquency occur when aspirations are blocked. Where they diverged from Cohen, was with the view that working class youth aspire to middle class values and suffer psychologically as a consequence. For these subcultural theorists, working-class youths certainly have aspirations beyond their means, but these are not necessarily middle-class. Consequently, they do not experience 'status frustration' or 'reaction formation'. In a view closer to Merton than Cohen, and by evoking Edwin Sutherland's (1939) 'differential association theory' which suggested that crime occurs when there is a surplus of justifications that validate it over those that promote law abiding behaviour, Cloward and Ohlin proffer a more rationalistic view of why working class young people might join gangs.

Like Merton, they also believe that delinquency occurs because there is a structural disjunction between what society defines as success and the social means made available to realise it. As the capitalist system is organised in ways that systematically preclude the poor who simply cannot compete equally for success it is inevitable that some young people will refuse to abide by its norms and conventions. Although they may experience strain, these young people are free (by virtue of structural inequality) from moral constraints, such as guilt and anxiety, and organise themselves into subcultural units that provide support, approval and ultimately a rationale for delinquent behaviour. Since deviant behaviour, like all behaviour, is learned behaviour (Sutherland, 1939). While for Cloward and Ohlin, social structure creates the preconditions for the formation of youth subculture, the precise form it takes is shaped by the pattern of already existing criminal networks operating around it. They argued that the more established the criminal a network is, that is if an area supports a stable, longstanding criminal fraternity that controls illegal activities provides role models and money-making opportunities for young people, the more organised the gang will be in relation to committing income generating offences. On the other hand, if no organised group exists, if little to no illegal opportunities are available or the older criminal fraternity are ineffective, it is likely that the gangs will be disorganised, fighting groups (Cloward and Ohlin, 1960).

What is strong about this subcultural tradition is that it attends more closely to a process than can be found in the macro sociology of Merton. Where it is weak and where it has been criticised lies in its assumption that entities such as gangs were populated by outsiders who had internalised or created value systems that departed in some significant way from that of mainstream society. In a powerful critique of this assumption Miller argued that many of the values celebrated by gang members were in fact embedded within the parent working class communities from which gang members derived (Miller, 1975). His work stressed the continuities that linked the gang member and the parent community more than the differences that separated them. Matza was also critical of the assumption that these outsiders were committed to a different value system (Matza, 1964). Because they engaged in 'techniques of neutralisation' this suggested that they accepted the dominant moral order, while their commitment to deviance was in most cases, he argued, short lived. It was something most would 'drift' into and drift away from. This did not, he thought, require fully fledged criminal careers.

THE BRITISH SUBCULTURAL TRADITION

America has a long standing gang research tradition, whereas Britain's enquiry into the gang has been much more limited; though this situation has changed with the contemporary rediscovery of the gang (Hallsworth and Young, 2008). There are a number of reasons that might explain the absence of the gang in British research, as well as the rediscovery of it, and these bear consideration. To begin with, it could be argued that the UK has always had its fair share of gangs but these have not been accorded due attention by a criminological establishment that remains, according to American gang researcher Malcolm Klein, in denial of them (Klein, 2002). A second and more plausible conjecture, holds that whilst there might well have been gangs present in British society, they were relatively rare and did not approximate to the numerous, large, organised fighting groups found in the US. As such, they did not warrant the attention the gang would receive in the US. Allied to this was the fact that while the gang literature might help explain the gang, it was unable, in and of itself, to help make sense of the most important, and visible, youth subcultures that prevailed in British society during the post-war period.

Subculture and parent culture

When British criminologists did get around to studying the nature of group-based delinquency what they found did not readily approximate the kind of gangs identified in the American subcultural tradition. It is this crucial difference that would lead the British research tradition along a different trajectory from that of the United States. It was however in the pioneering work of the British criminologist

David Downes that the real differences between the American and the British experience were clearly distinguished.

In a formative attempt to apply American subcultural theory to the British context, Downes studied adolescents in London's East End (Downes, 1966) and concluded that the British experience of gang formation did not mirror that of America. Young working-class males did not display problems of '*adjustment*' or '*status frustration*' as theorised by Cohen. On the contrary they were fully immersed in mainstream working-class culture and displayed little discontentment with their status. Cohen's notion of 'malicious', 'negativistic' behaviour as an expressive symbol of young people's frustration had, for Downes, no resonance in British East End life. As with Millar, the young people he studied did not display a morality at odds with the dominant culture but values they had derived from their working class parent culture. While these youths were clearly products of their class of origin they were however 'disassociated' from conventional middle class norms that governed the educational establishments they attended and the world of work. Early on in life, Downes argued, they came to recognise that the work available to them was inherently debased, boring and tedious. The more they recognised this as their allocated lot in life the more they would aspire to compensate by seeking in the sphere of leisure a place of freedom that the disciplines of wage labour could not provide. The result of this 'dissociation' was not organised street gangs but 'street-corner' groups. Whilst youth in street corner groups would engage in delinquency, they did so periodically and not as confirmation of a commitment to crime as an occupation. Their expressed deviance was an attempt to create excitement and autonomy that the labour market, by its nature, denied them (Downes, 1966).[1]

Though, by no means explicitly seeking to provide a theory of gang or youth delinquency, Paul Willis subsequently provided a more nuanced explanation of why certain working class males recurrently appeared attached to a delinquent set of norms that repudiated those in mainstream culture. In his influential book *Learning to Labour* (Willis, 1977), Willis attempted to explain how 'working class kids get working class jobs'. In a detailed ethnographic study of a school he showed how young working-class men, in opposition to a school environment structured around middle-class norms and values, rebelled by forming their own subculture that embraced values that consciously repudiated it. They would, for example, code intellectual work as 'feminised work' irrelevant to their material needs. In a school system whose value system stressed the importance of personal characteristics such as intellect, restraint and self-control, his 'lads' celebrated in opposition to these macho values such as toughness, aggression and immediate gratification, whilst also embracing a highly misogynistic and racist worldview. While the behaviours adopted by the working-class young men in Willis's study could be viewed as a rational response to a middle class educational environment (they perceived as) established to fail them, it was essentially a 'negative adaptation' as, ironically, what this rebellion ultimately accomplished was to readying them for the world of mundane, unskilled, low paid work capitalism they had identified as their destiny.

What the British research tradition found was not a disenfranchised American-style gang but a youth subculture which, while tolerating delinquency, was ultimately steeped in the mores of wider working class culture it also reproduced. What is common to these research studies is the picture they establish of group delinquency.

This is represented as a rational response to being born into a poor socio-economic class, in a milieu where upward mobility is limited and where available work is mundane. Young working class males in effect realise what life has in store for them and adopt a delinquent pose as a way of redeeming in leisure what the world of work with its disciplines denies.

Subculture and style

After an initial engagement with American gang research in the 1950s and 1960s, British criminology started to refocus its attention away from the gang and towards subculture and style. Though a focus still remained on accounting for what was perceived as problematic youth, the focus on territorial-based youth collectives had largely disappeared. This reflected, in part, an attempt to engage with the reality of a post-war world where gangs on the American model did not appear to exist, but this shift was also motivated by the need to make sense of an array of flamboyant youth subcultures that did. The shift in focus also reflected a growing recognition that the defining characteristics of post-war subcultural groups such as the Teddy Boys, Mods and Rockers, Skinheads and Punks could not be adequately understood in terms of classic subcultural theory: first, because the stylistic features of these subcultures were widely distributed across society and were not the sole property of a single group and; second, because most members of these groups did not routinely engage in overt delinquent behaviour associated with street-based fighting units.

In an attempt to grasp the motivational forces behind subcultures, British sociologists, particularly those associated with the Birmingham School of Cultural Studies, argued that subcultures could be understood as expressive of what Stuart Hall and Tony Jefferson would famously identify as 'resistance through ritual' (Hall and Jefferson, 1976). Far from seeing subculture as a product of the ecology of place alone, it was theorised instead as a rational (if imaginary) response to the material contradictions young people experienced living in the context of post-war capitalist society. What the subcultural response marked, specifically, was a symbolic attempt to resolve these lived contradictions through innovative cultural development. For example, the skinhead movement could be viewed as a pathological (and dramatic) response to the decline of the [white] working class community in a de-industrialising society. In the appropriation of artefacts such as Doctor Martin boots, Ben Sherman shirts (whose meanings changed in the process of appropriation), black bomber jackets, red braces, they symbolically resolved the crisis of their parent class in a creative subculture that accentuated naked machismo. At the symbolic level this could be viewed as an attempt to redeem and reclaim the virtues of a labour movement that was in the process of decline through de-industrialisation. As with Willis's 'lads' what was attempted, however, was no more than a symbolic gesture. The style revolt evident in the subculture of violence around which they constructed their identities did not address the objective problems of society that produced the conditions that they were responding to. For these subcultural theorists then, what the wider society typically coded as dangerous and threatening subcultures were in fact highly creative social movements, even if the solutions posed were often imaginary.

Drawing upon the labelling theory of Becker (1966), new sociologists of deviance such as Stan Cohen also drew attention to the pivotal role played by control agents in constructing the very deviant groups they recoiled from in outrage. In his study of the Mods and Rockers (Cohen, 1980), Cohen showed that subcultures were themselves as much products of media '*demonisation*' as they were spontaneous creators of their world. By constructing a '*folk devil*', through the medium of a '*moral panic*', the defining features of the subculture were constructed in the manner of a self-fulfilling prophecy. The social response – often evident in sensationalised media reporting, escalation in law enforcement activity and hysterical political over-reaction – created a context in which low level delinquency among a diffuse group of young people could be reconstructed as a major social problem. The social response also helped to provide an identifiable set of core themes around which the identity of the group in question could coalesce.

While subcultural theory has proved enduring and innovative it began to lose its popularity with the post-modern turn. In societies where identities forged through association with older class structures mutate towards forms of identity characterised increasingly by consumption, and in the context of a more hybridised culture, the preconditions in which the post-war subcultures flourished have been progressively dismantled. In post-modern fixed subcultures break up and endlessly mutate. Style culture replaces subculture in societies where identities become atomised and free-floating.

CONTEMPORARY RESEARCH

If we were to stand back and survey the history of contemporary research into group deviance as it has developed from the early twentieth century then one observation that could be made is that we are not looking at the development of a unitary research programme. On the contrary we are looking at a research domain, which is neither homogeneous nor unitary. If we look a little closer then this burgeoning industry can usefully be subdivided into three broad strands of enquiry: administrative criminology, cultural and critical criminology and gender. In what follows, we critically examine each of these research problematic, drawing attention to their respective strengths and weaknesses.

Administrative criminology

By far the most dominant areas of gang research in the US today is what could be classified as the administrative criminological tradition. Within this tradition the gang is considered to be a social problem that must be suppressed. At the heart of this enterprise we find a convergence of interests between academics and policy makers around the need for 'action' and 'evaluative' research dedicated to discovering 'what works'. Indeed, what has emerged within this tradition is an empirically based programme of research dedicated to the pragmatic goal of establishing the reality of gangs, identifying the prevalance of gang related offences and the efficacy of programmes designed to tackle the gang problem.

If we consider the research focus of the administrative tradition then its approach to the gang has involved: (i) typologising the gang; (ii) identifying the (risk) factors for gang membership; (iii) understanding structure and the factors that promote group integration; and (iv) evaluating the impact of various intervention programmes.

In antithesis to Thrasher, who defined the gang in a non-criminalising way, state sponsored gang researchers conceive the gang as an inherently criminogenic group and defined exclusively by reference to its engagement in crime and violence. From Thrasher's view of the gang as an interstitial entity formed spontaneously we thus move towards the contemporary view of the gang as a group defined by its delinquency. Klein (1971) offers one highly influential definition of the gang defined in these terms:

> Any detonable adolescent group of youngsters who (a) are generally perceived as a distinct aggregation by others in their neighbourhood; (b) recognise themselves as a detonable group (almost invariably with a group name); and (c) have been involved in a sufficient number of delinquent incidents to call forth a consistent negative response from neighbourhood residents, and/or law.
>
> (Klein 1971: 46)

Whereas the American subcultural tradition saw gang formation as a response to structural dislocations, the focus of administrative gang research has been directed at understanding the role that more proximate social forces perform in reproducing gang culture and integration. In his work on gangs in Los Angeles, Klein (1971) argued that gangs coalesced around a set of internal group mechanisms, which helped forge group solidarity. One of Klein's key assumptions was that the gang became stronger, and its solidarity more developed, in response to the 'external pressures' directed against it from outside agencies. Although he identified poverty, unemployment, weak family socialisation and the threat of violence, as key factors in forging group cohesion, he particularly emphasised the role that external pressures played in forging it. Quite controversially, by 'external influences' Klein did not mean other gangs and law-enforcement agencies; those he singled out were 'soft' services that were employed to help gang members; particularly detached youth work and community inclusion projects such as 'gang' events. Subsequently, Klein called for a 'lassiez-faire' approach to the problem of the gang and the complete withdrawal of all support services that worked with them (Decker and Van Winkle, 1997: 11). Klein's 'withdrawal' theory was tested with questionable success at a Group Guidance Project in Ladino Hills where the emergent findings was a decrease in group cohesion but an overall *increase* in delinquency particularly involving serious offences (Decker and Van Winkle, 1997: 11).

Much of the research conducted within the administrative research tradition has involved the use of questionnaires, often conducted in schools to develop risk profiles of gang members. Analysis in the area has been directed at profiling group structure, membership, delinquency and identifying (often through an analysis of various psychometric variables such as their relationship to authority figures), the factors that distinguish gang from non-gang affiliated young people. Such surveys have also been used to quantify the number of people who are gang affiliated and to assess gang distribution more generally. The findings of such studies reinforce the view of the gang member as a pathological outsider by showing that gang members are likely to have a more persistent and serious crime profile and to be exposed to more risk factors associated with criminal behaviour than non-gang-affiliated members (see Klein and Maxon, 1995).

Though the administrative tradition in gang research has provided some important empirical data on the formation and nature of gangs, much of the work conducted within this tradition is atheoretical and empiricist in focus. Another limitation of this tradition is its reductiveness and compulsion towards producing 'voodoo statistics' that reduce complex social issues into mathematical equations (Young, 2004: 13). Two further criticisms can also be made. First, though factors like poverty and unemployment are mentioned their analysis is often marginalised in the analysis. There is little attempt to theorise, how and why gang formation is shaped by wider socio-economic and political environments. When such factors are mentioned they are simply listed as background factors without being systematically studied; a position which, by default, leads to a representation of the gang as – literally – the sole author of its depravity. What this vision of the gang has also encouraged is an analysis that connects it with various visions of an urban underclass steeped in what Charles Murray would identify as 'moral turpitude' (Murray, 1990). Second, contemporary research projects are often restricted to narrow school-based comparative studies in communities where ethnic minorities are over-represented which creates the impression gangs are a social problem most readily associated with these groups. Within administrative criminology the lessons of the subcultural tradition that sought to humanise the gang member have largely disappeared in discipline that now imagines them instead as a pathological expression of a class which needs to be suppressed.

Cultural and critical criminology

As noted above, the administrative tradition tends to construct gangs as a serious social problem (to be coercively managed) and views the role of academics as collaborators to assist policy makers towards this end. However, it is not a position that is universally accepted. A number of scholars, influenced by different schools of thought such as phenomenology and Marxism, have established a very different perspective to the gang and law enforcement effort directed to suppress it. What distinguishes this tradition from its administrative adversary are a number of key differences. First, in contrast to the empiricism that prevails in administrative criminology, the critical tradition places greater emphasis upon grounded ethnographic research. Second, this tradition is more sensitive to the phenomenology of the delinquent and to delinquent behaviour. In this sense, cultural and critical criminology attempts to excavate the lived reality of those involved in street-based groups and, by so doing, sought to comprehend existential narratives. Third, this tradition differs in so far as it locates the analysis of the gang further within the wider socio-economic context which is understood to crucially shape and determine gang formation and persistence. Fourth, this tradition does not, necessarily, view law enforcement as benign. On the contrary, it conceives the effort of control agencies such as the police, the penal estate and 'punitive culture' as being as problematic as the gang menace it confronts. Lastly, the gang is theorised in ways that conceive it as an important social phenomenon which cannot simply be understood as, or reduced to, a crime and violence machine.

In what may be viewed as a critique of Klein's position (which conceived the gang as a fragile and temporal entity) longitudinal ethnographic has shown that many gangs are both longstanding and durable (see Campbell, 1984; Horowitz, 1983; Kontos *et al.* 2003; Moore *et al.* 1978; Moore, 1991; Padilla, 1992). For these ethnographic researchers the gang exists precisely because the social conditions which create it (poverty, marginalisation, criminalisation and chronic unemployment) persist.

These social conditions connect with the impact of wider socio-economic changes within American society; the impact of which has been to create the preconditions in which urban gangs have taken root and thrived.

In the space of two decades America has undergone a process of profound economic restructuring in its movement towards a service sector economy. This process has occasioned a decline and reduction in America's manufacturing industry that constituted the basis of employment for many people living in urban areas. This shift resulted in the loss of many manual and semi-skilled jobs for working class communities, and America's minority ethnic populations. In the face of entrenched economic decline that would see the economic base of many cities destroyed, the seeds were sown for the construction of urban ghettos whose populations were forced to exist in conditions of abject poverty, unemployment and underdevelopment (Huff, 1989). It is in areas subject to political and economic exclusion and hyper-ghettoisation (Wacquant, 2005), characterised by ever-decreasing employment opportunities, (Moore, 1978, 1991), multiple marginality (Virgil, 1988) and mass incarceration that gangs have prospered.

For cultural criminologists the gang appears in such environments precisely because the conditions of life within the ghetto compel young people to discover alternative ways to entertain, protect themselves, achieve respect and status, find economic security and escape the futility of life (Moore, 1978, 1991). In effect, far from being expressive of a crisis of social reproduction the gang meets a range of personal and social needs for its members in a harsh and unforgiving environment. While the 'codes of the street' (Anderson, 1999) to which the urban young live can cause and be used to justify extreme violence (for example in the case of drive by shootings and 'gang bangs' (see Saunders, 1994); as well as illegalities such as robbery, drug distribution and use, the gang also offers members a space for sociability and friendship as well as a space from which they can escape and transcend the boredom of everyday life.

The work of Jack Katz presents a unique interpretation of group behaviour in his analysis of what he termed the 'seductions of evil' (Katz, 1990). What makes his work relevant is that he provides an important series of insights into the inner world of young delinquents. This he does through an analysis of the phenomenology of crime. Intrinsic to his approach is a need to recognise that youth involvement in groups and delinquency cannot be readily understood by seeing it in rational and instrumental terms. Young men, he observes, enjoy 'walking the ways of the badd-ass' because they are seduced by the experience of appearing evil; it is something they take pleasure in. Reminiscent of the view adopted by Matza, Katz argues that in a monotonous existence where realistic exit strategies are limited, young men will creatively circumvent the mundanely of their life by reconstructing it in sensational ways. Run down estates take on the trappings of sovereign empires that must – like the nation state – be defended. By congregating in public young men take on the role of the urban street warrior defending their territory from outsiders. By engaging in violent acts and, as importantly, weaving extravagant legends around their violence, so the profane world is remade as a liminal space of excitement and danger. Conceived this way in the collective life of the gang the ordinary features of urban life can be spectacularly transcended. Subsequently, the gang member is less a calculating rational actor and far more a transgressive edge worker who dwells at and beyond the limits (Katz, 1990). Considered within a cultural criminological focus, the gang has been conceived as a rich and complex site of cultural production. Indeed, contemporary gang researchers have shown gangs to be more reminiscent of new social movements with a longstanding history, political trajectory of development, complex traditions and rituals. Over the last two decades David Brotherton and Luis Barrios have traced the development of the Almighty Latin King and Queen Nation (ALKQN). Their work has tracked how the ALKQN have attempted to evolve from a traditional fighting gang, heavily implicated in crime and drug distribution, into a social movement (Brotherton and Barrios, 2004). In this process, Brotherton and Barrios note how the gang have made a conscious attempt (continuously thwarted by law-enforcement), to reduce the level and type of violence and to encourage members to live in accordance to the principles of 'Kingism' in order to liberate themselves, and their community from oppression and poverty.[3]

In recent work studying gang formation in Kazan, Svetlana Stephenson also presents a profound challenge to the crisis of reproduction thesis (Stephenson, 2008). In what she terms the 'Kazan leviathan' Stephenson shows how a social crisis, precipitated by the break-up of the Soviet Union, created a power vacuum in the Kazan area and substantial rises in violent street crime. In part, the violence was driven by the transformation of volatile groups into territorially based street gangs but, paradoxically, it was also these street gangs that helped reduce the violence by their own mobilisation of this resource. In the first instance, street gangs eliminated the anomic predatory violence that the economic and political crisis provoked. Second, having gained sovereign control of their territory the groups came to exercise the rule of law within it particularly where this could not be guaranteed by the state. Truces between groups were established over time and rules of conduct were drawn up to regulate the way violence was utilised. Evoking the work of the political theorist Thomas Hobbes, Stephenson sought to demonstrate that the street gang emerged in much the way as the state did in the earlier stages of its formation. While in part a symptom of social breakdown in Kazan, its street gangs (the new Leviathan) themselves became vehicles through which governance from below was exercised in a disorganised period when it could no longer be guaranteed from above.

In conclusion, this rich and diverse research tradition has drawn attention to the harsh social conditions that provoke gang formation and has explored the consequences of the severe censure and repression members experience. In keeping with the subcultural tradition, in whose footsteps it follows, this tradition depicts the gang as a rational adaptation to hostile conditions, whilst not losing sight of the destructive consequences gang membership has on individuals and the community. This includes an analysis of the damage inflicted by inter and intra-gang rivalry, a sober appreciation of the relationship between gangs and drugs as well as identifying the effects of extreme repression in a law-and-order society with a mass incarceration agenda.

The gender turn

The final strand of research we consider in this chapter places at its centre the question of gender and considers how this important, but oft neglected variable, can help us understand group life and group offending.

Influenced by feminism, much of the early work undertaken within this tradition lay in re-evaluating the role of women in relation to the gang as this had been theorised by male gang researchers. This work was spurred by the recognition that, while male criminologists had made a number of important contributions to the task of understanding the world of the male gang member, whenever they spoke of women, what was said rarely extended beyond trite generalisations and crass stereotypes. To an extent this was fuelled by the belief that women were, as Sutherland and Cressey (1966) argued, essentially 'law-abiding' and were thus removed from a dominant male culture that bred gangs. Considered this way, the kind of crime a person committed was shaped by their gender. Men, being men, would tend towards committing crimes like violence and robbery while women being women would engage in sexual promiscuity, infanticide, fraud and shoplifting (Chesney-Lind and Hagedorn, 1999).

Considered through the stereotypical and sexist lens of this traditional male gaze, females in the 'gang' were typically considered 'bad girls' because, according to the assumptions these researchers typically brought to bear, 'good girls' did not normally join gangs. When female participation was considered worthy of analysis it was relegated to auxiliary 'bit parts' within the male experience (Campbell, 1984). In practice gang women were thought to exist either to gratify the sexual appetite of the males or act as their lowly assistants by providing them with shelter and alibis. Within this essentially negative and essentially misogynistic representation gang women were assumed to be either sexually permissive, cheap and available (in other words 'sluts'); or were alternatively construed as 'maladjusted tomboys' – in other words as women who had betrayed their 'normal' gender role by behaving like men (Chesney-Lind, 1997).

These works were essentially a child of their times in so far as they were composed in a social milieu that supported very traditional (white middle-class) views of femininity and female behaviour. Within the socio-cultural settings from which these writings were produced women were perceived as bound to the home and expected to behave in ways that were befitting of a 'lady'; i.e., possessing manners, being presentable, exercising chastity, expressing fragility and composure, and above all demonstrating a capacity to observe the rules. Any behaviour that ran contra to the traditional views was considered to be outside the realms of 'normal' femininity and, therefore, deviant. Like much of the early gang literature on male groups, female subjects were drawn from minority groups such as the Italians, Jewish, and Irish, but the predominant gaze was upon the African-American/African Caribbean and Mexican American communities. It is clear from reading these texts that there was at the least a clear lack of understanding about other cultures and cultural behaviours. What this meant, in practice, was that the behaviour of different ethnic groups was judged according to the traditional mores of white middle class America. Unsurprisingly this led to a proliferation of works that were entirely judgmental, ethnocentric and, at their worst, racist.

Inherent in the texts is the view that women minority ethnic groups did not conform to the dominant cultural ideal of femininity. Thus we find male researchers commenting extensively on the ways girls looked and dressed (their 'unruly hair', 'slouched behaviour'), where deportment and dress-style were considered evidence of gender violation and thus expressive of a deviant personality. Consider the comments of Rice (1963) who described a female gang called the Persian Queens as 'extraordinarily unqueenly queens', who were 'exceptionally unattractive' due to their 'slouching swagger' (Chesney-Lind and Hagedorn, 1999: 29). Note too, Waln Brown's (1977) depiction of the Holly Ho's in his work on Black female gangs in Philadelphia. He described them as 'football players with big shoulders and fight scarred faces who greatly resemble the warring Amazonian women referred to in ancient mythology. 'Like the Amazons', Brown concluded, 'the Holly Ho's appear to be fearless, aggressive women who will fight men and women alike'.[2] Unsurprisingly this way of thinking about women legitimated a bizarre series of responses designed to change gang women by restoring them to their 'appropriate' gender role. These included the construction of charm schools aimed at [re]socialising young women by re-educating them in manners and etiquette. In sum, the prevailing philosophy was that one could groom and coach young women from behaving like boys, and out of the gang, by turning them into 'real ladies'.

The classical [mis] interpretation of females in gangs paid little attention to why young women joined the gang, and where an explanation was offered it appeared in the form of a deficit. The deficit-model assumes that for maladjusted females gang membership provides them with a place where they can find the things they have lost. For example, the gang offers security, meaningful relationships, education, protection and friendship; in essence, the gang provides young women with meaning and identity. Gone are the notions of subterranean delinquent values, the search for excitement and wild transcendence that male researchers believe motivate and animate male gang members. Men, this line of thinking suggests, join gangs to get things and achieve things women – by contrast – join because they are sad and needy. From this position the analysis of female involvement in gang life is reduced to the psychosocial theoretical explanations and interventions, which, ultimately, simplify and misrepresent the female experience: it denies women their agency.

In opposition to this superficial and stereotypical way of thinking, contemporary female gang researchers have sought to present an analysis of women's involvement in the gang in ways that demonstrate that women are not the maladjusted agentic gender traitors they are too often presented as being. In her pioneering study of women in New York gangs, Anne Campbell was one of the first academics to present the gang from a female perspective. In her work *Girls in the gang* – and subsequent work – Campbell clearly illustrates the tumultuous lives of females gang members. She argues strongly that young women in the gang are not inherently 'bad girls' with deviant personalities (or deviant sexualities) but young women who are responding to the rejection of mainstream society. She asserts that female association with the gang 'is a public proclamation of their rejection of the lifestyle that the community expects from them (Campbell, in Chesney-Lind and Hagedorn, 1991: 116). More recently, scholars such as Miller (2002) and Joe-Laider and Hunt (2001) have sought to challenge the assumption that woman who fight in gangs are in some respect violating what it is to be female showing how women in gangs accomplish femininity within gang groups and experience themselves as women even when engaging in violence every bit as brutal as their male counterparts.

In a paper that challenges many of the stereotypical assumptions that tend to dog male research into female gang members, Young's work shows that while young women may congregate into groups, the groups into which they collect cannot readily be termed gangs read as pathological fighting machines (Young, 2009). While capable of violence and sometimes serious violence, such violence had less to do, she argues, with gang membership but reflected far deeper issues connected with chaotic lives often marked by serious trauma and victimisation.

The attempt to rethink the way in which women are positioned in relation to the gang has been accompanied by a parallel attempt to reconsider the nature and role of masculinity in defining why gang members behave in particular ways. Intrinsic to this research is that behaviour is shaped by a particular species of masculinity. Work conducted in this area has been particularly influenced by the pioneering work of Connell (1987, 1993, 1995). While observing that historically and contemporaneously masculinity has been defined in very different ways between social classes and different ethnic groups, Connell argued that within western culture there existed a particular dominant form of masculinity. This he termed 'hegemonic masculinity'. What made it hegemonic is that the values that characterise it dominate and prevail over other 'subordinate varieties' of masculinity, which are positioned as inferior to it. What guarantees its ascendancy is that most men within the west are beholden to the norms that define it. Because these are men who also exercise disproportionate power in society this also means that the vision of the world enshrined within it also prevails in defining how the world was ideally organised as well as specifying how men were positioned within this world. Unsurprisingly the vision of what it is to be male (i.e.) strong, independent, competitive, etc. is also the vision that has historically been mediated through the media.

Hegemonic masculinity is historically beholden to the belief that men are the dominant force within society. Their power in turn is believed to derive from the faculty of reason they uniquely possess and from their successful domination and subjugation of women (Connell, 1987). Historically, hegemonic masculinity is also defined by its commitment to heterosexuality and by its antagonism to other forms of subaltern masculinities, particular homosexuality.

Most men, Connell argues, are socialised into the norms and conventions of hegemonic masculinity, which in effect, establish the horizons through which they then come to see the world around them. It defines their expectations. In effect, to be a man is to be a person who possesses power of some kind, to possess a 'natural' desire for women and to look with contempt on and fear homosexuality. Because society is organised in ways that reproduce male power (men predominantly control and own the means and forces of production) so the implicit equation that conflates masculinity with power is naturalised and experienced by many men as a normal fact of life.

Though by no means a traditional gang researcher, James Messerschmidt (1993) has recently sought to use this way of thinking about masculinity in order to throw an important light on forms of group conflict. In particular he shows how the commitment to a culture organised in the image of hegemonic masculinity can help explain different patterns of delinquent group behaviour. In the case of males who are already powerful he shows how their commitment to a hegemonic masculine culture that already validates strong assertive males and which has traditionally excused those who breach and contest rules as something 'boys do' (a norm that has not historically been conceded to girls) can validate forms of delinquent group behaviour. Recent cases of group rape conducted by prominent footballers exemplify this, as do the rituals that have often been identified with various middle class 'frat' fraternities in American colleges (Sanday, 1990).

Whereas for powerful men their masculinity is never bought into question precisely because they hold positions of power which already validate it, the same cannot be said for socially excluded and marginalised males. This is particularly the case for males in multiply deprived populations who, while socialised into a culture that conflates power with masculinity, are born into a socio-economic context where their entrenched social and economic disadvantage renders them powerless. What Messerschmidt argues is that for some males in this situation masculinity, far from being something that they can readily claim or presume, is something they are forced to prove. In other words, unlike the business executive whose power is revealed in his position and the purchasing power this provides, this situation does not accrue to powerless males who have no embedded source of power at all. Messerschmidt argues that far from simply accepting their powerless status as natural, some young males respond to their experience by harnessing the one power resource they do possess – this the propensity for violence. By challenging each other through fighting rituals and by exemplifying in word and deed their manliness (what Katz terms 'the seductions of evil') so their masculinity is demonstrated, revealed and confirmed as a 'situational accomplishment'. By engaging in the rituals of the gang powerless young men 'do gender'. The example Messerschmidt cites as an illustration of this form of 'masculinity in crisis' is a group rape conducted by a gang of young black urban males on a middle class white female jogger in Central Park, New York. For Messerschmidt, what made the rape explicable, as well as the extreme violence that characterised it, was that it constituted a performance through which a group subject to extreme class and racial disadvantage could accomplish a viable male identity. Though an act of deviance in one respect on another level their acts are entirely legible according to the standards of hegemonic masculinity.

It could be argued that the turn towards examining gender has had a profound effect on the way in which group delinquency is theorised. As we have seen, feminist inspired theorists have successfully contested the often banal stereotypical assumptions that male criminologists often made about women whilst providing an alternative way of understanding the role of females in the gang. Likewise, for male criminologists influenced by feminism their attempt to study masculinity and its accomplishment has itself drawn attention to an important and historically undertheorised aspect of male group delinquency.

CONCLUSION: TOWARDS A SOCIOLOGY OF THE STREET

In the context of law and order societies like the USA and the UK, societies that tend to view any sign of collectivism on the part of young people as symptomatic of a malaise that needs to be suppressed, it is unlikely that wider social interest in young people congregating together will abate. Criminology and criminologists will no doubt continue to play a role, either in helping the state identify the delinquent groups it believes it confronts, or alternatively (and more progressively), challenging the resulting policies and intervention that lead to the widespread criminalisation of young people.

With this in mind, we draw this chapter to a close by briefly outlining what we believe constitute the primary lessons that this brief review of criminological thinking has to teach us about how we interpret our present.

Humanising the deviant

From the perspective of the kind of law and order societies in which we live, young people who congregate in public are typically conceived as pathological outsiders, driven to crime by some set of deficits they possess. A different and more humane picture emerges if we consider the sociologically grounded traditions profiled here. These work to demolish populist conceptions of street collectives as motivated outsiders addicted to evil. What the research we have covered here points to instead, is a different way of conceiving street collectives and those who belong to them.

This sociologically grounded tradition, far from conceiving the individual member of a subculture or gang as driven by some psychological deficit, considers them as rational individuals who make choices and decisions that are shaped by the socio-economic situation and environmental conditions in which they live. Group behaviour then is primarily a *social* phenomenon, not a *psychological* problem and needs to be studied as such. This does not mean that the choices gang members make are necessarily good or sensible, only to point out that the choices made are constrained by the world into which people are born which they had no say in creating.

If the pattern of adaptation selected is sometimes negative in so far as it licences collective violence and delinquency, there remains little evidence that group life and subcultural expressions associated with it mark the beginning of fully-fledged criminal careers for most young people. Group life, while often treated as pathological by the adult world, is often motivated by 'normal' and innocuous motives such as the desire to have a good time and 'hang out with friends' in order to alleviate boredom which ends, for most youngsters, in late teenage years or early twenties (Smith and Bradshaw, 2005).

At the same time group life and the 'subterranean values' that characterise it is less likely to involve organised criminality, so much as an attempt on the part of young people to transcend mundane existence through acts of collective transgression.

As subcultural theory reminds us, young people are not simply shaped by forces totally beyond their control. They respond creatively to their environment and their response to the world they confront is often expressed in the subcultural rituals which they develop and in which they engage. As the work of the Birmingham school has shown, in subculture young people often problematise and aspire to resolve the contradictions they experience, albeit magically as Phil Cohen observed. In the style of dress they adopt, the language they use, the music they listen to, and their social presentation of self, young people express and mediate a highly complex series of messages about the world in which they live. From the accentuated machismo of the skinhead and, more recently, the American hip hop ghetto warrior, through to the nihilism of punk, so young people dramatise their social situation and do so in highly creative ways.

As we also saw in the work of theorists like Barrios, Brotherton and Stephenson, far from conceiving collectives such as gangs as expressing a crisis of social reproduction, it is often the case that collectives like gangs emerge and develop not only in response to a wider social crisis, but as a force that will challenge and resolve the crisis that provokes their appearance. Be this the hyper-ghettoisation of the urban poor in the USA, or the breakdown of law and order in a Russian republic. What the work of these theorists also shows is that street collectives are more than style cultures. As Hagadorn (2008) observes, they are political actors in their own right, deliberating subjects, not passive agents and need to be engaged as such.

And the lesson of this for criminology is that when faced with societies that view youth collectives as pathological outsiders, it is necessary to contest such criminalisation by identifying the innate creativity that invariably informs the way young people respond to the world around them. It means treating them as sources of agency and as political units, not as passive actors to which various interventions and therapies can be directed.

Remembering the realist lesson

Whilst 'humanising the deviant', to use Cohen's (1981) expression, is as important today as it ever has been, this must not also distract criminologists (including critical criminologists) from registering the often self destructive ways of life that can also form part of the response young people can make to the predicament that confronts them. As Saunders (1994) study of the gang wars in the USA demonstrates, gangs can and do mobilise ultra violence and, too often, the victims of such violence are other people just like themselves: invariably poor, multiply marginalised, urban males. For critical traditions, such violence is often difficult to confront and explain. First, because to do so, may also work to inadvertently further criminalise already stigmatised outsiders. Second, because explaining carnage does not come easily to critical traditions more attuned to contesting criminalisation by drawing attention to the creative non-violent response young people manifest to the social problems that confront them. Third, because some critical criminologists often tend to treat crime among the urban poor as a social construction produced by control agents, not a phenomena that has a sui generic reality in its own right (see Hallsworth, 2008).

Whilst worthy reasons in and of themselves, not to study the more socially destructive aspects of youth collectives tends to leave the field of explanation open to less progressive currents in criminology who have no trouble identifying and explaining such violence. This invariably legitimates even greater state repression particularly when the research that is left works with deficit models of youth violence. The left realist mantra that the left need to be real about crime, specifically that perpetrated by the urban poor males, remains an important lesson (Lea and Young, 1984). We need to explain how and why the violence that often blights poor neighbourhoods occurs, and how explanations can be developed in ways that do not criminalise already criminalised males, or which racialise crime further, as some commentators such as Michael Keith (1993) and Paul Gilroy (1987) have argued.

Putting control in its place

Another important lesson the research traditions reviewed have to teach is that street collectives cannot be studied without reference to the social response directed against them. This works, as we have seen, at a number of different levels. As the British subcultural school demonstrated, the identity of groups, while always a creative response to the socio-economic conditions in which they are located, is never solely an autonomous creation of the group alone. Control agents including the mass media also perform very important roles in helping forge and sustain group solidarity, as well as helping forge group identity. As the American gang research tradition reminds us, the solidarity of the group is not least affirmed by its recognition as a group by control agents; while, British subcultural theorists have shown, the capacity of the media to amplify the deviant acts they otherwise condemn through the production of moral panics, itself remains an important source for creating cohesion among what would otherwise be a diffuse social body. An important lesson this poses for criminologists is that they must reflect on how far their actions may influence the conduct of the formations they wish to study. The second lesson this poses is that no group can meaningfully be studied without attending to the dialectical relationship between the forces of social control that aspire to define and control the collective and the collectives own response to these forces.

At the same time we need to remain aware of the persuasive role the media can perform in producing an alternative representation of the street realities. As the work of Cohen (1972) and Hall *et al.* (1978) powerfully demonstrate, through moral panics the media are often instrumental in producing and mobilising popular fears and anxieties. The problem of the street is therefore as much a problem of how it is defined and represented as it is a matter of deviant collectives out there. It is also important to recognise that research into street collectives is tied to social policies which themselves mirror wider media induced fears and anxieties and can work to confirm them. To take the case of gangs, there have been several surges of interest in them. Decker has shown that such public interest in the gang was evident in the 1890s, 1920s, 1960s 1980s, 1990s (Decker, 1996) and the recent rediscovery of the gang in the UK is but another instalment in a long history. The lesson we need to take away from this is that part of the critical academics role is to contest as opposed to pander to media [over]-reaction, Sober realistic reflection of the facts must always be affirmed.

A question of epistemology: understanding street worlds

Another important lesson that the British subcultural tradition poses in its focus on social control is in forcing us to recognise that the reality of group life and the way it is represented are often two very different things. The aim of good research must always be to represent what are often highly complex and fluid social relations in ways that do not distort what they claim to represent, and which work to represent them accurately as concrete in thought.

While it might be remarked here that surely everyone is beholden to the same ambition, this is by no means the case. As Stan Cohen (1984) reminds us, in 'control speak' we find a discourse which articulates what some control agents like to imagine they are doing, often when it is doing something altogether different. Part of the problem here is that for control agents to operate effectively, they need to know who their enemies are. Ideally they like them to be clearly discernible structured entities, and when they look to understand street collectives this is what they want to find; an organised enemy to suppress.

Where all this becomes problematic is that in order to locate and identify a suitable enemy, the messy, chaotic and fluid reality of the street is overlooked in favour of a more coherent structure that best defines formal bureaucratic organisations. The problem here is that street life is inherently volatile and cannot be grasped by applying to the street the epistemological categories we use to define formal organisations.

This does not preclude the fact that gangs may have organisational features, only it is rare for the organisation to exist in ways that fully determine and shape the deviance of the actors who inhabit them, at least as this is often imagined by practitioners. As Hallsworth and Silverstone's (2009) work on the violent street worlds of gun users in the UK found, firearms may be used in the context of a territorial fight between gangs but they are also used by individual members for reasons that bare no relation to their gang belonging. Far from group life being organised in ways that produced violent outcomes as practitioners often imagined, it is the social disorganisation of the streetworld that appears to be the problem.

The tendency towards imposing upon the street a coherence and organisation it may not possess, is a problem for academics as well, specifically those who uncritically accept the testimony of control agents. John Pitts' (2008) recent attempt to define the 'new face of youth crime' as a problem posed by the arrival and plenitude of organised gangs in the UK, is a paradigmatic exercise in misplaced thinking of this kind. The lesson here is that researchers studying the street must be sensitive to understanding its constitutive sui generic logic in a way that does not fall into this trap. This, it must be emphasised, does not mean seeing the street as a space of disorganisation but of grasping its constitutive organisation in ways that can grasp its its inherent and often unstable volatility.

On groups and gangs

An inherent problem with academic gang research is that it always works on the *a priori* assumption that the problem of the street is the problem of the gang. It works this way both because of the fixations of gang researchers (who do what they are programmed to do which is to find gangs); and because they are paid to do this by control agents who assume that the gang is the enemy they need to uncover. The problem with this gang fixation is that there are many street collectives that are not gangs, which as a consequence, fall under the gang radar and do not get studied; or who, by default, find themselves problematically labelled as gangs with all the criminalising implications that follow. Given that the gangs typically studied are overrepresented by poor urban males and ethnic minority groups, a knock-on effect of gang research is that it can inadvertently racialise crime even more than it already does. At the same time, by making the problem of street collectives a problem of an ethnic outside, so the forms of collective delinquency associated with middle class and the affluent are never researched.

The lessons this poses for researchers is that they really need to cast their research nets beyond the gang if they are to see the street world aright. As the empirical research we conducted in London demonstrated, while collectives like gangs certainly existed, these were different from what we identified as volatile peer groups (by far the most usual collective); and differed as well from what we came to call

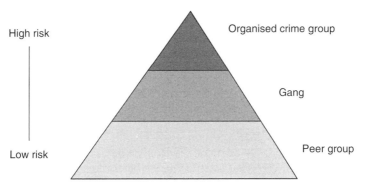

Figure 4.1   Pyramid of risk.

organised crime groups (see Hallsworth and Young, 2006). Each group posed a different level of risk and both, for the purposes of social control, needed to be treated very differently (see Figure 4.1).

While our approach points to the need to study different groups and how they intersect within a given locality, there remains a need to theorise more astutely how different collectives are organised and understand their different relationship to violence and to each other. Far more research effort also needs to be directed at understanding the collective delinquency and value systems of the peer groups into which more affluent groups coalesce.

Endnote

As we noted above, given young people's tendency to congregate, given the creative and often defiant cultural manifestations such collectives adopt, they will remain as much objects of fascination for the wider society and its control apparatus as they will for criminologists. As this chapter has attempted to show, the nature of street collectives are complex and this chapter has attempted to profile some of the ways social theorists often beholden to very different research methods and theories have approached studying them. Whilst understanding the changing nature of street collectives in a globalising world remains an ongoing task, it is one that will hopefully develop and be informed by the strength of the research traditions that precede it.

NOTES

1 For an excellent literary representation of this aspect of working class male culture see Alan Sillitoe's *Friday Night and Saturday Morning* [ref].

2 Brown, W. (1977) Black female gangs in Philadelphia. In Chesney-Lind and Hagedorn (1999) *Female Gangs in America*, p. 62.

3 Kingism could be understood as the code of conduct adhered to by membes of the ALKQN or a spiritual religion followed by members.

REFERENCES

Anderson, E. (1999) *Code of the Street: Decency, Violence, and the Moral Life of the Inner City.* New York/London: W. W. Norton and Company.

Becker, H. S. (1966) *Outsiders: Studies in the Sociology of Deviance,* Free Press; Collier-Macmillan.

Brotherton, D. C. and Barrios, L. (2004) *The Almighty Latin King and Queen Nation: Street Politics and the Transformation of a New York City Gang.* Columbia University Press.

Brown, W. K. (1977) Black female gangs in Philadelphia. *International Journal of Offender Therapy and Comparative Criminology,* 21: 221–228.

Campbell, A. (1984) The *Girls in the Gang.* Oxford: Basil Blackwell.

Chesney-Lind, M. (1997) *The Female Offender: Girl, Women and Crime.* Sage Publications Inc.

Chesney-Lind, M. and Hagedorn, J. M. (1999) *Female Gangs in America: Essays on Girls, Gangs and Gender.* Lake View Press.

Cloward, R. and Ohlin, L. (1960) *Delinquency and Opportunity.* NY: Free Press.

Cohen, A. K. (1955) *Delinquent Boys: The Culture of the Gang.* Glencoe, Ill: Free Press.

Cohen, P. (1972) Subcultural conflict and working class community. *Cultural Studies,* 1972: 25–52.

Cohen, S. (1980) *Folk Devil and Moral Panics.* London: Martin Robertson.

Cohen, S. (1981) Footprints in the Sand: A Further Report on Criminology and the Sociology of Deviance in Britain. In: M. Fitzgerald, G. McLennan and J. Pawson, *Crime and Society,* pp. 220–247.

Cohen, S. (1984) *Visions of Social Control: Crime, Punishment and Classification.* Cambridge: Polity.

Connell, R. W. (1987) *Gender and Power: Society, the Person and Sexual Politics* Cambridge: Polity.

Connell, R. W. (1993) *Schools and Social Justice.* Philadelphia: Temple University Press.

Connell, R. W. (1995) *Masculinities.* Cambridge: Polity.

Decker, S. and Van Winkle, B. (1997) *Life in the Gang: Family, Friends and Violence.* Cambridge University Press.

Downes, D. (1966) *The Delinquent Solution.* London, Routledge and Kegan Paul.

Downes, D. and Rock, P. (2003) *Understanding Deviance: a Guide to the Sociology of Crime and Rule Breaking.* Oxford: Oxford University Press.

Gilroy, P. (1987) The myth of black criminality. In P. Scraton (ed.), *Law, Order, and the Authoritarian State: Readings in Critical Criminology,* pp. 107–120. Milton Keynes and Philadelphia: Open University Press.

Hagedorn, J. (2008) *World of Gangs: Armed Young Men and Gangsta Culture.* University of Minnesota Press.

Hall, S. *et al.* (1976) *Resistance Through Rituals: Youth Subcultures in Post-war Britain.* London, Hutchinson [for] the Centre for Contemporary Cultural Studies, University of Birmingham.

Hall, S. *et al.* (1978) *Policing the Crisis: Mugging, the State, and Law and Order.* London: Macmillan.

Hallsworth, S. (2008) Street crime: interpretation and legacy in policing the crisis, *Crime, Media Culture* 4(1).

Hallsworth, S. and Silverstone, D. (2009) 'That's life innit': A British perspective on guns, crime and social order, *Criminology and Criminal Justice,* 9: 359.

Hallsworth, S. and Young, T. (2006) *Urban Collectives: Gangs and Other Groups,* Report for Operation Cruise, Metropolitan Police Service.

Hallsworth, S. and Young, T. (2008) Gang talk and gang talkers: a critique, *Crime Media Culture,* 4(2).

Horowitz, R. (1983) *Honor and the American Dream,* New Brunswick, New Jersey: Rutgers University Press.

Huff, C. R. (1989) Youth gangs and public policy, *Crime and Delinquency,* 35(4): 524–537.

Katz, J. (1990) *Seductions of Crime: Moral and Sensual Attractions of Doing Evil.* New York: Basic Books.

Keith, M. (1993) *Race, Riots and Policing: Lore and Disorder in a Multi-rascist Society.* London: UCL Press.

Klein, M. W. (1971) Street *Gangs and Street Workers.* Prentice-Hall.

Klein, M. W., Kerner, H. J., Maxson, C. and Weitekamp, E. (eds) (2002) *The Eurogang Paradox: Street Gangs and Youth Groups in US and Europe*. Kluwer Academic Publishers.

Kontos, L., Brotherton, D. and Barrios, L. (2003) *Gangs and Society: Alternative Perspectives*. Columbian University Press.

Laidler, K. J. and Hunt, G. (2001) Accomplishing femininity among the girls in the gang: *British Journal of Criminology*, Autumn 2001, Vol. 41, No. 4, pp. 656–678.

Lea, J. and Young, J. (1984) *What is to be Done About Law and Order?* (2nd edition) London: Pluto Press.

Matza, D. (1964) *Delinquency and Drift*, pp. x.199. New York: John Wiley and Sons.

Maxson, C. L. and Klein, M. W. (1995) Investigating gang structures. *Journal of Gang Research*, 3: 33–40.

Merton, R. K. (1938) Social structure and anomie, *American Sociological Review,* 3(5): 672–682.

Merton, R. K. (1968) *Social Theory and Structure*. MacMillan, USA.

Messerschmidt, J. (1993) *Masculinities and Crime*. Lanham, Md.: Rowman and Littlefield.

Miller, J. (2000) *One of the Guys*. New York: Oxford University Press.

Moore, J., Garcia, C., Garcia, L. and Valencia, F. (1978) *Homeboys: Gangs, Drugs, and Prison in the Barrios of Los Angeles*. Temple University Press.

Moore, J. (1991) *Going Down to the Barrio: Homeboys and Homegirls in Change*. Philadelphia: Temple University Press.

Murray, C. (1990) *The Emerging British Underclass*. London: Institute for Economic Affairs.

Padilla, F. (1992) *The Gang as American an Enterprise*. Rutgers University Press.

Pitts, J. (2008) *Reluctant Gangsters: the Changing Face of Youth Crime*. Cullompton: Willan.

Rice, R. (1963) A reporter at large: The Persian Queens, In: M. Chesney-Lind and J. Hagedorn, (1999) *Female Gangs in America: Essays on Girls, Gangs and Gender*. Lake View Press, pp. 27–44.

Sanday, P. R. (1990) *Fraternity Gang Rape: Sex, Brotherhood and Privilege on Campus*. New York University Press.

Saunders, W. B. (1994) *Gangbangs and Drive-bys*: *Grounded Culture and Juvenile Gang Violence*. New York: Aldine De Gruyter.

Shaw, C. and McKay, H. (1942) *Juvenile Delinquency in Urban Areas*. Chicago: University Chicago Press.

Shaw, C. R. and McKay, H. D. (1969) *Juvenile Delinquency in Urban Areas* (rev. ed). Chicago: University of Chicago Press.

Smith, D. J. and Bradshaw, P. (2005) *Gang Membership and Teenage Offending,* Centre for Law and Society, University of Edinburgh.

Stephenson, S. (2008) Russian gangs, in D. Brotherton and L. Kontos (eds), *Encyclopedia of Gangs,* Greenwood Press, pp. 214–216.

Sutherland, E. (1939) *Principles of criminology* 3rd ed. Philadelphia: J.B. Lippincott.

Sutherland, E. H. and Cressey, R. D. (1966) *Principles of Criminology*. Philadelphia: Lippincott.

Thrasher, F. M. (1927) *The Gang: A Study of 1,313 Gangs in Chicago*. Chicago III: University of Chicago Press.

Vigil, J. D. (1988) *Barrio Gangs: Street Life and Identity in Southern California*. Austin: University of Texas Press.

Wacquant, L. (2005) The great penal leap backwards, In: J. Pratt, M. Brown, D. Brown, S. Hallsworth and W. Morrison (eds), *The New Punitiveness, Issues Theories and Debates*, Willan Publishers.

Willis, P. E. (1977) *Learning to Labour: How Working Class Kids Get Working Class Jobs*. Farnborough, Hants: Saxon House.

Young, J. (2004) Voodoo Criminology and the Numbers Game, in J. Ferrell, K. Hayward, W. Morrison and M. Presdee (eds), *Cultural Criminology Unleashed*. London: Glass House.

Young, T. (2009) Girls and Gangs: 'Shemale' Gangsters in the UK? *Youth Justice,* 9(3): 224–238.

5

Strain Theories

Robert Agnew and Timothy Brezina

INTRODUCTION

Strain theory states that certain strains or stressors increase the likelihood of crime. There are several versions of strain theory, each of which describes; (a) those strains most conducive to crime; (b) why such strains increase the likelihood of crime; and (c) why some individuals are more likely than others to respond to strains with crime. This chapter begins with a brief historic overview of the different versions of strain theory, then focuses on the most recent and broadest version of strain theory: Agnew's general strain theory (GST). The major propositions of GST are described, along with the research on these propositions. There is then a discussion of how GST has been used to explain certain key issues in criminology, including gender and community differences in crime rates; as well as patterns of offending over the life course. Finally, future directions for research on GST are discussed.

HISTORIC OVERVIEW OF STRAIN THEORIES

Classic strain theories

Merton
Merton presented the first modern version of strain theory in 1938 (see Agnew, 1997a; Merton, 1938, 1968). His goal in developing this theory was to explain class differences in offending in the United States. He argued that all people in the United States – poor as well as rich – are encouraged to place a high relative emphasis on the goal of monetary success. At the same time, many lower-class individuals are prevented from achieving this goal through legal channels, such as getting a good education and then a good job. This inability to achieve monetary success was said to create much frustration among lower-class individuals. Merton described several ways of coping with this frustration, certain of which involve crime. Most notably,

individuals might attempt to achieve their monetary goals through illegitimate channels, such as theft, drug sales, and prostitution. Other methods of coping, however, are legal. Individuals, for example, might lower the emphasis they place on monetary success. Merton briefly discussed the factors that influence the choice of coping strategies. He noted, for example, that lower-class individuals are more likely to cope through crime because, being less well socialized, they have a lower commitment to conventional norms.

Surprisingly, Merton's theory has not been well tested. A proper test of the theory would require measures of the relative emphasis placed on monetary success and the extent to which individuals had achieved or expected to achieve such success. Most tests of the theory, however, fail to adequately measure these variables (see Agnew, 1997; Agnew *et al.*, 1996). Nevertheless, there is some evidence in support of Merton's theory (see Agnew *et al.*, 1996; Baron, 2004). Data suggest that crime is higher among individuals who are dissatisfied with their monetary situation and are experiencing a range of monetary problems. Qualitative studies confirm this, with criminals often reporting that their crimes were motivated by a desperate desire for money (e.g., Hagan and McCarthy, 1997; Topalli and Wright, 2004). Further, monetary problems and dissatisfaction are more common among members of the lower class.

The relationship between class and monetary dissatisfaction/problems, however, is only moderate in size. Merton himself anticipated this moderate relationship at certain points in his work, noting that many higher class individuals may come to pursue economic goals beyond their reach. Several criminologists have discussed the reasons for this. Passas (1997), for example, drew on Merton's reference group theory to argue that individuals in the United States frequently select comparison others who have more money than they do, thus leading to feelings of relative deprivation in all classes.

During the 1950s and 1960s, several theorists attempted to apply Merton's theory to what was perceived as a major problem at the time: juvenile gangs. Like Merton, they argued that crime was rooted in the inability of individuals to achieve their success goals. At the same time, they revised and extended Merton's theory in important ways – especially in their discussion of the factors that influence the reaction to strains.

Cohen

Cohen (1955) argued that lower-class juveniles were not simply interested in monetary success, but desired the somewhat broader goal of middle-class status. That is, they wanted the financial success, reputation, and lifestyle associated with the middle class. The families of lower-class juveniles, however, were often unable to equip them with the knowledge, values, and skills necessary to achieve middle-class status through legal channels. This became apparent in the school system, where lower-class juveniles were frequently unable to compete successfully against their middle-class peers and live up to the expectations of their middle class teachers. Lower class students, in fact, were often humiliated at school and defined as problems by school officials.

Lower-class juveniles could not cope with their frustration by trying to achieve middle class status through illegal channels. One cannot easily steal middle-class status.

Cohen, however, argued that if a sufficient number of lower-class juveniles are in regular contact with one another, they may cope by setting up an alternative status system in which they could successfully compete. Their hostility to the middle class, among other things, lead them to set up an "oppositional" status system that challenges middle-class values. In particular, these lower-class juveniles were said to form gangs that valued such things as toughness, fighting ability, theft, and vandalism. Strain, then, does not lead directly to crime. Rather, it leads to the formation of delinquent groups, which in turn provide the direct motivation for crime.

Parts of Cohen's theory have been criticized. In particular, research suggests that most delinquents do not unconditionally approve of all delinquent acts. However, many delinquents and delinquent groups do hold beliefs that are conducive to delinquency. For example, they may believe that violence is an acceptable response to a broad range of provocations or that theft is justified under certain conditions. Researchers who attempt to explain the origin of such beliefs often make arguments reminiscent of Cohen. That is, they explain such beliefs at least partly in terms of the strains individuals and groups experience. For example, Anderson (1999) argues that the inability to achieve status through legal channels leads some young people to 'campaign' for respect on the streets by adopting an aggressive demeanor and occasionally engaging in shows of violence. It also leads them to embrace a street code of conduct (or set of beliefs) that prescribes violent responses to shows of disrespect. This adaptation is said to be especially likely in economically-deprived neighborhoods, where conventional means to achieve status are limited (also see Brezina *et al.*, 2004: 311).

Cloward and Ohlin

Drawing on Merton, Cloward and Ohlin (1960) argue that many lower-class juveniles desire monetary success, but realize that they will be unable to achieve such success through legal channels. Drawing on Cohen, Cloward and Ohlin argue that such youth are most likely to turn to crime when they form or join delinquent gangs. The formation of delinquent gangs depends on the extent to which strained juveniles regularly interact with one another and blame their goal blockage on the larger society. Delinquent gangs are important because they provide juveniles with justifications and other support for crime. Cloward and Ohlin, however, argue that there are three major types of delinquent gangs. Certain gangs focus on fighting, others on theft, and still others on drug use. Much of Cloward and Ohlin's work focuses on explaining why strained youth form or join one type of gang as opposed to another.

In their most distinctive contribution, Cloward and Ohlin argue that the type of gang which forms depends on the 'illegitimate opportunities' that are available to youth. In some communities, for example, older individuals instruct and support juveniles in theft and other income-generating crimes. In other communities, strained youth are left to cope on their own, and violence-oriented gangs are more likely to develop. Cloward and Ohlin's arguments in this area have been challenged. Data suggest that most delinquent gangs tend to engage in a range of delinquent acts, including income-generating crimes, violence, and drug use (although see Hagedorn, 1994; Warr, 1996). Gangs are generally not as specialized as Cloward and Ohlin suggest. Nevertheless, the more general argument of Cloward and Ohlin – that crime is a function of both motivation and opportunities – has had a major impact on the discipline.

The legacy of classic strain theories

The classic strain theories of Merton, Cohen, and Cloward and Ohlin dominated criminology during the 1950s and 1960s. They were perhaps the leading explanations of crime and they had a major impact on public policy. The War on Poverty, initiated by President Kennedy and implemented by President Johnson, was in part inspired by these theories. In particular, a range of social programs were developed in order to make it easier for poor individuals to achieve economic success through legal channels. While a good many of these programs have since been dismantled, some still remain – such as Project Headstart and Job Corps. Further, data suggest that certain of these programs are effective in reducing crime (Agnew, 1995a, 2005).

Classic strain theories, however, came under attack in the late 1960s and 1970s. A number of studies attempted to test these theories, most often by examining the distinction between educational and occupational aspirations and expectations. Such tests found that "strain" – conceptualized in these studies as a disjunction between aspirations and expectations – had little relationship to criminal or delinquent behavior. These tests have been criticized, however (e.g., Agnew, 1992, 1995b, 1997a; Agnew *et al.*, 1996). Among other things, it has been pointed out that the primary focus of classic strain theory was on monetary success rather than educational attainment or occupational status. Also, the disjunction between aspirations or ideal goals and expectations is not likely to generate much strain. Rather, the disjunction between expectations and actual achievements – something not measured in the research – is most relevant to strain. Nevertheless, such research played an important role in reducing the influence of the classic strain theories.

At the same time, classic strain theories have helped stimulate recent research on the contribution of economic factors to crime. At the individual level, researchers have focused on the effect of socioeconomic status, economic dissatisfaction, and economic problems on crime (Agnew *et al.*, 1996; Agnew, 2006a, b). Studies suggest that crime is related to severe and chronic poverty, economic dissatisfaction, and the experience of economic problems such as trouble paying bills. Such problems, it should be noted, sometimes affect white-collar workers and may help to explain white collar crime (see Agnew *et al.*, 2009; Benson, 1985). The effect of these factors on crime can be explained in terms of theories other than strain theory, but these effects are certainly quite compatible with classic strain theories.

At the macro level, researchers have tried to explain community and societal differences in crime rates in terms of economic deprivation and inequality (for overviews see Agnew, 1999, 2006). Economic deprivation has emerged as the strongest correlate of community differences in crime within the United States. The effect of economic inequality is less clear. Economic inequality, however, is perhaps the strongest correlate of cross-national differences in crime. This is especially the case when the inequality results from discrimination based on race or religion. Further, economic inequality has an especially strong effect on crime in societies that provide low levels of social support, such as health benefits and welfare assistance. Again, such associations can be explained in terms of several theories, but they are quite compatible with strain theory.

Efforts to broaden the focus of classic strain theory

The classic strain theories of Merton, Cohen, and Cloward and Ohlin focus on one type of strain: the inability to achieve economic success or the somewhat broader goal of middle-class status. While this may be a potent source of strain in many cases, researchers in the 1970s and beyond began to focus on additional types of strain. This was especially true of efforts to explain delinquency. Here researchers argued that most adolescents are not overly concerned about their future economic or middle-class status. The revisions in classic strain theory, however, still focused on the blockage of goal seeking behavior – they simply expanded the range of goals that were examined.

Using strain theory, Greenberg (1977) attempted to explain the rise of delinquency during adolescence and its decline during adulthood. He argued that the structural position of adolescents in the US and many other societies leads them to pursue certain goals, but at the same time frequently prevents them from achieving these goals through legal channels. In particular, adolescents come to place great stress on popularity with peers, partly as a consequence of their isolation from adult society. Popularity with peers, however, requires money for such things as clothes and entertainment. Many youth lack sufficient money for such items and activities given their limited employment opportunities, leading some to resort to delinquency. Greenberg notes that qualitative data support this argument, although some quantitative data question it. In particular, data suggest that youths with more money are more – not less – likely to engage in delinquency (Wright *et al.*, 2001).

Greenberg also argues that adolescents come to pursue the goal of autonomy, which may be defined as "power over oneself," including the ability to resist the demands of others and to engage in action without the permission of others. This occurs because adolescents are encouraged by society to strive for independence as they grow older, their physical maturity fosters a desire for autonomy, and they witness other adolescents behaving in an autonomous manner. Adolescents, however, are frequently denied the autonomy they desire. Among other things, they are subject to close control in the school system and are legally forbidden from engaging in many 'adult' activities, such as sexual intercourse, drinking, and staying out late. Such adolescents may engage in delinquency in an effort to assert or obtain their autonomy, with truancy, curfew violation, and drinking being examples. Delinquency may also be a way of expressing their frustration with those who deny autonomy. Several other theorists have made similar arguments. Most notably, this argument is at the core of Moffitt's (1993) explanation of adolescence-limited offending. Certain data suggest that frustrated autonomy needs do in fact contribute to delinquency (Agnew, 1984a; Brezina, 2000).

Further, Greenberg argues that many male adolescents want to fulfill "conventional male role expectations," but are sometimes prevented from doing so through legal channels. For example, the requirement that students behave in a docile, submissive manner may challenge the desire of many males to act in an independent, assertive manner. These males may engage in delinquent acts such as assault in an effort to demonstrate masculinity and obtain revenge against those who threaten their masculinity. This argument has also been expressed in various forms by several theorists. Most notably, it is at the core of Messerschmidt's (1993) theory of masculinities and crime. According to Messerschmidt, attempts to "accomplish masculinity" through crime or delinquency are most likely to occur when traditional means of demonstrating masculinity (e.g., autonomy, income, steady full-time work) are blocked or unavailable. Qualitative studies provide some support for this argument and, although limited, certain quantitative data suggest that violence is more likely among young men who embrace traditional conceptions of masculinity but who have few traditional 'masculine-validating' resources or outlets (Krienert, 2003).

Still other types of goal blockage have been identified. Elliott *et al.* (1979) and others have argued that adolescents pursue a broad range of immediate goals – such as getting good grades, being a good athlete, and popularity with peers – and that these goals are often more important to young people than future educational or occupational success. According to this argument, then, it is the inability to achieve these immediate goals that is most relevant to delinquency. Data in this area are limited, but preliminary tests of this argument have not been encouraging (Agnew, 1984b; Elliott *et al.*, 1985).

GENERAL STRAIN THEORY

Classic strain theories – along with the revisions to these theories – focus on the blockage of goal-seeking behavior, with several relevant goals being identified. These theories also devote some attention to those factors that condition the effects of strains on crime, including level of social control and association with delinquent others. Agnew's (1992, 2006a, b) general strain theory (GST) draws on all of these theories, as well as several other literatures. In particular, GST draws on the stress literatures in sociology and psychology to identify new sources of strain beyond the blockage of goal-seeking behavior. GST draws on the justice and emotions literatures to more fully describe the types of strain most likely to result in crime and why certain strains increase crime. And GST draws on the coping, social support, and broader criminology literatures to more fully describe the factors that condition the effects of strains on crime. GST, therefore, is the most comprehensive or general version of strain theory.

In brief, GST states that a broad range of strains contribute to crime. These strains contribute to negative emotions, which in turn create pressure for corrective action. Individuals *may* cope with such strains and negative emotions through crime. Crime may be a means of reducing or escaping from strains, seeking revenge against those believed responsible for the strains or related targets, and alleviating the negative emotions associated with strains (e.g., through illicit drug use). A range of factors influence the choice of criminal versus legal coping strategies. The major arguments of GST are described below; GST is then used to explain gender and community differences in crime rates, as well as patterns of offending across the life course; and the chapter concludes with recommendations for further research on GST.

Strains conducive to crime

Definition of strain
GST defines a strain as an event or condition that is disliked by individuals. A distinction is made between subjective and objective strains. A subjective strain is one that is disliked by the particular individual experiencing it. An objective strain refers to an event or condition that is disliked by most people in a given group. The stress literature demonstrates that individuals often differ in their subjective evaluation of the same objective strains. For example, individuals differ greatly in their subjective

evaluation of an event such as divorce, with some people being devastated by the experience and others viewing it as a cause for celebration (Wheaton, 1990). We would expect subjective strains to be more strongly related to crime than objective strains (Froggio and Agnew, 2007). Nevertheless, most research on GST focuses on objective strains. That is, researchers ask individuals whether they have experienced events and conditions which are assumed to be disliked. They do not ask individuals how much they personally dislike such events/conditions. GST devotes some attention to those factors that influence the subjective evaluation of objective strains, a critical issue if we want to improve the explanation of crime and better link larger social forces to individual behavior.

Experienced, vicarious, and anticipated strains

The focus of GST is on personally experienced strains, since it is assumed that these will have the greatest impact on the individual. GST, however, also devotes some attention to vicarious and anticipated strains – which may sometimes contribute to crime as well. Vicarious strains refer to strains experienced by close others, such as family members and friends, and to members of the individual's major reference groups. A recent study indicates that individuals are more likely to engage in crime when their family members and friends are criminally victimized, even after we take account of the individual's own victimization experiences and prior level of crime (Agnew, 2002). Anticipated strains refer to strains that individuals anticipate they will experience in the future. Evidence suggests that crime is more likely among individuals who anticipate that they will experience violence in the near future, for example (Agnew, 2002).

Major categories of strains

GST points to three general types of strains: (1) the inability to achieve goals through legal channels, including monetary, autonomy, and status goals; (2) the loss of positively-valued stimuli, such as friends, romantic partners, and money; and (3) the presentation of negatively-valued stimuli, such as verbal and physical abuse. Many specific strains fall under each of these general categories. In fact, inventories of stressful life events, chronic stressors, and life hassles often list hundreds of specific strains – most of which fall into the latter two categories. Not all strains contribute to crime, however. As indicated above, GST draws on several literatures to describe the characteristics of those strains most likely to lead to crime.

Characteristics of strains conducive to crime

Those strains most conducive to crime have four characteristics. First, they are high in magnitude. Magnitude refers to the extent to which the strain is disliked and viewed as having a negative impact on one's life. Magnitude is influenced by the degree or size of the strain (e.g., a severe versus minor physical injury); the duration and frequency of the strain; and the extent to which the strain threatens the core goals, needs, values, activities, and/or identities of the person. Strains that are high in magnitude are more likely to lead to crime for several reasons, including the fact that they generate more intense negative emotions and are more difficult to cope with in a legal manner.

Second, the strain is seen as unjust. Unjust strains usually involve the voluntary and intentional violation of a relevant justice norm. To give a few examples, victims are more likely to perceive strains as unjust under the following circumstances: The strain is seen as undeserved (e.g., a child is punished for an offense she did not commit). The strain violates strongly held social norms or values (e.g., individuals are treated in ways generally seen as disrespectful or aggressive). The victim has no voice or say in the decision to inflict the strain and no rationale for the strain is provided. And the strain is very different from the victim's past treatment in similar circumstances and/or from the treatment of similar others (a teacher punishes the victim for talking in class, but ignores the talking of other students). Among other things, strains perceived as unjust provoke more intense negative emotions, especially anger.

Third, the strain is associated with low social control (see Chapter 6 in this volume). Social controls refer to the restraints against crime and may be of several types. Direct controls refer to the extent to which others set clear rules for the individual, monitor behavior, and consistently sanction rule violations. Stake in conformity refers to those things that the individual has to lose from crime. Some individuals, for example, have good grades, good jobs, and close relationships with others that would be jeopardized by crime. Internal control refers to the belief that crime is wrong. Certain strains are associated with low levels of social control. For example, this is the case with parental rejection, since juveniles rejected by their parents are probably subject to little direct parental control and do not care about jeopardizing their ties to parents. Such individuals are more likely to cope with this strain through crime since the costs of crime are lower for them. Other strains are associated with high social control and thus are less conducive to crime. This is the case, for example, with strains involving the care of young children or working long hours at a highly paid, prestigious job.

Fourth, the strain creates some pressure or incentive for criminal coping. Certain strains are more easily resolved through crime than others, and thus create more incentive for criminal coping. For example, it is easier to achieve one's monetary goals through crime than it is one's educational goals. Also, certain strains are associated with exposure to others who model crime, reinforce crime, teach beliefs favorable to crime, or otherwise try to pressure or entice the individual into crime. For example, individuals who are bullied by peers are regularly exposed to criminal models. These individuals are therefore more likely to cope through crime.

Drawing on the above, GST lists several strains that are especially conducive to crime.

- Parental rejection. Parents who reject their children do not express love or affection for them, show little interest in them, provide little support to them, and often display hostility toward them.
- Supervision/discipline that is erratic, excessive, and/or harsh (use of humiliation/insults, threats, screaming, and/or physical punishments).
- Child abuse and neglect. Child abuse and neglect include physical abuse; sexual abuse; and the failure to provide adequate food, shelter, medical care, and affection/attention (neglect).
- Negative secondary school experiences, including low grades, negative relations with teachers, and the experience of school as boring and a waste of time.
- Abusive peer relations, including insults, ridicule, threats, attempts to coerce, and physical assaults.

- Work at jobs in the secondary labor market. Such jobs commonly involve unpleasant tasks, little autonomy, coercive control, low pay, few benefits, little prestige, and very limited opportunities for advancement.
- Unemployment, especially when it is chronic and blamed on others.
- Marital problems, including frequent conflicts and verbal and physical abuse.
- The failure to achieve selected goals, including thrills/excitement, personal autonomy, masculine status, and the desire for much money in a short period of time.
- Criminal victimization.
- Residence in severely-deprived communities, which is associated with exposure to a host of strains – including criminal victimization and economic problems.
- Homelessness.
- Discrimination based on characteristics such as race/ethnicity, gender, and religion.

Data suggest that most of these strains are in fact associated with crime, with certain being among the best predictors of crime (Agnew, 2005, 2006a, b). Other of these strains, such as peer abuse, discrimination, and the failure to achieve goals, are just starting to receive research attention as causes of crime.

Why strains increase the likelihood of crime

GST states that the above strains lead to a range of negative emotions, including anger, frustration, and hopelessness. These emotions create pressure for corrective action, with crime being one possible response. Individuals may engage in crime to reduce or escape from strains (e.g., theft to obtain money, running away to escape abusive parents), seek revenge against the source of their strains or related targets, or alleviate their negative emotions. The few studies to properly test this idea have found some support for it. In particular, strains increase the experience of negative emotional states and these states mediate a good part of the effect of strains on crime, especially violent crime (Agnew, 2006a, b; Brezina, 1996, 1998). These studies focus on the emotion of anger, which plays a key role in GST. Anger energizes the individual for action, creates a desire for revenge, and reduces inhibitions. Strains, however, may lead to other negative emotions, such as frustration, malicious envy, depression, and fear. And these emotions may also contribute to crime. One intriguing possibility is that particular strains are more conducive to certain negative emotions than others, and that particular emotions are more conducive to some types of crime than others. For example, anger may be most conducive to violence, frustration to property crime, depression to drug use, and fear to illegal escape attempts such as running away and truancy. This is a ripe area for further research (Agnew, 2006a; Morgan, 2006).

While GST emphasizes the mediating role of negative emotions, the theory also states that strains may affect crime by reducing social control, increasing association with delinquent peers, fostering beliefs favorable to crime, and contributing to individual traits such as negative emotionality. Certain of these arguments, in fact, were at the core of the classic strain theories described above.

Strains may reduce social control in several ways. Many strains involve negative treatment by conventional others, such as parents, teachers, and employers. These strains reduce the individual's bond or attachment to these others. These strains may also reduce direct control by causing individuals to retreat from these others. Further, these strains may reduce the belief that crime is wrong, since the individual's ties to those who teach this belief are weakened. Some data support these arguments, suggesting that strains are negatively associated with several types of social control (e.g., Elliott *et al.*, 1985; Paternoster and Mazerolle, 1994). Further, several strains are synonymous with a weak investment in conventional society. Such strains include low grades, work in the secondary labor market, and chronic unemployment.

Strained individuals may form or join criminal groups in an effort to alleviate their strains. As several researchers have noted, individuals frequently join gangs with the hope of better achieving their goals, including their monetary and status goals. Individuals may also join gangs in an effort to escape bad home environments and obtain comfort and support. Further, they may join gangs in an effort to protect themselves from victimization. Interviews with gang members support these arguments, and quantitative studies suggest that strain increases the likelihood of association with delinquent peers (e.g., Paternoster and Mazerolle, 1994).

The experience of strains may also foster beliefs favorable to crime, particularly beliefs that define crime as a desirable, justifiable, or excusable response to strains. Imagine, for example, individuals who are regularly harassed by others in their neighborhood and are unable to obtain relief through legal channels, such as the police. These individuals may eventually come to believe that violence is a justifiable response to provocations. Limited ethnographic and quantitative data support this argument (Agnew and Peters, 1986; Anderson, 1999; Elliott *et al.*, 1985).

Finally, the chronic experience of strains may contribute to personality traits conducive to crime, particularly the trait of negative emotionality. People high in negative emotionality are easily upset, experience intense emotional reactions when upset, and have an aggressive interactional style. Some data suggest that chronic strain contributes to this trait, including several studies indicating that strains have a positive effect on trait anger or the tendency to become angry in response to a range of stressors (Agnew, 1997b; Bernard, 1990; Brezina, 1996).

In sum, strains increase the likelihood of crime for several reasons, with the key mechanism being the impact of strains on negative emotional states.

Factors that increase the likelihood of criminal coping

There are a variety of ways to cope with strains, only some of which involve crime. Among other things, individuals may engage in behavioral coping of a legal nature (e.g., negotiate with the peers who harass them), they may employ cognitive coping strategies that allow them to reinterpret objective strains in ways that minimize their subjective adversity (e.g., they may decide that monetary success is not that important), and they may employ emotional coping strategies of a legal nature (e.g., listening to music, exercising). GST lists those factors that increase the likelihood that individuals will engage in criminal coping.

Poor coping skills and resources
Criminal coping is said to be more likely among individuals with poor conventional coping skills and resources. This includes poor problem-solving and social skills,

personality traits such as negative emotionality and low constraint, low intelligence, low self-efficacy, and low socioeconomic status. Criminal coping is also more likely among those with good criminal coping skills and resources, including physical strength, fighting ability, and criminal self-efficacy (the belief that one can successfully engage in crime).

Low conventional social support

Criminal coping is more likely among people who cannot turn to others for support when they experience strains. These others include family members, friends, coworkers, and professionals such as social workers and attorneys. The support provided may include advice on how to cope, emotional support, financial assistance, and direct assistance in coping (e.g., helping someone find a job).

Low social control

Individuals who are low in the various types of social control are more likely to engage in criminal coping. They are less likely to be sanctioned for such coping, have less to lose if sanctioned, and do not define crime as wrong.

Association with criminal others/beliefs favorable to crime

Criminal coping is also more likely among those who associate with other criminals and hold beliefs favorable to crime. Criminal others are more likely to encourage, reinforce, model, and teach beliefs favorable to crime. Many of these beliefs define crime as a justifiable or excusable response to certain strains, such as severe financial need and provocations by others.

Exposure to situations where the costs of crime are seen as low and the benefits as high

Finally, criminal coping is more likely when strained individuals are in situations where the benefits of such coping are high and the costs low. Perceptions of benefits and costs are influenced by such things as the availability of capable guardians, attractive targets for crime, and drugs and alcohol (Agnew, 2005).

In sum, a range of factors are said to influence the likelihood that individuals will cope with strains in a criminal manner. Research in this area, however, has produced mixed results. Some studies, for example, indicate that criminal coping is more likely among those with delinquent peers, while other studies do not. These mixed results may stem from the difficulty of detecting conditioning effects with survey data, and Agnew (2006a, b) has suggested that researchers test for conditioning effects using experimental, vignette, and qualitative studies.

Applying GST to key issues in criminology

GST focuses on explaining why some individuals are more likely to engage in crime than others. The theory, however, has also been applied to the explanation of group differences in offending and offending over the life course. Brief discussions of certain of these applications are provided below. For additional applications of GST, including the use of GST to explain crime in countries other than the United States, see Agnew (2006a).

Gender and crime

GST states that males have higher rates of crime than females for two reasons (Broidy and Agnew, 1997). First, males are more likely to experience strains conducive to crime. While males do not experiences more strains overall than females, studies suggest that males are more likely to experience strains such as harsh discipline, negative secondary school experiences, abusive peer relations, criminal victimization, and homelessness. Also, males may be more likely to pursue and have trouble achieving several goals conducive to crime, including masculine status, autonomy, and monetary success. At the same time, females are more likely to experience certain strains that reduce the likelihood of many types of crime. Such strains include close supervision by parents and others, and the burdens associated with the care of others, such as children and spouses. This is not of course to say that females do not experience strains conducive to crime, only that they are less likely to do so than males.

Second, males are more likely than females to respond to strains with crime, particularly other-directed crime. Contrary to certain popular accounts, this is not because "men get angry, and women get depressed." Studies suggest that women are just as likely or somewhat more likely than males to get angry when they experience strains. However, the anger of males may differ from that of females. The anger of females is more often accompanied by emotions such as depression, guilt, fear, anxiety and shame. The anger of men, on the other hand, is more often characterized by moral outrage. These differences may reflect differences in socialization and social position. The moral outrage of males is more conducive to other-directed crime than is the anger of females, and this may partly explain gender differences in crime.

Males may also be more likely to react to strains with crime because they more often possess personality traits like low constraint and negative emotionality. Males are also lower in certain types of conventional social support, particularly emotional support. Males are lower in certain types of social control, including parental supervision, school ties, and beliefs regarding crime. Males are more likely to associate with other criminals, who reinforce, model, and otherwise encourage criminal responses to strains. And males are more likely to hold beliefs, including gender-related beliefs, conducive to crime.

Some data support these arguments (for a review, see Agnew, 2006a). Studies find that males are more likely to experience certain strains conducive to crime, such as criminal victimization, and that this difference partly explains gender differences in offending. Most, although not all, studies find that males are more likely to cope with strains through crime. And some data suggest that this is because of gender differences in certain of the factors that condition the effect of strains on crime. More research is needed in these areas, however, particularly research that examines a broad range of strains, emotions, and conditioning variables.

Communities and crime

The strongest correlate of community crime rates is economic deprivation. GST states that deprived communities have higher rates of crime because their residents are more likely to experience certain strains conducive to crime and to cope with these strains through crime (Agnew, 1999, 2006a).

Most notably, the residents of deprived communities have more trouble achieving their economic goals through legal channels, even after we take account of individual characteristics such as their education. They have less access to stable, high paying jobs – which are more often located in suburban areas. Relatively few individuals in the community have the types of job contacts or connections that might help others get jobs. There are fewer individuals in the community to teach and model the skills and attitudes necessary for successful job performance. And the schools in deprived communities are generally inferior.

Further, the residents of deprived communities are more likely to experience a host of other strains linked to poverty, including family, school, and peer problems. For example, economic problems increase the likelihood of a range of family problems, including divorce, abuse, harsh/erratic discipline, and parental rejection. The pervasiveness of strain in such communities also means that residents are more likely to come in contact with other strained/angry individuals. This, in turn, further increases the likelihood of negative treatment.

Individuals in deprived communities are also more likely to cope with the strains they experience with crime. This partly stems from their more limited coping skills and resources. They have fewer financial resources, for example. Also, there are fewer people in such communities to teach and model effective problem-solving skills. As social disorganization theorists point out, people in deprived communities are less able and willing to come to one another's assistance, partly because they are consumed with their own problems. They are also less able and willing to exercise social control over one another. And they are more likely to associate with other criminals and hold beliefs conducive to crime.

There has not been much research on the ability of GST to explain community differences in crime rates, although a few studies provide some support for the above arguments (Boardman *et al.*, 2001; Brezina *et al.*, 2001; Warner and Fowler, 2003).

Adolescence-limited offending

Most individuals increase their levels of offending as they move from childhood to adolescence, with a majority of adolescents occasionally engaging in minor offending. Most adolescents, in turn, drift out of offending as they enter adulthood. GST explains this adolescence-limited pattern of offending by stating that adolescents are more likely to (a) experience strains conducive to crime, and (b) cope with these strains through crime (Agnew, 1997b).

One reason that adolescents experience more strains is that they live in a larger, more demanding social world than do children and adults. As juveniles approach adolescence, they leave elementary school and enter secondary schools. Such schools are more demanding, which increases the likelihood of academic problems. They are also larger and more diverse, such that adolescents come into contact with many more students, including students from backgrounds different than their own. Adolescents also get involved in larger, more diverse peers groups; and spend much more time with peers in unsupervised settings. These changes increase the likelihood of negative treatment, since adolescents are interacting with large numbers of diverse others, often free from adult supervision. As adolescents become adults, however, their social world narrows and they have more control over the people they interact with – thus reducing the likelihood of negative treatment.

Adolescents are also more likely to experience strains because they come to desire many of the privileges of adulthood, but are often prevented from achieving these privileges through legitimate channels. Such privileges including increased autonomy, respect, a broader range of goods and services, and the right to engage in such "adult behaviors" as drinking and sexual activity. Adolescents, however, are frequently denied the privileges they desire. For example, they are often subject to strict controls at school, they lack legitimate sources of income, and they are legally forbidden to engage in many adult behaviors. As a consequence, adolescents may seek such adult privileges through illegal channels.

Adolescents are also more likely to cope with strains through crime. Adolescents have less experience at coping than adults, and so have poorer problem-solving and social skills. While adolescents do have more coping experience than children, adults usually keep a close watch over children and cope on their behalf. Further, adolescents lack many key coping resources, such as self-control, power, and money. Adolescents are lower in certain types of social control than children and adults. In particular, they are less well supervised and more likely to lack strong ties to conventional institutions, such as work and family. Finally, adolescents are more likely to associate with delinquent peers, who frequently encourage criminal coping.

Data provide some support for these arguments. Studies suggest that adolescents are more likely to experience certain strains than children and/or adults. For example, grades become worse during adolescence and victimization increases. And the stress literature suggests that adolescents are more likely to cope with strains in "immature" or maladaptive ways, including crime.

Life-course persistent offending
A small group of offenders tend to offend at high rates over much of their lives. It is critical to explain the offending of this group since they account for a large share of all crime, particularly serious crime. Not surprisingly, GST states that these individuals are more likely to experience strains conducive to crime and to cope with strains through crime (Agnew, 1997b).

These individuals are more likely to experience strains conducive to crime because they develop the traits of negative emotionality and low constraint early in life. As indicated, individuals with such traits are impulsive, have little concern for others, are especially sensitive to strains, and have an antagonistic interactional style. The development of these traits is partly a function of biological factors, including genetic inheritance and exposure to biological harms – such as head injuries and toxic substances. And these traits are partly a function of environmental factors, including a troubled family environment.

Individuals with the above traits are more likely to experience strains over the life course because: (a) they provoke negative reactions from others in given situations; (b) they alienate and frustrate those they regularly interact with, such as parents and teachers, creating an ongoing pattern of negative interaction; (c) they select themselves into environments where they are more likely to be treated in a negative manner, such as delinquent peer groups and bad jobs; and (d) they are more likely to perceive a given environment in a negative manner. Further, as indicated earlier, such individuals are more likely to cope with the strains they experience through crime.

CONCLUSIONS

Strain theory provides a unique explanation of crime. Unlike other theories, strain theory focuses explicitly on negative treatment by others and assigns a central role to negative emotions in the explanation of crime. At the same time, strain theory is intimately linked to other crime theories. GST, in particular, draws on other crime theories in describing the factors that condition the effects of strains on crime. Also, the strains identified by GST may reduce control, foster the social learning of crime, and contribute to personality traits conducive to crime. (And the factors identified by these other theories may contribute to strain, see Agnew (1995c, 2006a).

Research is generally supportive of strain theory, particularly GST. Numerous studies indicate that most of the strains identified by GST increase the likelihood of crime. More limited evidence suggests that the effect of these strains is partly explained by negative emotions. And, as indicated, research on those factors that condition the effects of strains on crime is mixed. More research on GST is needed, however.

Certain of the strains identified by GST have not been the subject of much research. This includes strains such as peer abuse, discrimination, and the inability to achieve monetary, autonomy, and masculinity goals. Further, strains are poorly measured in most of the existing research – reflecting the limitations of existing data sets for testing GST. Researchers typically focus on objective strains, even though we would expect subjective strains to be more strongly related to crime. Researchers often employ single-item measures that poorly index the nature and magnitude of strains. And researchers often group several strains together into summary scales, even though only certain of these strains are conducive to crime. In addition, researchers seldom examine the ways in which strains work together to impact crime. GST, in particular, states that strains are most likely to cause crime when they cluster together in time – thereby overwhelming the legal coping resources of the individual.

More research is also needed on the intervening mechanisms between strains and crime. Only a few studies have examined the impact of strains on the intervening variable of emotional states, with this research focusing on anger. More research is clearly needed in this area, including research on other negative emotions. In this area, researchers should explore whether certain strains are more conducive to some emotions than others, and whether certain emotions are more conducive to some types of crime than others. Also, researchers should devote more attention to the impact of strains on social control, the social learning of crime, and personality traits such as negative emotionality and low constraint.

In addition, researchers should devote more attention to those factors that condition the effect of strains on crime. As indicated, it is difficult to detect such conditioning effects using survey research. Researchers should therefore explore such effects using experiments, vignette studies, and observational studies. Researchers should also explore the ways in which conditioning variables work together to influence the reaction to strains. Conditioning variables are usually examined in isolation from one another. Those most likely to cope with crime, however, may be those who are deficient in all or most of the factors that favor legal coping.

Further, more research is needed on the ability of GST to explain group differences in offending and offending among particular groups. Most research in this area focuses on gender, and all of the research in this area is limited because it only focuses on a portion of those strains conducive to crime and those factors that increase the likelihood of criminal coping. Related to this, theorists should attempt to link GST with macro and psychobiological theories of crime. GST explains group differences in crime in terms of group differences in the exposure to strains conducive to crime and conditioning variables. GST, however, says little about the reasons for such differences. Macro and psychobiological theories of crime offer much insight here. Such theories include feminist, critical race, institutional anomie, conflict, and other theories.

Assuming that GST receives sufficient support in the above research, researchers should also examine the policy implications of the theory (Agnew, 2006a). Drawing on GST, we may reduce crime by: (a) eliminating strains conducive to crime; (b) altering strains so as to make them less conducive to crime (e.g., reducing their magnitude and perceived injustice); (c) removing individuals from strains conducive to crime; (d) equipping individuals with the traits and skills needed to avoid strains conducive to crime; (e) altering the perceptions, cognitions, or goals of individuals to reduce their subjective levels of strain; (f) improving coping skills and resources; (g) increasing conventional social support; (h) increasing social control; (i) reducing association with criminal peers and beliefs conducive to crime; and (j) reducing exposure to situations conducive to crime.

While the results of initial empirical tests have been encouraging, GST remains a 'work in progress.' Additional research in the above areas should facilitate the development and refinement of the theory. Such work may also help to solidify the status of strain theory, especially GST, as a leading explanation of crime and delinquency.

REFERENCES

Agnew, R. (1984a). Autonomy and delinquency. *Sociological Perspectives* 27: 219–240.

Agnew, R. (1984b). Goal achievement and delinquency. *Sociology and Social Research* 68: 435–451.

Agnew, R. (1992). Foundation for a general strain theory of crime and delinquency. *Criminology* 30: 47–87.

Agnew, R. (1995a). Controlling delinquency: recommendations from general strain theory. Pp. 43–70 in *Crime and Public Policy: Putting Theory to Work*, edited by H. D. Barlow. Boulder, CO: Westview.

Agnew, R. (1995b). The contribution of social-psychological strain theory to the explanation of crime and delinquency. Pp. 113–138 in *The Legacy of Anomie Theory: Advances in Criminological Theory*, Volume 6, edited by F. Adler and W. S. Laufer. New Brunswick, NJ: Transaction.

Agnew, R. (1995c). Testing the leading crime theories: an alternative strategy focusing on motivational processes. *Journal of Research in Crime and Delinquency* 32: 363–398.

Agnew, R. (1997a). The nature and determinants of strain: another look at Durkheim and Merton. In *The Future of Anomie Theory*. Edited by N. Passas and R. Agnew. Boston: Northeastern University Press.

Agnew, R. (1997b). Stability and change in crime over the life course: a strain theory explanation. Pp. 101–132 in *Developmental Theories of Crime and Delinquency: Advances in Criminological Theory*, Volume 7, edited by T. P. Thornberry. New Brunswick, NJ: Transaction.

Agnew, R. (1999). A general strain theory of community differences in crime rates. *Journal of Research in Crime and Delinquency* 36: 123–155.

Agnew, R. (2002). Experienced, vicarious, and anticipated strain: an exploratory study focusing on physical victimization and delinquency. *Justice Quarterly* 19: 603–632.

Agnew, R. (2005). *Juvenile Delinquency: Causes and Control.* Los Angeles: Roxbury.

Agnew, R. (2006a). *Pressured Into Crime: An Overview of General Strain Theory.* Los Angeles, CA: Roxbury.

Agnew, R. (2006b). General strain theory: current status and directions for further research. Pp. 101–123 in *Taking Stock: The Status of Criminological Theory: Advances in Criminological Theory,* Volume 15, edited by F. T. Cullen, J. P. Wright and K. R. Blevins. New Brunswick, NJ: Transaction.

Agnew, R., Cullen, F. T., Burton, V. S. Jr., Evans, T. S. and Dunaway, R. G. (1996). A new test of classic strain theory. *Justice Quarterly* 13: 681–704.

Agnew, R. and Peters, A. A. R. (1986). The techniques of neutralization: an analysis of predisposing and situational factors. *Criminal Justice and Behavior* 13: 81–97.

Agnew, R., Piquero, N. and Cullen, F. T. (2009). General strain theory and white-collar crime. In *The Criminology of White-Collar Offending*, edited by S. R. Simpson and D. Weisburd.

Anderson, E. (1999). *Code of the Street: Decency, Violence, and the Moral Life of the Inner City.* New York: Norton.

Baron, S. W. (2004). General strain theory, street youth, and crime: a test of Agnew's revised theory. *Criminology* 24: 457–483.

Benson, M. L. (1985). Denying the guilty mind: accounting for involvement in a white-collar crime. *Criminology* 23(4): 583–607.

Bernard, T. J. (1990). Angry aggression among the 'truly disadvantaged'. *Criminology* 28: 73–96.

Boardman, J. D., Finch, B. K. and Ellison, C. G. (2001). Neighborhood disadvantage, stress, and drug use among adults. *Journal of Health and Social Behavior* 42: 151–165.

Brezina, T. (1996). Adapting to strain: an examination of delinquent coping responses. *Criminology* 34: 39–60.

Brezina, T. (1998). Adolescent maltreatment and delinquency: the question of intervening processes. *Journal of Research in Crime and Delinquency* 35: 71–99.

Brezina, T. (2000). Delinquency, control maintenance, and the negation of fatalism. *Justice Quarterly* 17(4): 779–803.

Brezina, T., Agnew, R., Cullen, F. T. and Wright, J. P. (2004). The code of the street: a quantitative assessment of Elijah Anderson's subculture of violence thesis and its contribution to youth violence research. *Youth Violence and Juvenile Justice* 4(2): 303–328.

Brezina, T., Piquero, A. and Mazerolle, P. (2001). Student anger and aggressive behavior in school: an initial test of Agnew's macro-level strain theory. *Journal of Research in Crime and Delinquency* 38: 362–386.

Broidy, L. and Agnew, R. (1997). Gender and crime: a general strain theory perspective. *Journal of Research in Crime and Delinquency* 34: 275–306.

Cloward, R. A. and Ohlin, L. E. (1960). *Delinquency and Opportunity*. New York: Free Press.

Cohen, A. (1955). *Delinquent Boys*. New York: Free Press.

Elliott, D. S., Ageton, S. S. and Canter, R. J. (1979). An integrated theoretical perspective on delinquent behavior. *Journal of Research in Crime and Delinquency* 6: 3–27.

Elliott, D. S., Huizinga, D. and Ageton, S. S. (1985). *Explaining Delinquency and Drug Use*. Beverly Hill, CA: Sage.

Froggio, G. and Agnew, R. (2007). The relationship between crime and 'objective' versus 'subjective' strains.' *Journal of Criminal Justice,* 35: 81–87.

Greenberg, D. F. (1977). Delinquency and the age structure of society. *Contemporary Crises* 1: 189–223.

Hagan, J. and McCarthy, B. (1997). *Mean Streets: Youth Crime and Homelessness*. Cambridge: Cambridge University Press.

Hagedorn, J. (1994). Homeboys, dope fiends, legits, and new jacks. *Criminology* 32(2): 206–219.

Krienert, J. L. (2003). Masculinity and crime: a quantitative exploration of Messerschmidt's hypothesis. *The Electronic Journal of Sociology* 7(2).

Merton, R. (1938). Social structure and anomie. *American Sociological Review* 3: 672–682.

Merton, R. (1968). *Social Theory and Social Structure.* New York: Free Press.

Messerschmidt, J. W. (1993). *Masculinities and Crime: Critique and Reconceptuatlization of Theory.* Lanham, MD: Rowan and Littlefield Publishers, Inc.

Moffitt, T. E. (1993). Adolescence-limited and life-course-persistent antisocial behavior: a developmental taxonomy. *Psychological Review* 100: 674–701.

Morgan, N. (2006). *The Role of Negative Emotion in General Strain Theory.* PhD Dissertation, Emory University, Atlanta.

Passas, N. (1997). Anomie, reference groups, and relative deprivation. In *The Future of Anomie Theory*, edited by N. Passas and R. Agnew. Boston: Northeastern University Press.

Paternoster, R. and Mazerolle, P. (1994). General strain theory and delinquency: a replication and extension. *Journal of Research in Crime and Delinquency* 31(3): 235–263.

Topalli, V. and Wright, R. T. (2004). Dubs and dees, beats and rims: carjackers and urban violence. Pp. 149–160 in *Crime Types*, edited by D. A. Dabney. Belmont, CA: Wadsworth.

Warner, B. D. and Fowler, S. K. (2003). Strain and violence: testing a general strain theory model of community violence. *Journal of Criminal Justice* 31: 511–521.

Warr, M. (1996). Organization and Instigation in delinquent groups. *Criminology* 34: 11–38.

Wheaton, B. (1990). Life transitions, role histories, and mental health. *American Sociological Review* 55: 209–224.

Wright, J. P., Cullen, F. T., Agnew, R. and Brezina, T. (2001). The root of all evil? Money and delinquent involvement. *Justice Quarterly* 18: 239–268.

6

Control Theories

Ray Paternoster and Ronet Bachman

INTRODUCTION

As discussed in the last chapter of this volume, strain theories in criminology generally attempt to answer the question, "If human beings are adequately socialized and under normal circumstances they will comply with norms and laws, why do they sometimes commit crimes?" At the individual level, the answer to this question is that people commit crimes because they feel strain or experience some stressful or unpleasant experience which in turn motivates them to break the rules that they would normally comply with. Thus, strain theories begin with the assumption that conformity can be taken for granted because of normally effective socialization, and it is rule breaking or deviance that is in need of explanation. The explanation for rule-breaking lies in between-individual variation in criminal motivation of some sort.

Control theories, on the other hand, begin with a very different assumption of human nature. Control theories begin with the assumption that socialization is not fully adequate, and that a person's first inclination is to act on the basis of their own self interest, which may easily run them afoul of the law since the pursuit of self-interest through crime is very often the quickest and easiest way to need fulfillment.[1] Unlike strain theories, therefore, deviance or rule breaking is not problematic and needs no explanation. What must be explained, according to control theories, is restraint or compliance with rules.[2] In other words, in explaining why there is differential involvement in crime, strain theorists would contend that there are differences across persons in criminal motivation, while control theorists would argue that there are differences in restraints or controls.

For control theorists these inhibitions or controls over crime come in many different forms. They may be: (1) internal to the person (compliance to rules is enforced by self) or (2) external (compliance is enforced by others). In addition, control may be imposed (1) directly (feelings of guilt or shame imposed by self or control by the strict supervision or monitoring by others) or (2) indirectly as in a by-product of socialization (securing conventional commitments such as an intimate partner that may then be jeopardized by non-compliance) or as involvement in social relationships (the good will of others may be jeopardized). Variation across individuals in their vulnerability to rule breaking, control theorists would contend, can be explained by variation in the strength of these internal/external and direct/indirect controls (Nye, 1958).

In this chapter we will discuss two forms of control theory, control theory at the individual level (a control theory of individual offending) and control theory at the neighborhood or community level (a control theory of crime rates). Both types are control theories and begin with the two basic assumptions of control theory: (1) human beings are imperfectly socialized and are motivated by self-interest, and (2) self-interest must be restrained by a source of control than is external to the individual. Because much of the theoretical and empirical literature regarding community-level controls has been covered in the chapter on social disorganization, we will spend most of the essay discussing individual level control theory – its origins, key concepts and propositions, and current controversies.

COMMUNITY OR NEIGHBORHOOD LEVEL CONTROL THEORY

A brief history of neighborhood control theory

Although there certainly was earlier empirical work done on the relationship between neighborhoods and crime,[3] the origin of macro-level or community control theory in criminology is usually traced to the work of Clifford Shaw and Henry McKay in Chicago.[4] We all know that Shaw and McKay's empirical work revealed:

- Crime was neither randomly nor uniformly distributed throughout the city of Chicago. Some neighborhoods had very high rates of crime and delinquency, some had very low rates of crime and delinquency, with other areas falling between the two extremes.
- Rates of neighborhood crime and delinquency were relatively stable over time such that high crime neighborhoods in 1910 were also high in crime in 1920, 1930 and 1940.
- Areas characterized by high rates of crime and delinquency had high crime and delinquency rates regardless of the ethnic composition of the people who lived in them. In fact, different ethnic groups seemed to conform to the level of crime and delinquency that historically characterized the neighborhood in which they were living.
- Crime rates seemed to monotonically decrease with the distance from the central business district.
- Neighborhoods characterized by high crime and delinquency also had high rates of a host of other social ills including school truancy, infant mortality, poverty, mental illness, and tuberculosis.

These empirical regularities in Chicago convinced Shaw and McKay of two things: (1) high rates of crime and delinquency could not be due to the fact that urbanization or urban life itself was promoting crime, and (2) high rates of crime and delinquency could not be due to the biological deficiencies of immigrants and their children.

They concluded that there must be something about the *neighborhood* itself, some enduring community characteristic, which was responsible for stable delinquent areas. But what was it about these neighborhoods?

In arriving at an explanation, Shaw and McKay drew upon the work of other Chicago sociologists, notably the urban sociology and human ecology work of Robert E. Park and Ernest W. Burgess and the social psychology of W. I. Thomas. From Park and Burgess, Shaw and McKay characterized the growth of Chicago as one beginning at the center and oldest area of the city and then expanding outward. The expansion of cities, however, occurs through a particular social process initiated by competition over scarce space. Because of this Darwinian competition for space, newer areas are literally "invaded" by older areas, pushing those economically able to move out of the older area into the adjacent space and leaving the "weaker" behind (Park, 1936a).[5] There is a structural organization to the city produced by previous competition that is represented by different urban areas – the central business district, zone of transition, zone of working men's homes, etc. When the invasion of one area by another occurs (e.g., when the central business and industrial area expands and pushes into the adjacent zone of transition), Shaw and McKay contended that there was structural disorganization.

Structural disorganization does not run unhindered, however, for an invaded area adapts, adjusts and reorganizes itself along different lines. For example, parts of an old zone of transition may now become the fringe of the central business/industrial district, while the inner fringe of the old working men's residential area may become part of the zone of transition, and so on. While invasion starts with some structural organization, it inevitably brings with it structural disorganization, and then the communities reorganize themselves into new structural forms. Burgess (Park, *et al.*, 1967: 54) describes this process of organization → disorganization → reorganization as follows:

> Normally, the process of disorganization and organization may be thought of as in reciprocal relationship to each other, and as co-operating in a moving equilibrium of social order toward an end vague or definitely regarded as progressive. So far as disorganization points to reorganization and makes for more efficient adjustment, disorganization must be conceived not as pathological, but as normal.

It is this normal process of competition, invasion, disorganization and reorganization that produces the ecological distribution of population in the city that Shaw and McKay observed. One outcome of which is the "natural area":

> The general effect of the continuous process of invasions and accommodations is to give to the developed community well-defined areas, each having its own peculiar selective and cultural characteristics. Such units of communal life may be termed "natural areas" or formations, to use the term of the plant ecologist.

Natural areas are not, therefore, static but are dynamically ever-changing in response to processes of competition, invasion, disorganization and reorganization – processes summed up in the concepts of dominance and succession (Park, 1936 a, b).

Unlike the competition that goes on in the plant kingdom, however, the competition over scarce resources, including space, among human beings is not unregulated. Human society, what Darwin and human ecologists after him referred to as the "web of life," includes not only a biological level, but a cultural level as well. The cultural superstructure of society imposes an external order and restraint upon biological systems. Competition over scarce resources, and the pursuit of self-interest which biology drives, is restrained by culture. Social order, in fact, is only made possible to the extent to which natural competitive drives have been successfully harnessed:

> Society is everywhere a control organization. Its function is to organize, integrate, and direct the energies resident in the individuals of which it is composed. One might, perhaps, say that the function of society was everywhere to restrict competition and by so doing bring about a more effective co-operation of the organic units of which society is composed. Competition, on the biotic level, as we observe it in the plant and animal communities, seems to be relatively unrestricted. Society, so far as it exists, is anarchic and free. On the cultural level, this freedom of the individual to compete is restricted by conventions, understandings, and law.
>
> (Park, 1936b: 14)

Human culture, then, imposes constraints on the exercise of self-interest in the competitive struggle over available but relatively scarce resources. This does not mean, however, that culture eliminates competition and struggle between people, only that there is a sufficient balance or equilibrium produced to enable a social organization to exist.[6]

Since structure and culture are in symbiotic balance, disruptions of the structural order affect culture and the ability of culture to regulate competition. While normally society is in a state of organization and equilibrium, and the forces of competition are successfully constrained, there are times when structural dislocations upset this balance. In fact, periods of organization and equilibrium followed by a period of disorganization and then reorganization is a normal part of the growth processes of any urban area – domination and succession. A state of social disorganization is, then, only temporary – a prelude to a process of reorganization as individuals selectively adapt to change. The period of social disorganization, however, has both a group and an individual component. For the group, social disorganization brings with it collective inertia as the group cannot act collectively to realize its values or objectives. At the individual level, social disorganization leaves the individual with no controls or restraint on the exercise of self-interest.[7]

The question is, how does social disorganization arise and what are its consequences? For Shaw and McKay, the origin of social disorganization is natural urban growth – the invasion of neighborhoods by industry, and the arrival of new persons in these and adjacent communities with new and different cultures. The natural competition over space implies that industry will move into adjacent areas when they feel the economic need to expand. These areas adjacent to the central business and industrial area are in transition – landowners anticipating their take-over by industry fail to keep up housing or other services in the area and they become physically deteriorated and unsightly. In the struggle for survival, those who are economically able to flee the invaded neighborhood do so and move to better neighborhoods where they begin a process of reorganization. Those left behind, however, are confronted with: (1) high population mobility as "better" families depart and new arrivals appear, (2) cultural diversity as the new arrivals' norms and values may be different from those who remained behind, and (3) cultural obsolescence as the culture brought by the new arrivals does not adequately prepare them for their new life.[8]

There are several consequences for those living in these newly invaded areas undergoing a process of social disorganization:

- The diversity and obsolescence of culture means that self-interest cannot easily be regulated and there is no common value system.
- The cultural diversity and high mobility makes it difficult for community organizations to develop.
- Unconnected by a common value system, social institutions like schools and the family are unable to effectively and collectively organize to rid the community of social problems. Hence, these communities have high rates of crime, mental illness, illiteracy, infant mortality, truancy, poverty, illegitimate births, tuberculosis, etc.
- The power of social institutions like the family, neighbors, and the school over their members is weakened and individuals are able to work themselves free from control.

Essentially, then, the normal processes of urban growth – invasion, domination, and succession – weaken cultural and institutional controls in the neighborhood. There is a breakdown in both internal (culturally induced shame and guilt) and external (family, neighbors, schools) controls as well as direct (supervision by neighbors and family weakens) and indirect (organizations that bind people together and gives them common interests fail to develop) controls. This weakening of control among community institutions and the family gives individuals greater freedom. Freedom from control in turn brings high rates of crime and delinquency in particular neighborhoods ("delinquent areas") that persist over time. It is not until these communities can reorganize themselves that control over individuals will again be effectively exercised and crime/delinquency rates can begin to fall.

CURRENT VERSIONS OF NEIGHBORHOOD CONTROL THEORY

Neighborhood control theory or what has been called social disorganization theory was popular in the discipline from the late 1920s until well into the 1940s when its appeal began to decline and theories of individual offending began to take their place. The decline in interest in studying and trying to explain neighborhood rates of crime was due in some measure to conceptual and methodological problems within neighborhood crime research itself,[9] but the decline was also due to theoretical advances at the individual level and to the development of a persuasive and convenient approach (the self-report) to study individual variation in offending. Beginning approximately in the 1980s, however, empirical and theoretical interest in neighborhoods and crime reappeared (Reiss and Tonry, 1986). This theorizing and research was less focused on social disorganization *per se* than in understanding the intervening causal mechanisms that linked the structural properties of neighborhoods to crime rates. What was entirely consistent between the two periods of interest in neighborhood factors and crime was the belief that high crime in some communities was not due to motivational factors, but the absence of restraint or control.

Two of the most important theoretical/conceptual statements were made by Bursik and Grasmick (1993) and Sampson and colleagues (Sampson, *et al.*, 1997). In 1993

Bursik and Grasmick published an important theoretical extension of neighborhood control theory, which they referred to as a *systemic theory of community*. Bursik and Grasmick expanded the idea from Shaw and McKay that the failure of residents in a community to develop strong ties to each other was the impetus for a breakdown in social control. Their point was that neighborhood life was characterized by social ties among residents and by social ties that link residents to other institutions and organizations outside of but still part of community life. Taking social organization to be the ability of residents to regulate what behaviors take place within their community, Bursik and Grasmick argued that it arises out of dense social ties or the social capital that a community possesses (Bursik and Grasmick, 1993; Bursik, 1999). The capacity for social control exists on three levels: (1) the private – control exercised by close intimate others in the community, (2) the parochial – control exercised by neighborhood residents and institutions, and (3) the public – the capacity of the neighborhood to secure goods and services from larger political and economic institutions outside of the community. In the systemic theory of neighborhood control, strong social ties create effective informal and formal social control. Bursik and Grasmick (1993: 18) put it this way:

> ... the private, parochial, and public networks capable of social control do not develop instantaneously. Rather, they slowly emerge through interaction among the residents over a period of time. Therefore, the greater the level of residential instability that exists in a neighborhood, the less likely it is that such networks are able to control the threat of crime in an area ...

The key, then, to systemic neighborhood control is residential stability since such stability builds up dense social ties, which in turn facilitates the three levels of social control.

In what many have argued is the most comprehensive extension of neighborhood control theory since the Chicago school, Sampson and colleagues have argued that *collective efficacy* is the causal mechanism that links the structural characteristics of a neighborhood (population mobility, heterogeneity, poverty, family intactness) to the capacity to develop informal social control capable of inhibiting crime (Raudenbush and Sampson, 1999; Sampson, 2006a, b; Sampson *et al.*, 1997).[10] Collective efficacy is a combination of social trust/cohesion and the shared expectation that residents will do something about community problems. Communities high in collective efficacy are those wherein neighbors both trust one another and share a belief that the community can and will solve its problems, including problems of social control. Collective efficacy may grow out of shared interactions and dense social networks among residents but need not, and it is the causal mechanism linking the structural characteristics of a community to neighborhood rates of crime. A productive line of research has consistently shown that neighborhoods high in collective efficacy have lower rates of crime/delinquency and other social problems compared to neighborhoods low in collective efficacy (Sampson *et al.*,1997, 1999, 2002, 2005; Lowenkamp *et al.*, 2003; Pratt and Cullen, 2005; Silver and Miller, 2004; Wikström and Sampson, 2003).

In sum, although theorizing and empirical interest in social control at the neighborhood level has waxed and waned over the years, recent reformulations have advanced our understanding of the intervening causal mechanisms by which neighborhoods and communities can exert control over residents to inhibit crime and deviance.

As will be seen in the next section, theorizing at the individual level has also significantly evolved over the past four decades as well.

Individual level control theory

As we have seen, control theory at the neighborhood level has focused on explaining variation in crime rates, that is, why some communities have higher levels of crime than others. Notwithstanding the ecological fallacy, the causal processes that operate at the community or neighborhood level, however, are linked to individual level processes. That is, processes of organization, disorganization and reorganization ultimately occur at the individual level in response to structural characteristics of communities:

> Disorganization as preliminary to reorganization of attitudes and conduct is almost invariably the lot of the newcomer to the city, and the discarding of the habitual and often of what has been to him the moral, is not infrequently accompanied by sharp mental conflict and sense of personal loss. Oftener, perhaps, the change gives sooner or later a feeling of emancipation and an urge toward new goals.
>
> The mobility of city life, with its increase in the number and intensity of stimulations, tends inevitably to confuse and to demoralize the person. For an essential element in the mores and in personal morality is consistency, consistency of the type that is natural in the social control of the primary group. Where mobility is the greatest, and where in consequence primary controls break down completely, as in the zone of deterioration in the modern city, there develop areas of demoralization, of promiscuity, and of vice.
>
> (Burgess, 1967: 59)

The processes of organization → disorganization → reorganization occurs at the individual level as well as the community level. This theme was developed most extensively by W. I. Thomas and F. W. Znaniecki (1920) with his notion of the demoralization of the individual. Demoralization occurs when individuals find themselves in conditions where primary groups fail to provide for their needs and they are left with no restraint on self-interest (Thomas and Znaniecki, 1920: 166–167):

> In America, on the contrary, the moral progress due to the new organization created by the Polish immigrants is much less general and intense than the demoralization resulting from the fact that the old rules are losing their influence upon the individual isolated from his original social milieu. The new system here, even at its best, would be unable to control individual behavior as efficiently as did the old system in Poland, and thus the surprisingly rapid development of new institutions in Polish-American society, though checking the pace of demoralization, cannot prevent the average moral level of immigrants in general from slowly but unmistakably declining instead of rising, nor does it provide the society with adequate means of dealing with such radical cases of demoralization as those which we shall study presently. … We shall find overwhelming evidence that the natural tendencies of an individual, unless controlled and organized by social organization, inevitably lead to a behavior which must be judged as abnormal from the social standpoint.

Although Thomas was speaking specifically about Polish immigrants, his ideas can be generalized to all immigrant groups. In essence, he contends that in the absence of primary group controls, the individual becomes demoralized and until reorganization at the individual level occurs, this state can lead to such outcomes as economic dependency, marital disruption, sexual promiscuity, crime, and delinquency.

The history of individual-level control theory can reasonably be traced to the social psychology of Thomas and his efforts to explain the individual moral consequences of social change. Individual level control theory was, therefore, meant to initially explain variation in criminal/delinquent offending between individuals, and within recent years it has been expanded to include within-individual variation in offending over time.

One of the first expressions of an individual level control theory of crime/delinquency was a paper published in 1951 by Albert Reiss appropriately titled, "Delinquency as the Failure of Personal and Social Controls" (Reiss, 1951).[11] In the very first paragraph of this paper Reiss (1951: 196) delineates the individual control position, namely that delinquency is due to the *failure of restraint*:[12] "Delinquency may be defined as the behavior consequent to the failure of personal and social controls to produce behavior in conformity with the norms of the social system to which legal penalties are attached." One of the most important institutions in the development of social control of the individual is the family. Reiss argues that strong bonds of attachment between parents and children are important because when such a bond exists parents are more likely to exercise direct control over the child, children are more likely to identify with parents, and this identification, in turn, is necessary for the development of a sense of morality and personal control over self-interest. Another dimension of control is provided by community institutions whose ability to inhibit unwanted behavior is a function of the family's residential stability in the neighborhood.

Reiss also argued for logical extensions of control theory. For example, he contended that if delinquency was due to the absence of controls, then it was unlikely that contact with delinquent peers was causally necessary to provide delinquent motivation. Reiss stated (1951: 197) that "the delinquent peer group is here viewed as a *consequence* of the failure of personal and social controls in the social system" (emphasis added). Rather than cause delinquent behavior, then, those with weak personal and social controls seek out others like them and any relationship between delinquent behavior and delinquent peers is spurious – due to social selection.[13]

Jackson Toby (1957: 16) further advanced the control explanation. By his account, variation in delinquent offending could not be due to between-individual variation in the motivation to offend since "impulses to steal and murder and rape are universal." What accounts for differences in rule breaking is variation in the extent to which someone has something to lose by deviance, or what Toby (1957: 16) called variation in a "*stake in conformity*." He stated:

> … the differences between the law-abiding adolescent and the hoodlum is not that one has impulses to violate the rules of society while the other has not. Both are tempted to break laws at some time or other – because laws prohibit what circumstance may make attractive: driving an automobile at 80 miles an hour, beating up an enemy, taking what one wants without paying for it. The hoodlum yields to these temptations. The boy living in a middle-class neighborhood does not. How can this difference be accounted for? … youngsters vary in the extent to which they feel a stake in American society. For those with social honor, disgrace is a powerful sanction. For a boy disapproved of already, there is less incentive to resist the temptation to do what he wants when he wants to do it.

This "stake in conformity" not only includes material objects, but also things one aspires to such as a reputation as a good person, and a sense of right and wrong, all of which can be placed in jeopardy should one decide to break rules and become a "hoodlum." Toby (1957: 17) also notes that the kind of individual level theory of social control he was discussing should be viewed as complementary to a macro-level theory since:

> … the social disorganization approach can explain why community 'A' has a higher crime rate than community 'B' but not why Joe becomes a hoodlum and Jim does not. The differential stake in conformity of the individuals within a given community, on the other hand, can account for varying tendencies to become committed to an anti-social way of life.

Together, then, Reiss and Toby break control theory away from its macro origins in the social disorganization perspective of the Chicago urban sociologists and begin to develop a theory at the level of the individual.

The next significant theoretical advance in individual control theory did not appear for almost ten years, when Scott Briar and Irving Piliavin (1965) published a paper in *Social Problems*. What is important about the Briar and Piliavin paper is that they directly take what they call "motivational theories" of delinquency, such as cultural deviance theory, to the proverbial woodshed for their inadequacies. There are several problems with these motivational theories according to Briar and Piliavin. First there is the epistemological issue that motivational theories take the side of criminal differentiation (Taylor *et al.*, 1974) – that offenders are fundamentally different from non-offenders: "These theories regard the illegal acts of delinquents as the product of some enduring disposition or combination of dispositions unique to these youths" (Briar and Piliavin, 1965: 35). The second problem with these theories is that they suffer from what Matza (1964) referred to as "an abundance of riches" – they predict too much delinquency. Most delinquents do not engage in delinquency all the time and many youth exposed to commonly identified motivational influences do not commit crimes. Finally, Briar and Piliavin note that because motivational theories build in such strong compulsions to crime, they cannot account for the fact that virtually all youth eventually "age out" of delinquency on their own and desist from offending.

The control theory that Briar and Piliavin constructed was one that combined weak motivation with inhibitions or controls over delinquent conduct. The motivations that Briar and Piliavin appeal to are not, however, enduring individual dispositions formed in the early years of delinquent youth and unique to them, but are transient, situational and universal. What they refer to as "situationally induced desires experienced by all boys" are more like opportunities than motives (Briar and Piliavin, 1965: 36). Since these motives to offend are "experienced by all boys" we can assume that, in addition to being uniform in their effect, they are quite ubiquitous and cannot under the theory carry much explanatory weight. Whatever short-term inducements to crime the situation offers they are not enough by themselves to bring about crime. The act of crime requires that controls be eased: "whether or not the motives to deviate are situationally induced, the behavioral expression of them depends on the degree to which the individuals experiencing the motives also experience constraints against that behavior" (Briar and Piliavin, 1965: 38).

For Briar and Piliavin, the constraint that keeps ubiquitous but situationally-induced motives from being expressed in crime is termed a "*commitment to conformity*." This commitment to conformity is formed primarily through socialization by the family, school and other social institutions and include not only the possibility of material deprivations should one break rules, but also a loss of one's self-esteem, the good opinion of valued others, and anticipated but not yet enjoyed events, experiences, objects, and social positions, which may be placed in jeopardy. Having a high commitment to conformity not only restrains the situational and temporary motivation to break rules, but has other consequences as well, such as influencing the kind of peers a youth will hang out with. Rather than a cause of crime, as in cultural deviance theory, then, Briar and Piliavin like Reiss before them argued that such peers are a consequence of delinquency.[14] Finally, the kind of control theory that Briar and Piliavin envisioned is also able to explain within-individual offending over time. A youth with a strong commitment to conformity may gradually have those commitments reduced as a result of delinquent offending. In addition, those whose initial conventional commitments are weak "may encounter experiences which serve to increase their stakes, leading them, in turn, to more conventional behavior" (Briar and Piliavin, 1965: 41). Later life experiences can, therefore, strengthen initially weak commitments turning bad kids into good and can weaken initially strong commitments leading good kids to crime. Briar and Piliavin's theory is a very dynamic control theory that argues for the possibility of a great reshuffling of the good and the bad over time, an issue that has gained a great deal of recent theoretical attention (Gottfredson and Hirschi, 1990; Laub and Sampson, 2003; Sampson and Laub, 1993).[15]

Since Briar and Piliavin's groundbreaking paper, there have been at least three other important theoretical contributions to individual control theory. One of these was by the sociologist of the family F. Ivan Nye (1958). In a book entitled *Family Relationships and Delinquent Behavior*, Nye acknowledged that a minor share of delinquency might be due to the influence of strong motivation, an acknowledgment not entirely friendly to a "pure" control theory.[16] However, he also (1958: 4) readily acknowledged that such motivated conduct is rare in comparison to the lion's share of delinquency which he clearly stated "is the result of insufficient social control." Since control theorists uniformly agree that illegal/immoral means are often the quickest and most convenient way to satisfy one's needs, social order demands that self-interest be constrained in some way.[17] Nye articulated three main dimensions of social control that operate to inhibit delinquent conduct: (1) internal control: when delinquent conduct is inhibited by moral beliefs or one's conscience, and is what we might call shame today (Grasmick and Bursik, 1990); (2) indirect control: due to the fear of social censure from others particularly family members and is what we might call embarrassment today; and (3) direct control: due to the fear of formal sanctions. Similar to Reiss, the most important source of social control for Nye was the indirect control provided by the family. In an argument that would be more fully developed by Travis Hirschi, a healthy and emotionally close bond between parent and child, Nye contended, was the primary foundation of social control.

Another development in social control theory around this same time was Walter Reckless' Containment Theory (Reckless *et al.*, 1956, 1957; Reckless, 1967). Although considered a control theory, containment theory, like other individual level control theories before it, is a mixture of both motivations and restraints. According to the theory, youths are motivated to commit delinquent acts by inner and outer pushes and pulls. Examples of pushes or pressures to commit delinquent acts would include adverse living conditions, and a general lack of legitimate opportunities (in other words, strains), while pulls would include the allure of delinquent companions and delinquent/deviant subcultures. These pushes and pulls provide sufficient motivation to commit crime unless they are counteracted by the restraint provided by inner and outer controls or "*containment*." An important inner containment as specified in the theory is a positive self-concept. Outer containments essentially consist of emotional relationships with conventional primary groups (the family is of utmost importance) and material stakes in conformity.

At the time, perhaps both the most articulated and "pure" version of individual level control theory was developed by Travis Hirschi and presented in his classic book, *Causes of Delinquency* (1969). In *Causes* Hirschi showed no interest at all in the motivations for offending and argued that delinquent acts were inhibited only to the extent to which the individual has formed a social bond with conventional society. The social bond reflects how connected to or immersed the person is within a conventional life, and consists of four elements: attachments, commitments, involvements, and beliefs. The simple hypothesis derived from Hirschi's theory is that "delinquent acts result when an individual's bond to society is weak or broken" (Hirschi, 1969: 16).

Causes of Delinquency was more than an opportunity for Hirschi to present his version of social control theory. Anticipating his later position that the most productive avenue of theoretical development is competition among theories, *Causes* presented Hirschi with an opportunity to assess and comment on alternative explanations of delinquency.[18] The competition for the theory of the social bond at the time was primarily strain and differential association/cultural deviance theory. Hirschi contended that these were inferior to social bond theory in large part because they predicted too much delinquency and could not easily account for the age–crime curve. As theories of delinquent motivation, strain and cultural deviance theories could not easily account for periods when delinquent acts were not being committed (what happened to the motivation?). More importantly, once adolescents are bearing the full brunt of the strain and cultural pressure to break rules in early adulthood, empirical data demonstrates that they actually begin to "age-out" of offending and begin their downward trend toward conformity.[19] Hirschi believed that his social control theory was immune to these two criticisms.

Because Hirschi's social bond theory did not need to incorporate motivation for delinquency, since delinquent acts occur in the absence of restraint, his theory was spared the first criticism. Because the bond to conventional society is variable across individuals, there was variability in the extent to which bonds provided the inhibition to act on self-interest and commit crime. In explaining why delinquent acts occur, Hirschi in *Causes* adopts the classical view that the social bond, if formed, serves to inhibit the natural impulse to act solely in accord with one's self-interest primarily by making delinquent/criminal behavior costly. That is, in deciding whether or not to commit a given delinquent act, an individual weighs the immediate benefits of "quick and easy" delinquent behavior against the potential price of a damaged social bond: "…the theory holds that to the extent these factors [the elements of the social bond] have large values the individual is likely to conclude that the costs of crime are not worth the benefits" (Hirschi, 1986: 109). The social bond inhibits crime because an investment in conventional attachments, commitments, involvements, and beliefs makes it more costly than the immediate benefits of offending. The delinquent offender is a calculator, albeit imperfect, of the costs and benefits of behavior.

In dodging the second criticism of motivational theories, Hirschi also believed that his theory provided a better explanation of the process of maturational reform.

In explaining why delinquent acts decline with age, Hirschi adopted the view that changes in the social bond over time are related to changes in restraint over time. In *Causes* (1969: 87) he is critical of those control theories that place the source of inhibition in an internal, time-stable characteristic of the individual because a time-stable trait would be unable to account for the decline in offending with age:

> Explanations of the effects of attachment to the parents on delinquent behavior by reference to the internalization of norms (or, as is common in social control theories, by reference to "internal" or "personal" control) creates difficulties in explaining variations in delinquent activity over time. If the conscience is a relative constant built into the child at an early age, how do we explain the increase in delinquent activity in early adolescence and the decline in late adolescence?

In assuming that the decline in crime over time was variable, not everyone's offending declined and those that declined did not do so at the same rate, social bond theory could not attribute such variation in desistance to a stable individual difference. Instead, Hirschi's control theory accounted for variations in desistance over time by variations in the strength of the social bond over the life course. Some offenders desist, and some desist faster when their bonds become strengthened. Similarly, some formerly non-offenders begin to offend and offenders continue offending when their social bonds become or continue to be weak:

> These difficulties are avoided if we ignore internalization and assume that the moral element in attachment to parents resides directly in the attachment itself. If the bond to the parent is weakened, the probability of delinquent behavior increases; if this bond is strengthened, the probability of delinquent behavior declined. Attachment may easily be seen as *variable* over persons and over time for the same person.
>
> (Hirschi, 1969: 88, emphasis in original)

Variations in offending over time, therefore, are due to variations in the condition of the social bond – the experiences that people have over the life course which cause them to either lose or gain commitments, attachments, involvements or beliefs:

> Unlike more purely psychological theories, it [social control theory] emphasizes the significance of variation in group membership across the life cycle. With this latter emphasis, the theory can attempt to account for one of the major facts of crime ignored by other theories: the considerable variation in criminal behavior over the life of the "offender".
>
> (Hirschi and Rudisil, 1976: 21)

The theory of the social bond, then, was argued by Hirschi at the time to be able to account for many of the known facts of delinquency, and also seemed able to account for a troubling anomaly that befuddled motivational theories of crime – that delinquency seemed to decrease after the mid-teens and steadily declined to adulthood. The decline in crime seemed to be occurring when the social controls discussed by Hirschi in *Causes* seemed to be increasing (education, jobs, marriage), and there was very little optimism that delinquent motivation could have declined so progressively. When stated in 1969, Hirschi's social bond theory seemingly could explain how crime occurs in the first place (it occurs when the bond to society is poorly formed or weakened) and why crime declined over time at varying rates for different people (a once weak bond could later be strengthened, and a once strong bond could be later damaged). Social bond theory proved to be an immensely popular explanation of crime. It spawned scores of empirical studies, and it has been characterized as "the dominant theory of criminal and delinquent behavior for the past twenty-five years" (Akers, 1994: 115).

Although there have been literally hundreds of scholars who have commented on or empirically tested social bond theory, Hirschi himself remained virtually silent about his theory until 1990. In that year, his silence was broken with the publication of his book with Michael Gottfredson entitled, *A General Theory of Crime* (Gottfredson and Hirschi, 1990). Their general theory was not only a theory of crime and delinquency, but a theoretical explanation of criminal offending at all ages, in all places, as well as an explanation of non-criminal acts that were thought to share important conceptual ground with crime and delinquency (smoking, drinking, accidents, obesity, gambling).

The key theoretical construct in the general theory of crime is the attribute of self-control. Exactly what self-control is has changed slightly over the years, but one characteristic that was first stated in the 1990 book that has not changed over time is that self-control is a relatively time-stable trait of persons that consists of the inability to resist immediate gratification and avoid the long-term costs of one's behavior.[20] Like other forms of social control, self-control is something that has to be created. Like many control theorists before them, Gottfredson and Hirschi contended that restraint on self interest was formed primarily as a product of socialization in the family. Moreover, once formed, self-control is difficult to undo, and if not created early in life it is difficult to create later. As a result, differences in self-control, once established early in life, are relatively stable over the life course.

As an explanation, the general theory of crime truly was general. Much broader in scope than social bond theory, it was an account of "all crimes, at all times, and, for that matter, many forms of behavior that are not sanctioned by the state" (1990: 117). Ironically, though more general in scope than social bond theory, self-control theory was conceptually more parsimonious. Together with opportunity and age, self-control was "for all intents and purposes, *the* individual-level cause of crime (1990: 232). Moreover, unlike social control theory, the general theory of crime did not attempt to offer an explanation of maturational reform. According to the theory of self-control (Gottfredson and Hirschi, 1990: 136), maturational reform, the decline in delinquent and criminal offending with time, was just that – a decline in crime brought on by aging:

> An alternative interpretation of maturational reform or spontaneous desistance is that crime declines with with age. ... This explanation suggests that maturational reform is just that, change in behavior that comes with maturation; it suggests that spontaneous desistance is just that, change in behavior that cannot be explained, change that occurs regardless of what else happens.

In the general theory of crime, then, the decline in crime as a person grows older need not and cannot be explained by the theory; it is due to the "inexorable aging of the organism" (Gottfredson and Hirschi, 1990: 141).[21] The important implication of this is that offending declines for everyone at the same rate over time – maturational reform as reflected in the age–crime curve is invariant. It was this very point that was the impetus for the development of another individual-level social control theory – one that was perceived to be more faithful to the original version of social bond theory and at odds with self-control theory (Sampson and Laub, 1993).

Subsequent to *A General Theory of Crime*, Sampson and Laub (1993: 6) published their own version of social control theory, which they labeled "an age-graded theory of informal social control." Given the view by some that Hirschi had abandoned his earlier theory,[22] Sampson and Laub may be argued to be the true inheritors of social bonding theory. Like Hirschi's theory in 1969, their's was an attempt to explain both why people become involved in crime in the first place and, perhaps more importantly, how they get out of crime once involved. With respect to how crime originates in the first place, with only minor disagreements,[23] they essentially agree with Hirschi's view in *Causes* – crime occurs when the social bond that inhibits crime is weak. With respect to the second question, how maturational reform is explained, Sampson and Laub fairly dramatically part company with the Hirschi of 1990.[24] Sampson and Laub's position with respect to maturational reform is compatible with Hirschi's original view in *Causes* – variation over time in offending is due to variation in the strength of the social bond over time.

A major tenet of Sampson and Laub's informal social control theory is that while there is a great deal of stability in offending and conformity over time (on average that delinquent kids in the present are more likely to be adult offenders in the future), there is also a non-trivial amount of change over the life course that a theory needs to explain. That is, Sampson and Laub believed, as many control theorists including the Hirschi of *Causes* believed, that time can bring with it a reshuffling of people such that those who were formally offenders could later desist from crime and those who were formally non-offenders (or minor offenders) could later take up crime (Laub and Sampson, 2003; Sampson and Laub, 1993). What accounts for this reshuffling? In short, changes in the social bond. Former offenders can do things (either deliberately by their own actions or without their intention or awareness) whereby a previously weak bond can become strong. They can, for example, develop an intimate relationship with a spouse or partner who provides both greater external control via supervision and monitoring (a change in crime) and/or makes them change their character so that they are different people (a change in criminality – see, Laub and Sampson, 2001, 2003; Sampson and Laub, 1993, 2003, 2005a–c; Sampson *et al.*, 2006a, b). Former offenders can also take on steady employment which provides them with something substantial to lose should they succumb to temptation and commit more criminal acts. Or they could unwittingly just get in the habit of complying with rules and at some point realize that they have quit crime, what Laub and Sampson (2003) have described as desistance by default. On the other hand, those with previously strong bonds can for various reasons commit criminal or other acts in adulthood, acts which could cause a person to lose his family, his job or otherwise diminish his stake in conformity.

There are, then, two different versions of individual level control theory in the current literature. The key difference between Gottfredson and Hirschi's self-control theory and Sampson and Laub's age-graded theory of informal social control lies in the variance/invariance of the age–crime curve and whether or not changes in the social bond later in life are *causally related* to changes in criminal offending. In their self-control version of control theory, Hirschi (Gottfredson and Hirschi, 1990) abandons his belief in *Causes* that desistance in crime occurs at different times and different rates for different offenders, a position that Sampson and Laub pick up.

To fully understand the difference between Hirschi's social bond and self-control theory on this issue, we need to examine an article that appeared some seven years before the publication of *A General Theory of Crime*. In 1983, Hirschi and Gottfredson published a paper in the *American Journal of Sociology* entitled, "Age and the Explanation of Crime." In that article they made an important interpretation of an empirical observation. After presenting empirical distributions of the age–crime curve from different time periods, different countries, different crime types, and different demographic groups, they concluded that the distribution of crime over age was invariant. That is, criminal offending increases during adolescence, reaches a peak, and then consistently declines toward zero as people get older, and this increase in offending toward adolescence and steady decline throughout adulthood *is the same for everyone* – the age–crime curve is invariant: "… our thesis is that the age effect is invariant across social and cultural conditions" (Hirschi and Gottfredson, 1983: 560).

Although the invariance of the age–crime curve is an empirical observation or rather an interpretation of an empirical observation, its theoretical implication for social control theory is profound. If desistance from crime occurs for everyone, at roughly the same ages, and at roughly the same rate, then the variables of social control theory need not (indeed, cannot) explain it. For example, if maturational reform unfolds the same for everyone then it cannot really be explained by variations in the strength of the bond over time. Recall Hirschi's very different assumption in *Causes*, that the desistance from crime that occurs from adolescence into adulthood is variable – some desist/some do not, some desist faster than others and former non-offenders initiate crime later in life. This was one of the assumed "facts" of crime that any theory was supposed to, in fact, had to, explain in order to be taken seriously. The theory of social control outlined in *Causes* was crafted in part to account for the assumed fact that aging out of crime was variable. Social control theory explained the variability of desistance by hypothesizing that the strength of the social bond can change over time. The argument was that those adolescents with formally weak bonds could, for example, become attached to a conventional spouse or committed to a productive and satisfying job and reform thereafter. It also had to assume that adolescents with strong bonds could become detached from a conventional spouse (via divorce) or could become unemployed, thus loosening the bond and making late onset offending more likely. This is the argument in *Causes* and in only slightly modified form it is the argument by Sampson and Laub (1993; Laub and Sampson, 2003).

If, however, maturational reform is invariant, then Hirschi's criticism in *Causes* (1969: 87) of a time-stable source of control is invalid. The invariance of maturational reform is hostile to the position that changes in the condition of the social bond over time has a substantial effect on offending, but it is perfectly compatible with the notion of a time-stable difference in the capacity to restrain oneself from the temptation of the moment. What has changed with control theory from *Causes* to *A General Theory of Crime* is the interpretation of one particular "fact" about crime – the variance or invariance of the age–crime curve. The Hirschi in *Causes* certainly assumed that crime declines with age as did the Hirschi in *A General Theory*. The important difference between the two positions is that in *Causes* and in Sampson and Laub's more recent version of control theory, the age effect is different for different people and is explained by variations in the social bond. In contrast, in *A General Theory,* the age effect is approximately the same for everyone and is for the most part due to the direct effect of age. The presence of the age effect on crime is not in dispute between social control and self-control theory, the difference is a theoretical interpretation, and not an empirical fact.[25]

The critical question, then, is whether Hirschi, in taking a different theoretical direction in *A General Theory of Crime*, as Akers and Sellers (2004: 123–124) and Taylor (2001: 370, 382) contend, has abandoned the field of social control theory to Sampson and Laub. We argue that he has not. There is important common ground between Hirschi's theory of the social bond presented in *Causes* (and by implication that found in Sampson and Laub's work) and the general theory of crime. The common ground can be found in the importance of social relationships, particularly those early in life.

What is absolutely clear is that according to the general theory of crime, a prerequisite for the creation of self-control is that there exist a positive, caring *attachment* between the care giver and child. Gottfredson and Hirschi clearly delineate this importance:

> The traits composing low self-control are also not conducive to the achievement of long-term individual goals. … It follows that people who *care about* the interpersonal skill, educational and occupational achievement, and physical and economic well-being of those in their care will seek to rid them of these traits.
>
> (Gottfredson and Hirschi, 1990: 96, emphasis added)

> The person who *cares for* the child will watch his behavior, see him doing things he should not do, and correct him.
>
> (Gottfredson and Hirschi, 1990: 97, emphasis added)

> Our model states that parental concern for the welfare or behavior of the child is a necessary condition for successful child-rearing.
>
> (Gottfredson and Hirschi, 1990: 98)

> … learning to defer pleasures of mood, to attend to obligations, to wait one's turn in line, to negotiate needs with others, to respect the rights of the weak, requires diligent training and teaching, accomplished by someone who cares about the outcome.
>
> (Gottfredson and Hirschi, 2003: 7)

In both theories, the child's relationship with the person or persons entrusted to care for them is a critical factor in the creation of an inhibition over self-interested behavior. What the creation of self-control requires, therefore, is an important element of the social bond – an attachment between care giver and child. Furthermore, in the general theory of crime, the presence of emotionally attached care givers can be taken as an indicator of effective self-control:

> These measures of early parental attachment, which create self-control, are indistinguishable from measures of self-control in the child when applied later in life. If affection creates self-control, in large part through monitoring and appropriate sanctioning, then the child's affection for the parents, expressed as a desire to accommodate to their parent's wishes and expectations is essentially an indicator of self-control. If this is so, then commonly used indicators of attachment to parents (and by extension to other social institutions such as schools and religions) – the social bond – is at the same time a good measure of self-control – also a social bond. It seems logical to say that common measures of self-control for

adolescents are good proxies for attachment (both from the parent to child and child to parent).

(Gottfredson, 2005)

Effective attachment between care giver and child creates self-control and this is seen in part by the bond of affection between them and the child's desire to meet the expectations of the care giver.

The creation of self-control, then, requires that there be a bond of affection between care giver and child, that the care giver care enough both to inform the child of the expectations they have for good behavior, and care enough to do something about it when behavioral expectations are not met. The process of creating inhibition or restraint through the creation of self-control is identical to the role of attachment between parent and child in Hirschi's original social control theory. Social control theory argues that the key element of attachment is not the direct control or monitoring of the child's behavior, but the anticipated consequences on the part of the parent by the child – the "psychological presence of the parent" (Hirschi, 1969: 94). In other words, the child imagines the possible sanctions that the parent may impose (disappointment, guilt) and, given the fact that there is a bond of affection between them, the child restrains itself out of respect for that bond of affection. In order for the imagination of sanctions or consequences to be meaningful to the child, the parent must, at least initially, directly monitor the behavior of the child and sanction or react to behavior that is deemed inappropriate. Direct monitoring and correcting of the child's behavior is antecedent to "the psychological presence of the parent."

If the child does not communicate with his parents, if he does not tell them of his activities, then he does not have to concern himself with their imagined reactions to his behavior. If, by the same token, they do not tell him how they feel about his behavior, this too frees him from an important source of potential concern.

(Hirschi, 1969:108)

Both the creation of the social bond and self-control, then, requires a tie of affection between care giver and child, a tie of affection strong enough that the care giver makes the effort to both monitor the behavior of the child and to respond to it. Although conceptually distinct, in this way the social bond and self-control become empirically indistinguishable.

Clearly, then, we do not agree with Akers and Sellers' (2004: 123) argument that social control and self-control theories are incompatible in part because "there is no place for self-control as a separate element in Hirschi's (1969) social bonding version of control theory." Our view is that they are perfectly compatible because there is no need for separate elements of the social bond and self-control. Parents who have self-control are more likely to be attached to their children, they are more likely to care about them and how they behave, and they are more likely to watch over them and "correct" them when they behave inappropriately. They also are more likely to pass high self-control onto their children. Similarly children high in self-control are going to be more concerned about the opinion of their parents, they are going to care about what their parents think of them, and as a result, they will be more likely to do the kinds of things that parents would like them to do and refrain from doing the kinds of things parents disapprove of, however much immediate pleasure they may gain.

The important common ground that we contend exists between social bond and self-control theory, of course, should be not taken to mean that we believe the two theories are identical. We have already suggested that a major theoretical shift occurred with Hirschi about the invariance of the age–crime curve. Assuming that the age–crime curve crime is invariant implies that the distribution of crime over the life course is likely due to both some common process such as aging, and some time-stable characteristic of individuals. Accepting this, one must also accept the fact that there is only the barest amount of reshuffling of those with high and those with low criminal propensity. Consequently, it does not harmonize well with the view that adult social bonds nor many other events/experiences later in life can alter lives to such a degree that the good become bad and the bad become good.

THE FUTURE OF CONTROL THEORY

It is likely that control theory, both at the community or neighborhood level and at the individual level, will continue to dominate theoretical and empirical work in criminology. There are important puzzles for scholars in both areas to work on. One of these puzzles for those working on neighborhood level control theory is the origin of collective efficacy. While Bursik and his colleagues (Bursik and Grasmick, 1993; Bursik, 1999) have argued for the importance of strong social ties, collective efficacy theorists have argued that dense social ties might not be necessary for strong informal social control, and also that under the right conditions, such ties may serve to weaken informal community control (Sampson, 2006a, b). If frequent social interactions among the residents of a neighborhood are not a necessary basis for effective informal social control, then what is? Sampson (2006a) has suggested that the structural resources available within a community (mainly the economic wealth of an area), the density of non-profit organizations, and the density of technology may account for feelings of trust and efficacy in the absence of strong social relationships. It remains to be seen how these concepts can be interwoven into a formal control theory of neighborhood crime as antecedents to collective efficacy and whether such a theory has empirical support. Another important area of both theoretical and empirical work for neighborhood level control theorists is the likely reciprocal relationship between collective efficacy and crime. While it has been shown how feelings of trust and efficacy can effectively lower the crime in a neighborhood, it is equally reasonable to see that crime and discord can reduce both. What has to be examined is the empirical validity of such a reciprocal relationship and the specific causal mechanisms involved therein.

There are numerous and equally tantalizing areas of theoretical and empirical work for scholars interested in individual level control theory, particularly within the field of criminal desistance. While there is agreement within criminology that desistance or what used to be called maturational reform takes place, agreements end there. Some have argued that desistance is invariant, occurring approximately at the same rate and the same time for everyone. Others have argued that desistance from crime differentially occurs across individuals. As we have seen, there are important theoretical implications of this, but exactly what form empirical support for either position would take is not entirely clear. For those who would argue that desistance occurs through the biological process of aging, the burden is to "unpack" the precise events or changes that take place with age that bring about a change in crime. Does age change crime, the opportunity to offend, criminality, the propensity to offend, or both? Those who argue that desistance occurs at different times and at different rates for different people have the similar burden of arguing whether adult life events modify opportunity (does a good partner simply change our routine activities?) or propensity as well (does she/he change "us" into different people?). Moreover, recent control theorists have underscored the importance of human agency in the desistance process (Laub and Sampson, 2003) yet have not been entirely clear as to what role agency plays in the reduction of crime, how large a role it plays, nor exactly what agency is. Finally, control theorists have primarily focused on desistance from crime, but if there is, in fact, a non-trivial reshuffling of people over time, it is important to provide a theoretical account for how it is that formally law abiding people can become offenders in their adult years and demonstrate that such a process occurs.

Clearly, there is a great deal of work to do in exploring the efficacy of the various control theories in explaining offending over the life course, as well as the mechanisms by which the constructs within each theory actually work. It is hoped that the very brief research agenda of theoretical and empirical questions outlined above will be the catalyst for future work for decades to come.

NOTES

1 The observation that the pursuit of self-interest runs a high risk of rule breaking because both involve a quick and easy satisfaction of wants has been recently attributed by scholars and students of control theory to Gottfredson and Hirschi (1990) in their recent restatement of social control theory as a general theory of crime. Although it may easily pre-date him, F. Ivan Nye (1958: 5) noted nearly 60 years ago that "… in general behavior prescribed as delinquent or criminal need not be explained in any positive sense, since it usually results in quicker and easier achievement of goals than the normative behavior".

2 In the usually succinct words of Hirschi (1969: 34), "The question is, 'Why don't we do it? There is much evidence that we would if we dared".

3 Interest in the spatial distribution of crime can be traced at least as far back as the second decade of the nineteenth century with the publication in France of the annual *Compte General de L'administration de al Justice Criminelle en France*, first published in 1825. The *Compte* consisted of crime reports compiled by French prosecutors at the local level who then mailed in quarterly crime reports to the central government in Paris. The data included specific characteristics of the crime committed such as whether or not a suspect was arrested, the location of the crime, and other information. The data contained in the *Compte* was analyzed by the Belgian astronomer and mathematician Adolphe Quetelet and the French lawyer André-Michel Guerry (see Beirne, 1993; Taylor *et al.*, 1974). In England, comparable work on the spatial distribution of crime in England and London was conducted by Joseph Fletcher and Henry Mayhew (see Morris, 1957).

4 Perhaps the cleanest statement of social disorganization as control theory by the early Chicago theorists can be found in Shaw *et al.* (1929). As Kornhauser (1978) correctly argues, theoretical work by Shaw and McKay subsequent to that can best be described as a "mixed" model of delinquency where control theory notions were combined with concepts and causal processes from cultural deviance and even strain theory. If we ignore some of Shaw and McKay's later theorizing, therefore, it is reasonable to think that they are a good starting point for a discussion of neighborhood control theory. It is tempting to argue that Frederic Thrasher (1927) is the first neighborhood control theorist as he predates Shaw by two years. We agree with Kornhauser (1978), however, that Thrasher's is a theory of gang formation and is not as instructive as Shaw and McKay as a theory of crime and delinquency. There is a common thread here, however, as we believe that both

Thrasher and Shaw and McKay's neighborhood control theory was heavily influenced by Thomas (1928) and Thomas and Znaniecki's (1920) work.

5 That there is a very definite Darwinian process of competition, selection, and survival of the fittest cannot be understated. In describing the ecological process of the city McKenzie (Park *et al.*, 1967: 64) wrote that: "A great deal has been written about the biological, economical and social aspects of competition and selection, but little attention has been given to the distributive and spatial aspects of these processes. The plant ecologist is aware of the effect of the struggle for space, food, and light upon the nature of a plant formation, but the sociologist has failed to recognize that the same processes of competition and accommodation are at work determining the size and ecological organization of the human community."

6 Elsewhere, Park (1936a: 175) wrote that "The same biotic interdependence of individual and species, which has been observed and studied in plant and animal communities, seems to exist likewise on the human level, except for the fact that in human society competition and the struggle for existence are limited by custom, convention, and law".

7 Thomas and Znaniecki (1920: 165) referred to this breakdown of control at the individual level as "demoralization": "Demoralization is the decay of the personal life-organization of an individual member of a social group" (see Thomas, 1920: 165–171).

8 In describing the origins of the demoralization of the immigrant, Thomas and Znaniecki (1920; xi) note that: "For all these reasons, though the steady influx of new immigrants coming directly from Poland and full of old country memories prevents the interest in traditional institutions from disappearing entirely, the social organization which develops spontaneously here is necessarily only a very imperfect imitation of the old Polish original. It still centers around the family and the primary community, and the fundamental principles of direct personal solidarity and conformity with social opinion are still recognized; but of the many varied and coherent beliefs and customs which made these institutions so rich and vital most are either entirely forgotten or inefficient, or even ridiculous, and whatever new beliefs and customary forms of behavior may have developed in the new conditions are not sufficiently general, numerous, stable or binding to take adequately the place of the obliterated tradition."

9 For example, there were concerns about how exactly to measure social disorganization, whether things like poverty, population mobility and heterogeneity, and the presence of other problems in a neighborhood was social disorganization or indicators that social disorganization was present, and controversies about the "ecological fallacy" that seemed endemic to the theory (see Bursik, 1988; Kornhauser, 1978; Finestone, 1976).

10 Sampson and colleagues' work was anticipated by Sampson and Groves (1989) who made an important first step in describing the causal mechanisms behind social disorganization. Using the British Crime Survey, Sampson and Groves found that the structural characteristics of communities were connected to crime rates through three intervening mechanisms: community supervision of teenage peer groups, local friendship networks, and participation in community organizations.

11 Reiss's paper is an interesting bridge between neighborhood and individual level control theory. He argues (1951: 201) that "a major source of a person's control lies in the social controls of the community and its institutions". He seems to be suggesting that personal controls are easier to create within communities where social control is stronger and those where there is residential stability.

12 There is a hint in Reiss' paper that the motivation for rule breaking may not be entirely uniformly distributed. He argues that an important function of the family is to meet the needs of its members. He states (1951: 198) that the "economically dependent" family may be financially unable to meet the demands and needs of its members, and that this may engender feelings of anxiety and insecurity. This in turn may weaken the ability of the family to control its members. It is not unreasonable to think, however, that these feelings of anxiety and insecurity might provide a foci for motivation to commit crime. Unmet needs and wants as a source of criminal motivation may not, therefore, be equally distributed – an argument made by strain theories of crime.

13 The argument that low social control at the individual level has reverberations down the life course is a frequent, though until recently (Gottfredson and Hirschi, 1990), not fully appreciated component of individual-level social control theory.

14 Briar and Piliavin (1965: 40) argued that "... stakes in conformity will influence the youth's choice of friends. Those boys who have high stakes will tend not to befriend peers whose stakes are low since the latter are more likely to 'get into trouble'. Boys with low stakes, on the other

hand, will tend to avoid those who are 'chicken' and to seek out those with congruent interests and freedom to act."

15 Although it is possible for bad kids to become good, Briar and Piliavin (1965: 41) argue that it is not easy: "It is likely that failure to develop conformity commitments through the desire to satisfy parental expectations reduces the probability that the youth will develop such commitments in other social contexts." Compare this to Gottfredson and Hirschi (1990: 107): "It is difficult for subsequent institutions to make up for deficiencies, but socialization is a task that once successfully accomplished, appears to be largely irreversible."

16 Nye (1958: 4–5) argues that his is a general theory of crime that is "multi-causal." His multi-causal theory includes a large dose of the failure of control and a teaspoon of criminal/delinquent motivation.

17 In what is a common control theory theme, illegal behavior is perceived to be the quickest and easiest way to satisfy needs. Nye (1958: 4) put it as follows: "The laws of society protect the property and person of its individual members, but in the process society makes it impossible for most of its members to *quickly and conveniently* achieve their major goals. For example, the quickest way for a vice-president to become president would be to murder the president, but this is frowned upon."

18 "... [t]he first purpose of oppositional theory construction is to make the world safe for a theory contrary to currently accepted views. Unless this task is accomplished, there will be little hope for the survival of the theory and less hope for its development. Therefore, oppositional theorists should not make life easy for those interested in preserving the *status quo*. They should instead remain at all times blind to the weaknesses of their own position and stubborn in its defense. Finally, they should never smile" (Hirschi, 1989: 43).

19 In referring to the tendency of positivistic theories to build too much motivation into their theories, Hirsch noted that "... at the moment the offender is fully created, at the moment he is complete, he begins to do what he does less and less frequently, and the theory that created him cannot explain why he no longer does what he was designed to do" (Hirschi and Gottfredson, 1986: 55).

20 In *A General Theory of Crime* self-control was multidimensional, with a number of different "elements." Those with low self-control preferred an immediate and easy gratification of desires, they preferred acts that were risky and thrilling, were disinclined to pursue long-term objectives that required planning, and were indifferent to others and self-centered. In later writings, a smaller conceptual fence seemed to be built around the idea of self-control. Hirschi and Gottfredson began to think of self-control as a tendency to be tempted by behaviors that promised short-term pleasure at the expense of long-term cost –"People who engage in crime are people who tend to neglect long-term consequences" (Hirschi and Gotttfredson, 2001: 90).

21 In explaining maturational reform, Gottfredson and Hirschi draw a distinction between "crime" and "criminality." Crimes are events that occur only under specified conditions of opportunity, criminality is a relatively time stable propensity of persons to commit crimes. Differences in criminality are only imperfectly captured by differences in crime and criminal offending may change over time while criminality does not.

22 Since both social bond and self-control theory were written or co-written by the same theorist, and both were identified as a control theory of crime, it was inevitable that comparisons would be made between the two. For the most part those who have offered such comparisons of the theories have concluded that social control and self-control are very different, even contradictory, theories, and that Hirschi abandoned the former for the latter. For example, Akers and Sellers (2004: 123) argue that the two theories are incompatible in part because "there is no place for self-control as a separate element in Hirschi's (1969) social bonding version of control theory." Taylor (2001: 370, 382) similarly takes the position that "social control and self-control theory [citations omitted] are based on fundamentally different principles" and that they are "theoretically incompatible."

23 Though not so much a disagreement as a difference in emphasis, Sampson and Laub argue that exactly what people bond to changes over the life course (bonding to the family and school as youth – marriage and job as adults), hence their notion of age-graded social controls. In addition, they emphasize social control that arises from a bond with the family, school and neighbors, rather than inhibition due to the threat of legal punishment, hence their notion of *informal* control. When Hirschi was first writing *Causes*, developmental psychology was still in its infancy and had not yet

integrated itself into criminology. As a result, he did not direct himself to the issue of age-graded variation in the precise nature of the bonds. Nonetheless, it is fairly easy to agree with the position that precisely what we bond to (parents, peers, the school, partners, employment) changes somewhat as we age.

24 They also differ with respect to the role of opportunity in their respective theories. In their general theory of crime, Gottfredson and Hirschi (1990) argued that while low self-control is *the* individual factor involved in crime, another important consideration is the opportunity to commit crime. Even in the presence of low self-control, crime may not occur in the absence of opportunity. Initially, Sampson and Laub (1995) argued that opportunity cannot carry much theoretical weight in any explanation of crime since opportunities to act on self interest are ubiquitous. They have recently modified that position since routine activities or opportunities to commit crime now play at least a modest role in their theory of criminal desistance (Laub and Sampson, 2003).

25 The issue is empirical, as Hirschi (2002: xxxi) acknowledges. If it turned out that the distribution of crime over age was actually found to be different for different people, in different places, at different times then this might be just the empirical evidence to indicate that the age–crime curve is not invariant. We are not optimistic, however, that the debate between propensity theorists like Gottfredson and Hirschi and life-course theorists like Sampson and Laub and others will be so easily resolved on empirical grounds alone. Empirical observations are made sense of within some theoretical context, that is, not everybody "sees" the same thing when they look at the same data. For example, Figure 5.11 in Sampson and Laub (2003: 104) showed offending trajectories for what was called "total crime" from ages 7 to 70 from the Glueck data. The figure depicted the pattern of offending from age 7 to 70 for six different "types" of offenders identified in the data, from high-rate offenders to low-rate. Gottfredson and Hirschi looked at this figure from the vantage point of their age–crime invariance position and concluded that with minor perturbations, there is considerable relative consistency in the age crime curve for everybody – that offending (total crime) declines at approximately the same rate for everyone, and this constancy is due mainly to the fact that these subjects were getting old. Sampson and Laub, however, looked at the very same figure and claimed that clearly the distribution of crime over age is not invariant. They can point to the fact that at times formerly high risk offenders (moderate rate desisters) have lower levels of offending than formerly low risk offenders (low-rate chronic II). They would argue that this shows that offenders and non-offenders are "changing places" with each other over the life course, and that this changing of places is due to things like variations in the adult social bond. This seems to imply that the disagreement between these points of view will continue to be a theoretical rather than an empirical one. Even this description glosses over the fact that the "disposition" and "life course" camps are seeing anything close to the same thing when they view something like the data in that figure. Gottfredson and Hirschi might argue that what the figure reveals is a change in the commission of "crime" (an act) with age, but not a change or decline in "criminality" (a disposition to offend). In other words, that age results in a decline in crime without a necessary decline in criminality. In contrast, life course theorists might argue that social events and situations that people find themselves in change both their "criminality" and their involvement in "crime" – as a result of changing social situations.

REFERENCES

Akers, R. L. (1994) *Criminological Theories*. Los Angeles: Roxbury.

Akers, R. and Sellers, C. S. (2004) *Criminological Theories* (Fourth Edition). Los Angeles, CA: Roxbury Publishing.

Beirne, P. (1993) *Inventing Criminology: Essays on the Rise of "Homo Criminalis"*. Albany: State University of New York Press.

Briar, S. and Piliavin, I. (1965) Delinquency, situational inducements, and commitment to conformity. *Social Problems* 13: 35–45.

Burgess, E. W. (1967) The growth of the city: An introduction to a research project. Pp. 47–62 in *The City*. R. E. Park and E. W. Burgess (eds). Chicago: University of Chicago Press.

Bursik, R. J. Jr. (1988) Social disorganization and theories of crime and delinquency. *Criminology* 26: 519–551.

Bursik, R. J. Jr. (1999) The informal control of crime through neighborhood networks. *Sociological Focus* 32: 85–97.

Bursik, R. J., Jr. and Grasmick, H. G. (1993) *Neigborhoods and Crime: The Dimensions of Effective Community Control.* New York: Lexington.

Finestone, H. (1976) The delinquent and society: The Shaw and McKay tradition. Pp. 23–49, in *Delinquency, Crime and Society.* J. F. Short (ed.). Chicago: University of Chicago Press.

Gottfredson, M. R. (2005) The empirical status of control theory in criminology. Pp. 77–100, in *Taking Stock: The Status of Criminological Theory.* F. Cullen, J. P. Wright and K. Blevins (eds). Piscataway, NJ: Transaction Publishers.

Gottfredson, M. R. and Hirschi, T. (1990) *A General Theory of Crime.* Stanford, CA: Stanford University Press.

Gottfredson, M. R. and Hirschi, T. (2003) Self-control and opportunity. Pp. 5–19, in *Control Theories of Crime and Delinquency* (Advances in Criminological Theory, Volume 12). C. L. Britt and M. R. Gottfredson (eds). New Brunswick, NJ: Transaction Publishers.

Grasmick, H. G. and Bursik, R. J. Jr. (1990) Conscience, significant others, and rational choice: Extending the deterrence model. *Law and Society Review* 24: 837–861.

Hirschi, T. (1969) *Causes of Delinquency.* Berkeley, CA: University of California Press.

Hirschi, T. (1989) Exploring alternatives to integrated theory. Pp. 37–49, in *Theoretical Integration in the Study of Deviance and Crime: Problems and Prospects.* S. F. Messner, M. D. Krohn and A. E. Liska (eds). Albany, NY: State University of New York Press.

Hirschi, T. (1986) On the compatibility of rational choice and social control theories of crime. Pp. 105–118, in *The Reasoning Criminal: Rational Choice Perspectives on Offending.* D. B. Cornish and R. V. Clarke (eds). New York: Springer-Verlag.

Hirschi, T. (2002) *The Craft of Criminology.* New Brunswick, NJ: Transaction Publishers.

Hirschi, T. and Gottfredson, M. (1983) Age and the explanation of crime. *American Journal of Sociology* 89: 552–584.

Hirschi, T. and Gottfredson, M. (1986) The distinction between crime and criminality. Pp. 55–69, in *Critique and Explanation: Essays in Honor of Gwynne Nettler.* T. F. Hartnagel and R. A. Silverman (eds). New Brunswick, NJ: Transaction Books.

Hirschi, T. and Gottfredson, M. (2001) Self-control theory. Pp. 81–96, in *Explaining Criminals and Crime.* R. Paternoster and R. Bachman (eds). Los Angeles: Roxbury Publishing.

Hirschi, T. and Rudisil, D. (1976) The Great American Search: Causes of Crime 1876–1976. *Annals of the American Academy of Political and Social Scince* 423: 14–22.

Kornhauser, R. R. (1978) *Social Sources of Delinquency.* Chicago: University of Chicago Press.

Laub, J. H. and Sampson, R. J. (2001) Understanding desistance from crime. Pp. 1–69 in M. Tonry (ed.), *Crime and Justice: A Review of Research*, Volume 28. Chicago: University of Chicago Press.

Laub, J. H. and Sampson, R. J. (2003) *Shared Beginnings, Divergent Lives: Delinquent Boys to Age 70.* Cambridge, MA: Harvard University Press.

Lowenkamp, C. T., Cullen, F. T. and Pratt, T. C. (2003) Replicating Sampson and Grove's test of social disorganization theory: Revisiting a criminological classic. *Journal of Research in Crime and Delinquency* 40: 351–372.

Matza, D. (1964) *Delinquency and Drift.* New York: Wiley.

Morris, T. (1957) *The Criminal Area.* London: Routledge and Kegan Paul.

Nye, F. I. (1958) *Family Relationships and Delinquent Behavior.* New York: Wiley.

Park, R. E. (1936a) Human ecology. *American Journal of Sociology* 42: 1–15.

Park, R. E. (1936b) Succession, an ecological concept. *American Sociological Review* 1: 171–179.

Park, R. E., Burgess, E. W. and McKenzie (1967) *The City.* Chicago: University of Chicago Press.

Pratt, T. C. and Cullen, F. T. (2005) Assessing the relative effects of macro-level predictors of crime: A meta-analysis. Pp. 373–450 in M. Tonry (ed.), *Crime and Justice: A Review of Research*, Volume 32. Chicago: University of Chicago Press.

Raudenbush, S. W. and Sampson, R. J. (1999) Ecometrics: Toward a science of assessing ecological settings with an application to the systematic social observation of neighborhoods. *Sociological Methodology* 29:1–41.

Reckless, W. (1967) *The Crime Problem.* New York: Appleton, Century Crofts.

Reckless, W., Dinitz, S. and Murray, E. (1956) Self concept as an insulator against delinquency. *American Sociological Review* 21: 744–756.

Reckless, W., Dinitz, S. and Kay, B. (1957) The self component in potential delinquency and potential nondelinquency. *American Sociological Review* 25: 566–570.

Reiss, A. J. Jr. (1951) Delinquency as the failure of personal and social controls. *American Sociological Review* 16: 196–207.

Reiss, A. J. Jr. and Tonry, M. (1986) *Communities and Crime,* Volume 8, *Crime and Justice: An Annual Review of Research.* Chicago: University of Chicago Press.

Sampson, R. J. (2006a) How does community context matter? Social mechanisms and the explanation of crime. Pp. 60 in *The Explanation of Crime: Context, Mechanisms and Development.* P.-O. H. Wikströms and R. J. Sampson (eds). Cambridge: Cambridge University Press.

Sampson, R. J. (2006b) Collective efficacy theory: Lessons learned and directions for future inquiry. Pp. 149–167 in *Taking Stock: The Status of Criminological Theory.* F. T. Cullen, J. P. Wright and K. R. Blevins (eds). New Brunswick, NJ: Transaction.

Sampson, R. J. and Byron Groves, W. (1989) Community structure and crime: Testing social-disorganization theory. *American Journal of Sociology* 94: 774–802.

Sampson, R. J. and Laub, J. H. (1993) *Crime in the Making: Pathways and Turning Points Through Life.* Cambridge, MA: Harvard University Press.

Sampson, R. J. and Laub, J. H. (1995) Understanding variability in lives through time: Contributions of life-course criminology. *Studies on Crime and Crime Prevention* 4: 143–158.

Sampson, R. J. and Laub, J. H. (2003) Life-course desisters? Trajectories of crime among delinquent boys followed to age 70. *Criminology* 41: 301–339.

Sampson, R. J. and Laub, J. H. (2005a) A general age-graded theory of crime: Lessons learned and the future of life-course criminology. Pp. 165–181 in D. P. Farrington (ed.), *Integrated Developmental and Life Course Theories of Offending.* New Brunswick, NJ: Transaction.

Sampson, R. J. and Laub, J. H. (2005b) A life-course view of the development of crime. *The Annals* 602: 12–45.

Sampson, R. J. and Laub, J. H. (2005c) When prediction fails: From crime-prone boys to heterogeneity in adulthood. *The Annals* 602: 73–79.

Sampson, R. J., Laub, J. H. and Sweeten, G. A. (2006a) Assessing Sampson and Laub's life-course theory of crime. Pp. 313–333, in F. T. Cullen, J. P. Wright and K. R. Blevins (eds), *Taking Stock: The Status of Criminological Theory.* New Brunswick, NJ: Transaction.

Sampson, R. J., Laub, J. H. and Wimer, C. (2006b) Does marriage reduce crime? A counter-factual approach to within-individual causal effects. *Criminology* 44: 465–508.

Sampson, R. J., Morenoff, J. D. and Earls, F. (1999) Beyond social capital: Spatial dynamics of collective efficacy for children. *American Sociological Review* 64: 633–660.

Sampson, R. J., Morenoff, J. D. and Gannon-Rowley, T. (2002) Assessing neighborhood effects: Social processes and new directions in research. *Annual Review of Sociology* 28: 443–478.

Sampson, R. J., Morenoff, J. D. and Raudenbush, S. W. (2005) Social anatomy of racial and ethnic disparities in violence. *American Journal of Public Health* 95: 224–232.

Sampson, R. J., Raudenbush, S. W. and Earls, F. (1997) Neighborhoods and violent crime: A multi-level study of collective efficacy. *Science* 277: 918–924.

Shaw, C. R. with Zorbaugh, F. M., McKay, H. D. and Cottrell, L. S. (1929) *Delinquency Areas.* Chicago: University of Chicago Press.

Silver, E. and Miller, L. (2004) Sournces of informal social control in Chicago neighborhoods. *Criminology* 42: 551–583.

Taylor, C. (2001) The relationship between social and self-control: tracing Hirschi's Criminological career. *Theoretical Criminology* 5: 369–388.

Taylor, I., Walton, P. and Young, J. (1974) *The New Criminology*. New York: Harper and Row.

Thomas, W. I. (1928) *The Unadjusted Girl*. Boston: Little Brown and Company.

Thomas, W. I. and Znaniecki, F. (1920) *The Polish Peasant in Europe and America*. Volume V, Organization and Disorganization in America. Boston: Badger Publishing.

Thrasher, F. M. (1927) *The Gang*. (Abridged Edition, 1963) Chicago: University of Chicago Press.

Toby, J. (1957) Social disorganization and stake in conformity: Complementary factors in the predatory behavior of hoodlums. *Journal of Criminology, Criminal Law and Police Science*. 48: 12–17.

Wikström, P.-O. and Sampson, R. J. (2003) Social mechanisms of community influences on crime and pathways in criminality. Pp. 118–148 in B. Lahey, T. Moffitt and A. Caspi (eds), *Causes of Conduct Disorder and Serious Juvenile Delinquency*. New York: Guilford Press.

7

Labelling, Social Reaction and Social Constructionism

John Muncie

Deviance is not a property *inherent in* certain forms of behaviour; it is a property *conferred upon* these forms by the audiences which directly or indirectly witness them. Sociologically, then, the critical variable in the study of deviance is the social *audience*, rather than the individual *person* ....

Kai T. Erikson (1962, p. 308) *Notes on the Sociology of Deviance*

Deviance may be conceived as a process by which the members of a group, community, or society (1) interpret behavior as deviant, (2) define persons who so behave as a certain kind of deviant, and (3) accord them the treatment considered appropriate to such deviants.

John Kitsuse (1962, p. 248) *Societal Reaction to Deviant Behavior*

Deviance is *not* a quality of the act the person commits, but rather a consequence of the application by others of rules and sanctions to an 'offender'. The deviant is one to whom that label has successfully been applied; deviant behaviour is behaviour that people so label.

Howard Becker (1963, p. 9) *Outsiders: Studies in the Sociology of Deviance*

This is a large turn away from older sociology which tended to rest heavily upon the idea that deviance leads to social control. I have come to believe that the reverse idea, i.e., social control leads to deviance, is equally tenable and the potentially richer premise for studying deviance in modern society.

Edwin Lemert (1967, p. v) *Human Deviance, Social Problems and Social Control*

Today these classic statements are widely recognised as forming the central tenets of what has variously been described as labelling theory, the labelling perspective, neo-Chicagoan theory, the West Coast school of sociology, social reaction theory and new deviancy theory. The presence of labelling in most undergraduate socio-logical criminology courses is now almost taken for granted. Yet 40 years ago it marked a radical departure in criminological (or rather more typically 'sociology of deviance') studies. As a young undergraduate in 1970 when I first had the opportu-nity to study these texts it was as if 'common sense' was being turned on its head. Surely deviance was a self evident behavioural problem? How could deviance be created by those very forces that were designed for its control? Reversing these conventional logics was crucial in radicalising a discipline that for so long simply appeared to be an adjunct of, and in collusion with, state agencies. For myself, and I suspect many others, the discovery of labelling was a crucial first step in under-standing why and how it is that only certain troubling behaviours and acts are subject to criminalisation and why a host of other more serious social harms appear to be routinely practised with impunity. For many, labelling effectively began the process of politicising the study of deviance, crime and social control.

THEORETICAL TRACES

Unlike traditional approaches which assume that the causes of crime and deviance lie either within the biological or psychological characteristics of individual offenders or within their socio-economic circumstances, labelling argues that criminological analysis should begin with how people come to be defined as deviant and then examine the implications that such definitions hold for future offending behaviour. Such argument is now widely associated with the work of Howard Becker (1963) who famously claimed that behaviour only becomes deviant when it is labelled and treated as such and that labelling creates and perpetuates 'deviant careers'. Traces of such an approach, however, can be found throughout the nineteenth century. The penal reformer and utilitarian philosopher, Jeremy Bentham, for example, argued that certain social reactions to crime – the unreformed prison, for example – were more likely to promote offending than curtail it. Henry Mayhew, the social commentator, considered that over-zealous policing was a significant factor in the creation of juvenile delinquency in the mid nineteenth century. Such themes are now widely repeated in the perennial and popular claims that prisons are 'colleges of crime' and that when people are treated as criminal they are more likely to act in that fashion in the future.

   The formative *theoretical* traces of labelling, however, are to be found in the inter-actionist school of sociology of the 1930s. Labelling is not just concerned with the stigmatising 'power of the label', but also with how definitions of deviance are constructed through micro level interactions between rule violator and rule enforcer. In contrast to the then prevailing paradigm of positivism, interactionism presented a worldview which emphasised the flexibility of individual responses to social situations. Rather than viewing behaviour as determined by 'external' forces, inter-actionism centred questions about human choice, voluntarism and the variability of meaning in everyday life. Most famously, George Herbert Mead (1934) argued that 'the self' is a social construct and that the way in which individuals act and regard themselves is in part a consequence of the way others see and react to them. In this conception of human action it made no sense to depict the social order as held together though an uncontested moral consensus (as many a positivist would have it). Rather, that order was viewed as comprising a set of fluid pluralistic relationships embracing conflict, domination, exploitation and disagreement, as well as co-operation. Labelling took this approach to underline the importance of how rules and regulations cannot be accepted as 'givens' but as sites of negotiation and dispute. In one of the earliest formulations Frank Tannenbaum (1938) argued that deviance was created through a process of social interaction. Whilst a majority commit deviant acts only a minority come to be known as deviant. The known deviant is then targeted, identified, defined and treated as such even though their behaviour may be no different to those who have not been so identified. As a result certain people 'become deviant' through the imposition of social judgements on their behaviour: they *become* the essence of what is being complained of.

In the 1950s Edwin Lemert (1951) further developed this approach by distinguishing between primary and secondary deviation. He argued that primary deviance is often a temporary transgression in which perpetrators have no conception of themselves as deviant. Secondary deviance is created through the reaction of others to the initial deviance. Through name-calling, stereotyping and labelling, a deviant identity is established and confirmed. Often deviants resolve this personal crisis by accepting their deviant status and by reorganising their lives accordingly. They become more, rather than less, deviant. In a similar vein David Matza (1964) argued that delinquency is transient and intermittent. Juvenile delinquents are not that different from other juveniles. This is because, rather than being at polar extremes, conformist values and non-conformist values often intersect and propagate similar desires, such as for hedonism, fun and excitement. The delinquent is committed neither to the mainstream nor to a delinquent culture, but *chooses to drift* between one or the other. This granting of authenticity to deviants' own accounts of their activities and the concentration on processes of social interaction and social reaction led Muncie and Fitzgerald (1981) to argue that the major achievement of labelling was to have 'effectively humanised deviance'.

In these ways interactionism and labelling called into question positivism's rigid separation of what constituted the deviant and the conformist; the criminal and non-criminal. Notions of negotiated interaction, voluntarism, and pluralism became crucial reference points for labelling. Deviance could no longer be viewed simply as a pathological act that violated consensual norms, but as something created in a *process* of social interaction, in which some people who commit deviant acts come to be known as deviants whereas others do not. In particular Lemert's (1967) conclusion that *social control causes deviancy* was a crucial turning point in the politicisation of the sociology of deviance and the development of a radical criminological imagination.

The clearest formulation of labelling eventually emerged in the 1960s not only through the work of Howard Becker, but also through numerous studies designed to reveal the role of moral entrepreneurs in constructing social problems (for example Erikson (1966) on witchcraft; and Platt (1969) on delinquency). For each, the key to understanding the origins of deviance lay in the reactions of a social audience, rather than in the behaviour of individual actors. A number of ethnographic studies were also published in the 1960s and 1970s which revealed the processes of *becoming* a marijuana smoker, a prostitute, a homosexual, a prisoner and so on. In each it was the stigma attached to the label that was considered pivotal in informing future behaviour patterns. Defined as 'outsiders', it is such groups that came to epitomise what was considered to be criminal. A self-fulfilling prophesy ensues. Criminality is continually sought only in those identified as criminal. And the power of the label of 'criminal' ensures that 'criminal careers' are exacerbated.

In these ways labelling was concerned both with processes of social interaction and social reaction. It would be misleading though to describe this work as belonging to any one tightly defined 'school' or 'tradition of thought'. Lemert, for example, recalled that there was very little correspondence between himself and Becker and that labelling and social reaction theory were developed quite independently of each other (interview by John Laub in March 1979 accessible on http://www.sonoma.edu/cja/info/emljl.html). Nevertheless this refocusing of criminology dramatically shifted attention from the behaviours of those commonly thought to constitute a problem for society to those who conceive those behaviours as problems.

THE DEFINING CONCEPTS

A number of key concepts in contemporary criminology are traceable to labelling and interactionism. These include 'primary and secondary deviation', 'stigma', 'social reaction', 'deviation amplification', 'stereotyping', 'scapegoating', 'deviant career' and 'deviant identity'. Labelling also left its mark on criminal justice policy and practice within the movements for diversion, deinstitutionalisation and radical non-intervention in the 1970s.

Lemert (1967) distinguished between *primary deviance* – isolated, relatively insignificant rule-breaking (e.g., petty theft, classroom misbehaviour) – and *secondary deviance* – the construction of a deviant identity as a result of social reaction to the initial act. In making this distinction he emphasised first that deviance is a process, and second that social control is not simply a response to deviant activity, but plays an active and propelling role in the creation and promotion of deviance. Lemert (1951), for example, argued that whilst most youths commit some delinquent acts, it is only a few that are eventually labelled as delinquent. Official reactions (condemnation, treatment, punishment) to this few do not deter or reform but initiate processes that push the labelled delinquent towards further delinquent conduct. If there is no official reaction, delinquent behaviour may dissipate or at least will not accelerate, because the notion of a delinquent 'career' will not be established. Otherwise, difference is translated into undesirability or inferiority. The stigmatised are cast as not quite human. Reactions against the *stigma* of such castings are likely to be viewed as confirming the original defect. The stigmatised individual may attempt to correct the condition, but it can also affect self-esteem, self-concept and future behaviour. The stigmatised may come to resist their classifiers as unjustly exercising their power to deny them their full humanity. The stigma process cements rather than prevents the onset of *deviant careers*. Applied to prisoners and inmates of mental hospitals, for example, the stereotyping of them as 'spoiled' precludes their ability to return to the mainstream. Further deviance is entertained when opportunities are foreclosed by persistent readings of character as negative and by related feelings of estrangement, self-doubt or resistance. Schwartz and Skolnick's (1964) study of legal stigma, for example, found consistent discrimination by employers when considering job applications from unskilled workers with a criminal record. However stigma also varies according to social status. Examining the subsequent careers of doctors who had been accused of malpractice this research found almost no long term negative effect. As a result only a partial and distinct population of deviants emerges: a direct result not only of the stigma of imprisonment *but also* of a collective intolerance towards the relatively powerless. Stigma, too, can also be used for wider political purposes through which moral entrepreneurs engage in moral crusades (or 'stigma contests') to manipulate public opinion against specific groups, such as youth subcultures, asylum seekers, working mothers, teenage mothers, drug users and so on (Schur, 1980).

Leslie Wilkins (1964) first used the term *deviation amplification* to explore the relationship between levels of tolerance/intolerance and the reinforcement of *deviant identities*. He noted how societies which had developed an intolerant response to deviancy tended to define more acts as criminal and took more formal action against criminals. This in turn led to the increased alienation of deviants, more crime by deviant groups and a corresponding affirmation of intolerance of deviants by conforming groups. The production of intolerance is subject to a 'positive feedback loop' in which the identification of and reaction to deviancy becomes self perpetuating. The further an individual is defined as having moved away from the cultural norm the more they are likely to actually behave in a non-conformist fashion. As a result Wilkins argued that deviancy control is best achieved by building social systems which can tolerate difference and minimise the number of persons who are subject to formal criminal justice intervention. In the UK Jock Young (1971) applied the concept in his participant observation study of marijuana users in Notting Hill, London in the late 1960s. He showed how the relatively harmless social activity of marijuana smoking was transformed into a serious social problem through the combined reaction of the mass media, the police and the public. Through sensational reporting, users were portrayed by the media as sick, promiscuous and dangerous outsiders. Media and public pressure forced the police to take more direct action by increasing surveillance and rates of arrest. For the drug users what was once a peripheral activity became a symbol of their difference and a key part of their defiance of perceived social injustices. Police activity acted to amplify both the extent and the symbolic importance of drug usage for the users themselves. Moreover as drug taking was driven underground it moved from being a low key, low profit activity to one organised by a 'criminal underworld'. *Social reaction* amplified deviance in both mythical and actual terms. A vicious spiral of escalation ensued. Gary Marx (1981) reiterated many of these concerns by noting numerous ways – through escalation, non-enforcement and covert facilitation – in which the agencies of social control can in specific situations amplify or even generate the activities they are meant to control. Identifying those considered 'at risk' can create new categories of offenders and victims. The intervening presence of the police in some situations can lead to an increase in their seriousness, whilst a 'blind eye' may be turned to other similarly 'volatile' situations. The role of undercover police, say in participating in drug trafficking, may encourage such deviant activity to be initiated. In a wide variety of situations social control can ironically be a cause of primary as well as secondary deviance.

Armed with these novel concepts, labelling drew attention to some of the negative consequences of public perceptions, police actions and social reaction in general. It revealed how processes of reaction are also processes of invention and creation. It continues to force us to consider the possibility that criminality is not driven by any peculiar motivation or that criminals are always a species apart. Rather crime is often ordinary, natural and widespread and requires no more special an explanation than that which might be attached to any everyday activity. What remains in need of explanation is the complex process by which moral entrepreneurs and agencies of social control are able to realise the public identification of certain people as criminal; how social reaction and labelling can produce and reproduce a recognisable criminal population.

POLICY IMPLICATIONS

In contrast to reactive 'get tough' approaches, decriminalisation, diversion, deinstitutionalisation and radical non-intervention are the hallmarks of labelling. The phrase 'radical non-intervention' is widely attributed to Edwin Schur (1974). It is the logical policy implication of a labelling approach to understanding crime and deviance. If, as labelling theorists suggested, social reaction does not prevent offending but establishes deviant identities and careers then the reach of reaction should be reduced. If state intervention causes crime and is a significant agency in the creation of the crime problem, then steps must be taken to limit its powers. In particular Schur (1965) argued that a range of 'victimless crimes' should be removed from the remit of criminal law. Drug use, gambling, juvenile status offences (truancy, promiscuity), pornography and so on, he argued, may be undesirable, but tackling them with the full weight of the law is not only expensive, but also generally counter-productive. Criminalizing drug users, for instance, not only creates new classes of criminals, but may also encourage the development of organised crime and law enforcement corruption and redirect resources away from health and treatment programmes. In short, the removal of many troubling behaviours from criminal law sanction has the potential to be a highly effective measure of crime reduction.

Forms of radical non-intervention (and the labelling approach in general) grew in popularity during the 1960s and were in part a reflection of an emergent distrust of institutional intervention – particularly indeterminate sentencing in the name of 'treatment' – that developed throughout that decade. It had a profound impact on social policy (Empey, 1982). A series of measures – decriminalisation, diversion and deinstitutionalisation – designed to limit the extent of the state's intrusion into offenders lives have subsequently been implemented to varying degrees and with varying success in most western criminal justice systems. For example, in the UK the Labour Party's (1964) report *Crime: A Challenge to Us All*, argued that although all children misbehave, it is only working-class children that are likely to come to the attention of the authorities. It went on to argue that no child in early adolescence should face criminal proceedings, that criminal proceedings were unnecessary where the offence was trivial, and that serious offences indicated the child's need for skilled help and guidance. Hence the report proposed: *decriminalisation* by redefining the legitimate jurisdiction of the criminal court; *de-institutionalisation* by diversion away from the formal criminal justice system; *informality* in dealing with the problem overall; and the *de-stigmatisation* of working-class children. Indeed such strategies were employed to a remarkable effect particularly in the youth justice system of England and Wales during the 1980s which witnessed dramatic falls in the numbers being sent to court and to custody. They also continue to have a presence in some restorative justice initiatives, such as the more constructive forms of 're-integrative shaming' involved in various forms of family group conferencing, healing and sentencing circles that have emerged since the 1980s as alternatives to impersonal, stigmatising, formal court processes (Braithwaite, 1989).

MISGIVINGS

Because labelling constituted a radical critique of prevailing notions of moral consensus and presented an argument that official reaction to deviance probably did more harm than good, it was unsurprising to find it soon immersed in a wide range of controversies:

- Advocates of positivist criminology pointed out that motivations for primary deviance were either ignored or poorly explained. Labelling moved us little further forward in understanding why people commit criminal acts in the first place. For positivists its premises lacked empirical evidence and were un-testable. The usual riposte to this was that positivist criminology, whether individual or sociological, had also abjectly failed to discover a primary causative factor in over 100 years of its endeavour (Goode, 1975). Nevertheless attempts continue to be made to quantitatively measure how far criminal intervention curtails or accelerates future deviant careers (Bernburg *et al.*, 2006).
- By concentrating on 'victimless' crimes such as drug taking, homosexuality and so on, labelling appeared to insufficiently recognise the fundamental deviance attached to other 'serious crimes' such as murder, rape and institutional violence. For some it was simply indefensible to claim that 'no act is intrinsically criminal' (Wellford, 1975).
- It has been suggested that the origins of a 'deviant identity' do not primarily lie in processes of social reaction, but in local community and neighbourhood settings. The extent to which a real amplification of deviance is driven by its public identification also remains questionable (and probably unknowable). A complex of motivations may underlie the development of deviant careers, of which social reaction might play a relatively small part.
- From those who were also committed anti-positivists emerged a critique directed at the deterministic basis of the theory. Labelling may have rejected the determinism of psychological, biological and social factors as causes of crime, but seemed to have had simply replaced them with the determinism of social reaction. In both cases the deviant was depicted as 'driven' rather than acting voluntarily.
- Other radical authors have subsequently argued that the logic of labelling is limited when employed without any analysis of the social and political structures and inequalities in which such labels are constructed and upheld. Labelling fails to explain *why* it is only *some* behaviours that come to be defined in a historical and political context as deviant, whilst others have not. The key question – whose law and whose order is being protected? – was notably overlooked. As a result some critical criminologists in the 1970s argued that the insights of labelling needed to be wedded to a Marxist or conflict model of society and the state (Taylor *et al.*, 1973).

- The concept has been most commonly applied to explain escalations in expressive forms of deviancy. In 'humanising deviance', it has been accused of patronising, 'zoo keeping' and over-romanticising deviant behaviour (Gouldner, 1973; Lea and Young, 1984). Its wider applicability to other less publicised forms of rule-breaking is also less clear. It may remain the case that in other instances (for example domestic violence, denial of human rights) it is a *lack* of negative social reaction (intolerance) which provides a climate for its continuation.
- As a result of the above labelling has been critiqued as merely offering an *approach* and not meeting the requirements for a fully worked up criminological theory (Beirne and Messerschmidt, 1991).

The bulk of these criticisms appeared in the 1970s. Since then labelling has been incorporated by some as a primary tool in encouraging critical analysis whilst simply ignored by others. It has though remained influential in further theoretical renewal: first the development of conflict theory at the end of the 1960s, second moral panic and social control theory of the early 1970s, and third a reworking of many of its themes within broader social and ideological constructionist frameworks from the 1970s onwards.

LABELLING APPLIED: CONFLICT THEORY AND CRITICAL CRIMINOLOGY

Labelling clearly opened up new lines of critical enquiry by posing definitional rather than behavioural questions – 'who defines another as deviant?'; 'how does that person react to such designation?' 'why are some behaviours and not others defined as deviant? 'who has the power to define another as deviant?', and 'how are deviant roles subsequently adopted and played out?' (Cohen, 1973b). In addressing such questions it was necessary not only to begin to study how rules/laws were created, but to ask in whose interests they were enforced. In addition, labelling encouraged the development of an explicitly political position in the demand that mainstream social scientists acknowledge and address the issue of the correctionalist bias in their research. This 'politicisation of criminology' was indeed a logical extension of the critical questioning of social science and its role in research, teaching and policy-making that had emerged in the 1960s. Political developments growing out of the American civil rights campaigns, anti-Vietnam war movements and the radicalisation of student and countercultures had a direct impact on many academic disciplines and their role in either defending or critiquing the *status quo*. C. Wright Mills challenged the whole notion of scientific neutrality in academic research and Becker (1966) himself brought such questioning directly into criminology and the sociology of deviance by asking social scientists: 'Whose side are you on?'. Positivist criminology was charged with lending the state a spurious legitimacy and functioning as little more than a justification for oppressive power. This was the beginning of a radical reconstitution of criminology as part of a more comprehensive sociology of the state and political economy, in which questions of political and social control took precedence over behavioural and correctional issues. The key subject matter could no longer simply be crime and deviance and their control, but a critical understanding of the social order and the power to criminalise.

   Thus the subject matter of criminology was eventually to be considerably expanded to incorporate theories of power, social order and the state as well as processes of criminalisation, social control and resistance. Of note, both conflict theory in the USA (Quinney, 1970) and a 'new' or critical criminology in the UK (Taylor *et al.*, 1973) both utilised labelling as a core component of their more general theories about the 'power to criminalise'. In these ways labelling was pivotal in politicising the 'meaning of crime'.

LABELLING APPLIED: MORAL PANICS
AND SOCIAL CONTROL

The term 'moral panic' was first used by Jock Young in his study of 'drug-takers' published in 1971. But it was only from the following year when it appeared in the title of Stanley Cohen's (1973a) book *Folk Devils and Moral Panics: The Creation of the Mods and Rockers* that it became ubiquitous in criminology and the sociology of deviance. A third edition containing the original text with a new introduction was published exactly 30 years later. Cohen (1967; 1973a) had argued that relatively minor incidents between groups of youth over a bank holiday weekend were exaggerated by media reportage and magnified by subsequent police and judicial targeting. Their deviance was amplified through social reaction which in turn produced an actual amplification in real levels of deviancy as the mods and rockers took on aspects of their new publicly defined personas. Such youthful 'rowdyism' was of course by no means new (Pearson, 1983) but it was to receive front page outrage in the national press. The media spoke of a 'day of terror'; of youngsters who 'beat up an entire town'; of a town being invaded by a mob 'hell-bent on destruction'. Youths were presented as being engaged in a confrontation between easily recognisable rival gangs – 'mods' or 'rockers'. Cohen's research, on the other hand, found no evidence of any structured gangs. The typical offence throughout was not assault or malicious damage, but threatening behaviour. A few days after the event a journalist was forced to admit that the affair had been 'a little over-reported'.
   Cohen argued that this over-reporting set in train a series of interrelated responses. First, it initiated a wider public concern which obliged the police to step up their surveillance of the two groups. Second, an emphasis on the antagonism between the groups, and their stylistic differences, encouraged the youths to place themselves in one of the opposing camps. Third, continuing disturbances attracted more news coverage, increased police activity and further public concern. Exploring the socioeconomic background to these events Cohen argued that the mid-1960s was the time of a supposedly new permissiveness, a rise in working-class youth spending power, the onslaught of a new consumerism, and the decline of traditional working-class communities. Public anxiety, uncertainty and anomie circulating around these social changes were 'resolved' by identifying certain social groups as scapegoats or folk devils. They became the visual symbols of what was wrong with society. The more intractable and structural problems to do with relative deprivation and restricted opportunities were overlooked and passed by in a developing climate of pervasive social control.

Subsequently, as Cohen (2002) records, the concept has been used in a wide variety of forms to explore reactions not only to unruly working class youth but also school violence, drugs, single parenting, permissiveness, paedophilia, satanic abuse, asylum seekers and so on. Its use now appears ubiquitous, often ungrounded and employed as much by the media themselves as well as by radical scholars. Goode and Ben-Yehuda (1994) attempted a more precise definition by noting the five key characteristics of: concern, hostility, consensus, disproportionality and volatility. They concluded that moral panics serve as a mechanism for simultaneously strengthening and redrawing society's moral boundaries – the line between morality and immorality. When a society's moral boundaries are sharp, clear and secure and the central norms and values are strongly held by nearly everyone, moral panics rarely grip its members. However, when the moral boundaries are fuzzy and shifting and often seem to be contested, moral panics are far more likely to take hold.

Nevertheless the concept has been critiqued for a lack of any precise theoretical grounding (Plummer, 1979); for being a polemical rather than an analytical concept (Waddington, 1986); for ignoring the reality of crime (Lea and Young, 1984); and for simplifying complex processes of media representation, public perception and pressure group contestation (McRobbie and Thornton, 1995). Left realism maintained that crime and the fear of crime should be taken seriously and not dismissed as 'just' an expression of media over-reaction or panic. By the mid-1980s the theoretical integrity of 'moral panic' was to be seriously questioned. By then the term had become part of a normalised rhetoric rather than an exceptional intervention. McRobbie and Thornton (1995) were persuasive in their argument that moral panic, rather than necessarily being an unwanted label designed to denigrate youth cultural pursuits, had become something to be actively pursued by youth themselves. Indeed the growing prevalence of niche media, lobbies, pressure groups and commercial interests has made it virtually impossible to talk of discrete moral panics (or discrete youth cultures) as in Cohen's original use of the term. Rather we appear enmeshed in an endless debate about deviance, difference, and diversity in a climate of permanent public unease and fear (Feeley and Simon, 2007).

LABELLING APPLIED: SOCIAL AND IDEOLOGICAL CONSTRUCTIONISM

Realist perspectives in criminology tend to treat social problems as phenomena about whose existence we can all agree. The basis of social constructionism is rather that we should ask instead, who says this is a social problem? – and why do they say so? This approach affords a central role to the processes through which the meaning of social phenomena is constructed, produced and reproduced (Burr, 1996). All reality is mediated by meaning: what we experience is 'the social construction of reality' (Berger and Luckman, 1996). Social issues are not self evident, emerging from objective conditions: rather their identification as 'problematic' depends on individuals and/or organisations making 'certain truth claims' about the phenomena and being in a position to bring them to public awareness. How any social problem is named, defined and mapped is crucial in how it can subsequently be 'made sense' of.

Clearly the tools of social constructionism can be employed in a wide range of theoretical positions, typically ethnomethodology, and phenomenological sociology as well as labelling and moral panic, but their ability to reveal how processes of 'knowledge construction' inform relations of power has formed a key element of various forms of critical criminological analysis.

During the 1970s critical criminology developed the basic premise of interactionism and labelling (that crime only exists through the labelling of certain behaviours as such) by arguing that it is essential to ground such generalities in specific relations of power and domination. It is not simply a question of any number of interest groups acting in competition with each other (as in the interactionist and some constructionist versions), but of the systematic and consistent empowerment of some groups to the detriment of others. Some Marxist conceptions would, for example, emphasise class divisions in which those who own and control the means of production are in a position to assert their economic and political power by using the law to protect their own interests. Some feminist conceptions would, in contrast, emphasise gender divisions and the discriminatory implications of a patriarchal monopoly of political, economic and legal power. Each stresses the political nature of crime. Law supplies to some people both *the authority* and the means to criminalise the behaviour of others. Hall *et al.* (1978) in the classic critical criminological text *Policing the Crisis*, for example, trace the way in which definitions of 'mugging' in the UK in the 1970s were employed to justify not only a new category of crime, but also punitive sentencing and an image of a generalised breakdown of law and order in society. Working within a Gramscian framework they argued that the social construction of mugging achieved the prominence it did because its themes of 'race', crime and youth crystallised some of the broader political and economic shifts of the 1970s. New racial discourses emerged that identified young black males in particular as central to the problem of British society. Hall *et al.* argued that moral panic, now generalised, rather than discrete, underscored the onslaught of authoritarian populism in Britain. As was evident by the early 1980s, the enunciation of authoritarian policies, if repeated often enough, can come to form the terrain of any debate concerned with issues of law and order.

Crime is also a political and ideological construction in the sense that it involves and requires the deployment of the *power* to translate legal rules into action, to impose one's will on others and to enforce one's definition of another's behaviour as illegal. The Schwendingers' (1970) argument, that practices of law creation and enforcement are selective and partial, is underlined by Cohen's insistence that: 'damage, victimisation, exploitation, theft and destruction when carried out by the powerful are not only not punished, but are not called "crime"' (Cohen, 1973a: 624). The concept of 'crime' far from being value free, is a highly politicised ideological construction (Box, 1983). It has no 'objective' reality other than in the ways in which the powerful, including the state, construe 'criminality' for their own ends. Rather, it is argued, if the signifier of 'crime' is to be retained, it should be equally applied not only to 'ordinary crime' or behaviours that are not typically prosecuted (such as tax avoidance, environmental pollution and government corruption), but also to crimes of the state and mass political killings (such as the Holocaust, the genocide of the East Timorese and the 'ethnic cleansing' in Bosnia and Kosovo).

Sumner (1990) developed this line of argument by treating crime and deviance as matters of moral and political judgement – as social censures rooted in particular ideologies. The concept of crime, then, is neither a behavioural nor a legal category, but an expression of particular cultural and political conditions. Neither is 'crime' simply a label, but a generic term to describe a series of 'negative ideological categories with specific historical applications … categories of denunciation or abuse lodged within very complex, historically loaded practical conflicts and moral debates … these negative categories of moral ideology are social censures' (Sumner, 1990: 26, 28).

The most common critique of these constructionist and critical perspectives is that they trivialise the reality of crime and other social problems – implying that such issues are *merely* social or ideological constructions. But it is only through language, meaning, imagery and so on that we can apprehend and act on 'real life'. They reveal how constructions, ideologies and discourses become institutionalised; how constructions come to define the thinkable; and how alternatives can be dismissed as unthinkable, utopian, or politically motivated (Clarke, 2003). Constructionist and critical perspectives not only reveal how layers of 'commonsense', everyday wisdom, institutionalised norms, and forms of social power become institutionalised but also provide the means to begin their 'deconstruction' and challenge by 'replacement discourses'. By the 1990s such an approach had indeed significantly opened up what had been long-neglected topics for criminological investigation (Cohen, 2001) and had facilitated levels of analysis of social harms which encouraged us to go 'beyond criminology' itself (Hillyard *et al.*, 2004).

FUTURE PROSPECTS

Labelling remains distinctive because it begins from the assumption that no act is intrinsically criminal. What counts as crime and deviance is forever problematic because deviance only arises from the imposition of specific social judgements on others' behaviour. Such judgements are typically established by the powerful through the formulation of laws and their interpretation and enforcement by police, courts and other controlling institutions. But these formulations and interpretations are by no means constant: they change according to historical contingencies and individual discretion. Thus exactly what constitutes 'crime' and 'deviance' is subject to historical and social variability. Neither can be 'objectively' defined because their existence always depends on relations of power between rule-makers/enforcers and rule violators. Labelling continues to offer an important challenge to traditional criminological approaches even if we accept that it operates more at a level of offering sensitising concepts rather than a fully coherent theory. By focussing on definitional issues it is able to reveal how the concepts of 'crime' and 'deviance' are not universally agreed upon, but are always contingent and contestable. By drawing attention to the role of social reaction (and law enforcement in particular) it warns of the ways in which criminal justice may cause that which it is designed to curtail. These insights marked a dramatic radicalisation of criminology, particularly sociologically informed criminology, in the 1960s and despite the critiques of the 1970s and 1980s it still retains its original power to help students to begin thinking critically about their subject matter. Perhaps for this reason it also remains largely ignored or dismissed by those criminologies with a more conservative, technocratic and administrative focus.

As De Haan (1991: 208) put it 'what we need is not a better theory of crime, but a more powerful critique of crime'. This is an essential agenda for criminology that was first opened up by labelling and which a combination of social constructionism and critical criminology continues to make available to us.

REFERENCES

Becker, H. (1963) *Outsiders: Studies in the Sociology of Deviance.* New York: Free Press.

Becker, H. (1966) Whose side are you on? *Social Problems*, 14(3): 239–247.

Beirne, P. and Messerschmidt, J. (1991) *Criminology.* Fort Worth, TX: Harcourt Brace Jovanovich.

Berger, P. and Luckmann, T. (1966) *The Social Construction of Reality.* New York: Doubleday.

Bernburg, J. G., Krohn, M. and Rivera, C. (2006) Official labeling, criminal embeddedness and subsequent delinquency, *Journal of Research in Crime and Delinquency*, 43(1): 67–88.

Box, S. (1983) *Power, Crime and Mystification.* London: Tavistock.

Braithwaite, J. (1989) *Crime, Shame and Reintegration.* Cambridge: Cambridge University Press.

Burr, V. (1996) *An Introduction to Social Constructionism.* London: Routledge.

Clarke, J. (2003) Social constructionism, in McLaughlin, E. and Muncie, J. (eds), *The Sage Dictionary of Criminology*, second edition. London: Sage.

Cohen. S. (1967) Mods, rockers and the rest: Community reactions to juvenile delinquency, *The Howard Journal*, 12: 121–130.

Cohen, S. (1973a) *Folk Devils and Moral Panics.* London: MacGibbon and Kee.

Cohen, S. (1973b) The failures of criminology, *The Listener*, 8 November, pp. 622–625.

Cohen, S. (2001) *States of Denial.* Cambridge: Polity.

Cohen, S. (2002) *Folk Devils and Moral Panics*, third edition. London: Routledge.

De Haan, W. (1991) Abolitionism and crime control: a contradiction in terms, in Stenson, K. and Cowell, D. (eds), *The Politics of Crime Control.* London: Sage.

Empey, La Mar T. (1982) *American Delinquency: Its Meaning and Construction*, second edition. Chicago, Dorsey Press.

Erikson, K. T. (1962) Notes on the sociology of deviance, *Social Problems*, 9: 307–314.

Erikson, K. T. (1966) *Wayward Puritans: A Study in the Sociology of Deviance.* New York: Wiley.

Feeley, M. and Simon, J. (2007) Folk devils and moral panics: an appreciation from North America, in Downes, D. *et al.* (eds), *Crime, Social Control and Human Rights: Essays in Honour of Stanley Cohen.* Cullompton: Willan.

Goffman, E. (1963) *Stigma.* Englewood Cliffs, NJ: Prentice Hall.

Goode, E. (1975) On behalf of labeling theory, *Social Problems*, 22(5): 570–583.

Goode, E. and Ben-Yehuda, N. (1994) Moral Panics: The Social Construction of Deviance, Oxford: Blackwell.

Gouldner, A. W. (1973) *For Sociology: Renewal and Critique in Sociology Today.* New York: Basic Books.

Hall, S., Critcher, C., Jefferson, T., Clarke, J. and Roberts, B. (1978) *Policing the Crisis: Mugging, the State and Law and Order.* London: Macmillan.

Hillyard, P., Pantazis, C., Tombs, S. and Gordon, D. (eds) (2004) *Beyond Criminology: Taking Harm Seriously.* London: Pluto.

Kitsuse, J. (1962) Societal reaction to deviant behaviour, *Social Problems*, 9: 247–256.

Lea, J. and Young, J. (1984) *What Is To Be Done about Law and Order?* Harmondsworth: Penguin.

Lemert, E. (1951) *Social Pathology.* New York: McGraw-Hill.

Lemert, E. (1967) *Human Deviance, Social Problems and Social Control*. Englewood Cliffs, N.J.: Prentice Hall.

Lemert, E. (1974) Beyond Mead: The societal reaction to deviance, *Social Problems* 21(4): 457–468.

Marx, G. T. (1981) Ironies of social control: Authorities as contributors to deviance through escalation, nonenforcement and covert facilitation, *Social Problems*, 28(3): 221–246.

Matza, D. (1964) *Delinquency and Drift*, New York: Wiley.

McRobbie, A. and Thornton, S. (1995) Rethinking moral panic for multi-mediated social worlds, *British Journal of Sociology*, 46(4): 559–574.

Mead, G. H. (1934) *Mind, Self and Society*. Chicago: Chicago University Press.

Muncie, J. and Fitzgerald, M. (1981) Humanizing the deviant, in Fitzgerald, M., McLellan, G. and Pawson, J. (eds), *Crime and Society*. London: Routledge/Open University.

Pearson, G. (1983) *Hooligan: A History of Respectable Fears*. London: Macmillan.

Platt, A. (1969) *The Child Savers*, Chicago: Chicago University Press.

Plummer, K. (1979) Misunderstanding labelling perspectives, in Downes, D. and Rock, P. (eds), *Deviant Interpretations*. Oxford: Oxford University Press.

Quinney, R. (1970) *The Social Reality of Crime*. Boston: Little, Brown.

Schur, E. M. (1965) *Crime Without Victims*. Englewood Cliffs, N.J.: Prentice Hall.

Schur, E. M. (1971) *Labeling Deviant Behavior*. New York: Harper and Row.

Schur, E. M. (1974) *Radical Non Intervention: Rethinking the Delinquency Problem*. Englewood Cliffs, N.J.: Prentice Hall.

Schur, E. M. (1980) *The Politics of Deviance: Stigma Contests and the Uses of Power*. Englewood Cliffs, NJ: Prentice Hall.

Schwartz, R. and Skolnick, J. (1964) Two studies of legal stigma, in Becker, H. (ed.), *The Other Side*. New York: Free Press.

Schwendinger, H. and Schwendinger, J. (1970) Defenders of order or guardians of human rights?, *Issues in Criminology*, 5(2): 123–157.

Sumner, C. (ed.) (1990) *Censure, Politics and Criminal Justice*. Buckingham: Open University Press.

Sumner, C. (1994) *The Sociology of Deviance: an Obituary*. Buckingham: Open University Press.

Tannenbaum, F. (1938) *Crime and the Community*. New York: Colombia University Press.

Taylor, I., Walton, P. and Young, J. (1973) *The New Criminology*. London: Routledge.

Wellford, C. (1975) Labelling theory and criminology, *Social Problems*, 22(3): 332–345.

Waddington, P. A. J. (1986) Mugging as a moral panic: a question of proportion, *British Journal of Sociology*, 32(2): 245–259.

Wilkins, L. T. (1964) *Social Deviance*. London: Tavistock.

Young, J. (1971) The role of the police as amplifiers of deviancy, negotiators of reality and translators of fantasy, in Cohen, S. (ed.), *Images of Deviance*. Harmondsworth: Penguin.

8

Critical Criminology

Eugene McLaughlin

Stan Cohen (1971) provides a succinct outline of the reasons that led to the forma-tion of the National Deviancy Conference (NDC) in July 1968. A generation of young sociologists were radicalised through labelling theory with its questioning of how deviance is defined, processed and reproduced by control agencies and how conformity to social rules and norms is secured. In policy terms, the perennial 'criminological knowledge for what purpose?' question was, as a result of Becker (1967), re-posed as 'whose side are we on?'. This sceptical, deconstructionist, humanist approach to crime and deviance stood against 'correctional criminology' in terms of the latter's: connections with the re-socialisation' ideologies and prac-tices of penal-welfarism; conception of 'the criminal' as essentially different from 'the non criminal'; reliance on the criminal justice system for research data; desire to be an applied 'scientific' discipline closely involved in the identification and man-agement of offenders; empiricist acceptance of the dominant 'facts' of crime and deviance; and rejection of sociological perspectives. However, Cohen (1971: 15) cautioned against assuming that the re-sociologisation of criminology would provide a more intellectually supportive environment. Sociology as a discipline found 'crime' and 'deviance' to be 'too messy and devoid of significance' and in tandem with 'correctional criminology' operated with 'a depersonalized, dehumanized pic-ture of the deviant: he was simply part of the waste products of the system, the reject from the conveyor belt' (see also Rock, 1973: 11; Downes and Rock, 1982: 21).

For Cohen an additional problem was the difficulty for the NDC of constructing 'a more general position in regard to the study of deviance' because members 'are probably more agreed on what we are against than what we are for' (1971: 16). Those participating in the NDC could not agree on whether they were attempting to create an alternative criminology or an alternative to criminology in the form of a New Deviancy Theory (see also Cohen, 1974; 1988: x). This is not surprising given Young's (2002: 252) description of the NDC as 'anarchistic, set deep in the counter culture of the time ... hectic, irreverent, transgressive and, above all, fun. It took no notice of disciplinary boundaries ... it was the pluralism and social constructionism of deviancy theory that gave it such a pivotal role'. Nevertheless, Cohen does identify the common NDC themes that demonstrated 'that the accepted world did not stand for the world as it really was' (Cohen, 1988: 31), namely: revealing crime and deviance as social constructions; the complicated multi-stage process of 'becoming deviant'; the pro-active role of moral entrepreneurs in definitional processes; the crime generating functions of control agencies; the selective nature of law enforcement and criminal justice; and an 'appreciative' approach to understanding deviance that ruled out intellectual detachment:

> This involves abandoning correctionalism, and any attempts to get rid of deviant phenomenon, and instead favours attempts to empathize with and thus comprehend the subject of inquiry. This commitment to the phenomenon without violating its integrity has – as Matza is aware – dangers and absurdities. It means suspending some conventional standards of morality, but it also means avoiding romanticism … not denying or suppressing the distasteful features of the phenomenon.
>
> (Cohen and Taylor, 1976: 192)

Cohen argued that the unfolding situation called for intellectual honesty, with criminologists being explicit about their ideological values and their political aims. If criminologists 'want to be technologists to help solve the state's administrative and political problems, let them state this' (1971: 22). New Deviancy Theorists, on the other hand, needed to be honest in considering the implications of their activism re support for: decarceration, diversion, de-labelling, decriminalisation and de-professionalisation and in maintaining that deviant behaviour should be accorded political status and that the criminality of the powerful was more damaging than the criminality of the powerless. Equally important they needed to explain their affinity with radical social work and radical psychiatry.

This quick background summary provides the context for the rest of the chapter which evaluates the development and current state of what has become known as Critical Criminology. The first section details the initial radicalisation of New Deviancy Theory, then I move on to discuss the Marxisation of Critical Criminology whilst the third section discusses the theoretical co-ordinates of an orthodox Critical Criminology that took form in the course of the 1980s and 1990s. I need to acknowledge from the outset that, globally, there are of course several 'brands' and 'scattered citadel' (Cohen, 1990: xiii) of Critical Criminology. My primary geographical reference point is the UK as, for a unique set of reasons, it has generated an orthodox Critical Criminological position. Readers will also notice that I make periodic reference to the work of Nils Christie – one of the most consistent Critical Criminologists.

RADICALISATION

North American conflict criminologists, such as Chambliss, Quinney, Pepinsky, and Turk argued that the radical logic of labelling theory remained limited if employed without any analysis of the socio-economic and political structures in which such labels are constructed and upheld. Labelling failed to explain why some behaviour patterns have been defined in a historical and political context as 'deviant', and why others have not. Is deviance the result of a relatively unstructured cultural heterogeneity and diversity, or are certain classes and groups in society structurally afforded the power to be able to assert their definitions as the legally correct ones? A key question – 'whose law and what order is being protected?' was notably under-conceptualised by the labelling perspective as was the role of the state. Labelling theory was essentially 'stateless' in its analysis. To apply the insights of labelling theory to concrete situations, it was necessary to analyse how the abstract notion of 'social control' linked to the maintenance of political order. 'Crime', 'deviance', 'law and order' and 'criminal justice' need to be related to a general model of a class-based society and state. In this context, an instrumental Marxist analysis of crime and crime control took form:

- the state is organised to serve the interest of the capitalist ruling class
- criminal law is an instrument of the capitalist state and ruling class to maintain the *status quo* ('bourgeois legalism')
- capitalist crime control is accomplished through a variety of coercive and welfare institutions and agencies (the 'iron fist in the velvet glove')
- the criminal justice system concentrates on the detection and processing of minor offences committed by those at the bottom of the class system
- the capitalist economic system is criminogenic
- only with the transition to socialism will there be a solution to crime (see Quinney, 1974a; 1974b)

Schwendinger and Schwendinger (1970) proposed a 'human rights' rather than criminological perspective to define what is 'social injury' and 'public wrong'.

A pivotal moment in the growth of Critical Criminology in the UK occurred in 1973 with the publication of Cohen and Young's *Manufacture of the News*, Taylor, Walton and Young's *New Criminology* and Taylor and Taylor's *Politics and Deviance*. In addition there was the inaugural conference of the 'European Group for the Study of Deviance and Social Control'.

The *New Criminology* provided an 'immanent critique' of dominant criminological traditions and argued for a 'full social theory of deviance'. Taylor, *et al.* sought to synthesise an interactionist approach to deviancy with a structural approach grounded in political economy and class relations. Like labelling, they argued that crime and deviance should be understood as part of the processes of social control, but social control was determined by the needs of late capitalism. *The New Criminology* promoted a 'grand', fully politicised, criminological narrative. Its insistence that inequities and divisions in material production and ownership are intrinsically linked to the social factors producing crime brought notions of the possibility of a crime free society to the fore: a society based on principles of 'socialist diversity and tolerance of deviance' (1973: 281). This 'political criminology' was the logical extension of the critique of correctional criminology in which the questioning of political and social control would take precedence over behavioural and correctional issues. The key subject matter was no longer simply the causes of crime and deviance, but a critical understanding of the role of crime control in the maintenance of political order and the capacity of the capitalist state to criminalise problematical behaviour. Furthermore:

> For us, as for Marx, and for other new criminologists, *deviance* is normal in the sense that men are now consciously involved (in the prisons that are contemporary society and in the

real prisons) in asserting their human diversity. The task is not merely to 'penetrate' these
problems, not merely to question the stereotypes, or to act as 'alternative phenomenological
realities'. The task is to create a society in which the facts of human diversity, whether personal, organic or social, are not subject to the power to criminalise.

(Taylor *et al.*, 1973: 282)

MARXISATION

Taylor *et al.* (1975) *Critical Criminology* marked a striking shift in the politicisation
of critical criminology (see also Taylor and Taylor, 1973). According to the editors
the political priority was not to conduct empirical research but to build a rigorous
Marxist theoretical framework that would be able to interrogate 'the moral and ideological veneer of an unequal society', formulate meaningful progressive policies and
pose 'fundamental and consistent challenges to the everyday political assumptions,
practices and implications of one of the most influential and state dominated
branches of applied social 'science' – the 'science' of criminology' (p. 5):

radical criminology must move beyond the mere collection of further empirical data to the
construction of theories which make sense of the (measurable or not so easily measurable)
changes in the structure of social control, law and crime. The task is not simply to catalogue
inequalities but to create empirically grounded analyses which point the way out of inequality into a genuinely just and humane society.

(Taylor *et al.*, 1975b: 44)

With its critique of correctional criminology, Fabian criminology, New Deviancy
theory, US conflict theory and Scandinavian 'romanticism', Taylor *et al.* were determined to clear the decks once and for all. For example, the politically constrained
reformist orientation of Fabian criminology was dismissed as being part of the problem. However, it was the characterisation of New Deviancy Theory as idealistic and
politically naïve that was most significant. Its 'idealistic' conception of human
nature had resulted in 'a form of 'moral voyeurism', a celebration rather than an
analysis of the deviant form with which the deviancy theorist could vicariously identify (Taylor *et al.*, 1975b: 18). It had also generated an 'expose criminology' which
'ultimately is based on a mindless, and a-theoretical moral indignation. The guiding
theme appears to be one of feigned or real amazement at the double standards of
ruling groups' (ibid.: 30). A 'shock! horror! how could they' reaction to revelation of
instances of the 'crimes of the powerful' was not theoretically or politically adequate.
The task must be to generate systematic evidence of the class based 'organized practice of criminal and legal systems' and 'the disjunction between the imaginary
(ideological) social order and the real social order' (p. 37).

Young (1975) elaborated upon these themes in this argument for 'working class
criminology' where New Deviancy Theory was criticised for its 'Peter Pan' politics
and desire to romanticise 'hip and cool' illegality:

it is engaged in an astonishing accomplishment – the development of a criminology that
does not deal with property crime, and a criminology whose subjects live in a world not of
work, but of leisure. Expressive deviancy is the centre of attention ... marihuana-use rather
than burglary, prostitution rather than homicide, 'psychopathy' and 'schizophrenia' rather
than 'hysteria' or 'neurosis'. The emphasis is on 'crimes without victims' and the contention,

overall is that a big proportion of crime control involves undue and unnecessary interference in the liberty of the individual.

(Young, 1975: 68)

In addition, Left idealists were unwilling or unable to recognise that: there is a degree of public consensus concerning the core 'problem of crime'; close analysis of the official criminal statistics would demonstrate that crime was a serious social problem. A significant increase in crime and a multitude of invisible victims has damaging sociological effects on working class neighbourhoods. For Young:

> The working class does have a real stake in a genuine social order, however much it may be that conservative 'law and order' campaigns are a sham behind which particular interests advance themselves, and proclaim themselves to be acting in the interests of all. It is a simple fact that the majority of working class crime is *intra* and not *inter* class in its choice of target, area of activity and distribution. Working class people suffer from crime, confront daily the experience of material desperation, undergo the ravages of disorganization and competitive individualism.

(Young, 1975: 79)

Young argued that a credible Critical Criminology must develop a responsible political position. The risks of criminal victimization in working class communities must take priority over: celebrating the resistance of deviant subcultures and youth cultures; defending criminals on the grounds that they are the real victims; and an obsessive search for the injustices of the criminal justice system. This re-answered the question regarding 'whose side are we on?'

> It is unrealistic to suggest that the problem of crimes like mugging is merely the problem of mis-categorisation and concomitant moral panics. If we choose to embrace this liberal position, we leave the political arena open to conservative campaigns for law and order – for, however exaggerated and distorted the arguments conservatives may marshal, the reality of crime in the streets *can be* the reality of human suffering and personal disaster.

(Young, 1975: 89)

The practical task for a realistic Critical Criminology was 'not to help the courts to work, nor to design better prisons' but to 'aid and inform' working class communities against anti-social activities which in doing so will help them address their 'frequently disorganised and disintegrated' state.

This version of Marxist criminology opened up the debate. Hirst (1975: 203) ridiculed Taylor *et al.* for their amateurish attempt to construct a criminological theory out of, in the words of Paul Hirst, *ad hoc* 'scraps of Marx's writings'. For Hirst 'criminology', and its object of study was incompatible with the object of study and conceptual framework of Marxism:

> There is no 'Marxist theory of deviance', either in existence, or which can be developed within orthodox Marxism. Crime and deviance vanish into the general theoretical concerns and the specific scientific object of Marxism. Crime and deviance are no more a scientific field for Marxism than education, the family or sport. The objects of Marxism are specified by its own concepts.

(Hirst, 1975: 204)

Hirst was also critical for the lack of understanding that 'Marx and Engels strong language and their strong opposition to the criminal classes and the demi-monde, far

from expressing an idiosyncratic morality, stems from a definite theoretical-political
point of departure' (1975: 217). He also advocated a more sophisticated analysis of
law and common sense when it came to crime control:

> All societies outlaw certain categories of acts and punish. The operation of law or custom,
> however much it may be associated in some societies with injustice and oppression,
> is a necessary condition of existence in any social formation. Whether the social formation
> has a state or not, whether it is communist or not, it will control and coerce in certain
> ways the acts of its members. The police force in our own society is not *merely* an
> instrument of oppression, or of the maintenance of the capitalist economic system, but
> also a condition of a civilized existence under the present political-economic relations.
> One cannot imagine the absence of the control of the traffic or the absence of the suppres-
> sion of theft and murder, nor can one consider these controls to be purely oppressive.
> If Taylor and Walton do not disagree with this view, then we can only suppose they
> select the cause of the 'deviants' they support with some care. We presume they do not
> intend us to believe that they make common cause with professional thieves or cynical
> murderers. However, they offer us no clear theoretical basis on which they might base
> this separation.
>
> (1975: 241; see also Currie, 1974)

At a moment of unprecedented crisis in post-war British society, personified by
the election of a New Right government, Critical Criminology consolidated the
Marxist turn. This was evidenced in three texts: Hall *et al.*'s (1978) *Policing the
Crisis*, which emanated from the Birmingham Centre for Contemporary Cultural
Studies, and the last two NDC publications both published in 1979: *Capitalism and
the Rule of Law* and *Permissiveness and Control.*

THE CENTRE FOR CONTEMPORARY CULTURAL STUDIES

There is general agreement that the most sophisticated example of how Marxist
analysis could be applied to understand the specifics of 'crime' in a particular historical period was Hall *et al.*'s (1978) neo-Gramscian analysis of the crime of
'mugging' and the emergent crisis of hegemony in the British state in the early
1970s. This publication also represented a decisive theoretical and political intervention by the Birmingham CCCS in the emergent Marxist criminology. What was
remarkable given the intellectual ambitions of the authors, was the fact that Taylor
et al. provided no 'elaborated analysis of the state', capitalist or otherwise (Reiner,
1988: 149). *Policing the Crisis* addressed this theoretical and political absence
head on.

Hall *et al.* utilised the work of Pashukanis and Gramsci to examine the complexities of the 'state-crime-law-social control' nexus. These theorists had tempered the
determinist tendencies of instrumental Marxist theory of the state by arguing that the
law within the logic of capitalism, must also act as the guarantor of commodity-
exchange relations between capital and labour, and thus incorporate processes of
consensus as well as conflict. Within this view, consensus is not simply a 'false
consciousness', but an essential precondition for the existence of predictable
exchange relations between formally equal legal subjects. Coercion could not
logically be held to be the major support for ruling class domination. Rather the law
plays not only a co-ordinating function, but its own educative and ethical role.

Through the state, strategies are formulated and the whole of civil and moral life actively conforms to the needs not only of particular capitalists, but of the capitalist mode of production as a whole. This approach therefore stresses the strategic role of the law in managing consent, organising domination and securing hegemony. Hegemony, though, is rarely achieved, but is constantly struggled for and must be renewed and re-enacted. The primary task for the state in the 1970s was to manage a field of class struggle in an attempt to bring social relations into line with the structural tendencies set by the free market economy. This could not be achieved through coercion alone. The state also had to attempt to win the consent of the people, hence the critical notion of 'authoritarian populism'.

The nature of the state could not be derived, as Critical Criminologists assumed, from some general theory, but only by detailed analysis which remained alive to shifts in capital-state relations at particular historical moments. The state, faced by a crisis of hegemony, generated by Britain's post colonial economic decline and reflected in industrial disputes and working class resistance, was attempting to regain its legitimacy by defining the crisis in terms of 'law', 'order' and 'authority'. The crisis was deflected onto and manifested through a series of moral panics with a multitude of 'problems' defined as lack of respect for institutional authority and the rule of law. The solution lay in securing public acceptance for coercive measures – measures which ultimately had repercussions for whole populations and the way in which the social order was generally perceived.

Hall *et al.* began with an analysis of the 'moral panic' about 'mugging' which first surfaced in Britain in 1972, examining the label 'mugging' to reveal how the state was able to use concerns over law and order to divert public concern away from socio-economic and political crises. In this process the real problems facing Britain were defined solely as ones of criminality and lawlessness, rather than social depri-vation or class and racial inequalities. Above all, Hall *et al.* made it clear that crime can be defined differently at distinctive historical moments. This has little to do with actual events or incidents of crime, but reveals how the state uses 'crime' to prepare the ground for a general exercise of legal restraint and political control. Condemning the 'rising crime rate' as a product of 1960s permissiveness, the British state in the 1970s was able to construct public unease about historical recurring street crimes – now labelled as 'muggings' – into a popular mobilisation of fears and anxieties which were subsequently drawn upon to legitimate the development of an 'excep-tional' form of the 'authoritarian state', 'law and order' society and corresponding 'control cultures'. In an increasingly conflictual society, street crime – or in this case the 'perfect folk devil' of the 'black mugger' – became one of the few symbolic sources of unity. This analysis re-worked Cohen's concept of 'moral panic':

> 'moral panic' appears to us to be one of the principle forms of ideological consciousness by means of which a 'silent majority' is won over to the support of increasingly coercive measures on the part of the state, and lends its legitimacy to a 'more than usual' exercise of control.
>
> (Hall *et al.*, 1978: 221)

Through such analysis, Critical Criminology had moved a long way beyond the causes and labeling of criminal behaviour. The task is to explain why particular con-cepts of crime become so powerful at particular historical conjunctures and to understand the role of such conceptualisations in the development of disciplinary state practices. Stuart Hall's (1979) Cobden Trust Lecture *Drifting into a Law and*

Order Society hardened the 'authoritarian state' arguments of *Policing the Crisis* in the light of the law and order ideology that was constitutive of 'a deep and decisive movement towards a more disciplinary, authoritarian kind of society' (Hall, 1979: 4).

THE NATIONAL DEVIANCE CONFERENCE

Permissiveness and Control, the first NDC publication since 1976, reiterated that the Marxisation of Critical Criminology was essential to create a radical intellectual space in opposition to 'the arid criminological conferences at the Institute of Criminology at Cambridge, sponsored by the Home Office' (NDC, 1979: vii–viii). The chapters in the book reflected on, like parts of *Policing the Crisis*, the nature of the permissive society, the drug debate, delinquency, and race. The connecting theme was the idea of the 1960s being the 'age of permissiveness' was a mythology that had diverted public attention from increased state control and was used to justify a right wing backlash. The second NDC publication, *Capitalism and the Rule of Law* (Fine *et al.*, 1979), declared that it was 'the first thorough going Marxist analysis' of both Critical Criminology and Critical Legal Studies. Jock Young elaborated upon his emergent 'Left Realist' position dismissing Fabian criminology for being a 'mere mismash' of ideas and attacking Left idealist criminology for its 'capitalism is criminogenic' stance:

> Its stress on the illusory nature of appearances: the consensus masks coercion; the crime statistics are sheer fiction, hiding the criminality of the rich; treatment is a cloak for punishment; the universalism of law is a rhetoric which hides particularism; 'normality' and 'deviance' are concepts of ideology; the differences between different parts of the social control apparatus merely conceal an identity of purpose and a unity of form and discipline. In its most extreme form, idealism is unable to distinguish the factory from the prison, education from brainwashing, the anti-social from the social, fascism from democracy.
>
> (Young, 1979: 16)

Without naming the text, Young provides a critique of *Policing the Crisis*, berating the authors for their failure to recognise that public fear of 'street crime' cannot be theoretically or politically explained away as a police orchestrated 'moral panic' or state induced 'ideological mystification' (see, Young, 1979: 20–21; see also Matthews, 1979: 111).

So by now we have the basis for Young's revisionist 'Left Realist' criminology:

- the left has to take the rising official crime rate seriously because it is just the tip of an iceberg of 'unrecognized victims';
- criminal victimisation and fear of crime, because they are widespread, are socially destructive and politically dangerous;
- theoretical reflection must take second place to producing practical proposals that will reduce victimisation of the vulnerable and powerless (see also Young, 1992).

What is equally significant in *Capitalism and the Rule of Law* is that several chapters point towards a distinctive 'Marxist Legal Studies' (see also Hunt and Cain, 1979; Bierne, 1979). Other chapters represent the first engagement with Foucault's *Discipline and Punish* thesis (cf. Lea, 1979).

We also need to remind ourselves before leaving this critical historical moment that some NDC 'fellow travellers' condemned the departure from a humanist approach that emphasised tolerance, pluralism and diversity; the rejection of Fabian criminology and the misrepresentation of labelling theory (see the various contributions in Downes and Rock, 1979). Downes (1979: 12) censured Marxist criminology for its distortion of Fabian reformism and for not recognising the law and order needs of working class communities 'which would leave the poorer and more vulnerable sections of the working class far worst than now, reproducing a state of affairs that already prevails in the worst American ghettoes". Downes also criticised the Marxists for side stepping the vexed issue of authoritaritarian crime control in existing socialist societies.

For labeling theorists the theoretical basis was flawed. Rock (1979) argued that the grounding of Critical Criminology in the meta-theory of Marxism inevitably meant that it lost sight of micro meanings, motives and intentions of individuals. Marxisation was seen as a regression to a more impersonal and large scale level of analysis in which the radicalism of labelling theory's break with positivism was lost. It mattered little that a conservative view of the social order as consensual had been substituted by a conflict based account. Both acted to impose structuralist imperatives on social phenomena which, they argued, could only be understood at a micro level and in a pluralistic manner. Critical Criminology was a political posture rather than a rigorous social analysis of crime and deviance. In addition, this macro stance was a dispiriting mass of contradictions:

> The coalition of Marxists, anarchists, populists, conflict theorists and libertarians is prone to some internal dissension. Its future hinges on the resolution of internal contradictions. Anarchism and Marxism are not entirely complementary. Neither are libertarianism and structuralism, it is conceivable that radical criminology will shatter into a host of subordinate criminologies, each veering towards a parent world view.
>
> (Rock, 1979: 83)

It was also unstable because of its attempt to reconcile grand theory with partisan politics. Selectively supporting campaigning groups which were in themselves powerless and short-lived would generate 'the politics of the marginal [which] are marginal politics, drifting into inaction and expressive displays' (Rock, 1979: 84).

Cohen expressed disappointment that 'A large measure of the diversity and eccentricity which were so characteristic of the group's [National Deviance Conference] early years has now been exported out ... *consequently, the hard core of the remaining group has become more orthodox and homogenous* [italics added] (1981: 241). Marxisation had produced a move away from: ethnographic studies towards structural and historical research on the criminogenic aspects of capitalism; empirical studies of the operational practices of social control agencies towards 'totalising' macro-analysis of repressive law and order and welfare policies; a sociology of crime and deviance towards a political economy of crime, law and the state.

For Cohen (1979: 21) there could be a high political price to pay for over deliberation on arcane theoretical matters and neglect of the rapidly changing criminal justice scene: 'beyond filling in the picture of the system as *repressive*, the impact of the new theories has been slight. And while it would be politically naïve to assume that our writings in themselves could have much power, *it is important to construct an agenda which does not leave the debate to the Right*'. Cohen identified

James Q. Wilson's (1975) *Thinking About Crime* as symptomatic of a sea change from a liberal concern with crime causation to a conservative focus on the deterrent capacities of the criminal justice system (see also Platt and Takagi, 1977). The 'critical' in criminology was being redefined by the anti-sociological assault of neo-classicism! He also noted that correctional criminology had not been 'beheaded'. In fact its institutional capacities were being reinforced by empowered crime control agencies:

> The Home Office Research Unit, the research branches of the Prison Department, the Metropolitan Police and allied state agencies have all expanded and become more professional and productive. … In line with what happened in the United States over this decade, the content of this type of criminology has switched (and is likely to switch even more) in the direction of 'criminal justice', that is to say, an exclusive concern with the operation of the system. Research deals mainly with matters and decision-making, manpower, evaluation and classification.
>
> (Cohen, 1981: 236)

The hardening of political positions was producing 'an ambiguous no-man's-land' on either side of which correctional and Marxist criminologists could 'carry on with their private preoccupations' (Cohen, 1981: 238).

ORTHODOX THEORY AND APPLICATION

It cannot be over-emphasised how central the social conflicts of the early 1980s are to understanding the development of an orthodox Critical Criminology in the UK. This strategic 'moment of truth' is something that is increasingly forgotten in conventional histories. Addressing the 'whose side are we on?' question in this political conjuncture sharpened the schism between Left Realists championing a working class victimology that mandated state action to protect the vulnerable from the predatory criminality associated with acquisitive individualism and Critical Criminologists intent on monitoring and resisting the criminalisation practices of the 'authoritarian state'. The 'heightened indignation, zeal and emotional commitment' surrounding a 'politics of injustice', identified by Cohen (1988: 261), is reflected in various publications (see for example, Cowell *et al.*, 1982). From this point on I will leave the Left Realist part of the story to Roger Matthews (in this volume; see also Lea and Young, 1984; Jones *et al.*, 1986; Kinsey *et al.*, 1986; Matthews and Young, 1986; Matthews and Young, 1992a, b). As Cohen has noted, the emergence of a fully fledged Left Realism 'demands our most serious attention in the telling the story of anti-criminology' as it represents 'an almost complete reversal of the original enterprise' (1988: 17). The Left Realist turn received a considerable boost from feminist criminologists who wanted to use the 'criminalising power of the state for instrumental and symbolic ends' (Cohen, 1988: 245).

It needs also to be noted that a post-Marxist branch of Critical Criminology also developed during the 1980s which was to a large degree inspired by Foucault's (1977; 1978a, b) analysis of the shift from 'sovereign' to 'disciplinary' power and:

> its capillary form of existence, the point where power reaches into the very grain of individuals, touches their bodies and inserts itself into their actions and attitudes, their

discourses, learning processes and everyday life … a synaptic regime of power, a regime of its exercise within the soul and body rather than from above.

(Foucault, 1978a: 39)

This perspective preferred to examine the plurality of forms of social control, penality, survelliance and governance. Hence, the chain of Critical Criminological references premised as they were on the 'sovereign state' were viewed as too simplistic a base from which to explain the problematics of government associated with advanced neo-liberalism (see Abel, 1982; Cohen and Scull, 1983; Garland and Young, 1983; Cohen, 1985; Shearing and Stenning, 1985; see O'Malley in this volume).

In an ever worsening context of mutual hostility we see the construction of distinctive Critical Criminological and Left Realist positions. Hall *et al.*'s concept of the 'authoritarian state' was embedded in the neural wiring of Critical Criminology. However, it was also hard-edged via Poulantzas' (1978: 79) insistence on the 'the role of violence in the *grounding of power*'. The brutal reality of the ever-present 'iron fist' in 'the velvet glove' remains an unshakeable truth for Critical Criminology:

> Even if violence is not concretized in the daily exercise of power as it used to be, it still, and indeed more than ever, occupies a *determining* position. For its very monopolisation by the state induces forms of domination in which the numerous methods of establishing consent play the key role. … Physical violence and consent do not exist side by side like two calculable homogenous magnitudes, related in such a way that more consent corresponds to less violence. Violence-terror always occupies a *determining* place – and merely because it remains in reserve, coming into the open only in critical situations. State monopolised physical violence underlies the power and mechanisms of consent: it is inscribed in the web of disciplinary and ideological devices and even when not directly exercises, it shapes the materiality of the social body upon which domination is brought to bear. We need to grasp the material organisation of labour as a class relation whose condition of existence and guarantee of reproduction is organised physical violence.
>
> (Poulantzas, 1978: 80–83)

Critical Criminology's engagement with broader theoretical developments would be configured through this theoretical filter.

I would argue that nesting under 'the authoritarian state' thesis is a portfolio of five theoretical co-ordinates that would define the Critical Criminology research agenda: criminalisation; racialisation; ideological distortion; abolitionism (as a 'replacement discourse'); and praxis.

The primary concern was identifying the 'criminalisation' practices that emanated from and assisted the 'authoritarian state' in its management of structural contradictions (Scraton and Chadwick, 1991; see also Scraton, 1987). The overriding concern is to demonstrate how the application of the criminal label is not simply a matter of controlling 'criminality' but of containing political opposition and resistance. 'Criminalisation' is one of the most powerful disciplinary strategies available to the 'authoritarian state' because it mobilises the consent of the public who are more likely to support state action against particular groups if they are linked to criminal threats. The 'authoritarian state' is grounded in the interests of, not just of a particular class or of capital, but also in those of 'race' and gender. Classism, sexism, heterosexism and racism, it is argued, are not isolated phenomena, but become institutionalised as taken-for-granted relations of power, which constitute and determine the punitive policies and practices of the criminal justice system. 'Racialisation' is a second key co-ordinate. Gilroy (1982) re-iterated Hall *et al.*'s thesis that a carefully cultivated racialised fear of crime, especially when connected to the ideological construction of the 'young, black male criminal', justified both tough police and judical actions and fuelled 'tough on crime' legislation. As a consequence, not only were certain forms of crime racialised but whole communities criminalised.

Although it is more likely to be assumed rather than researched, the third co-ordinate is 'ideological distortion'. Hall *et al.*'s reworked 'moral panic' thesis, combined with Herman and Chomsky's (1988: 298) position on the mass media's role in 'manufacturing consent', became the default position for explaining rising crime rates, public fear of crime and popular punitiveness and electoral support for authoritarian law and order policies. 'Common sense' crime control ideologies are embedded in the mass media's processes and practices. Box (1983: 3) provides us with a classic example: 'Maybe what is stuffed into our consciousness as *the* crime problem is in fact an illusion, a trick to deflect attention away from other more serious crimes and victimising behaviours which objectively cause the vast bulk of avoidable death, injury and deprivation'.

The fourth theoretical coordinate is 'abolitionism'. This was first suggested by Mathiesen (1974). The starting point is that conventional thinking about crime, criminality and crime control is fundamentally flawed because the 'harms' associated with social life cannot, and should not be, regulated by the criminal justice system. The abolitionist insists that events and behaviours that are criminalised have nothing in common other than the fact that they have been usurped by the criminal justice system. Hence 'crime' has no ontological reality independent of the definitional processes of the criminal law and criminal justice system. Crime is not the object but the product of crime control philosophies and practices. Social problems, conflicts, harms and antagonisms are an inevitable part of everyday life and therefore cannot be delegated to professionals and experts 'promising' to provide 'solutions'. When professionals intervene, the essence of social problems and conflicts are effectively 'stolen' and re-presented in forms that only perpetuate the problems/conflicts (see Christie, 1977). This is why the criminal justice system is overwhelmingly counter-productive in relation to its objectives:

- it does not function according to the rationales and legitimations claimed by it, whether they be rehabilitation, deterrence or prevention.
- it does not attend to the needs of victims or offenders because it causes unnecessary suffering and offers little influence to those directly involved.
- it cannot protect people from being victimised and cannot control criminality.

Abolitionism is advocated for the following reasons. First, discursively, events can be reclassified. The organizational vocabulary of the traditional criminal justice system, especially the essentialising concepts of crime and criminality, should be eradicated because they distort and or simplify complex realities. This would in turn undermine other problematic concepts such as 'seriousness', 'dangerousness', 'evil', 'good', 'punishment', and 'guilt' as well as the philosophical premises of retribution, deterrence and rehabilitation (see De Folter, 1986: 43–44). We would do better to utilise notions of 'negligence' and 'accidents' rather than 'intent' and 'responsibility'. 'Crimes' could then be reclassified for what they really are – conflicts, troubles, disputes, problems, harms, etc. (see Christie, 1977; Bianchi and van Swaaningen, 1986).

Second, legislatively, we could also use other bodies of law – economic, administrative, environmental, health, labour – rather than the criminal law to conceptualise and resolve conflicts. This would result in extensive 'de-criminalisation' that is the process through which governments effectively legalise an act that was formerly a crime. De-criminalisation of 'victimless' offences such as drug taking, prostitution, etc. would allow the criminal justice system to concentrate on serious forms of inter-personal violence and the crimes of the powerful. Finally, in policy terms we should seek abolition of the apparatuses of the criminal justice system.

Nils Christie's (1993) *Crime Control as Industry* stands as an exemplar of this perspective in the 1990s. In this text Christie attempts to get to grips with the unfolding neo-liberalisation of crime control. His initial argument is familiar. His first move is to problematise 'crime': 'Acts are not, they become. So also with crime. Crime does not exist. Crime is created' (1993: 21). 'Acts' acquire different meanings within different social frameworks. Second, 'the major dangers of crime in modern societies are not the crime, but that the fight against them may lead societies towards totalitarian developments' (1993: 14). He notes the global tendency for states to declare war on 'internal enemies'. The rolling out of the 'war' against 'an unlimited reservoir of acts which can be defined as crimes' (1993: 22) would result in the development of Western style Gulags. Authoritarian tendencies are facilitated by an increasingly punitive law and order politics:

> The ground has been prepared. The media prepare it every day and night. Politicians join ranks with the media. It is impossible politically not to be against sin. This is a competition won by the highest bidder. To protect people from crime is a cause more just than any. At the same time, the producers of control are eagerly pushing for order. They have the capacity. There are no natural limits. A crime-free society is such a sacred goal for so many, that even money does not count. Who asks about costs in the middle of a total war?
>
> (Christie, 1993: 166)

The prison plays the crucial function in advanced capitalist societies of warehousing 'surplus populations' and the 'dangerous classes'. However, this classic carceral function has taken a novel turn because of privatisation. These particular commercial enterprises have a built in 'growth dynamic' because they have a vested interest in seeing the problem of crime growing. In addition, an extra 'profit motive' has been introduced in the utilisation of inmates as a cheap source of labour:

> Compared to most other industries, the crime control industry is in a most privileged position. There is no lack of raw material, crime seems to be in endless supply. Endless also are the demands for the service, as well as the willingness to pay for what is seen as security. And the usual industrial questions of contamination do not apply. On the contrary, this is an industry seen as cleaning up, removing unwanted elements from the social system. … This is an industry with particular advantages, providing weapons for what is often seen as a permanent war against crime.
>
> (Christie, 1993: 111)

The private sector is capable of building, equipping and running prisons for whatever purpose is deemed appropriate by the 'carceral state':

> the dangerous population will not be exterminated, except for those killed by capital punishment. But the risks are great that those seen as core members of the dangerous population may be confined, warehoused, stored away, and forced to live for their most active years as consumers of control. It can be done democratically, and under the strict control of the legal

institution ... it is democratic crime control by the voting majority. To this there are no
natural limits, as long as the actions do not hurt that majority.

(Christie, 1993: 171–173)

'Crime Control PLC' is an industry committed to developing, not reducing,
its 'core business' and in the process is producing extremely 'dangerous states' for
citizens.

The final theoretical co-ordinate is 'praxis'. Accompanying the abolitionist position, is commitment to a unity of theory and activism intended to transform personal
troubles into public issues (cf. Mills, 1959). This can be achieved through:

- working with pressure groups campaigning for reform of the criminal justice system or miscar-
  riages of justice produced by institutionalised racism, sexism and classism;
- campaigning and/or participating in inquiries into controversial criminal justice practices;
- interrogating official reports into state controversies (riots, industrial disputes, prison protests,
  police violence, etc.) in order to: expose accounts of 'what really happened'; attempts to dis-
  credit victims, survivors or campaigners; and/or manipulation and management of news media
  reporting;
- investigating the crimes of the economically powerful, state crimes and human rights violations
  (for fuller details see Scraton, 2002).

THINKING AFRESH? TWENTY-FIRST CENTURY
CRITICAL CRIMINOLOGY

The previous discussion sought to establish how the theoretical and political parameters of Critical Criminology hardened into an orthodoxy during the 1990s. So what
of the twenty-first century? A significant number of Critical Criminologists remain
confident that the theoretical co-ordinates of the orthodox paradigm are still relevant
to 'new times', particularly with the post 9/11 global 'war on terror'. Carrington and
Hogg (2002), Hillyard et al. (2004) and Barton et al. (2007) provide us with an
insight as to where Critical Criminology currently stands. Given their genealogy, it
is not surprising that the texts are remarkably similar in their endorsement of the
parameters of Critical Criminology:

1   the problematisation of 'crime' because it has no ontological reality;
2   the problematisation of criminalization processes as ineffective and counter-productive;
3   the priority research areas for critical criminology must be highlighting the social injustices
    associated with:
    • the relentless expansion of the crisis-prone criminal justice system
    • the crimes committed by the powerful.

The antipathy towards the 'dismal science' of conventional criminology in the
twenty-first century remains intense because its knowledge base is implicated in
the intensification of authoritarian crime control practices and the construction of
'suitable enemies' (Christie, 1986). This is most obvious in the case of state-
sponsored 'managerialist criminology' and 'crime science' whose stated aim is to

devise new crime control techniques. However, liberal criminologists are also criticised for continuing to work within the welfarist parts of the crime control complex that legitimise criminalisation and marginalisation practices. 'Criminology' is compromised by its institutionalisation as a 'relevant' rather than an independent academic discipline and its willingness to work within the state's criminological agenda and preferred methodologies in return for power in the form of funding, patronage and recognition:

> Since its inception, criminology has enjoyed an intimate relationship with the powerful, a relationship determined largely by its failure to subject to critique the category of crime – and disciplinary agendas set by this – which has been handed down by the state and around which the criminal justice system has been organised.
>
> (Hillyard and Tombs 2004: 18)

Hillyard and Tombs (2004: 28) acknowledge that 'it would be simply wrong to claim that criminology has not contributed to any progressive social change'. However:

> the efforts of over 100 years focus on the object of crime have been accompanied by: a depressing and almost cyclical tour around a series of cul-de-sacs in search of the 'causes' of crime; vastly expanded criminal justice systems which, at the same time, have proven unsuccessful on the basis of almost any publicly provided rationale for them; and ever increasing processes of criminalization, as a succession of critical criminologists have demonstrated. If criminology is now well established as a discipline, the costs of legitimacy and professionalisation have been, and continue to be, high when measured against any index of social justice.
>
> (Hillyard and Tombs, 2004: 28)

For them, 'all too often, the products of criminological reasoning have been used to bolster states, providing rationales for the extension of state activities in the name of more effective criminal justice' (Hillyard and Tombs, 2004: 25). In addition, the blindspot of conventional criminology retains its steadfast refusal to research victimization by the powerful, not least because the state does not recognize nor fund such research.

Throughout the three texts there remains an insistence on the 'unity' of Critical Criminological writing, research and transformative political practice. For Scraton (2002: 35) Critical Criminology must continue to challenge 'the political and ideological imperatives of official discourse, state sponsored evaluations of official policy initiatives and the correspondence of vocational training to the requirements of the crime control industry'. It must also be politically allied to 'those struggling for social justice' and 'those who endure institutionalised harm' at the hands of the state as a result of structural inequalities derived from and sustained by the 'determining contexts' of class, patriarchy, race and age:

> Critical analysis … turns individual cases and personal troubles into public issues. In challenging the social and political constructions of crime, disorder, terror, evil, power, critical analysis responds to Noam Chomsky's appeal for *intellectual responsibility*. … It is about bearing witness, gathering testimonies, sharing experiences, garnering the *view from below* and exposing the politics and discourses of authoritarianism. It moves beyond the resources of *theory* into *praxis*, recognising the self-as-academic as the *self-as-participant*. It takes political responsibility.
>
> (Scraton, 2005: 22)

Walters (2007; see also Hillyard *et al.*, 2004) builds on this position arguing that it is imperative for academic criminologists to distance themselves publicly from the state's criminological agenda rather than pandering to it:

> If all academics boycotted Home Office research and refused to provide such research with the credibility that academic credentials bring – then the Home Office would be forced either to change the existing agenda or to engage solely corporate researchers. If the latter was adopted, not only would Westminster begin to question the lack of 'expertise' informing policy but the emperor would also be without clothes. The policies and research of the Home office would be seen for what they are – nothing more than financial transactions to the lowest and most reliable bidder, researched and written as quickly as possible, and with the government's interests at heart in order to secure future deals.
>
> (Walters, 2007: 30)

This would also create the opportunity to 'name and shame' those 'entrepreneurial' criminologists who are willing to conduct 'quick and dirty' research on a tightly regulated contractual basis with no moral or political consideration of the implications of their work.

An age old question continues to unsettle twenty-first century Critical Criminology – should it abandon what it deems to be the compromised discipline of criminology to the managerial criminologists and crime scientists? Hillyard and Tombs (2004) advocate a 'social harm' or 'zemiological' perspective which would take in, physical, financial/economic and emotional/psychological harms. They recognise that 'harm is no more definable than crime, and that it too lacks any ontological reality' (Hillyard and Tombs, 2004: 20). It is also difficult to identify the range of issues to be encompassed by 'social harm'. However, their arguments in support of moving from a criminological to a 'social harm' approach are as follows:

- it acknowledges the multitude of harms that can affect people in the 'cradle to the grave' life cycle;
- it recognises of not just individual but corporate and collective responsibility for actions and non-actions;
- it prioritises a social policy rather than criminal justice policy response;
- it facilitates consideration of 'mass harms' which cannot be handled satisfactorily by the criminal justice process;
- it confronts powerful interests and power structures.

Before leaving this section I want to return to the work of Nils Christie. In a *Suitable Amount of Crime* (2004) he re-iterates many of his core themes but also presents an analysis obviously influenced by writers such as Zygmunt Bauman and Mike Davis. Neo-liberal market thinking is expanding and implanting itself across institutional arrangements, marginalising alternative ways of thinking, understanding and living. The defining feature of contemporary life for most people is living as individuals among strangers who have little knowledge or understanding of each other:

> People don't meet people to the extent they once did. This means increased reliance on the media for what happens and gives meaning to occurrences. It also means greater dependence on the state to cope with perceived dangers.
>
> (Christie, 2004: 67)

Individualisation combined with the decline in informal social controls makes it more likely that people will be suspicious and fearful of others. Consequently there is the tendency to categorise incidents as 'criminal'. This generates a fearful, insecure society which empowers both the self-serving and self-fulfilling criminal justice lobby and a burgeoning private security industry:

> What happens to the locks on the doors, to the gilded cities, and with those living in the midst of broken windows – this is just in miniature what whole states are doing these days. The rich protect their property by hiding behind walls. So do also the rich states, to keep citizens from the poor states out of their territory.
>
> (Christie, 2004: 31)

Globalization has also weakened the state and the democratic political process and this has led to the politicisation of crime: 'Crime, or rather the fight against crime, becomes indispensible in creating legitimacy in, and for, the suitably weakened state' (2004: 37). 'Acts' with the potential to be defined as 'crimes' are an unlimited natural resource that can be taken advantage of. The most extreme manifestation of this is the dramatisation of the war against organised crime and terrorism which is used to justify the introduction of new criminal justice legislation and practices that empower the criminal justice system. The inevitable result is mass incarceration.

For Christie, the alternative is maximizing informal, social controls and minimizing state controls. The starting point must be 'conflicts' rather than 'crimes':

> We have to live with sorrow and misery in the shadow of atrocities. But we must at the same time also try out some old-fashioned ways of solving conflict, maybe even before the culprits have moved so far as to ask for this. We do not want amnesia. But, after all the information has been brought to the surface, imprinted in all our minds and all human history, we might in the end have no better solution than forgiveness and restoration.
>
> (Christie, 2004: 100)

Hence, his support for truth-telling, reconciliation, mediation, restorative justice, and re-integrative shaming. Christie also voices his concerns about the discipline of criminology. Criminologists have a moral obligation to campaign against mass incarceration, normalisation of the 'war against crime' and securitisation practices. This also requires criminologists to challenge their US counterparts for being part of the shift from 'welfare criminology' to 'control criminology' and active involvement in the expansion of a punitive criminal justice system. Christie is also concerned about the pressure to work ever more closely with the criminal justice system and the development of professional managerial criminal justice knowledges that are independent of criminology.

CONCLUSION

The psycho-social dynamics that define contemporary society mean that the need for an agenda-setting Critical Criminological perspective has never been greater. Young (2002: 271) argues that it does, however, have to renew itself intellectually so that it can work on the 'fundamental *dislocations of justice* [italics added] that occur throughout our social order'. This is partly responsible for Young deciding that it was time to instigate a 'cultural criminology' suitable for the 'switchback' of 'liquid modernity' defined by:

> a world of broken narratives where economic and ontological insecurity abounds, where crime, far from being mundane and calculative is transgressive and sensual, where punishment is frequently vituperative and vindictive and where society, rather than being a one-dimensional scenario of rational contractual atoms, is divisive, contested, contradictory and ironic.
>
> (Young, 2002: 259)

This 'cultural turn' allowed Young to resurrect the radicalness of the NDC that had been rejected as politically irresponsible in the late 1970s. This turn also offers the possibility of re-connection with broader intellectual shifts associated with cultural studies.

And for Currie (2002: v) the *dislocations of justice* are global in nature:

> creating justice systems permeated by respect for human rights in a world where those rights are threatened at every turn by the proliferation of autocratic and/or failed regimes and of predatory and punitive ideologies; the challenge of creating and maintaining safe, vibrant and respectful communities in the face of global economic forces that threaten to erode communal stability and widen the inequality that is so often at the root of criminality; the challenge ... of effectively confronting new forms of global violence while simultaneously promoting democracy and accountability in our institutions of criminal justice; and more ... .

Being mandated to act as the 'book-keepers of the soul' (Horowitz, 1979: 1) continues to place a heavy burden on Critical Criminology. However, there are serious question marks as to whether orthodox Critical Criminology's portfolio of core theoretical coordinates are all that is needed to 'work' on these *dislocations of justice*. First, for understandable reasons, it remains committed to the 'authoritarian state' paradigm. There are of course limits to how much Critical Criminology can shift methodologically – and politically – in its conceptualisation of the state's practices. However, as Schwendinger and Schwendinger (1970: 57) noted concepts 'are brought to light and operationalised by the political struggles *of our time*' (italics added). Reification of the 1970s concept of the 'authoritarian state' – as a credo – rather than as twenty-first century sensitising concept, limits the possibilities for engaging in the rigorous examination of the contradictory evidence that is so vital to renewal. There is evidence that a self-referential orthodox Critical Criminology is deteriorating theoretically to the point where it is incapable of engaging with the complex of risks and uncertainties that define a rapidly changing sociological and political landscape. Stuart Hall's warning has never been more prescient:

> The purpose of theorizing is not to enhance one's intellectual or academic reputation but to enable us to grasp, understand, and explain – to produce a more adequate knowledge of – the historical world and its processes; and thereby to inform our practice so that we may transform it.
>
> (Hall, 1988: 36)

Second, allied to this, Critical Criminology has little access to the institutional sites of criminal justice and national security, As a consequence, with notable exceptions, it has increasing difficulty in generating primary research data and methodological innovation. Third, at an interventionist level, Critical Criminology remains, again for understandable reasons – normative and practical – highly selective in the social injustices it chooses to research and campaign around. For example, whilst it remains evangelical in its determination to unearth the crimes of the economically, politically and socially powerful, it continues to distance itself from the conventional crime problems that define public debate. With the demise of Left Realism, this has created a serious political problem. Fourth, Critical Criminology tends to construct itself as a victim of a reactionary state sponsored conventional criminology whilst at the same time marginalising or silencing those critical criminologists who express difference. Fifth, politically, Critical Criminology continues to have difficulty in identifying progressive practices. It has a public responsibility to provoke, irritate and exasperate as the bearer of 'unwelcome news' (Cohen, 2002: xiii), and to act as the adversary of the 'condescension of complacency' (Brabazon, 2009: 47). However, this has a tendency to slip into sweeping generalisations that push aside tensions and contradictions. Finally, as has been discussed through this chapter, from its inception, the 'scarlet thread' that runs through Critical Criminology is the quest for a 'replacement discourse' that will move beyond and/or dissolve both 'crime' and 'criminology'. This replacement discourse will of course provide intellectual replenishment. However, despite advocacy of 'abolitionism', 'social justice', 'zeimiology' and 'human rights' it has not, as yet, been possible to generate a satisfactory alternative to 'criminology'.

Cohen argues that there will always be a tension between the requirements of intellectual/academic and political life. The former 'thrive best and depend upon a spirit of scepticism, doubt and uncertainty. The answers are provisional; thought is ambiguous; irony is deliberate' (1989: 100). The latter 'calls for some immediate commitments' and 'values that are binding and encourage neither scepticism nor irony'. Cohen goes on to discuss the moral obligations of the Critical Criminologist. The 'over-riding obligation' must be to 'honest intellectual inquiry … (however sceptical, provisional, irrelevant and unrealistic)' (p. 122). The political commitment to social justice and responding to pressing and immediate demands for humanitarian help is never going to be easy:

> All we can do, is find the best guide to each one – then confront the tension that results. This is hard going. In the end the only guides are, first, our sense of social justice, and second whatever time we have in the 24 hour day … our task is seemingly impossible: to combine detachment with commitment. There is only one universal guide for this: not to use intellectual scepticism as an alibi for political inaction.
>
> (Cohen, 1989: 123 and 127)

And he reminds us of what he thinks is best in Michel Foucault's 'intellectual ethics': avoiding too many general injunctions; putting the 'little' pieces together in a careful manner; interrogating the self-evident, the accepted and familiar; and continual re-problematisation of the field of study.

REFERENCES

Abel, R. (ed.) (1982) *The Politics of Informal Justice.* New York: Academic Press.

Barton, A., Corteen, K., Scott, D. and Whyte, D. (eds) (2007) *Expanding the Criminological Imagination.* Cullompton: Willan.

Becker, H. (1967) Whose side are we on?, *Social Problems,* 14(3): 239–247.

Bianchi, H. and van Swaaningen, R. (eds) (1986) *Abolitionism: Towards a Non-Repressive Approach to Crime.* Amsterdam: Free University Press.

Bierne, P. (1979) Empiricism and the critique of Marxism on law and crime. *Social Problems,* 24(4): 373–85.

Box, S. (1983) *Power, Crime and Mystification.* London: Tavistock.

Brabazon, T. (2009) Review of E. P. Thompson, *The Making of the English Working Class. Times Higher Education,* 25 June–1st July, p. 47.

Carrington, K. and Hogg, R. (eds) (2002) *Critical Criminology: Issues, Debates, Challenges.* Cullompton: Willan.

Christie, N. (1977) Conflicts as property, *British Journal of Criminology,* 17(1): 1–15.

Christie, N. (1986) Suitable enemies, in H. Bianchi, and R. van Swaaningen (eds), *Abolitionism: Towards a Non-Repressive Approach to Crime.* Amsterdam: Free University Press.

Christie, N. (1993) *Crime Control as Industry: Towards Gulags Western Style.* London: Routledge.

Christie, N. (2004) *A Suitable Amount of Pain.* London: Routledge.

Cohen, S. (ed.) (1971) *Images of Deviance.* Harmondsworth: Penguin.

Cohen, S. (1974) Criminology and the sociology of deviance in Britain: a recent history and a current report, in P. Rock and M. McIntosh (eds), *Deviance and Social Control.* London: Tavistock.

Cohen, S. (1979) Guilt, justice and tolerance: some old concepts for a new criminology, in D. Downes and P. Rock (eds), *Deviant Interpretations.* London: Martin Robertson.

Cohen, S. (1981) Footprints on the sand: a further report on criminology and the sociology of deviance in Britain, in M. Fitzgerald *et al.* (eds), *Crime and Society: Readings in History and Theory.* London: Routledge.

Cohen, S. (1985) *Visions of Social Control: Crime Punishment and Classification.* Cambridge: Polity.

Cohen, S. (1988) *Against Criminology.* London: Transaction Books.

Cohen, S. (1989) Intellectual scepticism and political commitment: the case of radical criminology, in P. Walton *et al.* (eds) *New Criminology Revisited.*

Cohen, S. (1990) 'Preface' to W. de Haan, *The Politics of Redress.* London: Unwin Hyman.

Cohen, S. (2002) *States of Denial.* Cambridge: Polity.

Cohen, S. and Scull, A. (eds) (1983) *Social Control and the State: Historical and Comparative Essays,* Oxford: Martin Robertson.

Cohen, S. and Taylor, L. (1975) From psychopaths to outsiders: British criminology and the national deviancy conference, in Bianchi, H. *et al.* (eds), *Deviance and Control in Europe,* London: John Wiley and Sons.

Cohen, S. and Taylor, L. (1976) *Prison Attempts: the Theory and Practice of Resistance in Everyday Life,* London: Penguin.

Cowell, D., Jones, T. and Young, J. (eds) (1982) *Policing the Riots,* London: Junction Books.

Currie, E. (1974) The new criminology, *Crime and Social Justice,* pp. 109–113.

Currie, E. (2002) Preface, in K. Carrington and R. Hogg (eds), *Critical Criminology: Issues, Debates, Challenges.* Cullompton: Willan.

De Folter, R. S. (1986) On the methodological foundation of the abolitionist approach to criminal justice. *Contemporary Crises,* 10(2): 39–623.

Downes, D. (1988) The sociology of crime and social control in Britain, 1960–87, in P. Rock (ed.), *History of British Criminology.* Oxford: Oxford University Press.

Downes, D. and Rock, P. (eds) (1979) *Deviant Interpretations.* Oxford: Oxford University Press.

Fine, B., Kinsey, R., Lea, J., Picciotto, S. and Young, J. (eds) (1979) *Capitalism and the Rule of Law: from Deviancy to Marxism.* London: Hutchinson.

Foucault, M. (1977) *Discipline and Punish,* Harmondsworth: Penguin.

Foucault, M. (1978a) Governmentality, in G. Burchell, C. Gordon and P. Miller, *The Foucault Effect: Studies in Governmentality.* Chicago: University of Chicago Press.

Foucault, M. (1978b) Prison talk, in M. Foucault, *Power/Knowledge: Selected Interviews and Other Writings 1972–77.* Bristol: Harvester Wheatsheaf (edited by C. Gordon).

Garland, D. and Young, P. (eds) (1983) *The Power to Punish: Contemporary Penality and Social Analysis.* London: Heinemann.

Gilroy, P. (1983) The myth of black criminality, in M. Eve and D. Musson (eds), *The Socialist Register,* London: Merlin.

Hall, S. *et al.* (1978) *Policing the Crisis.* London: Hutchinson.

Hall, S. (1979) *Drifting into a Law and Order Society.* London: Cobden Trust.

Hall, S. (1988) The toad in the garden: Thatcherism among the theorists, in C. Nelson and L. Grossberg (eds), *Marxism and the Interpretation of Culture.* Basingstoke: MacMillan.

Herman, E. S. and Chomsky, H. (1988) *Manufacturing Consent: the Political Economy of Mass Media.* New York, Pantheon Books.

Hillyard, P. *et al.* (2004) *Beyond Criminology: Taking Harm Seriously.* London: Pluto.

Hillyard, P., Sim, J., Tombs, S. and Whyte, D. (2004) Leaving a stain on the silence, *British Journal of Criminology.*

Hirst, P. (1975) Marx and Engels on law, crime and morality, in I. Taylor *et al.* (eds), *Critical Criminology.* London: Routledge and Kegan Paul.

Hogg, R. and Carrington, K. (eds) (2002) *Critical Criminology: Issues, Debates and Challenges.* Cullompton: Willan.

Horowitz, I. L. (1979) *Constructing Policy.* New York: Praeger Press.

Hunt, A. and Cain, M. (eds) (1979) *Marx and Engels on Law,* London: Academic Press.

Kinsey, R., Lea, J. and Young, J. (1986) *Losing the Fight Against Crime.* Oxford: Blackwell.

Jones, T., MacLean, B. and Young, J. (1986) *The Islington Crime Survey.* Aldershot: Gower.

Lea, J. (1979) Discipline and capitalist development, in B. Fine *et al.* (eds), *Capitalism and the Rule of Law: from Deviancy to Marxism.* London: Hutchinson.

Lea, J. and Young, J. (1984) *What is to be Done about Law and Order?* Harmondsworth: Penguin.

Mathiesen, T. (1974) *The Politics of Abolition.* London: Martin Robertson.

Matthews, R. (1979) 'Decarceration' and the fiscal crisis in B. Fine *et al.* (eds), *Capitalism and the Rule of Law: From Deviancy Theory to Marxism.* London: Hutchinson.

Matthews, R. and Young, J. (eds) (1986) *Confronting Crime.* London: Sage.

Matthews, R. and Young, J. (eds) (1992a) *Rethinking Criminology: The Realist Debate.* London: Sage.

Matthews, R. and Young, J. (eds) (1992b) *Issues in Realist Criminology.* London: Sage.

Mills, C. W. (1959) *The Sociological Imagination.* New York: Oxford University Press.

National Deviance Conference (1979) *Permissiveness and Control: the Fate of Sixties Legislation.* Basingstoke: MacMillan.

Platt, A. and Takagi, T. (1977) Intellectuals for law and order: a critique of the 'new' realists, *Crime and Social Justice* 8 (Fall/Winter).

Poulantzas, N. (1978) *State, Power and Socialism.* London: Verso.

Quinney, R. (1974a) *The Social Reality of Crime.* Little, Brown.

Quinney, R. (1974b) *Critique of Legal Order.* Little, Brown.

Reiner, R. (1988) British criminology and the state, in P. Rock (ed.), *A History of British Criminology.* Oxford: Clarendon Press.

Rock, P. (1973) *Deviant Behaviour.* London: Hutchinson.

Rock, P. (1979) Sociology of deviance, in D. Downes and P. Rock (eds), *Deviant Interpretations.* Oxford: Oxford University Press.

Schwendinger, H. and Schwendinger, J. (1970) Defenders of order or guardians of human rights, *Issues in Criminology* 5: 123–157.

Scraton, P. (ed.) (1987) *Law, Order and the Authoritarian State: Readings in Critical Criminology.* Milton Keynes: Open University Press.

Scraton, P. and Chadwick, K. (1991) Challenging the new orthodoxies: the theoretical and political priorities of critical criminology, in K. Stenson and D. Cowell (eds), *The Politics of Crime Control.* London: Sage.

Scraton, P. (2002) Defining 'power' and challenging 'knowledge': critical analysis and resistance in the UK, in R. Hogg and K. Carrington (eds), *Critical Criminology: Issues, Debates and Challenges.* Cullompton: Willan.

Scraton, P. (2005) The authoritarian within: reflections on power, knowledge and resistance. http://www.statewatch.org/news/2005

Shearing, C. and Stenning, P. (1985) From the panopticon to the Disneyworld: the development of discipline, in A. N. Doob and E. L. Greenspan (eds), *Perspectives in Criminal Law*. Aurora: Canadian Law Book Co.

Taylor, I. (1982) *Law and Order: Arguments for Socialism*.

Taylor, I. (1999) *Crime in Context: a Critical Criminology of Market Societies*. Cambridge: Polity.

Taylor, I. and Walton, P. (1970) Values in deviancy theory and society, *The British Journal of Sociology*, 21(4): 362–74.

Taylor, I. and Taylor, L. (eds) (1973) *Politics and Deviance: Papers from the National Deviancy Conference*. Harmondsworth: Penguin.

Taylor, I., Walton, P. and Young, J. (1973) *The New Criminology*. London: Routledge and Kegan Paul.

Taylor, I., Walton, P. and Young, J. (1975a) *Critical Criminology*. London: Routledge and Kegan Paul.

Taylor, I., Walton, P. and Young, J. (1975b) Critical criminology in Britain: review and prospects, in I. Taylor *et al.* (1975a) *Critical Criminology*. London: Routledge and Kegan Paul.

Walters, R. (2007) Critical criminology and the intensification of the authoritarian state, in A. Barton *et al.* (2006) *Expanding the Criminological Imagination*. Cullompton: Willan.

Young, J. (1975) Working class criminology, in I. Taylor *et al.* (eds), *Critical Criminology*. London: Routledge.

Young, J. (1979) Left idealism, reformism and beyond: from new criminology to Marxism, in B. Fine *et al.* (eds), *Capitalism and the Rule of Law: from Deviancy to Marxism*. London: Hutchinson.

Young, J. (1992) Ten points of realism, in R. Matthews and J. Young (eds), *Rethinking Criminology: The Realist Debate*. London: Sage.

Young, J. (2002) Critical criminology in the twenty-first century: critique, irony and the always unfinished, in K. Carrington and R. Hogg (eds), *Critical Criminology: Issues, Debates, Challenges*. Cullompton: Willan.

9

Integrative Criminology

Gregg Barak

As a recently established and yet still emerging area of the criminological enterprise 'integrative criminology' means different things to different criminologists. In other words, working within, across, and beyond the classical, positivist, and critical traditions are diverse criminologists effectively integrating a myriad of related phenomena and social relations. Narrowly conceived, integrative criminology is commonly and falsely reduced to the praxis of theoretical integration. Broadly conceived, the praxis of integrative criminology includes of course theory integration, but it also represents the efforts of those criminologists who are creating and transforming an ever expanding 'inclusive' criminology, whether they are, for example, actively incorporating a 'feminist' criminology,[1] developing a 'global' criminology[2] or problematizing a 'green' criminology.[3] The point being, there are literally countless ways of doing integrative criminology that may or may not be directly related to theoretical integration. The only limitations to what integrative criminology can become are limited only by our lack of critical imaginations.

Hence, if criminology adopts a broader view of integration in general or if criminologists take a macro–micro approach to integrative criminology in particular[4] there is a synergy between these diverse yet related criminological endeavors that I argue are consistent with the very *raison d'etre* of integrative criminology: defined as an 'interdisciplinary approach to understanding crime and crime control which incorporates at least two disciplinary (or non-disciplinary) bodies of knowledge. This incorporation of criminologies and other bodies of knowledge aspire to encompass any and all data, theories and methods that shed light on the production of crime, criminals and social control, including the field of criminology itself'.[5]

Viewed comprehensively, multiple strands of investigation, examination, and incorporation constitute integrative criminology. Few integrative criminologists, however, work from the vantage point of trying to integrate these divergent practices of integrative criminology whose umbrella covers the more traditional modernist and the more critical post-modernist integrations, the former synthesizing theories and the latter synthesizing bodies of knowledge.[6] More generally, most criminologists when they think of criminological integration think primarily of combining single theories, or elements of those theories, into a more comprehensive statement. At the same time, the field of criminology is experiencing a 'hybridization' of sorts where integration has through a shared narrative discourse spawned and/or merged with other interactive, developmental, life-course, and reciprocal approaches to crime and justice, violence and nonviolence, or war and peace[7] that have yielded a resonating cadre of integrative analyses reflecting on what appears to be an ever expanding or evolving criminological perspective.

At the beginning of the twenty-first century the suggestion of an 'inclusive' criminology means critically integrating the extensive variety of theoretical positions, traditional, emergent and imaginative that constitutes the inter- and intra-disciplines of criminology. When broadly conceived, an integrative criminology also represents a part of the criminological enterprise engaged in the search for an allusive 'meta-narrative' or 'logical narrative' capable of accommodating the numerous criminologies at work. Philosophically, an integrative criminology can strive towards the 'transdisciplinary' integration of the natural and social sciences along with the arts, laws, and the humanities – including evolutionary biology and cognitive neuroscience, psychoanalysis and social psychology, visual representation and media consumption, politics of law and justice, and the political economy of the globalization of crime and social control.

A BRIEF HISTORICAL OVERVIEW

Some would claim that integrative criminology was instigated at the time that criminology began exploring beyond the boundaries of sociology in the 1970s:

> Our failure to achieve much in the way of understanding the causal sequences of crime is in part a reflection of our slowness in moving toward multidisciplinary, integrated theoretical structures. The fact is that for two-thirds of [the last] century, as criminology developed, we remained committed to a small number of sociological models for which there is extensive proof of their important but limited value. Fortunately in the last 20 years, this has begun to change. Today [1997] we see under way substantial research efforts that are based upon models of explanation that far exceed the traditional sociological approaches.[8]

Actually, the roots of integrative criminology may be traced back both to some of the earlier twentieth century sociological work done by Merton (1938), Sutherland (1947), Cohen (1955), and Cloward and Ohlin (1960) and to the social-psychological work done by Tarde (1890), Fromm (1931), Mead (1934), Maslow (1959), and Halleck (1967).[9]

However, it was not until C. Ray Jeffery made one of the earliest explicit cases for integration in his textbook *Criminology: An Interdisciplinary Approach* (1990) that integration moved beyond theories of causation and the debate over the value of integrating these theories to the field of criminology as a whole. Jeffery argued specifically that the time had come for criminology to integrate bodies of knowledge from biology, psychology, sociology, law and other fields. A few years later, he argued that what was required to facilitate the development of crime prevention was an integration of both a theory of crime and a theory of criminal behavior.[10] To accomplish this type of integrative criminology, Jeffery has maintained further that the field must develop an interdisciplinary theory of general behavior and then apply it to explanations of both crime and criminal behavior.

In *Integrating Criminologies* (1998) written during the 'gestation' period of the emerging integrative paradigm, Barak argued for a merging of the goals and objectives of conventional and critical criminologies. Similarly, he argued for an integration of modernist and postmodernist approaches to criminology. More recently, Mathew Robinson in his book, *Why Crime? An Integrated Systems Theory of Antisocial Behavior* (2004), argues for an interdisciplinary perspective that focuses 'on human behavior generally and maladaptive behaviors in particular, rather than those behaviors proscribed by law'. By utilizing an integrated systems perspective that examines factors at all levels of analysis, including the cell, organ, organism, group, community/organization, and society, and by also assuming that every behavior is a person–environment event or interaction, Robinson claims this 'allows various factors which have been identified by numerous academic disciplines to be discussed and meaningfully integrated or synthesized into a coherent theoretical explanation of behavior without reinforcing disciplinary boundaries'.[11]

Most recently, Anthony Walsh and Lee Ellis in *Criminology: An Interdisciplinary Approach* (2007) remind us that while criminology is the study of an interdisciplinary/multidisciplinary enterprise, it nevertheless 'has yet to integrate these disciplines in any comprehensive way'. At the same time, utilizing social, psychosocial, and biosocial perspectives they argue interactively that 'the probability of moving from law-abiding to law-breaking behavior' is a function of:

> Evolutionary forces lead to species-specific genomes. Each person has a unique genotype. These genotypes lead to differential central and peripheral nervous system functioning. This functioning is modified by the person's developmental history. Working together, the person's temperament and developmental history form his or her personality. This personality may often lead the person to different situations and lead him or her to appraise those situations differently from other persons. The behavior elicited from that appraisal is thus the result of every thing that preceded it, plus pure chance.

Additionally, Walsh and Ellis maintain that because crime rates change drastically from time to time without a corresponding change in the gene pool or personalities of the people, that 'changing sociocultural environments must be the only causes of changing crime rates';[12] supporting an analysis of integration that is implicitly quite similar or analogous to the two-prong model of crime and criminal behavior proposed by Jeffery.

CORE IDEAS AND KEY CONCEPTS

While the debates over the value of integrative criminology have subsided since the early 1990s, and integrative approaches have received legitimacy as they now provide for an obligatory chapter in most criminology textbooks, something that was clearly absent even a decade ago, there still does not seem to be much agreement over what exactly constitutes integration, let alone what the core ideas and key concepts are. Most integrationists, regardless of orientation, however, generally agree that integration may be 'specific', focusing on a single form of criminality like homicide or sexual predators, 'general', focusing on a broader range of criminality such as the 'crimes of the powerful' including governmental, corporate, and organized offenses, or 'specific-general', focusing on related offenses such as sexual harassment, rape, or pedophilia and sexual terrorism more generally.

Beyond this core idea or concept of what can be traditionally integrated, most criminologists when they consider integration, think primarily about theoretical integration or the combination of theories or elements of theories. Historically, these more 'comprehensive' formulations have reflected the positivistic biases of sociological criminology. A review of the criminological literature on theoretical integration in the early 1990s found a strong reliance on strain, followed closely by subcultural, conflict, and Marxist theories. Rarely included were theories of biology, personality, gender, economics or law.[13] Since then, two things have occurred to expand the boundaries of integrative criminology: First, there have actually been the development of new integrative theories, models, and frameworks that are not derivative of or a product of combining already existing theories from only sociology, like the work of Robinson or Walsh and Ellis mentioned above. Second, there has been a rethinking or reformulation of what constitutes integrative criminology to include allied or related models of life-course or developmental or reciprocal criminology.

Though a variety of intellectual (theoretical) strands of integrative criminology will be discussed in the next couple of sections, the different practices of integrative criminology can be dualistically divided between 'modernist' and 'postmodernist' forms of construction and reconstruction. The former, usually more formalistic and singular, takes a relatively narrow and parochial disciplinary-based approach to integration, preferring to integrate theories within sociology, psychology, or biology, for example, rather than across or between these disciplines. The latter, usually more relaxed and layered, takes a relatively broad-gauged and cosmopolitan multi-disciplinary approach to integration, preferring to integrate bodies of knowledge from an array of sites. While each of these forms of 'merging' may be both propositional and conceptual in their synthetic formulations, modern integrations emphasize the centrality of theory in the construction of 'causal models'[14] and postmodern integrations emphasize the changing 'voices of plurality' and reconstruction that provide meaning for the local sites of crime, justice, law, and community.[15]

More specifically, modernist formulations of criminological integration have tended to be either conceptual revealing how concepts from one theory are shown to overlap in meaning with concepts from another theory or they have been propositional underscoring the related propositions from different theories; the former arguing on behalf of shared or similar ideas, the latter linking separate theories by a common principle. Modernist theories may also be divided into those that assume a more static-oriented or consensus model and those that assume a more dynamic-oriented or conflict model:

> The 'static state' theories would include those emphasizing organized structures and objectively measurable social roles, containing individuals with limited internal attributes and a limited capacity for spontaneity, as in biological, early personality theories based on rational choice. The 'dynamic state' theories would include those giving more weight to subjective interpretation, negotiated and spontaneous interaction, informal and creative process, and conflicts between differences, such as labeling theory, social constructionism, and anarchist criminology.[16]

By contrast, postmodern integrationists are concerned less about theories than about knowledges. Rather than pursuing the cause–effect predictions of theoretical integration or the synthesis of theories of crime and/or social control within or between a couple of disciplines, these integrationists formulate explanatory models of crime and social control that connect, link, or cut across and through a whole range of multi- and interdisciplinary knowledges. For example, scholars of 'state-corporate' crime such as Ron Kramer, David Kauzlarich, and Rick Mathews take as their starting point 'an examination of the intersection of state and corporate actions on three levels of analysis: individual, institutional, and structural or societal'.[17] In brief, their integrative models or framework strives to 'unite the three levels of social experience that constitute the dialectical totality of human life'.[18]

Finally, postmodernist integrationists argue that crime and crime control are recursive productions or routinized activities that cannot be separated from historically and culturally specific discourses and structures that have retained a relative stability over time and place.[19] As such these integrationists argue that it is important to ground their integrations of crime and justice, war and peace, law and order, and so on and so forth, within the context of mass communications and globalization. In turn, these types of analysis or examination allow for an integration of theory and practice.[20]

CONTEMPORARY STRANDS OF INTEGRATIVE CRIMINOLOGY

Informal and formal integration today consists of the convergence of at least three recent theoretical strands within the criminological enterprise: 'developmental', 'life-course', and 'reciprocal' theories of human behavior. Stated affirmatively, each of these criminological strands or emerging 'schools' of criminological thinking exemplifies the indispensability of the integrative paradigm to criminology today. In fact, regardless of the similarities and dissimilarities between those theories associated with each of these strands, I would argue that what they all share fundamentally in common are their integrative approaches to the problem of individual–environment relationships and how these experiences set up pathways toward and/or away from antisocial behavior, deviance, delinquency, crime, or violence. Finally, each of these integrative schemata relies conceptually on notions of interaction and intersection, and operationally each of these explanatory models relies on a myriad of complexities and conditions. These are not simple 'cause-and-effect' analyses of antisocial behavior or crime because they are all contingent on a multiplicity of dynamic variables.

In the rest of this section I provide an overview of each of these related strands of integrative criminology, providing more cursory samplings from developmental and reciprocal criminologies than from life-course criminologies because the latter is better known and also because these seem to blend with the other two.

Developmental criminology

Gerald Patterson and colleagues have offered up a 'social-interactional' developmental model of delinquency where children and their environments are in constant interchange. According to this schema, when the actions of children elicit negative

reactions, children will in turn act in antisocial ways that elicit more counterproduc-
tive reactions causing a spiraling of 'action–reaction' sequences that over time
increase the risks for long-term social maladjustment and criminal behavior. In
explaining *early-onset delinquency*, Patterson, DeBarshy, and Ramsey observed that
antisocial behavior 'appears to be a developmental trait that begins early in life and
often continues into adolescence and adulthood'.[21] Their explanatory framework of
antisocial predispositions also relies on a social learning framework where they
contend that family members directly train children to perform antisocial behavior.
In turn, as these antisocial children move out into the world, they manifest 'child
conduct problems', performing poorly in school and often acting out aggressively
toward other children and suffering rejection from the 'normal peer group' which
propels these youths in late childhood and early adolescence toward 'deviant peer
group membership' that positively reinforces antisocial behavior, thereby consoli-
dating these youths' involvement in misconduct.[22]

While 'early starters' in antisocial behavior is largely a theory of continuity in
offending, in which social-interactional processes increasingly constrain individuals
to deviant life courses or pathways, Patterson and Karen Yoerger a few years later
proposed a developmental model for *late-onset delinquency* that they explain by way
of a 'marginality hypothesis'. In a nutshell, these children and youths do not grow
up in 'dysfunctional' families marked by extreme early deficits that set in motion
antisocial behavior during childhood. But rather these 'late starters' in antisocial
behavior, live primarily marginally disadvantaged lives with marginally effective
child-rearing techniques that meet their match or causal mechanism in the 'deviant
peer group'. Finally, Patterson and Yoerger contend that comparatively speaking,
late-onset delinquents are less likely to persist and more likely to desist from serious
offending than early-onset delinquents.[23]

Similarly, Terrie Moffitt's *life-course-persistent/adolescence-limited theory* is
another developmental model, which contends that antisocial behavior is by continuity or by change:

> For delinquents whose criminal activity is confined to the adolescent years, the casual factors
> may be proximal, specific to the period of adolescent development, and theory must account
> for the *dis*continuity in their lives. In contrast, for persons whose adolescent delinquency
> is merely one infliction in a continuous lifelong antisocial course, a theory of antisocial
> behavior must locate its causal factors in early childhood and must explain the continuity in
> their troubled lives.[24]

Moffitt argues further that each of these two distinct types of antisocial offenders
have unique natural histories and etiologies.

In the case of the life-course-persistent theory of antisocial behavior, 'children's
neuropsychological problems interact cumulatively with their criminogenic environments across development, culminating in a pathological personality'.[25] In the case
of the adolescence-limited theory of antisocial behavior, 'a contemporary maturity
gap encourages teens to mimic antisocial behavior in ways that are normative and
adjustive'.[26] Comparatively, the antisocial behavior of these teens is temporary, situational, and less extreme than the antisocial behavior of the adults who were children
with neuropsychological and environmental problems, represented by a relatively
small number of males whose behavioral problems are acute, stable, and persistent
over the life course.

A continuity of antisocial behavior throughout the life course is what constitutes the life-course-persistent antisocial persons. Moffitt locates the roots of stable anti-social behavior in factors that are present before or soon after birth. She hypothesizes that 'the etiological chain begins with some factor capable of producing individual differences in the neuropsychological functions of the infant nervous system'.[27] Moreover, Moffitt identifies three person–environment interactions that she believes are important in promoting an antisocial style and maintaining its continuity across the life course. These interactions include the most influential one, *evocative*, and two others, *reactive* and *proactive*.

Evocative interaction refers to that which occurs when a child's behavior evokes distinct responses from others, even the most resourceful, loving, and patient fami-lies. Moffitt continues that once the evocative interactions are set in motion, reactive and proactive interactions promote the further extension or continuity and pervasive-ness of antisocial behavior throughout the life course, as long as the same underlying constellation of traits that got a person into trouble as a child remain intact. Ultimately, at the core of her explanation of life-course-persistent antisocial behav-ior is a theory that 'emphasizes the constant process of reciprocal interaction between personal traits and environmental reactions to them'.[28]

Another developmental theory trajectory changes the emphases to the cognitive mind sets of the offenders over time and to their human agency and the ability to alter, change, desist, or transform their perceptions of their past, present, and future. In short, what do criminals think about themselves and their criminality? Shaad Maruna's *theory of redemption scripts* exemplifies this developmental perspective in life-course criminology.[29] What Maruna wanted to unravel was how and why did those individuals with dismal futures and multiple risk factors for antisocial behavior transcend their persistent long-term patterns of criminal behavior? In other words, despite a combination of 'criminogenic traits', 'criminogenic backgrounds', and 'criminogenic environments' there were those who were able to desist from contin-ued antisocial behavior.

Maruna argued that what separated desisting offenders from persisting offenders were different phenomenological orientations as well as markedly different cogni-tive understandings of their lives in crime. Like all of us, 'desisters' and 'persisters' also have life stories or narratives that give meaning to their lives. What separated these two groups of offenders, in other words, were the 'scripts' that each used to describe their long-term criminality. Persistent offenders spoke in terms of their being 'doomed to deviance' and of their being 'condemned' to lives of crime due to circumstances beyond their control. In contrast, offenders who had desisted and were 'making good' spoke in terms of a 'rhetoric of redemption' or 'redemption script' that distorts the 'grim realities of their past lives' while ignoring their struc-tural and situation realities.

In the end, although these redemption scripts circumscribe these desisters past criminal behavior as circumstantial and not derivative of their true natures, helping them to reconstruct their identifies as 'stronger' persons because of their ability to overcome their past conditions and take control of their lives, the proverbial chicken-and-egg question remains as to whether these scripts of redemption precipitate a movement away from crime or emerge after the fact, serving to reinforce a nascent prosocial experiment.[30]

Life-course criminology

Generally, the life-course perspectives aim to connect the social meanings of age throughout the lifespan, the intergenerational transmission of social patterns, and the effects of social history and social structure to the study of human behavior over time.[31] Applied to the study of criminal behavior, the life-course perspective through conceptualizations of 'trajectories' and 'transitions' allows for an understanding of the initiation, persistence, desistance, and/or changing nature of offending behavior over the course of a person's life. For a comprehensive review of life-course criminology, see the edited reader by Piquero and Mazerolle.[32] For probably the best-known example in criminology, I turn to the work of Robert Sampson and John Laub.

Overlapping with the developmental models explored by Patterson and his colleagues and by Huang *et al.,* is Sampson and Laub's theory of *informal social control and cumulative disadvantage* that challenged Moffitt's integrative schema by reframing the talk of a 'cascade' of secondary problems (e.g., school failure, peer rejection, depressed mood, and involvement with deviant peers) and of antisocial traits as a 'chimera' of socially constructed and interactive aspects of racial, socio-economic, and structural locations.[33] Their explanation of antisocial behavior argues that there are important events and conditions that alter and redirect deviant pathways. Initially, they introduced a *theory of age-graded informal social control* to explain the continuity of crime from childhood to adolescence to adulthood.[34] Their revised theory on desistance from law breaking in *Shared Beginnings, Divergent Lives* is built upon three related themes from their earlier work.

First, structural factors or conditions such as poverty or racism affect the development of social bonds. Second, a combination of social conditions and labeling processes can lead to cumulative disadvantage and the stability of the life span. Third, the development of social capital later in life, especially during adulthood, can alter antisocial trajectories toward conformity. What holds Sampson and Laub's theory of cumulative disadvantage together is 'a dynamic conceptualization of social control over the life course, integrated with' what they contend is 'the one theoretical perspective in criminology that is inherently developmental in nature – labeling theory'.[35]

Their theory also emphasizes the interactive nature of labeling, identity formation, the exclusion from normal routines and conventional opportunities, and the increased contact with and relative support from other deviant or antisocial subgroups. Together, these myriad of factors converge to create a cumulative disadvantage. More specifically, Sampson and Laub argue that 'the cumulative continuity of disadvantage is thus not only a result of stable individual differences in criminal propensity, but a dynamic process whereby childhood antisocial behavior and adolescent delinquency foster adult crime through the severance of adult social bonds'.[36] Similarly, the processes of desistance from offending or discontinuity are connected to the same trajectories or pathways of the causal sequential link in the chain of adversity between early childhood delinquency and adult criminal behavior as articulated in the constraints of four key institutions of social control: family, school, peers, and state sanctions.

What Sampson and Laub discovered by further studying the 500 males from the Gluecks' data was that first, as adults everyone sooner or later desists from breaking the law, and second, it is difficult to predict when desistance will occur.

Nevertheless, they do identify five aspects to the process of desisting during adulthood. Consistent with their earlier theorizing, they argue that structural 'turning points' like marriage and employment set the stage for change and that these, in turn, create social bonds that increase the informal controls over offenders. At the same time, their daily routine activities change from the unstructured and those focused on deviance or deviant locations to those structured and filled with prosocial responsibilities. And, in turn, there becomes a shifting in priorities away from deviancy and toward conformity or 'desistance by default'. These former offenders now possess investments and bonds of commitment that were previously lacking; thereby, weaning them off or away from their heretofore-criminogenic lifestyles. Finally, Sampson and Laub argue that what ultimately holds this transformation of their lives together is human agency or the choices they make, not the desistance process itself. In other words, interactively the desistance process may constrain, but it does not determine.[37]

Reciprocal criminology

One of the earliest reciprocal formulations within criminology was Terence Thornberry's *interactional theory of delinquency* that posited that 'adolescents interact with other people and institutions' and that their 'behavioral outcomes are formed by that interactive process'.[38] Thornberry's schema integrates social control and social learning theories and he argued, among other things, that social relationships between parents and children are dynamic rather than stable, that they could change over time, and that delinquents are not only influenced by their environments but that they, too, have an impact on others through their behavior. In short, like human behavior in general that occurs in social interaction, the same was true of delinquency, and as such both were a part of an 'interactive system'.[39] More importantly, Thornberry's model illustrated that relationships between variables are neither constant nor unidirectional. They could move in either direction. What's more he contended that delinquent relationships were *reciprocal* or 'embedded in a set of mutually reinforcing causal networks'. [40]

That is to say, Thornberry argued that the variables involved in social control and social learning had 'reciprocal effects' on the other. In other words, the two sets of variables interacted with each other so, for example, weak parental relations might make delinquent associations more likely, or delinquent associations might weaken attachments to parents. Similarly, peer associations may cause delinquent behavior; then again, delinquent behavior may affect friendship choices. Accordingly, Thornberry noted that these interactive or reciprocal processes were capable of creating a 'behavioral trajectory,' what life-course criminologists would ultimately refer to as 'cumulative disadvantage', that 'predicts increasing involvement in delinquency and crime' do to the reinforcing and combining factors of 'weak bonds', delinquent peer associations', and 'delinquency'.[41]

Thornberry also realized that during the life-course, variables may lose or gain importance and change over time. As parents become less important and peers become more important, as youths and adolescents succeed or fail in school, or as new variables emerge, such as work, college, military service, marriage, and so on and so forth, that one's bonds to conventional society ebb and flow determining whether delinquency will continue or desist.

Mark Colvin in *Crime and Coercion: An Integrated Theory of Chronic Criminality* (2000) argues that chronic criminals 'emerge from a developmental process that is punctuated by recurring erratic episodes of coercion. They become both the recipients and the perpetuators of coercion, entrapped in a dynamic that propels them along a pathway toward chronic criminality'.[42] Colvin's reciprocal *differential coercion theory* is not unlike a blending of Sutherland's *differential association* and Regoli and Hewitt's *differential oppression theory*[43] in that each of these models recognizes the variations in which people are exposed to sources of learning, oppression, coercion, and so on, and how these, in turn, reinforce and propel cumulative responses of chronic antisocial behavior. Differential coercion, Colvin argues, is key to understanding where a sense of unfairness and anger (general strain theory), weak or alienated bonds (social bond theory), coercive modeling (social learning theory), perceived control deficits with feelings of debasement (control balance theory), and low self-control (Gottfredson and Hirschi's general theory) come from, and where ultimately, these 'social psychological deficits' generate within individuals a *coercive ideation*.[44] In other words, Colvin's model maintains that coercive and erratic controls produce many of the factors that other theorists believe cause crime. His theory 'easily' integrates these allegedly competing explanations of crime and delinquency.

More specifically, Colvin distinguishes between those social environments where compliance is secured through noncoercive means and those where compliance is secured through coercive means. His argument in a nutshell is that those individuals over the life-course who are subjected to environments where coercion is harsh and inconsistent are more likely to develop strong criminal predispositions and to engage in chronic offending. In his four-cell model, controls can be either *coercive* or *noncoercive* and they can be either *consistent* or *erratic*. Combinations of consistent noncoercive controls create psychologically healthy youths, less likely to break the law. Combinations of coercive erratic controls create habitual offenders.

Importantly, Colvin defines coercion in a way that reflects both individual and structural realities and he operationalizes his model as an intergenerational one. First, he distinguishes between *interpersonal* and *impersonal* forms of coercion. The former referring to the 'threat of force and intimidation aimed at creating compliance through fear' and may involve not simply physical punishments, but the psychological withdrawal of love and support; the latter referring to the 'pressure arising from structural arrangements and circumstances that seem beyond individual control such as economic and social pressure caused by unemployment, poverty, or competition among businesses or other groups.[45] Moreover, interpersonal and impersonal forms of coercion often intersect in the same environment, increasing the likelihood of chronic offending.

Second, Colvin builds into his reciprocal causal model of chronic offending both a developmental and intergenerational integration succinctly captured in the fourth edition of *Criminological Theory: Context and Consequences* (2007) by Lilly, Cullen, and Ball:

> The process begins with parents who come from coercive backgrounds, are employed in coercive workplaces, and are buffeted by impersonal coercive forces (e.g., economic recessions, poverty, racism, harsh living conditions). Such parents then reproduce themselves, so to speak, by using coercive and erratic child-rearing techniques. Their social psychological deficits and coercive ideation are thus transmitted to their children. In turn, these youngsters

enter social environment – school, peer groups, and so on – where they experience harsh controls, further reinforcing their deficits and coercive thinking orientation. As they move into early adulthood, they tend to be employed in the secondary labor market, which fails to lift them out of poverty and exposes them to coercive working conditions. Often, they are ensnared in the criminal justice system, where they experience more coercive treatment. These factors across the life course continually nourish coercive ideation and criminal predispositions, thereby placing these individuals at risk for chronic criminality. Eventually, these offenders will reproduce their experiences in a subsequent generation of youths.[46]

Finally, I turn to my own integrative and *reciprocal theory of violence and nonviolence*. Initially introduced in *Violence and Nonviolence: Pathways to Understanding* (2003) and further refined in the edited volume, *The Essential Criminology Reader* (2006),[47] my model is derivative of all of the theories discussed and citations found in this section, and it is particularly informed by Huang *et al.'s* The Social Development Model of Prosocial and Antisocial Behavior and influenced by Charles Tittle's Control Balance Theory, original and fine-tuned, discussed in the next section.[48] Incorporating these divergent and intertwined newer epistemological approaches to prosocial and antisocial behavior, I assume a complexity of human, institutional, and structural interacting variables that cut across the full range of behavioral motivations and cultural constraints. At the same time, I add to these interacting models by treating the interactions between the interpersonal, institutional, and structural relations of violence and nonviolence.

I argue that it is not enough to examine the life-course or developmental trajectories of assets and deficits experienced by individuals leading to their 'prosocial' and 'antisocial' interactions, but that it is also necessary to examine the 'life-course', 'developmental', and 'reciprocal' interactions between the interpersonal histories of violence and nonviolence and the institutional and structural histories of violence and nonviolence. In other words, a comprehensive explanation of violence and nonviolence requires a model that can account for (1) the reciprocal and cumulative effects that lead to, sustain, or desist violent and nonviolent outcomes, and (2) the dynamic interactions between the dialectics of adversarialism and mutualism that commonly intersect virtually all individuals, groups, and nation-states alike. In short, my theoretical model is integrative because it not only addresses 'properties' of violence and nonviolence as two sides of the same fundamental set of relations, but it is also inclusive of virtually all of the 'pathways' to violent and nonviolent behavior or to the 'causal' agents or variables found in integrative and nonintegrative theories of crime and violence alike.

More specifically, I argue that when it comes to the reciprocity of violent and nonviolent properties and pathways, there are a diversity of expressions that operate across a two-sided continuum of interpersonal, institutional, and structural relations of social and cultural organization that simultaneously promote violence (adversarialism) and/or nonviolence (mutualism). I also argue that the interconnections between the interpersonal, institutional, and structural spheres constitute a reciprocal playing field where the pathways to violence and nonviolence are mutually reinforced, resisted, or negotiated by individuals and collectivities alike based on constellations and 'tipping points' on a two-sided continuum of or struggle within the properties for and against violence and nonviolence.

Properties of violence, both unsanctioned and sanctioned, refer to those attributes, characteristics, elements, factors, situations, routines, hot spots, and other conditions, including the negative emotional states involving feelings of alienation, shame, humiliation, mortification, rejection, abandonment, denial, depression, anger, hostility, projection, and displacement. Properties of violence may also include a lack of the emotional states associated with the properties of nonviolence such as empathy and compassion stemming from experiences of love, security, attachment, support, bonding, identification, altruism, and mutualism. Briefly, to the extent that individuals and groups feel abandoned by or bonded with their parents, peers, schools, communities, tribes, nations, and to other social groupings and subcultural stratifications based on age, gender, class, religion, ethnicity, and sexual orientation, or to the extent that people experience connection or disconnection, they are more or less likely to relate or not relate, to identify or not identify, to empathize or not empathize, to take or not take responsibility, to be anxious and uptight or contented and calm, to project or not project hostility/aggression, to engage in warmaking or peacemaking, or to make violence or nonviolence.

Pathways to violence and nonviolence refer to the 'familiar', 'subcultural', and 'cultural' transitions or trajectories that may coalesce around the constellations of violent and nonviolent properties. Hence, not only are each of the interpersonal, institutional, and structural spheres of violence and nonviolence capable of reinforcing and/or resisting the influences of each other, but an examination of the interactions of all three spheres reveals the possibility of nine divergent pathways to violence or nonviolence. Finally, the theory argues that as the interpersonal, institutional, and structural spheres of violence/nonviolence and as the three essential pathways to violence/nonviolence converge in time and space, then at least three things occur: (1) the severity or intensity of violence/nonviolence swells in magnitude; (2) the actions of violence/nonviolence become more or less prevalent; and (3) the distinguishing factors of the spheres of interpersonal, institutional, and structural violence/nonviolence became less distinct.

In sum, as the three spheres or levels of violence/nonviolence intersect, the reciprocal theory of violence and nonviolence hypothesizes three things. First, that the properties of violence and nonviolence are cumulative both 'in' and 'over' time. The more (or fewer) properties characteristic of violence and nonviolence, and the longer in the life-courses that either one is sustained, the more or less likely it is that violence or nonviolence will occur. Second, as the familiar, subcultural, and cultural pathways to violence and nonviolence combine, overlap, and intersect, expressions of violence/nonviolence will become more or less intense and, conversely, more or less common. Third, both the properties of and the pathways to violence and nonviolence are reciprocally and inversely related at the same time. In other words, properties and pathways are dialectically related, capable of reinforcing, resisting, and/or desisting from violence or nonviolence.

A CRITICAL REVIEW OF THE INCLUDED AND EXCLUDED STRANDS

To begin, I would argue that a 'critical review of the contemporary status of the perspective' of integrative criminology is problematic for at least three reasons. First, as I have already noted there is no agreement over what constitutes 'integrative criminology'.

Second, much of what I am arguing represents some of the most innovative, interesting and promising strands of integrative work in criminology has not been recognized as 'integrative criminology'. Third, until there is a definitional consensus or a paradigmatic recognition of what constitutes an 'inclusive' integrative criminology the status of the perspective will remain undervalued and underused.

My critique of the status of the perspective of integrative criminology revolves around the misunderstanding that reductively treats theoretical integration as the whole of integrative criminology when, in reality, theory development, propositional or conceptual, is only one significant expression or form of integration. Other forms of integrating crime, criminals, social control, history, political economy, human nature, evolutionary biology, mass communication, and globalization exist beyond theoretical integration, but not beyond theorizing or explanatory model building. This is an important distinction that I believe is lost on most criminologists at this point in time. Sure many criminologists today, post the integrative value and use debates still lingering in some quarters after some twenty years,[49] are now willing to include 'theory integration' at the criminological buffet, but there are other offerings that have not yet found a place in the integrative smorgasbord of criminology.

At the same time, since the 1970s to the present, there have been, for example, more than a few theories, some implicitly integrative such as Richard Quinney's conflict theory found in *The Social Reality of Crime* (1974) or his Marxist theories found in the first and second editions of *Class, State, and Crime: On the Theory and Practice of Criminal Justice* (1977, 1980), and some explicitly integrative like Stephen Box's *integrated theory of the crimes of the powerful* found in *Power, Crime, and Mystification* (1983) or Howard Kaplan's *self-esteem/self derogation theory* of adolescent deviance found in *Self-Attitudes and Deviant Behavior* (1975) or Becky Tatum's *neocolonial model of adolescent crime and violence* (1995, 1996)[50] or Kauzlarich and Kramer's 'integrated framework' found in *Crimes of the American Nuclear State: At Home and Abroad* (1998) that are rarely thought about and/or discussed when one entertains integrative theory or integrative criminology. More recently, however, I believe that this is beginning to change. For example, the first edition of *Class, Race, Gender, and Crime: The Social Realities of Justice in America* (2001)[51] was generally reviewed as either a *socially constructed* or *oppressive* theoretical orientation to criminal justice, and the second edition (2007)[52] has already been reviewed as an *integrated model of class, race, gender, and crime* which is exactly what it set out to become.

As part of my critique of the 'omission' or 'lack' when it comes to integrative theory in particular and to integrative criminology in general, I feel obliged to elaborate a bit more on the nature of the evaluative problem or status of the perspective by probing Tittle's *control balance theory* and the 'mixed' review, reception, or assessment that it has received. In my estimation, this mixture reflects whether or not one judges its theoretical value as 'predictive' or as 'heuristic'; the former assessment located within the domain of positivist theoretical integration, the latter assessment located within the domain of inclusive integrative criminology.

Perhaps Tittle's primary contribution to the field of control theories was to emphasize that people are not only 'objects' of control but also 'agents' of control. Each of us, in other words, is subject both to a certain amount of control that we are under and a certain amount of control that we exert. According to control balance theory, Tittle argued that some individuals experience a relative balance between the two countervailing forces of control. When this balance occurs, there is conforming behavior. Others experience what he called control 'deficits' or control 'surpluses'. These cases of control imbalance are associated with antisocial behavior, deviance, and crime. The *control ratio* or 'the amount of control to which an individual is subject, relative to the amount of control he or she can exercise, determines the probability of deviance occurring as well as the type of deviance likely to occur'.[53]

Now then, most criminologists would probably agree that Tittle's theory was innovative and not only added to the complexity of the traditional (e.g., Travis Hirschi) and newer (e.g., John Hagan) control theories that focus on the breakdown or lack of control by arguing, on the contrary, that too much control of a person could result in those crimes typically committed by the powerless or that a person with too much control could result in those crimes typically committed by the powerful. Not only does Tittle turn control theory on its head, but also more fundamentally he moves away from the simpler unidirectional or linearly based models to a two way directional or dialectically based model full of constraints and contingencies. However, as one sympathetic analysis has argued:

> If Tittle merely offered the thesis that control imbalance is criminogenic, then his theory would be *parsimonious* and easily understood. But for Tittle, the causal process of wayward conduct is complex and contingent on the intersection of an array of factors. Tittle's embrace of complexity is a double-edged sword: He sought to capture – not ignore – the multifaceted conditions that prompt misconduct, but his theory involves so many variables that interact in so many ways that it is difficult to test (emphasis added).[54]

So what's a 'positivist' criminologist to do, but reject complexity in favor of parsimony, testing, and predictability that taken together still do not account for most of the variance involved in criminal behavior? I have never been able to figure out why some degree of predictability over what amounts to not much of a 'total' explanation (without taking other partial explanations into account and combining them together) is preferable to a fuller, more comprehensive theory/model that perhaps lacks 'testability' and yet makes a lot more sense describing the phenomena involved. Finally, I do understand that had his theory claimed that control imbalance was criminogenic, that it may indeed have been parsimonious and easily understood, but would it have been more correct? Absolutely not, in fact, it would have been a different theory altogether.

On the other hand, if one thinks heuristically in terms of conceptual rather than propositional theory, then one can live with the nuances of crime and criminal behavior or with the complexity of the social reality that one is trying to explain, even if one cannot test it, easily or otherwise. After all, there are dialectical, reciprocal, and contradictory tendencies at work 'pushing' one both to and not to engage in social and antisocial behavior just as there are tendencies to be aggressive or non-aggressive as in Jeffrey Goldstein's *relational model of aggression*.[55] Criminologists should learn to deal with both sets of tendencies in time and space, whether or not we have historically figured out how to measure those interacting tendencies, for this is also what integrative criminology is all about.

Similarly, though the field has appreciated that Tittle sought to provide a general theory capable of explaining all forms of deviation, initially by way of a control balance continuum of 'repression' (deficits) at one end and of 'autonomy' (surpluses) at the other end,[56] and subsequently by way of a continuum of 'control balance desirability',[57] it has nevertheless devalued these continuums as once again they prove difficult to measure.

What's more there does not seem to be the proper appreciation that what makes Tittle's model a general one is that it is first and foremost an integrative model, seeking to address human nature and motivation as well as socialization and social control.

Folks may disagree with his emphasis on 'autonomy' or the proclivity of humans to escape the control that others might wish to impose on them, preferring, for example, those models that address self-gratification or the avoidance of pain, discomfort, and harm as each of these probably plays a role. Others may take issue with his model demoting the causal variables of self-control, social bonds, and social learning to the secondary role of constraints and contingencies, but it makes a whole lot of sense from an integrative point of view. Within the limited frame of positivist criminology, the challenge becomes to pit control balance theory in an empirical contest against other theories; within the more expansive frame of integrative criminology, the challenge becomes to appreciate the newer way of looking at social control and to build on that.

FUTURE PROSPECTS

I am optimistic about the future developments of integrative criminology whether viewed narrowly and exclusively as positivist theory integration and prediction, or broadly and inclusively as post-postmodern syntheses of incorporated bodies of knowledge. In terms of traditional or contemporary criminology theory, I believe that there will be an expansion of theoretical integrative models both within and across disciplines. I also believe that these integrative models will increasingly rely on disciplines other than sociology. I further believe there will be more emphasis on conceptual and heuristic models than predictive models whether non-integrative or integrative because when 'push comes to shove' the latter have not been all that worthwhile or productive anyway. Again, I still cannot understand why folks are bothered that they cannot test the complexity of 'good theory' like Tittle's control balance when theories like self-control or social bond even if empirically proven, don't really explain, once again most of the variance, and therefore, are not really an explanation of much of anything without linking, connecting, or integrating such other theories as social control, social learning, social ecology, differential association, opportunity, and so on and so forth.

In terms of the heuristically driven models, narratives, and modernist–postmodernist syntheses that may or may not be testable, I believe that historically criminology has always been an eclectic mix of all kinds and types of criminological strands or knowledges and that crime and crime control as socially constructed phenomena have always represented and will continue to represent that place of intersection where literally all of the bodies and disciplines of knowledge may 'theoretically' converge. In this sense, integration is really quite old, what most folks in the natural and social sciences were doing before the age of specialization came to life in the late nineteenth century. Marx, Weber, and Durkheim, for example, were integrationists in that their models of 'social behavior' were inclusive and certainly met the definition of integrative employed here.

As I noted at the beginning of this essay the only limits to an inclusive criminology are in our minds. In this context, I think criminologists will slowly but surely learn to see the conceptual if not the practical advantages of doing integrative criminology as opposed to 'sectarian' criminology. They will also come to accept and to reconceptualize integrative criminology from that of theory integration to the inclusion of all the different criminologies, including an embracement of the variety of criminological theories, old and new, found within these pages of *The Sage Handbook of Criminological Theory*, and which have had 'staying power' within criminological discourse whether or not they were parsimonious and provable.

NOTES

1 Hatty, S. (2000). *Masculinities, Violence, and Culture*. Thousand Oaks, CA: Sage Publications.

2 Morrison, W. (2006). *Criminology, Civilization and the New World Order*. New York: Routledge-Cavendish.

3 Beirne, P. and South, N. (2007). *Issues in Green Criminology: Confronting Harms against Environments, Humanity and Other Animals*. Portland, OR: Willan Publishing.

4 Barak, G. (2009). *Criminology: An Integrated Approach*, second edition. Lanham, MD: Rowman & Littlefield.

5 Barak, G. (2001). Integrative criminology. In: E. McLaughlin and J. Muncie (eds), *The Sage Dictionary of Criminology*, p. 153. London: Sage Publications.

6 Barak, G. (1998). *Integrating Criminologies*. Boston: Allyn and Bacon.

7 Barak, G. (2003). *Violence and Nonviolence: Pathway to Understanding*. Thousand Oaks, CA: Sage Publications.

8 Wellford, C. (1997). 1996 Presidential Address: Controlling crime and achieving justice, *Criminology*, 35: 1–11.

9 Merton, R. (1938). 'Social structure and anomie, *American Sociological Review*, 3: 672–682. Sutherland, E. (1947). *Criminology* fourth edition. Philadelphia: Lippincott. Cohen, A. (1955). *Delinquent Boys: The Culture of the Gang*. Glencoe, IL: Free Press. Cloward, R. and Ohlin, L. (1960). *Delinquency and Opportunity – A Theory of Delinquent Gangs*. New York: Free Press. Tarde, G. [1890] (1903). *The Laws of Imitation*. Translated by E. Parsons. New York: Henry Holt. Fromm, E. [1931] On the psychology of the criminal and the punitive society, reprinted (2000) in *Erich Fromm and Critical Criminology: Beyond the Punitive Society*, edited by K. Anderson and R. Quinney, pp. 129–56. Translated by H. Osterle and K. Anderson. Urbana and Chicago: University of Illinois Press. Mead, G. (1934). *Mind, Self, and Society*. C. Morris (ed.). Chicago: University of Chicago Press. Maslow, A. (ed.) (1959). *New Knowledge in Human Values*. New York: Harper. Halleck, S. (1967). *Psychiatry and the Dilemmas of Crime*. New York: Harper and Row.

10 Jeffery. C. (1994). Biological and Neuropsychiatric Approaches to Criminal Behavior. In: G. Barak (ed.), *Varieties of Criminology: Readings from a Dynamic Discipline*, pp. 15–28. Westport, CN: Praeger.

11 Robinson, M. (2004). *Why Crime? An Integrated Systems Theory of Antisocial Behavior*, pp. 10–11, 38–39. Upper Saddle River, NJ: Pearson Prentice Hall.

12 Walsh, A. and Ellis, L. (2007). *Criminology: An Interdisciplinary Approach*, pp. 21, 19, 18, and 19. Thousand Oaks, CA: Sage Publications.

13 Einstadter, W. and Henry, S. (1995). *Criminological Theory: An Analysis of Its Underlying Assumptions*. Fort Worth, Texas: Harcourt Brace College Publishers.

14 Messner, S., Krohn, M. and Liska, A. (eds) (1989). *Theoretical Integration in the Study of Deviance and Crime: Problems and Prospects*. Albany, NY: SUNY Press.

15 Henry, S. and Milovanovic, D. (1996). *Constitutive Criminology: Beyond Postmodernism*. London: Sage Publications.

16 Einstadter and Henry, op. cit., p. 308.

17 Green, P. and Ward, T. (2004). *State Crime: Governments, Violence and Corruption*, p. 29. London: Pluto Press.

18 Kramer, R. (1992). The space shuttle challenger explosion. In K. Schlegel and D. Weisburd (eds) *White-Collar Crime Reconsidered*, p. 216. Boston: Northeastern University Press.

19 Henry and Milovanovic, op. cit.

20 Barak, G. (2007). Mediatizing law and order: Applying Cottle's architecture of communicative frames to the social construction of crime and justice, *Crime Media Culture*. 3(1): 100–108.

21 Patterson, G., DeBarshy, B. and Ramsey, E. (1989). A developmental perspective on antisocial behavior, *American Psychologist*, 44: 329.

22 Op. cit., 330.

23 Patterson, G. and Yoerger, K. (1997). A developmental model for late-onset delinquency. In D. W. Osgood (ed.), *Motivation and Delinquency: Nebraska Symposium on Motivation* (Vol. 44, pp. 119–177. Lincoln, NB: University of Nebraska Press.

24 Moffitt, T. (2001). Adolescence-limited and life-course persistent antisocial behavior: a developmental taxonomy. In A. Piquero and P. Mazerolle (eds), *Life-Course Criminology: Contemporary and Classic Readings*, pp. 91–145. Belmont, CA: Wadsworth.

25 Ibid., p. 91.

26 Ibid.

27 Ibid., p. 102.

28 Ibid., p. 111.

29 Maruna, S. (2001). *Making Good: How Ex-convicts Reform and Rebuild their Lives*. Washington, DC: American Psychological Association.

30 Maruna, S. and Copes, H. (2005). What have we leaned from five decades of neutralization research? In: M. Tonry (ed.), *Crime and Justice: A Review of Research* (Vol. 32, pp. 221–320. Chicago: University of Chicago Press. See also, Huang, B. Kosterman, R. Catalano, R., Hawkins, J., and Abbot, R. (2001). Modeling mediation in the etiology of violent behavior in adolescence: A test of the social development model. *Criminology*, 39: 75–108.

31 Elder, G. (1992). The life-course. In E Borgatta and M. Borgatta (eds), *The Encyclopedia of Sociology* (Vol. 3). New York: Macmillan.

32 Piquero, A. and Mazerolle, P. (eds) (2001). *Life-Course Criminology: Contemporary and Classic Readings*, pp. 91–145. Belmont, CA: Wadsworth.

33 Sampson, R. and Laub, J. (2001). A life-course theory of cumulative disadvantage and the stability of delinquency. In A. Piquero and P. Mazerolle (eds), *Life-course Criminology: Contemporary and Classic Readings*, pp. 146–170. Belmont, CA: Wadsworth.

34 Sampson, R. and Laub, J. (1993). *Crime in the Making: Pathways and Turning Points Through Life*. Cambridge, MA: Harvard University Press.

35 Sampson and Laub. (2001), p. 147.

36 Sampson, R. and Laub, J. (2003). *Shared Beginnings, Divergent Lives: Delinquency and Boys to Age 70*. Cambridge, MA: Harvard University Press.

37 Sampson and Laub. (2001), p. 155.

38 Thornberry, T. (1987). Toward an interactional theory of delinquency. *Criminology*, 25: 864.

39 Ibid.

40 Thornberry, T. (1996). Empirical support for interactional theory: a review of the literature. In: J. D. Hawkins (ed.), *Delinquency and Crime: Current Theories*, pp. 198–235. New York: Cambridge University Press. See also Thornberry, T. and Krohn, M. (2005). Applying interactional theory to the explanation of continuity and change in antisocial behavior. In D. Farrington (ed.). *Integrated Development and Life-Course Theories of Offending* (Advances in Criminological Theory, Vol. 14, pp. 183–209). New Brunswick, NJl: Transaction Publishing.

41 Thornberry, T. (1987), p. 883.

42 Colvin, M. (2000). *Crime and Coercion: An Integrated Theory of Chronic Criminality*, p. 1. New York: St. Martin's.

43 Regoli, Regoli, R. and Hewitt, J. (1997). *Delinquency and Society* (third edition.). New York: McGraw-Hill.

44 Colvin, M. (2000), p. 43.

45 Ibid., p. 5.

46 Lilly, J., Cullen, F. and Ball, R. (2007). *Criminological Theory: Context and Consequences* (fourth edition), p. 118. Thousand Oaks, CA: Sage Publications.

47 Barak, G. (2006). Applying integrated theory: A reciprocal theory of violence and non-violence. In: S. Henry, and M. Lanier (eds). *The Essential Criminology Reader*, pp. 336–346. Boulder, CO: Westview Press.

48 Tittle, C. (1995). *Control Balance: Toward a General Theory of Deviance*. Boulder, CO: Westview Press. Tittle, C. (2004). Refining control balance theory. *Theoretical Criminology*, 20: 143–172.

49 Messner, S., Krohn, M. and Liska, A. (eds) (1989), op. cit.

50 Tatum, B. (1995. Race, class, alienation and delinquency: assessing motivational factors through the application of structural models. Doctoral Dissertation. Albany, NY: SUNY. (1996). 'The colonial model as a theoretical explanation of crime and delinquency'. In A. Sutton (ed.), *African–American Perspectives on Crime Causation, Criminal Justice Administration, and Crime Prevention*. Boston: Butterworth-Heinemann.

51 Barak, G., Flavin, J., and Leighton, P. (2001). *Class, Race, Gender, and Crime: The Social Realities of Justice in America*. Los Angeles: Roxbury Publishing.

52 Barak, G., Leighton, P. and Flavin, J. (2007). *Class, Race, Gender, and Crime: The Social Realities of Justice in America*. Lanham, MD: Rowman and Littlefield.

53 Tittle, C. (1995), op. cit., p. 135.

54 Lilly, J., Cullen, F., and Ball, R. (2007), op. cit., p. 114.

55 Goldstein, J. (1986). *Aggression and Crimes of Violence* (second edition). New York: Oxford University Press.

56 Tittle, C. (1995).

57 Tittle, C. (2004).

10

Realist Criminology Revisited

Roger Matthews

THE CONTINUING FAILURE OF CRIMINOLOGY

Just over twenty years ago Jock Young (1986) wrote a path breaking article which identified the failures of criminology and made the case for developing what became known as left, critical or radical realism. Over the past two decades however these failures have, if anything, become more entrenched. From a realist perspective the ongoing failures of academic criminology are seen to centre around its conceptual weaknesses, lack of methodological and analytic rigour and diminishing policy relevance. Among its most spectacular failures has been its inability to adequately conceptualise 'crime', explain the causes of crime or account for crime trends.

It has been suggested that as academic criminology has expanded that it has become more fragmented and diversified (Ericson and Carriere, 1994). However, it is not so much a fragmentation of the subject that has taken place as its division into a number of reasonably distinct groupings. These groupings can be demarcated along political lines, which embody differences of epistemology, theoretical orientation, and methodology. In essence, there are four major groupings. These include what has become known as 'right realism' or conservative criminology, administrative criminology and related pseudo-scientific criminologies, critical criminology or left idealism as it is sometimes known, and liberal criminology in its various forms.

Considerable shifts have occurred over the past twenty years in the size and influence of these different groupings. Whereas critical or radical criminology was extremely influential in the 1970s it fell into 'crisis' and became more marginalised in the 1980s. Although it has been effective in developing sustained critiques of mainstream criminology it was unable to articulate an alternative approach and present a viable alternative to mainstream criminology (Cohen, 1998; Van Swaaningen, 1999).

During the 1980s conservative criminology benefited from the demise of critical criminology and developed a relatively hard hitting approach towards 'law and order', providing a rationale for 'get tough' public order policing, the expansion of prisons, the more systematic regulation of incivilities, disorder and anti-social behaviour and provided a justification for focusing attention on the activities of ethnic minorities and the 'underclass' (Herrnstein and Murray, 1994; Wilson and Kelling, 1982; Wilson and Herrnstein, 1985; Murray, 1994).

A great deal of liberal criminology during the 1980s and early 1990s was directed at countering the conservative arguments about crime and punishment, arguing instead for limits to state power, respecting individual liberties, celebrating diversity and developing more welfare oriented policies. While the conservatives were claiming that 'prison works' and putting forward a case for its expansion, liberals were talking about the 'crisis of imprisonment' and arguing for reductionism. While conservatives were arguing for more intensive forms of public order and zero tolerance policing liberals were arguing for community policing and greater accountability. While some conservatives maintained that the disproportionate involvement of certain ethnic minority groups in the criminal justice system was a function of low IQs or inadequate socialisation, liberals were pointing to deprivation and marginalisation as precursors to criminal involvement. In broad terms conservatives tended to operate with a relatively abstract and at times a nostalgic notion of the 'community' while liberals tended to operate with an equally problematic notion of the autonomous individual.

During the 1990s, however, the influence of conservative criminology began to wane as a number of the leading conservative criminologists retired, while the influence of those who continued to publish decreased. The growing barrage of liberal criticism has no doubt dented the credibility of the conservatives. Consequently during the 1990s liberal criminology was in the ascendancy and increasingly academic criminology became dominated by a wide-ranging liberal consensus. Some conservative criminologists continued to influence crime policy directly and indirectly, while others moved into the pseudo scientific terrain of risk analysis and 'crime science'. However, it can reasonably be claimed the in relation to academic criminology that the subject is currently dominated by liberals, whether they be humanistic, pessimistic or radical (see for example Garland, 2001; Wacquant, 2001; Tonry, 2001).

The relative demise of conservative criminology, however, has meant that liberals are less able to develop policies and programmes simply in opposition, and are under increasing pressure to develop policies that are politically credible and that resonate with the general public. This is proving extremely difficult and many liberal criminologists as a consequence have turned their attention away from the formulation of criminal justice policies and have increasingly focused instead on exposing what is seen as the surge in punitiveness or vindictiveness (Pratt, 2007). Thus in a context in which liberals have little to say about the major issues of the day their attention is increasingly turned to what are seen as maverick and unscrupulous politicians who we are told are playing the 'law and order' card in order to win the votes of a gullible and anxious public who willingly absorb the punitive political rhetoric and allow politicians to increasingly 'govern through crime' (Ericson, 2007; Simon, 2007).

There is a form of social amnesia associated with this position. Liberal critics seem to have forgotten that twenty years ago during the Thatcher–Reagan era there was a significant body of political and public opinion calling for the reintroduction or greater use of capital punishment and for the more extensive use of imprisonment, not to mention the criminalisation of working class strikes and other forms of association. Currently, however, it is difficult in the UK, at least, to find much support for reintroducing the death penalty while on both sides of the Atlantic very few people are arguing for prison expansion. At the same time many of the 'get tough' policies introduced in the 1980s and early 1990s – zero tolerance policing, mandatory and determinate sentencing, boot camps, and other 'punitive' measures – are in decline or have been abandoned, in recent years. Correspondingly, there has been an increased emphasis on developing 'non-punitive' measures such as forms of crime prevention, community based alternatives to custody, new forms of surveillance and monitoring, 'reassurance' and 'community policing' as well as the significant international development of restorative justice (Matthews, 2005; Pitts, 2008).

This changing political and policy landscape however, provides a new challenge for criminologists and the dominance of liberalism in its various forms, with its limited policy relevance, suggests the need for the development of a criminology that is both critical and engaged. It is not surprising in this context that there should be growing concerns about the policy relevance of criminology (Currie, 2004; Burawoy, 2004; Matthews, 2008). This has occurred against an increase of what Elliot Currie has described as 'So What?' criminology, by which he means those forms of criminology that are a-theoretical, overly descriptive or generally unintelligible. Alongside these 'So What?' criminologies we might add those forms of liberal pessimism that claim either that nothing works, or that most interventions have negative and unintended effects and that it is better to try to less harm rather than do more good. There are also those pessimists that claim that we are moving ineluctably towards more oppressive and restrictive forms of social control (Zedner, 2002).

Even in its more radical variants liberalism tends to present a form of critique that is politically and professionally safe. Liberals conspicuously avoid difficult questions about who should go to prison and for how long, the role of retribution, the intra class and the intra racial nature of some forms of crime, and the interest that the poor and marginalised have in pursuing social and distributive justice and reducing victimisation. The steady growth of a criminology lacking policy relevance has created an expanding criminological industry that has become more obese and is, as they say nowadays in official circles, 'unfit for purpose'.

In responding to the flabby consensus in criminology, realism aims to develop an approach that is theory driven while being evidence based. It is practically and politically engaged and takes the concerns of the general public seriously, seeing them neither as dupes nor as irrational. In this way, it also aims to avoid the pitfalls of idealism, empiricism and the growing pessimism that is becoming increasingly prevalent in academic criminology. Most importantly it aims to develop an approach that is critical and stands in opposition to those forms of naïve realism that see the notion of 'crime' as unproblematic.

CRITICAL VS. NAÏVE REALISM

A pivotal distinction in relation to realism is that between critical realism, on one hand, and naïve realism, on the other. While critical realism sees the appropriation of social reality as problematic, naïve realism sees both social reality in general and crime in particular as pregiven and directly accessible (Bhaskar, 2002). Whereas critical realism sees crime as a complex social construction, naïve realism in its various forms – administrative criminology, descriptive criminologies and 'crime science' – tends to take the category of 'crime' for granted and believes that the aim of criminological investigation is simply to record, count, describe or map 'crime' and 'victimisation'. Although there may be some concerns about the accuracy and consistency of available data and the gaps between recorded, reported and unreported 'crime' there is little reflexivity or detailed investigation into the meaning of the general category of crime or indeed the sub-categories such as violence, robbery and theft.

Terms like 'violence' and 'robbery' are generic categories that cover a variety of actions which involve different offender–victim relations in different contexts. An initial task of inquiry therefore is to disaggregate these terms. Thus, in relation to robbery, for example, there is a need to differentiate between commercial and street robbery and if the aim is then to investigate street robbery this category in turn needs to be broken down into its component parts – mugging, theft from the person and snatch thefts. (Matthews, 2001; Young, 1988). This is critical for understanding the specificity and the causal processes involved which in turn will have more or less direct implications for the formulation of policy. The selection of categories and concepts that we use in carving up and defining our objects of study is crucial to the investigation. Unfortunately, much criminological investigation ignores this fundamental issue, as if it were simply a matter of intuition (Sayer, 1992).

The general lack of conceptual sophistication in both administrative and academic criminology is reflected in the blurring of the central categories of investigation, as for example, in the British Crime Survey which is not about 'crime' but 'victimisation'. Consequently, it would be more accurate to refer to it as the British Victimisation Survey. Many of the incidents reported in the British Crime Survey have little likelihood of being recorded as 'crimes'. The process of victimisation and the construction of crime are different. At the same time, the data presented in the British Crime Survey is too vague and insufficiently contextualised, on one level, and too individualistic and subjective, on the other. A major limitation of the British Crime Survey is its lack of specificity and its tendency to obscure significant local social and geographical variations in the distribution of victimisation (Jones *et al.*, 1986; Young, 1992). These problems are further compounded in the International Crime Victimisation survey which not only confuses 'crime' and 'victimisation' but also loses sight of the specificity and meaning of crime categories in different countries (Van Dijk, 2008). On one level the blurring of the distinction between crime and victimisation might appear to be trivial or inconsequential, however, it is indicative of the low level conceptualisation that pervades criminology.

In problematising crime and the mechanisms of crime control critical realists are interested in understanding the ways in which social reality is constructed and appropriated. Because social phenomena and human action involve meaning, social inquiry necessarily involves the process of interpretation. Meaning has to be understood. It cannot be simply measured or counted. Meaning is also related to the material circumstances and practical contexts in which communication takes place and therefore critical realists insist that there is a material non-discursive dimension to social life (Sayer, 2000; Manicas, 2006). Thus those forms of criminology that emulate the methods of the natural sciences and which exclude forms of interpretative understanding are always going to be of limited utility. Although social science can use the same methods as natural science regarding causal explanation, it necessarily involves an interpretative or hermeneutic dimension. Thus:

> While natural scientists necessarily have to enter the hermeneutic circle of their scientific community, social scientists also have to enter that of those whom they study. In other words, natural science operates in a single hermeneutic while social science operates in a double hermeneutic. These circles imply a two-way movement, a 'fusing of horizons' of listener and speaker, researcher and researched in which the latter's actions and texts never speak simply to themselves, and yet are not reducible to the researcher's interpretation of them either.
>
> (Sayer, 2000: 17)

Realist criminologists have consistently emphasised the need to engage with the lived reality of its subjects (Young, 1992a). There are three reasons for engaging directly with the subjects under study. First, it is necessary to understand the meanings, discourses and conceptions that are routinely employed in everyday social interaction. Second, to establish a congruence of meaning between the researcher and the researched. Third, to develop policies and forms of intervention that are appropriate and resonate with relevant groups. For these reasons realists also emphasise the importance of understanding subcultural processes and the important role that cultural politics can have in shaping social relations and influencing social interventions (Ferrell, 2007; Lea and Young, 1984; O'Brien, 2005).

For example, Orlando Patterson's (2006) analysis of how the cultural integration of black youths in America fuels their socio-economic marginalisation while at the same time serves to form identities centered around the generation of respect. Patterson argues that there is a need to develop a form of cultural politics that is able to understand and engage with the cultural attitudes of this group if they are to be reconnected with the socio-economic mainstream. Significantly, Patterson lays much of the blame for the failure to properly comprehend and respond to this situation on forms of analysis that are overly descriptive and subjective, on one hand, or overly statistical and impersonal, on the other.

Similarly, undertaking forms of ethnographic work can provide important insights into meanings, tacit assumptions and social relations but like other forms of qualitative research it can easily become purely descriptive lacking critical analysis and reflexivity. Where ethnographic work is a-theoretical or wholly descriptive it is unlikely to provide much of value. As Paul Willis (1977) demonstrated in his classic study 'Learning to Labour', good quality ethnographic work is typically based on a clear and significant problematic, the ability to penetrate beneath the surface of social interaction and develop forms of analysis that are able to evaluate and explain these social worlds, not only to the academic community, but also in some cases to the subjects themselves. Thus the aim of ethnographic work is not merely to empathise, rationalise or romanticise these social activities but rather to explore the issues, meanings, inconsistencies, misunderstandings and inherent contradictions against a background of the power relations in play (Anderson, 2002). As Sam Porter (1993) has argued the purpose of ethnographic investigation is not just to idiographically illuminate small-scale social events, but through the examination of human agency to shed light on the relationship between agency and structure. Uncritical acceptance of the subjects' own accounts leads predictably to analytic superficiality.

In engaging with the lived experience of subjects critical realism is committed to grounded empirical inquiry and the development of evidence-based policy. This approach, however, should be distinguished from the form of 'grounded theory' first outlined by Glaser and Strauss (1967). This form of 'grounded theory' involves a combination of American pragmatism and symbolic interactionism and is portrayed as a problem-solving endeavour concerned with understanding action from the per-spective of the human agent. Although placing emphasis on qualitative research 'grounded theory' embodies elements of naïve realism in that it begins from the col-lection of data and sees theory as inductively derived from the analysis of this data. It separates the phenomena under study from the data method and although has pre-tensions to rigour by emulating the accepted canons of scientific inquiry – consistency, reproducibility and generalisability – it attempts to do this through an inversion of the normal hypothetico – deductive methods of investigation (Haig, 1995).

Because all forms of social inquiry necessarily involve interpretation, critical real-ists in line with most critical criminologists, reject the inductivist assumption that 'facts speak for themselves'. Instead the aim of critical inquiry is to understand the causal processes involved in producing actions or events and thereby to move beyond immediate appearances. In realist terms this involves the search for genera-tive causes that produce observable outcomes. Thus the principle aim is to identify the mechanisms that operate 'below the surface' of social relations that create appearances. These causal processes may be conflicting, complex and contradictory since social phenomena are rarely the product of a single cause. Thus critical realism generally rejects one-dimensional, linear or reductionist accounts.

Neither is the aim of social investigation to search for regularities as positivists and empiricists tend to do. The aim of social inquiry is to distinguish the causal from the contingent. Distinguishing necessity from contingency and identifying the causal processes involved and how they work, rather than focus upon repetition, is why critical realists are sceptical of accounts that focus on correlations. Correlations, no matter how statistically significant they may be, make little or no contribution to an explanation of the processes involved in generating social change and at best provide an indication of possible causal links.

The difference in approach between critical and naïve realists is apparent when we compare the approaches of the recently developed 'crime science' and critical realist criminology. While both approaches want to place investigation on a sound and rigorous methodological base and aim to produce effective policies and programmes, they are in many respects oppositional. It is indicative that 'crime science' emulates the natural sciences in developing what is seen as new 'discipline' or a new 'paradigm'. Drawing on the methodical approach developed in medicine, Gloria Laycock (2005), for example, claims that; 'it is about reducing crime, as natural science is about reducing ill health'. But crime is a very different type of phenomena than illness. Consequently, the natural scientific methodological procedures adopted by medicine are less than adequate for criminological investigation. The forms of randomised testing and control trials that are frequently used in medicine have little purchase in criminology. Crime as a form of rule breaking necessarily involves an understanding of the motivation of the offender, the selection of victims and targets, the relation between offenders and victims as well as an assessment of the justness and appropriateness of rules (Hayward and Young, 2004). Consequently, the application of natural scientific methods to social phenomena like crime will always omit the critical explanatory framework needed to understand how programmes work. Moreover, the critical processes of discourse, negotiation and history tend to be ignored by 'crime science' limiting explanatory options.

In its attempt to overcome this narrow reliance on the methods of natural science 'crime science' aims to combine its interest in technology and biosocial criminology with rational choice theory, routine activities theory and crime mapping, thus producing an epistemological and methodological hotch-potch that generally adopts an uncritical concept of crime and its construction, a limited appreciation of the role of structures and 'deep causes', an ignorance of the role of power and the state in shaping and responding to crime and a dubious methodological approach that is not particularly suited to dealing with the messy nature of open systems. Because of its generally low level of theorisation and its unreflexive use of social categories it tends to dissolve into pragmatism and low-level policy formation.

THE SOCIAL CONSTRUCTION OF CRIME

It has been suggested that there is some serious conceptual confusion and slippage in relation to the central organising concept of 'crime'. This lack of clarity is indicative of the low level of theorisation and conceptual rigour in this subject area. These problems are further evident in the discussion about the meaning of 'crime' in most of the standard criminology textbooks. These discussions tend to be between empiricists on one hand who 'know' what crime is and focus their energies on collecting 'facts' about crime. On the other hand are idealists who argue that crime is a social construction and that it has no ontological reality (Hulsman, 1986). The realist approach to understanding the ways in which concepts like 'crime' come to be produced and appropriated is distinctly different from that of the empiricists and naïve realists on one hand and idealists on the other.

The attractiveness of the social constructionist approach is that it emphasises that the notion of crime is historically and culturally variable. In rejecting the uncritical, taken-for-granted conceptions of 'crime' adopted by naïve realists it stresses the role of human interaction and the ways in which through such interaction and discourse social categories are produced and reified (Berger and Luckman, 1984). The historical and cultural variability of social categories like 'crime' leaves them open to the possibility of transformation and at the same time opens them up to critical review. Not surprisingly, therefore, social constructionism finds its advocates amongst critical criminologists while traditional criminologists tend to adopt existing social categories uncritically. A key role for critical criminologists is the deconstruction of crime categories into its component parts in order to identify their meaning.

Up to a point we can go along with social constructionism and recognise the need to understand and problematise key concepts like 'crime'. However in its more extreme form social constructionism has a tendency to dissolve into relativism and to suggest that social categories like crime are arbitrary or fictional constructs and should be replaced by terms such as 'problematic situations'. The use of general terms such as 'problematic situations' by some critical criminologists, does not, however, solve the problem but replaces the concept of crime with a concept that not only has even less 'ontological reality', but also loses sight of the empirical and social significance of crime and the criminal justice process. Removing the concept of 'crime' also means that idealists find it difficult if not impossible to engage meaningfully in ongoing debates associated with crime and the operation of the criminal justice system and effectively become marginalised from important social and political debates. While criminologists and sociologists may critically engage with certain social concepts, and are prone on occasions to invent their own concepts, to completely dismiss substantive categories like 'crime' is untenable:

> For we simply cannot construct the world any old way we choose, and if we persistently attempt to do so we are ultimately more likely to come to the attention of psychiatric services than to gain academic approval. However, realising that our world is socially constructed need not force us to adopt promiscuous or unbridled relativism. Social constructions are all around us and include diverse features, such as racism, marriage and marriage guidance, government policies, governments themselves, child abuse, crime, disease, psychology including constructionist psychology, buildings, people and cities (to name but a few). *None of these things are any less real for being socially constructed*, although the dominance of the process of construction, as compared to other influences, may vary from one to the other.
>
> (Cromby and Nightingale, 1999: 9)

What is required, therefore, is a grounded social constructionism that recognises that social categories like 'crime' have an independence, objectivity and effects. Critical realism rejects the notion that everyone's views are equally valid and point out that when relativists argue this position their own position is compromised. It is also the case that social categories and perceptions are not reducible to language and discourse. Many problems are located in material conflicts and contradictions. The more hard line constructionists have found it difficult to offer normative theories that can be applied to a world ravaged by poverty, disease and social conflict. In a similar vein these constructionists tend to pay limited attention to 'structure' in shaping social meaning (Houston, 2001).

A primary example of the conceptual confusion and misunderstanding of the nature and significance of social categories in criminology is evident in approaches to the definition of 'crime' itself. The debate tends to centre around the legalists, on one side, who claim that crime involves actions that break the law and critical criminologists on the other side who claim that acts that come to be defined as 'crimes' can change significantly over time. In most criminology textbooks the debate remains unresolved and 'crime' is left as problematic and uncertain concept. Realist criminologists have argued that 'crime' should be seen as a process of action and reaction and that it is important to understand the nature of the social relations involved and the effects of power and social contexts. However, this response does not fully resolve the problem, although it does recognise that all of the approaches to the question of definition contain partial truths. The difficulty in understanding the construction and significance of the concept of crime is that it embodies a certain circularity and that for an act to become a crime several conditions must apply. First it has to be blameworthy and potentially interpreted as illegal. This presupposes the existence of the criminal law. Second, it needs legitimate and recognised actors (usually victims) to define the act as possible crime and report it to the authorities.

Third, there needs to be a normative structure in place that supports the definition of the type of act committed by relevant actors as being blameworthy and potentially a crime. Fourth, there has to be some recognition within the criminal justice system that the claims of the victim and the perceived blameworthiness of the offender are appropriate. In cases in which stages three and four are missing 'problematic situations' will not become 'crimes' although some form of transgression or victimisation may have taken place. There is also an important point that arises from this analysis about rules, norms and laws, which do not only regulate but are constitutive. Thus, in football, for example, if there were no rules there would be no 'football' – only people kicking a ball around. Thus without antecedently existing rules there is no sense in which their behaviour could be described as 'playing football'. The specification that 'they played football' presupposes the existence of such rules in the same way that the claim that they have committed crime presupposes the existence of the criminal law (Pires and Acosta, 1994). Thus it is in a sense correct to claim that the law 'creates' crime but it is not constitutive of the blameworthy act itself.

A significant contribution that realist criminology has made to an understanding of the process of the construction of 'crime' has been presented through its model of the 'square of crime' (Lea, 1992). In this form of analysis it has been argued that the construction of the concept of 'crime' involves at least four component parts – the offender, the victim, the state and state agencies, the general public and social norms. The fact that so few criminologists have recognised or adopted this or a similar model and that even fewer incorporate two or more dimensions of the 'square of crime' in their analysis is symptomatic of the narrow one-dimensional focus of much academic criminology. Very few criminologists who study crime also study punishment while there are divisions between those who study offenders and those who study victims. This division and fragmentation in the subject is further compounded by those who see themselves as theorists, methodologists and those who focus on policy developments. While some form of a division of labour and specialism is to be expected, the one-dimensional nature of much criminology reduces its potential impact and significance. The aim of critical realist criminology is to develop a more 'joined-up' approach that incorporates a grounded social constructionism that avoids the excesses of relativism and idealism.

WHAT IS CRITICAL ABOUT CRITICAL CRIMINOLOGY?

All criminological approaches are in a sense critical inasmuch as they involve explicit or implicit critiques of other approaches. Thus, the question arises of what makes 'critical criminology' critical? More specifically for our purposes is to explain why critical realism provides a more consistent and effective form of critical criminology than the more idealist versions and forms of radical liberalism that are currently circulating.

Is it a difference of perspectives on the purpose, significance of criminology, the different normative standpoints of the researchers, different theoretical orientations and assumptions that guide investigation, or does the distinguishing feature of critical criminology lie in its mode of analysis? In answering these questions we are drawn into issues about the proper nature of critical theory, the difference between critical and traditional theory and the significance of the standpoint from which we address these issues (Carlen, 2002; Young, 2002).

Probably the best place to begin to answer this question is the work of Karl Marx. In 1843, Marx defined critical theory as 'the self-clarification of the struggles and wishes of the age'. This fundamentally political definition locates critical theory at the centre of social conflict, aspirations and struggles. Thus for Marx critical theory is bound up with the struggle for emancipation. The central aim of critical theory is to shed light on current issues, to reveal their dynamics and explore the potential for change. In this process of self-clarification the aim it to demystify the basis of conflict. This necessarily involves going beyond appearances since capitalism, Marx believed, has the propensity to invert real relations and to present them in a mystified form (Fraser, 1977).

Following in the footsteps of Marx, Max Horkheimer (1937) directly addresses the question of the difference between critical and traditional theory. He argues that traditional theory tends to take the natural sciences as its point of reference and suggests that social sciences follow a similar approach. The formation of the natural sciences is Horkheimer argues a social product whose aim is to amass a body of knowledge that allows the physical manipulation of nature, the development of technology and the organisation of economic and social relations, by employing methods that are impersonal, abstract and autonomous, separating fact from and value and knowledge from action. In doing so it loses sight of the categories through which 'facts' are socially produced and tends to reify social relations.

In contrast, critical theory Horkheimer argues, must begin by examining and deconstructing the relevant social categories. Adopting a reflexive approach critical theory aims not just to gather knowledge but to link it to an emancipatory project. In doing so it does not focus on atomised individuals, on one hand, or on abstract society on the other. Instead, it aims to examine the ways in which society produces individual subjects and how those subjects constitute and potentially change society. Horkheimer argues that critical theory operates on the premise that the individual and society involves a contradictory and conflicting set of relations and claims that: 'critical thought has a concept of man as in conflict with himself until the opposition is removed'.

Thus, for Horkheimer and other critical theorists, it is important to engage in ideology critique since social reality, particularly in capitalist societies, tends to be presented in distorted or opaque forms. Indeed it is one of the distinguishing features of capitalist social relations according to Horkheimer is that ideology serves as a mechanism for masking real social relations and thereby concealing the process of exploitation and domination. The aim of inquiry therefore involves moving beyond ideological representations in order to reveal the underlying reality and to explain why appearances assume the form that they do. Thus engaging in ideology critique presupposes a reality independent of the forms of representation.

In many respects critical realism has a great deal in common with critical criminology inasmuch as it aims to unpack and unmask ideological representations of reality. Realism, however, differs from the more idealistic forms of critical criminology in two important respects. First, realism places great emphasis on engagement with policy and practice and is concerned with effecting social change. Although critical realists recognise the value of engaging in ideology critique they also emphasise the need to change practices and in some cases the material conditions that produce ideologies. Critique is not an end in itself. The second, and related, departure from most forms of critical criminology is the integration of theory, method and practice. Although realists are fairly flexible about the adoption of methods they stress that the selection of methods is not arbitrary or predetermined but is rather governed by the research question and the nature of the object under study. We should be suspicious, therefore, of 'cookbook criminologies' who have one preferred method for all occasions or alternatively a pre-established hierarchy of methods in which certain methodological approaches are deemed superior in all cases (Sherman, *et al.,* 2002). At the same time the integration of theory, method and practice is designed to overcome the separation of researchers into theorists, methodologists, and those dealing with policy and practice. On one level, this unnecessary division of labour amongst social scientists reflects the divisions that are a feature of 'traditional' theory, while on another level it detracts from the transformative and emancipatory potential of critical inquiry (Matthews, 2008).

One response to the uncertainties and disputes about the significance of criminology and the meaning of 'crime' has been to 'move beyond' or abandon criminology. There is a long and distinguished history of anti-criminology even amongst those who professionally identify themselves as criminologists (Cohen, 1998). The most recent variant of this anti-criminology is the attempt to broaden the focus beyond the boundaries crime and the criminal justice system and to establish a new discipline that examines different forms of harm. This new 'harmology' claims that criminology is too narrowly focused, that it makes little contribution to the achievement of social justice and pays little attention to how the state creates harms. Within this emerging form of anti-criminology there is an ambivalence about the status of crime. At one point crime is considered to be one of a number of identifiable harms, while at another it is claimed that it has no 'ontological reality' and is a 'myth'. However, similar problems of definition confront the notion of 'harms', which has even less ontological reality than crime. Not surprisingly, these critical criminologists present a fairly arbitrary set of criteria to identify 'harms' and provide little understanding of how they are caused. Ironically, this group of critical criminologists have historically paid scant attention to the impact of normal or social crime on its victims, but now want to mount a campaign to address all harms, as they define them (Hillyard and Tombs, 2004).

This approach, like much previous anti-criminology, fails to appreciate the historical and social significance of 'crime', law and the state and its role in relation to maintaining social order and discipline. Like the actuarial approach that they reject they see crime as one of a number of 'hazards' or 'risks' to be prevented, rather than see it as a unique area of investigation. Thus in addressing harms is general, particularly those seen to be perpetrated by the powerful, the state or the 'system' there is a real danger that this new form of critical theory, like its predecessors, will lose analytic and political focus and end up as a diatribe against various social problems, abuses and injustices ranging from environmental issues to poverty and political oppression.

A slightly different approach that is sceptical about the possibility of developing a critical criminology in either its idealist or realist forms has been presented by postmodernists, who claim that the changing nature of knowledge formation and power relations in late modernity has produced a climate in which critique is no longer tenable. Thus Pavlich, for example, writes:

> At stake here is not merely the issue of reviving Marxist, radical or critical traditions; it has to do with the increasingly problematic foundations of criticism. It is not that critical

> criminology in its utopian or realist moments has failed to deliver the goods; rather the
> rug has been pulled from underneath the critical practices that once seemed so integral
> to critical criminology. The very idea of a critical project has been problematised to a
> point where some critics now question whether the word 'critical' has any specific
> meaning.
>
> (Pavlich, 1999: 36)

Drawing on Lyotard's work on knowledge formation, Pavlich argues that critical
criminology has become unable to articulate an alternative discourse to the dominant
form of correctionalism. Lyotard argues that in postmodern social formations that
knowledge production has become more highly controlled and tied to forms of pragmatism. The problem with this defeatist postmodernism is that it engages in a
thoroughgoing critical attack on the nature of knowledge production while claiming
that the possibility of such a critique is no longer possible. At the same time Lyotard
and other postmodernists are critical of meta-narratives, particularly those associated
with Marxism, while developing elaborate meta-narratives of their own. Consequently,
they move towards a relativism and an idealism advocating 'local knowledge' and
the politics of fragmentation and conjuncture (Fraser and Nicholson, 1990).
Postmodernists like Lyotard tend to play down the importance of structural or social
determinants such as class, race or gender that should be central to any criminological inquiry. Moreover, it is not a choice between grand narratives and local
knowledge since the two are implicated in each other. As Nola and Irzik (2003)
argue Lyotard muddles epistemological matters about the definition of knowledge
with sociological information about how knowledge circulates in modern societies.
Inasmuch as Lyotard is correct that government agencies are becoming more directly
involved in the production and distribution of criminological knowledge it suggests
a greater need for critical engagement with this knowledge and the development of
alternative perspectives (Walters, 2003).

We encounter similar problems with postmodernism in relation to Carol Smart's
(1990) critique of 'grand narratives' and the situated nature of knowledge.
Understandably suspicious of a male-centred or male-constructed criminology,
Smart argues that the truth claims of criminology have to be deconstructed and challenged from a feminist standpoint. That is from the standpoint of what she calls 'the
new social subjects' by which she means 'lesbians and gays, black women and men,
Asian women and men'. However, as John Lea (1998) has pointed out the claim that
the dominated and marginalised have certain advantages in terms of understanding
of society and that as a result their social and economic exclusion they are able to
see things that are invisible to the dominant group, only serves to replace one form
of foundationalism with another.

> Suppose we agree that the concept of 'crime' is a male discourse insofar as it marginalises
> phenomena, which are at the core of gender relations in modern society. One solution is to
> say that it is 'true' that violence is a central ingredient of gender relations – good old fash-
> ioned foundationalism in which the truth of a statement is independent of the status of the
> speaker. But we know that such a truth is contaminated with (male) power. What Smart
> appears to be arguing is that the validity of the argument is to be found in the fact that it
> is being articulated by the groups she mentions. The point is surely that those groups come
> predesignated as progressive forces. Smart constructs her list of resisters from the stand-
> point of her own 'grand narrative' concerning what is progressive in the world.
>
> (Lea, 1998: 172)

Realism distinguishes between the discovery of knowledge and the justifications for knowledge. It realises that knowledge is in a sense always selective and consequently argues for critical reflexivity recognising that we stand in a certain position in relation to our objects of inquiry. The aim is to identify what influence our position has on our appreciation of the object (Sayer, 2000). Thus, although it is recognised that all knowledge is social, situated and contextual it does not follow that truth claims can only be applicable to the particular groups who propose them. Thus, if the study of crime reflects men's social position while presenting itself as universally applicable and gender neutral then the problem is not just that it is socially influenced but that the knowledge is inadequate, one-sided and misleading. Significantly, the concept of misrecognition and error requires the acceptance of the realist assumption of an independent reality about which we can be mistaken.

WHAT WORKS ?

As a result of their interest with practical issues and fostering social change, realists are often accused of pragmatism. This is a serious mischaracterisation and demonstrates a fundamental misunderstanding of the realist project (Pavlich, 1999). Although realists are interested in 'what works' they are more concerned with why and how things work.

Understanding how and why things work, critical realists argue, involves identifying the causal mechanisms that foster change (Pawson and Tilley, 1997). It is important, however, to distinguish between secessionist notions of causality, which is characteristic of positivistic modes of social inquiry, and generative notions of causality favoured by critical realists. Successionist models of causality focus on the frequency of association between two events. However, critical realists argue that what causes something to happen has nothing to do with the number of times we observe it happening. In order to understand causal connections we need to identify the causal mechanisms in play rather than focus on outcome regularities (Pawson, 2006). The aim of investigation is to understand the mechanisms that are inherent in systems, agents or structures that account for causal regularities. Ray Pawson provides two very different examples of the operation of generative mechanisms:

> Bureaucracies make things happen because of what they are. Because the workforce is organised in a hierarchy and because agreements are struck on responsibilities, work gets done in routinised ways. The structure generates the work pattern. Gunpowder has a tendency to go off because of what it is. Chemicals react and combine in different ways. Some combinations give off a large amount of energy under the application of heat (exothermic reactions) and it is this capacity that makes the mix of potassium, nitrate, charcoal and sulphur so excitable. The chemical composition generates the capacity to explode.
>
> (Pawson, 2006: 23)

Thus, a central claim of critical realism is that it is not something inherent in particular programmes that makes them work but the propensities and the capacities of the agents or objects that such programmes are directed towards that allow them to work. Thus, whether rehabilitation programmes, for example, work as intended will depend on whether the subjects go along with the programmes and choose to use the resources as intended (Pawson and Tilley, 1997). Thus, realists aim to look beneath

the surface of what works with the objective of identifying the generative mechanisms in play. It is this unique conception of causal processes and how they work
that distinguishes critical realism from pragmatism, empiricism and positivism.

It is also the case that generative mechanisms may operate differently in different
contexts. If gunpowder is not properly compacted or if the atmosphere is too damp
its capacity to explode may be prevented. Thus for critical realists there is a need to
examine how interventions may trigger certain mechanisms, which in turn may be
activated according to the characteristics and circumstances of subjects, and
that this, in turn, will be conditioned by the context in which implementation
takes place.

Critical realists also have a distinctive view of the nature and meaning of interventions. Interventions are not just practices but theories or hypotheses that postulate the
possibility of bringing about an improved outcome. Consequently, interventions are
potentially fallible, particularly since they deal with complex social realities, as well
as with different groups of subjects and may be implemented differently in different
contexts. Therefore, all of these elements must be considered when addressing the
question of what works in order to find out what works for whom under what circumstances. Thus, there are a number of different ways in which programmes may
be said to work.

Between the 1970s and 1990s we have moved from a 'nothing works' to a 'what
works?' agenda (Cullen and Gendrau, 2001). This has involved a shift from pessimism to pragmatism: the pessimism was initially a product of the form of
meta-analysis adopted by Robert Martinson (1974) while much of the current 'what
works?' agenda is based largely upon a-theoretical approaches associated with
administrative criminology. While this approach has a formal commitment to the
development of evidence-based policy there are issues about how this evidence is
gathered as well as the relation between evidence and politics. It has been suggested
that we are witnessing new forms of political management of criminological research
as well as the use and interpretation of findings (Walters, 2003). Criminological
research, it has been argued, has increasingly become a tool of legitimation to
uphold governmental truth claims. If this is the case, then the argument for the development of a critical and engaged criminology becomes even stronger.

CONCLUSION

The aim of this chapter has been to trace in fairly broad strokes the marginalisation
of critical criminology over the past two decades and the more recent demise of
conservative criminology. This has resulted in a woolly liberal consensus dominating academic criminology. Because of various (mis)conceptions about the nature of
'crime' and its inability to come to terms with the more challenging questions about
victimisation and punishment, liberalism has been unable to develop policies in relation to crime control that resonate politically or with the general public (Currie,
2007). Consequently, they have turned their attention to castigating what are seen as
unscrupulous politicians who apparently want to 'govern through crime' in order to
gain the support of a gullible but increasingly intolerant public. From this vantage
point crime control is reduced to a form of voluntarism, which provides a convenient

rationale for not properly examining the actual dynamics of contemporary forms of crime control or actively engaging in changing criminal justice policy.

At the same time we have witnessed the steady expansion of administrative criminology tied to largely a-theoretical and instrumental agenda. This approach has been supported by a range of pseudo scientific approaches including actuarial approaches focusing on risk management as well as 'crime science'. Although these approaches claim to be policy focused they are ultimately not very practical because the naive realist and empiricist approach on which it is based largely fails to comprehend the causal processes involved in producing the complex social phenomena of 'crime'. Indirectly, the knowledge produced tends to be non-cumulative and the conclusions often weak or ambivalent.

In this context there is an urgent need to develop a criminology that can begin to understand the causes of crime and the processes of crime control and which does not emulate the natural sciences with its emphases on successionist notions of causality or its reliance on statistical correlations. On the other hand, there is little point in developing an anti-criminology that is not engaged in the ongoing debates around normal or social crime. While not wanting to resurrect rigid disciplinary boundaries, the focus on crime and social control provides a unique and important field of study since it touches on key themes associated with the regulation of the social order, human rights, as well as social and distributive justice.

The task facing critical criminology is to engage in this issue and to develop a coherent and integrated approach that emphasises the role of a theoretical approach that is critical but grounded. The deployment of methods of investigation that are responsive to the object under study and are designed to identify how and why measures work and ultimately to fashion interventions that are aimed at making tangible improvements in the world and which are ultimately tied to an emancipatory project. In short, we need to develop a criminology that is theoretical but not theoreticist, critical but not negative or impossibilist, utopian but grounded in lived experience, joined up but targeted, methodologically flexible but rigorous, practical but not pragmatic and policy relevant rather than policy driven – if we are to overcome the continuing failure of criminology.

REFERENCES

Anderson, E. (2002) The ideologically driven critique, *American Journal of Sociology* No. 6: 1533–1560.

Berger, P. and Luckman, T. (1984) *The Social Construction of Reality: A Treatise in the Sociology of Knowledge.* London: Penguin.

Bhaskar, R. (1989) *Reclaiming Reality: A Critical Introduction to Contemporary Philosophy.* London: Verso.

Bhaskar, R. (2002) *From Science to Emancipation.* New Delhi: Sage.

Carlen, P. (2002) Critical criminology? In praise of oxymoron and its enemies, in K. Carrrington and R. Hogg (eds), *Critical Criminology: Issues, Debates, Challenges.* Cullompton: Willan.

Cohen, S. (1998) *Against Criminology.* New Jersey: Transaction Publishers.

Cromby, J. and Nighgtingale, D. (1999) What's wrong with Social Constructionism?, in J. Cromby and D. Nightingale (eds), *Social Constructionist Psychology: A Critical Analysis of Theory and Practice.* Buckingham: Open University Press.

Cullen, F. and Gendrau, R. (2001) From nothing works to what works: changing professional ideology in the 21st Century, *The Prison Journal,* 81(3): 313–338.

Currie, E. (2007) Against marginality: arguments for a public criminology, *Theoretical Criminology* 11(2): 175–190.

Ericson, R. (2007) *Crime in an Insecure World.* Cambridge: Polity.

Ericson, R. and Carriere, K. (1994) The fragmentation of criminology, in D. Nelken (ed.), *The Futures of Criminology,* London: Sage.

Ferrell, J. (2007) For a ruthless cultural criticism of everything existing, *Crime Media and Culture* 3(1): 91–100.

Fraser, N. (1987) What's critical about critical theory? The case of *Habermas and Gender?*, in S. Benhabib and D. Cornell (eds), *Feminism as Critique.* Oxford: Basil Blackwell.

Fraser, N. and Nicholson, L. (1990) Social criticism without philosophy, in L. Nicholson (ed.), *Feminism/ Postmodernism.* New York: Routledge.

Garland, D. (2001) *The Culture of Control.* Oxford University Press.

Glaser, B. and Strauss, A. (1967) *The Discovery of Grounded Theory.* Chicago: Aldine.

Haig, B. (1995) Grounded theory in scientific method, *Philosophy of Education.*

Hayward, K. and Young, J. (2004) Cultural criminology: some notes on a script, *Theoretical Criminology* 8(3): 259–285.

Herrnstein, R. and Murray, C. (1994) *The Bell Curve: Intelligence and Class Structure in American Life,* New York: Simon and Schuster.

Hillyard, P. and Tombs, S. (2004) Beyond criminology?, in P. Hillyard, C. Pantazis, S. Tombs and D. Gordon (eds), *Beyond Criminology: Taking Harm Seriously.* London: Pluto Press.

Hope, T. (2004) Pretend it works: evidence and governance in the evaluation of the reducing burglary initiative, *Criminal Justice* 4(3): 287–308.

Horkheimer, M. (1937) *Critical Theory: Selected Essays,* New York: Herder and Herder.

Houston, S. (2001) Beyond social constructionism: critical realism and social work, *British Journal of Social Work* 31: 845–861.

Hulsman, L. (1986) Critical criminology and the concept of crime, *Contemporary Crisis* 10(1): 63–80.

Jones, T., Maclean, B. and Young, J. (1986) *The Islington Crime Survey.* Aldershot: Gower.

Laycock, G. (2005) Defining crime science, in M. Smith and N. Tilley (eds), *Crime Science: New Approaches to Preventing and Detecting Crime.* Cullompton: Willan.

Lea, J. (1992) The analysis of the square of crime, in J. Young and R. Matthews (eds), *Rethinking Criminology.* London: Sage.

Lea, J. (1998) Criminology and postmodernism, in P. Walton and J. Young (eds), *The New Criminology Revisited.* London: Macmillan.

Lea, J. and Young, J. (1984) *What's to be Done About Law and Order?* Harmondsworth: Penguin.

Manicas, P. (2006) *A Realist Philosophy of Social Science: Explanation and Understanding,* Cambridge University Press.

Martinson, R. (1974) What works? Questions and answers about prison reform, *The Public Interest* 35: 22–54.

Matthews, R. (2001) *Armed Robbery.* Cullompton: Willan.

Matthews, R. (2005) The myth of punitiveness, *Theoretical Criminology* 9(2): 175–201.

Matthews, R. (2009) Beyond 'So What?' Criminology: Rediscovering Realism, *Theoretical Criminology* 13(3): 341–362.

Murray, C. (1994) *Underclass: The Crisis Deepens.* London: Institute of Economic Affairs.

Nola, R. and Irzik, G. (2003) Incredulity towards lyotard: a critique of postmodern accounts of science and knowledge, *Studies in the History and Philosophy of Science* 34: 391–421.

O'Brien, M. (2005) What's cultural about cultural criminology?, *British Journal of Criminology,* 45: 599–612.

Patterson, O. (2006) Poverty of the mind. *New York Times,* 26th March.

Pavlich, G. (1999) Criticism and criminology: in search of legitimacy, *Theoretical Criminology* 3(1): 29–53.

Pawson, R. (2006) *Evidence Based Policy: A Realist Perspective.* London: Sage.

Pawson, R. and Tilley, N. (1997) *Realistic Evaluation.* London: Sage.

Pires, A. and Acosta, F. (1994) What's real in realism? What's construction in constructionism? The case of criminology. *The Journal of Human Justice* 5(2): 6–33.

Pitts, J. (2008) Too grand, too bland, too abstract: the limitations of 'Youth Governance' as an explanatory schema for contemporary responses to socially deviant young people, *Youth and Policy*, Spring No. 99: 67–89.

Porter, S. (1993) Critical realist ethnography: the case of racism and professionalism in a medical setting, *Sociology* 27(4): 591–609.

Pratt, J. (2007) *Penal Populism,* London: Routledge.

Sayer, A. (1992) *Method in Social Science: A Realist Approach.* London: Routledge.

Sayer, A. (2000) *Realism and Social Science*, London: Sage.

Sherman, L., Farrington, D., Welsh, B. and Mackenzie, D. (2002) *Evidence Based Crime Prevention*, New York: Routledge.

Simon, J. (2007) *Governing Through Crime: How the War on Crime Transformed American Democracy and Created a Culture of Terror*, New York: Oxford University Press.

Smart, C. (1990) Feminist approaches to criminology or post-modern woman meets atavistic man, in L. Gelsthorpe and A. Morris (eds), *Feminist Perspectives in Criminology.* Buckingham: Open University Press.

Tonry, M. (2001) Symbol, Substance and Severity in Western Penal Policies, *Punishment and Society* 3(4): 517–536.

Van Dijk, J. (2008) *The World of Crime.* California: Sage.

van Swaaningen, R. (1999) Reclaiming critical criminology: social justice and the European tradition, *Theoretical Criminology* 3(1): 5–29.

Walters, R. (2003) New modes of governance and the commodification of criminological knowledge, *Social and Legal Studies* 12(1): 5–26.

Wacquant, L. (2001) Deadly Symbiosis: When Ghetto and Prisons Merge, *Punishment and Society* 3(1): 45–134.

Willis, P. (1977) *Learning to Labour: Why Working Class Kids Get Working Class Jobs.* Wexmead: Saxon House.

Wilson, J. and Hernstein, R. (1985) *Crime and Human Nature: The Definitive Study of the Causes of Crime.* New York: Simon and Schuster.

Wilson, J. and Kelling, G. (1982) Broken Windows: The Police and Neighborhood Safety, *Atlantic Monthly,* March: 29–38.

Young, J. (1986) The failure of criminology: the need for radical realism, in R. Matthews and J. Young (eds), *Confronting Crime.* London: Sage.

Young, J. (1988) Risk of crime and fear of crime: a realist critique of survey based assumptions, in M. Maguire and J. Pointing (eds), *Victims of Crime: A New Deal.* Milton Keynes: Open University Press.

Young, J. (1992) Realist research as a basis for local criminal justice policy, in J. Lowman and B. MacLean (eds), *Realist Criminology: Crime Control and Policing in the 1990s.* University of Toronto Press.

Young, J. (1992a) Ten points of realism, in J. Young and R. Matthews (eds), *Rethinking Criminology: The Realist Debate.* London: Sage.

Young, J. (2002) Critical criminology in the twenty-first century: critique, irony and the always unfinished, in D. Carrington and R. Hogg (eds), *Critical Criminology: Issues, Debates, Challenges.* Cullompton: Willan.

Zedner, L. (2002) Dangers of dystopias in penal theory, *Oxford Journal of Legal Studies* 22(3): 341–366.

11

Routine Activities

Sharon Chamard

INTRODUCTION

The routine activities approach is both a micro-level theory that states that crime happens when three elements – a likely offender, a suitable target, and the absence of a capable guardian – converge in time and space, and a macro-level theory that examines broad changes in society and how these lead to changes in community life that create new opportunities for crime. The approach is one of the "opportunity" theories of crime (along with rational choice and crime pattern theories), and also is included in the group of theories referred to as "environmental criminology" (which includes the three opportunity theories, situational crime prevention and victimization theories that focus on lifestyles). Unlike theories of *criminality*, which attempt to explain why some people have a propensity to commit crime while others do not, routine activities is a theory of *crime* – that is, it focuses both on broad and situational reasons for the occurrence of *crime events*.

The approach was first articulated in an article published in 1979 in the *American Sociological Review*. The authors, Lawrence Cohen and Marcus Felson, were colleagues in the Department of Sociology at the University of Illinois at Urbana-Champaign. Publication of the work did not come easily. It was rejected by six leading journals. Reviewers offered a great deal of resistance to the manuscript, for it was an "overt challenge to conventional criminology." Early critics declared the theory to be overly simplistic. They thought it would be best to integrate it into or subsume it under mainstream theories. They doubted it would ever amount to anything. Yet routine activities, despite the dire predictions of these critics, has gone on to be one of the most frequently cited and tested theories in criminology (Felson, 2008: 72).

This chapter begins by describing the main ideas and key concepts of the approach. Then, the theoretical foundation of routine activities is discussed. Just as early detractors urged incorporation into existing theories, there has been a steady stream of scholars who have argued for the integration of routine activities with social disorganization, social control, self-control, and neutralization theories, to name just a few. Routine activities has evolved considerably in the past three decades, partly because of integration into older theories, but more so because of new discoveries about crime. This process of evolution will be explored. Next, the standing of routine activities as a contemporary theory will be discussed. Finally, some thought will be given to the future of routine activities.

MAIN IDEAS AND KEY CONCEPTS

The main purpose of the 1979 *American Sociological Review* article was to explain why there were dramatic increases in crime, despite improvements during 1960–1975 in the social conditions that were thought to contribute to crime. Rather unexpectedly, although poverty and unemployment dropped in urban areas, and levels of education and income increased, rates of violent crime (robbery, aggravated assault, forcible rape, and homicide) grew between 164 per cent and 263 per cent, as did property crime – burglary alone increased 200 per cent (Cohen and Felson 1979: 588). It was clear that the mainstream theories used by criminologists to explain crime, theories which pointed to "root causes" such as poverty, blocked opportunities, and the like, were inadequate to explain these rapid increases in violent crime or property crime.

Cohen and Felson offered an alternative explanation. Drawing heavily from the work of the early human ecologist, Amos Hawley, and others (such as Roger Barker and O. D. Duncan) who looked at the relationship between humans and the environment, Cohen and Felson argued that the increase in crime rates could be attributed to changes in social and technological patterns. Specifically, they claimed that the routine activities of people, the "recurrent and prevalent activities" that people do to meet their needs, had changed. *Routine activities* refer to day-to-day things such as going to work or school, shopping, socializing, and playing. They can occur at home or away from home. During the 1960s, the routine activities of a large number of people in the American population changed in ways that resulted in a "dispersion of activities away from family and household" (Cohen and Felson 1979: 600). Specifically, more women entered the workforce or post-secondary education, and there were more households of only one person. People also traveled more.

The consequence of this shift in routine activities away from the home was that there was less guardianship of those homes, which made these homes more attractive targets for burglars. Children and teenagers were less supervised as mothers moved into the workplace in large numbers. This had two results. First, it increased the risk of victimization of youth because no adults were around to protect them, and second, it allowed youth to engage in criminal activity more readily because no adults were monitoring their behavior.

Not only did social changes appear on the home front, they were manifested in public life. Women who started working outside the home and going to school became more suitable targets for opportunistic offenders, as did private vehicles used in commuting.

Routine activities also addresses how crime rates are affected by technological changes. Cohen and Felson found that the characteristics of "durable goods" (such as television sets and cars) were strongly associated with levels of property crime.

Consumer goods became more widely owned, smaller, and lighter. Not only did the number of targets increase, the targets became more *suitable* to likely offenders. The way this increasing number of goods was sold changed too. The number of stores selling these durable goods remained fairly constant, and there were fewer salespeople on the floor to tend to customers. Also, retailing shifted to more of a self-service approach, which brought more customers in closer contact with more products. The result of decreased supervision of customers and greater customer access to a larger number of goods was increased shoplifting.

Original elements of the routine activities approach

The micro-level aspect of routine activities states that a crime event can only happen when a *likely offender* and a *suitable target* come together in a particular place and time, and there is no *capable guardian* there to prevent an interaction between the offender and the target. On the face of it, this is an extremely simplistic model for crime. But this is a strength of the theory, for it points to very straight-forward crime prevention measures. If even one of the three sides of the "crime triangle" can be removed, then the crime event does not occur.

Patterns of criminal behavior obviously vary from place to place. Where you park your car makes a big difference to the likelihood that it will be stolen or broken into. Your own locked garage is the safest place; a public parking lot is the most dangerous place. Risk varies across different time periods as well. Some places are safe during the day but dangerous at night, largely due to the nature of the land use and who is using the space. For example, there may be low rates of victimization in a downtown park during business hours. People using the park would be mostly engaged in benign activities, such as eating lunch, selling food and drink from carts, feeding pigeons, and so on. Although there are scores of suitable targets, there are also many capable guardians. Later in the day, when the offices close and the business people and vendors go home, a different group of people occupy the park. The staggering drunks and straggling commuters are suitable targets, and given the lack of capable guardians, victimization is much more likely. Crime can vary considerably in one place, even without taking into account the numbers of likely offenders or their motivations to commit crime.

This example illustrates one of the fundamental assumptions made by routine activities about human nature. Motivation and inclination to commit crime are seen as natural and given; individual tendencies towards crime are not addressed in a meaningful manner (Cohen and Felson 1979: 589). Instead, the role of temporal and spatial factors is stressed. Indeed, this theme underlies the constellation of theories associated with routine activities, which asserts that crime cannot be explained solely in terms of characteristics of offenders, but that environmental factors are as, or more, important. Felson (1986) explains that the organization of daily life in communities affects the amount of crime by changing the amount of criminal opportunity; crime can thus increase or decrease without any alteration in the motivations of offenders. A key difference between the routine activities approach and most explanations of crime is that very little emphasis is placed on offenders. With this in mind, we now turn to the specific elements of the micro-level version of routine activities.

Likely offender

A likely offender is someone who has both the propensity and the ability to commit a crime. If a crime actually happens, it is because the likely offender finds a situation where there is a suitable target and no capable guardian around to prevent the inter-action. The approach assumes that there is a ready supply of people who are likely offenders. Why some people are inclined to commit crime while others are not so predisposed is not a focus of routine activities (though it is not claimed, as many observers of the theory incorrectly assume, that inclination and predisposition are invariant). Attempting to reduce crime by making people "better" is explicitly rejected by routine activities.

Routine activities is often criticized for neglecting the "root causes" of crime (e.g., poor parenting, poverty, and blocked opportunities). In addition, because routine activities assume that offender motivation is irrelevant, opponents argue that it fails to take into account differences in disposition. However, it should be noted that the approach does not actually claim that everyone is equal in terms of proclivity towards crime; it just deems differences in levels of motivation not important.

Suitable target

A suitable target can be a person or an object. It is the characteristics of targets that make them attractive to likely offenders. Cohen and Felson introduced the acronym VIVA to simplify these qualities, which include value, inertia, visibility, and access.

Value   Objects that can be easily converted to cash are highly prized by thieves. Recognition of this has led crime prevention practitioners to disrupt markets for stolen goods (such as pawn shops, flea markets, and increasingly, Internet sites where people sell second-hand items) in an attempt to make it harder to exchange these goods for money. Similarly, programs like *Operation Identification*, wherein people mark their property with a unique code (like a driver's license number), are designed to reduce the value of objects to thieves because objects are harder to fence if they are marked.

For violent offenders, some potential victims have more value than others. For example, rapists tend to prefer younger women. A suitable target for an armed robber is someone who is expected to be carrying cash or other valuables.

Inertia   This refers generally to the size and weight of an item, and specifically, how easily the item can be removed from the area. The smaller and lighter an object, the more suitable it is to a thief, as less effort is needed to carry it away. Heavy objects are less desirable, though not if they have functioning wheels. Drivers who use devices that prevent their vehicles from being shifted into gear are relying on the principle of inertia – it is very difficult to move a car if the wheels cannot rotate. Retailers of expensive fur and leather clothing often chain the garments to the display racks, thus substantially increasing the inertia of the items.

Visibility   A potential thief has to see an object before assessing whether it is a suitable target. If the item is not visible, it is less vulnerable to be stolen. Around the holiday season, shoppers are warned to lock their purchases in the trunk; failure to do so alerts thieves to the presence of goods worth stealing, and can result in car break-ins. Pickpockets have been known to observe crowds in proximity to signs warning of pickpocketing. The instinct of many people is to check if their wallets are still there upon reading such a sign. This has the effect of making visible what was previously hidden in a pocket or handbag.

Access   The more easily a thief can get to an item, the more suitable that item is as a target. Stores lock their jewelry in display cases. Homeowners install solid-core doors and strong deadbolts. These are examples of target hardening, which reduces accessibility and the attractiveness of the target.

A subsequent variation of VIVA was offered by Ronald Clarke in a 1999 mono-graph entitled *Hot Products*, wherein he argued that crime prevention efforts can be more efficient if they focus on items that are most vulnerable to theft. Similar con-ceptually to repeat victimization and hot spots (locations where crime repeatedly occurs, and with some predictability), a "hot product" is a consumer good that is exceedingly desirable to thieves (Clarke, 1999: 1). Unlike VIVA, which was not intended to be a complete model of target suitability, Clarke's model takes into account research on hot products in the two decades subsequent to the first mention of VIVA, and more explicitly incorporates notions of offender decision-making. The more comprehensive model proposes that a target is attractive (or "CRAVED") if it has the quality of being concealable, removable, available, valuable, enjoyable, and disposable.

Capable guardian

A capable guardian is someone who prevents the convergence in time and space of a likely offender and a suitable target. Most often, we are capable guardians of our own belongings and property. Those around us, such as family, friends, and co-workers, can also function as capable guardians. It should be noted that the routine activities approach is very explicit in stating that police officers, because they so infrequently detect crime as it is happening, are rarely capable guardians.

Research on the effects of guardianship on crime and delinquency has typically measured how people spend their time, in particular in unstructured and unsuper-vised activities. Examples of this are given later in this chapter.

The absence of a capable guardian can result in a crime because the likely offender and suitable target are alone together. For crime prevention, increasing the capability of guardianship is important. In many university libraries, signs are posted warning patrons of the dangers of leaving belongings unattended. Some parents install hidden closed-circuit video cameras so as to better observe their children's babysitters.

Newer elements of the routine activities approach

Intimate handler

The 1979 *American Sociological Review* article, while acknowledging that guardians may supervise targets, offenders, or both (Cohen and Felson, 1979: 590 fn), did not elaborate on this distinction. Later iterations of the theory (Felson, 1986) incorpo-rated a fourth element – the *intimate handler* – based on concepts from Travis Hirschi's control theory. Control theory has four components – attachment, commitment, involvement, and belief – that together explain how families, communities, and society as a whole control people's behavior through informal ways. What makes this control effective is that people fear what will happen to their futures or relationships with friends and family if they behave badly. Also, encouraging participation in conventional activities puts limits on available options about how to spend one's time, and manipulating belief systems makes people feel guilty when they are bad.

The intimate handler is someone who exerts some influence over a likely offender by virtue of knowing the offender well enough to know what varieties of informal control will work best act as a curb on criminal behavior. Examples include parents, adults in the community, and even peers. The key is that the handler must know who the potential offender is. Offenders can easily avoid the influence of handlers by going to another part of the community where no one knows or recognizes them. The growth in human settlements from villages to large, sprawling urban areas, coupled with increased car ownership and part-time jobs that provide disposable income, have made it a simple matter for youth to escape the supervision of handlers.

In terms of crime prevention, much youth crime takes place after school but before parents get home from work when there is little supervision of teenagers. After-school programs are an example of increasing the capacity of handlers to exert control over their charges.

Place manager

A more recent addition to routine activities, the *place manager*, was suggested by the work of John Eck (1995). The place manager is someone who has responsibility over a particular space. This differs from the capable guardian in that it is not the target that the place manager is protecting, but the location where the suitable target and likely offender converge. The effectiveness of place managers varies by how much they feel responsible for the place. Those with diffuse responsibility are less effective than those who own the property or those who have contractual or employment-based duties to look over the space. To prevent crime in neighborhoods, there is much to be said for on-site managers in apartment buildings, particularly if the manager is motivated to keep the property free from crime. Resident owners are even better. Examples of place managers include doormen, receptionists, janitors, security guards, and building superintendents.

Adding place managers and intimate handlers to the original conception of routine activities (a likely offender and suitable target converging in time and space in the absence of a capable guardian) creates what is called "Eck's Triplets," wherein crime is discouraged when the likely offender is supervised by the intimate handler, the suitable target is protected by the capable guardian, and the time and space where the convergence occurs is monitored by the place manager.

THEORETICAL FOUNDATION OF ROUTINE ACTIVITIES

To understand the theoretical origin of routine activities is to understand the intellectual growth of Marcus Felson, because to a very large extent, the theory was developed in an incremental fashion, with bits and pieces from the work of others added to a chain of ideas that stretches over many years. These bits and pieces themselves are connected by a web of scholars who have studied and worked together; many of them influenced Felson directly because they were his teachers or his colleagues.

Before the seminal 1979 article that posited the main principles of routine activities, Felson and his colleague Kenneth Land (also at the University of Illinois at Urbana-Champaign) introduced "macro parameterization," which provided a method of using demographic data to represent changes in society directly in terms of other societal changes, and thus determine the extent of institutional interdependence among elements of society often measured by demographers (Land and Felson, 1976: 575–576). This research concluded that much of the variance in crime rates is systematically related to other measures of social and economic conditions and that further, these indicators actually reflect real changes in the structure of society (Land and Felson, 1976: 598).

This form of analysis was inspired by the prolific sociologist William Ogburn (1922), who believed that large-scale conditions, such as changes in business cycles, are better explanations of social phenomena (such as crime) than explanations that point to will power or personality characteristics. This approach, and the philosophy underlying it, is evident in the macro-level routine activities theory.

Another contribution of Ogburn was the theory of cultural lag and the importance of technology in shaping the direction of society. He argued that the various parts of society do not change all at the same time. Rather, "some parts are changing much more rapidly than others; and that since there is a correlation and interdependence of parts, a rapid change in one part of our culture requires readjustment through other changes in the various correlated parts of culture" (Ogburn 1922: 200–201). The important role of technological changes in determining macro-level patterns in crime is a repeating theme in Felson's work.

The central role of technology in shaping society was also addressed by renowned social demographer Otis Dudley Duncan, who was one of Ogburn's students at the University of Chicago. Duncan, whose major contributions were the introduction of path analysis and structural equation modeling to sociology and his work with Peter Blau on social stratification, would himself have an influence on Felson when the latter was one of his graduate students at the University of Michigan. In particular, Duncan built on the work of early "Chicago School" theorist Robert Park and promoted the incorporation of human ecology principles in demographic research. These principles – population, organization, environment, and technology (Duncan, 1959: 681) – were later referred to by Felson using the acronym "POET" (1994: 60). Duncan's contributions to routine activities theory are many: the dynamic way that human populations adapt to their environments (even if they be entirely urban and devoid of "natural" features), the idea that societies are organized primarily around "sustenance-producing" activities, the importance of technology in shaping the form of this organization, and the use of demographic variables as "indicators" of aspects of organization (Duncan, 1959). These themes run through routine activities.

Duncan himself relied heavily on the ideas of sociologist Amos Hawley, who is noted for describing the temporal components that underlie community structure. The first of these is rhythm, which refers to the regular periodicity with which events occur. Examples include commuting and other travel patterns. The second is tempo, or the number of events per unit of time. The third is timing – the coordination among different activities which are more or less independent (Hawley, 1950: 289). Hawley is cited by Cohen and Felson (1979), who then described research conducted by, among others, Amir and Wolfgang, who found significant differences in the distribution of predatory crime across various time periods, be they hours, days, or months. Cohen and Felson (1979: 592) recognized that these variations matched the tempos of the routine activities upon which the criminal activity feeds. This focus on the temporal dimensions of the distribution of criminal opportunities has helped make routine activities "one of criminology's more robust and enduring theoretical frameworks" (Wilcox *et al.*, 2003: 142).

A key concept in routine activities is the convergence in time and space of the three necessary elements. Where and when this coming together happens is essentially a "behavior setting," a concept developed by Roger Barker (1968) in his studies of human activities in small Midwestern towns. A behavior setting is a place where people gather to carry out relatively consistent activities, or as Cohen and Felson might say, "recurrent and prevalent activities which provide for basic population and individual needs" (1979: 592).

Barker's (1968) key observation was that while there are variations in individual human behavior – someone may be quiet in one moment and boisterous in the next, dominant with one person and submissive with another, interested in one classroom and bored in another – generally speaking, people in the same setting behave alike. While people's internal thoughts, motives, and so on may vary from person to person, behavior in given settings will be similar because of "forces operating within the behavior settings." These forces include physical constraints, social forces, and influence of behavior on the milieu (Barker, 1968: 29–31). In essence, "the setting constrains the *individuals* within it to behave appropriately" (Barker, 1978: 224).

Barker's discussion of the factors at play in settings that influence people's behavior is clearly one of the foundations of the concept of capable guardianship, for it is authority figures who determine to a large extent what behaviors are considered to be appropriate in settings. In addition, like many of the other theorists and researchers that contributed theoretically to the development of routine activities, Barker observed his research environment through the eyes of an ecologist more than as a sociologist. The theme of studying humans in their natural environment, taking into account spatial characteristics and temporal patterns, is something that runs through Felson's work. Early on, he argued that analyzing crime events is a "special case of the ecology of daily life" because it relies upon the "physical structure of social phenomena – where people are when and what they are doing" (1986: 120). In some of his later writing, in particular *Crime and Nature* (Felson, 2006), human ecology became much more central to the theory.

THE EVOLUTION OF ROUTINE ACTIVITIES THEORY

The routine activities approach has undergone somewhat of a revision since 1979 in response to contributions from other scholars and theorists. First, the approach has been broadened in recognition of the important theoretical links between routine activities and other approaches (such as rational choice and crime pattern theory), and at the same time, has moved away from its roots in sociology. There has also been an explicit introduction of ecological concepts. While the original version of routine activities had only micro- and macro-level aspects, recent iterations have taken into account offender decision-making, journey to crime, the geography of crime, and situational crime prevention. The second development has been the integration of routine activities with other theories. Theoretical integration is covered more fully in the next section of this chapter.

The three "opportunity" theories of routine activities, rational choice, and crime pattern theory work together to form a comprehensive model that begins with a society-level analysis (routine activities), follows with a focus on the local area (crime pattern theory), and ends with the individual (rational choice) (Felson and Clarke, 1998: 8).

The influence of rational choice on routine activities has led to greater recognition of the perception of likely offenders with respect to whether a target is seen as suitable or a guardian viewed as capable. A basic assumption of rational choice is that offenders weigh the costs and benefits of particular courses of action and choose those most likely to result in the greatest return on investment (be it in terms of time or effort). This simple idea, as applicable to crime as it is to cognitive linguistics, was famously described as the "principle of least effort" by George Zipf (1949).

In a co-authored work (1998), Felson partnered with his Rutgers' colleague (and one of the "inventors" of criminology's rational choice theory) Ronald Clarke to explain how opportunities to commit crime affect criminal motivation. In an echo of Barker's observations, they argued that "individual behavior is a product of an interaction between the person and setting" and that most criminological theories address only the person and ignore the setting almost entirely (1998: 1).

The significance of crime pattern theory is clear if one focuses on how settings create opportunities for crime. Crime pattern theory examines how people move about in space and time. How different actors converge in given settings involves looking at the "geographical distribution of crime and the daily rhythm of activity" (Felson and Clarke, 1998: 6). Key concepts include activity nodes (like the home, school, workplace, and shopping and recreation areas), paths between activity nodes, and edges – the boundaries of these nodes and paths. Like the other opportunity theories of routine activities and rational choice, crime pattern theory assumes there is variation in the motivation of offenders, but does not put primary focus on this element of the crime event. Yet it is not discounted either. Paul and Patricia Brantingham, the scholars behind crime pattern theory, predicted that one of the most fruitful lines of inquiry in environmental criminology in the 1990s would be the interaction between opportunity and motivation (1991: 250). As we shall see later in this chapter during the discussion of theoretical integration, that is indeed what has happened as there is increasing focus on the importance of "context" in explaining both individual-level and community-level variation in crime.

Finally, this section on the evolution of the theory will address the increasing role of ecology in the study of crime and how this has altered the routine activity approach. As has been previously described, much of the foundation of the approach is based on human ecology: Duncan, Hawley, and Barker could all be classified as social ecologists. The contribution of ecology *as a life science* to routine activities has been fleshed out considerably by Felson in the past decade or more. In his 2006 text, *Crime and Nature*, the potential contribution of both naturalists and ecologists to the study of crime science is explored. Felson structures this discussion about "crime in motion, its living processes" (2006: 3) around the seven special requirements of life: organization, adaptation, metabolism, movement, growth, reproduction, and irritability. Of these, only two – metabolism (i.e., rhythm in response to other rhythms) and motion – are clearly derived from the original micro-level formulation of routine activities.

Felson's early writings about routine activities largely concerned predatory or exploitative crime, that is, crime wherein not every party involved willingly chooses to participate. But clearly, a fair amount of crime is what is typically referred to as "victimless." To a social ecologist, such interactions between people, be they of a criminal nature or not, are called "symbiotic." Felson has more recently explored these interactions in the context of routine activities.

In elaborations of the macro-level components of the approach, Felson has discussed how increases in human density, from villages to small towns to large cities (or the "divergent metropolis"), have created new opportunities for crime. For example, changes in land use and zoning as cities got bigger and more complex have resulted in alterations to the urban form, such that residential areas are now typically located far away from job locations. This leads to people spending more time commuting (which reduces guardianship of their home and increases the risk of predation by strangers), and more people relying on personal vehicles, which are then parked for hours at a stretch in untended parking lots.

THE CURRENT STANDING OF ROUTINE ACTIVITIES

For the most part, research on the usefulness of routine activities with respect to its explanatory power has been supportive of the theory. It is also the case, however, that much of this research derives its variables from the initial 1979 version of the theory, and has failed to incorporate the changes to routine activities that have occurred over the past three decades. Beyond that, the majority of research testing routine activities has focused solely on the micro-level aspects of the theory and typically equates the approach with lifestyle theories of victimization, in particular that proposed by Hindelang and his colleagues (Hindelang *et al.*, 1978).

Routine activities, perhaps because of its apparent simplicity, has been tested extensively in the research literature. The main concepts of routine activities have been operationalized in a variety of ways. The first approach is to ask subjects how often they have been presented with criminal opportunities (this of course, is contrary to the approach taken by those who view routine activities as primarily a victimization theory). For example, Grasmick *et al.* (1993) included items asking how often respondents had been exposed to situations where acts of fraud or force would "be possible to do easily," "gratifying in the moment," or "without much chance that somebody who might do something about it would find out." As Hay and Forrest (2008) pointed out, while this strategy directly measures perceived opportunity, it is rarely used in research because few existing datasets include these types of measures.

Miethe and Meier (1990) were among the first to argue for the need for integration of routine activities with other theories. They asserted that previous studies supporting victimization theories (among them routine activities) were misspecified because relevant variables were not included in the model. They proposed a "structural-choice" theory of victimization that combined macro-level forces that lead to a criminal opportunity structure (these forces include demographic and other changes in society, not unlike what Cohen and Felson (1979) described) with micro-level processes that influence particular decision-making by offenders with respect to target selection. Miethe and Meier (1990: 245) presented this as a "union of criminal opportunity and lifestyle/exposure perspectives." Strictly speaking, this union does not merge disparate theories, but brings together the micro-level and macro-level aspects of routine activities into a single model. Most researchers, even today, tend to include in their models only the core concepts from the 1979 explication of routine activities (the convergence in time and space of a likely offender, a suitable target, and the lack of a capable guardian), while effectively ignoring contextual considerations. But it is not evident that incorporating these considerations is theoretical integration, because the matter of context has been discussed quite fully in the routine activities literature.

The Miethe and Meier (1990) study used data from the British Crime Survey and included four main independent variables, each of which had been validated in previous research by others. The first was proximity to high-crime areas, which was measured by (1) living in an inner-city area, (2) how safe the neighborhood was felt to be at night, and (3) the mean rate of offending in the respondent's community. Exposure to criminal opportunities was derived from various measures of the level of "nonhousehold primary activity" – in other words, how often the respondent left home during the day or evening. The third variable was target attractiveness. This was determined from the social class of the respondent and whether he or she owned a VCR. Guardianship, the fourth variable, was measured by whether the respondent lived with another adult and whether he or she either used a weapon for self-protection or had a burglar alarm.

Analyses included both main effects and interactive effects models. The results were, according to Miethe and Meier (1990: 258) "not anticipated from previous research or current theories of victimization." Physical guardianship (using a weapon or burglar alarm) and target attractiveness were not significant predictors of victimization risk. The researchers did concede that the operationalization of target attractiveness may have been lacking, possibly due to the subjective nature of target suitability and the primacy of other factors, such as risk of detection or apprehension, guiding offender selection (Miethe and Meier, 1990).

Most studies of routine activities have indirectly operationalized criminal opportunity by focusing on involvement in relationships or exposure to situations that promote crime. For example, Bratt (2008) compared cannabis and alcohol use in a group of Norwegian teenagers before and after social workers were introduced to the settings where youth gathered outside of homes. The guardians did not have a "substantial preventive effect" on use of alcohol, and may even have contributed to increased use of cannabis. He concluded that participation in unsupervised activities is not a sufficient cause of delinquent behavior, but it is a necessary cause (Bratt, 2008).

Osgood *et al.* (1996) proposed an individual-level perspective that focused in the effect of guardianship upon deviance. The argued that certain situations are conducive to deviance, and that being in the company of peers exposes a person to more of these situational inducements. They made a concerted effort to use indicators that were consistent with routine activities and less so with alternative theories. For example, items asking about involvement in deviant activities, like hanging out in pool halls, may actually operationalize social learning concepts, such as association with deviant peers. Likewise, it is inconsistent with routine activities to focus on behaviors that "carry connotations of deviance or virtue" (Osgood *et al.,* 1996: 637) because the approach is very clear in rejecting the notion that crime is caused by violations of norms and values. The Osgood *et al.* (1996) study of young adults measured time spent with peers in unstructured and unsupervised activities, using variables from the *Monitoring the Future* questionnaire, which included riding in a car for fun, visiting with friends, going to parties, and going out for the evening. They found strong support for the hypothesis that socializing with peers away from the home and authority figures was closely associated with deviant behavior. But just spending time in informal and unsupervised activities with peers does not predict deviance, they argued. This was only the case if the activity did not include a "structuring agenda" (1996: 651). Thus, activities like going on a date or playing sports, even if done away from home away from the watchful eyes of parents and other supervisory adults, do not significantly contribute to deviance. The conclusion that deviance is more likely among youth who spend more time "hanging out" with their friends in the absence of authority figures seems to be very robust – numerous other studies had similar findings.

The strong influence of context in determining what behaviors are deemed accept-able in a particular time and place is seen by many researchers as not fully explicated in the Cohen and Felson's 1979 *American Sociological Review* article. Attempts to integrate routine activities with other theories aim to address this apparent weakness.

Osgood and Anderson (2004), for example, tested whether the individual-level perspective advanced by Osgood *et al.* (1996) could be used to account for aggregate-level variation. They attempted to integrate routine activities with social disorganization theory by examining whether communities where a large proportion of youth spend much of their time in unstructured and unsupervised activities have higher levels of adolescent delinquency. The subjects of the study were over 4,000 eighth-grade students at schools where a school-based gang prevention program had been implemented. The measure of interest was an item which asked "In an average week, how many hours do you spend hanging around with your current friends, not doing anything in particular, where no adults are present?" (Osgood and Anderson 2004: 530). Questions were also asked concerning to what extent the respondent's parents know what he or she is doing, where, and with whom. Other explanatory variables included the school environment, commitment to school success, attach-ment to parents, impulsivity, risk taking, and various demographic characteristics, thus allowing for a comparison of routine activities against both social control and self control theories. The research supported the hypothesis – the higher the aggre-gate rates of unstructured socializing, the greater the opportunity for all teenagers in that group.

Using a different level of analysis (the face block – one side of a city block, but including locations on both sides of the street) Rice and Smith (2002) proposed to integrate routine activities and social disorganization theories as a means to explain the spatial distribution of auto theft. Social disorganization concepts were operationalized by the number of black people, the number of single-parent households, distance from the city center, and percentage below the property line. Routine activities variables focused on land use, and included the number of commercial places, the number of hotels and motels, the number of "youth places," the number of vacant lots and parking lots, the number of stores and shops, the number of multifamily buildings, and the average assessed apartment or office value. The measures simultaneously operationalized target availability and guardianship. For example, it was assumed that face blocks with large numbers of stores and shops will have more cars parked on the street compared to residential areas, and the cars will be less guarded as well. Rice and Smith (2002) concluded that the tandem occurrence of opportunity and motivated offenders on socially disorganized face blocks results in more auto theft than just opportunity or motivation taken individually. There was evidence of the value of an integrated approach – context is important.

Wilcox and colleagues (2003) developed a "dynamic, multicontextual criminal opportunity theory" in which they integrated routine activities with what they argued is often seen as the competing and contradictory social control theory. This more general model was specifically designed to support multilevel analysis, in particular techniques such as hierarchical linear models.

THE FUTURE OF ROUTINE ACTIVITIES

The research agenda focusing on connections between individual-level and context-specific variables is likely to continue. There is value in this approach, for the convergence in time and space of likely offender, suitable target, and lack of a capable guardian does not happen in a vacuum. But researchers need not look to other theories, such as social disorganization, for these measures. However, they do need to look beyond the 1979 *American Sociological Review* article for ideas about operationalizing routine activities concepts, because much has been written since then to expand the approach.

Routine activities has tremendous utility for crime prevention, largely because the straight-forward nature of the micro-level aspect of the approach points to specific measures that can be taken. Targets can be made less suitable, guardians more capable, place managers more observant, and handlers more effective, all without undertaking the difficult task of trying to make people better.

The close association between routine activities, rational choice, crime pattern theory, and situational crime prevention is continuing to be a source of practical research. The increasing popularity of this merged field, as evidenced by growing numbers of scholars who attend the annual Environmental Criminology and Crime Analysis symposium, as well as the recent formation of specialized research groups in England, bodes well for the future of routine activities. One would expect to see increased collaboration and an even deeper melding of these approaches into a comprehensive perspective. The incorporation of geographic information systems and agent-based modeling into the work of these "crime scientists" promises to ensure that the research will continue to be cutting-edge and attract the brightest young scholars in criminology and related disciplines.

REFERENCES

Barker, R. G. (1968). *Ecological Psychology: Concepts and Methods for Studying the Environment of Human Behavior.* Stanford, CA: Stanford University Press.

Barker, R. G. (1978). Theory of behavior settings. In R. G. Barker and Associates (eds), *Habitats, Environments, and Human Behavior* (pp. 213–228). San Francisco, CA: Jossey-Bass Publishers.

Brantingham, P. J. and Brantingham, P. L. (1991). Introduction: The dimensions of crime. In P. J. Brantingham and P. L. Brantingham (eds), *Environmental Criminology* (pp. 7–26). Prospect Heights, IL: Waveland Press.

Bratt, C. (2008). Guardians to counter adolescent drug use? Limitations of a routine activity approach. *Youth & Society* 39(3): 385–405.

Clarke, R. V. (1999). *Hot Products: Understanding, Anticipating and Reducing Demand for Stolen Goods.* Police Research Series, Paper 112. Policing and Reducing Crime Unit. London, UK: Home Office.

Cohen, L. and Felson, M. (1979). Social change and crime rate trends: a routine activity approach. *American Sociological Review* 44(4): 588–608.

Duncan, O. D. (1959). Human ecology and population studies. In P. M. Hauser and O. D. Duncan (eds), *The Study of Population: An Inventory and Appraisal* (pp. 678–716). Chicago, IL: University of Chicago Press.

Eck, J. E. and Weisburd, D. (1995). Crime places in crime theory. In J. E. Eck and D. Weisburd (eds), *Crime and Place*, Crime Prevention Studies, Vol. 4 (pp. 1–34). Monsey, NY: Willow Tree Press.

Felson, M. (1986). Linking criminal choices, routine activities, informal control, and criminal outcomes. In D. B. Cornish and R. V. Clarke (eds), *The Reasoning Criminal: Rational Choice Perspectives on Offending* (pp. 119–128). New York: Springer-Verlag.

Felson, M. (1994). *Crime and Everyday Life*. Thousand Oaks, CA: Pine Forge Press.

Felson, M. (2006). *Crime and Nature*. Thousand Oaks, CA: Sage Publications.

Felson, M. (2008). Routine activities approach. In R. Wortley and L. Mazerolle (eds), *Environmental Criminology and Crime Analysis* (pp. 70–77). Portland, OR: Willan Publishing.

Felson, M. and Clarke, R. V. (1998). *Opportunity Makes the Thief: Practical Theory for Crime Prevention.* Police Research Series, Paper 98. Policing and Reducing Crime Unit. London, UK: Home Office.

Grasmick, H., Tittle, C. R., Bursik, R. J. and Arneklev, B. J. (1993). Testing the core implications of Gottfredson and Hirschi's general theory of crime. *Journal of Research in Crime and Delinquency* 30(1): 5–29.

Hawley, A. (1950). *Human Ecology: A Theory of Community Structure.* New York, NY: Ronald Press Co.

Hay, C. and Forrest, W. (2008). Self-control theory and the concept of opportunity: The case for a more systematic union. *Criminology* 46(4): 1039–1072.

Hindelang, M., Gottfredson, M. and Garofalo, J. (1978). *Victims of Personal Crime*. Cambridge, MA: Ballinger.

Land, K. C. and Felson, M. (1976). A general framework for building dynamic macro social indicator models: Including an analysis of changes in crime rates and police expenditures. *American Journal of Sociology* 82(3): 565–604.

Miethe, T. D. and Meier, R. F. (1990). Opportunity, choice, and criminal victimization: A test of a theoretical model. *Journal of Research in Crime and Delinquency* 27(3): 243–266.

Ogburn, W. F. (1922) *Social Change with Respect to Culture and Original Nature*. New York: B. W. Huebsch.

Osgood, D. W. and Anderson, A. L. (2004). Unstructured socializing and rates of delinquency. *Criminology* 42(3): 519–549.

Osgood, D. W., Wilson, J. K., O'Malley, P. M., Bachman, J. G. and Johnston, L. D. (1996). Routine activities and individual deviant behavior. *American Sociological Review* 61(4): 635–655.

Rice, K. J. and Smith, W. R. (2002). Socioecological models of automotive theft: Integrating routine activity and social disorganization approaches. *Journal of Research in Crime and Delinquency* 39(3): 304–336.

Wilcox, P., Land, K. C. and Hunt, S. A. (2003). *Criminal Circumstance: A Dynamic Multi-Contextual Criminal Opportunity Theory.* New York: Aldine de Gruyter.

Zipf, G. (1949). *Human Behavior and the Principle of Least Effort: An Introduction to Human Ecology.* Cambridge, MA: Addison-Wesley.

12

Feminist Perspectives in Criminology: A Review with Gen Y in Mind

Kathleen Daly

What does *feminism* mean to Generation Y? Born in affluent western nations between 1980 and 1992, Gen Y is in their late teens and twenties, the age range of those reading texts like this.[1] A UK study suggests that for Gen Y members, 'the cultural and economic enfranchisement of women is deep rooted and irreversible', and Gen Y men and women hold similar attitudes 'not only to work and politics but even to feminism itself' (Wynter, 2006: 145, quoting Demos Foundation). In fact, many (most?) Gen Y women do not call themselves feminists. I am confronted, then, with a problem: what does a chapter on feminist perspectives in criminology mean to readers for whom feminism or feminist perspectives are viewed as irrelevant?

Another way to view the situation is to assume that popularised versions of feminist ideas have already been absorbed by Gen Y. For that reason, young women have no need to join a social movement or to brand their ideas a certain way. This phenomenon holds for criminology: popularised versions of feminist ideas and concepts have seeped into common knowledge. Students generally understand and appreciate the circumstances of partner and sexual violence; they realise that many offenders have also been victimised; and they are aware of the double standard of treatment for male and female prisoners. These ideas, which are commonplace today, were new 35 years ago, when they were first introduced by feminist movement activists and academics. Since then, more sophisticated theories have been put forward by feminist scholars, including those in criminology. Although feminist movement activity is more quiet today, theory and research with a focus on girls/boys, women/ men, and sex/gender continues to flourish.

In this chapter, I present and discuss key feminist conceptual breakthroughs in criminology. For those familiar with popularised understandings, these new concepts and theories may encourage an interest to dive deeper, and to embark on more sophisticated understandings of sex/gender in crime, victimisation, and justice. Although Gen Y members seem to be familiar, indeed appreciative, of feminist ideas, some may be uncertain about what it means to be 'a feminist' or what a 'feminist theory' is, or they may lack confidence in applying feminist concepts and ideas to criminological phenomena. If this chapter goes some way toward clearing up confusion and encouraging confidence, then it will have succeeded.

STUDENT ENGAGEMENT WITH FEMINIST IDEAS

I begin with two emails from students, who seek my views on feminism and criminology. Their questions show sources of confusion and a need for encouragement. I have preserved all the spelling, capitalisation, and misuses of grammar in their emails because this helps to see the mindset and emotion of the writer.

The first comes from L, a British female university student, in 2004. Following L's email is my response to her.

Hello,
My name is L and i attend the university of Lancaster in the UK. i am doing an essay on feminist approach to reconciliation instead of punishment within the criminal justice system. I came across an article you wrote on this topic, and i was wondering whether you are a feminist yourself. since you have a considerable knowledge on this area i was wondering if you could direct me to other feminist writers who are and who are not in flavor of it.

Thank you soooooooooooooo much, and your time.
L
****

L
See Oxford Handbook of Criminology for numerous references to my work on feminism and criminology. See my website (below) for articles on RJ and feminism, esp under part 2 of publications, forthcoming article in Violence Against Women on victim advocacy groups and the idea of RJ. I'm currently engaged in a major program of research on the race and gender politics of new justice practices, which includes RJ and Indigenous justice. I am surprised that you haven't heard of me and my work on feminism and criminology. I've been at it for over 20 years ...
Kathy

L surprises me with her question, 'I was wondering if you are a feminist yourself'. I wonder why she is uncertain. I like the image of being 'in flavor' of a particular view on a debate, and I smile when I see 'soooooooooooooo much'. That's real appreciation!

The second is from a male university student in California, whose home town, he tells me later, is near the Mexican border. We exchanged notes in 2007.

Hello Mrs. Daly,
   I was wondering if you could help me with a school project. I am currently enrolled in a Feminist Course and my professor asked us to select and research a feminist so i have decided to choose you:) I hope this is not an inconvenience for you. We are also required to select a film to study and i also chose ***MARIA FULL OF GRACE*** but in order to finish my project i need some information about you. ...

I was looking for information about you online but i just found books like Criminology at the crossroads: feminist readings in crime and justice. ... is there a homepage on you to get information. ...

BASICALLY i am going to apply the SOCIALIST FEMINISM VIEW for the film i saw and i just thought that maybe you can give me some FEEDBACK how you feel about SOCIALIST FEMINISM to help me write my paper. WHAT other special books have you written? How do you feel about SOCIALIST FEMINISM and opression in LATIN AMERICAN COUNTRIES? HOw do you feel about socialist feminism and opression???

PLEASE ANY INFORMATION IS GOOD... THANK YOU
G
****

Dear G
Socialist feminism was the start of a multi-ethnic analysis, but today, you should read more recent analysis in critical race feminism. There are several readers out, and they have essays on latinas and feminism, which are relevant to Maria Full of Grace. See the reader edited by Adrienne Wing.

As for information about me, attached is my latest cv and some recent bio blurbs. I have a website (see below), although the cv and bio blurbs are a bit out of date. The very first article on the website is relevant in giving some biographical stuff as to why I came to Australia.

Where are you writing from?
best wishes, Prof Daly

****

GOOD AFTERNOON,
THANK YOU VERY MUCH FOR ALL OF the information you provided. This will surely help my understandings of feminism and broaden my knowledge as well. I Appreciate everything that you have done for me. I am writing from CALIFORNIA STATE UNIVERSITY IN SAN BERNARDINO but i reside in a small little COMMUNITY named IMPERIAL, CALIFORNIA close to the border with MEXICALI, MEXICO adjacent to SAN DIEGO CALIFORNIA and TIJUANA MEXICO!!:) THANK YOU AGAIN FOR EVERYTHING ...
G

Several things strike me about G's note. He is taking a feminist course in a university, and he is using 'socialist feminism' and 'oppression' not distantly, but in ways that suggest the terms are meaningful to him. He wonders if they would be appropriate in analysing 'Maria Full of Grace'. He is right to think they would be because the film is about a Colombian girl, who, after being fired from her job at a flower factory, agrees to work as a drug mule, transporting cocaine to New York City. It is not surprising that G finds this film compelling, in light of where he lives. Finally, G is so appreciative of the small direction and advice I offer: he thanks me three times in the second email.

I draw four points about Gen Y and my exchanges with L and G. First, as Wynter (2006) suggests, feminism as a social movement in the 1960s and 1970s, has less visibility and salience to Gen Y. At the same time, a range of popularised ideas generated from feminism – about women and girls, men and boys, and sex/gender – has been absorbed into mainstream Gen Y thinking. But second, I would distinguish these *popularised* ideas from those *theories or concepts* that help us to understand how sex/gender works in complex ways in society and daily life. In other words, it is important to distinguish the *relevance of feminism as a social movement* from *conceptual frameworks to analyse sex/gender*. Although feminism as a social movement may have diminished, at least for some age groups living in affluent western nations, the relevance and need for the latter has not diminished.

Third, it can be difficult to 'spot the feminist' or 'a feminist analysis' because an author may not name the research or argument as 'feminist' or may be exploring domains that are not explicitly about sex/gender, even if the writer is known to be a feminist scholar. I suspect that the reason L asked me, are 'you a feminist yourself', despite my having produced a substantial body of feminist work for over two decades, was that in the article she was reading, I gave no explicit mention of feminist arguments or theories. She may have assumed that feminist scholars have to consistently brand themselves in certain ways, or announce themselves to the reader, or always focus their arguments on sex/gender. This is not necessary, of course, but it can be a source of confusion for those new to the field. Further confusion can arise because the criminological field today is characterised by both feminist and non-feminist analyses of men, women, and crime (see review in Daly, 1998). Thus, just because what you read may have gender content does not mean that the researcher is using, or is even aware of, feminist perspectives. Fourth, some men are comfortable using feminist perspectives in criminological research, and many have done so in analysing masculinities; whereas many women are not.[2] Unlike the 1970s and 1980s, where it was only women who were utilising and discussing feminist perspectives in criminology, this situation has changed. G is a good example of a man, who is struggling to understand race and gender oppression analytically. This would have been unimaginable when I was an undergraduate and graduate student in the 1970s and early 1980s.

FEMINIST THEORIES AND PERSPECTIVES TODAY

There is extraordinary range and sophistication in feminist work. This is a consequence, in part, of the generalist or specialist orientations of researchers (Davis, 2008), and in part, of the disciplinary breadth in feminist knowledge: it ranges across all the disciplines in the humanities, arts and performing arts, education, law, social sciences, natural sciences, engineering and technology, and medical and mental health. In the last 10 to 15 years, there has been considerable international expansion, i.e., beyond advanced capitalist societies of the developed world. Articles in English-language feminist journals such as *Signs, International Women's Studies International Forum* (formerly *Women's Studies International Quarterly*)*, European Journal of Women's Studies, Journal of International Women's Studies, Feminist Studies, Feminist Theory*, and *Feminist Review*, among others, show that areas of great growth today lie in feminist analyses of social conditions in the developing world. If some affluent western women of Gen Y think that feminism is largely irrelevant, women in the developing world do not. Equality and rights are very much on the agenda for most of the world's female population, although their analyses are shaped and coloured by varying conditions and contexts.

What, then, are the elements associated with feminism or feminist perspectives in criminology? Quoting Gelsthorpe (2002: 135, emphasis in original), they are as follows:[3]

- a focus on *sex/gender* as a central organizing principle in social life;
- recognition of the importance of *power* in shaping social relations;
- sensitivity to the influence of social *context* on behaviour;
- recognition that social reality is a *process* and that research methods need to reflect this;
- a political commitment to *social change*;
- personal and theoretical reflexivity on epistemological, methodological, and ethical choices and commitments; and
- openness and creativity in thinking about producing and evaluating knowledge.

When scanning this list, we see many points of overlap between feminist perspectives in criminology and those in critical criminology (Stubbs, 2008; see Anthony and Cunneen, 2008a, more generally). In fact, a significant impact of social movement politics of the 1960s and 1970s was the emergence, in the 1980s, of a cohort of students and researchers with shared interests to expose 'dominant crime discourse and interests it represents' (Anthony and Cunneen, 2008b: 2) and to identify alternatives for social change. There is a good deal of affinity and crossover between feminist perspectives in criminology and those termed critical, anti-racist, multi-ethnic, or cultural criminology. Differences do exist in the focus of research, theories used, and preferred epistemologies and methodologies. However, extrapolating from Cain's (1990a) vision of feminist criminology, the shared enterprise is 'transgressing' and 'transforming' the field of criminology.

FEMINIST PERSPECTIVES IN CRIMINOLOGY: A BRIEF CHRONOLOGY

Because the range and diversity of feminist contributions to criminology is large, those new to the field may feel overwhelmed with a sense of not knowing where to begin. A good place to start is to read retrospective reviews of the past three to four decades. These provide a story of the emergence and development of differing trajectories of feminist work in criminology, as they were informed by the wider field of feminist and other social theories. Recent reviews by scholars in Australia (Carrington, 2008; Daly, 1997, 1998; Daly and Maher, 1998b; Naffine, 1997; Stubbs, 2008), Britain (Gelsthorpe, 2002; Heidensohn and Gelsthorpe, 2007), the United States (Britton, 2000; Burgess-Proctor, 2006; Miller and Mullins, 2006), and Canada (Comack, 1999) contain schematics of differing types of feminist perspectives in, or engagements with, the field of criminology. The following schematizes the differing emphases and debates over time.

During the 1970s and early 1980s, a general aim was to bring girls, women, and gender difference into the criminological frame, to ask 'where are girls, women, and gender in theories of crime, victimisation, and justice?'[4] One focus was to redress the lack of empirical knowledge on female offending and criminalisation, but there was also keen interest to depict and politicize 'everyday violence' in women's lives (Kelly, 1988; Rafter and Stanko, 1982; Stanko, 1990). In the mid 1980s, this early focus gave way to reflecting upon and analysing *differences* among girls and women, particularly with respect to class, racial, and ethnic identities and subjectivities. This shift was prompted by a significant wave of critique by women of colour, beginning in the early 1980s, which argued for more complex analyses of race relations and positionalities between and among men and women. Their critique challenged any simple idea of a 'woman's perspective' and any unified feminist politics for change. Other sites and sources of difference among women were named and brought forward, including those related to sexual identities, nation, disabilities, among others. Connected to and running parallel with this critique, epistemological questions were raised about what constituted authoritative knowledge, or what Harding (1986) termed the 'science question' for feminism. For feminists in criminology, this meant a reflection on methodological assumptions and ethical questions in generating knowledge.

Gelsthorpe (2002) offers an accessible review of three methodological and epistemological orientations taken by feminist scholars: empiricism, standpointism, and deconstruction. Empiricism refers to studies of the 'real world out there', and it takes a variety of forms, ranging from non-critical to critical and post-positivist orientations, such as realism and social constructionism. Standpointism refers to knowledge that is explicitly generated from a 'point of view' or positionality, as for example, a 'black feminist standpoint' by Collins (1990) or a 'feminist standpoint' in criminology by Cain (1990b). Deconstruction refers to analyses that break down categorical thinking, challenge binary oppositions, and reveal meaning in language and discourse. By the end of the 1980s, it was no longer possible to speak of girls or women (or boys and men) as unified categories, nor was it possible to represent any group from one standpoint alone, and certainly not from a 'neutral' position. Binary thinking (as in strong claims of gender difference) and universalist claims (as in 'most girls act this way') became less tenable.

Several important streams of empirical and theoretical work began to emerge at the turn of the 1990s. One stream, informed by empirical research, was interested to depict ethnographically rich 'real women', i.e., the viewpoints, 'experience' (Scott, 1992), and life worlds of girls and women as offenders and victims (Daly, 1992; Daly and Maher, 1998b; Miller, 1998, 2001), including their treatment in criminal courts and prison systems (H. Allen, 1987; Daly, 1994a; Rafter, 1990). Reflecting broader currents in feminist theory to invest girls and women with greater 'agency', concerns were raised about the representation of girls and women as victims and volitional actors (Daly, 1992; Maher, 1997). A second stream drew upon emerging sociological, psychoanalytical, and feminist theories of masculinity to address more fully what J. Allen (1989) has termed the 'maleness of crime' (Messerschmidt, 1993) and to problematize the taken-for-granted subject of criminological theorising: boys and men (Collier, 1998; Jefferson, 1997). A third stream, which drew from poststructuralism and deconstructive approaches, focused on 'women of discourse', i.e., the ways in which women and sexual difference were constituted in and by criminological, legal, and social discourses (Howe, 1994; Smart, 1989; Worrall, 1990; Young, 1996). A related fourth stream, anticipated early by Smart (1990, 1995) explored women as 'sexed subjects' in law (Naffine and Owens, 1997) and 'the body' and 'sexed bodies' as discursively created (Collier, 1998).

SEX AND GENDER: A SEISMIC SHIFT IN FEMINIST THOUGHT

A significant shift occurred in feminist scholarship in the 1990s, with a rethinking of the relationship between sex and gender. To date, this shift has had a minimal impact on feminist work in criminology, but I expect that this will change. Because the shift is relatively recent, I consider the conceptual breakthroughs associated with it toward the end of the chapter. However, I outline it here because it informs my understanding of sex and gender today.

In the 1970s, the received feminist wisdom was that sex was a biological category, in the realm of the 'natural', which distinguished male and female. By comparison, gender was a social category, in the realm of the 'cultural', referencing a diversity of meanings, associations, and identities, that were connected to, but not simply derived from sex difference. As Harrison (2006: 35) suggests, the point of making a distinction between sex and gender 'was not to create two concepts, but to allow the concept of gender to take off'. By 'gender taking off', she means that while sex is typically conceived as male or female, i.e., two ways of being in nature, gender could reference a wider and more fluid field of relations, differences, and identities. Further, because sex differences in contemporary society are 'drawn into a dualistic frame of reference' (Smart, 1990: 204), where male and female 'traits' are arrayed hierarchically, with the male represented as the 'universal' and the female as the 'difference', or the 'mark of sex' (Harrison, 2006: 36–38, discussing Delphy, 1984), the concept of *gender* was a liberating force for change, a way to imagine 'overcoming' sex difference and inequality.

In the early 1990s, this conventional wisdom began to change. Rather then viewing sex as a pre-social biological concept, theorists argued it too was socially and discursively constructed (Butler, 1990, 1993). By this is meant that particular body parts and capacities (such as genitals and reproductive capacities) are given a particular social significance in language and culture; moreover, specific understandings of sex difference are not the same across time and culture, but variable. Associated with this shift in seeing both sex and gender as socially and discursively created, was a rethinking of 'the body'. Rather than seeing the body as a biological given, as residing on the subordinate side of a mind ('culture') and body ('nature') dualism, scholars wished to break this dualism by using terms such as 'embodied subjectivity', 'psychical corporeality' (Grosz, 1994: p. 22), and 'embodied experience' (Lacey, 1997: 74).

What are the benefits of making such a break? One is that we can imagine and recognise diverse 'embodied experiences' or subjectivities, not just two categories of male and female. Second, we may also recognise that sex and gender may 'in practice' be 'indistinguishable from one another' (Harrison, 2006: 46). Harrison draws from Wacquant's (2003) account of becoming a boxer, where training 'involves not only the creation of a particular kind of body but also the shaping of a whole moral and psychological universe inhabited by the boxer' (p. 47). She argues that we need to think of 'body and mind – musculature and skill, fantasy and conceptualization – [as] indivisible ... more than mere morphology. It has to be taken right through to the biochemistry of body and brain' (Harrison, 2006: 47). In so doing, there is an 'incorporation', perhaps a fusion, of the biological and cultural: there are particular ways of 'incarnating masculinity, femininity, or even a transgendered status, in the body. We shape ourselves at the very moment in which we are shaped' (p. 47).

Harrison (2006) is right, I think, to see sex and gender as 'incorporated': at times they may be 'indistinguishable', and at other times, incorporation can produce multiple subjectivities, subject positions, and sexed bodies.[5] To keep that complexity in mind, I use sex/gender to reference an incorporation, not a dualism or binary; and I use this term in writing from my current perspective as a feminist thinker. Up to the mid to late 1990s, however, virtually all feminist contributions to criminology, including mine, used terms such as gender, gender difference, and gendered phenomenon. Sex was absent, and there was a presumed separation of sex and gender. In my review of feminist conceptual breakthroughs, I present the terms as they were discussed at the time, i.e., with a sole focus on gender. However, be aware that sex/gender terms are now shifting in use and meaning.

FEMINIST CONCEPTUAL BREAKTHROUGHS IN CRIMINOLOGY

Few feminist scholars are interested to devise a grand theory of crime. Indeed, the trend across the criminological spectrum today is to view such a quest as misguided, a product of earlier modernist ideals in criminology (Garland, 2002). All researchers recognise that their work is part of a larger mosaic of knowledge and that one theory is incapable of explaining the complexity and diversity of individual, occupational, organisational, and state crime. I present a selected set of feminist concepts and conceptual breakthroughs, which give the feminist project in criminology its distinctive signature.[6] Some concepts reveal theoretical problems for criminology and how it constructs knowledge about women (or men) and sex/gender; whereas others may be applied in analysing crime, victimisation, justice, or institutions of social control. For simplicity, the examples I give focus largely on crime and offending.

The generalizability problem and the gender ratio problem

In 1988, two problems were identified in building theories of gender and crime (Daly and Chesney-Lind, 1988). One, the generalizability problem, asked if theories of crime, which at the time were drawn exclusively from research on boys/men, could be applied to girls/women. The second, the gender ratio problem, asked why boys/men were more likely to commit crime than girls/women. The conceptual breakthrough was to distinguish these as separate theoretical problems. For example, Merton's (1938) strain theory or elements in various social control theories may explain variation *among* girls' or women's rates of offending (although some terms and concepts would need to be changed), but they could not explain differences in the rates of men's and women's offending. By pointing out that the generalizability problem and the gender ratio problem were distinctive theoretical and empirical tasks, the ground was cleared for people to think more precisely about what they were trying to explain: variability within or differences between groups.

During the 1970s and early 1980s, feminist critiques exposed the omission of girls and women in so-called 'general' theories of crime; and when girls/women were studied, critics noted that biological explanations were more often used to explain women's than men's offending. Although critiques of crime theories formed one wedge of feminist inquiry in this early phase, of greater significance was bringing to light women's victimisation, in particular, physical and sexual violence by men they knew.

Blurred boundaries of victimisation and criminalisation

Connections began to be made between girls' and women's experiences of victimisation and their subsequent offending or criminalisation. It became clear that offender and victim groups were not distinctive, but often overlapped. The concept of 'blurred boundaries of victimisation and criminalisation', which collectively emerged in the 1980s and early 1990s (e.g., Carlen, 1987; Chesney-Lind and Rodriquez, 1983; Daly, 1992; Gilfus, 1992; Klein, 1988; Maher and Curtis, 1992) captures these ideas. For example, girls may run away from abusive homes to the streets, where their efforts to survive are criminalised (Chesney-Lind, 1989; Gilfus, 1992). Living rough on the street, young women are not only pulled into lawbreaking, but also they are subject to high levels of abuse and violence (Hatty, 1997: 212). Women in violent relationships may see killing an abusive partner as their only exit option (Browne, 1987); or they may fight back to protect themselves from abusive mates (Dobash and Dobash, 2004: 341–342).

The 'blurred boundaries' concept offers a more holistic picture of the developmental, biographical, and situational contexts of victimisation and offending. At the same time, it raises questions about the meaning of 'responsibility' or 'culpability' for crime when offending is viewed as arising, in part, from immediate or past victimisation. One potential problem with 'blurred boundaries' is that it may promote explanations for offending that focus mainly on victimization, which leaves little room for agency or responsibility (Daly, 1992: 48–49). Research is exploring the complex developmental relations of victimisation and offending (Simpson *et al.*, 2008; Teague *et al.*, 2008). Meanwhile, studies of imprisoned women show that victimisation is a dominant motif in their lives (Richie, 1996).

Woman of discourse and real women

During the late 1980s, two distinctive trajectories emerged within feminist research in criminology: 'woman of discourse' and 'real women' (Daly and Maher, 1998b). Both were prompted by major challenges to feminism in the 1980s: one, from within (black and racialized women's critiques of dominant white analyses in feminist thought); and the other, from without (poststructuralist critiques of positivist social science and dualisms in western thought) (see Daly, 1997). The terms 'woman of discourse' and 'real women' are metaphors to describe differing ways of theorising women (and men) in the social world. Although they are not incompatible, they reflect different emphases and theoretical orientations.

The woman of legal discourse, developed by Smart (1992), proposes that 'Woman is a gendered subject position which legal discourse brings into being' (p. 34). There is more to her argument and its implications than I have space to explore here. My aim here is to situate Smart's argument as one type of theoretical approach that is concerned with how women (or men and sex/gender) are constituted in and by legal, criminological, and social discourses; and with how disciplines themselves (e.g., law and criminology) discursively construct women, men, and sex/gender. (Other examples are Howe, 1994; Young, 1996: Chapter 2.) With respect to the male-centred or masculine-valued qualities in criminology, early feminist critiques were made by Klein (1973), Naffine (1987), and Smart (1976). However, Smart's (1992) more recent poststructuralist argument departs from these by suggesting that law (or criminology) is not 'monolithic and unitary' (p. 40), nor does it produce women in 'some predetermined, calculated, powerless form' (p. 41).

By 'real women' is meant feminist social science studies that explore women as agents in constructing their life worlds, including lawbreaking and victimisation. These may include interview, observational, or ethnographic studies of girls' or women's behaviour, 'talk', and 'accounts'. They include a range of critical empirical inquiries on the shifting constraints, material conditions, decisions and actions, and possibilities of girls' and women's lives. Examples are Carlen (1988), Maher (1997), Miller (2001), and selections in Daly and Maher (1998a).

One cannot fully depict 'real women' without reference to the discursive fields by which girls and women are constructed and construct themselves. Likewise, one cannot assume that analyses of 'women of discourse' necessarily reflect girls' and women's identities and the lives they lead. Ideally and depending on the focus of inquiry, theory and research should attempt to interpolate 'the discursive' and 'the real', as Smart (1995: 231) also acknowledges. The problem is that each approach comes with its own set of theoretical referents and specialized vocabularies, and researchers tend to specialize in one or the other. There are some exceptions (see, e.g., Bosworth, 1999; Maher, 1997; Mason, 2002; Miller, 2001), and we should see more in the future.

Gendered pathways, gendered crime, and gendered lives

Based on studies carried out in the 1980s and 1990s, which typically used a 'real women' frame of reference, I identified several directions of feminist research on crime (Daly, 1998). I suggested that gender differences in rates of arrest or criminalisation (the 'gender ratio problem') should not be the sole focus of inquiry. There were other directions (Daly, 1998: 94–95):

- *Gendered pathways to lawbreaking*: What is the nature of, and what explains the character of girls'/women's and boys'/men's pathways to lawbreaking? What brings people to the street, to use illegal drugs, to become involved in workplace crime, or to be arrested and prosecuted for crime? How do boys/men and girls/women move in and out of foster homes, conventional work, jails and prisons, hospitals, and halfway houses?
- *Gendered crime*: What are the contexts and qualities of boys'/men's and girls'/women's illegal acts? What is the social organization of specific offences (e.g., drug dealing, prostitution, and credit frauds)?

- *Gendered lives*: How does gender organize the ways in which men and women survive, take care of themselves and their children, and find shelter and food? How does gender structure thinkable courses of action and identities?

Miller and Mullins (2006) review and discuss this conceptual scheme, with an extended analysis of masculinities and crime, adding new references and research. I commend their review for those interested.

Gendered pathways emphasises biographical elements, life course trajectories, and developmental sequences. There are non-feminist versions of the pathways idea, for example, the life course analyses of Sampson and Laub (1993) and the criminal career orientation of Blumstein *et al.* (1988).[7] Feminist versions give analytical attention to girls' routes to the street, likely forms of income generation, and relationships with other women, men, and children, at times applying the 'blurred boundaries' theme. In Daly (1992), I identified a leading feminist scenario of women's lawbreaking, that of 'street women', who run from abusive families, whose efforts to survive on the street are criminalised, and who may use illegal drugs, which leads to further lawbreaking and time spent in and out of jail. From a review of defendants' files in a New Haven felony court, I found that 'street women' was one of several major pathways to court, but there were others. Simpson *et al.* (2008) applied my pathways typology to over 350 women awaiting trial in a Baltimore Detention Centre. Their study found 'substantial overlap' (p. 102) in several New Haven and Baltimore women's pathways; but they also identified new pathways and differences in pathways, depending on when a woman first offended (in childhood, adolescence, or adulthood).

Gendered crime refers to (1) the ways in which street life, drugs and sex markets, informal economies, crime opportunities, and crime groups are ordered by gender and other social relations and (2) variation in the sequencing and contexts of boys'/men's and girls'/women's lawbreaking, including their offence roles, accounts of themselves, and how their acts are translated into official crime categories.[8] There are several ways to research gendered crime. Offence elements, such as the size of the crime group and a person's role in the offence can be counted and compared, although we know that elements alone do not grasp the subtleties and gestalt of crime (Daly, 1994a: 96, 99, 108). Ethnographies of 'the street' and the informal drug economy can show its sexed and gendered character (Maher, 1997). By taking a 'doing gender' approach, one can analyse crime as a flexible repertoire of situated and structured actions (see section below on 'doing gender').

Gendered lives refers to the different ways that men and women experience society. Fineman (1990) developed the concept of women's gendered lives to counter gender-neutral legal theories. She observes that women's existences are constituted by a variety of experiences: material, psychological, physical, social, and cultural. Some have a biological basis, and others are rooted in culture and custom (Fineman, 1995: 45). Applying this idea to criminology means to examine the wider picture of how the 'gender-related conditions of life' (Bottcher, 1995: 37) create the potential for delinquent and non-delinquent actions and identities. Using this approach, one is also likely to explore gendered pathways, gendered crime, or both.

In her first study, Bottcher (1995) conceptualised gender 'as social control', using individuals as the unit of analysis; but in a later study, she shifted her focus by conceptualising gender as a 'process of social life', using 'social practices of gender as a unit of analysis' (Bottcher, 2001: 924), drawing from Giddens (1984). Bottcher's 'social practices of gender' shares affinities with gender as situated action ('doing gender'), but it identifies a particular set of social practices that create and reproduce the 'gender ratio of crime'. Specifically, three significant areas in young people's lives are explored: 'making friends and having fun, relating sexually and becoming parents, and surviving hardship and finding purpose' (Bottcher, 2001: 905), each of which is associated with sub-sets of social practices. She identifies the following dimensions as most salient in explaining gender differences in 'high risk' youths' delinquency:

> ... teenage children and parental responsibilities, assumed largely by the females; highly sex-segregated friendship groups; more crime-prone activities for males than for females; male dominance in virtually all adolescent activities; differences in the timing of transition to adult-hood; and limited social support for female delinquency, compared with male delinquency.
> (Bottcher, 2001: 923)

Her findings were drawn from interviewing young people, asking them about their daily routines, what they did, who they spent time with, and what their most danger-ous experience was, among other items.

Bottcher's theory and method departs significantly from standard criminological approaches that attempt to devise and test theories of the gender ratio of crime. Such efforts are limited because they display little understanding of girls'/women's or boys'/men's day-to-day routines and life worlds, they contain poorly conceived or popularised ideas about gender, or there is little or no attention is paid to gender practices and power relations. Her approach shows the value of building theories from 'outside' criminology and from the bottom up: starting from gendered social practices (or other theories of sex/gender) and relating these to delinquency and crime. This approach is more promising than starting with existing criminological theories and attempting, then, to 'add' girls, women, or sex/gender. These latter approaches often have ill-founded assumptions about sex/gender, use variables that are not dynamic or interactive, or employ quantitative-only designs that are not ame-nable to interpreting social processes.

Class–race–gender and intersectionality

A significant body of work emerged in the 1980s that addressed the multiple, cross-cutting, and contingent influences of class, race, gender, and other relations in social phenomenon (Daly, 1993, 1997). In time, the theoretical concept came to be termed 'intersectional analysis' or 'intersectionality'. It is used widely today in all areas of feminist inquiry, including criminology, becoming as Davis (2008: 75) suggests, a 'buzzword' for feminist inquiry. The editors of a special issue of the *European Journal of Women's Studies* on 'intersectionality' (Phoenix and Pattynama, 2006: 187) suggest that the concept is popular because it is 'a handy catchall phrase that aims to make visible the multiple positioning that constitutes everyday life and the power relations that are central to it'.

An intersectionality perspective assumes that everyone is located in a matrix of multiple social relations, and that these operate at different levels: macro (society or institutions), meso (neighbourhoods, streets), and micro (individual). Particular social relations or identities may be more salient in one context than another. Structural relations are not additive, but interactive, contingent, and inflected by other social relations. Because everyone is located in a social matrix, an intersectional analysis is just as relevant to middle-class white men as it is to working-class black women. Intersectional analyses can also be used to politicise and problematize the construction of knowledge, in light of the different world views or lenses that participants bring to encounters.

In criminology, as in other fields, researchers may conceptualise intersectionality in different ways. Some foreground structure and multiple inequalities, whereas others examine context and contingency of multiple identities. These different approaches have been termed, respectively, 'systemic intersectionality' and 'constructionist intersectionality' (Prins, 2006), but they do not exhaust the range of approaches taken (Phoenix and Pattynama, 2006: 188). How one conducts an intersectional analysis – what methods to use – is open to debate (compare, e.g., Davis, 2008; McCall, 2005; and Simpson and Gibbs, 2006), as is the potential for intersectional analyses to 'inspire political action and policy development' (Phoenix and Pattynama, 2006: 189).

Intersectionality is a significant conceptual development in feminist criminology. Although many analysts *advocate* taking an intersectional perspective (see, e.g., Burgess-Proctor, 2006: 39–43), *actually doing so* is harder and more challenging (Daly, 1993: 64–66; Daly, 1994b: 433). With some notable exceptions (e.g., Maher, 1997; Chapter 7), intersectional analyses in criminology are more an aspiration for the future than a research practice today.

Doing gender

Drawing from social theories of 'situated action', West and Zimmerman (1987) popularised the concept of 'doing gender', which describes gender as a 'situated accomplishment' (p. 126). Rather than seeing gender as a trait, role, or variable (p. 129), they conceptualised it as 'an emergent feature of social situations':

> [It is] an outcome of and a rationale for ... social arrangements ... a means of legitimating [a] fundamental division ... of society. [Gender is] a routine, methodical, and recurring accomplishment.
>
> (p. 126)

Gender is thus socially constructed and 'produced' in interaction. It is behaviourally generated, involving action, movement, and accomplishment, along with attributions of that behaviour by onlookers. West and Zimmerman's conceptualisation, while sharing some affinities with Smart (1992) in seeing gender as 'produced', differs from hers because Smart is concerned with law's *discursive* production of sex/gender.

Miller (2002) reviews research that takes a 'doing gender' in criminology, clarifying theoretical elements, and critiquing some applications of the concept. Her review essay, coupled with Miller and Mullins (2006), offers a comprehensive analysis of theoretical developments in this area, including recent sociological theories of gender (e.g., Connell, 2002a). Miller (2002) takes a 'situated/structured action' to 'doing gender', which means she is interested not only in gender difference and inequalities, but also those based on 'race, sexuality, and generation' (p. 439).

The first empirical applications of 'doing gender' in criminology focused on masculinities and crime (Messerschmidt, 1993), drawing on Connell's (1987) theorisations of gender. Messerschdmit's (1993: 85) early argument, in a nutshell, was that crime may be 'invoked as a practice through which masculinities (and men and women) are differentiated from one another. Moreover, crime is a resource that may be summoned when men lack other resources to accomplish gender'. Messerschmidt identified a range of masculinities: hegemonic, accommodating, and oppositional, to account for the fact that boys and men are differently positioned (by race, class, and age) in the social order. However, one major problem with his early formulation was that hegemonic masculinity[9] was used as both a cause and an effect of crime (Collier, 1998: 21). A second problem was that crime as 'doing masculinity' over-determined men's offending. Hood-Williams (2001: 44) puts it this way:

> In the famous phrases that echo around the masculinities literature, doing crime is doing masculinity; crime is a resource for doing gender; crime is men's work. The question remains, however, why it is that only a minority of men need to produce masculinity through crime rather than through other, non-criminal, means? Messerschmidt's theoretical scheme offers no formal mechanism that makes the discrimination.[10]

To be fair, the analogous problem occurs when it is said that 'poverty causes crime'. Although higher proportions of economically dispossessed than affluent people may commit common crime, most do not. Likewise for gender: a higher share of men than women commit crime, but most men do not. On this, I would add that whereas 'doing masculinity' has intuitive appeal, most people would find 'doing poverty' to be in bad taste. This anticipates a third major problem with doing gender: how to apply the concept to people who are differently arrayed 'within hierarchies of structural position' (e.g., gender, race, class, sexuality) (Miller, 2002: 439).

The problem is addressed by Miller (2002: 441–449) in some detail, and I can only gloss it here. She explores how 'doing masculinity' and crime may apply to girls and women, in particular, to the girls in the 'majority-male, mixed-gender youth gangs' (p. 445) she studied. She finds that those gang girls who are accorded the most respect are 'one of the guys'. They achieve this status by 'gender crossing', more specifically by distancing themselves from a 'denigrated sexual identity' as 'ho' or 'slut' (p. 446). For example, one girl, Latisha, described herself as 'like a dude in a girl's body'. Latisha emphasised that the boys respected her (and other girls) '*as females* ..., [but] we just so much like dudes that they just don't trip off of it' (p. 446, emphasis in original). Being treated 'like a dude' meant that the girls were not treated in 'overly sexualised ways' (p. 446); this status was actively sought by the girls to address gender inequalities, not to accomplish 'femininity'. Because gender relations and constructs of masculinity and femininity are not symmetrical but are based on an organising principle of men's superiority, 'there are greater rewards and incentives for women to "cross" into culturally defined masculine terrain than there are for men to cross into feminine terrain' (p. 445). The implications of this point are crucial for understanding girls' and women's 'situated action', including crime. Miller suggests that 'it is as much a response to and negotiation with gender inequality as it is a resource for accomplishing gender', drawing on Kandiyoti's (1988) evocative phrase of 'bargaining with patriarchy' (p. 452). Specifically, we may see a range of 'gender strategies for navigating within male-dominated terrains'

(p. 452) that are used by girls and women in participating (or not) in crime. For example, in committing robberies, some women may explicitly 'use' female sexuality (as when they feign sexual interest in a man); whereas others may hide their bodies and instead dress 'like a man' (see Miller, 1998). In the mixed gang context, girls may participate with boys as a way to reduce police suspicion of the boys' criminal activity; and they may rely on the boys 'for protection' in dangerous environments, despite their status as 'one of the guys'.

Miller's (2002) analysis shows that girls and women use a flexible repertoire of situated actions that may (or may not) be principally concerned with accomplishing normative femininity. She argues that gender dualisms should be avoided because they limit an appreciation of gender 'crossing', and that doing gender does not occur in a symmetrical way for boys/men and girls/women in light of gender inequalities. Although the application of 'doing gender' and crime was initiated in the early 1990s as one way to theorise boys and men, masculinities, and crime,[11] it has moved further, with greater theoretical complexity, when applied to girls and women, femininities, and crime.

Sexed bodies and sexed subjects

The concepts of 'sexed bodies' and 'sexed subjects' emerged at the turn of the 1990s as feminist scholars re-examined sex and gender (the 'seismic shift' above). These concepts are used in different, and often complex ways, which I shall try to simplify. Although I sketch different approaches, a common element is to view sex/gender not as a dualism, where one is 'biological' and the other 'cultural', but rather as a socially produced embodiment.

One approach uses 'sexed bodies' to explore the 'sexed subjectivity' of men: 'subjectivity understood as embodiment, subjectivity as the lived experience of a (specifically masculine) body as it is socially and culturally inscribed' (Collier, 1998: 32). Collier is critical of Messerschmidt's 'doing gender' approach to masculinities and crime because it ignores the 'specificities of male and female bodies' (p. 25). He argues that 'sexed bodies' is a more satisfactory way to depict and theorise men's crime because it explicitly addresses 'ideas of the body, sexual difference, and subjectivities' (p. 33) which are otherwise 'silenced' in debates on masculinities and crime. He argues that we should analyse the particular 'system of signification' within which 'particular sexed bodies of men [are] valorised', rather than the behaviourally-oriented approaches, which examine gender only, not sex/gender as 'embodied subjectivity'.

Another approach, taken by Smart (1990), argues that law, as one of several major discourses, constructs 'taken-for-granted natural differences [that] reinforce our "experience" as men and women' (p. 204). What appears to be 'natural' or biological sex difference is, in fact, socially produced through language. Smart further suggests that women are constructed in legal discourse, *as* 'the sexed body', as 'biological womanness' ... 'in a sexualized and subjugated form' (1990: 203, 204). She calls for the need 'to deconstruct the biological/sexed woman' (p. 208), although she recognises that this will be difficult. In a more recent essay, Smart (1995: Chapter 13) describes legal practices as 'gendering practices' which work alongside 'sexing practices' (pp. 228–229). She views the body as 'the site of both sex and gender: bodies do not exist which have not already been subject to both sexing and gendering' (p. 229). (This is how I view sex/gender, as incorporation.) Likewise, Smart (1995: 231) reflects on the need to analyse both the woman of legal discourse and real women (although she does not use these terms).

Whereas Collier is concerned with analysing the 'embodied subjectivity' of men, Smart analyses the discursive construction of sexed (and gendered) bodies in law. Other feminist legal scholars are analysing the 'sexed subjects' of law (see contributors to Naffine and Owens, 1997), with varied concerns and emphases (e.g., Davies, 1997; Lacey, 1997).

'Sexed bodies' and 'doing gender' emphasise differing elements of sex/gender: the former focuses on embodied subjectivities and the discursive construction of sex/gender; and the latter focuses on the performance and accomplishment of gender. In practice, however, we know that it is difficult to separate the two, whether in our daily lives or the study of crime. Recall the examples above of the two women committing robbery: one 'used' sexual difference, her 'sexual appeal' as a woman to a man; whereas the other hid sexual difference. Common to both perspectives is that theorists call attention to a wider social and culture sphere which, in a sense, regulates or conditions our understandings and interpretations of sex/gender. Those employing 'sexed bodies' use the term 'system of signification' to reference the ways in which bodies and sex difference are imbued with specific meanings, which are historically and culturally variable. 'Doing gender' analysts use the term 'gender attribution' to reference the selective perception and interpretation by individuals (an audience) of what others are 'doing' when doing gender (see Miller, 2002: 455). Thus, adherents of both perspectives would say that we cannot contemplate 'bodies', 'accomplishments', or sex/gender outside of the language we use or the culture and time we live in.

REFLECTIONS AND DIRECTIONS: DIVING DEEPER

This chapter reveals considerable scope and variety in applying feminist and related theories to criminology. There are significant differences in how feminist scholars conceptualise sex/gender and conduct research, which I have endeavoured to highlight in an accessible way. Crime, victimisation, justice, and law – the stuff of criminology – are productive sites to analyse sex/gender *in* society. And, as we have learned from an intersectional perspective, these sites are structured by multiple social relations and identities (including gender, class, race-ethnicity, age, sexuality), which may assume more or less salience, depending on context. Girls/women, boys/men, and sex/gender cannot be grasped as 'real' entities unmediated by culture, history, or language. Sexed/gendered meanings and behaviours are constituted in the fibre of society, culture, and social institutions; and at the same time, they are enacted and created, produced and reproduced, and contested and subverted by 'real' individuals, groups, and institutions.

Popularised understandings of sex/gender play at the surface of 'real' boys/men and girls/women, and 'discursive' constructions of sex/gender. The astute student of criminology will need to move from popularised understandings that play at the surface, diving deeper and using a more sophisticated set of conceptual tools. Those in Gen Y are well conditioned to take the plunge.

Within the broad church of feminist approaches in criminology, differences are apparent in theoretical and methodological preferences, e.g., positivist, phenomeno-logical (or social constructionist), post-positivist realist, and poststructuralist. Because the feminist enterprise is creative and open to new ideas, there is interest to apply new concepts and to be in the forefront of theoretical developments. There is also interest to display a synthetic knowledge, which may weave together disparate theoretical strands. All of this bodes well for energetic, dynamic, and transformative theories and research. At the same time, there are dangers in not respecting the epis-temological and methodological assumptions inhering in some concepts, i.e., they can be misused or misappropriated. This occurs when researchers have large datasets and attempt to apply quantitative analyses to concepts that in fact require a qualita-tive understanding of process and interaction. For example, Heimer (1995) argues for an 'interactionist' model of delinquency that attends to how the 'meaning of behaviour ... varies across gender' (p. 167), but she tries to develop it with a multi-variate analysis of survey data. Simpson and Elis (1995) attempt to employ a 'doing gender' perspective from a quantitative analysis of self-reported delinquency. In each case, the desired theoretical objective (to depict social interaction or doing gender) is not congruent with the chosen method of data gathering and analysis.

That is not to say that quantitative studies are not relevant to feminist work in criminology because they are. It is to say that such studies can tell us little about social processes and how meaning is produced in interaction. Theoretical development may be better served by using mixed research designs (Creswell and Clark, 2007) or researcher partnerships, which try to balance or mediate conflicting epistemological assumptions, if that is the aim. This may help to overcome theoretical incoherence of the sort evinced by Steffensmeier and Allen (1996: 100), who call for a 'gendered approach' to theories of crime, but one that is 'gender-neutral'. It is difficult to fathom what this means: if crime is gendered, how is a gender-neutral theory possible?

Criminology is dominated by quantitative and experimental research designs that value large datasets, categorical variables, and predictive models; and many students are encouraged in this direction (see McElrath, 2001). Among the many challenges that feminist perspectives pose to criminology is to suspend belief on superficial, popularised understandings of sex/gender, which are often embedded in quantitative and experimental designs. The need to dive deeper is not confined to Gen Y.

NOTES

1 Many would resist the categories of Boomer, Gen X, and Gen Y because they imply a homo-geneity of outlook and perspective, when there is a good deal of diversity within age cohorts. I appreciate this view, but want to reflect on the relevance of feminist ideas, which were formed from social movement activism of the 1960s and 1970s, to criminology students today (that is, in 2008, the time of this writing). See Snyder's (2008) review essay on third-wave feminism, the practices of Gen Y feminists.

2 One reason for this discomfort, particularly for Gen Y heterosexual women, is that being a 'feminist' may be associated with man-hating women who wear horns or other negative elements that may make them unattractive to men.

3 See also Daly and Chesney-Lind (1988: 504) for a set of elements that can be used to distin-guish feminist from non-feminist inquiry. I have changed gender to sex/gender in Gelsthorpe's list; this is explained below in the 'seismic shift' section.

4 I would emphasise here that the focus was on *gender* difference, not sex/gender or sex and gender difference. See discussion under 'seismic shift'.

5 This is one of a variety of ways that scholars are re-conceptualising sex/gender; see, e.g., the contributors to Naffine and Owens (1997). Griffin (2006) discusses the implications of sex/gender for 'gender bending' and considers the impact of the biological destabilisation of 'the body'.

6 This is a selected set of conceptual breakthroughs. Others that I do not include are women's different voice and the ethic of care (see reviews in Davis, 1992; Tronto, 1987); the difference and dominance debates in feminist legal theory (beginning with Marcus *et al.*, 1985); gendered organisations (Acker, 1990); and law as sexist, white, gendered, and gendering strategy (Smart, 1992). I use the term concepts rather than constructs or theories for simplicity. Ultimately, all concepts are, in a sense, theoretical.

7 The more recent developmental pathways literature pays greater attention to sex/gender, although not necessarily through a feminist lens (see, e.g., France and Homel, 2006).

8 The term 'gendered crime' is also misleadingly used to reference simple male–female differences in rates of arrest, when it is more properly used to reference the myriad ways in which sex/gender structures crime groups, street life, informal economies, crime as situated action, among other examples given above.

9 This term cannot be defined simply. As elaborated by Connell (2002b: 90–91), the term recognises 'the connection between two social patterns, hierarchy between men and women, and hierarchy among men; ... the historically mutable character of these relationships, the possibility of struggle for the hegemonic position, and contestation of hegemony ...' As a relational concept to 'marginalized, subordinated, or complicit masculinities ... the most visible form of [the dynamic of hegemonic masculinity] is the circulation of models of admired masculine conduct, which may be exalted by churches, narrated by mass media, celebrated by the state, or embedded informally in local cultures [although these] distort the everyday realities of social practice'. Hegemonic and other masculinities 'do not occur in ... generalized imagery' alone but also in institutions such as families, schools, and corporations.

10 In response to early critiques, Messerschmidt (2000, 2004) has since revised his ideas.

11 There are other ways to theorise masculinities and crime than 'doing gender'. See, e.g., Gadd and Farrall (2004) and Jefferson (1994, 1997, 2002).

REFERENCES

Acker, Joan (1990). Hierarchies, jobs, bodies: A theory of gendered organizations. *Gender and Society*, 4: 139–158.

Allen, Hilary (1987). Rendering them harmless: The professional portrayal of women charged with serious violent crimes. In Pat Carlen and Anne Worrall (eds), *Gender, Crime and Justice* (pp. 81–94). Buckingham: Open University Press.

Allen, Judith (1989). Men, crime and criminology: Recasting the questions. *International Journal of the Sociology of Law,* 17(1): 19–39.

Anthony, Thalia and Cunneen, Chris (eds) (2008a). *The Critical Criminology Companion.* Sydney: Federation Press.

Anthony, Thalia and Cunneen, Chris (2008b). Introduction. In Thalia Anthony and Chris Cunneen (eds), *The Critical Criminology Companion* (pp. 1– 4). Sydney: Federation Press.

Blumstein, Alfred, Cohen, Jacqueline, and Farrington, David (1988). Criminal career research: Its value for criminology. *Criminology,* 26: 1–35.

Bosworth, Mary (1999). *Engendering Resistance: Agency and Power in Women's Prisons.* Aldershot: Ashgate/Dartmouth.

Bottcher, Jean (1995). Gender as social control. *Justice Quarterly,* 12: 33–57.

Bottcher, Jean (2001). Social practices of gender: How gender relates to delinquency in the everyday lives of high-risk youths. *Criminology,* 39(4): 893–931.

Britton, Dana M. (2000). Feminism in criminology: Engendering the outlaw. *Annals of the American Academy of Political and Social Science,* 571(1): 57–76.

Browne, Angela (1987). *When Battered Women Kill.* New York: The Free Press.

Burgess-Proctor, Amanda (2006). Intersections of race, class, gender, and crime: Future directions for feminist criminology. *Feminist Criminology,* 1(1): 27–47.

Butler, Judith (1990). *Gender Trouble: Feminism and the Subversion of Identity.* New York: Routledge.

Butler, Judith (1993). *Bodies That Matter: On the Discursive Limits of 'Sex'.* New York: Routledge.

Cain, Maureen (1990a). Towards transgression: New directions in feminist criminology. *International Journal of the Sociology of Law,* 18: 1–18.

Cain, Maureen (1990b). Realist philosophy and standpoint epistemologies or feminist criminology as a successor science. In Loraine Gelsthorpe and Allison Morris (eds), *Feminist Perspectives in Criminology* (pp. 124–140). Buckingham: Open University Press.

Carlen, Pat (1987). Out of care, into custody: Dimensions and deconstructions of the state's regulation of twenty-two young working-class women. In Pat Carlen and Anne Worrall (eds), *Gender, Crime and Justice* (pp. 126–160). Milton Keynes: Open University Press.

Carlen, Pat (1988). *Women, Crime and Poverty.* Philadelphia: Open University Press.

Carrington, Kerry (2008). Critical reflections on feminist criminologies. In Thallia Anthony and Chris Cunneen (eds), *The Critical Criminology Companion* (pp. 82–93). Sydney: Federation Press.

Chesney-Lind, Meda (1989). Girls' crime and woman's place: Toward a feminist model of female delinquency. *Crime and Delinquency,* 35: 5–29.

Chesney-Lind, Meda and Rodriguez, Noelie (1983). Women under lock and key: A view from the inside. *The Prison Journal,* 63: 47–65.

Collier, Richard (1998). *Masculinities, Crime and Criminology: Men, Heterosexuality and the Criminal(ised) Other.* London: Sage.

Collins, Patricia H. (1990). *Black Feminist Thought: Knowledge, Consciousness, and the Politics of Empowerment.* London: Unwin Hyman.

Comack, Elizabeth (1999). New possibilities for a feminism 'in' criminology? From dualism to diversity. *Canadian Journal of Criminology,* (41): 161–170.

Connell, Robert W. (1987). *Gender and Power.* Stanford: Stanford University Press.

Connell, Robert W. (2002a). *Gender.* Cambridge: Polity Press.

Connell, Robert W. (2002b). On hegemonic masculinity and violence: Response to Jefferson and Hall. *Theoretical Criminology,* 6(1): 89–99.

Creswell, John W. and Clark, Vicki P. (2007). *Designing and Conducting Mixed Methods Research.* London: Sage.

Daly, Kathleen (1992). Women's pathways to felony court: Feminist theories of lawbreaking and problems of representation. *Southern California Review of Law and Women's Studies,* 2(1): 11–52.

Daly, Kathleen (1993). Class-race-gender: Sloganeering in search of meaning. *Social Justice,* 20(1–2): 56–71.

Daly, Kathleen (1994a). *Gender, Crime, and Punishment.* New Haven: Yale University Press.

Daly, Kathleen (1994b). Criminal law and justice system practices as racist, white, and racialized. *Washington and Lee Law Review,* 51: 431–464.

Daly, Kathleen (1997). Different ways of conceptualising sex/gender in feminist theories and their implications for criminology. *Theoretical Criminology,* 1(1): 25–51.

Daly, Kathleen (1998). Gender, crime, and criminology. In Michael Tonry (ed.), *The Handbook of Crime and Punishment* (pp. 85–108). Oxford: Oxford University Press.

Daly, Kathleen and Chesney-Lind, Meda (1988). Feminism and criminology. *Justice Quarterly,* 5(4): 497–538.

Daly, Kathleen and Maher, Lisa (eds) (1998a). *Criminology at the Crossroads: Feminist Readings in Crime and Justice.* New York: Oxford University Press.

Daly, Kathleen and Maher, Lisa (1998b). Crossroads and intersections: Building from feminist critique. In Kathleen Daly and Lisa Maher (eds), *Criminology at the Crossroads: Feminist Readings in Crime and Justice* (pp. 1–17). New York: Oxford University Press.

Davies, Margaret (1997). Taking the inside out: Sex and gender in the legal subject. In Ngaire Naffine and Rosemary J. Owens (eds), *Sexing the Subject of Law* (pp. 25–46). Sydney: LBC Information Services.

Davis, Kathy (1992). Toward a feminist rhetoric: The Gilligan debate revisited. *Women's Studies International Forum,* 15(2): 219–231.

Davis, Kathy (2008). Intersectionality as a buzzword. *Feminist Theory,* 9(1): 67–85.

Delphy, Christine (1984). *Close to Home: A Materialist Analysis of Women's Oppression* (translated by D. Leonard). London: Hutchinson.

Dobash, Russell P. and Dobash, R. Emerson (2004). Women's violence to men in intimate relationships: Working on a puzzle. *British Journal of Criminology,* 44(3): 324–349.

Fineman, Martha (1990). Challenging law, establishing differences: The future of feminist legal scholarship. *Florida Law Review,* 42: 25–43.

Fineman, Martha (1995). *The Neutered Mother, the Sexual Family, and Other Twentieth Century Tragedies.* New York: Routledge.

France, Alan and Homel, Ross (eds) (2006). Pathways and prevention. Special issue of *Australian and New Zealand Journal of Criminology,* 39(3).

Gadd, David and Farrall, Stephen (2004). Criminal careers, desistance and subjectivity. *Theoretical Criminology,* 8(2): 123–156.

Garland, David (2002). Of crimes and criminals: The development of criminology in Britain. In Mike Maguire, Rod Morgan, and Robert Reiner (eds), *The Oxford Handbook of Criminology* (third edition, pp. 7–50). Oxford: Oxford University Press.

Gelsthorpe, Loraine (2002). Feminism and criminology. In Mike Maguire, Rod Morgan, and Robert Reiner (eds), *The Oxford Handbook of Criminology* (third edition, pp. 112–143). Oxford: Oxford University Press.

Giddens, Anthony (1984). *The Constitution of Society.* Berkeley: University of California Press.

Gilfus, Mary E. (1992). From victims to survivors to offenders: Women's routes of entry and immersion into street crime. *Women and Criminal Justice,* 4: 63–90.

Griffin, Gabriele (2006). Gendered cultures. In Kathy Davis, Mary Evans, and Judith Lorber (eds), *Handbook of Gender and Women's Studies* (pp. 73–91). London: Sage.

Grosz, Elizabeth (1994). *Volatile Bodies: Toward a Corporeal Feminism.* St Leonards: Allen and Unwin.

Harding, Sandra (1986). *The Science Question in Feminism.* Ithaca: Cornell University Press.

Harrison, Wendy (2006). The shadow and the substance: The sex/gender debate. In Kathy Davis, Mary Evans, and Judith Lorber (eds), *Handbook of Gender and Women's Studies* (pp. 35–52). London: Sage.

Hatty, Suzanne (1997). The violence of displacement: The problematics of survival for homeless young women. In Sandy Cook and Judith Bessant (eds), *Women's Encounters with Violence: Australian Experiences* (pp. 203–218). Thousand Oaks: Sage.

Heidensohn, Frances and Gelsthorpe, Loraine (2007). Gender and crime. In Mike Maguire, Rod Morgan, and Robert Reiner (eds), *The Oxford Handbook of Criminology* (fourth edition, pp. 381–420). Oxford: Oxford University Press.

Heimer, Karen (1995). Gender, race, and the pathways to delinquency: An interactionist explanation. In John Hagan and Ruth Peterson (eds), *Crime and Inequality* (pp. 140–173). Palo Alto: Stanford University Press.

Hood-Williams, John (2001). Gender, masculinities and crime: From structures to psyches. *Theoretical Criminology,* 5(1): 37–60.

Howe, Adrian (1994). *Punish and Critique: Towards a Feminist Analysis of Penality.* New York: Routlegde.

Jefferson, Tony (1994). Theorizing masculine subjectivity. In Tim Newburn and Elizabeth A. Stanko (eds), *Just Boys Doing Business? Men, Masculinities and Crime* (pp. 10–31). New York: Routledge.

Jefferson, Tony (1997). Masculinities and crime. In Mike Maguire, Rod Morgan, and Robert Reiner (eds), *The Oxford Handbook of Criminology* (second edition, pp. 535–558). Oxford: Clarendon Press.

Jefferson, Tony (2002). Subordinating hegemonic masculinity. *Theoretical Criminology,* 6(1): 63–88.

Kandiyoti, Deniz (1988). Bargaining with patriarchy. *Gender and Society,* 2: 274–290.

Kelly, Liz (1988). *Surviving Sexual Violence.* London: Polity Press.

Klein, Dorie (1973). The Etiology of Female Crime: A Review of the Literature. *Issues in Criminology,* 8: 3–30.

Klein, Dorie (1988). Women offenders, victims and false labels. Paper presented at the *Tenth International Congress on Criminology*, Hamburg, September.

Lacey, Nicola (1997). On the subject of sexing the subject. … In Ngaire Naffine and Rosemary J. Owens (eds), *Sexing the Subject of Law* (pp. 65–76). Sydney: LBC Information Services.

Maher, Lisa (1997). *Sexed Work: Gender, Race and Resistance in a Brooklyn Drug Market.* Oxford: Clarendon Press.

Maher, Lisa, and Curtis, Richard (1992). Women on the edge of crime: Crack cocaine and the changing contexts of street level sex work in New York City. *Crime, Law, and Social Change*, 18: 221–258.

Marcus, Isabel, Spiegelman, Paul, DuBois, Ellen, Dunlap, Mary, Gilligan, Carol, MacKinnon Catharine, and Menkel-Meadow, Carrie (1985). Feminist discourse, moral values, and the law: A conversation. *Buffalo Law Review*, 34: 11–87.

Mason, Gail (2002). *The Spectacle of Violence: Homophobia, Gender, and Knowledge.* New York: Routledge.

McCall, Leslie (2005). The complexity of intersectionality. *Signs: Journal of Women in Culture and Society*, 30(31): 1771–1802.

McElrath, Karen (2001). Confessions of a quantitative criminologist. *ACJS Today*, 24(4): 1, 3–7.

Merton, Robert (1938). Social structure and anomie. *American Sociological Review*, 3: 672–682.

Messerschmidt, James W. (1993). *Masculinities and Crime: Critique, and Reconceptualization of Theory.* Lanham: Rowman and Littlefield.

Messerschmidt, James W. (2000). *Nine Lives: Adolescent Masculinities, the Body, and Violence.* Boulder: Westview Press.

Messerschmidt, James W. (2004). *Flesh and Blood: Adolescent Gender Diversity and Violence.* Lanham: Rowman and Littlefield.

Miller, Jody (1998). Up it up: Gender and the accomplishment of street robbery. *Criminology*, 36(1): 37–65.

Miller, Jody (2001). *One of the Guys: Girls, Gangs and Gender.* New York: Oxford University Press.

Miller, Jody (2002). The strengths and limits of "doing gender" for understanding street crime. *Theoretical Criminology,* 6(4): 433–460.

Miller, Jody and Mullins, Christopher (2006). The status of feminist theories in criminology. In Francis T. Cullen, John Wright, and Kristie Blevins (eds), *Taking Stock: The Status of Criminological Theory* (pp. 217–249). New Brunswick: Transaction Publishers.

Naffine, Ngaire (1987). *Female Crime: The Construction of Women in Criminology.* Sydney: Allen and Allen.

Naffine, Ngaire (1997). *Feminism and Criminology.* St. Leonards: Allen and Unwin.

Naffine, Ngaire and Owens, Rosemary J. (eds) (1997). *Sexing the Subject of Law.* Sydney: LBC Information Services.

Phoenix, Ann and Pattynama, Pamela (2006). Intersectionality. *European Journal of Women's Studies,* 13(3): 187–192.

Prins, Baukje (2006). Narrative accounts of origins: A blind spot in the intersectional approach. *European Journal of Women's Studies,* 13(3): 277–290.

Rafter, Nicole H. (1990). *Partial Justice: Women, Prisons, and Social Control* (second edition). New Brunswick: Transaction Publishers.

Rafter, Nicole H. and Stanko, Elizabeth (eds) (1982). *Judge, Lawyer, Victim, Thief.* Boston: Northeastern University Press.

Richie, Beth (1996). *Compelled to Crime: The Gender Entrapment of Battered Black Women.* New York: Routledge.

Sampson, Robert J. and Laub, John (1993). *Crime in the Making: Pathways and Turning Points Through Life*. Cambridge: Harvard University Press.

Scott, Joan W. (1992). 'Experience'. In Judith Butler and Joan W. Scott (eds), *Feminists Theorize the Political* (pp. 22–40). New York: Routledge.

Simpson, Sally and Elis, Lori (1995). Doing gender: Sorting out the caste and crime conundrum. *Criminology*, 33(1): 47–81.

Simpson, Sally and Gibbs, Carole (2006). Making sense of intersections. In Karen Heimer and Candace Kruttschnitt (eds), *Gender and Crime: Patterns in Victimization and Offending* (pp. 269–302). New York: New York University Press.

Simpson, Sally, Yahner, Jennifer, and Dugan, Laura (2008). Understanding women's pathways to jail: Analysing the lives of incarcerated women. *Australian and New Zealand Journal of Criminology*, 41(1): 84–108.

Smart, Carol (1976). *Women, Crime and Criminology: A Feminist Critique*. Boston: Routledge and Kegan Paul.

Smart, Carol (1989). *Feminism and the Power of Law*. New York: Routledge.

Smart, Carol (1990). Law's power, the sexed body, and feminist discourse. *Journal of Law and Society*, 17: 194–210.

Smart, Carol (1992). The woman of legal discourse. *Social and Legal Studies*, 1(1): 29–44.

Smart, Carol (1995). *Law, Crime and Sexuality: Essays in Feminism*. London: Sage.

Snyder, Claire (2008). What is third-wave feminism? A new directions essay. *Signs: Journal of Women in Culture and Society*, 34(1): 175–196.

Stanko, Elizabeth (1990). *Everyday Violence: How Women and Men Experience Sexual and Physical Danger*. London, Pandora.

Steffensmeier, Darrell and Allan, Emilie (1996). Gender and crime: Toward a gendered theory of female offending. *Annual Review of Sociology*, 22: 459–487.

Stubbs, Julie (2008). Critical criminology research. In Thallia Anthony and Chris Cunneen (eds), *The Critical Criminology Companion* (pp. 6–17). Sydney: Federation Press.

Teague, Rosie, Mazerolle, Paul, Legosz, Margot, and Sanderson, Jennifer (2008). Linking childhood exposure to physical abuse and adult offending: Examining mediating factors and gendered relationships. *Justice Quarterly*, 25(2): 318–348.

Tronto, Joan (1987). Beyond gender difference to a theory of care. *Signs: Journal of Women in Culture and Society*, 12(4): 644–663.

Wacquant, Loic (2003). *Body and Soul: Notebooks of an Apprentice Boxer*. New York: Oxford University Press.

West, Candace and Zimmerman, Don (1987). Doing gender. *Gender and Society*, 1(2): 125–151.

Worrall, Anne (1990). *Offending Women*. New York: Routledge.

Wynter, Vivienne (2006). They're not stupid girls. *Griffith Review*, 13: 141–145.

Young, Alison (1996). *Imagining Crime*. London: Sage.

PART II

New Directions

13

Life-Course and Developmental Theories in Criminology

David P. Farrington

Developmental and life-course criminology (DLC) is concerned mainly with three topics: (a) the development of offending and antisocial behaviour from the womb to the tomb; (b) the influence of risk and protective factors at different ages; and (c) the effects of life events on the course of development. In this chapter, I will first briefly review the current state of knowledge on these topics, then I will briefly review seven major DLC theories, and finally I will present my own DLC theory, called the Integrated Cognitive-Antisocial Potential (ICAP) theory.

DLC theories aim to explain offending by individuals (as opposed to crime rates of areas, for example). 'Offending' refers to the most common crimes of theft, burglary, robbery, violence, vandalism, minor fraud, and drug use, and to behaviour that in principle might lead to a conviction in Western industrialized societies such as the United States and the United Kingdom. These theories aim to explain results on offending obtained with both official records and self-reports. Generally, DLC findings and theories particularly apply to offending by lower class urban males in developed countries in the last 80 years or so. To what extent they apply to other types of persons (e.g., middle class rural females) or offences (e.g., white collar crimes or sex offences against children) are important empirical questions that I will not attempt to address here.

In conducting research on development, risk and protective factors, life events and DLC theories, it is essential to carry out prospective longitudinal surveys. I have directed the Cambridge Study in Delinquent Development, which is a prospective longitudinal survey of over 400 London males from age 8 to age 48 (Farrington *et al.*, 2006, 2009c). The main reason why developmental and life course criminology became important during the 1990s was because of the enormous volume and significance of longitudinal research on offending that was published during this decade. Particularly influential were the three 'Causes and Correlates' studies originally mounted by the U.S. Office of Juvenile Justice and Delinquency Prevention in Denver, Pittsburgh and Rochester (Huizinga *et al.*, 2003; Loeber *et al.*, 2003; Thornberry *et al.*, 2003). Other important longitudinal projects that came to prominence in the 1990s were the Seattle Social Development Project (Hawkins *et al.*, 2003), the Dunedin study in New Zealand (Moffitt *et al.*, 2001) the Montreal Longitudinal-Experimental study (Tremblay *et al.*, 2003), and the further analyses by Laub and Sampson (2003) of the classic Gluecks' study.

WHAT DO WE KNOW?

I begin with 10 widely accepted conclusions about the development of offending that any DLC theory must be able to explain. First, the prevalence of offending peaks in the late teenage years – between ages 15 and 19 (Farrington, 1986). Second, the peak age of onset of offending is between 8 and 14, and the peak age of desistance from offending is between 20 and 29 (Farrington, 1992). Third, an early age of onset predicts a relatively long criminal career duration and the commission of relatively many offences (Farrington *et al.*, 1998).

Fourth, there is marked continuity in offending and antisocial behaviour from childhood to the teenage years and to adulthood (Farrington, 1989, 1992). What this means is that there is relative stability of the ordering of people on some measure of antisocial behaviour over time, and that people who commit relatively many offences during one age range have a high probability of also committing relatively many offences during another age range. However, neither of these statements is incompatible with the assertion that the prevalence of offending varies with age or that many antisocial children become conforming adults. Between-individual stability in antisocial ordering is perfectly compatible with within-individual change in behaviour over time (Farrington, 1990). For example, people may graduate from cruelty to animals at age 6 to shoplifting at age 10, burglary at age 15, robbery at age 20, and eventually spouse assault and child abuse later in life. Generally, continuity in offending reflects persistent heterogeneity (the persistence of between-individual differences) rather than state dependence (a facilitating effect of earlier offending on later offending), although both processes can occur (Nagin and Farrington, 1992). There is also continuity in offending from one generation to the next (Farrington *et al.*, 2009a).

Fifth, a small fraction of the population (the 'chronic' offenders) commit a large fraction of all crimes (Farrington and West, 1993). In general, these chronic offenders have an early onset, a high individual offending frequency, and a long criminal career. Sixth, offending is versatile rather than specialized. For example, violent offenders are indistinguishable from frequent offenders in childhood, adolescent, and adult risk factors (Farrington, 1991b). Seventh, the types of acts defined as offences are elements of a larger syndrome of antisocial behaviour, including heavy drinking, reckless driving, sexual promiscuity, bullying, and truancy. Offenders tend to be versatile not only in committing several types of crimes but also in committing several types of antisocial behaviour (Farrington, 1991a).

Eighth, most offences up to the late teenage years are committed with others, whereas most offences from age 20 onwards are committed alone (Reiss and Farrington, 1991). This aggregate change is not caused by dropping out processes, or group offenders desisting earlier than lone offenders. Instead, there is change within individuals; people change from group offending to lone offending as they get older. Ninth, the reasons given for offending up to the late teenage years are quite variable, including utilitarian ones (e.g., to obtain material goods or for revenge), for excitement or enjoyment (or to relieve boredom), or because people get angry (in the case of violent crimes). In contrast, from age 20 onwards, utilitarian motives become increasingly dominant (Farrington, 1993). Tenth, different types of offences tend to be first committed at distinctively different ages. For example, shoplifting is typically committed before burglary, which in turn is typically committed before robbery (LeBlanc and Frechette, 1989). In general, there is increasing diversification of offending up to age 20; as each new type of crime is added, previously committed crimes continue to be committed. Conversely, after age 20, diversification decreases and specialization increases (Piquero *et al.*, 1999).

The main risk factors for the early onset of offending before age 20 are well known (Farrington, 2009): individual factors (low intelligence, low school achievement, hyperactivity-impulsiveness and risk-taking, antisocial child behaviour including aggression and bullying), family factors (poor parental supervision, harsh discipline and child physical abuse, inconsistent discipline, a cold parental attitude and child neglect, low involvement of parents with children, parental conflict, broken families, criminal parents, delinquent siblings), socio-economic factors (low family income, large family size), peer factors (delinquent peers, peer rejection and low popularity), school factors (a high delinquency rate school) and neighbourhood factors (a high crime neighbourhood). Less is known about promotive and protective factors (see Loeber *et al.*, 2008).

The main life events that encourage desistance after age 20 are getting married, getting a satisfying job, moving to a better area and joining the military (Farrington and West, 1995; Horney *et al.*, 1995; Laub and Sampson, 2001). The distinction between risk factors and life events is not clear-cut, since some life events may be continuing experiences whose duration is important (e.g., a marriage or a job), while some risk factors may occur at a particular time (e.g., loss of a parent). Other life events (e.g., converting to religion) may be important but have been studied less.

While the focus in DLC is on the development of offenders, it is important not to lose sight of factors that influence the commission of offences. It is plausible to assume that offences arise out of an interaction between the person (with a certain degree of criminal potential) and the environment (including opportunities and victims). Existing evidence suggests that people faced with criminal opportunities take account of the subjectively perceived benefits and costs of offending (compared with other possible activities) in deciding whether or not to offend (Clarke and Cornish, 1985). DLC theories should explain the commission of offences as well as the development of offenders.

LIFE EVENTS AND CHANGES WITHIN INDIVIDUALS

Developmental and life-course criminology aims to investigate the effects of life events on the course of development of antisocial behaviour. In the Cambridge Study, going to a high delinquency-rate school at age 11 did not seem to amplify the risk of offending, since badly behaved boys tended to go to high delinquency-rate schools (Farrington, 1972). However, getting convicted did lead to an increase in offending, according to the boys' self-reports, and a plausible intervening mechanism was increased hostility to the police (Farrington, 1977). Unemployment also caused an increase in offending, but only for crimes leading to financial gain, such as theft, burglary, robbery and fraud. There was no effect of unemployment on other offences such as violence, vandalism or drug use, suggesting that the link between unemployment and offending was mediated by lack of money rather than boredom (Farrington *et al.,* 1986).

It is often believed that marriage to a good woman is one of the most effective treatments for male offending, and indeed Farrington and West (1995) found that getting married led to a decrease in offending compared with staying single. Also, later separation from a wife led to an increase in offending compared with staying married, and the separated men were particularly likely to be violent. Another protective life event was moving out of London, which led to a decrease in self-reported violence (Osborn, 1980). This was probably because of the effect of the move in breaking up delinquent groups.

Studies of the effects of life events on the course of development usually involve within-individual analyses. A major problem with most research in criminology is that knowledge about risk factors is based on between-individual differences. For example, it is demonstrated that children who receive poor parental supervision are more likely to offend than other children who receive good parental supervision, after controlling for other between-individual factors that influence both parental supervision and offending. However, within-individual variations are more relevant to the concept of cause, as well as to prevention or intervention research (which requires within-individual change). For example, if it was demonstrated that children were more likely to offend during time periods when they were receiving poor parental supervision than during time periods when they were receiving good parental supervision, this would be more compelling evidence that poor parental supervision caused offending. Since the same individuals are followed up over time, many extraneous influences on offending are controlled (Farrington, 1988).

Research is also needed that systematically compares results obtained in within-individual analyses and between-individual analyses. In the Pittsburgh Youth Study, which is a prospective longitudinal survey of over 1,500 Pittsburgh boys, Farrington *et al.* (2002) found that poor parental supervision predicted a boy's delinquency both between and within individuals, but peer delinquency predicted a boy's delinquency between individuals but not within individuals. In other words, changes in peer delinquency within individuals (from one assessment to the next) did not predict changes in a boy's delinquency over time. This suggested that peer delinquency might not be a cause of a boy's delinquency but might instead be measuring the same underlying construct (perhaps reflecting co-offending). The message is that risk factors that predict offending between individuals may not predict offending within individuals, so that implications drawn from between-individual comparisons about causes and interventions may not be valid.

DEVELOPMENTAL AND LIFE-COURSE THEORIES

I now summarize some of the key features of seven leading DLC theories, ordered roughly from the more psychological to the more sociological. More details about all of these theories can be found in Farrington (2005a). Whereas traditional criminological theories aimed to explain between-individual differences in offending, such as why lower-class boys commit more offences than upper-class boys, DLC theories aim to explain within-individual changes in offending over time.

Lahey and Waldman

Lahey and Waldman (2005) aimed to explain the development of conduct disorder and juvenile delinquency, focussing particularly on childhood and adolescence. Their developmental propensity theory is influenced by data collected in the Developmental Trends Study (Loeber *et al.,* 2000). They do not address adult life events or attempt to explain desistance in the adult years, for example. They assume that it is desirable to distinguish different types of people, but they propose a continuum of developmental trajectories rather than only two categories of adolescence-limited and life-course-persistent offenders, for example.

Their key construct is antisocial propensity, which tends to persist over time and has a wide variety of behavioural manifestations, reflecting the versatility and comorbidity of antisocial behaviour. The most important factors that contribute to antisocial propensity are low cognitive ability (especially verbal ability), and three dispositional dimensions: prosociality (including sympathy and empathy, as opposed to callous-unemotional traits), daring (uninhibited or poorly controlled), and negative emotionality (e.g., easily frustrated, bored, or annoyed). These four factors are said to have a genetic basis, and Lahey and Waldman discuss gene–environment interactions.

In an important empirical test of this theory, Lahey *et al.* (2006) analysed data collected in the Pittsburgh Youth Study and found that prosociality (negatively), daring and negative emotionality at age 7 independently predicted self-reported delinquency between ages 11 and 17. Furthermore, these predictions held up after controlling for major demographic predictors of delinquency such as family income, the mother's education and ethnicity. In the latest test, Lahey *et al.* (2008) developed the Child and Adolescent Dispositions Scale (CADS) to measure the three dimensions and showed that these predicted conduct disorder in three samples in Georgia, Chicago and Pittsburgh.

Moffitt

Moffitt (1993) proposed that there are two qualitatively different categories of anti-social people (differing in kind rather than in degree), namely life-course-persistent

(LCP) and adolescence-limited (AL) offenders. As indicated by these terms, the LCPs start offending at an early age and persist beyond their twenties, while the ALs have a short criminal career largely limited to their teenage years. The LCPs commit a wide range of offences including violence, whereas the ALs commit predominantly 'rebellious' non-violent offences such as vandalism. This theory aims to explain findings in the Dunedin longitudinal study (Moffitt *et al.*, 2001).

The main factors that encourage offending by the LCPs are cognitive deficits, an undercontrolled temperament, hyperactivity, poor parenting, disrupted families, teenage parents, poverty, and low SES. Genetic and biological factors, such as a low heart rate, are important. There is not much discussion of neighbourhood factors, but it is proposed that the neuropsychological risk of the LCPs interacts multiplicatively with a disadvantaged environment. The theory does not propose that neuropsychological deficits and a disadvantaged environment influence an underlying construct such as antisocial propensity; rather, it suggests that neuropsychological and environmental factors are the key constructs underlying antisocial behaviour.

The main factors that encourage offending by the ALs are the 'maturity gap' (their inability to achieve adult rewards such as material goods during their teenage years) and peer influence (especially from the LCPs). Consequently, the ALs stop offending when they enter legitimate adult roles and can achieve their desires legally. The ALs can easily stop because they have few neuropsychological deficits.

The theory assumes that there can be labelling effects of 'snares' such as a criminal record, incarceration, drug or alcohol addiction, and (for girls) unwanted pregnancy, especially for the ALs. However, the observed continuity in offending over time is largely driven by the LCPs. The theory focusses mainly on the development of offenders and does not attempt to explain why offences are committed. However, it suggests that the presence of delinquent peers is an important situational influence on ALs, and that LCPs seek out opportunities and victims.

Decision-making in criminal opportunities is supposed to be rational for the ALs (who weigh likely costs against likely benefits) but not for the LCPs (who largely follow well-learned 'automatic' behavioural repertoires without thinking). However, the LCPs are mainly influenced by utilitarian motives, whereas the ALs are influenced by teenage boredom. Adult life events such as getting a job or getting married are hypothesized to be of little importance, because the LCPs are too committed to an antisocial life-style and the ALs desist naturally as they age into adult roles.

Possibly because it is arguably the earliest and most famous DLC theory, there has been more empirical research on this theory than on any others. Moffitt (2006) published a very impressive review of 10 years of research on her theory. While many of the predictions were confirmed, she discussed the need for additional categories of individuals: abstainers (who were overcontrolled, fearful, sexually timid, and unpopular), low-level chronics (who were undercontrolled like the LCPs, with family adversity, parental psychopathology, and low intelligence) and adult-onset offenders (whose existence was doubtful according to Moffitt). She argued that the abstainers in adolescence did not become adult-onset offenders, but Zara and Farrington (2009) found that adult-onset offenders in the Cambridge Study tended to be nervous and to have few friends at age 8–10, as well as still being sexual virgins at age 18. In one of the latest papers on the Moffitt theory, Odgers *et al.* (2008)

reported similar trajectories (and associated childhood origins and adult consequences) for males and females in the Dunedin study: LCP, adolescent-onset, childhood-limited, and low-level problems.

Catalano and Hawkins

According to Catalano *et al.* (2005), the Social Development Model (SDM) integrates social control/bonding, social learning and differential association theories, but does not include strain theory postulates. Their key construct is bonding to society (or socializing agents), consisting of attachment and commitment. The key construct underlying offending is the balance between antisocial and prosocial bonding. Continuity in antisocial behaviour over time depends on continuity in this balance. The main motivation that leads to offending and antisocial behaviour is the hedonistic desire to seek satisfaction and follow self-interest. This is opposed by the bond to society. Offending is essentially a rational decision in which people weigh the benefits against the costs. There is no assumption about different types of offenders. This theory aims to explain findings in the Seattle Social Development Project (Hawkins *et al.*, 2003).

There are two causal pathways, leading to antisocial or prosocial bonding. On the prosocial pathway, opportunities for prosocial interaction lead to involvement in prosocial behaviour; involvement and skills for prosocial behaviour lead to rewards for prosocial behaviour, which lead to prosocial bonding and beliefs. On the antisocial pathway, opportunities for antisocial interaction lead to involvement in antisocial behaviour; involvement and skills for antisocial behaviour lead to rewards for antisocial behaviour, which lead to antisocial bonding and beliefs. Hence, the antisocial pathway specifies factors encouraging offending and the prosocial pathway specifies factors inhibiting offending. Opportunities, involvement, skills and rewards are part of a socialization process. People learn prosocial and antisocial behaviour according to socialization by families, peers, schools and communities.

The SDM specifies that demographic factors (such as age, race, gender, and social class) and biological factors (such as difficult temperament, cognitive ability, low arousal and hyperactivity) influence opportunities and skills in the socialization process. There are somewhat different models for different developmental periods (preschool, elementary school, middle school, high school, young adulthood). For example, in the first two periods interaction with prosocial or antisocial family members is the most important, while in the other two periods interaction with prosocial or antisocial peers is the most important.

The development of offending and the commission of offences are not explicitly distinguished in the SDM. However, the theory includes prosocial and antisocial opportunities as situational factors and suggests that the perceived rewards and costs of antisocial behaviour influence the decision to offend. Motives for offending (e.g., utilitarian or excitement) are included under the heading of perceived rewards and costs. Neighbourhood factors, official labelling, and life events are important only insofar as they influence the key constructs of opportunities, involvement, skills, rewards, and bonding. For example, official labelling may increase involvement with antisocial people and marriage may increase prosocial opportunities and involvement.

In an empirical test of the SDM, Brown *et al.* (2005) found that not all relationships were fully mediated by SDM constructs. In particular, cognitive and socio-emotional skills influenced antisocial behaviour directly rather than through bonding and beliefs. The SDM has inspired an intervention programme called *Communities That Care* or CTC (Hawkins and Catalano, 1992). The effectiveness of this programme in reducing antisocial behaviour is being tested in an ambitious experiment (the Community Youth Development Study or CYDS) in which 24 communities have been randomly assigned to experimental or control conditions. Early results suggest that the CYDS is effective in reducing risk factors and delinquency (Hawkins *et al.*, 2008). CTC was evaluated in three UK sites by Crow *et al.* (2004) but implementation problems make it difficult to draw firm conclusions about its effectiveness from this evaluation.

LeBlanc

LeBlanc (1997, 2005) proposed an integrative multilayered control theory that explains the development of offending, the occurrence of criminal events, and community crime rates. This is undoubtedly the most complex of the DLC theories. The key construct underlying offending is general deviance, and LeBlanc discusses its structure and how it changes over time. According to his theory, the development of offending depends on four mechanisms of control: bonding to society (including family, school, peers, marriage and work), psychological development over time (especially away from egocentrism and towards 'allocentrism'), modelling (prosocial or antisocial), and constraints (external, including socialization, and internal, including beliefs).

LeBlanc assumes that environmental factors (e.g., social class and neighbourhood) influence bonding while biological capacity (including difficult temperament) influences psychological development. Bonding and psychological development influence modelling and constraints, which are proximate influences on general deviance and hence on offending. There is continuity in offending because the relative ordering of people on control mechanisms stays fairly consistent over time. This theory aims to explain findings in LeBlanc's Montreal longitudinal surveys of adolescents and delinquents (e.g., LeBlanc and Frechette, 1989).

LeBlanc proposes that there are three types of offenders: persistent, transitory, and common. Persistent offenders are most extreme on weak bonding, egocentrism, antisocial modelling, and low constraints. Common offenders are largely influenced by opportunities, while transitory offenders are in the middle (in having moderate control and being moderately influenced by opportunities). His theory includes biological and neighbourhood factors, but they are assumed to have indirect effects on offending through their effects on the constructs of bonding and psychological development. Similarly, he assumes that life events have effects via the constructs and that labelling influences external constraints. The theory includes learning processes and socialization but does not include strain theory assumptions.

LeBlanc's (1997) theory of criminal events suggests that they depend on community control (e.g., social disorganization), personal control (rational choice ideas of decision-making), self-control (impulsiveness, vulnerability to temptations), opportunities, routine activities and guardianship (e.g., physical protection).

People are viewed as hedonistic, and motives (e.g. excitement or utilitarian) are considered.

LeBlanc (2009) has provided the latest statement of this theory, which increasingly focusses on the 'chaos-order' paradigm. According to this, the complexity of deviant behaviour increases over time, from two types in early childhood to nine types at the end of adolescence. At all points, there are reciprocal relationships between types of deviance, with one type leading to another. Analyses of the Montreal surveys were presented to show how types of delinquency and substance use were inter-related within and between different ages.

Thornberry and Krohn

The interactional theory of Thornberry and Krohn (2005) particularly focusses on factors encouraging antisocial behaviour at different ages. It is influenced by findings in the Rochester Youth Development Study (Thornberry et al., 2003).They do not propose types of offenders but suggest that the causes of antisocial behaviour vary for children who start at different ages. At the earliest ages (birth to 6), the three most important factors are neuropsychological deficit and difficult temperament (e.g., impulsiveness, negative emotionality, fearlessness, poor emotion regulation), parenting deficits (e.g., poor monitoring, low affective ties, inconsistent discipline, physical punishment), and structural adversity (e.g., poverty, unemployment, welfare dependency, a disorganized neighbourhood). They also suggest that structural adversity might cause poor parenting.

Neuropsychological deficits are less important for children who start antisocial behaviour at older ages. At ages 6–12, neighbourhood and family factors are particularly salient, while at ages 12–18 school and peer factors dominate. Thornberry and Krohn also suggest that deviant opportunities, gangs, and deviant social networks are important for onset at ages 12–18. They propose that late starters (ages 18–25) have cognitive deficits such as low IQ and poor school performance but that they were protected from antisocial behaviour at earlier ages by a supportive family and school environment. At ages 18–25, they find it hard to make a successful transition to adult roles such as employment and marriage.

The most distinctive feature of this interactional theory is its emphasis on reciprocal causation. For example, it is proposed that the child's antisocial behaviour elicits coercive responses from parents and rejection by peers and makes antisocial behaviour more likely in the future. The theory does not postulate a single key construct underlying offending but suggests that children who start early tend to continue because of the persistence of neuropsychological and parenting deficits and structural adversity. Interestingly, Thornberry and Krohn predict that late starters (ages 18–25) will show more continuity over time than earlier starters (ages 12–18) because the late starters have more cognitive deficits. In an earlier exposition of the theory (Thornberry and Krohn, 2001), they proposed that desistance was caused by changing social influences (e.g., stronger family bonding), protective factors (e.g., high IQ and school success), and intervention programmes. Hence, they do think that criminal justice processing has an effect on future offending.

Recently, Thornberry (2005) has extended this theory to explain the intergenerational transmission of antisocial behaviour. He suggested that the parent's prosocial or antisocial bonding, structural adversity, stressors and ineffective parenting mediated the link between the parent's antisocial behaviour and the child's antisocial behaviour. Thornberry *et al.* (2009) tested these ideas in the Rochester Intergenerational Study and concluded that parental stress and ineffective parenting were the most important mediating factors.

Wikström

Wikström (2005) proposed a developmental ecological action theory that aims to explain moral rule breaking. The key construct underlying offending is individual criminal propensity, which depends on moral judgement and self-control. In turn, moral values influence moral judgement, and executive functions influence self-control. Wikström does not propose types of offenders. The motivation to offend arises from the interaction between the individual and the setting. For example, if individual propensity is low, features of the setting (persons, objects, and events) become more important. Continuity or change in offending over time depends on continuity or change in moral values, executive functions, and settings.

Situational factors are important in Wikström's theory, which aims to explain the commission of offences as well as the development of offenders. Opportunities cause temptation, friction produces provocation, and monitoring or the risk of sanctions has a deterrent effect. The theory emphasizes perception, choice, and human agency in deciding to offend. Learning processes are included in the theory, since it is suggested that moral values are taught by instruction and observation in a socialization process and that nurturing (the promotion of cognitive skills) influences executive functions. Life events also matter, since it is proposed that starting school, getting married (etc.) can trigger changes in constructs such as moral teaching and monitoring and hence influence moral rule breaking.

In the most recent statement of his 'Situational Action Theory', Wikström (2010) emphasizes that criminal acts (moral rule-breaking) arise from the interaction between individual (propensity) and environmental (moral context) factors. The main motivating factors are temptation and provocation. Whether criminal acts are committed depends partly on well-entrenched habits and partly on rational deliberation. The choice process, which Wikström terms a 'situational mechanism' depends on free will and on the action alternatives as perceived by a person. Wikström intends to test this theory in his Peterborough Adolescent and Young Adult Development Study (PADS).

Sampson and Laub

The key construct in Sampson and Laub's (2005) theory is age-graded informal social control, which means the strength of bonding to family, peers, schools, and later adult social institutions such as marriages and jobs. Sampson and Laub primarily aimed to explain why people do not commit offences, on the assumption that why people want to offend is unproblematic (presumably caused by hedonistic desires) and that offending is inhibited by the strength of bonding to society. Their theory is influenced by their analyses of the Glueck follow-up study of male delinquents and non-delinquents (Laub and Sampson, 2003; Sampson and Laub, 1993).

The strength of bonding depends on attachments to parents, schools, delinquent friends, and delinquent siblings, and also on parental socialization processes such as discipline and supervision. Structural background variables (e.g., social class, ethnicity, large family size, criminal parents, disrupted families) and individual difference factors (e.g., low intelligence, difficult temperament, early conduct disorder) have indirect effects on offending through their effects on informal social control (attachment and socialization processes).

Sampson and Laub are concerned with the whole life course. They emphasize change over time rather than consistency, and the poor ability of early childhood risk factors to predict later life outcomes. They focus on the importance of later life events (adult turning points) such as joining the military, getting a stable job, and getting married in fostering desistance and 'knifing off' the past from the present. They also suggest that neighbourhood changes can cause changes in offending. Because of their emphasis on change and unpredictability, they deny the importance of types of offenders such as 'life-course-persisters'. They suggest that offending decreases with age for all types of offenders (Sampson and Laub, 2003).

Sampson and Laub do not explicitly include immediate situational influences on criminal events in their theory, and believe that opportunities are not important because they are ubiquitous (Sampson and Laub, 1995). However, they do suggest that having few structured routine activities is conducive to offending. They focus on why people do not offend rather than on why people offend, and emphasize the importance of individual free will and purposeful choice ('human agency') in the decision to desist. They do not include strain theory ideas, but they propose that official labelling influences offending through its effects on job instability and unemployment. They argue that early delinquency can cause weak adult social bonds, which in turn fail to inhibit adult offending.

In their latest exposition of their theory, Sampson and Laub (2009) again argue against offender typologies and in favour of 'noisy, unpredictable development'. They contend that long-term patterns of offending cannot be explained by individual differences or childhood or adolescent characteristics, and that childhood variables are 'modest prognostic devices'. They further argue against the concept of 'developmental criminology' which they take to mean a 'predetermined unfolding' and in favour of the idea of 'life-course criminology' which (they say) refers to the constant interaction between the individual and the environment.

Happily, Sampson and Laub's predictions can be tested empirically. My own view is that childhood risk factors are better than 'modest' predictors of later offending. For example, in the Cambridge Study, the percentage of boys who were convicted increased from 20 per cent of those with no childhood risk factors to 85 per cent of those with five or six childhood risk factors (Farrington et al., 2009c). Similarly, in predicting adult offending, Sampson and Laub might expect that childhood variables would not predict independently of adult variables, but Farrington et al. (2009b) found several age 8–10 variables that predicted either onset or persistence in offending after age 21. More research is clearly needed, especially contrasting the polar opposite predictions of Moffitt (1993) and Sampson and Laub (2009).

THE ICAP THEORY

This theory was primarily designed to explain offending by lower class males, and it was influenced by results obtained in the Cambridge Study. I have called it the 'Integrated Cognitive Antisocial Potential' (ICAP) theory (see Farrington, 2005b). It integrates ideas from many other theories, including strain, control, learning, labelling and rational choice approaches; its key construct is antisocial potential (AP); and it assumes that the translation from antisocial potential to antisocial behaviour depends on cognitive (thinking and decision-making) processes that take account of opportunities and victims. Figure 13.1 is deliberately simplified in order to show the key elements of the ICAP theory on one page; for example, it does not show how the processes operate differently for onset compared with desistance or at different ages.

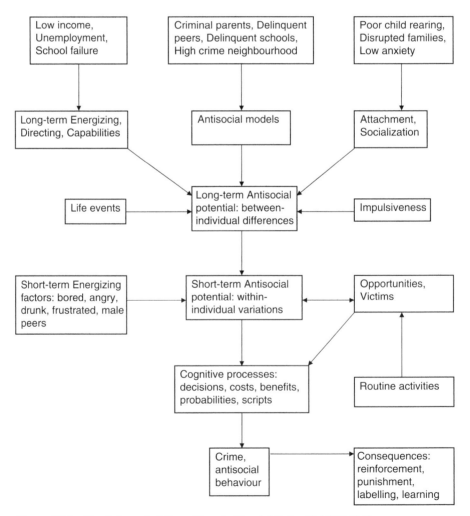

Figure 13.1   The Integrated Cognitive-Antisocial Potential (ICAP) theory.

The key construct underlying offending is antisocial potential (AP), which refers to the potential to commit antisocial acts. I prefer the term 'potential' rather than 'propensity', because propensity has more biological connotations. 'Offending' refers to the most common crimes of theft, burglary, robbery, violence, vandalism, minor fraud and drug use, and to behaviour that in principle might lead to a conviction in Western industrialized societies such as the United States and the United Kingdom. Long-term persisting between-individual differences in AP are distinguished from short-term within-individual variations in AP. Long-term AP depends on impulsiveness, on strain, modelling and socialization processes, and on life events, while short-term variations in AP depend on motivating and situational factors.

Regarding long-term AP, people can be ordered on a continuum from low to high. The distribution of AP in the population at any age is highly skewed; relatively few people have relatively high levels of AP. People with high AP are more likely to commit many different types of antisocial acts including different types of offences. Therefore, offending and antisocial behaviour are versatile not specialized. The relative ordering of people on AP (long-term between-individual variation) tends to be consistent over time, but absolute levels of AP vary with age, peaking in the teenage years, because of changes within individuals in the factors that influence long-term AP (e.g., from childhood to adolescence, the increasing importance of peers and decreasing importance of parents).

A key issue is whether the model should be the same for all types of crimes or whether different models are needed for different types of crimes. Because of their focus on the development of offenders, DLC researchers have concluded that, because offenders are versatile rather than specialized, it is not necessary to have different models for different types of crimes. For example, it is believed that the risk factors for violence are essentially the same as for property crime or substance abuse. However, researchers who have focussed on situational influences (e.g., Clarke and Cornish, 1985) have argued that different models are needed for different types of crimes. It is suggested that situational influences on burglary may be very different from situational influences on violence.

One possible way to resolve these differing viewpoints would be to assume that long-term potential was very general (e.g., a long-term potential for antisocial behaviour), whereas short-term potential was more specific (e.g., a short-term potential for violence). The top half of the model in Figure 13.1 could be the same for all types of crimes, whereas the bottom half could be different (with different situational influences) for different types of crimes.

In the interests of simplification, Figure 13.1 makes the DLC theory appear static rather than dynamic. For example, it does not explain changes in offending at different ages. Since it might be expected that different factors would be important at different ages or life stages, it seems likely that different models would be needed at different ages. Perhaps parents are more important in influencing children, peers are more important in influencing adolescents, and spouses and partners are more important in influencing adults.

Long-term risk factors

A great deal is known about risk factors that predict long-term persisting between-individual differences in antisocial potential. For example, in the Cambridge Study, the most important childhood risk factors for later offending were hyperactivity–impulsivity–attention deficit, low intelligence or low school attainment, family criminality, family poverty, large family size, poor child-rearing, and disrupted families (Farrington, 2003). Figure 13.1 shows how risk factors are hypothesized to influence long-term AP. This figure could be expanded to specify promotive and protective factors and study different influences on onset, persistence, escalation, de-escalation and desistance.

I have not included measures of antisocial behaviour (e.g., aggressiveness or dishonesty) as risk factors because of my concern with explanation, prevention and treatment. These measures do not cause offending; they predict offending because of the underlying continuity over time in AP. Measures of antisocial behaviour are useful in identifying risk groups but less useful in identifying causal factors to be targeted by interventions. Similarly, I have not included variables that cannot be changed, such as gender or ethnicity. I assume that their relationships with offending are mediated by changeable risk factors.

A major problem is to decide which risk factors are causes and which are merely markers or correlated with causes (see Murray *et al.*, 2009). Ideally, interventions should be targeted on risk factors that are causes. Interventions targeted on risk factors that are merely markers will not necessarily lead to any decrease in offending. Unfortunately, when risk factors are highly intercorrelated (as is usual), it is very difficult to establish which are causes in between-individual research. For example, the particular factors that appear to be independently important as predictors in any analysis may be greatly affected by measurement error and by essentially random variations between samples.

It is also important to establish how risk factors or causes have sequential or interactive effects on offending. Following strain theory, the main energizing factors that potentially lead to high long-term AP are desires for material goods, status among intimates, excitement, and sexual satisfaction. However, these motivations only lead to high AP if antisocial methods of satisfying them are habitually chosen. Antisocial methods tend to be chosen by people who find it difficult to satisfy their needs legitimately, such as people with low income, unemployed people, and those who fail at school. However, the methods chosen also depend on physical capabilities and behavioural skills; for example, a 5-year-old would have difficulty in stealing a car. For simplicity, energizing and directing processes and capabilities are shown in one box in Figure 13.1.

Long-term AP also depends on attachment and socialization processes. AP will be low if parents consistently and contingently reward good behaviour and punish bad behaviour. (Withdrawal of love may be a more effective method of socialization than hitting children.) Children with low anxiety will be less well socialized, because they care less about parental punishment. AP will be high if children are not attached to (prosocial) parents, for example if parents are cold and rejecting. Disrupted families (broken homes) may impair both attachment and socialization processes.

Long-term AP will also be high if people are exposed to and influenced by antisocial models, such as criminal parents, delinquent siblings, and delinquent peers, for example in high crime schools and neighbourhoods. Long-term AP will also be high for impulsive people, because they tend to act without thinking about the consequences. Also, life events affect AP; it decreases (at least for males) after people get married or move out of high crime areas, and it increases after separation from a partner.

There may also be interaction effects between the influences on long-term AP. For example, people who experience strain or poor socialization may be disproportionally antisocial if they are also exposed to antisocial models. In the interests of simplicity, Figure 13.1 does not attempt to show such interactions.

Figure 13.1 shows some of the processes by which risk factors have effects on AP. It does not show biological factors but these could be incorporated in the theory at various points. For example, the children of criminal parents could have high AP partly because of genetic transmission, excitement-seeking could be driven by low cortical arousal, school failure could depend partly on low intelligence, and high impulsiveness and low anxiety could both reflect biological processes.

Many researchers have measured only one risk factor (e.g., impulsivity) and have shown that it predicts or correlates with offending after controlling for a few other 'confounding factors', often including social class. The message of Figure 13.1 is: Don't forget the big picture. The particular causal linkages shown in Figure 13.1 may not be correct, but it is important to measure and analyse all important risk (and promotive and protective) factors in trying to draw conclusions about the causes of offending or the development of offenders.

Explaining the commission of crimes

According to the ICAP theory, the commission of offences and other types of antisocial acts depends on the interaction between the individual (with his immediate level of AP) and the social environment (especially criminal opportunities and victims). Short-term AP varies within individuals according to short-term energizing factors such as being bored, angry, drunk, or frustrated, or being encouraged by male peers. Criminal opportunities and the availability of victims depend on routine activities. Encountering a tempting opportunity or victim may cause a short-term increase in AP, just as a short-term increase in AP may motivate a person to seek out criminal opportunities and victims.

Whether a person with a certain level of AP commits a crime in a given situation depends on cognitive processes, including considering the subjective benefits, costs and probabilities of the different outcomes and stored behavioural repertoires or scripts (Huesmann, 1997). The subjective benefits and costs include immediate situational factors such as the material goods that can be stolen and the likelihood and consequences of being caught by the police. They also include social factors such as likely disapproval by parents or female partners, and encouragement or reinforcement from peers. In general, people tend to make decisions that seem rational to them, but those with low levels of AP will not commit offences even when (on the basis of subjective expected utilities) it appears rational to do so. Equally, high short-term levels of AP (e.g., caused by anger or drunkenness) may induce people to commit offences when it is not rational for them to do so.

The consequences of offending may, as a result of a learning process, lead to changes in long-term AP and in future cognitive decision-making processes. This is especially likely if the consequences are reinforcing (e.g., gaining material goods or peer approval) or punishing (e.g., receiving legal sanctions or parental disapproval).

Also, if the consequences involve labelling or stigmatizing the offender, this may make it more difficult for him to achieve his aims legally, and hence may lead to an increase in AP. (It is difficult to show these feedback effects in Figure 13.1 without making it very complex.)

A further issue that needs to be addressed is to what extent types of offenders might be distinguished. Perhaps some people commit crimes primarily because of their high long-term AP (e.g., the life-course-persistent offenders of Moffitt, 1993) and others primarily because of situational influences and high short-term AP. Perhaps some people commit offences primarily because of situational influences (e.g., getting drunk frequently) while others offend primarily because of the way they think and make decisions when faced with criminal opportunities. From the viewpoint of both explanation and prevention, research is needed to classify types of people according to their most influential risk factors and most important reasons for committing crimes.

CONCLUSIONS

More efforts should be made to compare and contrast the different DLC theories point-by-point in regard to their predictions and their agreement with empirical results (see Farrington, 2006). For example, Farrington *et al.* (2009b) studied the development of adolescence-limited, late-onset, and persistent offenders from age 8 to age 48 in the Cambridge Study. They found that, contrary to Moffitt's theory, adolescence-limited offenders had several of the same risk factors as persistent offenders. Contrary to Sampson and Laub's theory, early risk factors were important in predicting which offenders would persist or desist after age 21. Many other results were relevant to DLC theories, but there is not space here to review the empirical adequacy of these theories in more detail.

In order to advance knowledge about DLC theories and test them, new prospective longitudinal studies are needed with repeated self-report and official record measures of offending. Future longitudinal studies should follow people up to later ages and focus on desistance processes. Past studies have generally focussed on onset and on ages up to 30 (Farrington and Pulkkinen, 2009). Future studies should compare risk factors for early onset, continuation after onset (compared with early desistance), frequency, seriousness, later onset, and later persistence versus desistance. DLC theories should make explicit predictions about all these topics. Also, future studies should make more effort to investigate promotive and protective factors, and biological, peer, school, and neighbourhood risk factors, since most is known about individual and family factors. And future research should compare development, risk factors, and life events for males versus females and for different ethnic and racial groups in different countries.

Because most previous analyses of risk factors for offending involve between-individual comparisons, more within-individual analyses of offending are needed in longitudinal studies. These should investigate to what extent within-individual changes in risk and promotive factors are followed by within-individual changes in offending and other life outcomes. These analyses should provide compelling evidence about causal mechanisms. More information is needed about developmental sequences and about the predictability of future criminal careers, in order to know when and how it is best to intervene.

DLC findings and theories have many policy implications for the reduction of crime. First, it is clear that children at risk can be identified with reasonable accuracy at an early age. The worst offenders tend to start early and have long criminal careers. Often, offending is preceded by earlier types of antisocial behaviour in a developmental sequence, including cruelty to animals, bullying, truancy, and disruptive school behaviour. It is desirable to intervene early to reduce the later escalation into chronic or life-course-persistent offending. For example, programmes to prevent bullying in schools are generally effective (Ttofi and Farrington, 2009). It is desirable to develop risk–needs assessment devices to identify children at risk of becoming chronic offenders, who are usually children with specific needs. These devices could be implemented soon after school entry, at ages 6–8.

It would be desirable to derive implications for intervention from DLC theories, and to test these in randomized experiments. In principle, conclusions about causes can be drawn more convincingly in experimental research than in non-experimental longitudinal studies. The results summarized here have clear implications for intervention (Farrington, 2007). The main idea of risk-focussed prevention is to identify key risk factors for antisocial behaviour and implement prevention methods designed to counteract them. In addition, attempts should be made to enhance key promotive and protective factors.

As a further example of policy implications from DLC theories, Moffitt's (1993) theory suggests that different programmes are needed for adolescence-limited and life-course-persistent offenders. For adolescence-limited offenders, it is especially important to limit contact with delinquent peers. This is one of the main aims of Treatment Foster Care programmes (Chamberlain and Reid, 1998). Research on co-offending (Reiss and Farrington, 1991) suggests that it is important to identify and target 'recruiters', who are offenders who repeatedly commit crimes with younger, less experienced offenders, and who seem to be dragging more and more young people into the net of offending. Programmes that put antisocial peers together may have harmful effects (Dodge *et al.*, 2006). Moffitt also suggests that, in order to target the maturity gap of adolescence-limited offenders, it is important to provide opportunities for them to achieve status and material goods by legitimate means.

The main implication of Sampson and Laub's (2005) theory is that bonding to the family, the school and the community should be increased, for example by providing job training and structured routine activities in adulthood. They also suggest that desistance can be encouraged by fostering bonding to adult institutions such as employment and marriage. Another suggestion is that informal social control in communities could be improved by increasing community cohesiveness or 'collective efficacy' (Sampson *et al.*, 1997). They also argue that it is important to minimize labelling or stigmatization of offenders by minimizing the use of incarceration.

Because of their emphasis on development through life, DLC theories suggest that it is 'never too early, never too late' (Loeber and Farrington, 1998) to intervene successfully to reduce offending. In other words, it is highly desirable to focus not only on early intervention to prevent the adolescent onset of offending, but also on later programmes to prevent adult onset and to prevent continuation and encourage early desistance.

The fact that offenders tend to be antisocial in many aspects of their lives means that any measure that succeeds in reducing offending will probably have wide-ranging benefits in reducing, for example, accommodation problems, relationship problems, employment problems, alcohol and drug problems, and aggressive behaviour. Consequently, it is very likely that the financial benefits of successful programmes will greatly outweigh their financial costs. The time is ripe to mount a new programme of research to compare, contrast, and test predictions from different DLC theories, in the interests of developing more accurate theories and more effective policies.

ACKNOWLEDGMENTS

I am very grateful to Rico Catalano, Ben Lahey, Marc LeBlanc, Temi Moffitt, Rob Sampson, Terry Thornberry and P.-O. Wikström for providing recent papers.

REFERENCES

Brown, E. C., Catalano, R. F., Fleming, C. B., Haggerty, K. P., Abbott, R. D.,Cortes, R. R. and Park, J. (2005) Mediator effects on the social development model: An examination of constituent theories. *Criminal Behaviour and Mental Health,* 15: 221–235.

Catalano, R. F., Park, J., Harachi, T. W., Haggerty, K. P., Abbott, R. D. and Hawkins, J. D. (2005) Mediating the effects of poverty, gender, individual characteristics, and external constraints on antisocial behavior: A test of the Social Development Model and implications for developmental life-course theory. In D. P. Farrington (ed.), *Integrated Developmental and Life-Course Theories of Offending* (pp. 93–123). New Brunswick, NJ: Transaction.

Chamberlain, P. and Reid, J. B. (1998) Comparison of two community alternatives to incarceration for chronic juvenile offenders. *Journal of Consulting and Clinical Psychology,* 66: 624–633.

Clarke, R. V. and Cornish, D. B. (1985) Modeling offenders' decisions: A framework for research and policy. In M. Tonry and N. Morris (eds), *Crime and Justice,* Vol. 6 (pp. 147–185). Chicago: University of Chicago Press.

Crow, I., France, A., Hacking, S. and Hart, M. (2004) *Does Communities That Care Work? An Evaluation of a Community-Based Risk Prevention Programme in Three Neighbourhoods.* York: Joseph Rowntree Foundation.

Dodge, K. A., Dishion, T. J. and Lansford, J. E. (eds) (2006) *Deviant Peer Influences in Programs for Youth.* New York: Guilford.

Farrington, D. P. (1972) Delinquency begins at home. *New Society,* 21: 495–497.

Farrington, D. P. (1977) The effects of public labelling. *British Journal of Criminology,* 17: 112–125.

Farrington, D. P. (1986) Age and crime. In M. Tonry and N. Morris (eds), *Crime and Justice,* Vol. 7 (pp. 189–250). Chicago: University of Chicago Press.

Farrington, D. P. (1988) Studying changes within individuals: The causes of offending. In M. Rutter (ed.), *Studies of Psychosocial Risk: The Power of Longitudinal Data* (pp. 158–183). Cambridge: Cambridge University Press.

Farrington, D. P. (1989) Self-reported and official offending from adolescence to adulthood. In M. W. Klein (ed.), *Cross-National Research in Self-Reported Crime and Delinquency* (pp. 399–423). Dordrecht, Netherlands: Kluwer.

Farrington, D. P. (1990) Age, period, cohort, and offending. In D. M. Gottfredson and R. V. Clarke (eds), *Policy and Theory in Criminal Justice: Contributions in Honour of Leslie T. Wilkins (*pp. 51–75*).* Aldershot: Avebury.

Farrington, D. P. (1991a) Antisocial personality from childhood to adulthood. *The Psychologist,* 4: 389–394.

Farrington, D. P. (1991b) Childhood aggression and adult violence: Early precursors and later life outcomes. In D. J. Pepler and K. H. Rubin (eds), *The Development and Treatment of Childhood Aggression* (pp. 5–29). Hillsdale, NJ: Erlbaum.

Farrington, D. P. (1992) Criminal career research in the United Kingdom. *British Journal of Criminology,* 32: 521–536.

Farrington, D. P. (1993) Motivations for conduct disorder and delinquency. *Development and Psychopathology,* 5: 225–241.

Farrington, D. P. (2003) Key result from the first 40 years of the Cambridge Study in Delinquent Development. In T. P. Thornberry and M. D. Krohn (eds), *Taking Stock of Delinquency: An Overview of Findings from Contemporary Longitudinal Studies* (pp. 137–183). New York: Klumer/Plenum.

Farrington, D. P. (ed.) (2005a) *Integrated Developmental and Life-Course Theories of Offending.* (Advances in Criminological Theory, Vol. 14.) New Brunswick, NJ: Transaction.

Farrington, D. P. (2005b) The Integrated Cognitive Antisocial Potential (ICAP) theory. In D. P. Farrington (ed.), *Integrated Developmental and Life-Course Theories of Offending* (pp. 73–92). New Brunswick, NJ: Transaction.

Farrington, D. P. (2006) Building developmental and life-course theories of offending. In F. T. Cullen, J. P. Wright and K. R. Blevins (eds), *Taking Stock: The Status of Criminological Theory* (pp. 335–364). New Brunswick, NJ: Transaction.

Farrington, D. P. (2007) Childhood risk factors and risk-focussed prevention. In M. Maguire, R. Morgan and R. Reiner (eds), *The Oxford Handbook of Criminology* (fourth edition, pp. 602–640). Oxford: Oxford University press.

Farrington, D. P. (2009) Conduct disorder, aggression and delinquency. In R. M. Lerner and L. Steinberg (eds), *Handbook of Adolescent Psychology, Vol. 1: Individual Bases of Adolescent Development* (third edition, pp. 683–722). Hoboken, NJ: Wiley.

Farrington, D. P. and Pulkkinen, L. (2009) Introduction: The unusualness and contribution of life span longitudinal studies of aggressive and criminal behavior. *Aggressive Behavior,* 35: 115–116.

Farrington, D. P. and West, D. J. (1993) Criminal, penal, and life histories of chronic offenders: Risk and protective factors and early identification. *Criminal Behaviour and Mental Health,* 3: 492–523.

Farrington, D. P. and West, D. J. (1995) Effects of marriage, separation and children on offending by adult males. In J. Hagan (ed.), *Current Perspectives on Aging and the Life Cycle. Vol. 4: Delinquency and Disrepute in the Life Course* (pp. 249–281). Greenwich, CT: JAI Press.

Farrington, D. P., Gallagher, B., Morley, L., St. Ledger, R. J. and West, D. J. (1986) Unemployment, school leaving and crime. *British Journal of Criminology,* 26: 335–356.

Farrington, D. P., Lambert, S., and West, D. J. (1998) Criminal careers of two generations of family members in the Cambridge Study in Delinquent Development. *Studies on Crime and Crime Prevention,* 7: 85–106.

Farrington, D. P., Loeber, R., Yin, Y. and Anderson, S. J. (2002) Are within-individual causes of delinquency the same as between-individual causes? *Criminal Behaviour and Mental Health,* 12: 53–68.

Farrington, D. P., Coid, J. W., Harnett, L., Jolliffe, D., Soteriou, N., Turner, R. and West, D. J. (2006) *Criminal Careers up to age 50 and Life Success up to age 48: New Findings from the Cambridge Study in Delinquent Development.* London: Home Office (Research Study No. 299).

Farrington, D. P., Coid, J. W. and Murray, J. (2009a) Family factors in the intergenerational transmission of offending. *Criminal Behaviour and Mental Health,* 19: 109–124.

Farrington, D. P., Ttofi, M. M. and Coid, J. W. (2009b) Development of adolescence-limited, late-onset and persistent offenders from age 8 to age 48. *Aggressive Behavior,* 35: 150–163.

Farrington, D. P., Coid, J. W. and West, D. J. (2009c) The development of offending from age 8 to age 50: Recent results from the Cambridge Study in Delinquent Development. *Monatsschrift fur Kriminologie und Strafrechtsreform (Journal of Criminology and Penal Reform),* 92: 160–173.

Hawkins J. D. and Catalano, R. F. (1992) *Communities That Care.* San Francisco: Jossey-Bass.

Hawkins, J. D., Smith, B. H., Hill, K. G., Kosterman, R., Catalano, R. F. and Abbott, R. D. (2003) Understanding and preventing crime and violence: Findings from the Seattle Social Development Project. In T. P. Thornberry and M. D. Krohn (eds), *Taking Stock of Delinquency: An Overview of Findings from Contemporary Longitudinal Studies* (pp. 255–312). New York: Kluwer/ Plenum.

Hawkins, J. D., Brown, E. C., Oesterle, S., Arthur, M. W., Abbott, R. D. and Catalano, R. F. (2008) Early effects of Communities That Care on targeted risks and initiation of delinquent behavior and substance use. *Journal of Adolescent Health,* 43: 15–22.

Horney, J., Osgood, D. W. and Marshall, I. H. (1995) Criminal careers in the short-term: Intra-individual variability in crime and its relation to local life circumstances. *American Sociological Review,* 60: 655–673.

Huesmann, L. R. (1997) Observational learning of violent behavior: Social and biosocial processes. In A. Raine, P. A. Brennan, D. P. Farrington, and S. A. Mednick (eds), *Biosocial Bases of Violence* (pp. 69–88). New York: Plenum.

Huizinga, D., Weiher, A. W., Espiritu, R. and Esbensen, F. (2003) Delinquency and crime: Some highlights from the Denver Youth Survey. In T. P. Thornberry and M. D. Krohn (eds), *Taking Stock of Delinquency: An Overview of Findings from Contemporary Longitudinal Studies* (pp. 47–91). New York: Kluwer/Plenum.

Lahey, B. B. and Waldman, I. D. (2005) A developmental model of the propensity to offend during childhood and adolescence. In D. P. Farrington (ed.), *Integrated Developmental and Life-Course Theories of Offending* (pp. 15–50). New Brunswick, NJ: Transaction.

Lahey, B. B., Loeber, R., Waldman, I. D. and Farrington, D. P. (2006) Child socioemotional dispositions at school entry that predict adolescent delinquency and violence. *Impuls: Tidsskrift for Psykologi,* 3: 40–51.

Lahey, B. B., Applegate, B., Chronis, A. M., Jones, H. A., Williams, S. H., Loney, J. and Waldman, I. D. (2008) Psychometric characteristics of a measure of emotional dispositions developed to test a developmental propensity model of conduct disorder. *Journal of Clinical Child and Adolescent Psychology,* 37: 794–807.

Laub, J. H. and Sampson, R. J. (2001) Understanding desistance from crime. In M. Tonry (ed.), *Crime and Justice,* Vol. 28 (pp. 1–69). Chicago: University of Chicago Press.

Laub, J. H. and Sampson, R. J. (2003) *Shared Beginnings, Divergent Lives: Delinquent Boys to Age 70.* Cambridge, MA: Harvard University Press.

LeBlanc, M. (1997) A generic control theory of the criminal phenomenon: The structural and dynamic statements of an integrated multilayered control theory. In T. P. Thornberry (ed.), *Developmental Theories of Crime and Delinquency* (pp. 215–285). New Brunswick, NJ: Transaction.

LeBlanc, M. (2005) An integrated personal control theory of deviant behavior: Answers to contemporary empirical and theoretical developmental criminology issues. In D. P. Farrington (ed.), *Integrated Developmental and Life-Course Theories of Offending* (pp. 125–163). New Brunswick, NJ: Transaction.

LeBlanc, M. (2009) The development of deviant behavior, and its self-regulation. *Monatsschrift fur Kriminologie und Strafrechtsreform (Journal of Criminology and Penal Reform),* 92: 117–136.

LeBlanc, M. and Frechette, M. (1989) *Male Criminal Activity from Childhood through Youth.* New York: Springer-Verlag.

Loeber, R. and Farrington, D.P. (1998) Never too early, never too late: Risk factors and successful interventions for serious and violent juvenile offenders. *Studies on Crime and Crime Prevention,* 7: 7–30.

Loeber, R., Green, S. M., Lahey, B. B., Frick, P. J. and McBurnett, K. (2000) Findings on disruptive behavior disorders from the first decade of the Developmental Trends Study. *Clinical Child and Family Psychology Review,* 3: 37–60.

Loeber, R., Farrington, D. P., Stouthamer-Loeber, M., Moffitt, T. E., Caspi, A., White, H. R., Wei, E. H. and Beyers, J. M. (2003) The development of male offending: Key findings from fourteen years of the Pittsburgh Youth Study. In T. P. Thornberry and M. D. Krohn (eds), *Taking Stock of Delinquency: An Overview of Findings from Contemporary Longitudinal Studies* (pp. 93–136), New York: Kluwer/Plenum.

Loeber, R., Farrington, D. P., Stouthamer-Loeber, M. and White, H. R. (2008) *Violence and Serious Theft: Development and Prediction from Childhood to Adulthood.* New York: Routledge.

Moffitt, T. E. (1993) Adolescence-limited and life-course-persistent antisocial behavior: A developmental taxonomy. *Psychological Review,* 100: 674–701.

Moffitt, T. E. (2006) Life-course persistent and adolescent-limited antisocial behavior. In D. Cicchetti and D. J. Cohen (eds), *Developmental Psychopathology, Vol. 3: Risk, Disorder, and Adaptation* (pp. 570–598). New York: Wiley.

Moffitt, T. E., Caspi, A., Rutter, M. and Silva, P. A. (2001) *Sex Differences in Antisocial Behaviour: Conduct Disorder, Delinquency, and Violence in the Dunedin Longitudinal Study.* Cambridge: Cambridge University Press.

Murray, J., Farrington, D. P. and Eisner, M. P. (2009) Drawing conclusions about causes from systematic reviews of risk factors: The Cambridge Quality Checklists. *Journal of Experimental Criminology,* 5: 1–23.

Nagin, D. S. and Farrington, D. P. (1992) The stability of criminal potential from childhood to adulthood. *Criminology,* 30: 235–260.

Odgers, C. L., Moffitt, T. E., Broadbent, J. M., Dickson, N., Hancox, R. J., Harrington, H., Poulton, R., Sears, M. R., Thomson, W. M. and Caspi, A. (2008) Female and male antisocial trajectories: From childhood origins to adult outcomes. *Development and Psychopathology,* 20: 673–716.

Osborn, S. G. (1980) Moving home, leaving London, and delinquent trends. *British Journal of Criminology,* 20: 54–61.

Piquero, A., Paternoster, R., Mazerolle, P., Brame, R. and Dean, C. W. (1999) Onset age and offense specialization. *Journal of Research in Crime and Delinquency,* 36: 275–299.

Reiss, A. J. and Farrington, D. P. (1991) Advancing knowledge about co-offending: Results from a prospective longitudinal survey of London males. *Journal of Criminal Law and Criminology,* 82: 360–395.

Sampson, R. J. and Laub, J. H. (1993) *Crime in the Making: Pathways and Turning Points Through Life.* Cambridge, MA: Harvard University Press.

Sampson, R. J. and Laub, J. H. (1995) Understanding variability in lives through time: Contributions of life-course criminology. *Studies on Crime and Crime Prevention,* 4: 143–158.

Sampson, R. J. and Laub, J. H. (2003) Life-course desisters? Trajectories of crime among delinquent boys followed to age 70. *Criminology,* 41: 555–592.

Sampson, R. J. and Laub, J. H. (2005) A general age-graded theory of crime: Lessons learned and the future of life-course criminology. In D. P. Farrington (ed.), *Integrated Developmental and Life-Course Theories of Offending* (pp. 165–181). New Brunswick, NJ: Transaction.

Sampson, R. J. and Laub, J. H. (2009) A life-course theory and long-term project on trajectories of crime. *Monatsschrift fur Kriminologie und Strafrechtsreform (Journal of Criminology and Penal Reform),* 92: 226–239.

Sampson, R. J., Raudenbush, S. W. and Earls, F. (1997) Neighborhoods and violent crime: A multilevel study of collective efficacy. *Science,* 277: 918–924.

Thornberry, T. P. and Krohn, M. D. (2001) The development of delinquency: An interactional perspective. In S. O. White (ed.), *Handbook of Youth and Justice* (pp. 289–305). New York: Plenum.

Thornberry, T. P. (2005) Explaining multiple patterns of offending across the life course and across generations. *Annals of the American Academy of Political and Social Science,* 602: 156–195.

Thornberry, T. P., Lizotte, A. J., Krohn, M. D., Smith, C. A. and Porter, P. K. (2003) Causes and consequences of delinquency: Findings from the Rochester Youth Development Study. In T. P. Thornberry and M. D. Krohn (eds), *Taking Stock of Delinquency: An Overview of Findings from Contemporary Longitudinal Studies* (pp. 11–46). New York: Kluwer/Plenum.

Thornberry, T. P. and Krohn, M. D. (2005) Applying interactional theory to the explanation of continuity and change in antisocial behavior. In D. P. Farrington (ed.), *Integrated Developmental and Life-Course Theories of Offending* (pp. 183–209). New Brunswick, NJ: Transaction.

Thornberry, T. P., Freeman-Gallant, A. and Lovegrove, P. J. (2009) Intergenerational linkages in antisocial behaviour. *Criminal Behaviour and Mental Health,* 19: 80–93.

Tremblay, R. E., Vitaro, F., Nagin, D., Pagani, L. and Seguin, J. R. (2003) The Montreal Longitudinal and Experimental study: Rediscovering the power of descriptions. In T. P. Thornberry and M. D. Krohn (eds), *Taking Stock of Delinquency: An Overview of Findings from Contemporary Longitudinal Studies* (pp. 205–254). New York: Kluwer/Plenum.

Ttofi, M. M. and Farrington, D. P. (2009) What works in preventing bullying? Effective elements of anti-bullying programmes. *Journal of Aggression, Conflict and Peace Research,* 1: 13–23.

Wikström, P-O. H. (2005) The social origins of pathways in crime: Towards a developmental ecological action theory of crime involvement and its changes. In D. P. Farrington (ed.), *Integrated Developmental and Life-Course Theories of Offending* (pp. 211–245). New Brunswick, NJ: Transaction.

Wikström, P-O. H. (2010) Situational action theory. In F. T. Cullen and P. Wilcox (eds), *Encyclopedia of Criminological Theory.* Thousand Oaks, CA: Sage, in press.

Zara, G. and Farrington, D. P. (2009) Childhood and adolescent predictors of late onset criminal careers. *Journal of Youth and Adolescence,* 38: 287–300.

14

Crime Science

Ronald V. Clarke

INTRODUCTION

Crime science is a very recent addition to the criminological lexicon. It lacks a standard definition, few criminologists use the term routinely and even fewer might think of themselves as crime scientists. In fact, the term was created by Nick Ross, the presenter of BBC TV's monthly 'Crimewatch' program, who incorporated it in the name of the institute – The Jill Dando Institute of Crime Science – that he founded in 2001 at University College London (UCL) in memory of his murdered colleague. He chose the term crime science, not criminology, because he wanted the new institute to be focused exclusively on crime reduction, not merely on understanding and explaining crime, the traditional focus of criminology. And he chose UCL, not only because of its stellar reputation, but specifically because it did not have a department of criminology that might inhibit the growth and functioning of the new institute.

While crime science is a new term, it is closely affiliated with environmental criminology, a well-established sub-discipline comprising the "criminologies of everyday life" (Garland, 2001).[1] These theories and preventive applications "share a common interest in criminal events and the immediate circumstances in which they occur" (Wortley and Mazerolle, 2008: 1), which distinguishes them from most other criminological theories that are focused on offenders and the factors giving rise to delinquent or criminal dispositions. The best known theories and preventive applications of environmental criminology are listed in Table 14.1.

Many of those who now call themselves crime scientists (such as Ken Pease, Gloria Laycock and Nick Tilley) have already made substantial contributions to environmental criminology, and their more recent writings in the name of crime science could just as readily be encompassed by the original term. However, Nick Ross chose not to use environmental criminology in the institute's name perhaps

Table 14.1 Chronology of environmental criminology: theories and applications

Theories	Applications
The urban village (Jane Jacobs, 1961)	Defensible space (Newman, 1972)
Crime prevention through environmental design (Jeffery, 1971)	Problem-oriented policing (Goldstein, 1979)
	Situational prevention (Clarke, 1980)
Crime as opportunity (Mayhew et al., 1976)	Broken windows (Wilson and Kelling, 1982)
Routine activity approach (Cohen and Felson, 1979)	CPTED (Crowe, 1991)
Environmental criminology (Brantinghams, 1981)	Repeat victimization (Farrell and Pease, 1993)
Rational choice (Cornish and Clarke, 1986)	Pulling levers/Focused deterrence (Kennedy, 1997)
Situational deterrence (Cusson, 1993)	Geographic profiling (Rossmo, 2000 and earlier)
Crime pattern theory (Brantinghams, 1993)	Third party policing (Green Mazerolle and Roehl 1998)
Criminology of place (Eck, Weisburd, Sherman)*	The 5 I's (Ekblom, 2002)
Conjunction of criminal opportunity (Ekblom, 2000)	Crime-free products (Ekblom, Pease, Clarke,
Situational precipitators (Wortley, 2001)	Newman)**

*Various publications in late 1980s/early 1990s.
**Various publications in late 1990s/early 2000s.

because it is often confused with the study of environmental crime, but more important, because he wanted to draw attention to the mission of the new institute. First and foremost, as mentioned above, he wanted it to be focused exclusively on crime reduction. Second, he wanted it to be as much focused on deterrence (through improving methods of identifying and arresting offenders) as on opportunity reduction, which has been the main focus to date of environmental criminology. As described on the Jill Dando Institute's web site (accessed July 9, 2008), "(crime science's) emphasis is on crime reduction – both preventing crimes from happening and catching offenders more quickly after the event." Third, he supported the objective, much emphasized by Ken Pease (2005, 2008) who advised him in setting up the institute, to enlist the help of a wider range of scientific disciplines in the crime reduction enterprise.

New strands of environmental criminology commonly emerge, which are labeled to signal their differences from existing strands (see Table 14.1). So, is it the case that crime science is merely one of the many variants of environmental criminology, or does it represent something genuinely new? In fact, neither of these might be the best way to characterize crime science. Rather, it can be regarded an attractive new way to market environmental criminology, which at the same time broadens its focus to include a much wider range of scientific disciplines and a greater emphasis on deterrence. This raises an important question for the discipline of criminology: Should crime science be recognized as an integral and central component of criminology, or should it be regarded as a related, but different discipline, much like criminal justice, that will and that should go its own way?

The remainder of this chapter will, (1) identify the central theoretical premises of environmental criminology, (2) show that crime science shares these premises and, as said, that it might be a better descriptor than environmental criminology, (3) explore in more depth whether crime science should be treated as a separate discipline from criminology, and (4) consider the implications of such a separation.

THE PREMISES OF ENVIRONMENTAL CRIMINOLOGY

While they share a common interest in criminal events, there is little competition among the theories and the preventive applications of environmental criminology. For example, routine activity theory, crime pattern theory and the rational choice perspective operate at different levels of explanation (Felson and Clarke, 1998): routine activity theory is a *macro* theory dealing primarily with the ways that opportunities for crime rise or decline with broad changes in society; crime pattern theory is a *meso* theory dealing with the ways that offenders search for or discover crime opportunities in the course of their everyday lives; and the rational choice perspective is a *micro* theory dealing with the ways that offenders make decisions to take advantage of criminal opportunities. There is equal variety among the crime prevention approaches. For example, some of these seek to "design out" anticipated opportunities for crime (e.g., defensible space and CTED) whereas others, including problem-oriented policing and situational crime prevention, are conceived of as problem solving approaches, the former reserved for the police while the latter to be employed by any organization confronted with a crime problem.

Each of the theories and preventive applications of environmental criminology has a large literature, but they share a number of common premises, which, building on Wortley and Mazerolle's (2008) discussion, are enumerated below.

1 *Crime is the outcome of the interaction between dispositions and situations.* To put it another way, crime results from the interplay of criminal motivation and crime opportunities. A criminal disposition can only lead to crime when circumstances permit it, while a criminal opportunity will result in crime only if perceived and acted upon. A criminal disposition can sensitize an individual to perceive criminal opportunities, but it also the case that a mostly law-abiding person can be drawn into crime by encountering a criminal opportunity. Thus, at a macro, societal level, an abundance of easy crime opportunities can help to create a population of people who follow a life of crime. The interaction between dispositions and situations does not mean that they cannot be separately studied. Indeed, for the past hundred years criminology has studied dispositions while almost entirely ignoring situations, and environmental criminology chooses to focus on situations while leaving dispositions aside. Nor does the interaction imply that both dispositions and situations must be equally addressed in prevention. Indeed, the preventive implications of focusing upon one or the other are profoundly different.

2 *Crime is always the product of choice.* Offenders are always seeking to benefit themselves by crime even if the choice is heavily "bounded" by limitations of information, by emotion, by drugs or alcohol and by a host of other factors that result in offenders making less than optimal decisions. This is the theory of "bounded rationality" (Simon, 1955, 1978) that underpins increasing proportions of economics and other social sciences (Kahneman, 2003). It is at the heart of environmental criminology even when this is not explicitly acknowledged in the discussions of its different versions. It implies that most offenders are much the same as everybody else. Even those few offenders whose motivations are clearly pathological – serial murders, for example – show considerable evidence of "rationality" in their planning and efforts to avoid capture.

3 *A crime-specific focus is fundamental to understanding the role of situational factors in crime.* A focus on dispositions, supported by evidence that persistent offenders commit a variety of different crimes, has allowed traditional criminology to neglect the very important differences

among crimes. Thus, the dependent variable in much criminological research has been "crime" or "delinquency". This ignores entirely the subjective experience of offenders, who commit rape for very different reasons than they have for committing burglary or stealing cars. It also ignores the decisions they make in committing these crimes: how to achieve their objectives in the simplest, easiest and least risky ways. These decisions are largely driven by the features of the situation – features that offenders perceive and evaluate – which vary greatly from crime to crime. In fact, it is not enough in making distinctions between crimes to rely on broad legal definitions such as burglary and auto theft, since these categories include within them quite different forms of crime. This is illustrated by research on residential burglary undertaken by Poyner and Webb (1991) in one British city. They found that residential burglaries committed in the suburbs were quite different from those committed in the city center and that these two kinds of burglaries required different solutions. Thus, city center burglaries were committed by offenders on foot, looking for cash and jewelry. Because most of the housing was built in terraces they could only get in through the front door or a front window. To prevent these burglaries Poyner and Webb suggested improving security and surveillance at the front of the house. Suburban burglars, on the other hand, used cars and were looking for electronic goods such as videocassette players and TVs. They were more likely to break in at the back of the house than the front. They needed cars to get to the suburbs and to transport the stolen goods. The cars had to be parked near to the house, but not so close as to attract attention. Poyner and Webb's preventive suggestions included better surveillance of parking places and improved security at the back of houses. They also suggested that the police should crack down on fencing of stolen goods, particularly electronic items – a tactic that would have little effect on the inner city burglars who were primarily targeting cash and jewelry.

4   *Crime is heavily concentrated.* Opportunities for crime are not uniformly distributed over crime and space. They follow the distribution and routine movements of populations and they are heavily restricted by formal and informal security. However, there are still many situations in which opportunities for crime are easy and tempting. This results in the concentration of crime at particular places ("hot spots", Sherman *et al.*, 1989) on particular people ("repeat victims", Farrell and Pease, 1993), on particular products ("hot products", Clarke, 1999) and at particular establishments, premises and facilities ("risky facilities", Eck *et al.*, 2007). Focusing on crime concentrations enables those designing situational interventions to obtain the greatest preventive benefits from their actions.

5   *Crime can be reduced (often immediately and dramatically) by environmental changes that reduce opportunities and modify precipitators.* More specifically, crime can be reduced by increasing the difficulties and risks of crime, by reducing the rewards, and by removing provocations and excuses (Cornish and Clarke, 2003). This is true of every form of crime, however serious. There is little doubt, for example, that stringent gun controls are responsible for the much lower rate of homicide in the United Kingdom than in the United States. In fact, it is often easier to change the situations giving rise to crime than to prevent the development of criminal dispositions tendencies (or, using Ekblom's (2000) distinction, it is easier to change the near rather than the distant causes of crime). In addition, situational changes can result in immediate reductions in crime, whereas attempts to prevent the development of dispositions might take many years to bear fruit, if they ever do. It is often argued, however, that environmental crime prevention cannot work because it does not attempt to understand or change motivation. While a fuller understanding of motives can often assist environmental prevention, this is not always necessary. For example, an outbreak of random murders in the 1980s resulting from people buying painkillers that had been laced with cyanide was eliminated by the

introduction of tamper-proof packaging for all medicines and foods. The murderers were never arrested and their motivation remains obscure, but a straightforward opportunity-reducing initiative eliminated future occurrences (Clarke and Newman, 2005).

THE FIT BETWEEN CRIME SCIENCE AND ENVIRONMENTAL CRIMINOLOGY

It is clear from published descriptions to date (Clarke 2004; Laycock, 2001; Pease 2005; Ross 2003; Tilley in Smith and Tilley 2005) that crime science shares the premises listed above, but it also has some distinct features, the most important of which is its starting point of crime reduction. Second, in pursuing crime reduction, crime science explicitly includes methods of detecting and arresting prolific offenders. Most other forms of environmental criminology focus simply on opportunity-reduction, though there are some important exceptions. For example, an important element of many problem-oriented policing projects is the arrest of repeat offenders responsible for the specific problem being addressed. In addition, one of the main techniques of situational prevention is increasing the risks of detection (though not necessarily of arrest and punishment). Finally, David Kennedy has described his "focused deterrence/pulling levers" approach employed in the Boston Gun Project as a variant of situational crime prevention (Skubak Tillyer and Kennedy, 2008) and thus of environmental criminology.

A third difference between crime science and environmental criminology is the avowed intention of the former to recruit a broader range of sciences – particularly the "hard" sciences and engineering – to the crime reduction enterprise. This is not simply to increase the range and effectiveness of possible interventions or to sharpen the distinction between crime science and criminology. Rather it is to draw attention to the need for scientific rigor in studying crime – rigor which Nick Ross believes is generally lacking in criminology. But multi-disciplinarity and rigor are also components of environmental criminology, as shown by the following extract from a recent authoritative review:

> Across (the) three domains of theory, analysis and practice, the environmental perspective is multi-disciplinary in its foundations, empirical in its methods and utilitarian in its mission. The environmental perspective draws on the ideas and expertise of sociologists, psychologists, geographers, architects, town planners, industrial designers, computer scientists, demographers, political scientists and economists. It embraces measurement and the scientific method, and it is committed to building theories and providing advice based on rigorous analysis of the available data.
>
> (Wortley and Mazerolle, 2008: 3)

The differences in emphasis between crime science and environmental criminology are therefore relatively minor and crime science can readily be classified as a variant of environmental criminology. Equally easily, however, it could provide a new, and possibly more suitable, substitute term for environmental criminology. It shares the latter's theoretical premises, it encompasses both theory and preventive approaches, it signals more sharply a break with traditional criminology, it emphasizes scientific method, and it avoids the awkward association with environmental crimes. This association is likely to become even more confusing with the growth of criminological interest in these crimes. A new book on *Crimes against Nature* even uses the term "environmental criminology" in its subtitle (White, 2008).

Despite the advantages of the new term, the idea of substituting it for the existing term was rejected at the 13th Annual ECCA (Environmental Criminology and Crime Analysis) Symposiums held in Chile in July 2005.[2] The reasons were, first, that most participants valued their identity as criminologists. They thought that environmental criminology was at last becoming a recognized sub-field of the discipline and re-labeling it could jeopardize this hard-won standing. Second, they felt that the substitution was unwarranted because crime science was merely another variant of environmental criminology.

These are both good reasons for retaining environmental criminology as the descriptor of event-focused criminology, but they might also be the expression of some natural human tendencies. Environmental criminologists have led an uncomfortable existence on the edges of criminology for many years. They are now coming in from the cold and it is tempting for them to settle for being respected, if minor players in criminology, while still hoping that its continuing dispositional bias will gradually be corrected by greater infusions of situational thinking. Pushing too hard for a more central place in the discipline could lead to a backlash resulting in more fractiousness and disappointment.

To go one step further and break entirely with criminology by establishing an independent discipline of "crime science", carries much greater risks of discomfort and failure and perhaps only a newcomer, such as Nick Ross, could propose this. For established criminologists to turn their backs on their discipline would be like breaking with their parents or being disloyal to their country. Even so, there are good reasons for thinking about crime science as a separate discipline, loosely related to criminology, and these are examined below.

CRIME SCIENCE AND CRIMINOLOGY – SEPARATE DISCIPLINES?

As discussed above, the core difference between crime science and criminology is that crime science focuses on events and situations, while criminology focuses on offenders and dispositions. Criminology's dispositional focus can be traced back at least to Edwin Sutherland. In his introduction to *Principles of Criminology* (3rd edn, 1947), often considered criminology's "bible", he opined:

> The problem in criminology is to explain the criminality of behavior, not the behavior, as such.
>
> (p. 4)

> The situation operates in many ways, of which perhaps the least important is the provision of an opportunity for a criminal act.
>
> (p. 5)

In fact, the dispositional bias of criminology now runs so deep that it might never be corrected by an infusion of situational thinking. This would be a source of continuing frustration for crime scientists who chose to remain in criminology's fold, particularly for those acutely aware of the advantages of their own approach. Despite its short history, crime science has acquired an unparalleled record of success in crime prevention[3] and the different theories and applications which it encompasses share a coherent and largely integrated set of theoretical assumptions. These assumptions represent a different paradigm for the study and control of crime. Indeed, the division between crime science and criminology rests upon the classic nature/nurture divide in explaining behaviour. This is why crime science diverges more radically from criminology as a whole than any of the other versions of criminology described in this book.

Consistent with their different paradigms, many other differences exist between crime science and criminology in their research approaches, missions and constituencies served (see Table 14.2). Regarding research, the focus on offenders and dispositions has meant that certain research approaches and methodologies have come to dominate criminology. Much energy has been spent in the past several decades on testing theories (Weisburd and Piquero, 2008) and in undertaking research into criminal careers. To support this research an array of methodologies has been developed which have come to dominate the journals, including longitudinal cohort studies, self-reported delinquency measures, psychological assessments, measures of educational attainment and multivariate statistical analysis. In crime science, much more use is made of action research models designed to assist the solution of specific crime problems, in which problems are analysed, hypotheses are developed and potential solutions are identified and evaluated. The methods used include victimization surveys, risk assessments, crime audits, and analysis of hot spots and repeat victimization. GIS and crime mapping have proved to be especially important tools (Chainey and Ratcliffe, 2005).

Even when similar methods are employed by both groups of researchers the focus might be quite different. For example, criminologists use offender interviews to obtain information about offenders' backgrounds and criminal careers, while crime scientists use them to study how offenders choose their crimes and targets (Decker, 2005).

Sharp as the differences might be between crime science and criminology, they may be no greater than in some other academic disciplines. Indeed, universities are quite accustomed to dealing with radical differences of outlook among faculty members within particular departments. These differences can sometimes lead to the establishment of new departments, but in most cases not – the department is expected to achieve an accommodation among the different schools of thought. It is only when universities can see important advantages in terms of attracting students and research grants, or providing training and education for previously un-served constituencies, that they will be moved to establish new departments. This occurred in the early 1970s when colleges and universities throughout America, stimulated by the availability of considerable federal funds, began to establish departments of criminal justice. These were intended to fill two needs not properly served by criminology departments: (1) the need for operational studies of the criminal justice system and, (2) the need to provide relevant education background for the thousands

Table 14.2 Differences between crime science and criminology

Criminology	Crime science
Mission	
Understand criminals	Understand crime
Prevent delinquency and reform offenders	Control crime
Long-term social reform	Immediate crime reduction
Help the criminal underdog	Protect victims
Enlighten policy	Steer policy
Contributory disciplines	
Sociology, psychiatry, law, biology and genetics	Environmental criminology, geography, ecology, behavioral psychology, economics, architecture, town planning, computer science, engineering, design
Constituencies	
Criminal justice system	Police and the security industry
Social policy makers	Crime policy makers
Social workers/probation officers	Architects, town planners, city managers
Intellectuals/social commentators	Business, industry and designers
College and university teachers	Crime and intelligence analysts
Theory	
Causes of delinquency and criminality	Causes of crime
Distant causes pre-eminent in explanation	Near causes equally important
Preventive focus: distant causes	Preventive focus: near causes
Opportunity secondary	Opportunity central
Crime pathological	Crime normal
The WHY of crime	The HOW of crime
Criminal dispositions, criminal motivation	Criminal choice, the rewards of crime
Research	
Tests of theory	Hypothesis testing
Dependent variable: crime/delinquency	Dependent variable: specific crime problem
Street crime, violence	Street crime, disorder, violence, organized crime, transnational crime, terrorism, Internet crimes, corruption, fraud
Cohort studies	Crime analysis
Criminal careers, repeat offenders	Hot spots, repeat victims, hot products
Multivariate statistical analysis	Crime mapping
Self-reported delinquency	Victim surveys
Long term studies in depth	Rapid appraisal techniques

Adapted from Clarke (2004).

of jobs in the system filled by probation and parole officers, prison administrators, police officers and federal agents.

The same story could be repeated for crime science because neither criminology nor criminal justice aspires to meet its principal objective – that of securing immediate drops in crime through the reduction of criminal opportunities. Even the police are more interested in bringing offenders to justice than in preventing crime – and when they do focus on crime prevention, they are likely to use "broken windows" or problem-oriented policing approaches, both of which fall under crime science.

In fact, the professions that could play a role in reducing opportunities for crime are not served at all by criminology or criminal justice. They fall into two groups both of which operate "upstream" from the criminal justice system. The first group includes professions whose principal role is the provision of security and crime prevention. These include: security personnel, whether employed by security firms or the security departments of businesses, industries or large organizations, such as hospitals, ports and transport systems; and variety of other specialists such as compliance regulators and fraud controllers in banks, insurance firms and investment agencies. The second group comprises those professions whose role is not directly related to security, but whose work can materially affect the supply of crime opportunities. They include architects, town planners and city managers; facility managers; the designers and manufacturers of everyday objects that become targets or tools for crime; software engineers and system designers.

For the first group, security professionals, crime science offers a coherent body of theory to underpin their policies and practices (now mostly based on common sense) as well as extensive methodological expertise in evaluating and strengthening these practices (Gill, 2006). Thus, at present, whole swathes of the security industry make their living by providing guards or alarm services, but there is very little critical evaluation of either guards or alarms and little experimentation in ways of improving their efficiency. This has implications not just for the security firms providing the services and the businesses and organizations purchasing them, but also for the police and the public since more effective private security can benefit the community at large. These benefits, and more generally the overlapping roles of private and public policing, have been neglected by governments and academics alike. Thus, there are very few university departments of security administration in the United States and none in a major research university.

As for the second group of professions, those whose work can materially affect the supply of crime opportunities, the principal needs are to educate them about their role in generating or preventing crime, to persuade them to take some responsibility for reducing crime, and to provide them with tools and knowledge to do this. This implies a considerable agenda of research and outreach. Even most architects, the group which environmental criminologists have tried hardest to reach, have probably not heard of CPTED and would therefore need to be persuaded that they could and should do something to prevent crime.[4] If this is true of architects, it is even more likely to be the case for members of the other professions mentioned above, who have had little exposure to environmental criminology. They will argue that it is not their responsibility to prevent crime; that crime prevention is the job of welfare agencies, the police and the criminal justice system; that the courts should imprison more criminals and for longer periods of time; that reducing opportunities for crime will simply displace crime elsewhere, and so forth.

If the limited experience to date is any guide, one of the most difficult but important groups to influence will be manufacturers of criminogenic products (Clarke and Newman, 2005). For example, despite decades of research implicating poor vehicle security in high rates of car theft, car manufacturers have until recently been very resistant to the suggestion that they should improve the security of their products (Newman, 2004). In the United Kingdom, car manufacturers only began to make serious efforts to improve car security when the government began to publish statistics showing which models were most vulnerable to theft (Laycock, 2004), while in the EU vehicle manufacturers were compelled by law to fit electronic immobilisers to all new cars from 1998 (Webb, 2005). In fact, the tasks of engaging architects and manufacturers are so different that it implies the need for different groups of crime scientists, who specialize in the domains of the various professions mentioned above. This again underlines the need for a considerable educational and training agenda, not just for the target professions, but also for crime science students.

CONCLUSIONS

This chapter began by asking whether crime science is merely another version of environmental criminology, or whether it provides a better lable for the theories and preventive applications falling under that term, all of which focus on the criminal event. It argued in favor of the second of these alternatives and went on to argue that crime science offers a paradigm for the study and control of crime that is quite different from that of criminology. It concluded that crime science should therefore be regarded as a distinct discipline in its own right, one that serves important needs of crime control education and policy.

Splitting off crime science from criminology would entail few risks for the latter because people are continually fascinated by criminals and students enjoy studying the subject. In addition, policy makers will continue to demand an improved understanding and explanation of the sources of criminal motivation. Finally, there are vastly more criminologists than crime scientists so that the departure of the latter would make barely a dent in the discipline. The risks for crime science of splitting from criminology are greater and include the difficulties of establishing a new disciplinary label in public discourse, effectively communicating its domain and distinguishing it from criminology, and attracting a sufficiently large body of students. The greatest risk of a split for both disciplines is that university resources would not expand to accommodate their different needs and they might become embroiled in debilitating competitions for research and teaching funds.

On the other hand, separating crime science from criminology would leave them both free to focus on their essentially different missions. No doubt there would continue to be cross-fertilization of ideas between the disciplines, but without the implicit subordination of crime science. Students with an interest in crime would have a broader choice of rewarding career paths – either the more practical pursuits of crime science, or the more cerebral pursuits of criminology. Indeed, many students who enrol in courses in criminology might be little attracted to crime science's crime control mission and they might have little interest in developing the expertise needed in telecommunications, transport, retailing, housing, entertainment and the other arenas of everyday life where crime needs to be prevented. Rather, they might be motivated by the ideals of criminology – of enlightening society about crime, of helping to fashion a humane criminal justice system and of helping to reform criminals.

Universities have long recognized that an interest in crime and its control can take different forms that need to be served in different ways – that is why there already exist university departments of law, criminology, criminal justice and forensic science. Adding crime science to this mix would probably result in attracting a new group of students to universities who would otherwise have gone straight into the police or the security industry. It would not mean simply redistributing the same pool of students between the new and the established disciplines. Perhaps universities should now give formal recognition to this diversity of disciplines by establishing faculties of "crime and legal studies", which would encompass the disciplines and underline their importance as separate but related fields of study, offering very different but rewarding careers.

NOTES

1 By common consent, the origins of modern environmental criminology can be traced to 1971/2 with the publication of seminal works by C. Ray Jeffery (1971) and Oscar Newman (1972), though the term was not coined until ten years later (Brantingham and Brantingham, 1981).

2 ECCA Symposiums have been held annually since 1992 (Bichler and Malm, 2008).

3 The web site of the Center for Problem-oriented Policing (www.popcenter.org) lists more than 200 evaluated case studies of situational crime prevention, the great majority of which show substantial reductions in the specific forms of crime addressed (see also Guerette and Bowers, 2009).

4 Unfortunately, more convincing evidence is also needed of CPTED's effectiveness if more architects are to be persuaded of its value.

REFERENCES

Bichler, G. and Malm, A. (2008) A social network analysis of the evolution of Environmental Criminology and Crime Analysis (ECCA) Symposiums. *Crime Patterns and Analysis,* 1: 5–22.

Brantingham, P. J. and Brantingham, P. L. (eds) (1981) *Environmental Criminology.* Beverly Hills: Sage.

Brantingham, P. L. and Brantingham, P. L. (1993) Environment, routine and situation: toward a pattern theory of crime. In: R. V. Clarke and M. Felson (eds), *Routine Activity and Rational Choice.* New Brunswick, NJ: Transaction Press.

Chainey, S. and Ratcliffe, J. (2005) *GIS and Crime Mapping.* New York: Wiley.

Clarke, R. V. (1980) Situational crime prevention: theory and practice. *British Journal of Criminology,* 20: 136–47.

Clarke, R. V. (1999) *Hot Products: Understanding, Anticipating and Reducing the Demand for Stolen Goods.* Police Research Series. Paper 98. London: Home Office.

Clarke, R. V. (2004) Technology, criminology and crime science. *European Journal on Criminal Policy and Research,* XXX: 1–9.

Clarke, R. V. and Newman, G. R. (2005) Modifying criminogenic products: what role for government? In: R. V. Clarke, and G. R. Newman (eds), *Designing out Crime from Products and Systems.* Crime Prevention Studies, Volume 18. Monsey, NY: Criminal Justice Press.

Cohen, L. E. and Felson, M. (1979) social change and crime rate trends: a routine activity approach. *American Sociological Review,* 44: 588–608.

Cornish, D. B. and Clarke, R. V. (eds) (1986) *The Reasoning Criminal: Rational Choice Perspectives on Offending.* New York: Springer-Verlag.

Cornish, D. B. and Clarke, R. V. (2003) *Opportunities, Precipitators and Criminal Decisions.* Crime Prevention Studies, Vol 16. Monsey, NY: Criminal Justice Press. (accessible at www.popcenter.org)

Crowe, T. (1991) *Crime Prevention through Environmental Design. Applications of Architectural Design and Space Management Concepts.* Boston: Butterworth-Heinemann.

Cusson, M. (1993) *Situational Deterrence: Fear During the Criminal Event.* Crime Prevention Studies, vol. 1. Monsey, NY: Criminal Justice Press.

Decker, S. H. (2005) *Using Offender Interviews to Inform Police Problem Solving. Problem-Oriented Guides for Police.* Problem Solving Tools Series, No 3. Office of Community Oriented Policing Services. Washington, DC: U.S. Dept. of Justice. (accessible at www.popcenter.org)

Eck, J., Clarke, R. V. and Guerette, R. (2007) Risky facilities: crime concentrations in homogeneous sets of establishments and facilities. In Graham Farrell *et al.* (eds), *Imagination for Crime Prevention.* Crime Prevention Studies, Vol 21. Monsey, NY: Criminal Justice Press. (accessible at www.popcenter.org)

Ekblom, P. (2000) The conjunction of criminal opportunity. In: S. Ballintyne, K. Pease and V. McClaren (eds), *Secure Foundations. Key Issues in Crime Prevention, Crime Reduction and Community Safety.* London: Institute for Public Policy Research.

Ekblom, P. (2002) Towards a European knowledge base – the 5 Is. Unpublished paper prepared for the EU Crime Prevention Network Conference, Aalborg, Denmark.

Farrell, G. and Pease, K. (1993) *Once Bitten, Twice Bitten: Repeat Victimisation and its Implications for Crime Prevention.* Crime Prevention Unit Series, Paper 46. Police Research Group. London: Home Office.

Felson, M. and Clarke, R. V. (1998) *Opportunity Makes the Thief: Practical Theory for Crime Prevention.* Police Research Series, Paper 98. London: Home Office.

Garland, D. (2001) *The Culture of Control: Crime and Social Order in Contemporary Society.* Chicago: University of Chicago Press.

Gill, M. (2006) Introduction. In M. Gill (ed.), The Handbook of Security. Basingstoke, UK: Palgrave Macmillan.

Goldstein, H. (1979) Improving policing: a problem-oriented approach. *Crime and Delinquency,* 25: 236–258.

Green Mazerolle, L. and Roehl, J. (1998) *Civil Remedies and Crime Prevention.* Crime Prevention Studies, Vol. 9. Monsey, NY: Criminal Justice Press.

Guerette, R. T. and Bowers, K. J. (2009) Assessing the extent of crime displacement and difffusion of benefits: a review of situational crime prevention evaluations. *Criminology,* 47(4): 1311–1368.

Jacobs, J. (1961) *The Death and Life of Great American Cities.* New York: Random House.

Jeffery, C. R. (1971) *Crime Prevention through Environmental Design.* Beverly Hills: Sage.

Kahneman, D. (2003) A perspective on judgment and choice. mapping bounded rationality. *American Psychologist,* 58 (9): 697–720.

Kennedy, D. M. (1997) Pulling levers: chronic offenders, high crime settings and a theory of prevention. *Valparaiso University Law Review,* 31: 449–484.

Laycock, G. (2001) *Scientists or Politicians – Who Has the Answer to Crime.* Inaugural Lecture at the Jill Dando Institute of Crime Science. (http://www.jdi.ucl.ac.uk/publications/presentations/inaugural_lecture_2001.php, accessed August 3, 2008).

Laycock, G. (2004) The UK car theft index: an example of government leverage. In: M. G. Maxfield and R. V. Clarke (eds) *Understanding and Preventing Car Theft.* Crime Prevention Studies, Vol. 17. Monsey, NY: Criminal Justice Press (and Willan Publishing).

Mayhew, P. M., Clarke, R. V. G., Sturman, A. and Hough, J. M. (1976) *Crime as Opportunity.* Home Office Research Study, No 34. London: H.M.S.O.

Newman, G. R. (2004) Car safety and car security: an historical comparison. In: M. G. Maxfield and R. V. Clarke (eds), *Understanding and Preventing Car Theft.* Crime Prevention Studies, Vol. 17. Monsey, NY: Criminal Justice Press (and Willan Publishing).

Newman, O. (1972) *Defensible Space: Crime Prevention through Urban Design.* New York: MacMillan.

Pease, K. (2005) Science in the service of crime reduction. In: N. Tilley (ed.), *Handbook of Crime Prevention and Community Safety.* Cullompton, UK: Willan Publishing.

Pease, K. (2008) How to behave like a scientist. *Policing* 2(2): 154–159.

Poyner, B. and Webb, B. (1991) *Crime Free Housing.* Oxford UK: Butterworth Architect.

Ross, N. (2003) Foreword. In: Clarke, R. V. and Eck, J. *Become a Problem-Solving Crime Analyst – In 55 Steps.* London: Jill Dando Institute of Crime Science, UCL.

Rossmo, D. K. (2000) *Geographic Profiling.* Boca Raton, FL: CRC Press.

Sherman, L., Gartin, P. and Buerger, M. (1989) Hot spots of predatory crime: routine activities and the criminology of place. *Criminology,* 27: 27–55.

Simon, H. A. (1955) A behavioral model of rational choice. *Quarterly Journal of Economics,* 69: 99–118.

Simon, H. A. (1978) Rationality as process and product of thought. *American Economic Review,* 8(21): 1–11.

Skubak Tillyer, M. and Kennedy, D. (2008) Locating focused deterrence approaches within a situational crime prevention framework. *Crime Prevention and Community Safety* 10: 75–84.

Smith, M. J. and Tilley, N. (eds) (2005) *Crime Science. New Approaches to Preventing and Detecting Crime.* Cullompton, UK: Willan Publishing.

Sutherland, E. (1947) *Principles of Criminology* (3rd edition). New York: J. B. Lippincott company.

Webb, B. (2005) Preventing vehicle crime. In: Nick Tilley (ed.) *Handbook of Crime Prevention and Community Safety.* Cullompton, UK: Willan Publishing.

Weisburd, D. and Piquero, A. R. (2008) How well do criminologists explain crime? Statistical modeling in published studies. In: M. Tonry (ed.), *Crime and Justice: A Review of Research, Vol. 37.* Chicago: University of Chicago Press, Pp. 453–502.

White, R. (2008) *Crimes against Nature: Environmental Criminology and Ecological Justice.* Cullompton, UK: Willan Publishing.

Wilson, J. Q. and Kelling, G. L. (1982) Broken windows: the police and neighborhood safety. *The Atlantic Monthly,* March: 29–38.

Wortley, R. (2001) A classification of techniques for controlling situational precipitators of crime. *Security Journal,* 14: 63–82.

Wortley, R. and Mazerolle, L. (2008) Environmental criminology and crime analysis: situating the theory, analytic approach and application. In: R. Wortley, and L. Mazerolle (eds), *Environmental Criminology and Crime Analysis.* Cullompton, UK: Willan Publishing.

15

Psychosocial Criminology

Tony Jefferson

Criminology has always been psychosocial, in the sense that it has had an interest in both the psychic and the social dimensions of crime from its origins over two centuries ago. More directly, there has been a social psychology of offending behaviour at least since the 1920s. But, mostly the psyche and the social have been kept apart, or utilised without a definite notion of what might be entailed in attempting to bring them together, to think of them as always simultaneously operative on human behaviour, which means to think psychosocially about the object of enquiry. In the last decade or so, the term psychosocial has been explicitly defined as a particular way of theorizing the relationship between psychic and social factors, and its relevance for understanding a variety of criminological topics has been explored (Jefferson, 2002; Gadd and Jefferson, 2007a; Jones, 2008). As we shall see, this is not the same thing as a social psychology (or a psychological sociology, for that matter). This entry aims to tell the story of criminology from this early interest in the psychological and the social as distinctive approaches to the present deliberate naming of the psychosocial as a necessary approach; spell out why this matters; offer an outline of the principles involved in thinking psychosocially and a theoretical sketch of the subject based on such principles; explore the methodological implications of this psychosocial turn; and conclude with some of the unresolved theoretical issues.

CRIMINOLOGY AND ITS MULTI-DISCIPLINARY ORIGINS

There are a number of ways of telling criminology's story. In offering his account of 'the development of criminology in Britain', Garland (2002: 7) differentiates between a 'governmentality project' – which, from the eighteenth century onwards, was interested in crime patterns and how the various elements, such as the police and prisons, of what we would now call the criminal justice system, were working – and the 'Lombrosian' one – which, from the nineteenth century onwards, was interested in the nature of offenders and the etiology of offending. Add into the mix the eclectic, practical work of British doctors and psychiatrists in prisons in the late nineteenth and early twentieth centuries, diagnosing, classifying and treating prisoners, and the 'new science of criminology' (ibid.: 26) was born. Twenty years earlier, Heathcote (1981) chose to emphasize how the early social approaches to studying crime and deviance, the early nineteenth century work of the 'moral statisticians' in France and the later ecological studies of crime and poverty of philanthropic campaigners like Booth, Mayhew and Rowntree in Britain were 'overshadowed' by individualistic explanations after 1876, the year Lombroso published his 'L'Uomo Delinquente'. Thereafter, 'Durkeim … the first professional sociologist, attempted to reassert the merits of social explanation' (ibid: 346). Most recently, Jones (2008) tells the story in terms of Beccaria's eighteenth century classicist account of crime and punishment, with its conception of the freely-willed individual rationally calculating the cost–benefit ratios of crime commission versus likely punishment if caught, versus the new nineteenth century 'science' of positivism, with its conception of individuals variously at the mercy of forces beyond their control. This new 'scientific' approach united those for whom behaviour was 'determined' by forces from within (individual character in the case of psychological positivism) with those for whom behaviour was 'determined' by forces from without (social circumstances in the case of sociological positivism). But whatever the different emphases in how criminology's story is told – governmentality project versus Lombrosian project, social versus individualistic, classicism versus positivism – what unites these (and all the attempts that I know of) is an acknowledgement of the diversity of criminology's original objects of inquiry and its resulting multi-disciplinarity.

Initially, the key disciplines were biology, given the genetically-based theories of Lombroso, and a fledgling sociology. But as the Lombrosian idea of the born criminal fell into disfavour, especially with the treatment-minded forensic psychiatrists forging the new discipline in Britain, psychology became the other key discipline. Thereafter, criminology's story can partly be told in terms of which discipline, psychology or sociology, is in the ascendancy. In Britain, up until the Second World War, the focus on individual offenders and their treatment meant psychology was in the ascendancy. This broadly continued after the war and into the 1950s, although predictive studies became more dominant than the clinically-based ones of the inter-war years. The 1960s, in criminology as in so many areas of life, radically changed everything: the National Deviancy Conference emerged to challenge the criminological mainstream, which it saw as positivistic, policy-driven, correctionalist and narrowly focussed on predicting and treating offenders. Its weapons were sociological ideas imported from the US (where sociology had played a more prominent role in the emergence and development of criminology) and neo-Marxist ideas from continental Europe. Thereafter, psychological approaches have remained the subordinate partner in the criminological enterprise. Only in the last decade or so has there been anything resembling a resurgence of interest in the psychological dimension of crime, but still very much a minority one in terms of theoretical significance within criminology.

Although this multi-disciplinary nature of the field is acknowledged, it is, for the most part, accompanied by ignorance, perhaps especially within the dominant discipline.

Thus, sociologists today tend to be ignorant of, and uninterested in, the work of psychologists in the field, just as there was little interest in Durkheim and the Chicago School among the psychiatrists and psychologists dominating early British criminology. The disciplinary allegiances resulting from what gets taught (and, no doubt, disciplinary imperialism) have certainly played a part in sustaining this ignorance. It is also undeniable that much traditional, mainstream work within both disciplines is neither interesting nor helpful enough to tempt scholars and researchers beyond their own disciplinary boundaries. There is also the increasing problem of too much getting written in any one of the many sub-specialisms of the field for even the most committed of scholars to keep up with their own area of interest, never mind wander across disciplinary boundaries. However, it is hard from a theoretical point of view to sustain this rigid separation since to do so presupposes that sociology or psychology alone are adequate to answer criminological questions. For the most part, this is not a tenable position. To the extent that criminological theorizing is attempting to say anything about crime, control or punishment, some presumption about human subjectivity – as individuals or within groups – is inevitable. If the structure-agency debate teaches us nothing else, it should remind us that systems do not reproduce themselves. From that starting point, we have to have some conception of agency, the acting individual, as well as of structure, since agents are always operating within a specific social context. Since structures are only comprehensible through available discourses (systems of meaning), we need some conception of the discursive too.

However, there is a an important sub-theme within criminology that did recognize the importance of working across the disciplinary divide, namely, the social psychology of offending. On the face of it, this work appears to have recognized the importance of a psychosocial approach. Being concerned with the question, 'what differentiates offenders from non-offenders', the human subject was an unavoidable pre-supposition. Unfortunately, the methodological approach underpinning this work, with its focus on *typical* cases, fatally undermined the importance of *individual* biographies, and hence the psychic dimension. The result was increased knowledge about the sorts of psychosocial factors associated with offending, but continuing ignorance about the causes of offending.

THE SOCIAL PSYCHOLOGY OF OFFENDING

This body of work unites Cyril Burt's 1925 study of *The Young Delinquent*, Rutter and Giller's (1983) synthesizing volume on *Juvenile Delinquency* and David Farrington's (2002) long-running, longitudinal study of offending, to name three significant examples from different time periods. Here, an avowedly social psychological approach meant that neither discipline could be ignored. However, the crucial question of their integration, how both the psychic and the social dimensions were to be conceptualized as simultaneously operative on behaviour, was either never addressed theoretically, or in an unsatisfactory way, as we shall see.

Burt's study has been seen by some 'as the first major work of modern British criminology' (Garland, 2002: 37). Basically, it involved a variety of tests and reports on 400 school children (some delinquent, some not) utilizing measures of the sorts of psychological and social factors (e.g., intelligence, temperament, family circumstances) presumed to be related to delinquency. Combining statistical methods and psychoanalytic and social inquiries, it identified 'some 170 causative factors that were in some way associated with delinquency and ... [showed], by way of narrative case histories, how each factor might typically operate' (ibid.: 37). The findings that 'defective discipline, defective family relationships, and particular types of temperament, were highly correlated with delinquency' (ibid.: 38), however novel they might have been then, were to become a familiar mantra of such work. (Interestingly, poverty and low intelligence were found to be much less significant.) The problem endemic to all work of this kind is the attempt to produce causal explanations from factors gleaned from all the cases (i.e., using cross-sectional analysis) and then to use these within cases to show how they 'might typically operate'. What such an approach implicitly presumes about individual subjects is that they can be thought of as the amalgams of psychological and social factors that 'typically operate'. This precludes the possibility that the same factors operate differently for different individuals (a presupposition based on the axiomatic psychological notion of the uniqueness of individual lives) and thus essentially reduces the subject to a social type (however psychological the factors identified).

Nearly 60 years and countless research studies later, Rutter and Giller (1983: 219) sought to assess what was then known on the topic of juvenile delinquency. Their conclusions on the 'psycho-social variables ... associated with delinquency' were depressingly familiar: 'The family characteristics most strongly associated with delinquency are: parental criminality, ineffective supervision and discipline, familial discord and disharmony, weak parent–child relationships, large family size, and psychosocial disadvantage'. They go on to say that 'Less is known abut the precise mechanisms by which these family variables have their effects'. Once again, much is known about typical factors associated with those at 'high-risk' of offending – typical offenders – little about the 'precise mechanisms': how such factors actually operate in particular families, and thus, once again, about how the same factors might operate differently depending on the particular case. It is not that Rutter and Giller (1983: 221) are unaware of the issue because they go on to acknowledge that the 'two main findings' of prediction studies say much the same thing, namely, that 'many young people from a 'high-risk' background do *not* become delinquent; and ... a number of those who lack high-risk features *do* become delinquent' (emphases in original). Had they presupposed human subjects with unique biographies, these 'findings' would have been self-evident.

Farrington's longitudinal Cambridge Study of 411 mostly white, working class boys born in the 1950s has clear echoes of the Burt study, both in terms of sample size and findings. However, it has greater theoretical pretensions. Somewhat heroically, his 'Farrington theory' attempts to integrate the five key risk factors the Cambridge Study had identified, namely, 'impulsivity, low intelligence, poor parenting, a criminal family and socio-economic deprivation' (Farrington, 2002: 680) within a psychosocial theory drawing on diverse elements from existing developmental and situational theories to produce a dynamic, processual model of becoming delinquent. The problem, as we have argued at greater length elsewhere (Gadd and Jefferson, 2007a: 22–23), is that the different stages in the process ('energising', 'directing', 'inhibiting' and 'decision-making') all presume a different

subject: sometimes socially constrained, sometimes lacking self-control and sometimes rationally calculating. This is possible (and presumably why it passes
unnoticed by Farrington) because the study, like Burt's, attempts to build a subject
from cross-sectional factor analysis, ultimately to produce that will of the wisp, the
typical offender, rather than start with cases in all their specificities and begin to
spell out how developmental processes actually work, *in situ*. Daunting and tiring as
this might sound, it is the only way if we are ever to move beyond such eclectic,
theoretical generalizations. Rutter and Giller's (1983: 219) call for more observational research into the 'precise mechanisms' again went unanswered.

ONE-SIDED PSYCHOSOCIAL APPROACHES

One further way in which criminologists have thought psychosocially, but inade-
quately, has been to recognize the importance of both psychic and social factors but
then produce a theory that effectively eliminates one set of factors. The resulting
subject is reductive: either a psychological subject or a social subject, but no longer
a psychosocial one. Eysenck's (1964) personality-based theory is an example of the
former kind of reduction, Katz's (1988) *Seductions of Crime* an example of the latter.
Strictly speaking, Eysenck's theory is a biopsychosocial theory since it includes a
genetic component. His basic idea is that behaviour is a function of social conditioning. Conditioning produces a conscience, our internalized sense of right and wrong.
Different personality types (conceptualized in terms of extraversion, neuroticism and
psychoticism) condition more or less well and are thus more or less likely to offend.
Underpinning all this for Eysenck is the genetic component since this is what
explains personality: 'genetic differences in the way that the cortical and autonomic
nervous systems function underpin individual differences in personality' (Gadd and
Jefferson, 2007a: 20). Thus, the 'impulsive, risky and thrill-seeking' (and potentially
unlawful) activities characteristic of extraverts are all attempts 'to increase cortical
stimulation' since extraverts 'suffer from cortical under-arousal' (ibid.). It is this that
'makes them difficult to "condition"'(ibid.). The subject has thereby been reduced to
his or her neural biology since this, ultimately, explains 'both personality and conditionability' (ibid.: 21)

Katz's influential thesis about the 'seductions' of crime could not be more
different, lodging its explanation as it does in the phenomenology of the moment
when the crime is actually committed. Katz's insistence on the 'foreground' of crime
is pitted against all explanations based on 'background' factors. However, he is not
only interested in explaining individual crimes ('the causal process of commiting a
crime', Katz, 1988: 312); his 'systematic empirical theory' is also an attempt to
explain what we know about crime more generally: one 'that accounts at the aggregate level for recurrently documented correlations with biographical and ecological
background factors' (ibid.). If the focus on the actual act is unavoidably social, the
importance given to what Katz calls the 'moral emotions' (ibid.), such as shame and
humiliation, necessarily implicates psychology. The resulting scenarios of how
shame and humiliation are implicated in different crimes are brilliantly and compel-
lingly executed. Moreover, he is aware that different people respond differently to

feelings of humiliation; it is not always transformed, via rage, for example, into criminality (ibid.: 22). In other words, he knows that different people have different psychological resources for dealing with shame and humiliation. However, these are not allowed to enter the explanation. By insisting on the primacy of the situational dynamics, the explanation effectively reduces to them. Talking about what he calls 'righteous slaughter' he says: 'Whatever the deeper psychological sources of his aggression, he does not kill until and unless he can fashion violence to convey the situational meaning of defending his rights' (ibid.: 31). Thus, the question of who is likely to transform 'humiliation into rage' and who simply to 'endure humiliation' (ibid.: 22), surely the crucial question for criminologists since it differentiates merely confrontational situations from actually violent ones, is not addressed, and thus the theory's psychosocial promise remains unfulfilled. In the moment of the act the subject becomes purely social, for all his (since usually male in Katz's examples) implied psychological complexity.

THE EXISTING SUBJECT WITHIN CRIMINOLOGICAL THEORY

This overview of the unfortunate stand-off between psychology and sociology culminating in sociology's contemporary ascendancy that characterizes criminology's history, the limited body of work on the social psychology of delinquency, and the examples of work that start out psychosocial but end up uni-dimensional, either (bio) psychological or social, has revealed a failure to give proper psychosocial attention to the human subject at the heart of many questions of interest to criminologists, with dire results for understanding criminal behaviour. The contemporary ascendancy of sociology is responsible for the considerable loss of interest in the topic as control and criminalization – the social reaction to crime – emerged as an exciting, new, radical topic out of the politicizing maelstrom of the 1960s. Foucault's (1979) massively influential *Discipline and Punish*, for example, with its novel ideas about the disciplinary society produced much on the normalization of 'docile bodies', but little on the resistance to such processes by active subjects: the rather less docile bodies of offenders. Work specifically on the social psychology of offending, as we saw, allowed the methodological tail – large samples, cross-sectional analysis, statistical correlations – to wag the theoretical dog, with the result that the offender became a bundle of 'risk factors': a generalized type. And the work on offending that started out psychosocial, like that of Eysenck and Katz, ends up, as we saw, with a reductive explanation of offending, as each gives explanatory primacy to their core discipline.

This failure matters because many criminological topics that are not directly or obviously about individuals nevertheless depend on a presumption about subjectivity. Theories of criminal behaviour, whether psychological or sociological, personality-based or Marxist, depend on an assumption about the offending subject; victimological studies presume a (more or less) fearing subject; restorative justice studies an ashamed or shameable subject; masculinity and crime studies a gendered subject; gang studies presume gang members; and so on. In the absence of an adequately theorized subject, criminology has become saddled with a host of incompatible subjects. When I first argued the case 'for a psychosocial criminology' (Jefferson, 2002), I summarized these competing versions as follows:

- 'rational-unitary': 'the self-interested, cognitively-driven, rational, unitary subject of classical criminology, traditional psychology and contemporary economics' (ibid.: 151). This is the presumptive subject of theories as otherwise diverse as Charles Murray's underclass thesis, left realism and some versions of feminism;
- 'traditional Freudian': the individualistic notion of 'the self as a unique product of instincts, drives, learning and developmental processes, anxieties and the resulting defences' (ibid.: 150). This is now somewhat out-dated in academic criminology, thus not much in evidence, a point to which I return below;
- 'social-constructionist': the idea of 'the self as essentially a product of social forces' which presumptively underpins all social theories, be they structural, discursive or interactionist.

Expressed thus, in that order, we can discern something of criminology's history from its origins in classicism, through the ascendancy of a psychology in which Freud was still influential, to the present ascendancy of sociology. Although David Gadd and I (Gadd and Jefferson, 2007a: 15–40) later had a more detailed look at the nature of the subject presumed in key psychological, sociological and 'in between' (control theory and life-course) approaches, these broad conclusions remained intact. So, rather than rehearse the critiques and, through these, tease out the elements that would prove serviceable in 'constructing the theoretical contours of a properly psychosocial subject' (ibid.: 41), a route that would take far too much space, I intend, in the following section, to define the principles of thinking psychosocially about subjectivity, especially as these refer to criminology, justify each in turn, and finish with a brief outline theory of the psychosocial subject.

THINKING PSYCHOSOCIALLY ABOUT SUBJECTIVITY: CORE PRINCIPLES

First Principle: criticisms of mainstream academic criminology should not lead to a dismissal of the psychological as such: the psychological dimension of subjectivity matters.

Given criminology's heavy sociological emphasis, it is necessary to distinguish between what currently passes for psychological knowledge and the importance of the psychological as such. George Herbert Mead ([1934] 1964), a psychologist who is generally quoted approvingly in criminological circles as the father figure of symbolic interactionism and labelling theory, is usually remembered for his idea that we see ourselves as others do, the self as socially formed through our interactions with others (what he called the 'me'). However, he also had a notion of what he called the 'I' (the unique response of individuals to how others see them). This is often forgotten, or ignored (perhaps because he never successfully resolved how to integrate these two notions, remaining, as he did, trapped within his social starting point; see Gadd and Jefferson, 2007a: 33–37).

Second Principle: 'Human subjects' are 'simultaneously, the products of their own unique psychic worlds and *a shared social world' (Gadd and Jefferson, 2007a: 4; emphasis in original).*

The important word here is 'simultaneously'. This means that we are always already psychosocial with neither dimension having priority: the psyche orients our conception of the social at the same time as the social is constantly influencing the nature of our psyches.

Third Principle: The psyche must not be reduced to the social, nor the social to the psyche: 'the complexities of both the inner and the outer worlds' must be 'taken seriously' (ibid.).

This third principle begins to spell out the implications of the second. Proceeding non-reductively and recognizing the complexities of both inner and outer worlds is necessary because the external world is never simply internalized, as social constructionism implies. The self is never a simple copy of the social. Rather, what we take in of the social world depends on our pre-existing inner world, which is as personal to us as our biography is unique. By the same token, our unique inner worlds constantly affect how we make sense of the social; how the same situation can be perceived as safe or dangerous (to think of examples from fear of crime research); how the same situation can produce endurable humiliation or unendurable rage, to return to earlier examples from Katz.

Fourth Principle: 'Taking the social world seriously means thinking about questions to do with structure, power and discourse … taking the inner world seriously involves an engagement with contemporary psychoanalytic theorizing because only there … are unconscious as well as conscious processes, and the resulting conflicts and contradictions among reason, anxiety and desire, subjected to any sustained, critical attention' (Gadd and Jefferson, 2007a: 4).

For an audience of contemporary criminologists, the first part of this principle will be less problematic than the second. However, the relations among the terms structure, power and discourse are not self-evident although often deployed as if they were. Broadly speaking, social structure refers to the constraints operative in any given social environment, power refers to our ability to do something. Thus, the powerful, however defined, are less constrained by the social order than the less powerful since they can 'do' more. In the social sciences, the main power differences taken into account have been those of class, gender, race and age. This notion of a world principally structured by these differences of power has produced the corollary that we are but the sum of our structured positionings (although how these multiple structures operate in concert to produce a subject, the issue of intersectionality, has produced more theoretical heat than light)[1]. However, power is not only structurally based, it is also contingent upon the situation. Thus, in any given social situation, the dominant social order can be reversed: a woman getting the better of a man in verbal argument, for example, thus contravening the established gender order – sometimes with violent, even fatal results, as the man attempts to reassert his gendered power. Many of Katz's examples are of the structurally powerless upsetting the existing social order in this situationally-specific way: a poor black man robbing an older white one, for example.

Given the difficulties of thinking about multiple structures and the situationally-specific nature of power, attention has shifted to discourse – the systems of meaning that construct the social world. Because of the centrality of language to systems of meaning, this is sometimes referred to as the 'linguistic turn' in the social sciences. Massively influenced by the seminal work of Foucault, the starting assumption is that 'nothing has any meaning outside of discourse' (Foucault, 1972). Thus, structures have no meaning in themselves, but only acquire meaning within available discourses. Moreover, since knowledge is always implicated in regulating conduct – defining what constitutes madness, crime or acceptable sexuality, for example – there is always a power struggle over meaning. This renders the available discourses (what is knowable and what constitutes 'truth') historically specific, the outcome at any given time of prevailing power/knowledge relations.

This move from structural to discursive analysis has reinvigorated much writing in the social sciences, including much within criminology. However, the notion that 'nothing has any meaning outside of discourse' has sometimes slipped into the idea that nothing exists outside discourse. This error can lead to an exclusive focus on discursive analysis, and to the idea of the subject being purely the product of available discourses – the discursive subject. Despite the move from structures to discourses, the subject is still one-dimensional, still purely social. However, since meaning is not a given but the product of ongoing struggles (power/knowledge relations), it follows that not everyone finds the same meaning in the discourses that have achieved dominance at any historical moment. As Stuart Hall (2001: 80) puts it, 'we – must locate ourselves in the position from which the discourse makes most sense'. From this idea of discourses offering up subject positions that make more or less sense to us, we need to ask the question: to whom do particular discursive positions make sense? Who is attracted to the discursive position of religious fundamentalism, martyrdom and suicide bombing, who to that of racial hatred, and who to the idea that men should never show signs of weakness and vulnerability but respond to any challenge, however potentially destructive – to note just three examples with obvious criminological relevance. Having identified to whom such discursive positions appeal, the next question has to be: why? At this point, we are forced to 'take seriously' the inner world, and that means engaging with psychoanalysis. Let me try to justify that statement.

Of all the principles, the idea of needing to engage with contemporary psychoanalytic theorizing is perhaps the most contentious. Given this, I will need to spend a little time making the case. One core problem is historical. That is to say, the almost blanket dismissal of psychoanalysis by criminologists is based on a very outdated, often risible, notion of what are psychoanalytic ideas. It is as if there have been no new ideas in the discipline since before the Second World War, the last time psychoanalytic ideas had any currency in criminology. One reason for this is the present dominance of sociology within criminology; the other is the hostility to psychoanalysis within psychology, with its pretensions to being a proper science and the current dominance of cognitive and behavioural approaches. The result of all this is that most text book writers don't have a clue as to what is going on within psychoanalysis today. By way of example, let me take a contemporary American text-book called *Criminal Behavior* (Bartol and Bartol, 2005). Since it espouses, in the words of its sub-title, 'A Psychosocial Approach', it looked promising. Being in its seventh edition suggests it has been read by generations of American criminology students. Here (in 2005, remember) is its summary of the 'Freudian, psychoanalytic and psychodynamic positions' on criminal behaviour: 'criminal behavior is believed to spring from within, primarily dictated by the biological urges of the unconscious' (ibid.: 10). I have seen (too) many similar depictions. However, the authors go on to say that this is the traditional view and that 'Contemporary psychiatric criminology is far more diverse, increasingly research-based, and considerably less-steeped in the traditional belief that criminals are acting out their uncontrolled animalistic, unconscious or biological urges' (ibid.). Moreover, we are assured that 'Wherever possible' (ibid.) this more contemporary view will be relied upon in the text. Perhaps amends are about to be made. But, when I looked in the references for psychoanalytic theorists of contemporary relevance for thinking about offenders and offending, broadly those associated with an object relations approach, like Klein, Winnicott, Bion, Benjamin and Chodorow, for example, or attachment theory, like Bowlby, I find none mentioned (although space can be found for 10 entries for the very traditional bio-psychologist Eysenck). And neither 'object relations' nor 'attachment theory' appears as an entry in either the lengthy 15 page glossary or the 18 page index. Given that both of these notions represent important shifts away from traditional, drive-based psychoanalytic theorizing towards accounts in which the child's early social environment has significant developmental implications, especially its relationship with its first 'object', the mother, it is hard to see how they could not be included in 'contemporary psychiatric criminology'.

A more direct justification of the importance of psychoanalytic ideas is that its view of human subjectivity has always aspired to match the complexity that we know to be the reality of our lives. It offers sophisticated, case-based ideas about the development of emotional life, for example, and thus of the origins of painful feelings of humiliation, guilt and shame, that have rightly now become an important part of the criminological agenda. Crucially, it presumes a conflicted, non-unitary self, where the conscious mind is often contradicted by desires and anxieties emanating from a dynamic unconscious. These desires and anxieties, when they are too difficult or painful to acknowledge, will be defended against in various ways, classically by repressing them, sometimes by splitting them off and projecting them onto others, or, perhaps most commonly, by simple denial. Or they might make an appearance symptomatically. Think about childhood sexual abuse. Adult survivors often have limited or incomplete memory of this. This is because such memories are too painful, disempowering and invoke too much anxiety for the conscious mind to bear, so they are repressed. But, they never 'go away' (indeed, they may well manifest in a host of disabling symptoms). Under certain circumstances, it is of course possible for such memories to be brought to conscious awareness and successfully, if still painfully, held in mind – which would be the general therapeutic goal in such cases.

Here, hopefully, it is possible to glimpse the importance of the differential appeal of positions in discourse. How the subject positions available in contemporary discourses of sexuality will make more or less sense depending on how conscious and unconscious processes, including the defensive strategies put in place, have managed to deal with the abuse. There is nothing automatic about these processes and thus predicting outcomes is an impossible science. But more can be said about the general processes implicated in the construction of inner worlds; which brings us to our fifth and final principle.

Fifth Principle: Fantasy is what links 'the psychoanalytic subject to the social domain of structured power and discourse' (Gadd and Jefferson, 2007a: 4)

For certain purposes it might be useful to distinguish between conscious fantasies and unconscious ones (where some would argue the need for a change of spelling, to 'phantasies'); but not here. In using the term 'fantasy' here, it is partly to mark a strong contrast to 'reality', partly to capture the sense of a *dynamic* inner world: constantly imaginatively processing conflictual thoughts and feelings, desires and anxieties, in the face of constant demands from the external world; an inner world with conscious and unconscious aspects. Although this meaning will include fantasies in the conventional sense of the word, it is much broader; more like our imagination, plus what cannot be thought but still marks us. I am also deliberately echoing Frosh's (2003: 1554) usage when he says 'fantasy is not "just" something that occupies an internal space as a kind of mediation of reality, but … it also has material effects'. He, too, seems to be using the term as a catch-all for the internal world, but in a way that hangs on to its dynamism as a mediator of reality.

In summarising the importance of fantasy to how we see the social world, Frosh also uses the term 'invested' ('the social is psychically invested'). This is particularly useful for thinking about the focus of fantasies, since it implies potential rewards or profits. More directly, as Wendy Hollway (2001: 278) has shown in her influential work on subjectivity, it enables us to grasp how individuals come to adopt the particular positions in discourse that they do, the position 'from which the discourse makes most sense': 'By claiming that people have investments … in taking up certain positions in discourses … I mean that there will be some satisfaction or pay-off or reward … for that person'. She goes on to say that 'satisfaction … is not necessarily conscious or rational. But there is a reason' (ibid.). Perhaps the key reason, as she goes on to show, using numerous examples from her research into sexuality and relationships, is the attempt to avoid feeling powerless and vulnerable. Since such feelings make us feel anxious, a state which is uncomfortable, sometimes painfully so, they will activate unconscious defences in the effort to suppress, displace or deny them. Such feelings are also extremely important for understanding contemporary masculinity, being the antithesis of perhaps the still dominant discourse of masculinity in which 'real' men (often more in fantasy than reality) are powerful and strong, up for any challenge. And if there is one thing we know for sure it is that crime is largely men's work; which makes it important for contemporary criminology to understand just how feelings of vulnerability, unconscious defences against anxiety and masculinity are connected.

I can only offer a sketch of these connections. But, hopefully, it will be sufficient to demonstrate their theoretical importance for criminology. The human infant at first has no sense of self but is boundary-less in relation to its mother. Acquiring a sense of self as separate from that of its mother is thus a key, unavoidable developmental task. Such a process is inevitably conflictual and anxiety provoking since the price of independence is the (painful) recognition that a mother has (sometimes differing) needs too, and is powerful enough to impose these, regardless of the baby's 'protests'. How well the mother manages to recognize and think about such conflicts and protests, or 'contain' them as Bion (1984) puts it, will affect how the baby learns to manage anxiety, frustration and threat. But when anxiety becomes unbearable it is unconsciously defended against.

Klein (1988a, b) argues that the earliest defences against anxiety involve splitting off the bad, painful feelings and projecting them elsewhere where they can be safely hated, thus protecting the good, loving feelings from contamination. She called this the paranoid-schizoid position. At this moment, the 'object' – first the breast, then, when the baby can take in whole objects, the mother – that was 'good' has become 'bad'. Once the baby can perceive that the same mother can be sometimes good and sometimes bad, a notion that entails living with ambivalence, Klein talks of it entering the depressive position.

Although the depressive position is a developmental achievement, it is neither static nor fixed: paranoid-schizoid defences can be remobilized throughout the life-course, whenever the self feels sufficiently threatened. This has significant implications for offending behaviour, for one of the characteristics of paranoid-schizoid thinking is an inability to identify with the other, the hated object, for fear of contaminating the good. The other becomes just that: 'other', dissimilar, not like you and me, not like 'us' but one of 'them', an appropriate receptacle for all our fears, fantasies and hatreds. One can think of all kinds of crimes, from simple assaults to hate crimes, that become more likely when paranoid-schizoid defences are 'in command'. The issue of who is more or less likely to operate largely from the paranoid-schizoid position (and when), who from the depressive (and when) ultimately depends on historical biographical elements – how anxiety has been experienced and handled in the past – as well as contemporary contingent ones – how it is experienced and handled in the present. Such a question is too particularistic to be addressed here. But what should follow from the above is the importance of anxiety; if this becomes too painful too often when one is too young, or is not recognized, contained or otherwise de-toxified, it is likely to produce (painfully) negative outcomes, although not necessarily criminal.

A second, inevitable developmental task is coming to terms with our sexuality and finding our place in the gender order, the position from which who we are as sexed and gendered individuals 'makes most sense'. A key term for understanding how this takes place is 'identification'. To identify with someone is to imagine oneself, consciously or unconsciously, in their place. From this perspective, identity is achieved through such imaginings, fuelled by a desire to be like someone. Most commonly, the first person with whom children have an opportunity to identify is their mother. Before they become aware of sexual and gender difference and how this is implicated in social differences in the treatment of girls and boys, this need not present problems. In a world where sexual and gender difference matters, things become more complicated. For Freud ([1924] 1977), the awareness of sexual difference broadly coincides with a new set of anxieties consequent upon the entry of the father into the otherwise exclusive world of the mother–child dyad. For boy children, the father is both a large and powerful competitor for his mother's love and attention, but, being of a different sex than his mother, and usually doing rather different things, can offer new and rather different possibilities for identification. What Freud argues, essentially, is that the threat posed by the father provokes sufficient anxiety for the boy child unconsciously to defend against it by repressing his desire to replace the father in his mother's affections and to settle instead for a desire to be like him: to identify with him, and with the (gendered, as we would now say) cultural order he represents. In this account, what Freud talked of as the boy's Oedipal crisis, the boy's achievement of a gendered identity is fuelled by anxiety, enabled by giving up his desire for his mother, which gets repressed, and resolved through identification with his father. It is an imaginative solution to a vexing issue. But, among other problems, it is far too general. In order to be able to explain differential outcomes – those boys who, through an excess of fear or guilt, for example, fail to identify with their father, as well as those who do, i.e., negative as well as positive Oedipal outcomes (the possibility of which Freud ([1924] 1977: 322) was well aware) – the account needs to become more social.

Jessica Benjamin (1998), an analyst in the object relational tradition, and social theorist, took up this idea that Freud's positive outcome is not the only possible one. She argues, essentially, that Freud's distinction between pre-Oedipal object love (the desire for the mother) and post-Oedipal identificatory love (desire to be like the father) overlooks the fact that all pre-Oedipal children, boys and girls, identify with both mothers and fathers. Thus, she reconceptualizes Freud's positive Oedipal outcome as an example of the boy-child repudiating his identifications with his mother and projecting all those elements he associates with being dependent on her care on to girls. In Klein's terms, this is a paranoid-schizoid defensive manoeuvre. However, Benjamin suggests an alternative, less defensive, outcome is possible if boys manage to hang on to their identifications with their mother (even as they recognize and 'renounce' the fact that they cannot be the same sex as her). In other words, the issue for her is: what identifications are given up in becoming aware of gendered oppositions during the Oedipal process? When these multiple, bisexual, cross gender (since mothers' and fathers' sexual differences are culturally encoded), 'overinclusive' identifications are decisively given up, the result is the boy becomes conventionally masculine, an outcome that Benjamin sees as a defensive repudiation (Benjamin, 1998: 60). But when overinclusive identifications are not given up, it becomes possible to accept gender difference in a non-defensive way and tolerate ambiguity and uncertainty. Freud's singular, hence incipiently universal, Father, terrifying boys into giving up mother love to be like father, gets replaced by Benjamin with actual parental couples in variable relationships: some highly gender differentiated, some not. Where parents are happy with gender ambiguity and can tolerate gender uncertainty, the Oedipal outcome for their children will be different from those whose gender boundaries are rigidly exclusive.

In reconceptualizing babies as object relating creatures from the outset, object relational psychoanalysis not only made a significant move away from traditional, drive-based Freudian theorizing, but it laid the basis for an irreducibly psychosocial theory of the self. The mother's breast, then the 'whole' mother, provide the initial social context for the child; the fantasies of 'good' and 'bad' breasts/mothers start to shape how that social world is (uniquely) perceived. How the mother experiences the social world – breezily optimistic or perennially depressed, happy or sad, fulfilled or unfulfilled, distracted or attentive, able to sense her baby's needs or insensitive to them, 'good enough' or not good enough, etc., etc. – will affect how the child experiences her. Similar points can be made about the father. These experiences will have psychic consequences, good or bad. Anxiety and how this is coped with is crucial here. If unbearable anxiety remains too often uncontained, the unconscious defences used may become all but constant too, with consequences for how the world comes to be seen: safe or scary; peaceful or violent; supportive or 'out to get you'. The different behavioural consequences of such different perceptions should not be hard to imagine.

What the above sketch has attempted is to provide the theoretical contours of a psychosocial subject. It has focussed on the early years because so much of emotional significance, our characteristic ways of defending against anxiety, particular identifications, sexuality, and basic capacities for trust, empathy, toleration, sociability, and so on, our psychic template (or 'idiom', to use a term coined by Bollas, 1989), has been laid down here. In doing so, it has focussed on two unavoidable, hence universal, developmental tasks: tasks that are the same for all, but experienced differently (hence not universalistic). This psychic template is never fixed, given the capacity of everyday life to throw up new conflicts, traumas and threats sufficient to 'unfix' even the stablest of personalities. But, we cannot make headway on the psychic side of the psychosocial without taking these early years and the resulting psychic template seriously.

METHODOLOGICAL IMPLICATIONS

If we assume a psychosocial subject such as I have just sketched, we will need to ensure that the particularities of biography, which are always unique, are not reduced to a general set of psychosocial factors, and we will have to learn how to read lives, and accounts of lives, symptomatically – through the defensive strategies – and not assume that initial appearances, or the story as told, is the whole story (Hollway and Jefferson, 2000). This immediately problematizes the usual approach in the field: large, matched samples analysed cross-sectionally to identify the psychosocial factors correlated with delinquency. No matter how large the sample or how good the correlations, as every methodology text-book reminds us, correlations are not causes. Yet, as we have seen, such studies get endlessly repeated, with depressingly similar results. It's as if size of sample, strength of correlation and repetition of results will somehow produce the Holy Grail of causation.

To make headway here will require closely observed and carefully analysed cases, designed to advance our theoretical understanding: not just what is associated with what but how, and under what set of circumstances, particular lives take the courses they do. This means that we can learn as much from one 'atypical' case as from any other; indeed, from this perspective, all cases are atypical to some extent since no two will be identical. Generalization from this perspective is designed to advance theory: to see how well the processes uncovered, the causal connections inferred, hold up in other cases: to use new cases to modify the theory accordingly. How often all this is the case, the question of typicality that is the goal of statistically-based generalizations, is simply not the issue for case-study based work (Mitchell, 2000). But, unless and until the difference between these two forms of generalization is understood, as well as the need to fund more theoretically-driven case studies, students and researchers are going to be driven constantly to increase their sample size (thus wasting valuable time producing and analysing far more data than they can properly handle), however inappropriate it is to their research goal.

Researching defended subjectivity requires a research strategy that can get behind appearances. From this perspective, the research interview will echo features of the psychoanalytic interview, becoming alert to what is unsaid as much as to what is said, to how things are said, their emotional tone and to changes in these, to apparent contradictions between different parts of an interview or sudden shifts in focus, as well as to how all this felt to the interviewer (what in psychoanalysis is called the counter-transference). This requires that the interviewee sets the agenda, is allowed to 'freely associate', with the interviewer a careful listener, enabling the interviewee to continue when he or she dries up with gentle requests to expand on what has already been raised, nudging him or her along their self-chosen tracks, sticking to their priorities, ordering, phrasing, resisting the temptation to get the interviewee to explain him or herself. A follow up interview can help clarify ideas that emerge after listening to tapes of the initial interview. One approach that attempts this is the Free Association Narrative Interview method (Hollway and Jefferson, 2000). More recently, Wendy Hollway (with colleagues) has added psychoanalytic observation, based on the infant observation methods developed at the Tavistock clinic, to FANI-style interviewing in their study of 'becoming a mother' in London (cf. Urwin, 2007). As with psychoanalytically-informed interviewing, what gets noticed increases substantially.

CONCLUSION: UNRESOLVED THEORETICAL ISSUES

In attempting this overview, I have concentrated on a particular way of thinking about criminology. Historically, this involved charting the divide between psychology and sociology within criminology and its effects on theorizing subjectivity. Theoretically, it involved offering up a particular conception of the psychosocial subject, and of the social and psychoanalytic ideas implicated in this conception. Politically, the need was to show that such an approach to subjectivity was required, if any headway was to be made in understanding offending behaviour other than in terms of multiple 'risk factors'. However, it is important not to end on this note since to do so suggests matters are more tidily resolved than they are. At the risk of (further) simplification, there seem to me to be at least three big issues that are not only unresolved but possibly unresolvable, if the goal is to achieve some consensus on 'thinking psychosocially'.

The first is the issue of theoretical starting points and conceptual tool kits, and, relatedly, that of the objects of enquiry. Given the widespread renewal of interest in emotions, personal life and psychoanalysis across the social sciences, there is now a whole body of work that, in drawing on ideas from sociology, cultural studies, critical psychology and psychoanalysis, could be seen as broadly psychosocial. This has been recognized institutionally in the setting up of degrees and research networks claiming the mantle psychosocial (see Frosh, 2003). But, there is no agreement on the theories and methodologies necessary to do psychosocial work. Take, by way of a recent example in criminology, the special issue of *Theoretical Criminology* devoted to psychosocial re-readings of Clifford Shaw's (1930) famous study of

The Jack-Roller. The initial idea was to bring different psychosocial approaches, with their different theoretical starting points and inflections, to bear on the same case. The hope was that this might clarify theoretical differences; might even lead to the identification of the most promising. However, because authors chose to focus on different aspects of the case, i.e., had slightly different objects of enquiry in view, this hope was never realized. Thus, the relation between the articles that start from a broadly Kleinian, object relations starting point (Brown, 2007; Gadd and Jefferson, 2007b) and those based in the psychoanalytical hermeneutic tradition of the sociologist analyst Alfred Lorenzer (Bereswill, 2007; Koesling and Neuber, 2007) is not entirely clear. This is not to say that these different theoretical starting points produced contrary interpretations. Indeed, the focus on homosexuality in both Bereswill (2007) and Gadd and Jefferson (2007b) would seem to be encouraging on this score, the more so since apparently unnoticed until this point in time. However, the larger question of whether the same object of enquiry seen through different theoretical lenses can produce substantially similar if differently accented ideas about offending behaviour is not clear. If developments elsewhere in the psychosocial world are anything to go by, where Klein and Lacan have become somewhat conflicting starting points (see the special issue of *Psychoanalysis, Culture and Society*, 2008), the answer is not promising. As with all new theoretical developments in our post-Kuhnian world, conflicts over appropriate theoretical tools and theoretical schism generally would appear to be the order of the day. Perhaps the question now might be: is a workable or 'good enough' theoretical consensus achievable?

The second issue is that of reflexivity, or, the role of the researcher in both the production and interpretation of data. While all good social scientists are now aware of this research injunction, the addition of a psychoanalytic dimension to the process complicates the issue immeasureably. Over the years, the practice of psychoanalysis has shifted its emphasis from the analyst as expert interpreter of a client's unconscious motivations – a reader of symptoms – towards one in which the relationship between the two, analyst and analysand (for us, researcher and the researched), and the feelings generated in the session, are what is crucial. These feelings are thought to arise from the unconscious transferring of emotionally significant relationships between the two. This addition of the need to interrogate feelings and their unconscious origins in order to interpret what is being said lends to the interpretative endeavour a whole new level of difficulty. Given this, it might be important to hang on to Aron's (1996: 29) words: 'Just because ... both patient and analyst play a substantial role in constructing what they agree to be the truth, we need not deny that reality has its own structure apart from that which we impose on it'. Once again, the issue of how to work towards workable generalizations *via* transferential relations might be the question.

The third issue, and for me the trickiest, is the question of levels. In my account of the psychosocial, I have distinguished between an 'inner world', for which psychoanalytic concepts are needed to comprehend it (the individual level), an 'external' one, where sociological ideas are needed (the social level), and, crucially, the concepts (fantasy, investment, identification) needed to think about how the two levels are related. However, there are many examples in contemporary social science (and in the world of journalistic common sense) where psychoanalytic ideas, appropriate to the individual level, are used directly (and inappropriately in my view) in relation to the socio-cultural level (cf: Garland, 2001; Young, 1999). For some, such usage might constitute a psychosocial approach (although I suspect neither Garland nor Young would claim the mantle). Unfortunately, this erasure of the distinction between levels (as I see this issue) bedevils even the most sustained attempt to discuss how to link the psychic and the social (Cavalletto, 2007). After a thorough examination of Freud, Weber, Adorno and Elias as psycho-social theorists, Cavalletto offers four principles of 'psycho-social' (with a hyphen in his case) work. The fourth suggests that in order for 'sociological and psychological analyses' to be aligned, 'they need to occur at similar levels of abstraction' (Cavalletto, 2007: 265). In other words, to think psycho-socially, he says we need our concepts to operate in relation 'to a population group of similarly situated individuals' (ibid.). What this means for Cavalletto is ideal types, like the Authoritarian personality, where 'particular individuals … serve as exemplars of social group characteristics'. For me, this is an example of erasing the difference between the individual and the social levels with the consequence that we are still left with the unanswered question, namely, how to explain those who do not conform to type. Adorno (1950: 753) and his colleagues were well aware of the issue since they also found 'conventional' types. So we return to my question: how do particular individuals, with their unique biographies, relate to social types like the authoritarian personality? Whether this is a question that can be answered in that way, I am not sure.

Maruna and Matravers (2007: 429) introduce the special issue of *TC* on '*The Jack-Roller* at 100' with a challenge: 'Some readers may see in this glimpse of a future for criminology that merges the rigor and transparency of social scientific methods with the insight and empathic imagination of the great works of fiction'. For me the challenge is how to translate 'the insight and empathic imagination of the great works of fiction' into something the social sciences – with their legitimate concerns with replicability and verifiability – can use.

NOTE

1 There have been attempts (e.g., Messerschmidt's work on masculinity. See Messerschmidt, 1993, 1997) to break with this structural reproduction model of subjectivity by proposing a structured action model in which actors are said variously to accomplish or 'do' gender, race, class by appropriate, or accountable, performances in particular situations. For reasons I have no space to elaborate here (but have much to do with an untheorised notion of the subject), the theory ends up looking very similar to a structural reproduction model – and with the same problems (Gadd and Jefferson, 2007a: 41–42).

REFERENCES

Adorno, T. W., Frenkel-Brunswik, E., Levinson, D. J. and Sanford, R. N. (1950) *The Authoritarian Personality.* New York: Harper and Row.
Aron, L. (1996) *The Meeting of Minds.* Hillsdale, NJ: The Analytic Press.
Bartol, C. R. and Bartol, A. M. (2005) *Criminal Behavior: A Psychosocial Approach,* seventh edition. USR, NJ: Pearson Prentice Hall.

Benjamin, J. (1998) *Shadow of the Other.* London: Routledge.

Bereswill, M. (2007) Fighting like a wildcat: a deep hermeneutic interpretation of *The Jack-Roller, Theoretical Criminology* 11(4): 469–484.

Bion, W. (1984) *Learning From Experience,* second edition. London: Maresfield.

Bollas, C. (1989) *Forces of Destiny: Psychoanalysis and Human Idiom.* London: Free Association Press.

Brown, A. P. (2007) Interpretation and the case study: the challenge of a relational approach, *Theoretical Criminology* 11(4): 485–500.

Burt, C. (1925) *The Young Delinquent.* London: University of London Press.

Cavalletto, G. (2007) *Crossing the Psycho-Social Divide: Freud, Weber, Adorno and Elias.* Aldershot, Hants, UK: Ashgate.

Eysenck, H. J. (1964) *Crime and Personality.* London: Routledge and Kegan Paul.

Farrington, D. (2002) Developmental criminology and risk-focused prevention, in M. Maguire, R. Morgan and R. Reiner (eds), *The Oxford Handbook of Criminology,* third edition. Oxford: Oxford University Press, pp. 657–701.

Foucault, M. (1972) *The Archaeology of Knowledge.* London: Tavistock.

Foucault, M. (1979) *Discipline and Punish.* Harmondsworth: Peregrine.

Freud, S. [1924] (1977) The dissolution of the Oedipus Complex, in S. Freud, *The Pelican Freud Library, volume 7: On Sexuality.* Harmondsworth: Penguin, pp. 313–322.

Frosh, S. (2003) Psychosocial studies and psychology: is a critical approach emerging?, *Human Relations* 56(12): 1545–1567.

Gadd, D. and Jefferson, T. (2007a) *Psychosocial Criminology.* London: Sage.

Gadd, D. and Jefferson, T. (2007b) On the defensive: a psychoanalytically informed psychosocial reading of *The Jack-Roller, Theoretical Criminology* 11(4): 443–467.

Garland, D. (2001) *The Culture of Control.* Oxford: Oxford University Press.

Garland, D. (2002) Of crimes and criminals, in M. Maguire, R. Morgan and R. Reiner (eds), *The Oxford Handbook of Criminology,* third edition. Oxford: Oxford University Press, pp. 7–50.

Hall, S. (2001) Foucault: power, knowledge and discourse, in M. Wetherell, S. Taylor and S. J. Yates (eds), *Discourse, Theory and Practice.* London: Sage, pp. 72–81.

Heathcote, F. (1981) Social disorganisation theories, in M. Fitzgerald, G. McLennan and J. Pawson (eds), *Crime and Society.* London: Routledge & Kegan Paul, pp. 31–70.

Hollway, W. (2001) Gender difference and the production of sexuality, in M. Wetherell, S. Taylor and S. J. Yates (eds), *Discourse, Theory and Practice.* London: Sage, pp. 272–283.

Hollway, W. and Jefferson, T. (2000) *Doing Qualitative Research Differently.* London: Sage.

Jefferson, T. (2002) 'For a psychosocial criminology', in K. Carrington and R. Hogg (eds), *Critical Criminology: Issues, Debates, Challenges.* Cullompton, Devon, Willan, pp. 145–167.

Jones, D. W. (2008) *Understanding Criminal Behaviour: Psychosocial Approaches to Criminality.* Cullompton, Devon: Willan.

Katz, J. (1988) *Seductions of Crime.* New York: Basic Books.

Klein, M. (1988a) *Love, Guilt and Reparation and Other Works, 1921–1945.* London: Virago.

Klein, M. (1988b) *Envy and Gratitude and Other Works, 1946–1963.* London: Virago.

Koesling, A. and Neuber, A. (2007) The 'homesickness' of *The Jack-Roller, Theoretical Criminology* 11(4): 501–513.

Maruna, S. and Matravers, A. (2007) *N*=1: criminology and the person, *Theoretical Criminology* 11(4): 427–442.

Mead, G. H. [1934](1967) *Mind, Self and Society.* Chicago, Il: University of Chicago Press.

Messerschmidt, J. W. (1993) *Masculinities and Crime.* Lanham, MD: Rowman and Littlefield.

Messerschmidt, J. W. (1997) *Crime as Structured Action.* London: Sage.

Mitchell, J. C. (2000) Case and situation analysis, in R. Gomm, P. Hammersley and P. Foster (eds), *Case Study Method.* London: Sage, pp. 165–86.

Psychoanalysis, Culture and Society (2008) Special Issue: British Psycho(-)Social Studies, *Psychoanalysis, Culture and Society* 13(4).

Rutter, M. and Giller, H. (1983) *Juvenile Delinquency.* Harmondsworth: Penguin.

Shaw, C. R. (1930) *The Jack-Roller.* Chicago, Il: University of Chicago Press.

Urwin, C. (2007) Doing infant observation differently? Researching the formation of mothering identities in an inner London borough, *Infant Observation* 10(3): 239–251.

Young, J. (1999) *The Exclusive Society.* London: Sage.

16

Cultural Criminology:
The Loose Can[n]on

Jeff Ferrell

Of late I and other cultural criminologists have found ourselves negotiating a long sequence of assignments aimed at defining cultural criminology (e.g., Ferrell, 2007a, 2009; Hayward and Young, 2007). This isn't a complaint, by the way; these assignments constitute an appropriate and predictable disciplinary endeavor at this stage in cultural criminology's development. Dating to Ferrell and Sanders' (1995) *Cultural Criminology*, and taking on increasing disciplinary visibility over the course of the following 15 years, cultural criminology now seems the sort of established criminological theory that merits widespread explication in textbooks, edited collections, and encyclopedia.

Still, if this definitional project reflects a welcome degree of disciplinary engagement with cultural criminology, it strikes me nonetheless that too much definition can come to signal a sort of intellectual death. Definition denotes a certain closing down of debate, a solidification of intellectual orientation – and so a dangerous balance between the explication of a perspective and the extermination of its vitality. To use a political analogy, this tendency toward definition and delimitation recalls the fatal flaw that generally afflicts 'successful' revolutions: the desire to consolidate gains, to replace the fiery uncertainty of upheaval with the careful management of empowerment. Such a strategy of course risks – or assures – extinguishing the very fire out of which it is forged. Maybe Trotsky was right – maybe the revolution, whether one of politics or of intellectual perspective, must be permanent.

As regards criminological theory, it seems that moments of solid definition and careful demarcation often mark the beginning of caricature as well. Ten years, twenty years after a theoretical orientation emerges, and many a scholar or student seems to know it only *as* its summary definition.[1] Labeling theory reduced to the truism that 'deviance … is created by society', Becker's (1963/1973: 8, 177–212) protestations notwithstanding; left realism boxed inside a simple square of crime;

subcultural theory reacted to as little more than delinquent boys and their shared reaction formations – these thin caricatures flow from thick textbooks and shallow readings, certainly, but perhaps also originate in theorists' own attempts at self-definition and summation. Definition, it seems, easily enough becomes complexity's undoing.

Definitional closure and over-simplification would seem especially unfortunate, or at least ironic, in the case of cultural criminology. From the first cultural criminology has self-avowedly been as much an attempt to open theoretical space as it has been a conventional theory as such; cultural criminology's oppositional stance toward orthodox criminology has emerged in part from this very sensibility, from the sense that orthodox criminology today largely constitutes a closing down of theory and critique in the interest of quantification and criminal justice. Likewise, cultural criminology has embraced the ambiguous status attributed to it by those who wonder whether it is a fully developed theory or more a 'collection of individuals sharing some issues in common' (Webber, 2007: 140), answering that cultural criminology can perhaps best be thought of as 'a loose federation of outlaw intellectual critiques attuned to the cultural dynamics of late capitalism, open to the human construction of collective meaning, aware of both the harm and the hope of that transgression can offer' (Ferrell, 2007b: 99).

This resistance to conceptual closure certainly comes in part from the anarchist politics, theory, and epistemology that animate much of cultural criminology. An anarchist epistemology draws on philosopher of science Paul Feyerabend's (1975) sense that dominant paradigms mask their exercise of power and exclusion within ideologies of common sense and conventional wisdom, and so must be attacked counter-intuitively, subversively, and continuously if they are to be dislodged. This sort of approach likewise denies the value of intellectual certainty; as with the post-modern deconstruction of metanarratives, an anarchist epistemology argues that any 'answer' is false the moment we stop the process of inquiry by arriving at it. In this light it is also no accident that Situationist-inspired, anarchic intellectual and political orientations crop up often in cultural criminology (e.g., Ferrell, 2004, 2006; Ferrell *et al.*, 2008). The Situationist strategy of *detournement* – the stealing away of every-day meaning in the interest of decentering certainty and launching a 'revolution of everyday life' – echoes in cultural criminology's strategy of unraveling the taken-for-granted authority of orthodox criminological theory and method in the interest of a progressive, open-ended revolution in criminological practice. An approach that con-ceptualizes itself in these terms hardly lends itself to definitional closure.

But for all that, it seems to me that it is precisely cultural criminology's focus on *the cultural* that most strongly disinclines it to close theoretical definition. To under-stand cultural dynamics as a motor force in everyday life is not simply to notice the importance of image, style, and representation; it is also to understand that the very meaning of social life remains always under construction. Paying attention to the multiplicity of symbolic interactions and interpretations that shape this fluidity of meaning, a further insight emerges, and with it a subtle but significant shift in ana-lytic focus: the subject of criminology is not the criminal act or the experience of victimization or the court decision, but rather the *ongoing cultural processes* by which the meanings of such events are negotiated and their consequences contested. But if this is true for the subject of our analysis, it is true for the tools of our analysis as well; the theoretical models by which we make sense of the world are in practice surely less definable conceptual entities than they are blurry processes of intellectual and cultural engagement.

Definition, then, is inevitably an act of fiction – unless it isn't. So in the following sections I'll do my best to avoid defining cultural criminology, arguing instead that it constitutes a distinctively useful criminological theory precisely because it denies the validity of closure and definition. This undertaking will of course likely serve to create for cultural criminology yet another sort of definition. Calling for moral engagement and political activism, the theologian Harvey Cox once warned that, after all, not to decide is to decide. Likewise, I suspect, not to define is to define – but on we go.

CULTURAL CRIMINOLOGY: THE LOOSE CANNON

Today the term 'loose cannon' is generally used metaphorically to denote someone who can't be trusted to abide by the programme of a particular group, a person whose reckless words or behaviour may well do the collective more harm than good. Often, it seems, the term is used in particular to suggest an inappropriately scatter-shot approach – a loose cannon firing off in all directions, and so again, as likely to hit friend as foe. The etymology of the term, though, reveals a different sort of historical foundation for the metaphor – one a good bit more subtle but no less dangerous. As described by nineteenth-century writers, a 'loose cannon' was one that had come free from its moorings along the flanks of a wooden battleship during a sea storm. Unsecured, careening and skidding across the decks with the tossing of the ship, the massive cannon now constituted a grave danger to the ship and its sailors; put in motion, its sheer weight was such that it couldn't be restrained, and so might crush on-deck sailors, smash through decks or walls, even sink the ship itself. Witness the awful scene that Victor Hugo (1908 [1874]: 34) describes in his novel *Ninety-Three*:

> The carronade, hurled forward by the pitching, dashed into this knot of men, and crushed four at the first blow; then, flung back and shot out anew by the rolling, it cut in two a fifth poor fellow, glanced off to the larboard side, and struck a piece of the battery with such force as to unship it. … The enormous cannon was left alone. She was given up to herself. She was her own mistress, and mistress of the vessel. She could do what she willed with both. This whole crew, accustomed to laugh in battle, trembled now.

Dangerous business indeed – so dangerous that in Hugo's novel, the man responsible for the cannon's coming loose is later put to death for his mistake.

This sort of loose cannon introduces a dangerous and provocative irony as well. Carefully engineered and situated to defend the ship and to attack its enemies, the cannon now becomes the ship's own self-made enemy, attacking it and its occupants as it slides across the decks. Positioned to aim the ship's deadly force outward, it now turns the assault inwards. Secured, kept in its proper place, the cannon serves the interests of the ship and its owners; cut loose, free of restraints, the cannon serves itself, or perhaps no one at all. And worse yet: the bigger and heavier the cannon, the greater the danger of a crushing blow.

At least some of the time, cultural criminology operates as just such a cannon. By design it has come loose from orthodox criminology, torn itself away from the moorings of conventional criminological practice. By intention, it aims its fusillade of critique outward, at targets of crime, violence, and injustice – but it also aims inward, skidding across the decks of orthodox criminology, meaning to wreak havoc inside the ship itself. And for cultural criminologists, this internecine attack is necessitated by yet another irony: The ship of orthodox criminology, allegedly built to help understand social problems of crime and violence and so to move us toward a better world, is in fact today mostly an *impediment* to scholarly understanding and progressive social justice.

The reasons for this are clear enough. The ship, cultural criminologists argue, has been taken over by statisticians and survey researchers able only to sail the ship in the shallow waters of second-hand analysis, trolling along the shoals of 'predicted property reconviction probabilities for four age and race groups' (Mears *et al.*, 2008: 325) and 'regression coefficients representing the effects of self-control and morality on projections of future crime' (Antonaccio and Tittle, 2008: 499). Ownership of the ship seems to be changing as well; increasingly it is not guided by its own intellectual rudder, but mortgaged instead to granting agencies and criminal justice organizations. Because of this, the ship remains most of the time on a wandering course at best, unequipped to navigate the swirling waters of late modernity and its discontents. Other times the ship goes nowhere at all, consigned to an intellectual backwater of its own making – or it simply sits, tucked away in one institutional safe harbor or another. From the view of cultural criminology, the task is to save the ship or to sink it – but certainly not to assist in staying the course.

This present course degrades criminology both as an academic discipline and as a mode of intellectual engagement with the larger social world. Disciplinarily, the dominance of survey research, governmental records, statistical abstraction, and desiccated theory denies criminology's rich cultural and intellectual history. Under the present regime, the manifold sociological, criminological, and methodological insights of the Chicago School researchers, of American interactionists and ethnographers, of British cultural theorists and 'new criminologists', of critical intellectuals and Continental theorists are shriveled into logistic regression models and asocial 'theories' of self control and rational choice.

The relative intellectual and disciplinary independence embodied in these earlier forms of criminology erodes as well, with the discipline increasingly a paid-for adjunct of one criminal justice industrial complex or another. The blathering obfuscation that accompanies this endeavor – the two-page tables and talk of the 'joint zero-inflated Poisson latent class growth model: four-class solution' (McGloin *et al.*, 2008: 172) – largely precludes criminology's participation in critical public debate, save in the service of bureaucratic mystification. A discipline crafted historically around the most incendiary and important of subjects – crime and transgression, violence and victimization, justice and injustice – now excludes itself from the task of intellectual and human engagement. The ship stalls amidst its own stagnation.

Under such circumstances, cultural criminology's loose cannon gladly careens towards a number of targets. As a starting point, cultural criminologists attempt to punch holes in the already shoddy methodological framework on which the ship is built. Upon close inspection, they note, the ship of contemporary criminology reveals itself to be an oddly top-heavy craft, its towering abstractions of statistical manipulation built atop a lightweight framework of suspect governmental statistics and survey research responses. The statistics may be dazzling, but time and again the 'data' undergirding them is found to derive from simplistic surveys beset by low response rates, from governmental arrest or conviction records uncritically incorporated – even from 'convenience samples' of undergraduate students held captive in introductory criminology classes. Such methods offer no real engagement with the experiential reality of crime and victimization, cultural criminologists contend, nor any sense of the looping referentiality by which contemporary images of crime and justice interplay with such lived experiences (Ferrell *et al.*, 2008). Mostly, they're meant to produce numbers – per cent who answered 'yes' to question seventeen, number of arrests for burglary per thousand – and so to churn out the sort of culturally cleansed 'data' necessary for efficient statistical manipulation. Below the waterline, ignored amidst the ship-shape tables and sharp agency reports, the ship of criminology rides on a rotten methodological foundation.

The loose cannon that is cultural criminology likewise aims to collide head-on with what passes for theory in much of mainstream criminology. The popular 'broken windows' theory of crime (Wilson and Kelling, 1982), for example, seems in reality less a theory than a simplistic justification for policies of urban exclusion and low-level 'order maintenance policing'. But if it is a theory at all, it is one predicated on a series of untenable and unexamined assumptions. Proponents of the theory argue that phenomena like broken windows and street graffiti operate as signs of public disorder and neglect, and so as invitations to worsening criminality; residents perceive from them that crime is on the increase, criminals perceive them as signaling the ease with which crime can be committed, and a downward spiral of criminality and discouragement ensues. Yet the broken windows approach doesn't conceptualize these complex cultural dynamics of display, symbolism and perception so much as it simply assumes them, constructing a series of one-dimensional meanings and then arbitrarily assigning them to physical phenomena and imagined public audiences. Compounding this problem, as Kubrin (2008: 207, emphasis added) notes, 'most studies testing the broken windows thesis have relied on objective indictors of disorder, which fail to capture the *social meaning* ascribed to disorder by community residents that may trigger the broken windows process.' This, she adds, is 'somewhat ironic given that individuals' perceptions of their communities – not necessarily objective reality – are central to the theory.' Ironic, yes ... or indefensible. Presenting itself as a practically grounded 'theory' of crime, broken windows in fact strays into the waters explored by cultural criminology – into deeper domains of cultural communication and contested social meaning – and sinks.

Rational choice theory presents another ready target for the unsecured cannon, and for much the same reasons. Like the broken windows approach, rational choice theory largely excludes from analysis the large-scale social and cultural inequalities within which crime takes shape; fails even to account adequately for the smaller personal and interpersonal dynamics which are the theory's focus; and then offers all of this as a ready-made justification for individually punitive social policy and as a template for 'situational crime prevention'. In brief, rational choice theory posits that criminals follow a linear 'sequence of choices made at each stage of the criminal act – for example, preparation, target selection, commission of the act, escape, and aftermath,' and that these choices remain 'rational, albeit imperfect' even when 'made quickly [and] revised hastily', even when made 'in a fog of alcohol and drugs' (Cornish and Clarke, 2006: 19–21). Given this, situational crime prevention entails manipulating the social and physical environment in such a way as to interrupt this rational sequence by, for example, reducing the opportunities or rewards for crime. Cultural criminology argues on the other hand that this is more a tautology than a theory – all choices remain rational because all choices are rational – and moreover a tautology astoundingly out of tune with a late modern world ever more suffused with irrationalities of personal affect, cultural expressivity, and sensual gratification (Young, 2007). As Hayward (2007: 232, 238) points out, rational choice-inspired situational crime prevention strategies may well succeed at times in reducing certain types of property crime – but as a criminological *theory* of crime and its causes, rational choice presents a 'sociologically hollow narrative' that fails to satisfy even its own proponents, who note that it may well be unable to explain 'emotionally charged states'. These, of course, are precisely the states that increasingly circulate amidst the anomic immediacy of liquid modernity (Bauman, 2000), suffusing popular culture and street life alike. These are the states that likewise animate crimes of all sorts, from domestic violence to binge drinking and prison abuse. And so these are the states that merit the interest of cultural criminology (Ferrell, 1997).

A final strategy replicates precisely the reflexive motion of the loose cannon – that is, the turning inward of the assault that is commonly pointed outward. It also embodies the spirit of *detournement* in its attempt to upset certainty and steal away taken-for-granted meaning by interrogating that which generally remains unnoticed and unquestioned. Put simply, this strategy is to rotate cultural criminology's distinctively *cultural* analysis of crime and crime control inward, toward criminology itself. Certainly a hallmark of cultural criminological theory is the notion that symbolic codes and mediated communication matter; cultural criminology rests on an understanding that the reality of crime and control – their meanings and consequences – emerges from an interplay of representation, interpretation, and emotion. Given this, cultural criminologists carefully 'read' subtle symbolic cues of language, style, and ritualized representation for insights into the values and practices of those they study, whether they be neo-Nazi skinheads, newspaper page designers, corporate marketers, street gang members, or graffiti writers. That is, they regularly point their critical, cultural analysis outward, towards any number of groups and institutions. But what if this cultural interrogation broke loose, spun around, and so came to be pointed at the institution of orthodox criminology?

Cultural criminologists argue that it would reveal a discipline constipated by its own self-importance, a discipline hiding its human and political disengagement behind the trappings of objective research and abstract scholarship. The culture of orthodox criminology – its representational cues and symbolic practices – are after all easily enough read. The blandness of passive, third-person writing; the reliance on specialized, pseudo-scientific terminology; the tyranny of long equations and large tables; the mania for ever-longer lists of in-text citations; the disinclination toward art and the image – all suggest a discipline more interested in talking to itself, or in selling itself as an objectivist adjunct to institutionalized politics, than in engaging with the dangerous dynamics of crime, power, and transgression. The symbolic codes of orthodox criminology offer mostly objectification and obfuscation, read as ugly and dehumanizing, and so reveal much about the ship and its style of sailing. The ship-board songs the sailors sing are distinctly short on rhythm and passion; and when the sailors assemble on the deck, they seem more interested in starched uniforms and straight lines than nautical adventure.

And so the loose cannon continues, hurling forward into conventional methodologies, dashing into popular theoretical orientations, glancing off the culture of institutionalized criminology itself. Left long enough to its concussive work, cultural criminologists hope, it might even crack the closed canon of orthodox criminology, and so open criminology to innovations in cultural analysis and engagement.

CULTURAL CRIMINOLOGY: THE LOOSE CANON

> The horrible cannon flings itself about, advances, recoils, strikes to the right, strikes to the left, flees, passes. … The great danger of the situation is in the mobility of its base. … The ship, so to speak, has lightening imprisoned in its womb which seeks to escape; it is like thunder rolling above an earthquake.
>
> Victor Hugo, *Ninety-Three*

To speak of a canon – here, the canon of criminology – is to suggest a code of law and method, and with it a repository of shared learning and wisdom, that lies at the core of a discipline and so defines it. Often, and for very good world historical reasons, 'the canon' carries with it also the odor of ecclesiastic authority – the sense that this canon merits the sort of faithful adherence that transcends individual judgment. Already, cultural criminologists have caught a whiff of this in considering criminology's contemporary canon. Ferrell *et al.*, (2008: 167), for example, argue that many criminologists' blind faith in the social scientific stalwarts of survey research methods and statistical analysis constitutes a type of fundamentalism, a fundamentalism characterized by claims of innate superiority and transcendental objectivity, and by in-group pride in incomprehensibility to outsiders. 'And so', they conclude, 'possessed by the spirit of social science, orthodox criminologists speak in a sort of fundamentalist glossolalia, a private prayer language of logistic odds ratios and intercept models, their tongues tied by their own ineptitude in appreciating other ways of seeing the world.'

To characterize orthodox criminologists and their canon in this cavalier way is of course to engage, once again, in *detournement* – to undermine taken-for-granted understanding, to subvert carefully constructed meanings, in the interest of opening the world to new possibilities. To put it another way: Reconceptualizing criminological 'social scientists' and their canon as an obscurant cult of religious fundamentalists is not meant to be rude – its meant to be revolutionary.[2] The goal is to steal away what we think we know about criminology and its canon, and so to force a radical reconsideration of criminology itself. And this, I would argue, is the real potential of cultural criminology: not simply to flush into orthodox criminology a few new theories or subjects of study, but to *undefine* it, and so to create what would currently seem an inherent contradiction: a loose canon.

Understandably, many orthodox criminologists might well counter that this sort of characterization *is* in fact rude, and disingenuous to boot; the canon of criminology, they would say, is not constituted by surveys or statistics as such, but by a broader dedication to the scientific analysis of crime and criminals that dates to August Comte, Adolphe Quetelet, and especially the nineteenth century positivism of

Cesare Lombroso, with his 'systemic, empirical-observational, scientific research' (Einstadter and Henry, 1995: 75) into criminality. In this sense, they would contend, there certainly is a valid criminological canon, a long-accumulated and widely shared wisdom regarding the disciplinary value of (social) scientific inquiry and analysis. And, they would add that since 'the positivist approach has strong connections with statistical analysis' (Morrison, 1995: 165) – that is, since 'positivist modes of study tend to discover various *correlations* between crime and extraneous conditions but can rarely if ever claim to have specified direct *causes*' (Muncie, 2006: 303, emphasis in original) – today's surveys and statistics emerge naturally from this canon.

From the view of cultural criminology, they would be wrong on two counts.

First, as Wayne Morrison (2004: 67) has demonstrated, the early positivism of Lombroso and others was more a matter of staged performance and intellectual sleight-of-hand than of criminological science; as he says, 'positivist criminology was born amidst a dazzling and seductive spectacle' of displayed human skulls, gelatinized brains, tattoo collections, ersatz wall maps, and prison tours. In this sense, Morrison argues, early positivism was a 'cultural production' whose success rested not on the innate superiority of its scientific method but on its ability to *display itself* as an advancement in human knowledge. Worse, the spectacle of early positivism was an imperial one; it was 'performance art in the service of European power' (Morrison, 2004: 79), a form of cultural imperialism by which Lombroso and his associates could 'discover' inherent linkages between Aboriginal art, Maori tattoos, and criminality by *ignoring* their situated cultural meanings. The mythology of criminological positivism – the mythology of the social scientific criminological canon – is that criminologists today reject the suspect, sloped-forehead findings of early positivism while retaining its scientific methodology. The reality reveals another sort of retention – one already glimpsed in the cultural analysis of contemporary orthodox criminology. Positivist criminology – the social scientific criminology of control groups, surveys, and statistics – was and is disciplinary performance art, and by its own objectivist standards and statistical measures (Weisburd and Piquero, 2008; Young, 2004) a carefully staged fraud.

Second, the history of criminology from Lombroso forward hardly reveals widely shared canonical allegiance in any case. Peter Kropotkin was a renowned geographer who in his lifetime was offered both the Secretary of the Russian Geographical Society and the Chair of Geography at Cambridge University – but his groundbreaking criminologies of law and the prison were meant more as revolutionary calls to justice than as dispassionate social science. Born Meyer Schkolnick, changing his name to Robert K. Merlin during an early career as a magician and again later to the name we now know, Robert K. Merton considered himself both a social scientist and a sociologist of science – but he emphasized that 'typically, the scientific paper or monograph presents an immaculate appearance which reproduces little or nothing of the intuitive leaps, false starts, mistakes, loose ends, and happy accidents that actually cluttered up the inquiry'. Echoing Stinchcombe's comments on the importance of a theory's 'esthetic style' for its intellectual popularity, Merton also noted the stylish irony inherent in his work on social structure and its anomic tendencies, adding, 'that to me was both, what shall I say, the analytic interest and the esthetic interest' (in Cullen and Messner, 2007: 6, 12). A first generation of Chicago School sociologists like Robert Park, Frederic Thrasher, Clifford Shaw, and

Nels Anderson, and after them a second Chicago School-influenced generation including Howard Becker, Erving Goffman, and Ned Polsky, laid the substantive and theoretical foundations for significant segments of contemporary criminology – but their criminological approach was largely embodied in ethnographic field work that was 'unencumbered by legal restrictions, disciplinary codes, or stultifying customs', and in fact frequently illegal (Adler and Adler, 1998: xii; Chapoulie, 1996; Ferrell, 1997).

These few examples of course hardly constitute a comprehensive history of modern criminology – but they do suggest that the criminological canon is neither as solid nor as widely shared as orthodox criminology would have it. In fact, they suggest that Feyerabend (1975) was right – that the keepers of an intellectual domain construct artifices of 'truth' or 'common sense' or 'the canon' as part of the process by which their dominance is made to seem innate, if not inevitable. 'As a social system', Fuchs (1986: 126, 133) notes, 'science needs to coordinate patterns of knowledge so as to establish social order' – and so 'truth' comes to fit not 'into nature' but 'into the cultural possession of particular groups of professional knowledge producers.' Feyerabend emphasizes in turn that these artifices of canonical truth carry a deceptive historical trajectory as well. As he carefully documents, the history of natural science has necessarily been much as Morrison and Merton suggest: a series of intuitive/counter-intuitive leaps and intellectual tricks, a hodgepodge of political intrigue, public performance, and private persuasion. Yet afterwards, after one scientific paradigm replaces another, *post hoc* reifications emerge by which the tricks and the intrigue are forgotten; now the older paradigms seem to be seamlessly subsumed in the new, and the whole stumbling process is retrospectively made to appear a single, uninterrupted march toward scientific truth.

Orthodox, 'social scientific' criminology today engages in the same sort of *post hoc* revisionism–engages, we might say, in its own form of retrospective interpretation (Schur, 1971). Criminology's dicey history – the long drunk's stagger of pseudo-scientific performance and fraudulent persuasion, the shift from field research to statistical analysis in response to a new 'market for sociological studies' in the 1930s and 1940s (Chapoulie, 1996: 10), the competing periods of intellectual Dark Age and scholarly Renaissance (Adler and Adler, 1998) – is repackaged as a positivist canon, and presented as scientific progress toward criminological insight, with the latest probability model its apex.[3] Incorporated in introductory criminology textbooks, insinuated into the language of 'random samples' and 'control groups', employed by the keepers of flagship journals and federal grant money, this canon is made to close down on itself.[4] And in this, we see again the power and importance of orthodox criminology's culture: all those control groups, in-text citations, and long equations are essential props in the illusion, all devices by which criminology doth, perhaps, protest too much.

But if this is so – if the canonical core of orthodox criminology is in fact a performance and a political accomplishment, masking long-standing differences and largely inhibiting criminology's human and cultural engagement with contemporary circumstances – then the implication seems clear: set the loose cannon upon it and smash it open. Put differently, our job as criminologists is not to abide by the canon, but to move beyond it and the mythology that sustains it. Cultural criminology undertakes this move. Attuned to the culturally constructed reality of both criminology and that which it studies, embracing an array of alternative theoretical and

methodological approaches, investigating topics conventionally omitted from criminological analysis, it is particularly well positioned to reimagine the criminological
enterprise.

In fact, this reimagination was already underway in the earlier theoretical strands
that subsequently intertwined to help shape contemporary cultural criminology. In
the 1970s the Birmingham School for Cultural Studies and the National Deviancy
Conference in Great Britain developed a culturally informed 'new criminology'
(Taylor *et al.*, 1973) that challenged both orthodox criminology and conventional
understandings of social class, crime and crime control. Arguing that 'a social individual, born into a particular set of institutions and relations, is at the same moment
born into a particular configuration of meanings, which give her access to and locate
her within "a culture"' (Clarke *et al.*, 1976: 11), these theorists closely analyzed the
leisure aesthetics and symbolic practices of working class youth and others so as to
demonstrate the interconnections between these practices and larger dynamics of
resistance, transgression, and ideology. But altering criminology's substantive focus
to include aesthetics, symbolic representation, and cultural conflict required new
sorts of theoretical models, too – and so these theorists turned to an eclectic range of
literary writers, cultural theorists, and critical commentators, from Antonio Gramsci
and Jean Genet to Raymond Williams, Roland Barthes, and Louis Althusser. A sensitivity to aesthetics and ideology, and with it an innovative amalgam of intellectual
perspectives geared to precise aesthetic and ideological analysis, pushed hard against
the accepted core of criminology, maybe even began to crack it in places.

Around this same time, the advent of labeling theory in the United States likewise
changed … everything. While the debate over labeling theory's larger political implications has been ongoing since at least Becker's (1973: 177–208) 'labeling theory
reconsidered' addendum to *Outsiders*, its implications for criminology, I would
argue, are undeniably radical. With labeling theory, there is nothing to study, at least
in conventional criminological terms; the subject matter of orthodox criminology
disappears. The positivist sense of crime as an objective phenomenon amenable to
measurement and calculation evaporates, replaced by a complex, continuing process
through which the meaning of crime is socially negotiated and culturally contested.
And more radical yet: While 'crime' no longer constitutes the subject matter of
criminology, the statistics on which orthodox criminology relies now do. If for
labeling theory the criminologist's job is to investigate the processes by which crime
and criminals are constructed, then this investigation must surely include crime statistics employed by law makers and moral entrepreneurs, official arrest rates that
mask complex interactional dynamics while promoting institutional crime control
agendas – even the regression coefficients by which orthodox criminologists
themselves construct the numeric reality of their subject matter. If, to paraphrase
Becker's famous formulation, social groups create deviance by making and enforcing rules, doesn't criminology in part create its own criminality by way of the
theories and methods that define it?

Canon-loosening indeed, and cultural criminology continues this process by integrating the insights of cultural studies, the 'new criminology', and labeling theory
with other expansive orientations. Cultural criminologists like Stephanie Kane
(1998, 2004) not only draw on anthropological understandings of cultural dynamics
and anthropological methods of field research, but suggest embracing, perhaps even
engineering, on-the-street situations of surprise and serendipity as moments of

uncontrolled criminological insight. Beginning from a different intellectual tradition, cultural criminologist and 'philosopher-cop' Jonathan Wender (2004: 49–50) comes to a similar conclusion: that criminologists must escape the bureaucratic ethos of orthodox criminology and rediscover the phenomenology of crime – specifically, a 'phenomenological aesthetic of encounter' – if they are to reclaim their astonishment at the 'fullness and mystery of human existence.' Building from the pioneering work of Dwight Conquergood (2002) and others in the field of performance studies, Robert Garot (2007) echoes labeling theory in examining a conventional criminological subject like 'gang membership' not as an objective and quantifiable phenomenon, but as a series of slippery performances and transactional accomplishments (see similarly Hallsworth and Young, 2008). Likewise, Maggie O'Neill (2004: 219) subverts the objectivist mythology of orthodox criminology by engaging in forms of participatory action research and 'performative praxis' for the purpose of 'representing the lived experiences of those on the borders, at the margins, and in the liminal spaces'. In exploring crime and crime control as urban phenomena, other cultural criminologists (Ferrell, 2002; Hayward, 2004) utilize especially alternative forms of spatial analysis derived from cultural geography and related fields.

Out of these and other extra-canonical orientations a variety of specific theoretical models have also developed within cultural criminology, each of them an analytic counterpoint to orthodox criminology's aridly asocial models of rational choice, routine activities, and broken windows. As developed by Steve Lyng (1990, 2005), Jeff Ferrell (1996), and others (Ferrell *et al.*, 2001), the theory of *edgework*, for example, integrates symbolic interactionism and critical theory in proposing that many forms of illegal activity are characterized by extremes of collective risk-taking. These forms of criminality, edgework theorists argue, allow participants to reclaim a sense of self through an exhilarating mix of risk and skill, and so to counter the dehumanizing hyper-rationality and deskilled tedium enforced in their daily lives and daily work. The dangerous dialectic of risk and skill in turn spirals participants closer to the seductions (Katz, 1988) of 'the edge', and sets in motion an ironic dynamic between edgeworkers and agents of crime control: Given that edgework spawns an addictive 'adrenalin rush' as participants utilize self-made skills to survive ever more risky situations, aggressive law enforcement strategies designed to stop illegal edgework mostly serve to heighten the risk, to force the development of further skills – and thereby to amplify the very experience that participants seek and legal authorities seek to stop.

Similarly, Mike Presdee (2000) develops from the work of Mikhail Bakhtin a theory of crime as *carnival*, positing that contemporary phenomena such as drug taking, gang rituals, arson, and 'hotting' or 'joyriding' in stolen cars can be understood as free-floating historical residues of the carnivalesque excesses that were once contained inside ritualized times and events. Now, with the historical practice of carnival as a time of culturally ritualized excess and desire largely destroyed – outlawed in some cases, converted into legally regulated and commercialized spectacle in others – the remnants today circulate in different form. Many are now commodified and consumed as degrading 'reality television' shows or sadomasochistic pornography; others are enacted as crimes of vulgarity or destruction, made all the more dangerous because now cut loose from their containment within community ritual.

Both the theory of edgework and of carnival in this way counter orthodox criminology's reduction of crime to a rational, instrumental undertaking, while also
situating an understanding of emotionally charged criminality within a contemporary context of alienated work, commercialization, consumerism, and control. Two
other theoretical models in cultural criminology likewise move beyond orthodox
criminology in attempting to attune criminology to contemporary circumstances,
and to the distinctly late modern dynamics that shape contemporary emotion, experience, and perception. Jock Young's (1999) theory of *exclusion/inclusion* notes the
increasing economic and legal exclusion of large populations from mainstream
society by way of job loss, low-wage work, urban decay, and mass incarceration. Yet
at the same time, Young notes, these same populations are aggressively and increasingly *culturally* included; through the saturating power of the mass media and mass
advertising, they are socialized into the same world of consumer goods and consumer desires as are others. Echoing Merton's (1938; see Young, 2003) famous
formulation of adaptations to socially-induced strain, Young argues that this late
modern strain between economic exclusion and cultural inclusion spawns frustration, resentment, insecurity, and humiliation, and with it crimes of passion,
retaliation, and illicit acquisition.

Ferrell *et al.*'s (2007) theory of *media loops and spirals* likewise focuses on the
mediated saturation of late modernity, and links this cultural world of image
and representation to the dynamics of late modern crime and crime control.
According to their model, everyday life is now so suffused with media technologies
and mediated images that any clear demarcation between an event and its image
is largely lost. In place of the traditional positivist distinction between a phenomenon and its representation, representation now constitutes in many cases the
phenomenon itself; in place of the linear sequencing of crime followed by its mediated representation, crime and its representation now loop back on one another,
further confounding image, event, and perception. Violent gang assaults are not just
caught on camera, but staged for the camera and later sold on websites; 'reality'
television programmes not only distort existing legal proceedings, but spawn later
legal proceedings; police car cameras not only capture the police at work, but alter
the way in which they work. Over time, these loops become spirals, bending back
on themselves time and again, with, for example, police videotapes later emerging
as court evidence and later still, as part of television compilations, or as police
instructional videos. In this light, the canon can indeed be seen to crumble; even the
most basic of criminological subjects – street crime, everyday policing, court procedures – seem not so much objectively measurable phenomena as entanglements of
emergent image.

The methods by which cultural criminologists engage with this late modern world
of ephemeral emotions, spiralling images, and cultural excess continue the erosion
of criminology's social scientific mythology. In one sense cultural criminology constitutes a straightforward attempt to revitalize the Chicago School tradition of
in-depth ethnographic fieldwork, and to re-establish the historical role of this methodological orientation as a viable alternative to survey research and statistical
analysis (Adler and Adler, 1998; Chapoulie, 1996). Indeed, some of cultural criminology's most visible and visibly criticized (O'Brien, 2005) work has emerged from
long-term, participatory ethnography (Ferrell, 1996, 2006) and auto-ethnography
(Ferrell, 2002; Presdee, 2000). But cultural criminologists are also intent on

reinventing this tradition, on synchronizing its existing strengths with the late modern dynamics suggested by cultural criminology's theoretical models. Ferrell *et al*. (2008: 174–190) in fact propose that a variety of these innovative methodologies are now emerging in and around cultural criminology. 'Instant ethnography' blends traditional ethnography's attentiveness to cultural meaning and emotion with a contemporary sensitivity to situated performance and immediate communication, so as to engage with ephemeral moments of edgework, violence, or transgression. 'Liquid ethnography' likewise suggests that, in many contemporary cases, the subject matter of criminological ethnography will not be a static subculture or fixed situation, but rather transitory communities, shifting populations, and the flow of contested images by which they know and are known. Overturning the social scientific hierarchy of word over image, 'visual criminology' situates the criminologist in this flow of images doubly, first as a critical analyst of existing mediated representations, and second as a producer of alternative visual representation (Hayward and Presdee, 2009).

While these latest innovations in ethnographic methodology certainly continue to undermine criminology's canon of quantitative analysis, they also usefully begin to undermine what I would call criminology's 'shadow canon' as well. That is, they abandon any residual mythology that ethnography, by creating a comprehensive account of a particular, self-contained phenomenon, serves as an *almost* social science, a shadow canon and 'loyal opposition' to survey research and statistics that at least shares the canonical faith in full, objective comprehension and totalizing narrative. Alternative styles of argument and presentation in cultural criminology serve this purpose as well; uninterested in hiding behind orthodox criminology's pseudo-scientific façade of bland objectivity, cultural criminologists instead experiment with the evocative power of word and image. Auto-ethnography – the criminologist's own experiences and emotions as a subject of critical analysis – has already been mentioned. In addition, cultural criminological texts now include photographic essays, photographic dyptichs, and other representational juxtapositions as forms of visual analysis. They incorporate manifestos, 'true fiction' – that is, fictionalized narratives built from factual information – and other modes of alternative criminological discourse (Ferrell *et al*., 2008; Ferrell, 2003). And, as seen especially in the journal *Crime, Media, Culture*, they embrace narrative and visual styles ranging from poetry and graphic art to short stories and polemics.[5] If criminology is performance, the thinking goes, why not perform it in ways that are potentially more engaging, more creative, and more conversant with contemporary circumstances than is the long-running objectivist tragedy of orthodox criminology?

In loosening the canon of orthodox criminology, these various alternative theoretical models, methods, and presentational styles in turn encourage a reconsideration and expansion of criminology's subject matter – an expansive rethinking entirely necessary if criminology is to account for the mix of media dynamics, cultural representation, and shared emotion that animates contemporary circumstances of crime and crime control. Recent work in cultural criminology has, for example, broadened the analysis of criminal justice practices to include complex issues of cultural and multi-cultural identity; reconceptualized victimization in terms of public display, mediated image, and virtual community; recontextualized urban crime within the ambiguous cultural dynamics of the city and consumption; redefined gangs, sex workers, and other marginalized communities as contested manifestations of street activism, global migration, and official discourse; investigated the cultural and commercial politics of drug use; traced the flow of people and representation between the prison and the community; reconsidered a host of public anti-crime campaigns, popular films, television programmes, comic books, and video games as exercises in narrative development and ideological control; and examined terrorism and torture as contested cultural accomplishments, towards the goal of developing a cultural criminology of the state.[6] And with this loosening of criminology's conventional subject matter, who knows what might come next? A cultural analysis of DC Comics (1993) superhero Loose Cannon, once a police Special Crimes Unit officer, later to morph into a raging superhuman crime-fighter until his heart is stolen by ... organ thieves? Or a critical interrogation of the 3D action-adventure game Loose Cannon, set in a future world where 'crime and vigilante rule have taken over, and the few remaining law agencies have taken to hiring bounty hunters to help carry out their work' – and where, Blackwater-style, 'you'll play as a mercenary named Ashe, a recent hire of the authorities and a total bad ass'?[7]

Wherever it next goes, the loose cannon of cultural criminology does seem a powerful intellectual force for loosening the stultifying canon of orthodox criminology. We might hope, as with Victor Hugo, that the 'great danger' that cultural criminology's loose cannon poses for orthodox criminology is precisely 'in the mobility of its base' – that is, in the willingness and ability of cultural criminology to explore emerging contours of crime and crime control, and to move toward subjects and styles of analysis now excluded from criminology's canon. If this mobility can in fact serve to create for criminology a loose canon – a shared orientation toward the critical analysis of crime, transgression, and control, but one wide open to alternative approaches and understandings – then perhaps the lightning now imprisoned in the womb of criminology can indeed escape. Perhaps criminology can indeed rediscover its potential for coruscating insight, and so embrace a loose canon less attuned to disciplinary definition than to the rolling thunder of analysis and critique.

NOTES

1 With apologies to Carl Sandburg (1970: 136) and his commentary on war and the ephemeral glory of its battlefields: 'Two years, ten years, and passengers ask the conductor: What place is this? Where are we now?'

2 On the Situationist and proto-Situationist defiling of churches and sacred texts, see Marcus (1989).

3 Chapoulie's (1996: 11) characterization of American sociology in the 1940s would seem to apply as well to contemporary criminology – and certainly to contemporary criminal justice: 'Use of statistical instruments and the language of proof of the natural sciences was clearly a way to increase the scientific legitimacy of a discipline fully recognized neither in the university nor outside it.'

4 Criminology 'uses scientific methods to study the nature, extent, cause, and control of criminal behavior' (Seigel, 2008: 2); criminology is 'an interdisciplinary profession built around the scientific study of crime and criminal behavior ...' (Schmalleger, 2004: 14); criminologists 'scientifically study the nature and extent of crime ...'. (Glick, 2005: 5)

5 When in 2006 Crime, Media, Culture won the Association of Learned and Professional Society Publishers (ALPSP)/Charlesworth Award for Best New Journal, the award panel noted especially its design features and visual content.

6 These studies can be found in Ferrell *et al.* (2004); Ferrell *et al.* (2008); and in recent issues of the journal *Crime, Media, Culture.*

7 www.gamestats.com, visited 5 September 2008.

REFERENCES

Adler, P. and Adler, P. (1998). Foreword: moving backward, in J. Ferrell and M. Hamm (eds), *Ethnography at the Edge*. Boston: Northeastern University Press, pp. xii–xvi.

Antonaccio, O. and Tittle, C. (2008). Morality, self-control and crime, *Criminology* 46(2): 479–510.

Bauman, Z. (2000). *Liquid Modernity*. Cambridge, UK: Polity.

Becker, H. (1963/1973). *Outsiders*. New York: Free Press.

Chapoulie, J.-M. (1996). Everett Hughes and the Chicago tradition, *Sociological Theory* 14(1): 3–29.

Clarke, J., Hall, S., Jefferson, T. and Roberts, B. (1976). Subcultures, cultures and class, in S. Hall and T. Jefferson (eds), *Resistance through Ritual*. London: Harper Collins, pp. 9–74.

Conquergood, D. (2002). Lethal theatre: performance, punishment, and the death penalty. *Theatre Journal* 54(3): 339–367.

Cornish, D. and Clarke, R. (2006). The rational choice perspective, in S. Henry and M. Lanier (eds), *The Essential Criminology Reader*. Boulder, CO: Westview, pp. 18–29.

Cullen, F. and Messner, S. (2007). The making of criminology revisited, *Theoretical Criminology* 11(1): 5–37.

DC Comics (1993). *Action Comics Annual #5*. Los Angeles: Warner Bros.

Einstadter, W. and Henry, S. (1995). *Criminological Theory*. Ft. Worth, TX: Harcourt Brace.

Ferrell, J. (1996). *Crimes of Style*. Boston: Northeastern University Press.

Ferrell, J. (1997). Criminological Verstehen, *Justice Quarterly* 14(1): 3–23.

Ferrell, J. (2002). *Tearing Down the Streets*. New York: St. Martin's/Palgrave.

Ferrell, J. (2003). Speed kills, *Critical Criminology* 11(3): 185–198.

Ferrell, J. (2004). Boredom, crime and criminology, *Theoretical Criminology* 8(3): 287–302.

Ferrell, J. (2006). *Empire of Scrounge*. New York: New York University Press.

Ferrell, J. (2007a). Cultural criminology, in G. Ritzer (ed.), *The Blackwell Encyclopedia of Sociology*. New York: Blackwell, pp. 892–896.

Ferrell, J. (2007b). For a ruthless cultural criticism of everything existing, *Crime, Media, Culture* 3(1): 91–100.

Ferrell, J. (2009). Cultural criminology, in F. Cullen and P. Wilcox (eds), *Encyclopedia of Criminological Theory*. Thousand Oaks, CA: SAGE.

Ferrell, J., Hayward, K., Morrison, W. and Presdee, M. (eds) (2004). *Cultural Criminology Unleashed*. London: Glasshouse/Routledge.

Ferrell, J., Hayward, K. and Young, J. (2008). *Cultural criminology: An invitation*. London: SAGE.

Ferrell, J., Milovanovic, D. and Lyng, S. (2001). Edgework, media practices, and the elongation of meaning, *Theoretical Criminology* 5(2): 177–202.

Ferrell, J. and Sanders, C. (eds) (1995). *Cultural Criminology*. Boston: Northeastern University Press.

Feyerabend, P. (1975). *Against Method*. London: Verso.

Fuchs, S. (1986). The social organization of scientific knowledge, *Sociological Theory* 4(2): 126–142.

Garot, R. (2007). "Where You From!": Gang Identity as Performance, *Journal of Contemporary Ethnography* 36(1): 50–84.

Glick, L. (2005). *Criminology*. Boston: Pearson.

Hallsworth, S. and Young, T. (2008). Gang talk and gang talkers: a critique, *Crime, Media, Culture* 4(2): 175–195.

Hayward, K. (2004). *City Limits*. London: Routledge/Glasshouse.

Hayward, K. (2007). Situational crime prevention and its discontents, *Social Policy and Administration*, 41(3): 232–250.

Hayward, K. and Presdee, M. (eds) (2010). *Framing Crime: Cultural Criminology and the Image*. London: Routledge.

Hayward, K. and Young, J. (2007). Cultural criminology, in M. Maguire, R. Morgan and R. Reiner (eds), *The Oxford Handbook of Criminology*. Oxford: Oxford University Press.

Hugo, V. (1908 [1874]). *Ninety Three*. Boston: Dana Estes & Co.

Kane, S. (1998). Reversing the ethnographic gaze, in J. Ferrell and M. Hamm (eds), *Ethnography at the Edge*. Boston: Northeastern University Press, pp. 132–45.

Kane, S. (2004). The unconventional methods of cultural criminology, *Theoretical Criminology* 8(3): 303–321.

Katz, J. (1988). *Seductions of Crime*. New York: Basic Books.

Kubrin, C. (2008). Making order of disorder, *Criminology and Public Policy* 7(2): 203–214.

Lyng, S. (1990). Edgework, *American Journal of Sociology* 95(4): 851–886.

Lyng, S. (ed.) (2005). *Edgework*. New York: Routledge.

Marcus, G. (1989). *Lipstick Traces*. Cambridge, MA: Harvard University Press.

McGloin, J., Sullivan, C., Piquero, A. and Bacon, S. (2008). Investigating the stability of co-offending and co-offenders among a sample of youthful offenders, *Criminology* 46(1): 155–187.

Mears, D., Wang, X., Hay, C. and Bales, W. (2008). Social ecology and recidivism, *Criminology* 46(2): 301–339.

Merton, R. K. (1938). Social structure and anomie, *American Sociological Review* 3: 672–682.

Morrison, W. (1995). *Theoretical Criminology*, London: Cavendish.

Morrison, W. (2004). Lombroso and the birth of criminological positivism, in J Ferrell *et al.* (eds), *Cultural Criminology Unleashed*. London: GlassHouse, pp. 67–80.

Muncie, J. (2006). Positivism, in E. McLaughlin and J. Muncie (eds), *The SAGE Dictionary of Criminology*. London: SAGE, pp. 302–304.

O'Brien, M. (2005). What is *cultural* about cultural criminology? *British Journal of Criminology* 45: 599–612.

O'Neill, M. (2004). Crime, culture and visual methodologies, in J. Ferrell *et al.* (eds), *Cultural Criminology Unleashed*. London: GlassHouse, pp. 219–230.

Presdee, M. (2000). *Cultural Criminology and the Carnival of Crime*. London: Routledge.

Sandburg, C. (1970). *The Collected Poems of Carl Sandburg*. New York: Harcourt Brace Jovanovich.

Schmalleger, F. (2004). *Criminology Today*, 3rd ed. Upper Saddle River, NJ: Pearson.

Schur, E. (1971). *Labeling Deviant Behavior*. New York: Harper and Row.

Siegel, L. (2008). *Criminology: The Core*, third edition. Belmont, CA: Thompson.

Taylor, I., Walton, P. and Young, J. (1973). *The New Criminology*. New York: Harper and Row.

Webber, C. (2007). Background, foreground, foresight: The third dimension of cultural criminology?, *Crime, Media, Culture* 3(2): 139–157.

Weisburd, D. and Piquero, A. (2008). How well do criminologists explain crime? Statistical Modeling in Published Studies, *Crime and Justice* 37: 453–502.

Wender, J. (2004). Phenomenology, cultural criminology, and the return to astonishment, in J. Ferrell *et al.* (eds), *Cultural Criminology Unleashed*. London: GlassHouse/Routledge, pp. 49–60.

Wilson, J. and Kelling, G. (1982). Broken windows, *The Atlantic Monthly*, March, 29–38.

Young, J. (1999). *The Exclusive Society*. London: SAGE.

Young, J. (2003). Merton with energy, Katz with structure. *Theoretical Criminology* 7(3): 389–414.

Young, J. (2004). Voodoo Criminology and the Numbers Game, in J. Ferrell *et al.* (eds), *Cultural Criminology Unleashed*. London: Routledge/GlassHouse, pp. 13–27.

Young, J. (2007). *The Vertigo of Late Modernity*. London: SAGE.

17

Governmental Criminology

Pat O'Malley

The term 'governmental criminology' immediately conjures up rather jaundiced visions of the tame criminology developed, promulgated and often effected by government institutions such as the British Home Office. Here, however, it refers simply to a rather variable approach to criminology influenced by Foucault's work on governmentality and the work of social theorists who have elaborated this into an analytical framework. Its origins lie in the splash created when Foucault's *Discipline and Punish* (1977) was parachuted into a critical criminology dominated by Marxist and symbolic interactionist approaches. That it quickly had a major effect is hard to deny, although perhaps Stan Cohen was exaggerating when he argued that by 1985 'to write today about punishment and classification without Foucault, is like talking about the unconscious without Freud' (1985: 10). Like most new frameworks of thought, it was taken up in criminology in forms that were heavily and unevenly accented by the prevailing theoretical environment. Garland's (1985) *Punishment and Welfare*, and Melossi and Pavarini's (1981) *The Prison and the Factory* both deploy Foucault, but both end up broadly rejecting his approach.

Nevertheless, it offered an immediate challenge to the existing critical orthodoxies. The shock of this new approach may nowadays be hard to appreciate. In particular, official knowledges and practices in relation to the governance of crime were no longer to be regarded as illusory and distorting 'ideologies', indeed the term largely disappears. Class would be dissolved, race and – for a while – gender almost never mentioned, and power would be radically reformulated as the articulation of rationalities and techniques. Government would largely cease to be 'the state' and become something that states and many other agencies and subjectivities 'do'. The questions to be asked would no longer be about the truth concealed beneath the surface, but about the truth *at* the surface: the 'truths' that government regimes claim to speak. In the process, 'critique' would disappear, if by that we mean the theoretically guided revelation of truth and of the route to true freedom through theoretically guided government. In fact, both freedom and government would become problems rather than answers. Clearly, to the extent that such a Foucaultian criminology took hold, existing critical criminology would have to be rethought. It is this new criminological project, which took well over a decade to take definite shape, that I refer to as a governmental criminology – a criminology informed by a Foucaultian 'analytic of government'.

THE DISCOVERY OF DISCIPLINE

In 1977, Foucault's *Discipline and Punish: the Birth of the Prison*, appeared in English translation. Its focus was on discipline as a form of power: on the ways in which the body was worked upon to effect normalisation – the closure of a gap between the individual in question and a norm created as the proper or desired condition. In contrast to sovereignty, which worked erratically but spectacularly to illustrate to power of the sovereign command and the necessity of obedience, discipline worked through an economy of force. With as light a touch as possible discipline sought to create docile but 'free' subjects, whose learned self-discipline and self-reliance would make external intervention unnecessary. Class and capitalism were rarely mentioned as factors in discipline's move to being a central configuration of power (although they were given *a* role). Rather, its emergence was argued to be historically contingent, the effect of a genealogical convergence of ideas, interests, inventions, plans, architectures. In *Discipline and Punish*, no theory explained the rise of disciplinary power; not much interest was shown in any powerful interest that promoted it; and no functional necessity explained its position of dominance by the nineteenth century. Not surprisingly, this thesis met with very mixed reception in the critical criminological environment of the late seventies. I will consider two such leading responses in detail, one hostile, the other cautiously favourable.

A typical response from Marxist criminologists was the hostile critique provided by Dario Melossi in his 'Addendum' to the widely acclaimed *The Prison and the Factory* (Melossi and Pavarini, 1981). His principal objections were twofold. On the one hand, predictably, was 'the book's almost total disinterest (*sic*) in the relationship between discipline and the capitalist organisation of work'. In turn this was a problem because for Melossi 'the process of exploitation/accumulation … is at the core of the microphysics of power', that is, of discipline. Given that Foucault certainly did give the rise of capitalism some role in the promotion of discipline, Melossi's concern evidently was that Foucault did not place capital logic 'at the core' of discipline's form and ascendancy. In his view, Foucault misses the point that 'power works within determinate conditions of which it is itself a product' (1981: 192–194). Discipline in this view arises because of its role in creating and reproducing labour power. Melossi accepted grudgingly that 'perhaps' Foucault had usefully clarified and defined the form of power. But by failing to assert its underlying determinants in production relations, he was creating a political as well as theoretical error, merely adopting an anti-materialist position that had become 'a general discourse of our epoch' (Melossi, 1981: 193).

The second and related objection was that Foucault virtually ignored the question of resistance and especially class struggle. Foucault's focus on Jeremy Bentham's Panopticon is seen to reveal him as something of a 'map maker' (Melossi, 1981: 196).

By this Melossi meant that Foucault focuses only on the ideal plan of the panopticon, not on what actually occurred in the prison and the factory. Melossi argued that in failing to consider the impact of resistance and struggle, Foucault had merely provided a misleading and two-dimensional account that represented history as if plans were simply and straightforwardly realised. 'Draw a map' says Melossi but 'at least pose the question: what clashes of war, what struggles have left their mark on the paper, what forces keep changing and redrawing contours' (1981: 196). This criticism has proven remarkably durable, and late in the chapter I will return to consider its accuracy and value.[1]

If Melossi found *Discipline and Punish* unpalatable from a Marxist point of view, a rather different gloss was placed on things by Stan Cohen. Cohen had already established himself as possibly the most creative and least orthodox of the critical criminologists, retaining rather more of the interactionist legacy of that approach and never really embracing Marxist theory. It was probably easier, but not without difficulties, for him to accept much of the Foucaultian framework. As he expressed it himself:

> It is little wonder that theorizing about Foucault is so difficult … for many of his critics he is not at all a Marxist but the most extreme idealist imaginable. I will refrain from all such debate except to note here that what orthodox Marxists see as Foucault's greatest weakness – his conception of power as a 'thing' not reducible to the workings of labour and capital – is, for my purposes, his greatest strength. So I will use Foucault more or less uncritically, even though I am altogether unsympathetic to the intellectual climate in which his work flourishes and (being exactly the type of 'humanist' he is always attacking) totally opposed to his structuralist denial of human agency'.
>
> (Cohen 1985:10)

The passage is interesting for several reasons, not least being the common interpretation at the time that Foucault denied human agency as opposed to (as I would see it) not wishing to descend into the sterile squabbles over the structure-agency binary. It could instead be argued that Foucault gives an inordinate amount of space to human creativity, as his stress on the invention of the Panopticon suggests. Likewise, Cohen raises another sociological binary, that between idealism and materialism, from which Foucault was careful to distance himself and about which few critics would now be overly concerned. It was, then, very difficult to untangle oneself from the prevailing shibboleths of social theory, even for a criminologist of Cohen's independence of thought. Yet Cohen had detected exactly what was to appeal about Foucault. At this time, critical criminology was deeply concerned with the rise of 'community corrections', interpreting it in terms of the spreading tentacles of the expanding state (Abel, 1981), or conversely as a sign of 'decarceration', an economising retreat driven by the fiscal crisis of the state (Scull, 1978). It was a familiar, often contradictory, and always paranoid and pessimistic tale that by the 1980s was beginning to wear thin. For Cohen (1985: 8) in 'Foucault's extraordinary "archaeology" of deviancy control systems (w)e have here at last a vocabulary with which to comprehend recent changes'.

Still, it was not to be an easy escape from prevailing orthodoxies of critical criminology. Difficulties are illustrated in Cohen's own breakout, which had occurred with his pioneering and influential 1979 piece 'The Punitive City: Notes on the Dispersal of Social Control'. This began with a telling epigram from *Discipline and Punish*: 'This, then, is how one must imagine the punitive city. At the cross-roads, in the gardens, at the side of the roads being repaired or bridges built, in workshops open to all, in the depths of mines that may be visited, will be hundreds of tiny theatres of punishment' (Foucault quoted by Cohen 1979: 339). Foucault's shifting of attention from who was wielding power, and from the problematic of whose interests power was wielded in, allowed Cohen and others to move criminology toward understanding that the prison, indeed state itself, is not necessarily the principal target of critique. For Cohen, retaining the language of interactionism, this target was to become 'social control'. Yet in 'The Punitive City', and at more length in his already foreshadowed book *Visions of Social Control* (Cohen, 1985), social control appeared in two new lights.

First, while most criminologists' attention (then as now) had focused on the prison, Cohen's contribution was that he used the new vocabulary of discipline to make sense of the rise of community sanctions, community policing, and the 're-integrative' project that was already coming to his attention. If Foucault had written of the punitive city, Cohen argued, this had never been fully realised in practice, for discipline had been largely contained in institutional contexts such as the prison (Cohen, 1979: 359). What characterised the present era of 'community corrections' was the dispersal of discipline into what Marxists had termed 'civil society'.

Cohen pressed this further with his extraordinarily influential idea that the reach of justice was characterised by an 'expansion of the net and a thinning of the mesh' of social control. Critical criminologists were quite ready to accept this analysis which still gelled with traditional concerns with the domination of the powerful. But in another respect he was not so influential. The focus on power as technique freed analysis from the assumption that the task of a critical criminology was to reveal the 'real' politically repressive social interests and 'system' at work beneath the visible surface. Cohen introduced a surprising argument, in the context of current critical criminology. If power were a process or technique, rather than something possessed by groups, then we could not automatically assume that power was 'bad'. Now came the possibility that the agents of social control were not 'after all disguised paratroopers of the state', but 'might be able to deploy vastly improved opportunities and resources to offer help and service to groups, which desperately need them. These possibilities must not be ignored for a minute ...' (Cohen, 1979: 360). While Cohen's point was usually recognised, in many respects it remained the case that the rush to condemnation is the hallmark of critical criminology. Arguably this is still true even of what would become a 'governmental criminology': to detect positive possibilities and lines of flight in governmental practice (for example techniques of risk) still appears almost bad faith.

My focus on Cohen, and Melossi and Pavarini follows from their leading roles, but they are only exemplars of a much broader sea change that was beginning to take hold in the shadow of the discovery of discipline. Deploying the model of the Panopticon in analysis of the prison and of surveillance and control beyond the prison walls rapidly became a new orthodoxy of sorts in the mid to late eighties. Many criminological studies sought to identify the operations of discipline in the institutions of criminal justice. In practice it could often appear that the pervasive ethos of the old critical criminology had not been disrupted, but merely translated: if once class domination had been the devil in the machine revealed by theory, now discipline took its place. To reveal and delineate the contours of disciplinary power became almost an end in itself.

FROM DISCIPLINE TO A GOVERNMENTAL CRIMINOLOGY

In considerable degree, and despite some largely overlooked contributions that pointed elsewhere (Bottoms, 1983; Simon, 1987, 1988), critical criminology in the period up to the early 1990s basically understood Foucault's work in terms of *Discipline and Punish*. Thus while David Garland's (1991) overview of *Punishment and Modern Social Theory* registered the significance of Foucault's impact by assigning it two lengthy chapters, reference to Foucault's later and more sophisticated contributions with respect to security and governmentality, and to the interrelationships between discipline and other techniques of power, were peripheral and fragmentary. This is not a reflection on Garland, but more precisely is an index of the state of critical criminology at the time. All this was to change quite dramatically in the following year with the appearance of two papers – Feeley and Simon's "The New Penology" (1992) and O'Malley's (1992) "Risk, Power and Crime Prevention".

In his pioneering work on risk and governmentality in civil law and the risk society, Simon (1987, 1988) had argued that actuarial techniques were already displacing disciplinary governance. However, this development had largely escaped analytical attention partly because, as in insurance, they were already familiar. More importantly, he suggested, it was because actuarial techniques are unobtrusive. In Simon's view 'the unobtrusiveness is precisely why they have become so important; they make power more effective and efficient by diminishing moral and political fallout' (1988: 771). Simon argued that whereas disciplines focus on the bodies and 'souls' of individuals in institutions such as the prison, school or factory, actuarial practices usually operate on populations that are 'much less institutionally or spatially defined'. Instead of seeking to bring individuals closer to an established norm through the application of corrective interventions, actuarialism 'alters the physical and social structures within which individuals behave'. Examples of this range from the humble speed hump to more elaborate technologies such as electronic tagging and situational crime prevention. In its turn this 'increases the efficiency of power because changing people is difficult and expensive' (Simon, 1988: 773). In this sense, actuarialism continued the work of discipline but at lesser cost to power. 'It is cheaper to know and plan around people's failings than to normalise them' (Simon 1988: 774).

While actuarial technologies had clearly been in existence for well over a century, Simon suggested that their widespread application required the prior pacification of the 'dangerous classes' of the nineteenth century. This had been the task of the disciplines. Once the population has been rendered docile, and once it was no longer necessary to exploit labour intensively, then the more 'tolerant' but more 'efficient' actuarial practices could be substituted (1988: 744). Finally, following Ewald (1986) Simon suggested that actuarial practices have effects on subjectification. That is, actuarialism groups individuals together according to categories that do not derive from everyday life and experience, forming solidarities that are more politically passive than, say, traditional forms of worker solidarity (see also Defert, 1991; Ewald, 1991). The emergent subjectivities are thus more isolated and politically vulnerable because as identity with others diminishes, so do the possibilities or probabilities of collective resistance.

> For most of our history, power has negated resistance by the subjectivities it creates as a by-product in the very people on whom it is exercised. Without any formal suspension of political rights our institutions are becoming more immune from invoking political engagement. Actuarial practices are gradually forming a surface over our institutions and social policy arrangements that a make them nonconductive of political and moral charge.
>
> (Simon, 1988: 798)

There is much more of value in Simon's two pioneering papers from the 1980s, still largely overlooked by criminology. For the moment however, from the viewpoint of a governmental criminology a key concern is how these ideas were picked up and launched into the discipline four years later.

While the impact of Foucault had been widely registered in British, Australian and Canadian criminological work (Rose *et al.*, 2006), this was much less the case in the United States. Feeley and Simon's twin papers (1992, 1994) on the 'new penology' and 'actuarial justice' went some way to changing this. They argued that criminal justice developments since the 1970s were coalescing into a penology that was characterised by three features. First was a shift away from therapeutic and retributive discourses toward risk-based talk of probabilities and distributions. Second, these new discourses were linked to changes in techniques that included abandoning the old principles of proportionality between offence and sentence and inserting a new rationale of sentencing according to the risk that offenders represent. These techniques no longer attempted to understand individuals' pathologies, motivations and so on, but were concerned only with behaviours. The new actuarial justice aimed at classifying and incapacitating high risk offenders through either prison warehousing or newly merging techniques such as electronic monitoring and house arrest. Third, in line with this, a new form of managerialism entered official discourse. The old social science discourses linked to corrections were being replaced by systems analysis. 'Success' was no longer measured in terms of low rates of recidivism and implied rates of reform. Recidivism merely indicated that the high-risk offenders had been correctly identified, that the parole system had returned them efficiently, and that incapacitation had 'worked' because it had removed these ongoing risks from society. In a way, the problem was that they had to be released. It followed that longer periods of incarceration were justifiable in the name of public safety. What had emerged was understood as a 'pure risk' approach, because it emphasised neither reform, punishment or deterrence. It was concerned only with risk reduction.

In turn, Feeley and Simon began to piece together a genealogy of this actuarial justice. At the broadest level, following Foucault, they regarded this as part of a move toward governmentality, in which 'the population itself, in its biological and demographic sense is taken as the target of power' (1994: 177). Security, with its insurantial techniques and focus on population distributions was becoming central to governance. Within the field of justice, they linked this trend to shifts in tort law – toward its reliance on no-fault, strict liability and insurance models. To this they added influences from the development of the law and economics movement, with its utilitarian and quantitative reframing of criminal justice. This undermined the morally and individually focused traditions, as also did the related influence of systems and operations research as pervasive frameworks in managerial practice. In all of this, Feeley and Simon moved analysis away from any simple vision of determination by nebulous 'powerful interests' or requirements of a productive order, toward a contingent genealogical focus. But this did not mean, as Cohen might have objected, an 'idealist' focus, for they equally suggested that a key factor in this genealogy had been the development of an 'underclass'. Largely Black and Hispanic, this class had been rendered surplus by changes in the economy, particularly the export of much heavy industry to the Third World. Actuarial justice reflected the abandonment of the welfare ethos that all members of society were recoverable. The new rationality abandoned the project of 'penal modernism', for in its vision there was nothing left in economy and society into which these people could be reintegrated.

The papers on 'new penology' and 'actuarial justice' had an enormous impact, especially but not only in the United States. Feeley and Simon had been careful to stress that this was not an epochal change – that it was just one trend in justice. Indeed, they pointed specifically to factors that limited its reach (Simon and Feeley, 1995). But in the way of things, for many critical criminologists actuarial justice became the new touchstone. A hunt for actuarial justice was set up, and of course found it in many contexts making actuarial justice into something Feeley and Simon never intended to suggest it was – a new 'hegemonic' formation (e.g., Kempf-Leonard and Peterson, 2000; Miller, 2001).

Almost at the same moment that the new penology hit the US criminological newsstands, 'Risk, power and crime prevention' (O'Malley, 1992) appeared in the British theoretical journal *Economy and Society* – at that time the theoretical test-bed for governmentality studies. While (like Simon) relying extensively on Foucault's writings on governmentality, O'Malley's work was more explicitly influenced by the 'Anglo-Foucaultian' approach that was being developed by Nikolas Rose, Colin Gordon, Graeme Burchell and others (Burchell *et al.*, 1991; Gordon, 1991; Miller and O'Leary, 1987; Miller and Rose, 1988, 1990). Such work had begun to map out a more explicit analytical schema that reframed 'power' as 'government'. Government was understood as the articulation of political rationalities with the technologies they deployed in order to resolve problems. Rationalities are the more or less schematic theories or 'imaginaries' of society which map out the nature of problems, how they are to be identified, what their causes are, what kinds of subjects are involved and what the ideal outcome of intervention would be.

Miller and Rose (1990) had argued that it was precisely this articulation of rationalities and technologies that transformed discourse into government: government sought to change the world, not just think about it. In turn because government rationalities and techniques are closely integrated, they suggested it would be difficult to evaluate programs of government in terms whether they 'worked'. Because governmental rationalities set up different desired outcomes, and envisaged the world in such diverse ways, it was usually difficult or impossible to find a criterion upon which 'success' could be judged *between* rationalities. Hence, rising crime rates could register 'failure' for one rationality because they indicate more crime is occurring, or 'success' for another rationality because rates indicate the greater

willingness of the public to report crime and the greater efficiency of police in dealing with it. Given this, O'Malley (1992) argued, it could not simply be that where
actuarialism was displacing discipline, it was because of its demonstrable success or
efficiency as Simon had argued. Rather, the shift from one technology to another
suggested that, in a way reminiscent of a Kuhnian paradigm shift, one vision of 'the
problem' of crime was being replaced by another – in turn changing the nature of
crime control techniques used, and providing new criteria of success or failure.

For 'Risk, power and crime prevention' (O'Malley, 1992) the answer to this
conundrum came in a recognition that it was not that risk was new, but that its
configuration was changing. Risk technologies had been central to the welfare
state – particularly social insurance. But these were not the risk technologies being
promoted by the 1980s and 1990s. Quite to the contrary, these 'social' risk technologies were under assault. It was argued that we were witnessing the emergence of a
newly ascendant technology of risk linked to political rationalities hostile to the
welfare state: neo-liberalism. Whereas welfare liberalism had regarded problems of
government as requiring intervention at the 'social level' neo-liberals emphasised the
need to restore individuals to the centre. Social governance and social technologies
of risk management were regarded by neo-liberals as creating a dependent population that had lost its enterprise. Neo-liberalism therefore generated a 'new
prudentialism' in which risk management increasingly became a private sector
responsibility, and particularly a responsibility of individuals. This approach to risk
also reflected neo-liberals' emphasis on business principles, foregrounding prevention rather than moral retribution after the event (O'Malley, 1992).

The ascendancy of crime prevention in crime control politics could thus be understood in political terms rather than in terms of the relative efficiency of power.
Consequently, what was being promoted politically was not the traditional crime
prevention focusing on relative deprivation and linked to sociological criminology.
Neo-liberals rejected this as another 'social' response that weakened individual
responsibility. Instead, contractual 'partnerships' and 'contracts' between communities and police were promoted, such as Neighbourhood Watch, and private security
was fostered. Individuals were to be 'empowered': educated about crime risks and
how to minimise them. In the process reliance on the state supposedly diminished
and responsibility for crime victimisation shifted toward individuals. This 'responsibilisation' of individuals was likewise linked to a change in the theory of penology.
In place of sociological explanations of crime, the business and insurance model of
the rational choice actor were favoured. In this imaginary, offenders appeared as
responsible for their actions and deserving of punishment. In turn, correctionalism
would be evacuated from prisons both because in business cost–benefit terms it had
'failed', and because this perpetuated the disabling mythology that individuals were
victims of social circumstance. Finally, victims, as the 'customers' of crime control,
would be valorised. Some of the burden of risk would be shifted from their shoulders, and offenders would bear the burden instead, in the form of longer sentences
that would punish, deter and incapacitate.

In this way, the emergence of a new political rationality, with its particular vision
of the world and its problems, began a process of assembling new ways of understanding and talking about crime. Novel techniques and routines were created or
adapted for managing it. Subjectivities were invented and borrowed, subjects who

perform, suffer and resist crime. Even new architectures and streetscapes, new devices and new knowledges were mobilised to put it into effect. To talk of whether this 'imaginary' of crime was 'real' or not was thus seen to be slightly to one side of things in governmental criminology. The plan was empirically real enough, and an ascendant governmental rationality attempted to make its elements real in practice, while its opponents attempted to prevent and deny this. No matter whether governmental criminologists liked any of these developments – and clearly none of the above commentators much liked what was happening – a governmental criminology had no business imposing its own reality: for it could claim no privileged access to the truth that allowed it to determine what was 'in fact' right. This would prove frustrating to many who looked to criminology to arbitrate and establish a political program.

GOVERNING CRIME AT THE *FIN DE SIECLE*

The growing importance of governmentality in social theory, and the impact of governmental studies of neo-liberalism and of risk in governance, meant that the latter part of the 1990s was one of considerable development and elaboration in governmental criminology. Risk was to prove one of the more active areas of such growth, owing much to the landmark publication of Ericson and Haggerty's (1997) *Policing the Risk Society*. There had been a number of governmental analyses of police in the period leading up to this (e.g., O'Malley and Palmer, 1996; Stenson, 1993), but by and large these worked over threads that were familiar with respect to risk and to neo-liberalism. *Policing the Risk Society*, however, was iconoclastic, attempting to merge the governmental approach with the 'risk society' thesis of Ulrich Beck (1992). Beck's thesis could be seen as almost diametrically opposed to the tenets of governmentality, for it put forward a quasi-Marxist theory in which the alliance of capital and science was producing catastrophic global risks, which in turn created a mass 'risk consciousness'. This risk consciousness was said to generate both a heightened sense of insecurity, as more risks were identified, and a popular demand for increased guarantees of security.

Ericson and Haggerty's analysis began from this *sociological* foundation. Rather than being focused upon governmental maps or imaginaries, Beck's thesis presents itself as a sociological account of the world, linking a social theory to an empirical account of consciousness and action among the population. As would be becoming clear, governmentality distanced itself from such 'grand' theory, from the epochal model implied by the 'risk society', and from empirical sociologies – focusing instead on what Melossi contemptuously described as 'maps'. Undeterred, Ericson and Haggerty carried out a sociological fieldwork analysis of how policing was performed in the risk regime. Explicitly regarding this as a governmental analysis, they brought to the fore such things as the ways in which risk-based incident forms compelled police to record offences in terms of risk and security, the ways in which car-mounted computers regulated police movements and so on. These developments, particularly the incident report forms, in turn, were argued to be shaped by the governmental rationality of the insurance industry with its concerns for security and its insatiable need for risk-based information. In the process, crime was shown to be governmentally recoded as risk. In short, Ericson and Haggerty saw themselves as providing a governmentality 'in action' – the enacting of the techniques, imaginaries, discourses, subjectivities and so on. While all aspects of this was not necessarily accepted by others (e.g., O'Malley, 1999a), it nevertheless demonstrated that a governmental criminology could be treated (in Foucault's famous phrase) as part of a 'toolbox' for investigation. Governmental criminology already was beginning to be articulated with rather different approaches that supplied analysts with what its earlier exponents couldn't or wouldn't do.

At the same time, the approach was proving attractive to various feminist criminologists (Hannah-Moffatt, 1999, 2001; Merry, 1999; Valverde, 1998). Hannah-Moffatt's work has been particularly influential in this respect, taking as her focus women's imprisonment. Following the Foucaultian view of power as productive rather than merely negative (cf. Cohen 1985), she examined the governmental rationalities associated with a Canadian attempt to create 'woman-centred' prisons that would be more responsive to women's needs and concerns. As she is at pains to point out, these programs emerge not just from state sources, but in significant ways from blueprints that 'adhered unequivocally to a feminist philosophy' (Hannah-Moffatt, 2001: 143). As Lorna Weir (1996) had pointed out before her, programs of government have to be regarded not simply as, for example, 'neo-liberal' or 'feminist', as if these are antithetical and incapable of being assembled together. Rather, rationalities are multivocal. That is, the genealogical form of analysis takes into account the ways in which unexpected convergences and unanticipated hybrids are assembled together and 'rationalised'. Specific programs should be understood as such complex formations. In this way, there is a movement away from what David Garland (1997) has pointed to as an 'ideal typical' tendency in governmental criminology: a tendency to regard models of government rationalities as expressing an integrated logical form. At the same time, Hannah-Moffatt suggests that this is a key process whereby government programs take on their own life and produce unanticipated consequences. For example, how it could be that a program informed by 'progressive' agendas, one that set out to provide women with 'empowerment', 'choice' and 'healing', could generate institutions that 'inflict their own type of pain' (2001: 189)?. She suggests while the 'feminized' prison is less repressive than its predecessors, 'the darker side of the institutionalization of women's concerns is the unanticipated redefining of women's issues to make them compatible with the existing institutional arrangements of incarceration.' (Hannah-Moffatt, 2001: 161). For example, the treatment of low self esteem was held to reaffirm women-centredness, particularly women's shared disempowerment and marginalisation. However, in the penal context a 'critical feminist criminology of the self' was translated into a prudential prisoner who can 'take responsibility' for her criminal behaviour, for managing her own needs and minimising risks to others (Hannah-Moffatt, 2001: 171–172). In turn, women who refuse this 'empowerment', or are unable to comply, are defined as uncooperative, defiant and more at risk.

CRITICISMS AND ADVANCES

This work suggests that while it had been the case that criticism was relatively muted in governmental criminology (O'Malley *et al.*, 1997), its articulation with a feminist analytic generates an approach that creates critical possibilities without at the same time assuming an independent and privileged access to truth. Instead, the critical potential emerges from what Burchell (1993) refers to as diagnosis. Rather than resorting to revelation of the truth through theory, there is a reading of what are termed 'the costs to existence' of being governed in certain ways. Reading from Hannah-Moffatt's work, it is not that an underlying truth is revealed by theoretically recasting what is happening, finding the concealed interests beneath the surface, or searching the discourses for contradictions. It is the exposition of the rationales of government that makes clear which forms of subjectification are created and envisaged, what techniques and routines these mobilise, and thus what forms of existence the women-centred prison seeks to deliver. In a sense, the analytical truth remains that truth claimed by the rationality under examination, and by taking this seriously – or at least allowing a willing suspension of disbelief – its implications are made visible through the analytical grid that governmental criminology provides.

In such examples I suggest that the governmental analytic does not itself provide the frame of reference in terms of which to evaluate this penal assemblage. If, as suggested above, this is because evaluation is an approach internal to government (Miller and Rose, 1990); then it could be argued that ethical evaluation must therefore be provided from outside the framework. This would follow because the analytic itself is only an attempt to render government intelligible in its own terms. The evaluation in Hannah-Moffatt's case, by implication, comes from a feminist problematic. However, it is not clear that such a process of articulation between governmental criminology and a 'critical' approach such as feminism, is necessary to the production of what could be termed a *critical governmentality*. It is not difficult to point to examples of governmental criminology in which critical arguments are made apparently from within the governmental analytic. For example, in his study of crime prevention in New Zealand, Pavlich (1999: 125) has pointed to a series of 'dangers':

> It is difficult to see how the neo-liberal reliance on enterprising, prudential and egotistic selves can be reconciled with their postulated altruism in technically engineered and managed 'communities'. This is especially the case in regulatory environments that nurture parochialism of exclusion rather than compassion and reconciliation, and which rely upon entrepreneurial self interests for their very operations. In all this one may legitimately ponder the plight of justice.

Perhaps we could engage in an exercise of dissecting Pavlich's arguments in order to detect some point at which an 'outside' framework of criticism has been inserted into a governmental analytic – for example via the terms 'compassion' and 'reconciliation' – although what end this would serve is not immediately clear. The alternative seems to be the essentialising of the approach by claiming that only instances where such analysis has not been linked to criticism are to be taken as 'correct'. It could be argued less obsessively that governmental analytic is capable of taking on a diversity of forms, as has been seen already, and that no-one can legislate how it must be performed and what it must or must not be articulated with. In any case, criminologists will and should use it as they see fit. In such future innovative and iconoclastic usage, rather than in the endless refinement and ossifying of its technique, is doubtlessly to be found the best measure of its contribution to the discipline.

Indeed, the articulation of a governmental analytic to other approaches does seem to answer a number of other criticisms that have been levelled against it. Garland (1997: 185), for example, complained that while governmental analytics mapped out the assumptions and problematics of the governing agencies, 'alongside this knowledge of the authorities' knowledge I also want to be able to propose a different reading of what causes crime, why controls are failing, and why penal-welfare measures no longer seem adequate.' Probably most advocates of governmental criminology would wonder what there is in the approach that would prevent this. After all, governmentality does not pretend to offer any kind of analysis of crime, only of its governance. There is no obvious reason why a sociological analysis cannot be articulated with a governmental criminology in the way Garland proposes. Garland's (2001) own work provides an example of exactly this project in his *Culture of Control*. There, frequent resort to governmental analysis (e.g., 2001: 117–131) is linked to analyses of why penal-welfare programs do not seem adequate (2001: 77–116).[2]

Much the same point could be raised with respect to Melossi's now standard criticism that a governmental criminology refuses to look at the implementation of policies. There are certainly some statements to the effect that this is not a concern of governmental analysis (Barry *et al.*, 1996; Miller and Rose, 1990). But it is not clear how to interpret this. In my reading, the concern of such commentators was that governmental analysis should not become an empiricist sociology of the sort that does nothing other than map failures to implement, at least if the sole purpose is to map out the current state of affairs in some institutional context. As Miller and Rose (1990) accept from the outset, governmental programs routinely fail to be implemented as planned, so this would not be an insight alien to the approach. I would stress that, in any case, there is no problem with articulating a governmental analysis of the program and a sociological analysis of implementation in this way, and some excellent examples exist. (e.g., Kemshall, 1998; Kemshall and Maguire, 2001).

Perhaps Melossi's concern, and the concern of similar critics, is based on an assumption that a governmental analysis *necessarily* should examine plan and implementation: that somehow the analysis of the plan alone is incomplete analysis. Certainly this fits with the passages from his critique cited earlier in this paper. But this criticism misapprehends the purpose of Foucault's original analysis, which was about a technology and a telos of government that would have been taken up and translated in many different ways in many different contexts. We could take this for granted without having to study a multitude of examples, which in any case would reveal (as with sociology in general) that in different contexts different specific patterns emerge. The concern of writers such as Barry and his colleagues (Barry *et al.*, 1996), I suspect, was that such analysis takes us away from the identification of the general framework of this kind of 'power', not that such analysis is invalid or even useless in itself. Indeed, as Miller and Rose were at pains to argue, in one of the governmental analytic's formative papers:

> unplanned outcomes emerge from the intersection of one technology with another, or from the unexpected consequences of putting a technique to work. Contrariwise, techniques invented for one purpose may find their governmental role for another, and the unplanned conjunction of techniques and conditions arising from very different aspirations may allow something to work without or despite its explicit rationale.
>
> (1990: 11)

This is, of course, nothing other than genealogical analysis focused in the govern-mental domain, but it makes clear that a governmental criminology cannot and does not deny the importance of the kind of work Melossi favours. Rose (1998) himself has tracked the ways in which psychiatrists resisted the introduction of risk sched-ules and in the process created a new non-numerate register of risk, a new technology. Thus while Castel (1991) had argued that risk would lead to the subordination of clinical to actuarial knowledge, Rose found that there is rarely a comparison of patients' risk scores to statistical tables in order to generate probabilistic predictions.

> Rather it entails calculating the consequences of a concatenation of indicators or factors co-occurring in certain regular patterns. Even if clinical diagnosis has become probabilistic and factoral, however, it is seldom numerical ... mental health professionals tend to resist the use of numerical risk assessment schedules and classifications. They stress that assess-ment of risk is a clinical matter, and has to take place within a clinical assessment of mental disorder ...
>
> (Rose, 1998: 196–197)

More significantly, Feeley and Simon (1994) deployed exactly this approach in developing their work on actuarial justice. In examining the impact of this govern-ment program, they were forced to ask the question of why the success of the 'new penology' among criminal justice specialists had not been followed by a commensu-rate influence on public discourse. Broadly speaking, they argued that the new penology failed in this respect because its cool, risk-based, systems-analysis approach did not take account of public discourse and the 'irrational' demand for punishment and retribution. This answer would have warmed the hearts of critics such as Garland (1991) who decried the failure of governmentality to recognise the emotive side of the reaction to crime. Fortunately the story does not end here.

Feeley and Simon's point in carrying through their analysis of implementation was succinctly put: 'we are writing a history of the present. Our aim is not to describe a completed historical change' (1995: 149). It is highly significant therefore that Simon (1998, 2001) went on to analyse the rise of new techniques for governing crime through risk, risk techniques that *did* embrace this 'missing' emotive response. In such developments as Megan's Laws, he argues, the 'technical' and dispassionate character of risk techniques was assembled together with elements that were consist-ent with a 'politics of vengeance' that had been salient in public discourses. In a nutshell, if it were ever the case that governmentality ignored 'resistance', or did not take cognisance of emotive aspects of crime, this blind spot has been overcome. More than this, such work reveals that – as Durkheim would doubtlessly have rec-ognised – there is no discontinuity between governance and the irrational (see also Pratt, 2000a, b). Simply because there is a focus on the technologies of power – which Simon continues to embrace – this does not mean that such technologies may not incorporate, even mobilise, appeals and responses to the emotions. Simon (1998) makes this point explicitly when he refers to the processes of incapacitation and community notification in Megan's laws and the like as 'managing the monstrous'. In the 'monstrous', a new feared and hated subjectivity is created (or borrowed) and assembled together into a governmental problematic that makes such techniques as community notification justifiable and plausible 'solutions'.

Indeed, Garland (1996) himself sowed the seeds in this respect, when creating his distinction between 'criminologies of the self' and 'criminologies of the other'. On the one side, is a governmental imaginary in which crimes are normal, capable of being committed by anyone – in the subjectivity of the rational choice offender. As such, these criminologies of the self are linked with government techniques that incorporate offenders – for example through 'enterprising prisoner' schemes that seek to give self-governing responsibilities to inmates (Garland, 1997). On the other side are those 'criminologies of the other' that constitute offenders as outside the realm of normality, offending subjects that government cannot tolerate and that must be met with repression, incapacitation and denunciation. Moreover, as O'Malley argued (1999b) such criminologies and the technologies to which they are linked, can be aligned in the present era with broader political rationalities. Criminologies of the self meld with neo-liberalism and its rational choice offender and cost–benefit analysis of programs, while criminologies of the other resonate with neo-conservatism and its moral crusade – the two forming an uneasy alliance in New Right regimes.

In this way, a governmental criminology is brought back to an interest in ongoing politics as struggle and genealogy that it may on occasions forget. Here, the arguably too-monolithic and encompassing rationality of neo-liberalism has to be analytically reconsidered, decomposed into components that are in tension, alliances that are fragile, penologies that are 'volatile and contradictory' (O'Malley, 1999b). It had probably become the case that the construct of neo-liberalism presented a too-convenient, and too internally consistent an anchor to which could be moored many techniques, subjectivities, discourses and so on.[3] Perhaps its fragmentation is an important step in moving toward a politics in which governmental criminology may play an active role.

A GOVERNMENTAL POLITICS OF CRIME?

For reasons suggested already, a governmental criminology fits most uncomfortably with a programmatic politics, a politics with a clear program driven by a 'liberating' theory. Too often these theories and programs have become just another layer of domination. Part of the difficulty facing a governmental criminology, therefore, appears to be that it can only generate a politics from the sidelines rather than one that is engaged in *constructing* something 'better'. A decade ago, voices were raised from within governmentality that complained about its tendency to abandon political engagement, of the sort associated with Foucault himself. Instead it was seen to favour an overly abstracted and academic approach, linked to its emphasis on politics as mentalities of rule – with a concomitant weakening of emphasis on, and an engagement with, conflict and contestation. To some degree, as this chapter has indicated, aspects of this criticism have been overcome. It is clear that the ongoing struggles around the formation and implementation of political programs have been built into the approach. But probably the most influential and considered call was that while this should not lead to a programmatic politics, for which academics probably are ill-suited in any case, it should form a knowledge that will assist social contestation. (O'Malley *et al.*, 1997: 512). Such a modest goal takes its direction from

Foucault's own emphasis on an agonistic politics, a politics that maximises contestation and thus a politics that seeks to minimise domination (Foucault, 1982).

Arguably, in this respect, there has been remarkably little progress. Despite the fact that the central call for such work – by O'Malley, Weir and Shearing (O'Malley *et al.*, 1997) – is almost routinely cited in critical assessments, its message has been honoured primarily in the breach. O'Malley (2000) has indicated directions that can be taken with respect to risk and criminal justice, most specifically by challenging the expert-dominated definition of risks, and pointing to ways in which risk can be democratised. This would include forming consultative bodies drawing together drug users, householders, emergency workers, health agencies and so on. While it has to be said that it is not clear how far such moves take us far past the neo-liberal strategy of a stakeholder politics there has been little or no response to this intervention in the governmental literature. By far the most significant contribution has been from another sympathetic critic, Clifford Shearing. Following broadly similar 'democratising' lines, Shearing has experimented with models loosely based on restorative justice. For example, in South African townships, the definition and practice of security has been passed to local Peace Committees, bound only by certain procedural rules such as proscribing exclusion. Here, the expectation is that contestation will arise, and a diversity of views aired, simply because various subjects will appear at various times as complainants and defendants (Shearing and Brogden, 1993; Shearing and Johnston, 2006). There are clearly similar dangers here to those voiced in relation to restorative justice. However debate and development on Shearing's very high profile experiments, from within the governmentality literature, likewise has been minimal.

This is not encouraging. Even a strongly critical response to such initiatives might generate a debate within governmental criminology that would lead to further experimentation or, at worst, a clear exposition of why such forms of political engagement are beyond the approach or inconsistent with its tenets. Is this silence a freezing of political will and engagement brought on by the approach's mode of analysis, is it a politically wise refusal, or is it just another accident of history that can be changed? I think and hope it is the last of these, but perhaps in the last instance it doesn't matter so very much. If it is an analytical approach, then it can be deployed without a project of its own. It has already had its impact on other 'criminologies' such as feminist analysis, and the burgeoning surveillance literature that bundles it in with Deleuze, Baudrillard and others, and as David Garland's work exemplifies, it has had a substantial impact on that fairly encompassing but dynamic school of thought that still goes under the title 'critical criminology'. A 'governmental criminology' may thus have run its course as a distinct entity and in a suitably genealogical way be morphing into other, as yet nameless, criminologies.

NOTES

1 For other examples of this criticism, see for instance Garland (1991: 170–173) and Frankel (1997).

2 Indeed, it could probably be argued that *Culture of Control* exhibits close parallels with *Discipline and* Punish which likewise mobilises questions of governmental genealogy and historical interpretation – for example in its discussion of why sovereign responses began to be seen as

inadequate in the face of rising protests from the populace at the end of the eighteenth century. It could be argued, in this light, that Garland has provided a genealogy of the current crime control scene which is itself in almost all respects compatible with a governmental criminology. Thus when he refers to the 'culture' of control, it appears to be a governmental rationality of control, as seems clear in the following summation: 'The new culture of crime control has formed around three central elements: (a) a recoded penal-welfarism; (b) a criminology of control; (c) an economic style of reasoning. (Garland 2001: 175). Virtually all, if not indeed all, of the last chapter of this book could be read as a governmentality of current crime control. A sociology of this topic, on the other hand, would have raised such critical features as the impact of the War on Drugs on changing imprisonment patterns and sentencing assumptions, and even more so, the impact of a racialised economy. Neither is given *any* attention in the book, for which omission I suspect any self confessed governmental criminologist would have been subjected to lacerating critique.

3 It has to be noted that while this criticism is vital, my own work has done much to create its target.

REFERENCES

Abel, R. (1981) The political economy of informal justice, in R. Abel (ed.), *The Politics of Informal Justice*, Vol 1. New York: Academic Press, pp. 1–52.

Barry, A., Osborne, T. and Rose, N. (1993) Liberalism, neo-liberalism and governmentality: an introduction, *Economy and Society* 22: 265–266.

Beck, U. (1992) *Risk Society: Toward a New Modernity*. New York: Sage.

Bottoms, A. (1983) Neglected features of contemporary penal systems, in D. Garland and P. Young (eds) *The Power to Punish*. London: Heinemann, pp. 166–202.

Burchell, G., Gordon, C. *et al.* (1991) *The Foucault Effect. Studies in Governmentality*. London: Harvester/Wheatsheaf.

Castel, B. (1991) From dangerousness to risk, in G. Burchell, C. Gordon and P. Miller (eds), *The Foucault Effect. Studies in Governmentality*, London: Harvester/Wheatsheaf, pp. 281–298.

Cohen, S. (1979) 'The Punitive City: Notes on the Dispersal of Social Control', *Contemporary Crises,* 3: 339–363.

Defert, D. (1991) Popular life and insurance technology, in G. Burchell, C. Gordon and P. Miller (eds), *Foucault Effect, Studies in Governmentality*, London: Harvester Press, pp. 211–234.

Donzelot, J. (1979) The poverty of political culture, *Ideology and Consciousness*, 5: 71–86.

Ericson, R. and Haggerty, K. (1997) *Policing the Risk Society*. Toronto: University of Toronto Press.

Ewald, F. (1986) *L'Etat Providence*. Paris: Grasset et Fasquelle.

Ewald, F. (1991) Insurance and risk, in G. Burchell, C. Gordon and P. Miller (eds), *The Foucault Effect. Studies in Governmentality*, London: Harvester/Wheatsheaf, pp. 197–210.

Feeley, M. and Simon, J. (1992) The new penology: notes on the emerging strategy of corrections and its implications, *Criminology,* 30: 449–474.

Feeley, M. and Simon, J. (1994) 'Actuarial justice: the emerging new criminal law, in D. Nelken (ed.), *The Futures of Criminology*. New York: Sage, pp. 173–201.

Foucault, M. (1977) *Discipline and Punish*. London: Peregrine Books.

Foucault, M. (1979, 1984) *The History of Sexuality* (volume 1). London: Peregrine Books.

Foucault, M. (1978, 1991) Governmentality, in G. Burchell, C. Gordon and P. Miller (eds), *The Foucault Effect, Studies in Governmentality*, London: Harvester/Wheatsheaf, pp. 87–104.

Foucault, M. (1982) The subject and power, in H. Dreyfus and P. Rabinow (eds), *Michel Foucault. Beyond Structuralism and Hermeneutics* (pp. 208–226). Chicago: Chicago University Press.

Frankel, B. (1997) Confronting neoliberal regimes. The post-Marxist embrace of populism and realpolitik. *New Left Review,* 226: 57–92.

Garland, D. (1985) *Punishment and Welfare*. London: Ashgate.

Garland, D. (1991) *Punishment and Modern Society*. Oxford: Clarenson.

Garland, D. (1996) The limits of the sovereign state: strategies of crime control in contemporary society, *British Journal of Criminology*, 36: 445–471.

Garland, D. (1997) Governmentality and the problem of crime, *Theoretical Criminology*, 1: 173–214.

Garland, D. (2001) *The Culture of Control*. Oxford: Oxford University Press.

Gordon, C. (1991) Governmental rationality: an introduction, in G. Burchell, C. Gordon and P. Miller (eds), *The Foucault Effect. Studies in Governmentality*, Chicago: Chicago University Press, pp. 1–53.

Hannah-Moffatt, K. (1999) Moral agent or actuarial subject. Risk and Canadian women's imprisonment, *Theoretical Criminology*, 3: 71–95.

Hannah-Moffatt, K. (2001) *Punishment in Disguise. Penal Governance and Canadian Women's Imprisonment*. Toronto: University of Toronto Press.

Kempf-Leonard, K. and Peterson, E. (2000) Expanding realms of the new penology. The advent of actuarial justice for juveniles, *Punishment and Society*, 2: 66–96.

Kemshall, H. (1998) *Risk in Probation Practice*, Aldershot: Dartmouth.

Kemshall, H. and Maguire, M. (2001) Public protection, 'partnership' and risk penality, *Punishment and Society* 3: 237–254.

Melossi, D. (1981) Addendum, in D. Melossi and M. Pavariani (eds), *The Prison and the Factory. Origins of the Penitentiary System*. London: MacMillan, pp. 189–196.

Melossi, D. and Pavariani, M. (1981) *The Prison and the Factory. Origins of the Penitentiary System*. London: MacMillan, pp. 189–196.

Merry, S. (1999) Criminalization and gender. The changing governance of sexuality and gender violence. In R. Smandych (ed.), *Governable Places. Readings on Governmentality and Crime Control*. Aldershot: Dartmouth, pp. 75–102.

Miller, L. (2001) Looking for postmodernism in all the wrong places. Implementing a new penology, *British Journal of Criminology*, 41: 168–184.

Miller, P. and O'Leary, T. (1987) Accounting and the construction of the governable person, *Accounting, Organization and Society*, 12: 235–265.

Miller, P. and Rose, N. (1988). The Tavistock program – the government of subjectivity and social life, *Sociology*, 22: 171–192.

Miller, P. and Rose, N. (1990) Governing economic life, *Economy and Society*, 19: 1–31.

O'Malley, P. (1992) Risk, power and crime prevention, *Economy and Society*, 21: 252–275.

O'Malley, P. (1999a) Governmentality and the risk society, *Economy and Society*, 28: 138–148.

O'Malley, P. (1999b) Volatile and contradictory punishment, *Theoretical Criminology*, 3: 175–196.

O'Malley, P. (2000) Genealogy, rationalisation and resistance in 'Advanced Liberalism', In G. Pavlich and G. Wickham (eds), *Rethinking Law, Society and Governance: Foucault's Bequest*. Oxford: Hart, pp. 38–62.

O'Malley, P. and Palmer, D. (1996) Post-Keynesian policing, *Economy and Society*, 25: 137–155.

O'Malley, P., Weir, L. and Shearing, C. (1997) Governmentality, criticism, politics, *Economy and Society*, 26: 501–517.

Pavlich, G. (1999) Preventing crime. Social versus community governance in Aotearoa/New Zealand, in R. Smandych (ed.), *Governable Places. Readings on Governmentality and Crime Control*. Aldershot: Dartmouth, pp. 102–132.

Pratt, J. (2000a) Emotive and ostentatious punishment. Its decline and resurgence in modern society, *Punishment and Society*, 2: 417–441.

Pratt, J. (2000b) The return of the Wheelbarrow Man. Or the arrival of postmodern penality. *British Journal of Criminology*, 40: 127–145.

Rose, N. (1998) Governing risky individuals: The role of psychiatry in new regimes of control, *Psychiatry, Psychology and Law*, 5: 177–195.

Rose, N., O'Malley, P. and Valverde, M. (2006) Governmentality, *Annual Review of Law and Social Science*, 2: 83–104.

Scull, A. (1978) *Decarceration*. New York: Prentice-Hall.

Shearing, C. and Brogden, M. (1993) *Policing for a New South Africa*. London: Routledge.

Shearing, C. and Johnston, L. (2006) *Governing Security. Explorations in Policing and Justice.* London: Routledge.

Simon, J. (1987) The emergence of a risk society: insurance, law, and the state, *Socialist Review*, 95: 61–89.

Simon, J. (1988) The ideological effects of actuarial practices, *Law and Society Review*, 22: 771–800.

Simon, J. (1997) Governing through crime, in Friedman, L. and Fisher, G. (eds), *The Crime Conundrum. Essays in Criminal Justice.* Boulder, CO: Westview Press, pp. 171–189.

Simon, J. (1998) Managing the monstrous. Sex offenders and the new penology, *Psychology, Public Policy and Law*, 4: 452–467.

Simon, J. and Feeley, M. (1995) True crime. The new penology and public discourse on crime, in T. Blomberg and S. Cohen (eds), *Law, Punishment and Social Control: Essays in Honor of Sheldon Messinger.* New York: Aldine de Gruyter, pp. 147–180.

Stenson, K. (1993) Community policing as a governmental technology, *Economy and Society*, 22: 373–389.

Valverde, M. (1998) *Diseases of the Will. Alcohol and the Dilemmas of Freedom.* Cambridge: Cambridge University Press.

Weir, L. (1996) Recent developments in the government of pregnancy, *Economy and Society*, 25: 372–392.

18

New Institutionalism in Criminology: Approaches, Theories and Themes

Susanne Karstedt

(RE)INTRODUCING INSTITUTIONAL PERSPECTIVES TO CRIMINOLOGY

Criminology seeks an understanding of crime, criminality and criminal justice. The range of themes and the obvious divide between the strands of "crime" and "justice" have produced an abundance of theories that target either crime or justice, and occasionally both. This has led to scarcity amid abundance as criminologists are reluctant to agree on one single general theory of crime, and even less willing to agree on a general theory of justice. However, the characteristics of its subject(s) have made criminology a seedbed for *perspectives* rather than fully fledged general theories. Perspectives provide researchers with a framework rather than a set of hypotheses, with concepts that guide questions rather than give answers, and with paradigms rather than a more circumscribed theoretical account.

Throughout its recent history as a discipline criminology has profited immensely from such perspectives. The labelling approach – note: not labelling theory – was one of the most successful adaptations of constructivist paradigms in the social sciences, and criminology congenially lent itself to a widespread adoption of the framework of the "risk society". Criminology also changed its perspectives and henceforth paradigms considerably – partially concomitantly with its neighbouring social sciences, partially following the logic of its own inquiry. These perspectives had the virtue of providing a framework that linked criminology's different strands of inquiry, in particular those on crime with those on criminal justice. The labelling approach is unrivalled as to its framing – if not theorizing – of the links between justice and crime, as well as criminality.

In this chapter, I will (re)introduce a *(neo-) institutional perspective* to criminology, and outline the contours of a "New Institutional Criminology". Such an enterprise has to be aware that as a discipline criminology has always been a stronghold of institutional analysis. According to Edwin Sutherland's definition (1947), the analysis of the "making of laws" as well as of "reactions to the breaking of laws" both imply the systematic analysis of the setting, the structure and the functioning of the institutions of criminal justice. The system of criminal justice whether being perceived as one overarching or as a multitude of institutions, has traditionally occupied the core of disciplinary activities, and in criminology's branch of penology, criminologists explore criminal justice and law in their wider institutional contexts. Even if to a lesser extent, "the breaking of laws" has been theorized from institutional perspectives, with political economy and anomie theory certainly the most influential in the history of the discipline. Criminology has its roots in the study of institutions and their impact on "law making", "law breaking" and "reactions to law breaking"; criminologists have looked at institutions from an instrumentalist and outcome perspective when studying crime prevention. In these ways criminology has always adopted institutional perspectives in its different branches.

Further to this, criminology has a remarkable history in approaching institutions and making use of institutional perspectives. First, it has transcended the narrow institutional realm of penal law and criminal justice, and contextualized it within the wider institutional framework of society. Perhaps the most compelling institutional narrative of this kind is Foucault's "Discipline and Punish: the Birth of the Prison" (1977/1995) that links the invention and spread of the prison to changes in the core institutions of society.[1] Rusche and Kirchheimer's (1939/2003) political economy of punishment that contextualized the history of penal institutions within labour markets and economic institutions has been a predecessor of hardly less influence (see Reiner, 2007a). Second, notwithstanding the seductive lure of making dysfunctional and non-functioning institutions responsible for criminal action, criminologists have turned to the *normality* of institutional patterns and structures and the *routine working* of institutions in society as explanations for crime and punishment. This applies to the political economy of criminal action and punishment as well as to anomie theory. Here, criminologists have focused on the integrative and inclusionary potential of the institutional setting in its various corollaries for crime and penal justice. Third, criminologists have increasingly become aware that societies rely on plural forms of regulation and institutions when ensuring social order. Within this plurality that encompasses families, schools and communities, criminal justice functions as a "last resort" rather than operating as a routine mechanism of creating and maintaining social order.

Nonetheless, its outreach into the wider realm of institutional ensembles and transcending its own narrower remit has fostered tendencies in criminology to overrate the role of criminal justice in the context of societal institutions, and also to overstatethe impact of institutions other than legal and criminal justice institutions. The first of these tendencies partially followed outcome-oriented government policies in that it assumed a necessary and substantial impact of new institutional designs of policing, criminal justice and penal institutions on criminal action and criminality itself (instead of merely counting it). More influential was the strand of elevating criminal justice institutions, and in particular penal institutions to a decisive and functional core in society's ensemble of institutions. Even if one concedes that the conflict between good and bad functions as a strong internal dynamic within the institutional setting of societies, the often assumed centrality of criminal justice institutions can be doubted particularly because the implicit tendency toward explaining the centre from the margins and marginality. Rusche and Kirchheimer in a way laid the foundations for such a "deformation professionelle" by treating criminal justice as a central and seminal part of the political economy, and contemporary criminologists like Wacquant (2001, 2009), Simon (2007) and Melossi (2008, chapt. 9 and 10) have assigned a major role to penal institutions in managing pressures on the framework of social institutions. On the other hand, criminologists have readily claimed a particular institutional ensemble like "neo-liberalism" as responsible for rising crime rates, violence and increasing imprisonment across the globe (see Nelken, 2009; O'Malley, 2004; Reiner, 2007a,b) without scrutinizing the different shapes of institutional arrangements that are all painted with a broad brush as "neo-liberal".

Does criminology really need a 'new institutionalism' given the continuous success of its 'old institutionalism'? During the past decades criminology was under a "pincer pressure" (Reiner, 2007a: 345; 2007b) from two differing strands of theorizing and research, which were united in 'crowding out' institutional approaches. The rational choice perspective, routine activity theory and situational crime prevention were based on the application of neo-classical economics to crime and crime prevention. The "interpretative turn" (Reiner, 2007a: 344) focussed on the cultural and symbolic dimensions of crime (and justice) and clearly established the perspective of offenders. Both strands were inimical to institutional perspectives, which were deemed "deterministic" (ibid.), in that they stressed individual choice and agency in contrast to an assumed direct and determining impact of institutions. In this respect, criminology did not differ from its neighbouring social sciences, particularly sociology and political science. Notwithstanding the strength of the existentialist or "naturalist" appreciation of offender perspectives that kept reductionist and utilitarian models at bay in criminology, likewise as in political science and sociology, institutions were portrayed simply as arenas within which criminal behaviour and reactions to it occurred. Theories and ideas that embedded morality in institutions and communities gave way to moral individualism at best, and purely utilitarian individualism at worst. Further to this, criminal justice "managerialism" and its instrumental and outcome-oriented perspectives were mainly based on rational choice models of actors and politics as rational competition (for an account in political science, see March and Olsen, 1989, ch. 1).

Criminology therefore was a latecomer to the "institutional turn" that started at the end of the 1980s when "neo-institutionalism" took hold in economics, political science and sociology. In these disciplines neo-institutionalism tends to emphasize "the role of norms, trust and reciprocity in economic transactions" (Lambsdorff *et al.*, 2005: 5), and accordingly the role of "non-market institutions" (Crouch, 2007: 262). Neo-institutionalism thus emerged as a dialectic movement and strong challenge to neo-liberal ideas in these disciplines as well as in politics and government (see Crouch, 2007), and at its most extreme, is epitomized by communitarianism. However, the resurgence of institutional thinking in these disciplines was also a "cumulative consequence of the modern transformation of social institutions" (March and Olson, 1989: 1), and due to the experience of institutional change and its impact on all realms of social life.

In criminology, the invasion of neo-institutionalism proved to be of a less contentious nature (see Crouch (2007) for sociology and political science). Neo-institutionalism to some extent entered criminology via the pathways of 'old institutionalism' as in Institutional Anomie Theory (see below), or in the revival of a political economy of punishment (see Reiner, 2007a). Another route was the introduction of concepts like 'trust', 'collective efficacy' (Sampson *et al.*, 1997) and 'social capital' into the analysis of the social order of communities that took up communitarian ideas in the widest sense and contested models of situational crime prevention based solely on rational choice (see Hope and Karstedt (2003) for an overview; and for a critical review see Carson (2004)). Perhaps the most innovative contribution of neo-institutionalism were new themes that were added to the criminological agenda, and which reflected their increasing importance in neighbouring disciplines: trust in institutions, the role of procedural justice (Tyler, 1990/2006), and the importance of cooperation of citizens in the production of social order. In sum, neo-institutional perspectives are presently thriving in criminology without the term explicitly being used or their provenance from general developments in the social sciences being acknowledged (exceptions: Lambsdorf, 2007; Lambsdorf *et al.*, 2005).

In the following sections of this chapter I wish to explore neo-institutional perspectives in criminology. The next part will give a brief overview of the core arguments of neo-institutionalism in economics, politics and sociology and proceed to an abbreviated history of neo-institutional perspectives in criminology since the beginning of the 1990s. The third section will provide a detailed presentation of neo-institutional perspectives in theories of crime and deviance, and the fourth section will do the same for theories of punishment. Finally commitment to institutions will be examined as to its contribution to social order. The conclusion will assess the significance and the prospects of neo-institutional perspectives in contemporary criminology.

THE EMERGENCE OF NEW INSTITUTIONALISM: CONTEXTUALISING CRIMINOLOGY

Durkheim's ([1893] 1984: 21) observation that there is a non-contractual basis of contract and that the "… links between [economic actors] function not only in the brief moments when they engage in exchange or service, but extend considerably beyond" was at the roots of the emergence of neo-institutionalism in economics, sociology and political science. Its "central alternative contentions" against neo-classical economics and its influence on political science and sociology situated market activity within "a context of institutions" and thus within "non-market institutions". This was in stark contrast to neo-classical economics that assumed market mechanisms at work in "non-market institutions". According to the neo-institutional account the market is not privileged "in the sense that other institutions are … comprehended solely as market distortions or as necessarily inferior to it" (Crouch, 2007: 265). From the perspective of new institutional economics this translates into conceptualizing institutions as safeguarding transactions against "opportunistic", i.e., purely self-interested behaviour, and acknowledging the role of norms, morality and fairness. New institutionalism established a trend in theorizing that weakened "the sharp boundaries between economics and sociology" (Smelser and Swedberg, 1994: 17) and thus opened up routes towards a new political economy of our times that proved to become influential in criminology.

The founding father of new institutionalism in economics, D. C. North (1990), who had "discovered" the role of institutions when researching economic development in the Global South defined institutions in a way most sociologists could subscribe to. Institutions are the rules of the game, both formal rules and informal constraints; these are laws, conventions, norms of behaviour, self-imposed codes of conduct as well as the ways in which these are enforced. As such, institutions include our moral codes as well as our formal laws (North, 1990, 1996). He emphasized the inertia of institutions and path-dependence of institutional regimes rather than their capacity for change, their interdependence rather than their independence. Perhaps his most seminal contribution was the importance that he assigned to commitment in a society of strangers: commitment is created by institutions, but it includes commitment to institutions. Commitment is the foundation of compliance. Accordingly, he opened up the route for economists to discover the rule of law as decisive for economic development (Trebilcock and Daniels, 2008).

Even if all new institutionalists subscribe to a general definition of institutions as safeguards against opportunistic behaviour, and acknowledge their role in ensuring cooperation and soliciting commitment, the various strands of new institutionalism differ according to the role they assign to instrumental behaviour, i.e., rational choice, and with regard to conceptualizations of the "relationship between market and non-market institutions" (Crouch, 2007: 262). New institutionalists have in common that they "seek to elucidate the role that institutions play in the determination of social and political outcomes" (Hall and Taylor, 1996: 936), however they paint quite different pictures of the institutional world. New Institutional Economics (NIE) emphasize how individuals shape their institutional environment and the ways in which norms and trust result from rational choices and individual optimization (Lambsdorff et al., 2005: 5). In contrast to this "rational choice institutionalism" both "historical and sociological institutionalism" (Hall and Taylor, 1996: 936) conceive of institutions as socially constructed and primordial to the instrumental behaviour that takes account of the constraints that they impose.

Both types of institutionalism tend to emphasize the role of norms, trust and reciprocity in transactions, albeit in different ways. Rational choice institutionalism focuses on ways in which individuals shape their institutional environment, and how norms and trust result form optimizing behaviour. In contrast, historical and sociological institutionalism both focus on institutions as preconditions for individual behaviour, as they "provide moral or cognitive templates for interpretation and action" (Hall and Taylor, 1996: 939). It is from this perspective, that path dependency of institutional change as well as a focus on power and asymmetrical relations of power become seminal for institutional analysis. Granovetter (1992) summarized these differences. Sociological institutionalism (a) defines the pursuit of (economic) goals as accompanied by non-economic ones such as sociability, status and power; (b) assumes that all action (including economic action) is embedded in personal relations and networks; and (c) views all institutions (including economic institutions) as socially constructed rather than made inevitable by external circumstances (see also Lambsdorff et al., 2005: 6).

When embarking on neo-institutional perspectives criminologists tended to be more attracted to sociological institutionalism rather than "rational choice institutionalism", though both strands are present in contemporary criminological thinking (see, e.g., on corruption, Lambsdorff, 2007). Reasons for adopting the new institutional approach were as convincing in criminology as they were in the other social sciences, namely discontent with rational choice and market models as overarching explanatory tools of crime, criminality and justice (see, e.g., Hope and Karstedt, 2003). It seemed as if criminology had become oblivious to the earlier insight that crime in its relation to law "is best understood through its 'necessary' connection with morality" (Hart, 1961: 17), and moral rather than rational choices needed to be understood by criminologists (see Wikström (2004) for a revival of moral choice in his Situated Action Theory of Crime (SAT)). Risks of victimization and related fears of crime resisted transformation into purely actuarial concepts, and rather were imbued with moral meaning (Ericson and Doyle, 2003). Social order (or disorder) was not squarely the outcome of multiple rational decisions by multiple actors, who were strangers to each other, but were embedded in encompassing institutional arrangements, and based on trust, cooperation and solidarity. The creation of social order again became a question of institutional outcomes and efficiency of a wide range of institutions beyond the realm of criminal justice institutions (see Institutional Anomie Theory (IAT) in the next section).

Richard Ericson and Clifford Shearing were the first to take up the challenge and to give contour to an "Institutional Approach to Criminology" in 1991. They give an encompassing understanding of this approach: "An institutional approach to criminology entails a conception of criminal law and justice as an ordering system that functions to allocate resources (e.g., by guaranteeing and protecting relationships; …); to regulate and resolve conflict (e.g., by providing principles and procedures for doing so); and to keep peace (e.g., by establishing rules of behaviour and enforcing violations with sanctions)" (ibid., p. 8). These definitions of criminal law and justice quite closely follow the neo-institutional framework as outlined above, even if the authors never refer to it, and its contours are further visible in their concern to understand how the "institutional arrangements, and inter-institutional relations" of criminal justice contribute to social order and disorder (ibid.: 5).

Criminal justice institutions provide the starting point for an institutional criminology that situates them within the context of political, economic and cultural institutions and practices. Importantly the authors conceptualize social order in terms of three fundamental components or pillars of any institutional order as it guides and shapes behaviour: morality, procedure and hierarchy (ibid.: 6). With its focus on institutionalized values – morality, institutionalized commitment and legitimacy, on procedure – the "rules of the game" (North, 1990), and hierarchy – asymmetrical relations of power, inequality and domination, Ericson and Shearing's institutional approach comprises all of the seminal features of neo-institutional approaches in other social science disciplines. However, in making criminal justice institutions their core and starting point, they considerably narrow the scope of their institutional approach by ignoring the potential of institutional analyses for the causation of crime. They seek an "understanding of the mechanisms of criminal law and justice in their wider institutional contexts", whilst crime causation mainly figures as resulting from struggles and conflicts around political, economic, cultural and social dominance (1991: 9).

Messner and Rosenfeld's "Crime and the American Dream" (1994) and Gary LaFree's "Losing Legitimacy" (1998) were milestones in the institutional analysis of the causation of crime and criminality. With anomie theory as the most powerful legacy of the old institutionalism in criminology, its reconfiguration as "institutional anomie theory" by Messner and Rosenfeld can be deemed as one of the mayor developments of criminological theory during the past decades. Criminology proved capable of developing not only institutional *frameworks* for understanding crime and justice, but in addition institutional *theories* in their fullest and strictest sense; Messner and Rosenfeld's Institutional-Anomie Theory (IAT) is by far the most advanced of these.

Joan McCord's collection "Beyond Empiricism" (2004) further signified the return of institutions as a major theoretical concept in criminological thinking. The concepts of "institutions and intentions" – as the subtitle reads – should open up criminological theorizing for the mechanisms of change and choice that are guided by institutional contexts and moral values. Wikström's (2004) Situational Action Theory integrates instrumental and moral decision making in the dynamics of crime and juvenile delinquency. Messner and Rosenfeld (2004) in particular aimed at integrating institutional analysis into "etiological analyses" of crime, where they identified considerable neglect and underdevelopment. In his theory of "public/private interaction" Peter Grabosky (2004) theorized the interface of criminal justice and other non-market institutions in the production of social order.

In their work on comparative analyses of punishment, scholars like Michael Cavadino and James Dignan (2006) or Nicola Lacey (2008) have critically changed and extended the institutional horizon of criminology. They explore penal systems and their development within the broader institutional context of welfare states and democratic regimes, and one could also count David Garland's (2001) analysis of the transformation of the penal welfare state as a major contribution to an institutional approach. James Whitman (2003) contextualized punishment within the institutions of status hierarchies in the US, France and Germany in his historical and comparative study.

Finally, Jonathan Simon's (2007) study of how political institutions use crime and "govern" through it, reverses the prevailing causal chain by demonstrating in which ways crime and criminal justice institutions are capable of impacting on the institutional ensemble of societies. His and other studies transcend and give a new meaning to the more traditional perspective that criminal justice 'affirms' asymmetries of power, existing hierarchies, and inequality. Criminal justice institutions have a number of distinct outcomes that shape the institutional order of society; besides well-established detrimental effects on communities and families, more recent research has analysed the political fall-out of the disenfranchisement of felons in the US (Manza and Uggen, 2006), and thus a critical impact on political institutions. In flagging transitional democracies organized crime and corruption are seen as major threats to the development of political institutions (see Karstedt and LaFree, 2006).

This brief outline testifies to the influx and influence of new institutional thinking in criminology. Surprisingly, criminology has yet not adopted the term as such with the exception of Institutional Anomie Theory, and though new institutional economics have been applied to the study of corruption (Lambsdorff, 2007; Lambsdorff *et al.*, 2005). The following chapters will give a more detailed account of theoretical strands, themes and areas of research that combine into a New Institutional Approach in criminology.

INSTITUTIONS AND THE CAUSATION OF CRIME

The paradoxes of institutional change: LaFree's "Losing Legitimacy"

Gary LaFree's (1998) analysis of "street crime and the decline of social institutions in America" was and is one of the most compelling accounts of the role of institutions in the causation of crime waves. The main thesis of his book is that "historical and social changes created a crisis in institutional legitimacy that was responsible for the post-war wave of street crime in the US". March and Olson (1989:1) had named "cumulative consequences of the modern transformation of social institutions" as an incentive for neo-institutional thinking, and likewise, LaFree linked rapid institutional change in the US in the post-war period to the simultaneous wave of street crime. He argues and demonstrates through a wealth of empirical data that institutional change and the resulting loss in the legitimacy of political and economic institutions, as well as the family were at the roots of rising rates crime, in particular street robberies. He shows in which ways political events, distrust in government and collective action in the course of the civil rights movement co-vary with crime rates in a systematic way. Crime rates soar when economic institutions are "under stress" and cannot fulfil expectations and aspirations, as corroborated by rising inequality and increasing gaps in earnings between different social and ethnic groups. LaFree identifies the most thorough institutional change of all in the family with ever increasing divorce rates and simultaneously new forms of familial life developing. He assumes the strongest impact on crime from the loss of legitimacy of this institution, a hypothesis that has recently got considerable support from cross-national studies on institutional anomie and violence (Messner *et al.*, 2008a).

  LaFree's analysis focuses on the interdependence of institutions and in particular on "institutional responses" to their declining legitimacy (1998: 87). The interdependence between institutions accelerates upward, but possibly mainly downward spirals. Thus, distrust of government among the public in turn affected distrust of big business, and economic life more generally (ibid.: 177). The dynamics of institutional impact, outcome and change are actually "the genius of institutionalization" (ibid.: 151) as he exemplifies in his analysis of changing family patterns. "Blended, dual-career, male-household manager, single-parent, and even gay family forms are becoming increasingly institutionalized. As these alternatives to the traditional family become routinized, their ability to prevent crime and deviance should increase." It is the inherent dynamic of institutions and their malleability that needs to be acknowledged rather than their inertia and resistance to change. Paradoxically, the rapid decline and change that he observes in post-war American social institutions actually indicates that institutions are capable of rapid change, and in either direction. As an outcome of institutional change crime indicates the demise of existing institutional patterns and a lack of adaptation and innovation within institutions.

Gary LaFree's study reflects a number of seminal guidelines of new institutionalist approaches and demonstrates their potential for the analysis of crime and criminality: the importance of institutional outcomes and institutional dynamics, the interdependence of market and non-market institutions, and the adaptive characteristics of institutions. Like new institutionalists he transcends economic determinism, as often implied in a purist political economy of crime. With its focus on institutions and little recourse to traditional criminology, it has a unique position within the emerging field of new institutional criminology.

Institutional imbalance: Messner and Rosenfeld's Institutional Anomie Theory

With the title of their book "Crime and the American Dream" (1994, fourth edition, 2007) Steven Messner and Richard Rosenfeld attach themselves to the most influential tradition of institutional analysis in criminology, anomie theory, and aptly conceive of their theory as "Institutional Anomie Theory" (IAT). This "felicitous label" (Messner and Rosenfeld, 2006: 127)[2] actually designates a 'new' institutional theory, as their theory embodies seminal features of the new institutionalism. In line with traditions of anomie theory as conceived by Durkheim, these include the notion that institutions are safeguarding against opportunistic, i.e., self-interested and self-serving behaviour, the contention that non-market institutions are neither inferior to markets nor a distortion of it, and the assumption that institutional interdependency is characterized by relations of power and dominance between institutions. In fact their theory conceptualizes the relationship between market and non-market institutions in terms of institutional outcomes for levels of crime comprising the range from violence to property and white collar crime.

The core of their argument is based on Merton's (1938) adaptation of Durkheim's concept of anomie. Where market institutions dominate social life, non-market institutions lose their capacity to hold opportunistic behaviour at bay, i.e., they are losing a core function of institutions generally. If market institutions crowd out non-market institutions and put pressure on these to operate on market terms, severe institutional imbalances arise. Instead of attenuating the impact of market institutions on individuals, and of restricting opportunistic behaviour to these institutional realms, non-market institutions to the contrary are pervaded by opportunistic behaviour and assimilate themselves to the mechanisms of market institutions. The requisite balance in the relationship between market and non-market institutions is severely disrupted, and the interdependency between institutions induces a downward spiral of pervasive opportunistic behaviour, and an erosion of commitment to institutional norms that equally affect markets themselves as white collar crime and fraud are rising. "Institutional anomie" causes criminal behaviour of all types and in all realms of life, violence, property crime, and white collar crime.

Such "economic dominance" manifests itself in three ways (Messner *et al.*, 2008b: 168). *Devaluation* implies a decreasing value of non-economic institutions and roles relative to market institutions (and roles). In the process of *accommodation* individuals sacrifice non-market roles in favour of market roles. *Penetration* takes place when "the logic of the marketplace" intrudes into other realms of social life, and non-market institutions succumb to the rationale of market institutions. Messner and Rosenfeld analyse non-market institutions like education, the family

and importantly, welfare institutions, as these are explicitly designed to accommodate (negative) outcomes of market institutions like inequality. The "commodification"
of non-market institutions that supersedes their own institutional mechanisms of
solidarity, trust and reciprocity with opportunistic behaviour becomes most visible
in the demise of social welfare initiated by neo-liberal policies, and changes in
family patterns. 'Commodification' weakens institutional controls in family and
schools, and decreases the support they might give to those who are affected by
market institutions (Messner and Rosenfeld, 2006: 130).

Merton's legacy is obvious in the distinction between the cultural and structural
dimension of institutions (for new institutionalism see Hall and Taylor, 1996: 939).
Opportunistic behaviour is induced by the "moral or cognitive template(s)" (ibid.)
that are at the core of US American institutions. Achievement orientation, (egotistic)
individualism, universalism and "pecuniary materialism" (Messner and Rosenfeld,
2006: 131) provide institutionally built-in incentives for such behaviour, and decrease
commitment to institutional rules, in addition to a lack of solidarity and reciprocity.
Whether conceived of as distinct institutions or not (Messner and Rosenfeld, 2004;
Messner et al., 2008b), the interdependency between both institutional dimensions
induces a dynamic process of institutional disequilibrium that accounts for rising
rates of crime and violence. Both institutional dimensions/realms can be linked
"with criminal behaviour via both internalized normative controls and informal controls" (Messner et al., 2008b: 168) amounting to a lack of commitment to the
institutions of the market as well as non-market institutions.

IAT "has subsequently been interpreted more broadly as a macro-sociological
theory of crime" (Messner and Rosenfeld, 2006: 127). In recent explications of their
theory, Messner and Rosenfeld (2004, 2006) have turned towards institutional
outcomes on the individual, behavioural level. Again they relate back to traditional
anomie theory in analysing the role of social stratification. Low economic status and
exclusion inhibit access to properly functioning non-market institutions that might
buffer the impact of market institutions, leave individuals vulnerable to the pressures
of the American Dream, and impede commitment to institutions, their norms and
rules. On the individual level, economic dominance thus translates into preferences
for a 'calculus approach' towards means of action instead of a rule-oriented
approach. The authors contend that this mechanism links violence to institutional
anomie (Messner et al., 2008b).

It could be assumed that IAT would be best situated in explaining property,
acquisitive and high level economic crimes. In fact, violent crime (homicide) has
equal weight in the list of empirical studies that have been conducted since 1995
(see for an overview of studies, Messner and Rosenfeld, 2006: 137). The 'outcomes'
of institutional anomie comprise a broad range of deviant and criminal behaviours,
from property and violent crime, homicides to everyday crimes of middle classes
(Karstedt and Farrall, 2006) and ethical reasoning of managers (Cullen et al., 2004).
Given that IAT is a macro-sociological theory of crime, tests of the theory have
mainly used aggregate data and cross-national samples, as well as samples of US
states, counties and cities (see, e.g., Baumer and Gustafson, 2007). The moderating
effect of non-market institutions that IAT posits has been corroborated in a number
of studies, whilst "American exceptionalism" has not been supported in cross-national research (Cao, 2004; Jensen, 2002). Karstedt and Farrall (2006) use
individual-level data from three regions of distinct economic and institutional changes

(England and Wales, West and East Germany) and analyse crimes of everyday life and morally dubious actions in the market place. They identify a "syndrome of market anomie" comprising of lack of trust in others in the market place, fear of becoming a victim of the opportunistic behaviour of others and legal cynicism as a lack of commitment to legal norms, which reflect on trust, reciprocity and institutional commitment even in the realm of market institutions. Their findings corroborate a strong link between the syndrome of market anomie and intentions to engage in such dubious practices.

IAT particularly applies to transitional societies and their crime problems. The transition to a market economy and democracy naturally is an institutional transition that affects the institutional ensemble of market and non-market institutions alike, and thoroughly shifts the weight and role of institutions – economy, education, family, welfare and the polity. They provide an ideal setting for the study of market dominance and the ensuing institutional dynamics and "outcomes" in terms of criminal behaviour and violence. Pridemore's (2006; Pridemore and Kim, 2007) studies on violence and crime in Russia demonstrate – if not directly testing IAT – the potential of IAT as a theory of choice for such institutional settings.

IAT links 'old' and 'new' institutionalism in criminology, and by incorporating new institutional perspectives it has become one of the most innovative approaches in recent criminological theorising. IAT testifies to the continuous importance of institutional approaches in criminology, and to their adaptability and flexibility to incorporate new developments from other disciplines. It seems to be particularly suitable to analyse the impact of neo-liberal policies on crime rates – a much debated, however rarely tested, contention of contemporary criminology.

Comparative institutional (dis)advantage: democracy and crime

The transition to democracy and market economy was fraught with soaring rates of property and white collar crime, corruption and fraud, and increasing violence in all of the Eastern and Central European countries (Hagan and Radoeva, 1998; Karstedt, 2003, 2008; Neumayer, 2003). This raised the question whether democracies and the institutions that they create and nourish were in fact criminogenic, or whether the booms in violence and crime were caused by the transition itself, where the short-comings of transitional democracies and incomplete democratization account for the accompanying wave of crime and violence (Karstedt, 2006, 2008; Karstedt and LaFree, 2006). However, given the fact that established and mature western democracies had experienced waves of violence since the 1960s, led by the US (see Eisner, 2008; LaFree and Drass, 2002), answers to this question do not seem to be straight-forward. Democracies on the one hand "appear to carry with them the possibility of high levels of individual and collective violence in contrast to more autocratic 'law and order' regimes", while on the other hand they have built-in mechanisms that make them capable of returning to and retaining lower levels of violence (and crime) (Karstedt, 2006: 52).

What institutions, institutional outcomes and practices of citizens contribute to this volatile nature of democracies with regard to crime and violence? With the exception of the obvious crime of corruption (Lambsdorff, 2007: 39; Uslaner, 2008), criminologists have rarely taken political institutions and their outcome in terms of crime and violence into account. However, as new institutionalist approaches take a broader view on political and particularly democratic institutions, they incorporate democratic practices and values beyond a unilaterally formal perspective of the institutions and mechanisms of democracy. "Strong democratic institutions produce strong democratic practices", as Jaggers and Gurr (1995: 446) found in their empirical study, and this applies vice versa. Recent studies by Inglehart and Welzel (2005) found that the existence of democratic values in the population increases "the probability of the development of democratic institutions, that these reach high levels in established democracies and that they develop concomitantly" with the establishment of democratic institutions in the process of democratisation (Karstedt, 2006: 52–53).

The concept of "comparative institutional advantage(s)" (Hall and Soskice, 2001), which has been forwarded by new institutionalists in order to compare "varieties of capitalism" seems to be equally suitable for comparing political institutions and their institutional outcomes in terms of social order (or disorder). Comparative institutional advantages for economies are accumulated where markets are supported by institutions, both market and non-market institutions (Hall and Soskice, 2001: 38). In a similar vein the comparative institutional advantages for democracies ensue from their particular institutional ensemble and the practices they foster, when contrasted with more autocratic institutional regimes. Using a distinction between "liberal inclusion" that characterizes democratic institutions, and "repressive inclusion" as representative of more autocratic regimes, institutional features of democracies can be identified that are either conducive to lower levels of violence (and other crime), or in the case of "comparative disadvantages" to higher levels of violence and other forms of disorder (Karstedt, 2006: 62). Karstedt (2006: 63) lists as comparative advantages of democracies *value patterns* like individualism, egalitarianism and tolerance; *democratic practices* like generalized trust, pragmatic dissent and civic engagement; and institutions like rule of law, procedural justice, mobility and inclusion through welfare. Comparative institutional advantages are neutralized by respective comparative disadvantages, including expressive values not balanced by self-control, a general lack of social control in terms of practices, and institutional imbalances between market and welfare institutions, egalitarian values and inequality or discrimination against groups. Comparative advantages of autocracies include egalitarianism and welfare solidarity, pervasive social control, and institutions that produce high levels of social control though welfare inclusion and corporatism. Their comparative disadvantages are characterized by the use of violent means of social control by state agencies, arbitrary treatment of citizens, lack of trust, tolerance and civic engagement.

The results of an empirical study of homicide rates in a cross-national sample confirm comparative institutional advantages and disadvantages for both democracies and autocracies. Where democratic values and institutions cluster, levels of lethal violence are lower than in autocracies; however, egalitarian structures need to underpin respective values and practices. Where egalitarian values are at odds with discriminatory practices, and cause imbalances in the institutional ensemble, levels of such violence are higher, pointing toward comparative disadvantages of democracies. In contrast, the institutional cluster and specific values of autocracies that combine collectivistic and authoritarian values with consistently higher levels of inequality generate higher levels of violence than the majority of democracies. However, these patterns also produce a comparative advantage for autocracies in the case of high economic discrimination (Karstedt, 2006: 72–73). Similar results have been obtained in a study on the impact of democratic policies on homicide rates (Neumayer, 2003), though no support was given to the role of policies improving equality.

The concept of comparative institutional advantages certainly lends itself to the study of different institutions and their outcome in terms of social order, and in addition to studying comparative institutional advantages below the level of the nation state as in the studies named above. Sampson and his colleagues' research on "collective efficacy" (1997) that reduces violent crime in neighbourhoods, can be cast in terms of comparative institutional advantages of neighbourhoods, communities and cities, given the level of variation between them. Carr's (2005) ethnographic study of a neighbourhood lends further credibility to the concept as he identifies typical patterns of interdependency between formal and informal institutions of social control and welfare, which give advantages to neighbourhoods in the production of social order.

NEW INSTITUTIONALISM AND CRIMINAL PUNISHMENT

Besides anomie theory, the political economy of punishment can be identified as the other and equally strong strand of institutional approaches in criminological theorizing. From its early days, the political economy of punishment aimed at understanding the links between market institutions and the institutions of criminal justice, and thus at "understanding (of) the mechanisms of criminal law and justice in their wider institutional contexts", as Ericson and Shearing (1991: 9) define their institutional approach to criminology. It signifies a "more complex approach than simply spotlighting the significance of the economic, let alone economic determinism" (Reiner, 2007a: 341). As political economy proper developed into different strands of new institutionalism during the past decades, the political economy of punishment picked up on these and incorporated them into seminal studies. Likewise new institutionalist approaches, political economy positioned itself as a critique of neo-liberal approaches and policies, though in a more substantive way. Contemporary political economies of punishment (and also crime, see Reiner, 2007a for an overview) link the institutional outcomes of criminal justice to markets as well as non-market institutions. They particularly focus on the impact of neo-liberal policies as these shift the weight and role of market and non-market institutions by favouring the former over the latter.

As a matter of course, rates of imprisonment, the distribution of different types of sanctions across different social groups, or conditions in prison, primarily and at first instance are institutional outcomes of the respective penal system and the penal law as an institution (MacCormick, 2007). However, as Zimring and Johnson (2006) have pointed out, these institutional outcomes depend on the degree to which the criminal justice system and its institutional design are open respectively "insulated" from other institutions, predominantly political institutions. Less "insulation", they contend, will make the criminal justice system more receptive to populist demands for punishment and imprisonment, whilst a professional body of judges, and principled and individualized punishment decisions restrict popular impulses towards harsher punishment that otherwise can flow freely into the criminal justice system. In a similar way, Garland (2001) argues that the demise of the body of professionals and welfare bureaucrats, who ran the "penal welfare state", and their loss of legitimacy was seminal in the increase of imprisonment rates and the legislation of harsher punishment that define the "culture of control" at the turn of the century (see also Garland, 1985).

The concept of institutional insulation exemplifies the contingencies that characterize contemporary relationships between criminal justice institutions and their wider institutional environment across jurisdictions. These are equally visible in the huge differences in indicators of criminal punishment – like rates of imprisonment, sentences actually served, proportion of life-long imprisonment and general conditions of living for prisoners – across the generally similar political economies of western democracies (Karstedt, forthcoming). The notions of a more in-depth variety in the contemporary institutional ensemble of market and non-market institutions in these countries, and of institutional contingencies in their links to criminal justice clearly reject any kind of economic determinism.

Rusche and Kirchheimer's (1939/2003) historical study on the nexus between labour markets and punishment was a most significant contribution to the political economy of punishment. Its basic argument is still influential today, e.g., in the work of Loïc Wacquant (2001, 2009). Melossi (2008) and di Giorgi (2006) both argue that as the contemporary underclass to which both institutions refer, are immigrants, imprisonment rates are boosted by high numbers of economic migrants; as the labour market and the production regime of Post-Fordism fail to integrate and thus control immigrants, they are complemented by criminal punishment. These political economies of punishment combine the structuralism implicit in institutions with a more 'functionalist' view, as the needs of the system are deemed to dictate the combined institutional outcome of harsher or more lenient punishment and levels of punitiveness.[3]

The new historical institutionalism rather focuses on a more strictly defined structuralism of institutions and their outcomes. An exemplary study in this respect is James Whitman's "Harsh Justice" (2003), where he compares the historical development of punishment as it is shaped by institutions of status and asymmetrical relations of power in the US, France and Germany from the end of the eighteenth century. He demonstrates that the comparatively harsher punishment in the US is the result of equalizing status politics and institutions that receive their "moral and cognitive template" from the lowest status group, first from the institution of slavery and later from the most recent and most discriminated immigrant group. In contrast, the institutional ensembles in both France and Germany were characterized by more unequal relations of power and status, while their institutional moral templates of criminal justice were defined by higher status groups and their treatment, in particular the aristocratic or bourgeois 'political prisoner'; this accounts for the generally lower punitiveness and better prison conditions in both countries. The revolutions that decisively changed the institutions of status and concomitantly criminal justice rejected the older, status-based society with its implication for degrading punishment in both European countries. In the US, no such society existed, and consequently, the existing and pervading status hierarchy was defined by the institution of slavery. Whilst the institutions of criminal punishment were equalizing 'bottom-up' in the case of the US, they did so 'top-down' in both European countries, accounting for lasting and even increasing differences in the treatment of prisoners.

In particular, new institutional perspectives have informed recent studies of penal systems that seek to explore the impact of neo-liberal policies on criminal punishment. Contemporary capitalist economies have developed different models of the relationship between market and non-market institutions, and they differ as well according to regulatory institutions within markets themselves. In different ways they combine welfare institutions with corporatist labour markets, and strengthen non-market institutions tasked with attenuating the impact of markets on different social groups. Esping-Anderson's (1990) typology of welfare capitalism is based on distinct relations between (labour) market and non-market (welfare) institutions, and has been influential in reconfiguring the political economy of punishment. In their seminal study of 12 countries, comprising of the US, Australia and New Zealand, South Africa, West and North European countries, and Japan, Michael Cavadino and James Dignan (2006) compared neo-liberal institutional regimes (the US, Australia and New Zealand, England and Wales, South Africa), with neo-corporatist (West and South European countries), social democratic (Sweden and Finland) and one oriental corporatist (Japan) country. In contrast to Esping-Andersen, they incorporate institutions of status and citizenship into their typology, and also use attitudes towards punishment in the population in their "radical pluralist explanatory framework". They categorize the dimensions of criminal justice institutions in terms of the dominant penal ideology, modes of punishment, imprisonment rates and receptiveness to prison privatization. The different types of welfare-market institutionalizations are linked to distinct differences in "penal tendencies". Neo-liberal institutional regimes have the highest imprisonment rates, are dominated by 'law and order' ideologies, are most exclusionary in their modes of punishment, and most receptive to prison privatization. Scandinavian social democratic corporatism and oriental corporatism are situated at the opposite pole with low imprisonment rates, inclusionary modes of punishment and penal ideologies based on rights and restoration/rehabilitation.

Cavadino and Dignan base their study on a small selection of in-depth case studies that cluster evidence around the different dimensions and variables that they use. Sutton (2004) partially corroborates their findings with a cross-national sample and quantitative analyses. He bases his analysis of the relation between business cycles and imprisonment in affluent western democracies on evidence that non-market institutions – strong welfare states and neo-corporatist labour-market institutions – do not weaken economic performance as much as neo-liberal analysis assumes, but to the contrary (see also Crouch, 2007: 263). Imprisonment rates are significantly lower for neo-corporatist institutional regimes, and the business cycle – imprisonment nexus seems to be the result of antecedent differences between neoliberal and corporatist societies.

Nicola Lacey (2008) turns to the institutional framework of democracies. In her exploration of the "Prisoners' Dilemma" in contemporary democracies, she links institutional welfare regimes to the institutional framework of democracies, within which consensus and support for these regimes are elicited, and transformed into political decision making. Liberal and co-ordinated market economies (Hall and Sokice, 2001) do not emerge independently of characteristics of the political system that produces and fosters them. Liberal market economies generally are linked to majoritarian rule, single party governments, partisanship and more adversarial styles of politics. In contrast, co-ordinated market economies more often evolve in political

systems with proportionate representation, coalition governments, and more consensual styles of politics. As much as these institutional frameworks account for the
strength and role of non-market institutions and more egalitarian distribution of
wealth and income, they independently produce institutional outcomes in terms of
penal policies and systems. Using Zimring's concept of insulation, one might say
that proportionate representation and coalition governments are not only more insulated from popular demands and attitudes conducive to penal severity; in addition,
the combination of proportionate presentation and coalition governments slows and
waters down any demands from small, single issue groups, whilst majoritarian rule
and single-party governments have a built-in dynamic towards enhancing such
issues and spreading them throughout the electorate. Where the political system is
further dominated by complex patterns of federalism like in Germany (see Karstedt,
2002), insulation is even stronger, as the public, issue groups and politicians know
that changes to the criminal justice system are hard to achieve.

   Lacey's account adds necessary complexity to the institutional analysis of criminal punishment. It is difficult to assess the relative weight and importance of these
institutional "pillars" as well as their interactive effects and institutional outcomes
on criminal punishment and penal severity (see figures on pages 62 and 90). It is a
particular merit of her sophisticated account that she draws attention to "small
institutional differences (that) can lead to highly variable outcomes" in terms of
penal policies and penal severity, inclusion and redistribution, which both in turn
affect penal severity (ibid.: 163–164). Consequently, fairly large differences of
penal severity between contemporary mature democracies might be accounted for by
small and seemingly insignificant institutional differences rather than by institutional 'clusters' that independently and jointly are supposed to produce large
differences.[4] If small institutional differences in institutional regimes can account for
fairly large differences in terms of institutional outcomes, this indicates a high interdependency of institutions, as well as strong path dependency in their joint
development. Institutional interdependency and "clustering" might also account for
different growth rates of imprisonment and distinct pathways towards the build-
ing-up of large prison populations, when "comparative disadvantages" accumulate
that make criminal justice institutions and policies susceptible and vulnerable to
public demands for more severe penalty, as might have been the case in the US over
the past decades (Simon, 2007).

THE STRENGTH OF INSTITUTIONS: LEGITIMACY
AND COMPLIANCE

In order to function as providers of the 'rules of the game', and to establish safeguards against opportunistic behaviour through norms, trust and reciprocity,
institutions require commitment. LaFree's (1998) account of the loss of legitimacy
of vital institutions can be equally read as loss of commitment to the institutions of
the family, education and the economy. Karstedt and Farrall (2006) demonstrate
that lack of trust in market institutions, fear that others will not reciprocate and a
general decline of commitment to legal norms ('legal cynicism') gives way to unre-
stricted self-interested and opportunistic behaviour in the market place, resulting
in strong intentions to take advantage of opportunities even in illegal and morally

dubious ways. Commitment to institutions embodies the acceptance of and voluntary compliance with the 'rules of the game' that institutions establish, and thus links institutions to individuals.

Trust in institutions, as well as their legitimacy became a major focus for new institutionalist approaches in economics, political science and sociology (see, e.g., Braithwaite and Levi, 1998). Criminology was extremely receptive to these new themes for several reasons. Population surveys indicated a major loss of trust in criminal justice across western democracies (Ministry of Justice, 2008), which is deemed a major social problem and "contemporary evil" (Joseph Rowntree Foundation, 2009). Further, research on procedural justice demonstrated that procedural fairness not only leads to acceptance of the outcomes of criminal justice, but also could secure compliance with rules and norms in the long run (Tyler, 1990/2006; Tyler and Huo, 2002). Finally, it was acknowledged that social order is produced through willing cooperation with criminal justice as well as other institutions. Sampson and his colleagues' (1997) studies on 'collective efficacy' clearly demonstrate that such voluntary and active cooperation as well as a sense that it is effective contributes to social order even in highly deprived neighbourhoods. Institutional commitment mainly elicits those types of compliance that Bottoms defines as "normative compliance" in his typology comprising of the acceptance of the norm, attachment to it and its perceived legitimacy (2002: 30). This does not rule out that institutions will also produce two other types, namely "instrumental" or "prudential compliance", and compliance "based on habit or routine" (ibid.), as they include opportunistic behaviour, and actually provide strong incentives for habitual and routine behaviour. However, both these types depend on the strength of those institutions that establish the norm, and can muster at least some legitimacy and reciprocity, so that sanctions are credible and habitual behaviour is not punished by a lack of reciprocal routines from others (see Karstedt and Farrall, 2006).

Criminal justice institutions are legal authorities, and as such they are endowed with power and means to make others comply with their decisions and directives. Legitimacy is therefore crucial for criminal justice institutions in order to fulfil their tasks, and to elicit compliance as well as cooperation. Cooperating with legal authorities differs in many respects from cooperation in markets where institutions facilitate cooperation between equals or protect the more powerless. Legitimacy of all institutions and of criminal justice institutions in particular is based on acceptance of norms, rules and directives, and consequently relies on shared values, further on trust and confidence in an institution and its agents, and finally, though not decisively on how well these fulfil their task. More often than not, people seek help from legal authorities like the police or the courts, when they are unable to solve their conflicts (see Tyler, 1990/2006; Tyler and Fagan, 2008). Legitimacy of institutions and procedures increases acceptance of the decisions by legal authorities, even for adverse outcomes.

Most institutions rely on voluntary cooperation and compliance, and they need legitimacy and commitment to shared institutional values in order to achieve compliance and cooperation to a sufficient extent. Criminal justice institutions are different and even exceptional as they step in when compliance and cooperation fail in other institutions, and they try to achieve compliance predominantly through the deterrent threat of sanctions. However, they have also to rely on acceptance of and compliance with their decisions. Criminal justice institutions (like other institutions) achieve legitimacy and create and maintain commitment to shared values through procedural justice, i.e., fair procedures through which their decisions are delivered. Procedural justice broadly includes two types of issues: fairness of decision making, i.e., neutral, consistent, rule based, transparent, and fair treatment, involving respect for people and their rights, concern from authorities, and dignity and courtesy. Fair procedures achieve three institutional outcomes: voluntary acceptance of outcomes even when adverse to the interests of the claimant, enhanced legitimacy for the institution and their agents, and long-term (voluntary) compliance. Procedural justice is further seminal in creating trust and confidence in legal authorities generally and criminal justice institutions in particular (see, e.g., for courts Tyler, 2001; Rottmann, 2007; for police Tyler and Fagan, 2008). It emerges thus as the predominant mechanism through which criminal justice institutions can achieve legitimacy and commitment, resulting in voluntary acceptance of decisions of legal authorities and long-term compliance. It is also a major institutional safeguard against opportunistic behaviour, as it encourages individuals to accept outcomes that are against their own interest, and to comply with rules and norms; consequently procedural justice is used in a broad range of organizations and procedures beyond the realm of legal institutions.[5]

As criminal justice agencies acknowledge the importance of voluntary compliance, and seek the voluntary cooperation of citizens, reliance on sanction-based compliance has been seen as less effective generally and more costly then compliance based on institutional commitment and "deference-based legitimacy" (Tyler *et al.*, 2007: 14). It has been argued that overly relying on sanction-based compliance, including meticulous and stifling rules and regulations and close supervision will crowd out voluntary compliance by decreasing the motivation that springs from voluntary institutional commitments. This has much in common with the neoclassical argument that strong and paternalistic welfare states decrease the motivation to save and enter the labour market, which does not seem to be the case (see Crouch, 2007: 263; Svallfors, 2007). From a new institutionalist perspective, this is not a necessary consequence, and criminal justice institutions will give space to merely sanction-based "instrumental compliance" (Bottoms, 2002) as well as to those mechanisms that secure voluntary compliance. Communities seem to demand both from criminal justice institutions (Carr, 2005). Importantly the legitimacy of both types of mechanisms depends on procedural justice.

CONCLUSION: THE FUTURE OF A NEW INSTITUTIONAL CRIMINOLOGY

Institutions are the software of societies: they provide a framework and mechanisms, and the rules of the game, they are flexible and adaptable, and they establish links and guide action. As LaFree (1998: 151) phrased it, the genius of institutions is their adaptability. It is exactly this adaptability, interdependency and contingency that new institutionalist perspectives emphasize. In doing so, they equally reject the 'market-determinism' of neo-liberal approaches and the account of linear progress and convergent modernization where all institutional regimes will be ultimately assimilated. Instead, they stress the dynamics of comparatively small differences, and explore the comparative advantages of institutional clusters and ensembles. As such new institutional perspectives are capable of countering the grand narratives of neoliberalism – both as culprit and as remedy – that presently seem so dominant in criminology.

New institutionalist perspectives have changed traditional approaches in criminology in distinct ways. However, they have entered criminology more stealthily, and have been acknowledged by name only in Institutional Anomie Theory. They were hugely influential in recreating Durkheim's institutional legacy. Besides IAT, new institutionalist approaches in the analysis of punishment have replaced previous overarching narratives of modernization as well as of political economies (see Karstedt, 2007a). Crime and justice policies do not develop along a model of convergence; instead, they travel, and often reach new shores in quite distorted and changed shapes (Newburn and Sparks, 2004; Jones and Newburn, 2007). Criminal justice institutions do neither travel easily, and they need mechanism to link to existing institutions and settle in an environment that is receptive to the values on which they rely (see Karstedt, 2007b). New institutionalists in criminology would also reject the notion that neo-liberal crime policies travel everywhere, even where neo-liberal economic policies seem to be acceptable (O'Malley, 2004).

New institutional approaches conceptualize crime and justice as institutional outcomes of specific arrangements and clusters of institutions that exist in societies. They draw attention to their normalcy, as well as to imbalances and anomalies in their overall structure. They suggest shifting the institutional outcomes of criminal justice and legal authorities to more voluntary forms of compliance and cooperation with criminal justice institutions, based on legitimacy, fair procedures and trust. Most of this research has been done – with rare exceptions (Fischer *et al.*, 2007) – in societies where the apparatus of institutions functions, institutions are capable of setting the rules of the game and are accepted in this capacity. Institutional perspectives will be equally capable of framing the exploration of dysfunctional institutions in "disjunct democracies" (Caldeira and Holston, 1999), or the capture of criminal justice institutions by ruling elites and for their self-serving behaviour. They have already proven valuable in explaining corruption and improving prevention (Lambsdorff, 2007). In the global arena, we observe the total failure of major institutions, which is the defining characteristic of so-called failed states. In these countries, rates of violence reach the highest levels, and most of the world's corruption and terrorism is concentrated here (LaFree *et al.*, 2007). In which ways severely failing institutions can be strengthened, substituted by others or traditional institutions can be revitalized in order to reduce crime, install justice and increase safety is a challenging task for institutional criminologist.[6] They do not offer remedies from a holistic approach, but from one that is built more incrementally. This is not necessarily a disadvantage for an unfolding conceptual framework.

NOTES

1 Even if it was written as a sociological text, its triumph and influence as well as its adoption as a classic speak to criminology's embracing it as its own.

2 Actually, the term was coined by Chamlin and Cochran in a widely cited article in *Criminology* in 1995. Messner and Rosenfeld adopted it, and it is now the accepted name of their theory.

3 Punitiveness is a multi-faceted concept, that refers to 'objective measures' like imprisonment rates, prison conditions, etc. and thus to jurisdictions, as well as to 'subjective' measures of attitudes toward the punishment of criminals among social groups and total populations.

4 See Nelken (2009) who warns against such tendencies in comparative research on crime and punishment, and reminds us of our bias to look for the good causes of the outcomes that we want.

5 There is an abundant literature on procedural justice and its impact in other institutions and organisations, as well as on auditing, bargaining and other procedures.

6 The area of policing has proven to be the field where criminologists have taken up these challenging tasks (see Hinton and Newburn, 2009).

REFERENCES

Baumer, E. P., Gustafson, R. (2007) Social organization and instrumental crime: assessing the empirical validity of classic and contemporary anomie theories, *Criminology* 45(3): 617–663.

Bottoms, A. E. (2001) Compliance and community penalties, in A. E. Bottoms, L. Gelsthorpe and S. Rex (eds), *Community Penalties: Change and Challenges* (Cambridge Criminal Justice Series). Cullompton: Willan Publishing, pp. 87–16.

Bottoms, A. E. (2002) Morality, crime, compliance and public policy, in A. E. Bottoms and M. Tonry (eds), *Ideology, Crime and Criminal Justice* (Cambridge Criminal Justice Series). Cullompton: Willan Publishing. pp. 20–53.

Braithwaite, V. and Levi, M. (eds) (1998) *Trust and Governance*. New York: Russell Sage Foundation.

Caldeira, T. and Holston, J. (1999) Democracy and violence in Brazil, *Comparative Studies in Society and History* 41(4): 691–729.

Cao, L. (2004) Is American society more anomic? A test of Merton's theory with cross-national data, *International Journal of Comparative and Applied Criminal Justice* 28: 17–31.

Carr, P. J. (2005) Clean Streets. *Controlling Crime, Maintaining Order and Building Community Activism*. New York, London: New York University Press.

Carson, W. G. (2004) Is communalism dead? Reflections on the present and future directions of crime prevention. Part one, *The Australian and New Zealand Journal of Criminology* 37(1): 1–21; Part two, *The Australian and New Zealand Journal of Criminology* 37(2): 192–210.

Cavadino, M. and Dignan, J. (2006) *Penal Systems. A Comparative Approach*. London: Sage.

Crouch, C. (2007) Neoinstitutionalism: Still no intellectual hegemony?, Regulation and Governance 1: 261–270.

Cullen, J. B., Parboteeah, P. K. and Hoegl, M. (2004) Cross-national differences in managers, willingness to justify ethically suspect behaviors: a test of institutional anomie theory. *Academy of Management Journal* 47: 411–421.

Di Georgi, A. (2006) *Rethinking the Political Economy of Punishment: Perspectives on Post-Fordism and Penal Politics*. Aldershot: Ashgate.

Durkheim, E. (1893/1984) *The Division of Labour in Society*. New York.

Eisner, M. (2008) Modernity strikes back? A historical perspective an the latest increase in interpersonal violence (1960–1990), *International Journal of Conflict and Violence* 2(2): 288–316.

Ericson, R. V. and Shearing, C. D. (1991) Introduction: An institutional approach to criminology, in J. Gladstone, R. V. Ericson and C. D. Shearing (eds), *Criminology: A Reader's Guide*. Toronto: Centre of Criminology. pp. 3–19.

Ericson, R. V. and Doyle, A. (2003) Risk and morality, in R. V. Ericson and A. Doyle (eds), *Risk and Morality*. Toronto: University of Toronto Press, pp. 1–10.

Esping-Andersen, G. (1990) *The Three Worlds of Welfare Capitalism*. Cambridge: Polity Press.

Fischer, R., Harb, C., Al-Sarraf, S. and Nachabe, O. (2007) Support for resistance among Iraqi students, *Basic and Applied Social Psychology* 30: 1–9.

Foucault, M. (1977/1995) *Discipline and Punish: The Birth of the Prison*. NewYork: Random House.

Garland, D. (1985) *Punishment and Welfare. A History of Penal Strategies*. Aldershot: Gower.

Garland, D. (2001) *The Culture of Control*. Oxford: Oxford University Press.

Grabosky, P. (2004) Towards a theory of public/private interaction in policing, in J. McCord, *Beyond Empiricism. Institutions and Intentions in the Study of Crime*. Advances in Criminological Theory, vol. 13. New Brunswick, London: Transaction Publishers, pp. 69–82.

Granovetter, M. (1992) Economic institutions as social constructions: A framework for analysis, *Acta Sociologica* 35: 3–11.

Hagan, J. and Radoeva, D. (1998) Both too much and too little: From elite to street crime in the transformation of the Czech Republic, *Crime, Law and Social Change* 28: 195–211.

Hall, P. A. and Soskice, D. (2001) An introduction to varieties of capitalism, in P. A. Hall and D. Soskice (eds), *Varieties of Capitalism*. Oxford: Oxford University Press, pp. 1–68.

Hall, P. A. and Soskice, D. (eds) (2001) *Varieties of Capitalism*. Oxford: Oxford University Press.

Hall, P. A. and Taylor, R. C. (1996) Political science and the three new institutionalisms, *Political Studies* 44: 936–957.

Hart, H. L. A. (1961) *The Concept of Law*. Oxford: Clarendon.

Hinton, M. and Newburn, T. (eds) (2009) *Policing Developing Democracies*. London: Routledge.

Hope, T. and Karstedt, S. (2003) Towards a new social crime prevention. In *Crime Prevention. New Approaches*, edited by H. Kury and J. Obergfell-Fuchs. (*Mainzer Schriften zur Situation von Kriminalitaetsopfern*). Mainz, Germany: Weisser Ring.

Inglehart, R. and Welzel, C. (2005) *Modernization, Cultural Change and Democracy*. Cambridge: Cambridge University Press.

Iversen, T. and Soskice, D. (2006) Electoral institutions and the politics of coalitions: Why some democracies redistribute more than others, *American Political Science Review* 100: 165–181.

Jaggers, K. and Gurr, T. (1995) Tracking democracy's third wave with polity III data. *Journal of Peace Research* 32: 469–482.

Jensen, G. (2002) Institutional anomie and societal variation in crime: a critical appraisal, *International Journal of Sociology and Social Policy* 22: 45–74.

Jones, T. and Newburn, T. (2007) *Policy Transfer and Criminal Justice. Exploring US Influence over British Crime Control Policy*. Maidenhead: Open University Press.

Joseph Rowntree Foundation (ed.) (2009) *Contemporary Social Evils*. Bristol: The Policy Press.

Karstedt, S. (2002) Emotions and criminal justice. *Theoretical Criminology* 6: 299–317.

Karstedt, S. (2003) Legacies of a culture of inequality: The janus-face of crime in post-communist societies, *Crime, Law and Social Change* 40: 295–320.

Karstedt, S. (2006) Democracy, values and violence: Paradoxes, tensions and comparative advantages of liberal inclusion. In S. Karstedt and G. LaFree (eds), *Democracy, Crime and Justice*. Special Issue of The Annals of the American Academy of Political Science, vol. 605, pp. 50–81.

Karstedt, S. (2007a) Explorations into the sociology of criminal justice and punishment: Leaving the modernist project behind, *History of the Human Sciences*, 20(2): 51–70.

Karstedt, S. (2007b) Creating institutions: Linking the local and the global in the travel of crime policies, *Police Practice and Research* 8(2): 145–158.

Karstedt, S. (2008) Democratization and violence: European and international perspectives, in S. Body-Gendrot and P. Spierenburg (eds), *Cultures of Violence: Historical and Contemporary Perspectives*. Amsterdam: Kluwer, pp. 205–226.

Karstedt, S. (forthcoming) Liberty, equality and justice: Democratic culture and punishment, in A. Crawford (ed.), *International and Comparative Criminal Justice and Urban Governance*. Cambridge: Cambridge University Press.

Karstedt, S. and Farrall, S. (2006) The moral economy of everyday crime: markets, consumers and citizens, *British Journal of Criminology* 46: 1011–1036.

Karstedt, S. and LaFree, G. (2006) Democracy, crime and justice, in S. Karstedt and G. LaFree (eds), *Democracy, Crime and Justice*. Special Issue of The Annals of the American Academy of Political Science, vol. 605, pp. 6–25.

Lacey, N. (2008) *The Prisoners' Dilemma. Political Economy and Punishment in Contemporary Democracies*. Cambridge: Cambridge University Press.

LaFree, G. (1998) *Losing Legitimacy.* Boulder: Westview.

LaFree, G. and Drass, K. A. (2002) Counting crime booms among nations: Evidence for homicide victimization rates 1956–1998, *Criminology* 40: 769–800.

LaFree, G. Dugan, L. and Fahey, S. (2007) Global terrorism and failed states, in J. J. Hewitt, J. Wilkenfeld and T. Gurr (eds), *Peace and Conflict.* Boulder: Paradigm Publishers, pp. 39–54.

Lambsdorff, J. G. (2007) *The Institutional Economics of Corruption and Reform.* Cambridge: Cambridge University Press.

Lambsdorff, J. G., Taube, M. and Schramm, M. (2005) Corrupt contracting: Exploring the analytical capacity of New Institutional Economics and New Economic Sociology, in J. G. Lambsdorff, M. Taube, and M. Schramm (eds), *The New Institutional Economics of Corruption.* London: Routledge, pp. 1–15.

MacCormick, N. (2007) *Institutions of Law.* Oxford: Oxford University Press.

Manza, J. and Uggen, C. (2006) *Locked Out. Felon Disenfranchisement and American Democracy.* Oxford: Oxford University Press.

March, J. G. and Olsen, J. P. (1989) *Rediscovering Institutions. The Organizational Basis of Politics.* New York/London: The Free Press.

McCord, J. (ed.) (2004) *Beyond Empiricism. Institutions and Intentions in the Study of Crime.* Advances in Criminological Theory, vol. 13. New Brunswick, London: Transaction Publishers.

Melossi, D. (2008) *Controlling Crime, Controlling Society. Thinking about Crime in Europe and America.* Cambridge: Polity.

Merton, R. K. (1938) Social structure and anomie, *American Sociological Review* 3(5): 672–682.

Messner, S. and Rosenfeld, R. (2004) 'Institutionalizing' criminological theory, in J. McCord (ed.), *Beyond Empiricism. Institutions and Intentions in the Study of Crime.* Advances in Criminological Theory, vol. 13. New Brunswick, London: Transaction Publishers, pp. 83–106.

Messner, S. and Rosenfeld, R. (2006) The present and the /future of institutional anomie theory, in F. T. Cullen, J. P. Wright and K. R. Blevins (eds), *Taking Stock. The Status of Criminological Theory.* Advances in Criminological Theory. New Brunswick: Transaction Publishers, pp. 127–148.

Messner, S. and Rosenfeld, R. (2007/1994) *Crime and the American Dream*, fourth edition. Belmont: Thomson and Wadsworth.

Messner, S. F., Pearson-Nelson, B., Raffalovich, L. and Miner, Z. (2008a) Cross-national homicide trends in the latter decades of the 20th centruy: Losses and gains in institutional control? *Conference 'Control of Violence'* Centre for Interdisciplinary Research, University of Bielefeld, September 2008.

Messner, S., Thome, H. and Rosenfeld, R. (2008b) Institutions, anomie and violent crime: Clarifying and elaborating institutional anomie theory, *International Journal of Conflict and Violence* 2(2): 163–181.

Ministry of Justice (2008) *Explaining Attitudes towards the Justice System in the UK and Europe.* Ministry of Justice Research Series 9/08, June 2008.

Nelken, D. (2009) Comparative criminal justice: Beyond ethnocentrism and relativism, *European Journal of Criminology* 6(4): 291–312.

Neumayer, Eric (2003) Good policy can lower violent crime: Evidence from a cross-national panel of homicide rates 1980–1997, *Journal of Peace Research* 40(6): 619–640.

Newburn, T. and Sparks, R. (eds) (2004) *Criminal Justice and Political Cultures.* Cullompton: Willan Publishing.

North, D. C. (1990) *Institutions, Institutional Change and Economic Performance.* Cambridge: Cambridge University Press.

North, D. C. (1996) 'Where Have We Been And Where Are We Going? Economic History, Economics Working Paper Archive at WUSTL', Washington University, St. Louis.

O'Malley, P. (2004) Globalising risk? Distinguishing styles of 'neoliberal' criminal justice in Australia and the USA, in T. Newburn and R. Sparks (eds), *Criminal Justice and Political Cultures.* Cullompton: Willan Publishing, pp. 30–48.

Pridemore, W. (2006) 'Change and stability in the characteristics of homicide victims, offenders and incidents during rapid social change, *British Journal of Criminology* 46.

Pridemore, W. and Kim, S. W. (2007) Socioeconomic change and homicide in a transitional society, *The Sociological Quarterly* 48: 229–251.

Reiner, R. (2007a) Political economy, crime and criminal justice, in M. Maguire, R. Morgan and R. Reiner (eds), *The Oxford Handbook of Criminology*. Oxford: Oxford University Press, pp. 341–380.

Reiner, R. (2007b) *Law and Order. An Honest Citizen's Guide to Crime and Control*. Cambridge: Polity Press.

Rottmann, D. B. (2007) Adhere to procedural fairness in the justice system, *Criminology and Public Policy* 6: 835–842.

Rusche, G. and Kirchheimer, O. (1939/2003) *Punishment and social Structure.*1939: New York: Russell and Russell; 2003: New Brunswick, N.J.: Transaction Publishers.

Sampson, R., Raudenbusch, S. and Earls, F. (1997) Neighborhoods and violent crime: A multilevel study of collective efficacy, *Science* 277: 918–924.

Simon, J. (2007) *Governing through Crime*: *How the War on Crime Transformed American Democracy and Created a Culture of Fear*. New York: Oxford University Press.

Smelser, N. J. and Swedberg, R. (1994) The sociological perspective on the economy, in N. J. Smelser and R. Swedberg (eds), *The Handbook of Economic Sociology*. New Haven: Princeton, pp. 166–180.

Sutherland, E. (1947) *Principles of Criminology*. fourth edition. Philadelphia: J.B. Lippincott.

Sutton, J. R. (2004) The political economy of imprisonment in affluent western democracies, 1960–1990, American Sociological Review 69(2): 170–189.

Svallfors, S. (ed.) (2007) *The Political Sociology of the Welfare State*. Stanford: Stanford University Press.

Trebilcock, M. J. and Daniels, R. (2008) *Rule of Law Reform and Development*. Cheltenham: Edward Elgar.

Tyler, T. R. (1990/2006) *Why People Obey the Law*. New Haven: Yale University Press. 2006: Princeton: Princeton University Press.

Tyler, T. (2001) Public trust and confidence in legal authorities: What do majority and minority group members want from the law and legal institutions, *Behavioural Science and the Law* 19: 215–235.

Tyler, T. and Fagan, J. (2008) Legitimacy and cooperation: Why do people help the police fight crime in their communities, *Ohio State Journal of Criminal Law* 6: 231–275.

Tyler, T. and Huo, Y. (2002) *Trust in the Law*. *Encouraging Public/Cooperation with the Police and Courts*. New York: Russell Sage Foundation.

Tyler, T. R., Braga, A., Fagan, J., Meares, T., Sampson, R. and Winship, C. (2007) Legitimacy and criminal justice: International perspectives, in T. Tyler (ed.), *Legitimacy and Criminal Justice*: *International Perspectives*. New York: Russell Sage Foundation.

Uslaner, E. M. (2008) *Corruption, Inequality and the Rule of Law*. Cambridge: Cambridge University Press.

Wacquant, L. (2001) Deadly symbiosis: When ghetto and prison meet and mesh, *Punishment and Society* 3: 95–133.

Wacquant, L. (2009) Punishing the Poor. The Neoliberal Government of Social Insecurity. Durhamm, London: Duke University Press.

Whitman, J. (2003) *Harsh Justice. Criminal Punishment and the Widening Divide between America and Europe*. Oxford: Oxford University Press.

Wikström, P.-O. (2004) Crime as alternative: Towards a cross-level situational action theory of crime causation, in J. McCord (ed.), *Beyond Empiricism. Institutions and Intentions in the Study of Crime*. Advances in Criminological Theory vol. 13. New Brunswick, London: Transaction Publishers, pp. 1–38.

Zimring, F. E. and Johnson, D. T. (2006) 'Public opinion and the governance of punishment in democratic political systems, in S. Karstedt and G. LaFree (eds), *Democracy, Crime and Justice*. Special Issue of The Annals of the American Academy of Political Science, vol. 605, pp. 266–280.

19

Defiance, Compliance and Consilience: A General Theory of Criminology[1]

Lawrence W. Sherman

You are not required to obey any court which passes out such a ruling *[Brown]*. In fact, you are obligated to defy it.

U.S. Senator James Eastland, as quoted by Klarman (2004: 413)

INTRODUCTION

This chapter restates "defiance" (Sherman, 1993) as the independent variable in a general theory of all three domains of criminology: law-making, law-breaking and reactions to law-breaking (Sutherland, 1934: 3). The theory predicts behaviour in all three domains on the basis of emotion-driven moral obligations to *defy the status quo*, which can be dampened by "moral numbness" or heavily constructed through social networks of "rhetorical asymmetry" (Sunstein, 2009). Using the criminology of race in the US from 1619 to 2009 as case in point, the chapter shows how defiance theory achieves "consilience" of predictions in one class of events with similar predictions in other classes of events, all pointing to the same causal mechanism. An unceasing contest for the emotional "hearts and minds" of a society drives its perceived moral obligations, shaping moral indignation and empathy in causing crime, law, and punishment. Defiance theory, restated, provides a more comprehensive account than its earlier version of the failures of deterrence and retribution theories as the principal basis for strategies to obtain compliance with criminal laws.

DEFIANCE AS AN INDEPENDENT VARIABLE

The central idea of defiance theory is the emotional intuition of moral obligation to defy the status quo (Sherman, 1993, 1999, 2003). That emotion is a major independent variable predicting behaviour across all three domains of criminology, uniting them as no other theory has been able to do. The science of defiance contributes to explanations of law-making, law-breaking, and reactions to law-breaking (Sutherland, 1934: 3). This emotional sense of moral obligation or justification, rather than of wrong-doing, can be tested as a proximate cause beyond its initial scope of offender reactions to criminal sanctions (Sherman, 1993). These emotions of defiant moral obligation in relation to law, which social scientists and citizens often call *illegitimacy*, comprise a general causal force in criminology wherever definitions of right and wrong are contested. It can even predict desistance from crime when offenders, in effect, defy themselves, or the status quo of their previous identity, in response to a perceived moral obligation to become a new kind of person. Defiance is thus an independent variable that can be deployed across all three classes of events in criminology, rather than just as an "effect" (i.e., a dependent variable's response to an independent variable) found only in events of law-breaking.

Examples

Moral obligation was what Mississippi Senator James O. Eastland apparently had in mind when he declared "illegal" the 1954 U.S. Supreme Court decision in Brown v. Board of Education of Topeka Kansas. That decision required all public schools in the US to be de-segregated by race. "*Resistance to tyranny is obedience to God*," as the Senator told his constituents (Klarman, 2004: 427), borrowing an almost identical statement often misattributed to the primary author of the US Declaration of Independence, President Thomas Jefferson. The "tyranny" statement was also quoted by Susan Anthony (1900: 415), the leading campaigner for women's rights to vote in the US. The earliest record of the quotation attributes it to the Massachusetts Governor who took power after King James II was overthrown in the "Glorious Revolution" of 1688 (Massachusetts Constitutional Convention, 1853: 502).

Senator Eastland, it seems, was not alone in his view that morality trumps law. Even the University of Pennsylvania enshrines the sentiment in its University seal, a blend of the family coats of arms of Quaker William Penn and Deist Benjamin Franklin, the Latin motto of which is usually translated as:

Laws without morals are useless.

Moral obligation is also what Sudanese journalist Lubna Ahmed al-Hussein expressed in 2009 after a large group of police officers arrested her and 12 other women in a Khartoum restaurant for wearing trousers, in alleged violation of Islamic Sharia law. Several women who pled guilty to "dressing indecently" were flogged immediately with ten lashes, but Ms. Hussein pled not guilty and consulted a lawyer (BBC News, 2009a). When she was told she would not be prosecuted because she worked for the United Nations, she resigned her UN post and demanded that she be tried – so that the world would condemn the police actions as immoral. She told the BBC that "she wants a public flogging to make a point about the treatment of women in Sudan. She even sent out 500 invitations to witness her lashings" and scores of protesters rallied outside the courthouse when her case was heard. "I'm not afraid from pain, al-Hussein said, "... but flog is not pain, flog is (an) insult, insult to humans, insult to women" (CNN, 2009a).

Moral obligation is what R. Dwayne Betts (2009) expressed when he was sentenced to prison for an armed car-jacking, contradicting his character witnesses who said he committed crime because he was fatherless. He told the court and the victim that he committed the crime because he was wrong. The moment was an epiphany of defiance of his prior criminal behaviour and the street culture in which it arose, triggering remorse and a hope of redemption.

Overview

These and many other examples illustrate the challenge that criminology faces as a science whose empirical boundaries are defined by the precise content of the criminal law and the social mores – in any society, at any given moment. Meeting that challenge requires criminology to explain why people *create, enforce* or *nullify* laws, at the same time that criminology explains its favourite questions of why laws are broken or obeyed. This much has not been tried, at least not in a single coherent theory. Despite nearly a century of widespread acceptance of Sutherland's (1934: 3) definition of criminology as encompassing all of these questions, no theory has yet offered to use a single framework to link answers to them. The result has been three criminologies, one for each class of events. The challenge is to explore whether one theory can work in all three classes.

This chapter attempts to meet that challenge by offering a re-statement of defiance theory (Sherman, 1993). The original version of that theory was confined to explaining variation in responses of individuals and societies to criminal sanctions and sanction threats. That formulation focused on just one of Sutherland's three domains of criminology (law-breaking). Yet as sometimes happens in science, inductions from evidence in one class of events turn out to apply to inductions in another class of events – a pattern of testing theories that scientists historically called *consilience*. The goal of this chapter is to support the claim that inductions presented in the initial defiance theory can now be broadened in formulation, and then extended to the other domains of criminology as a coherent theory.

The chapter begins by reviewing the initial statement of defiance theory (Sherman, 1993), adding ten conceptual elaborations as the basis for re-formulating it as a general theory of criminology. It then introduces the concept of "consilience," as the standard a general theory must attempt to meet. The chapter then defines key terms and concepts for a *restated* construction of defiance theory. A formal re-statement of defiance theory follows, with some links to other theories in criminology. The chapter then illustrates the restated theory's consilience of predictions in the three classes of criminological phenomena with a brief outline of the criminology of race in the US from 1619 to 2009. The chapter concludes with a reflection on the implications of defiance theory for public policy.

DEFIANCE: VERSION 1.0

The initial version of defiance theory was an explanation of law-breaking caused by law-enforcing. Its purpose was to account for the variable effects of criminal sanctions on future criminal behaviour. "Defiance" was presented as one possible *effect* of criminal sanctions, which predictably occurs under certain conditions of sanction administration and the state of the person(s) subject to a sanction or sanction threat (Sherman, 1993: 459):

> Defiance is the net increase in the prevalence, incidence, or seriousness of future offending against a sanctioning community caused by a proud, shameless reaction to the administration of a criminal sanction.

Defiance theory integrated J. Braithwaite's (1989) theory of reintegrative shaming, Tyler's (1990) theory of procedural justice, Scheff and Retzinger's (1991) perspectives on emotions and violence, Black's (1983), Katz's (1988) and Weisburd's (1989) theories of what I called "displaced just deserts." Using key concepts from these theories, the initial defiance theory identified four conditions under which a "defiant effect" results from a criminal sanction or sanction threat (Sherman, 1993: 460):

> Defiance occurs under four conditions, all of which are necessary.
>
> 1 The offender defines a criminal sanction as unfair
> 2 The offender is poorly bonded to or alienated from the sanctioning agent or the community the agent represents.
> 3 The offender defines the sanction as stigmatizing and rejecting a person, not a lawbreaking act.
> 4 The offender denies or refuses to acknowledge the shame the sanction has actually caused him to suffer.

The initial statement of defiance identified two alternative conditions under which offenders would define sanctions as unfair (Sherman, 1993: 460):

> 1 The sanctioning agent behaves with disrespect for the offender, or for the group to which the offender belongs, regardless of how fair the sanction is on substantive grounds.
> 2 The sanction is substantively arbitrary, discriminatory, excessive, undeserved, or otherwise objectively unjust.

These building blocks then predicted three reactions to punishment that offenders define as unfair (Sherman, 1993: 461); point 2 in what follows can be seen as a "defiance effect":

> 1 When poorly bonded offenders accept the shame an unfair stigmatizing sanction provokes, the sanction will be *irrelevant* or possibly even deterrent to future rates of offending.
> 2 When poorly bonded offenders deny the shame they feel and respond with rage, the unfair stigmatizing sanction will *increase* their future rates of offending. This unacknowledged shame leads to an emotion of angry pride at defying the punishment. That pride predisposes the defiant offender to repeat the sanctioned conduct, symbolically labelling the sanctions or sanctioners, and not the offender's own acts, as truly shameful and morally deserving of punishment … .

3 The full shame-crime sequence does not occur, however, when a well-bonded offender defines a sanction as unfair … .

Elaborations on Version 1.0

Space does not permit a systematic review of the tests of this version of defiance theory, or "Defiance 1.0." That version is summarized here not to assess it on its own merits, but to extend its leverage into a general theory of criminology. In order to take the theory to that point of explaining behaviour in law-making and law-enforcing as well as in law-breaking (as "Defiance 2.0"), the following elaborations of the theory are necessary:

1 "Defiance" must be defined more broadly as a moral intuition (Sunstein, 2009) of an obligation or justification to defy the status quo, and not just as an effect of the administration of justice. That effect is included in the range of behaviour that defiance can explain as a general theory of criminology.
2 Defiance is therefore an independent variable, an emotional state of "angry pride," vengeance, sorrow, empathy or cold determination to disagree that can cause behaviour against the status quo.
3 Deterrence must also be seen as an independent variable located in the perspective of those attempting to resist challenges to the status quo, as an emotional intuition of moral obligation to deter comparable to the obligation to defy.
4 Both defiance and deterrence as *emotional predispositions* may or may not cause behaviour, which may or may not succeed in evoking the *effects* named after their intentions. Thus deterrent emotions may produce sanctioning behaviour that is "deterrent" by intent, but which encounters defiant emotions and produces defiant effects.
5 Whether defiant emotions lead to defiant behaviour (or deterrent emotions to deterrent behaviour) depends on a continuous contest between defiant and deterrent actors for winning the hearts and minds of any group of people. This contest depends on the success of any one of potentially numerous factions of actors in evoking moral indignation, empathy, or both by appealing to different principles of legitimation. Further elaborations of defiance theory must specify, then unify, the great range of these techniques and social processes.
6 Defiant emotions may cause a wide range of behaviours in law-making, law-breaking, and reactions to law-breaking. These can include lawful and unlawful efforts to change law itself (legislation versus revolution), lawful and unlawful use of powers delegated to agents of law, and nonviolent as well as violent confrontations by law-breakers with law-enforcers.
7 Both defiance and deterrence, as independent variables, must overcome predispositions to "moral numbness" associated with the routines of everyday life (Sunstein, 2009).
8 Moral intuitions of defiance are subject to rapid change and inconsistency, both individually and collectively, contingent on situational context and the "rhetorical asymmetry" of group dynamics and social networks (Sunstein, 2009).
9 Individuals, communities and nations can therefore defy themselves, rejecting their previous behaviour, condemning an old morality and embracing a new one (Braithwaite, 1989; Strang, 2002).
10 Defiance as a general theory of criminology therefore gives equal attention to the emotional intuitions of law-enforcers and law-breakers, of law-changers and law-change opponents, and especially the processes of reciprocal causation across the different classes of events in relation to criminal law.

The tenth elaboration summarizes the difference between the initial statement of defiance theory and the present restatement. It goes one giant step beyond the more-limited initial analysis of how sanctions are seen as unfair from the standpoint of the defiers of law enforcement (Sherman, 1993: 464), with an example of a disorderly conduct arrest that illustrated this general point:

> Those who approach authority with defiant attitudes are often punished for their speech rather than for any substantive offense. ... There is no written law against "contempt of cop," of course, but it is perhaps the most consistently enforced de facto law in the country. All systematic observation studies of police decision making (Sherman, 1980; Smith and Visher, 1981) have found that disrespect toward police powerfully increases the odds of being arrested.

Defiance, restated as a general theory, can now incorporate the emotions of *both* police and suspects in ways that the initial statement of the theory did not. It is just as important for criminology to understand why police punish disrespect as it is to understand why citizens often express it. If a single theory is able to explain both classes of events, then that extends the reach and explanatory power of criminology.

An elaboration of the initial defiance theory can also make problematic the moral contest within the wider *public audience* and divided opinions about encounters between citizens and police. The concept of a moral contest in elaboration number 5 above, for example, is clearly evident in the July, 2009 national debate in the United States over the Cambridge (Massachusetts) Police Department's arrest of Harvard Professor Henry Louis Gates in his own home (Seelye, 2009). This act of law-enforcement can be predicted by an elaborated defiance theory, but not by the original (Sherman, 1993) as formally stated.

Professor Gates was apparently feeling a defiant moral obligation to criticize intensely a police officer who demanded that Gates prove his ownership of his own home. In response, the police officer was apparently moved by deterrent emotions of obligation to insure that police would not be subjected to citizens criticizing police. The result was a Harvard professor photographed in handcuffs as he was led away from his own home for disorderly conduct (with the charges later dropped). The fact that the President of the United States then described the police conduct as "acting stupidly" ignited a firestorm of controversy in the US, culminating in a White House meeting "over a beer" in order to try to forget about the conflict – which was a moral contest between two people that mobilized a broader contest between two (or more) sides on the question in a nation of 300 million.

Forgetting about the conflict may have been good politics for the President, but it would not be a good path for criminology. Criminology needs to make such cases central to theories of law-making, law-breaking, and enforcing. The initial defiance theory stopped at the point of explaining why some law-making provokes law-breaking. But the concept of defiance can be applied well beyond that problem, in ways the elaboration above now makes possible.

DEFIANCE AND CONSILIENCE

While moral obligation is not the only factor predicting criminal behaviour, it is arguably one of the most important. Alone among many theories in criminology, defiance theory predicts phenomena in all three classes of events criminology must study: law-making, law-breaking and responses to law-breaking (Sutherland, 1934: 3). By making this claim, defiance theory must meet a higher standard of testing than mere prediction, as suggested by the nineteenth century polymath William Whewell – who invented the word "scientist" and set a stage for Darwin's general theory of evolution (Butts (ed.), 1989; Stanford Encyclopaedia of Philosophy, 2006). By Whewell's standard, any *general* theory must demonstrate the *consilience* (Whewell, 1840: 230) of inductions based on one class of events, such as law-making, with inductions based on another class of events, such as law-breaking. (Whewell also required a test of *coherence*, but conceded that consilience alone was sufficient evidence of a theory's coherence.)

Consilience, as Whewell (1840, 1847) defined it, is achieved when a range of observations and inductions "leap to the same point" of explanation by one common cause. As a primary example, Whewell (1840: 230–232) used Newton's law of universal gravitation as (1840: 230–232). He showed how Newton linked diverse observations about tides, falling objects, planetary orbits and other phenomena, demonstrating that they all pointed to the same general theory of gravitational force. That general theory of physics used a precise equation to fit all phenomena affected by gravity, both on earth and in outer space.

With the same goal of consilience, but with far less precision, defiance is now offered as a general theory of criminology. It mobilizes the growing intellectual consensus about moral intuitions (Sunstein, 2009) to make claims of causality in different classes of criminological phenomena. It predicts that *criminal laws are more likely to be made, broken, obeyed and enforced when people intuitively feel that their actions are morally founded*. It claims, in turn, that these moral judgments are reciprocally constructed across the domains of law-enforcing, law-breaking and law-making. The theory locates the causes of these moral judgments in both the "agency" of individual and collective actors as well as in the "unseen hand" of neuro-social dynamics – such as moral panics (Cohen, 1972), or the "identifiable victim" empathy and indignation advantage over harms to nameless victims of greater number.

Defiance theory does not attempt to provide a complete explanation for all aspects of crime and justice. Nor does it claim to be the only *general* theory criminology needs. Rather, it uses one powerful force – intuitions of moral obligation – to unify the causality of different classes of events in crime and justice on the basis of a single set of inductions.

A "general" criminological theory is not necessarily a "crime-general" one that attempts to explain all kinds of crime with a single hypothesis, as Gottfredson and Hirschi (1990) suggested. Rather, this chapter uses a conception of general theory more in keeping with the usage of the term in physics and biology: one that can explain a general problem found in different classes of events and at multiple levels of analysis.

The general problem of criminology is to explain and predict the reciprocal system of the content, enforcement and compliance with criminal law (Figure 19.1). This problem comprises three elements identified by Edwin Sutherland (1934: 3): criminal law-making, law-breaking, and responses to law-breaking. A *general* theory of criminology cannot be limited to any one of those questions, but must provide a link across the answers to all three. This requirement poses a higher standard of

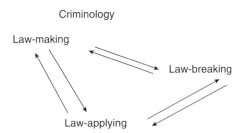

Figure 19.1   The general problem.

testing for a general theory than for more specific theories limited to one of the three questions, such as persistence or desistence in law-breaking over the life-course.

The importance of general theory is that it can yield predictions that would otherwise not be possible. Newton's theory led to the prediction that another planet must be in the universe beyond the eight that had been observed up to the time when the prediction was made. In 1846, the prediction was verified: Neptune was found on the basis of inductive equations yielding a precise guide to where astronomers should look for it (Sheehan *et al.*, 2004).

Such surprising predictions can also occur in criminology, although they have been harder to test. Braithwaite (2005), for example, applies hypotheses about restorative justice for individual criminality at the level of nation-states. His prediction at both levels is for the same result: less harm from redemptive managing of shame and pride than by pure retribution. He also post-dicts (Braithwaite, 2009) that restorative justice for the financial industry after the Enron collapse of 2001 could have prevented the financial collapse of 2008.

By taking consilience seriously, criminology may be able to advance more rapidly than by working on only one class of event at a time. Defiance should not remain the only theory that seeks to achieve consilience across classes, nor will it necessarily survive systematic testing to falsify it. What it may do best is to illustrate the potential for consilience in a field that has claimed to study three kinds of events, but invests almost all of its energy in only one.

DEFINING DEFIANCE: KEY CONCEPTS

In the fell clutch of circumstance
I have not winced nor cried aloud.
Under the bludgeonings of chance
My head is bloodied, but unbowed.

It matters not how straight the gate,
How charged with punishments the scroll,
I am the master of my fate.
I am the captain of my soul.

William Ernest Henley, 1875
"Invictus" [Unconquered]

The key concept of defiance as a general theory of criminology is a moral intuition to defy or resist the status quo – even with a head bloodied (but unbowed) from punishment for that resistance. This intuitive moral obligation may be driven by indignation, by empathy, or by some other powerful emotion that is experienced as right and righteous. This can occur while going on a hunger strike in prison, while killing a baby (Katz, 1988), or while desisting from criminal behaviour after release from prison (Maruna, 2001). The sense of moral obligation may explain why attempts by authorities to clamp down on efforts to change the status quo may result in even more efforts to effect that change – or why efforts by authorities to *create* change may amplify *resistance* to change. In either direction, the meaning of defiance is to fight back against a (so-far) dominant moral force. This includes both defiant effects and defiance as a cause of those effects, as well as several varieties of defiance.

Defiant effects vs. defiance causes

The initial statement of defiance theory (Sherman, 1993) implied two different criminological definitions of "defiance," but failed to clarify the distinctions. One meaning described defiance as a particular pattern of *effect* of criminal sancions. The other meaning described defiance as the *cause* of that effect. The particular effect is that crime sometimes expands in the aftermath of sanctions (Sherman, 1993: 448), as indicated in the words italicized in this chapter but not the original:

> Sanctions provoke defiance of the law (*persistence, more frequent or severe violations*) to the extent that offenders experience sanctioning conduct as illegitimate, that offenders have weak bonds to the sanctioning agent and community, and that offenders deny their shame and become proud of their isolation from the sanctioning community.

While the definition was followed immediately by a summary of the hypothesized causes of the effect, in the above quotation the italicized definition clearly refers to the criminal behaviour itself. In contrast, the second definition offered in the article refers clearly to the *causes* of that behaviour. But it unfortunately redefines the *defiance effect* of the sanctions by limiting it to that portion of criminal acts attributable to the causes specified by defiance theory (Sherman, 1993: 459):

> Defiance is the net increase in the prevalence, incidence, or seriousness of future offending against a sanctioning community caused by a proud, shameless reaction to the administration of a criminal sanction.

This is a clear flaw of contradiction in the definitions used in the initial theory. In retrospect, it would have been clearer to distinguish a defiant *effect* as an *observation* of a dependent variable (an expansion of crime) in response to the independent variable of sanctioning, and defiance *theory* as the algorithm of independent variables accounting for defiance effects. Such a distinction would track common usage of the concept of *"deterrent effects"* to mean any reduction in crime after sanctions are imposed, even without evidence that the reduction was caused by the hypothesized mechanisms (such as fear or utility) of deterrence doctrine (Gibbs, 1975). Such clarity might, for example, have allowed LaFree to use consistent language between his first report on a "defiance effect" in Northern Ireland (LaFree, 2007) and what anonymous peer reviewers required him (LaFree, 2009) to re-name a "backlash effect" in a subsequent article in the same journal (Lafree, *et al.*, 2009). The initial failure to use a single, consistent definition of defiant effect (Sherman, 1993) is the source of this confusion.

This restatement now presents a single definition of a *defiant effect* as the clear opposite of a *deterrent effect*. Even in publications subject to extensive peer review, the term "deterrent effect" is generally used without any evidence that a theoretical mechanism of deterrence caused a reduction in crime after a sanction (see, e.g., Sherman, 1990). The same can be said for what are called deterrent effects reported in LaFree and his colleagues' (2009) report on sanctions against terrorism in Northern Ireland. It is reasonable to call these observations "deterrent effects" because the pattern is consistent with the facts that deterrence theory can explain, even if the connecting links of that theory (inside the "black box") are not measured. The same should be true, by extension, for defiant effects.

For a general theory of criminology, there is a further consideration in the choice of words. A defiant effect needs to be defined as something that is possible in all three realms of criminology. We can define a *"defiant effect"* in a general theory of criminology as a form of *active resistance to a countervailing force*. A defiant effect must not only be seen in a decision to increase offending. It must also be seen in attempts to change law itself, or in a decision *not* to enforce law when enforcers defy their legal duty (as police have done while watching lynchings; see Garland (2005) and below). All classes of defiant effects have such behaviours that are observable.

We can then hypothesize what will be much harder to measure: the cause of that active resistance. That is the general sense in which *"defiance" as a cause* of any defiant effect can be described as an *individual or collective sense of moral obligation, including indignation and empathy*. The connection of defiance theory to indignation was clear in its original statement (Sherman, 1993). Since then, the work on restorative justice (Strang, 2002) and, more generally, on the criminology of emotions has pointed to empathy as a gateway to the feelings of remorse, repentance, redemption and reconciliation. To the extent that empathy can both cause and mitigate moral indignation, it is a central pillar of the larger concept of moral obligation.

The work of Valerie Braithwaite on the *attitudinal and behavioural signals* of defiance can also be incorporated into this framework. It is difficult to distinguish the attitudes she has measured in relation to tax law compliance (Braithwaite, V., 2009a) from the moral intuitions (Sunstein, 2009) that cause behaviour in all three criminological domains, but they clearly tap similar causes of crime-related behaviour. Valerie Braithwaite (2009b) defines defiance as:

> a signal that individuals express attitudinally or behaviourally towards an authority (and share with others) that communicates an unwillingness to follow the authority's prescribed path without question or protest.

The great virtue of this definition for a general theory of criminology is that it could describe defiant effects on "the authority's prescribed path" for law-making (status quo, for example), law-enforcing (less of it, a nicer treatment for suspects, or other dimension) and law-obeying (which anyone from war protesters to terrorists feel morally obligated to refuse to do).

Other concepts for defiance theory

Extending a defiance theory of law-breaking into a general theory of criminology requires redefinition of several other concepts from the last version of the theory, as well as some new concepts. These concepts include specific vs. general defiance, direct vs. displaced defiance, concealed vs. identifiable defiance, active vs. passive defiance, and (from V. Braithwaite, 2009b) resistant vs. dismissive defiance. These ten concepts form five dimensions of behaviour in relation to criminal law.

1. Specific vs. general defiance

This dimension is an analogue to specific vs. general deterrence. Specific defiance describes a single individual; general defiance describes a collectivity. Specific defiance (both cause and effect) is thus an oppositional reaction of an individual to an encounter with the status quo – of the content, violation or enforcement of law. The reaction could be law-enforcing, law-making or law-breaking. For example, if I become indignant about the widespread non-enforcement of the dog-walking leash law in my village, I could demand that the local police increase enforcement of the law through patrols, or I could videotape offenders and make citizens' arrests (*specific defiant law-enforcing*). I would be defiant of the status quo out of moral indignation. Or I could demand that the County Council triple the fine for walking a dog without a leash (*specific defiant law-making*). Or I could even take the law into my own hands, shooting the dogs or their owners (*specific defiant law-breaking*). All that would fall under the heading of "specific defiance" of the status quo.

  General defiance would occur if I organized the "Greater Respect for Rural Runners (GRRR)" as a national lobby against dog leash law violations, and local chapters of GRRR sprang up around the country. The collective actions of these groups would constitute general defiance in law-enforcing and law-making. If GRRR or others followed the path of some animal rights groups, we would smash the windows or even burn the houses of dog-leash law violators (*general defiant law-breaking*). Or if we followed the path of anti-abortion groups in the US, we would plan strategic assassinations of very flagrant violators of leash laws, perhaps owners of pit bulls who kill children.

2. Direct vs. displaced defiance

This dimension was originally described as direct versus indirect (Sherman, 1993), but with ample use of the concept of displacement.

  Defiant Law-Breaking is easily divided into at least these two categories. As Black (1983) has noted, much crime is committed with the moral intuition that the act is not crime but punishment. Some of this crime is directly aimed at persons who have committed a moral wrong in the eyes of the "punisher" (who is legally an offender). A crime committed against such a person – such as the 2009 murder of Kansas abortion doctor George Tiller in the lobby of his church – may be called "direct defiance." Displaced defiance is a crime committed against someone who is not personally known to the "punisher" to be immoral but who is a member of the same identity group to which a known immoral direct target belongs (the person who is the real focus of the moral indignation) – such as the murders of New York City police officers in 1971 by the Black Liberation Army.

Defiant law-enforcing can be equally direct when police "kettle" or restrain for hours every person who was actually demonstrating in the 1st April 2009 protests in London. Or it can be displaced, as in the videotaped attack by a riot squad police constable on a non-protesting bystander, Ian Tomlinson, who may have died as a result of his injuries (Edwards and Smith, 2009).

Defiant law-making can be directly aimed at a particular target of indignation, such as police chiefs Daryl Gates of Los Angeles (in 1992), Harold Breier of Milwaukee (in 1984) and Public Safety Commissioner "Bull" Connor of Birmingham, Alabama (in 1963). All three of these police executives lost their long-term control over large police agencies as a result of legislation or referendum changing the law. In all three cases, the purpose was to punish these police leaders for their hostility to African-Americans. Law-making can also constitute displaced defiance. One example may be the banning of head cover for female students in French schools in 2004, perhaps in moral indignation at the violent actions of a tiny fraction of all Muslims world-wide.

3. Concealed vs. identifiable defiance

This new classification of defiance is a continuum indicating how much a defiant actor is willing to sacrifice for the moral cause she defends.

Concealed and identified defiant law-breaking

Suicide bombers are the most extreme example of identifiable defiance, especially those bombers who look forward to a memorial videotape about them celebrating their bravery, one that will be watched for many years after their deaths. Identification is essential in such cases. Less identifiable was the accused killer of abortion doctor George Tiller, who made little effort to conceal his identity as he fled the church – but fled nonetheless. Less identifiable yet was Timothy McVeigh, the 1995 Oklahoma City Federal building bomber who went to his death proclaiming his crime to be an act of war against an illegitimate government – yet he fled the scene of the crime with an excellent chance of continued concealment. This dimension locates the protestors of the 2009 Iranian elections, who risked being shot on the streets of Teheran and ultimately stopped their daily marches. Yet they continued their defiance in a concealed way, just as their predecessors had in the 1979 revolution against the Shah: wailing on the rooftops after dark, where law enforcement cannot identify them. This form of "crime" against the orders of the regime to stop protesting is surely defiance, but with an eye towards a long-term project of resistance against unjust authority.

Concealed and identifiable defiant law-enforcing

The Iranian case also illustrates the necessity of concealment even for governments in power. The Iranian government in 2009 made every effort to conceal what is widely alleged to be cheating in the counting of votes – a form of corrupt law-enforcement that could be seen as a defiant reaction to the emergence of a strong opposition candidate to incumbent President Achmed Amadinejad. Unlike Iraqi President Saddam Hussein's absurd (and identifiable) announcement that he had been re-elected by 104 per cent of the vote, the Iranian government went through all the motions of an appeal and review of the ballot counts. They made an effort, at least, to deny any wrongdoing, rather than flaunting a theft of the vote.

Concealed and identifiable defiant law-making   Lawmakers or candidates for election often face a risk of murder in their campaigns, especially if they campaign against fanaticism – like Benazir Bhutto – or if they are themselves seen as fanatical (like George Wallace). Others are at the mercy of the governments against which they campaign, like Burma's Aung San Suu Kyi, who remains in confinement many years after her arrest during an election. Some may remain identifiable but retreat from the scene of struggle, like the Dalai Lama. Still other defiant law-makers may remain entirely hidden, like the allegedly corrupt control of the US Senate during the early twentieth century by heads of large corporations who could buy entire state legislatures that (at that time) elected all US Senators.

4. Active vs. passive defiance
This dichotomy connects to its close companions of concealment (above) and resistance (below). The distinction here is that active defiance requires action, while passive defiance requires withholding of action. Both may entail risks of confrontation, but in some situations a passive strategy may be more effective in changing the status quo.

Passive vs. active defiant lawmaking   The phrase "boycott" denotes a passive withholding of action, as in a failure to purchase a product that you may need but will forego as a passive statement of defiance. The origin of the word "boycott" in Ireland referred to a British land agent, Captain Charles Cunningham Boycott, from whom Irish farmers decided to withhold their labour in 1880 in collective defiance of agrarian land laws. Not even local shops would serve Captain Boycott; the British Army eventually came to harvest his crop for him. Even then, the concept of such passive defiance (without using Boycott's name) was at least a century old. Hundreds of thousands of British households, for example, stopped buying sugar in the late eighteenth century as in collective defiance of the laws allowing the Atlantic Slave trade to continue, even as it made Britain wealthy (Hochschild, 2005). But when Quakers and other religious groups obtained 390,000 signatures petitioning the parliament to abolish the slave trade in 1792, their defiance of the status quo of slavery – but not of the system of government – was manifestly active (Hochschild, 2005: 230).

Passive vs. active defiant law-enforcing   Law-enforcing can passively resist the status quo by ignoring the law. This is the larger meaning of police discretion, as described in Wilson (1968), Westley (1970), Reiss (1971), Black (1980), and other field studies. When police under-enforce the law, they resist the "zero tolerance" letter of the law in order to allow their own sense of moral obligation to be met. Why, they may feel, should they arrest a man for slapping his wife if they themselves have done the same thing? Why should they arrest some kids for "kid stuff" like stealing apples from a fruit stand if they did it at the same age? Why should they arrest young men for possessing pot when they smoked some last weekend? But moral indignation has also spurred police into defiant law-enforcement, doing more than is required or even allowed by law when they are morally outraged at the alleged lawbreakers – such as Rodney King in Los Angeles in 1991 or Abner Louima in New York in 1997.

Passive vs. active defiant lawbreaking Passive defiance of income tax laws is probably as old as income tax, which was introduced to Britain early in Queen Victoria's reign. The simple failure to report any and all income constitutes doing nothing – which is a crime. Failure to buy a ticket before boarding a train, failure to put on a seat belt in a car, failure to get enough sleep before driving a car – these and many other inactions constitute crimes by definition. Yet they are also very hard to detect. If your moral intuitions tell you that a "nanny state" should not be making you do all these things, you can take your stand with Melville's (1853) character called Bartleby, the scrivener, who wound up in prison in a descent from lower middle-class respectability by successively reciting the phrase "I would prefer not to."

As for active defiance while law-breaking, there may be no better example than attacking a law-maker. One example in 2009 was a UK citizen who was angry at Alan Duncan, M.P., for some expenses the M.P. was reimbursed for by the House of Commons. The citizen expressed his defiance by digging up a part of the M.P.'s lawn – in the shape of the £ sign for UK money. A far more deadly example is the 1984 bombing of the Conservative Party conference in Brighton by the Irish Republican Army, which almost killed the entire Cabinet of a nation's government.

5. Resistant vs. dismissive defiance

This final distinction is taken from Valerie Braithwaite (2009b), who notes two different purposes of defiant behaviours or attitudes towards tax authorities: "resistant" and "dismissive" defiance. *Resistant defiance* for Braithwaite appears when:

> the purpose is to change the course of action that the authority is taking but not destroy the authority itself. 'I don't like the way you are doing this and I want you to change, but I don't dispute that we need an authority to regulate us in this area.

This idea lies at the heart of procedural justice (Tyler, 1990), and all theories of legitimacy that address the manners or fairness of law enforcement. It is at the core of the initial statement of defiance theory (Sherman, 1993). In V. Braithwaite's formulation, it includes substantive justice ("change the course of action") as well as procedural (I don't like *the way* you are doing this), but it accepts the government's moral right to rule.

The *resistant* form of defiance might better be called an "engaged" defiance, in which defiers are willing to engage and work with those they defy or contradict. This stands in sharp contrast to the "disengaged" stance of dismissive defiance, in which the defiers do not accept the right of authority to exist; they just want to be left alone. As Braithwaite defines it, *dismissive defiance* is manifested by the defier when:

> the purpose is to disable the authority, to prevent the authority from intervening in this aspect of life. 'You have no business telling me what to do – no one should have the authority that you have over me.

V. Braithwaite's (2009b) data on Australian taxpayers revealed the same divisions over the distinction found in the US between the quest for fair treatment and the quest to destroy government. Dismissive defiance is amply expressed, for example, in the libertarian views of families like the authors *Little House on the Prairie* series, Laura Ingalls Wilder and her daughter-editor, Rose Lane (Thurman, 2009). Rose Lane's 1943 book, *The Discovery of Freedom: Man's Struggle Against Authority*, was a classic tract of the anti-statist movement that reacted defiantly to President Roosevelt's New Deal (and its taxes). As Thurman (2009) describes Lane's romantic view of an independent grandfather who illegally settled on a reservation set aside for Native-Americans:

> Her vision was of a quasi-anarchic democracy, with minimal taxes, limited government, and no entitlements, regulated only by the principle of personal responsibility. Its citizens would be equal in their absolute freedom to flourish or to fail.

Ironically, this vision came from the Wilder women as descendants of a New England Puritan family. Before living almost alone in the American West, that family lived in a culture founded on a vision of tight social control and a high level of governmental intrusiveness. This same New England culture had also produced an intrusive moral sentiment for abolition of slavery, defying the status quo settlement at Philadelphia in 1787 which allowed slave and free states to form the Union. For these and other reasons, no case study is more relevant for inducing a general theory of criminology than the history of race and criminal law in the US. But first we must provide a formal statement of defiance theory to apply to that history.

DEFIANCE THEORY: A RESTATEMENT

Premises

1 Defiance theory is an explanation (*explanans*) for what can be called defiant "effects" (*explananda*) on law-breaking, law-making and law-enforcing.
2 Defiance theory explains defiant behaviour, defined as morally-justified challenges to the status quo, by reference to variation in emotional intuitions of moral obligation.
3 People selectively perceive some harm caused by humans against others.
4 Moral intuitions about that harm may create emotions of empathy, indignation, or both.
5 These emotions may create a moral obligation to defy the status quo as illegitimate (by lacking a moral basis).
6 Defiance may be resistant (engaged) or dismissive (disengaged).
7 All defiance is a contest for audience approval of a claimed moral obligation, even when the audience is a single individual engaged in personal choice.
8 The dynamics of moral contests may predict the rates at which people act on their moral intuitions, repress them, or remain "morally numb," especially in the face of countervailing deterrent threats.
9 Resistant defiance can change or maintain outcomes of law-making, lawbreaking, and responses to lawbreaking.
10 Dismissive defiance by lawbreakers can cause regime change, lawbreaking, or increased severity of punishment for lawbreaking.
11 Defiance in any class of events may persist for decades or centuries.
12 Defiance can occur at macro, mezzo and micro levels, including individual conduct.

Predictions

1 Conduct will be criminalized to the extent that opponents of the conduct promote a feeling of moral obligation to oppose that conduct as illegitimate.

2 Laws will be enforced to the extent that enforcement agencies collectively and individually accept the legitimacy of the moral obligation to do so.

3 Laws will be broken to the extent that potential offenders feel a moral obligation to defy agents making and enforcing laws as illegitimate.

4 Morally infused campaigns of law-breaking can lead to changes in law, to the extent that the violations promote a feeling of moral obligation to allow them.

5 Law-makers and enforcers will also break laws, or re-make them, to the extent that they feel moral indignation, empathy, or a moral obligation to do so.

6 Changes in moral indignation or empathy can be fostered by events causing an epiphany revealing the harm caused by some conduct, law or punishment.

7 All of these predictions must be qualified by the possible interaction of other factors, such as invasions or massive armed force used to repress civilians, as well as other known causes of crime and social control.

Defiance and other theories

Defiance theory, as restated, explains the behavioural systems tied to criminal law as *symbolic contests* for the highest moral ground: the claim to *legitimacy*. These contests are performed for audiences whose moral intuitions (Sunstein, 2009) may provisionally decide who wins. Their decisions may be reversed, however, by appeals to wider audiences (as by women in the Sudan) or by repeated rematches on the same issue with the same audience but different contestants. Whether we see these contests in a sports metaphor, or use the dramaturgical metaphor of morality plays (Manning, 1977), we know the audiences engaged in watching the contests vary widely in their size and influence. Setting the stage for defiance theory locates the most important intuitions of moral obligation in these audiences, in ways that deeply affect the behaviour of the direct participants: the offenders, the law-enforcers, and law-makers.

This contest for the emotional "hearts and minds" can be as much a matter of skill as of power. Growing research suggests the effectiveness of some strategies over others for communicating outrage and organizing defiant actions. These strategic differences include emphasizing identifiable victims (e.g., "Megan's Law") over unidentified "statistical victims" (Heinzerling, 2000, as cited in Sunstein, 2009), victims close to home rather than far away, and the "rhetorical asymmetry" of readier group acceptance of a moral panic (Cohen, 1972) than of arguments that the alleged harm is overblown (Sunstein, 2009: 432). Similarly, organized strategies of fostering "moral numbness" may prevent societies from criminalizing or punishing very harmful behaviour (such as causes of global warming) even as they severely punish trivial behaviour. The strategic mechanisms for winning over hearts and minds on these issues appear quite basic. The neuro-social pathways (Borg *et al.*, 2006; Sinnott-Armstrong, 2008) of moral intuition link brain patterns and group context in ways that shape all phenomena of interest to criminology.

Defiance theory is therefore a complement to conflict theories in criminology that see criminal law as a struggle shaped by resources of *material* power of police and prisons. Defiance theory recognizes the material force of that power, but also predicts the long-term control of that force will fall into the hands of actors and social networks skilful enough to shape the *moral* intuitive power of electoral majorities (Gladwell, 2009; Ranulf, 1938).

Defiance theory also complements one of its major inspirations, the "techniques of neutralization" theory (Sykes and Matza, 1957). Defiance theory accepts that much lawbreaking may occur by neutralizing the moral force in favour of criminal laws, but suggests that offenders are often moved by an affirmative moral obligation to offend. Its initial argument rooted that hypothesis in theories of reintegrative shaming (Braithwaite, 1989), procedural justice (Tyler, 1990), and the Scheff and Retzinger (1991) analysis of emotions – all of which defiance theory continues to complement in the restatement below.

Defiance also still shares with subcultural theories the concept of competing systems of morality. But defiance theory can be far more flexible about where moral judgments come from. It does not require an entire moral system engulfing a distinct culture to predict a moral obligation to offend, or to punish, or to fight to change laws. Rather, defiance theory includes situational observations of emotions of moral obligation emerging in the spur of a moment (Collins, 2008; Wikstrom, 2006). In these moments, law-breakers may acknowledge the general moral legitimacy of law but feel in that a particular situation they had no choice but to break the law, either because they lacked control or because some higher moral imperative made it obligatory (Rock, 2009).

Defiance theory can complement all these and other theories by focusing on the central factor of moral intuitions that links them in their effects on law, crime and punishment. Defiance can meet the challenge of a general theory by only claiming to be a *partial* explanation for behaviour in any of criminology's domains. Its ambition is not to answer every question in criminology, but rather to reveal the theoretical connections that may advance the development of other theories as well.

Defiance and legitimacy

Defiance theory, as re-stated, uses the idea of moral obligation to predict illegitimacy, rather than to define it. By this distinction, it narrowly avoids tautology. To the extent that people who break the law may say that the law is illegitimate, it can be difficult to measure lawbreaking separately from an emotional sense of moral obligation. Even measures of procedural justice, by which people tell interviewers their opinions about how the law has treated them, may in fact be measuring underlying predispositions against law – and for crime. Defiance theory does not claim that all lawbreaking is caused by emotions of moral obligation – just some crime, and some law-making and some law-enforcing. The challenge is our measurement capacity to observe the distinctions between behaviour during acceptance of the status quo and behaviour while defying the status quo.

Police scholars may point the way to solving the tautology problem with their concept of "righteous cause corruption." Their concept distinguishes between police who break the law for their own personal reward, and police who break the law to satisfy a defensible moral obligation. Acts such as torture or beating people who would otherwise escape justice are frequently in the headlines in our post 9–11 world. Police in developing nations, such as Brazil and India, are often accused of executing suspects without trial or judicial authority. Developed nations are currently engaging in what may be the most serious contest about the morality of torture since Beccaria (1764) changed the moral sentiments of monarchs. The outcome of the contest is not clear, but the role of moral obligation in that conversation is manifest.

To the extent possible, tests of defiance theory as restated will depend on measuring *substantive principles of legitimation*. By focusing on intuitive sentiments (Sunstein, 2009) of moral obligation as the source of these principles, the concept of legitimacy is freed to vary independently of those principles. The principle of private property, for example, may not have been (in contemporary opinion) a legitimate consideration for the British government to consider when abolishing slavery in 1833, at least in the sentiments of New England abolitionists. But Parliamentary records make very clear that the moral principle of protecting private property won legitimacy (and compensation) in London when the UK banned slavery. Thus the same principle may succeed in some settings or periods and fail in others. What defiance does to explain these differences is to inject the crucial role of emotion into the dynamic of a contest among competing principles, even in societies that are not democratic.

Thus rehabilitation was once seen as the "right" thing to do with criminals, because every person has the potential to lead a good and honest life. Yet that principle of legitimation was strongly rejected in the US in the 1970s, in order to argue that parole boards were illegitimate – either from the right, which preferred legitimacy based on "truth in sentencing," or on the left, which sought legitimacy in personal freedom to hold anti-social attitudes beyond the review of parole boards. Indeterminate sentencing fast became illegitimate under this moral reconstruction project, and it was defiantly replaced by morally-inspired guidelines and flat sentences.

To say that people change laws, or commit crime, because they see the law as illegitimate is therefore not enough. Absent an independent measurement of moral principles that support or undermine legitimacy, explaining defiance with illegitimacy *alone* risks a circular argument: that people define law as illegitimate because they commit crime. To say, however, that a law was made (or broken, or enforced) because one principle of legitimation won a battle for emotional "hearts and minds" with a conflicting principle is a different matter entirely. Once the moral principle is specified, it can be measured and used, if the data indicate, to falsify defiance theory.

The issues of measurement are beyond the scope of this chapter, but one concluding example may help to support the claims about measuring moral obligation. The work of Paul Ekman (2007) has made great progress in measuring emotions in facial expressions that have been found universal across cultures. His micro-expression training tool (METT) is available on-line at www.mettonline.com. In principle, that tool could be used to measure emotions related to moral obligation by filming faces, and then coding the facial expressions of emotions. Even laboratory simulations of responses to discussions of morally contested issues of criminal law might offer tests of defiance theory as restated.

As a first test of the restated theory, this chapter uses the single most violently contested moral issue in the history of domestic rule of law in the US: the morality of using force to enslave, restrain and repress black people.

AN OUTLINE OF THE CRIMINOLOGY OF RACE IN THE US: 1619–2009

The making, enforcing and breaking of criminal laws in relation to the races of black and white in the United States preceded its Declaration of Independence by 157 years. In August of 1619, a document recorded the arrival in Jamestowne, Virginia, of "20 and odd" blacks on a Dutch trading ship (National Park Service, 2009). There is reportedly no evidence that the new arrivals were enslaved. Nor was slavery yet a well-established British institution, in the Caribbean or elsewhere, even though black slaves first came to England in 1555 (Hochschild, 2005: 13). Not until 1662 was slavery recognized in the Virginia colony's statutory law. By 1670 free blacks could no longer own white indentured servants. By 1691 blacks and whites were banned from marrying. By 1692 blacks could no longer own horses, cattle or hogs; slaves were deprived of trial by jury in capital crimes (National Park Service, 2009).

There is no criminological research on the law-making that established slavery in early Virginia or other colonies, but there is a hypothesis from defiance theory: that the moral sentiments of whites led them to conclude that it "felt right" to buy and use people who had already been enslaved by others. These sentiments were supported by ethicists such as John Locke (a slave-owner who famously wrote about the "consent of the governed") and George Whitefield (the Methodist evangelist who stirred the Great Awakening, and also owned 50 Georgia slaves). The Reverend Mr. Whitefield even implied it was a duty to do so, since "hot countries cannot be cultivated without negroes" (Hochschild, 2005: 87).

The reasons stated to morally justify slavery could be attributed to techniques of neutralization (Sykes and Matza, 1957), or to quasi-Aristotelian ideas that slaves are servile by nature and deserve no better – redolent of the way in which the staff of the concentration camps denied the full humanity of the Jews in the final solution (Rock, 2009). But the reasons people articulate for their behaviours are not necessarily causes (Sunstein, 2009). Many theories, economic and sociological, can be invoked to explain the rise of slavery. Most of them would fail, however, in explaining its demise – let alone other aspects of law enforcement and crime.

Defiance theory arguably explains all these dimensions of the problem by reference to a *public contest of moral obligations*. Moreover, it explains the legal demise of slavery, using the very different pathways in the US and UK to demonstrate a consilience of inductions. Defiance further explains the growing legal equality of African-Americans in the late twentieth century, even while explaining police brutality against blacks and rising rates of black crime among blacks, culminating in an imprisoned legion of blacks in a nation with a half-black President.

Defiant law-making on race

Britons largely ignored slavery for two centuries, morally numbed to it because slavery was beyond their daily experience. Slaves were kept almost entirely out of Britain until after the American Revolution. The British colonials who saw slavery in person were a tiny fraction of all of His Majesty's subjects, and most of those had an enormous economic stake in enslavement. It was not until Quakers encountered large numbers of slaves in the urban setting of Philadelphia that any British subjects denounced slavery in writing. In 1760 the Huguenot Anthony Benezet, who taught slaves in a Philadelphia Quaker School, published his *Observations on the enslaving, importing, and purchasing of negroes*. He also founded the first abolitionist society, continued by strong leaders (such as Dr. Benjamin Rush) after Beenzet's death. As the title page of an early biography (Vaux, 1817) summarizes Benezet's life, he exemplified the rise of empathy in the moral intuitions of the age,

> He was the offspring of humanity,
> And every child of sorrow was his brother.

The power of the printed word spread opposition in England. In 1774 John Wesley published his *Thoughts Upon Slavery*, which fed the ban on slave-owning preachers established by American Methodists in 1780 (Matlack, 1849). These writings combined with a rapid influx of American ex-slaves in London after the revolution – freed in recognition of their fighting for the Crown against the rebels – to create a dry forest that could be hit by a forest fire of moral sentiment (Gladwell, 2000). The tipping point was the *Zong* case that so shocked with British moral sentiments in 1783: 130 slaves had been thrown from a ship into the sea in an attempt to earn more money for their insurance than they would likely have fetched at market in the Carribbean. The case ruled only on whether the insurance company had to pay the ship owner for the full value of the slaves his Captain murdered (it did), not whether mass murder had been committed. That ruling shocked the Vice Chancellor of Cambridge University into setting a prize essay competition on whether it is "lawful to make slaves of others against their will" (Hochschild, 2005: 87).

The winner of that essay prize, an Anglican priest in training named Thomas Clarkson, devoted the rest of his life to the abolition of slavery. Together with the more famous William Wilberforce, MP, and an unsung band of organizers in hundreds of British cities and towns, Clarkson set the stage for a non-violent abolition of slavery. The complex history of the process ultimately depended on Clarkson fanning middle-class *empathy* for slaves and *indignation* at slave owners. Its success ultimately depended on larger political shifts in Britain, culminating in the Reform Act of 1832 that substantially increased votes by the middle class. Fifty-two years after he began, the British government enacted a law in 1833 that abolished slavery on 31 July, 1838 throughout the Empire. The largely non-violent solution worked by providing massive compensation to slave-owners for their loss of "property". The price was enormous: 40 per cent of the annual national budget. But compared to the price paid in the US, it was a bargain.

American abolitionists were inspired by the same moral sentiments, and with greater political power in their home states. But as a federal government, America had vested more political power in slave-owners than Britain ever had. Both north and south, it seems, were morally convinced they were right, but on opposite principles of moral legitimation. In the north, the principle was universal human rights of individuals. In the south, the principle was the right of states to freedom from an external authority. Both sides were morally indignant against the status quo: the north against slavery, the south against the greater political and industrial power of the north. In the end, the resolution was by massive bloodshed. Over 600,000 people died, or some 2 per cent of the US population (Faust, 2008). That did not begin to equal the 16 million slaves who may have died in transportation or extreme working conditions (Stannard, 1993). But the price of the American resolution by force vastly exceeded the price of the English "hearts and minds" (and money) resolution.

Only there was no resolution. The old form of slavery was gone, but the rise of "Jim Crow" laws created an American Apartheid that grew steadily over the next century. (Much the same happened in the British colonies). Criminal law-making repressed black rights. Disenfranchisement flourished along with lynchings. Segregated eating and public facilities were introduced in Washington for the first time as late as the Woodrow Wilson administration of 1913–1921. While some northerners expressed indignation, the Progressive movement was focused more on votes for women, protection of children from forced labour, and other visible harms in the everyday life of northern cities. Former slaves were still largely confined to the south, with a few big-city exceptions. Southern states defied the 1870s legislation (and Constitutional Amendment) giving equal rights to blacks, and northern states didn't care – or notice.

Then another war put black people into contact with whites, whose moral numbness was replaced by empathy. The great northern migration of blacks to work in defence factories during World War II combined with the anomaly of a segregated Army dying in battle against the racist Nazis. This all helped to make race law a subject of renewed moral indignation. As late as the 1930s Franklin Roosevelt had angrily refused his wife's demand to increase racial equality by speaking in pure pragmatism: "go make me," he said, meaning that Eleanor should create political pressure on him that he could use as leverage (Goodwin, 1995). She did not, but the War did. When it was over, President Truman de-segregated the armed forces.

By the early 1950s, it seems, cultural changes were increasing equality in the south (Klarman, 2004, 2007). Edwin "Bull" Connor, the racist elected Commissioner of Public Safety in Birmingham, Alabama, was defeated at the polls after almost two decades in office (Baggett, 2009). Racially moderate governors like Alabama's James Folsom were in ascendancy, trying to bring the races together. With no external pressure from the "illegitimate" national government, a new moral consensus may – or may not – have been reached on race (Gladwell, 2009). But moral indignation from the national elites re-opened the Civil War, provoking massive defiance in the south.

The 1954 Supreme Court case of Brown v. Board of Education was a tipping point of moral struggle over race and law. The plaintiffs defied the status quo, and the court agreed – declaring that separate services by race were inherently unequal. In response, southern politics turned reactionary. Moderate leaders were defeated, to be replaced by those who showed moral indignation against the law of the land. Bull

Connor came back into power, in time to put police brutality against black and white civil rights protestors on televisions screens around the world. Murders of protestors, and ultimately of black children, sickened people in both north and south. The excesses empowered the moderates to pass major new laws in Washington; they also lost many middle-class supporters of extreme defiance, just as Pape's (2005) theory predicts about moral sentiments in conflicts where suicide terrorist bombings begin.

In the final wave of defiant law-making, a new hyper-segregation developed in northern cities (Massey and Denton, 1992). White majorities fled to the suburbs with the black middle classes, leaving major cities to elect black mayors and appoint black police chiefs and judges. Affirmative action policies produced majority black police agencies in some cities, even while police and courts sent blacks to prison in record numbers. Many of these developments were unintended consequences of well-meant laws. All of them combined to shape law-enforcing with eaves of moral indignation.

Defiant law-enforcing on race

For the first century after the Civil War, law-enforcement defied the US Constitution to discriminate by race. Iowa police met many trains heading north to tell Southern blacks not to get off the train; blacks kept going towards Chicago, leaving Iowa with one of the whitest populations (95 per cent in 2000) of any state. Police stood by with passive defiance of law *de jure* to allow law *de facto* rule (Garland, 2005) as white mobs, primarily in the South, lynched 3,445 blacks from 1882 to 1968 (Tuskegee University Archives). In the summer of 1966, in Washington, Chicago and Boston, several thousand police decisions to arrest or not (when the facts allowed arrest) were observed by 36 trained observers trained in law, social science and law enforcement. They found blacks were substantially more likely than whites to be arrested (Black, 1980; Reiss, 1971). The 1960s saw America rocked by race riots, largely in response to perceived police abuses, especially against blacks (Rossi *et al.*, 1974). Police fought back against criticism by opposing civilian review boards, campaigning against the Supreme Court (with bumper stickers calling for the impeachment of the Chief Justice) and seeking public office. Police chiefs were elected Mayor in Philadelphia, Minneapolis and many smaller cities, promising (in effect) to put the blacks back in their place.

Even after police ranks became far more diverse by race and gender, police continued to be charged with racial bias. In the 1970s a major academic campaign documented race differences in police shootings and killings of suspects (Sherman, 1980). By 1985 the Supreme Court abolished police powers to kill unarmed fleeing suspects, the kind of killing that had seen the greatest racial disproportionality. But in1991, the Rodney King incident exploded on the nation's consciousness. The 1992 nation-wide race riots in protest of the acquittal of some of the officers accused in the Rodney King beating heightened police defiance; in LA itself, police became so passively defiant in ignoring the riot that a blue ribbon commission was formed to investigate. Persistent allegations of "racial profiling" dogged police around the US, leading the Justice Department to seek consent decrees for external oversight of police agencies placed, effectively, in moral bankruptcy.

The inauguration of President George W. Bush and the terrorist attacks of 11 September, 2001 put a damper on issues of race and law enforcement. But it did not stop the steady growth of racial disproportionality in the nation's prison population. Whether by unseen hands or otherwise, the US prison population rose by over 300 per cent from 1980 to 2006, from 200 per 100,000 population to over 750 per 100,000. At the same time, the black–white ratio of prison admissions has risen from blacks being imprisoned at a rate five times higher than whites in 1980 to almost seven times higher by 2000, mainly due to increasing prison sentences for drug-related crime.

While the process of punishing black people today is far more legalistic than it was a century ago, the result appears far more punitive. The institutions of reaction to crime now mete out more punishment per person to black people than at any time in US history. In mid-2008, almost 1 in 20 black American males (4,777 per 100,000) were incarcerated in prisons or local jails (Bureau of Justice Statistics, 2009a). This compared to 727 per 100,000 for white males. Whatever the reasons that can be given to support the legality of this result, the appearance of bias – on top of 300 years of more open discrimination – may deeply affect the moral sentiments of both blacks and whites about crime, law and punishment.

Defiant crime and race

A great mystery for defiance theory to solve is why more blacks don't kill or victimize more whites. This is true not only in the US, but among disproportionately punished minorities around the world. Australian Aborigines, for example, who are incarcerated at a rate that is 15 times higher than Australian whites, are very rarely charged with murder or other serious crimes against whites (Strang, 1991). In the US, a slightly higher black-on-white murder rate than white-on-black has remained largely unchanged for three decades, despite sharp rises (and declines) in the rates of black on black homicide (Bureau of Justice Statistics, 2009b). Inter-racial homicide is so rare in the UK that racial statistics are not even reported.

Compounding the mystery is the evidence that African-American crime rates remained lower than in other demographic groups during much of the first century after emancipation. Contrary to a direct link between slavery and violence, the blacks who lived in northern cities were less violent than many immigrant groups that had not been enslaved (Lane, 1986). They became steadily more violent against each other, however, in the face of race discrimination that de-stabilized their employment patterns and family lives. Yet that still does not explain why they should direct their frustration at other blacks, rather than the whites who inflicted the greatest harm on them.

The solution to this mystery may lie in the kind of defiant crime that moral indignation provokes. If young males, who commit most homicide, live their lives in minimal contact with people of other races, then they may have little provocation from whites for the sudden explosions of anger characteristic of homicide. Rather than engaging in "resistant" defiance, as Braithwaite (2009) describes it, they could instead adopt the dis-engagement of dismissive defiance. As Anderson (1999) describes the attitudes of young black males to the (largely black) police in Philadelphia's black ghettoes, they see police as essentially "not there" – and certainly not there to protect them. Instead, they see themselves in a kind of "Little Neighbourhood on the Prairie" where everyone must rely on their own wits for protection – from the police (Goffman, 2009) as well as from each other.

An alternative path to dismissive defiance of police comes not from substantive police ineffectiveness, but from moral intuitions of police procedural unfairness. Tankebe's (2009) survey of citizens in Ghana measured (among other things) their support for self-help vigilantism, their perceptions of police effectiveness, and perceptions of procedural justice. He found that a perceived lack of procedural justice predicted support for vigilantism, but not perceived ineffectiveness of police. If this finding applies to the US, it would suggest a different route to the same result: some people may dismissively defy the police because they are untrustworthy, regardless of their effectiveness.

Either way that defiance is caused, defiance theory predicts an indirect path from moral indignation at police (or mainstream society) to high rates of black-on-black homicide. It is not the obvious path that blacks kill whites out of moral indignation for past oppression – although that has happened in some African nations in post-colonial times. Rather, it is more likely that oppressed people suffer by refusing to accept institutions of law enforcement that were previously – and presently – oppressive.

By withdrawing legitimacy from the mainstream institutions of law enforcement, young black men in US poverty ghettoes expose themselves to a war-like "Code of the Street" that is a vestige of the murderous habits of Renaissance Gentlemen (Eisner, 2003; Matza and Sykes, 1961). This, in turn, causes them to carry weapons at a much higher rate for self-defence: guns in the US, and increasingly knives in the UK. With weapons at hand in any moments of insult or disrespect, they commit serious violent crimes at rates far higher than young men (of both races) who live in the mainstream population. The young men who accept law enforcement, rather than dismissing it, turn out to live a lot longer.

As for white murders of blacks, these surely outnumbered black murders of whites for centuries, at least since the 130 murders in 1782 on the slave ship *Zong*. These murders reflected a moral sentiment that blacks were property, and later that they were an enemy with a great potential to harm whites. But these moral sentiments are always subject to change. Such change can become especially likely if they appear unacceptable when held up to scrutiny in mainstream middle class institutions. If people who consider themselves "mainstream" begin to think that the mainstream disapproves of such conduct, their sense of not wanting to be different could create an intuition of moral obligation that would change their behaviour.

Defiance theory therefore predicts that southern white attitudes toward lynching blacks would change in response to a Hollywood movie making lynching look shameful. That shame would alter intuitions of moral obligation in relation to lynch mobs, perhaps increasing the pressures of informal social control on adult men not to join in lynch mobs. As defiance theory predicts, there was a sudden and large drop in lynchings of blacks across the US after the actor Spencer Tracy played the victim of a lynch mob in Fritz Lang's 1936 MGM movie *Fury*. As a movie shown in theatres all over the US – including the south – at a time when few other sources of entertainment competed with the cinema, it was able to penetrate deeply into popular culture. No one could watch that movie and come away feeling that lynching was morally justified – especially since the Spencer Tracy character was innocent. Anyone who had thought lynching was morally right might at least reconsider. As Garland (2005) observes:

> However much local support they attracted, public torture lynchings were always highly controversial. If many locals saw them as necessary, even admirable, expressions of popular justice, people there and elsewhere saw them as scandalous affronts to a civilized nation. And if their moral status was essentially contested, their legal status was no less unsettled.

In an ongoing moral contest such as the Southern struggle against lynchings, the opportunity to see one's self or community in a "mirror" like *Fury* can be a moral epiphany, a turning point in defying and rejecting a previous morality now seen as evil (Laub and Sampson, 2001). Moreover, very strong evidence from an entirely different class of events predicts exactly the same result. In a randomized controlled experiment on the effects of letters to Minnesota taxpayers encouraging them to pay taxes, the only version of the letters that increased tax payments was the one that said "93 per cent of taxpayers" pay all the taxes they owe – thus combating a view that tax cheating is widespread (Coleman, 1996). In both lynching and taxpaying, it seems, the "herd mentality" can create a sense of moral obligation to do what the others are doing, thereby defying the status quo moral rhetoric supporting defiance of law.

Absent such independent (experimental) testing of the same hypothesis and a consilient result, the causal inference about the effect of the movie *Fury* on lynching is admittedly not strong; few historical claims can be. The long-term record of lynchings shows an ongoing decline after the resurgence of the Ku Klux Klan in the 1920s (Tuskegee University Archives). Nonetheless, the speed of the decline appeared to accelerate just as the movie *Fury* was released. In the five years before the movie appeared, there were 75 lynchings of blacks; in five years after, there were just 38 – a 37 per cent drop. The ten year before/after difference was a 29 per cent drop. Three years after the movie came out, President Roosevelt created a special office in the US Department of Justice to investigate and prosecute lynchings, heavily concentrated in the South. By 1950, lynchings had virtually stopped.

By 2008, Barack Obama was elected president of the United States.

But the moral contest for legitimacy never stops. By 2009, 12 Congressmen introduced a bill requiring presidents to produce the originals of their birth certificates – reflecting a defiant social movement claiming that Obama's presidency is illegitimate because he was allegedly "not born in the US" (Aaronovitch, 2009). The same movement claims that Obama is reforming health care as a covert form of reparations to blacks for slavery, a longstanding race question in the US. The history of race in the US continues to intersect with fundamental differences in moral sentiments about the role of government in society.

Summary

In schematic form, this outline of a criminology of race in the US provides sufficient facts for several inductions, each in a different class of events, each using the same fundamental cause: an individual or collective intuitive sense of *moral obligation* leading to some form of defiance of the *legitimacy* of the status quo. While we cannot measure such intuitions directly in this chapter, we can infer them indirectly from statements and actions.

The criminological outline begins with abolitionists feeling a moral obligation, from empathy with slaves, to denounce the law as illegitimate. This leads them to end slavery by force of violence. In sum:

Defiant law-making: Why Was Slavery Criminalized?

Observed harm of slavery→empathy→moral obligation to defy slavery→illegitimacy of law→moral indignation→resistant defiance→civil war→emancipation

The outline moves on to the discrimination practiced by police and courts against blacks for much of the period 1865 to 1965, and beyond. This too is related to a sense of harm that creates a moral obligation to defy the law as illegitimate:

Defiant law-enforcing: Why did criminal justice violate the Constitution?

Observed harm at loss of state's rights or white supremacy→moral obligation to defy→illegitimacy of law→moral indignation→resistant defiance→racist justice

At the same time, poor blacks began to commit crimes against each other at increasing rates. Here the mechanism is more complex, with many poor blacks adopting the disengagement of dismissive defiance – denying the moral right of an illegitimate government to have any authority over them:

Defiant law-breaking: Why did black crime rates rise slowly after the civil war?

Observed harm at unfair treatment by law→moral indignation→moral obligation to defy→dismissive defiance of police and law by young men→loss of legal protection→self-help→higher crime rates among young men

At this point there is cyclical pattern in the outline, returning to the first question, defiant law-making – this time by the political right. The defiance was against a "soft-on-crime" view that had led imprisonment rates downwards throughout much of the 1950s and 60s until a turning point occurred in 1975. In that year there is evidence from political and cultural sources that there was a rising moral sentiment against rehabilitation, against get-out-early-on-parole, and against other aspects of law which meant prison terms were not "tough" enough. At the same time, the urban riots and rising crime indicated exactly the dismissive defiance among poor young blacks which threatened the legal system. All this arguably provoked a major change in the status quo that imposed huge increases in punishment on blacks, and only to a lesser extent on whites.

Defiant law-making: Why did rates of imprisonment of blacks soar after 1975?

Observed harm from rising crime→moral obligation to resist dismissiveness→illegitimacy of "soft on crime" laws→new laws increasing prison terms→disproportionate impact on blacks

What makes these inductions consilient is that they all feature the same key link in a chain of causation: an observed harm that somehow provokes a strong sense of moral obligation, feeding empathy, indignation, or both, that undermines the legitimacy of the status quo. Thus, as framed here, the outline of race, law, crime and punishment offers a demonstration of the consilience of defiance theory. In each class of events, the explanation leaps to the same place as in the other class of events. By doing so, the inductions provide preliminary evidence in support of a general theory of criminology.

DEFIANCE THEORY AND PUBLIC POLICY

There may be little connection between the state of criminological theory and the state of public policy. Few scholars would describe deterrence, for example, as a leading theory of criminology, but the deterrence doctrine has reigned supreme for over three decades in the US and UK. The cost of that policy, however, is now presenting taxpayers with a bill they may prefer not to pay. That preference might be enhanced by the suggestion that a pure deterrence policy is not just ineffective, but morally wrong.

In the early nineteenth century, when deterrence theorist Jeremy Bentham (1748–1832) was still warm in his grave, the UK's Prime Minister wrote this to the Lieutenant-Governor of Ireland in 1841:

> … when a country is tolerably quiet it is better for a government to be hard of hearing than to be very agile in prosecuting
>
> (quoted in Hurd, 2007: 319)

The Prime Minister was Sir Robert Peel, who had founded both the Royal Irish Constabulary and the Metropolitan Police to increase compliance – and abolished the death penalty for most offences, to reduce defiance (Hurd, 2007). Peel spent much of his career in government trying to avoid the kind of violent uprisings that continental Europe suffered in 1848. His nuanced view of when to use sanctions and when to use inducements lost him much support in the Tory Party – especially when he defied the right wing to let Irish Catholics sit in the House of Commons. Then as now, hard-liners drove politics towards confrontation and retribution. But Peel remained steadfast in support of harm reduction and crime prevention, by constant attention to building legitimacy: winning over hearts and minds to a sense of moral obligation to obey the law.

The North Atlantic world in the early twenty-first century seems oblivious to Peel's lessons. Just as his Lieutenant Governor of Ireland refused Peel's pleas to use persuasion rather than punishment, contemporary governments seem to refuse pleas from criminologists to change course on crime policy. Not even bankruptcy of US states has been able to reduce record prison populations. Not even a major recession in the UK has stopped a major program of prison construction. More punishment, rather than less, is widely justified by a potent moral intuition that retribution is "right" and deterrence will "work."

Much evidence is sadly to the contrary. A report on offenders given short prison sentences in Holland shows that prison tripled their reconviction rates over similar offenders given non-custodial sentences (Nieuwbeerta *et al.*, 2009). A report on adult prisoners in Maryland shows that short prison sentences leave them much angrier and more ready to commit crime when they leave prison than when they arrived (MacKenzie *et al.*, 2007). While social networks supporting higher prison populations fan the flames with each new horrible tragedy of an identifiable crime victim, prison may just cause more victims. One study suggests that incarcerating non-violent offenders only increases, rather than decreases, their likelihood of their next conviction being for a violent crime (Haney and Zimbardo, 1998: 13).

How much of this result is due to the hegemony of deterrence and retribution theory is not clear. This much is clear: for three decades, the alternative to tough sentencing has been presented as "rehabilitation." No matter how powerful the evidence in favour of rehabilitation, it seems unlikely that the word "rehabilitation" itself can be rehabilitated in the near future. That word has been destroyed by defiant social networks endorsing the moral obligation to punish severely; they help insure that for many people, "rehabilitation" just does not feel "right."

For people who are convinced that prison "works," even without access to rehabilitation services, a new word may be needed to shock them into a new intuition. It could be a word like the title of the movie that may have killed off lynching ("*Fury*"). It could be a word that sounds plausible enough to take seriously, even if it is about a contradictory theory of punishment. They may even need a word that strikes fear into their own hearts, much as Sir Robert Peel spent his adult life in fear of mobs burning down factories.

The word that will work is not likely to come from the traditional name in sociology for reverse effects of punishment ("labelling"). The words "backlash" or "backfire" fail to provide a clear opposite to "deterrence" in the minds of the general public. Nor will those words get much traction in Parliament or state legislatures.

The emotion-laden word that may stand a chance at competing with the intuitive appeal of deterrence is one that can get the facts – and criminology – a fair hearing in public policy. The word that could work is one that resonates with an intuition many people already feel. That word is one that might stir a moral obligation to resist the status quo.

That word is "defiance."

NOTE

1 The author is grateful to Tim Newburn, Justice Tankebe, John Braithwaite, Heather Strang, John MacDonald and Paul Rock for their comments on earlier drafts of this chapter.

REFERENCES

Aaronovitch, D. (2009) Obama gives birth to some genuine hatred: Why does the American Right insist that its opponents are not just wrong, but illegitimate? *The Times*, August 11, p. 20.

Anderson, E. (1999) *Code of the Street: Decency, Violence, and the Moral Life of the Inner City.* New York: W. W. Norton.

Anthony, S. B. (1900) *Woman: Her Position, Influence and Achievement Throughout the Civilized World.*

Baggett, J. L. (2009) Eugene 'Bull' Connor, *Encyclopedia of Alabama.* Downloaded 9 August, 2009 at http://www.encyclopediaofalabama.org/

BBC News (2009a) Sudan women 'lashed for trousers'. 13 July. http://news.bbc.co.uk/1/hi/world/africa/8147329.stm

Betts, R. D. (2009) *A Question of Freedom: A Memoir of Learning, Survival, and Coming of Age in Prison.* NY: Avery/Penguin.

Black, D. (1980) *The Manners and Customs of the Police.* NY: Academic Press.

Black, D. (1983) Crime as social control. *American Sociological Review* 48: 34–45.

Borg, J. S., Hynes, C., Van Horn, J., Grafton, S. and Sinnott-Armstrong, W. (2006) Consequences, action, and intention as factors in moral judgments: An fMRI investigation, *Journal of Cognitive Neuroscience* 18: 803–817.

Braithwaite, J. (2005) Between proportionality and impunity: confrontation → truth → prevention, *Criminology* 43: 283–306.

Braithwaite, J. (1989) *Crime, Shame and Reintegration.* Cambridge: Cambridge University Press.

Braithwaite, J. (2009) Restorative justice for banks through negative licensing, *British Journal of Criminology* 49: 439–450).

Braithwaite, V. (2009a) *Defiance in Taxation and Government.* Cheltenham: Edward Elgar.

Braithwaite, V. (2009b) *Values, Hope and Defiance.* Presentation to the Second International NPIA-Cambridge Conference on Evidence-Based Policing, Cambridge University, 1–3 July. Powerpoint posted at http://vab.anu.edu.au/present/VHD_Cambridge.ppt

Bureau of Justice Statistics (2009a) *Prison Inmates at Midyear 2008 – Statistical Tables.* Downloaded on August 11, 2009 from http://www.ojp.usdoj.gov/bjs/abstract/pim08st.htm

Bureau of Justice Statistics (2009b) *Homicide Trends in the US.* Downloaded on August 11, 2009 from http://www.ojp.usdoj.gov/bjs/homicide/race.htm

Butts, R. E. (ed.) (1989) *William Whewell: Theory of Scientific Method second edition.* Indianapolis: Hackett.

CNN (2009a) Protests as Sudan 'tight pants' trial delayed, 4 August. http://edition.cnn.com/2009/WORLD/africa/08/04/sudan.journalist.lashings/index.html?iref=hpmostpop

Cohen, S. (1972) *Folk Devils and Moral Panics: The Creation of the Mods and Rockers.* St. Albans: Paladin.

Coleman, S. (1996) *The Minnesota Income Tax Compliance Experiment State Tax Results.* St. Paul, MN: Minnesota State Department of Revenue. Downloaded 15 August 2009 from http://www.taxes.state.mn.us/legal_policy/research_reports/content/complnce.pdf

Collins, R. C. (2008) *Violence: A Micro-Sociological Theory.* Princeton, NJ: Princeton University Press.

Edwards, R. and Smith, R. (2009) Ian Tomlinson G20 protests death: police officer faces manslaughter charge … . after a second post mortem found that he died from internal bleeding. *The Telegraph*, April 17. http://www.telegraph.co.uk/finance/financetopics/g20-summit/5172206/Ian-Tomlinson-G20-protests-death-police-office-faces-manslaughter-charge.html

Ekman, P. (2007) *Emotions Revealed second edition.* NY: Owl.

Eisner, M. (2003) Long-term historcial trends in violent crime. Pp. 83–142 in M. Tonry (ed.), *Crime and Justice: A Review of Research.* Chicago: University of Chicago Press.

Faust, D. G. (2008) *This Republic of Suffering: Death and the American Civil War.* New York: Alfred A. Knopf.

Garland, D. (2005) Penal excess and surplus meaning: public torture lynchings in twentieth-century America, *Law and Society Review* 39: 793–834.

Gibbs, J. D. (1975) *Crime, Punishment and Deterrence.* N.Y.: Elsevier.

Gladwell, M. (2000) *The Tipping Point.* Boston: Little, Brown.

Gladwell, M. (2009) The courthouse ring: Atticus finch and the limits of southern liberalism. *The New Yorker,* August 10 and 17, pp. 26–32.

Goffman, A. (2009) On the run: Wanted men in a Philadelphia ghetto, *American Sociological Review* 74: 339–357.

Goodwin, D. K. (1995) *No Ordinary Time.* NY: Simon and Schuster.

Gottfredson, M. and Hirschi, T. (1990) *A General Theory of Crime.* Stanford, CA: Stanford University Press.

Haney, C. and Zimbardo, P. (1998) The past and future of U.S. prison policy twenty-five years after the Stanford prison experiment, *The American Psychologist* 53: 709–727 (pp. 1–24 on APA Psyc Articles, quotation to p. 13).

Heinzerling, L. (2000) The rights of statistical people, *Harvard Environmental Law Review* 24: 189.

Hochschild, A. (2005) *Bury the Chains.* NY: Houghton-Mifflin.

Hurd, D. (2007) *Robert Peel: A Biography.* London: Weidenfield & Nicolson.

Katz, J. (1988) *Seductions of Crime: Moral and Sensual Attractions of Doing Evil.* NY: Basic Books.

Klarman, M. J. (2004) *From Jim Crow to Civil Rights: The Supreme Court and the Struggle for Racial Equality.* NY: Oxford University Press.

Klarman, M. J. (2007) *Brown v. Board of Education and the Civil Rights Movement.* Abridged edition. NY: Oxford.

LaFree, G. (2007) Expanding criminology's domain: The American Society of Criminology 2006 Presidential Address. *Criminology* 45: 1–31.

LaFree, G. (2009) Personal communication, April 27.

LaFree, G., Dugan, L. and Korte, R. (2009) The impact of British counterterrorist strategies on political violence in Northern Ireland: Comparing deterrence and backlash models, *Criminology* 47: 17–45.

Lane, R. (1986) *Roots of Violence in Black Philadelphia, 1860–1900.* Cambridge, MA: Harvard University Press.

Laub, J. and Sampson, R. (2001) Understanding desistance from crime, *Crime and Justice* 28: 1–69.

MacKenzie, D., Bierie, D. and Mitchell, O. (2007) An experimental study of a therapeutic boot camp: Impact on impulses, attitudes and recidivism, *Journal of Experimental Criminology* 3: 221–246.

Manning, P. K. (1977) *Police Work: The Social Organization of Policing.* Cambridge: MIT Press.

Maruna, S. (2001) *Making Good: How Ex-Convicts Rebuild and Reform Their Lives.* Washington, DC: American Psychological Association.

Massachusetts Constitutional Convention (1853) *Official Report of the Debates and Proceedings in the State Convention: assembled May 4th, 1853.*

Massey, D. and Denton, P. (1992) *American Apartheid.* Cambridge, MA: Harvard University Press.

Matlack, L. C. (1849) *The History of American Slavery and Methodism, From 1780 to 1849; and History of the Wesleyan American Connection.* New York: Author.

Matza, D. and Sykes, G. (1961) Juvenile delinquency and subterranean values, *American Sociological Review* 22: 664–670.

Melville, H. (1853) *Bartleby, the Scrivener: A Story of Wall Street.* New York.

National Park Service (2009) African Americans at Jamestowne. Historic Jamestowne Website. Downloaded August 10, 2009 from http://www.nps.gov/jame/

Nieuwbeerta, P., Nagin, D. S. and Blokland, A. A. J. (2009) Assessing the impact of first-time imprisonment on offenders' subsequent criminal career development: a matched samples comparison, *Journal of Quantitative Criminology*, published on-line, June.

Pape, R. (2005) *Dying to Win.* New York: Random House.

Ranulf, S. (1938) *Moral Indignation and Middle Class Psychology.* Copenhagen: Levin & Munksgaard.

Reiss, A. J., Jr. (1971) *The Police and the Public.* New Haven: Yale University Press.

Rock, P. (2009) Personal communication, August 22.

Rossi, P., Berk, R. and Eidson, B. K. (1974) *The Roots of Urban Discontent.* NY: Wiley.

Scheff, T. and Retzinger, S. (1991) *Emotions and Violence: Shame and Rage in Destructive Conflicts.* Lexington, MA: Lexington Books.

Seelye, K. (2009) Obama wades into a volatile racial issue. *The New York Times*, July 23.

Sheehan, W., Kollerstrom, N. and Waff, C. B. (2004) The case of the pilfered planet: Did the British steal Neptune? *Scientific American*, December: 92–99.

Sherman, L. W. (ed.) (1980) Police and violence. *Annals of the American Academy of Political and Social Science*, p. 452.

Sherman, L. W. (1990) Police crackdowns: Initial and residual deterrence, pp. 1–48 in M. Tonry (ed.), *Crime and Justice: A Review of Research*, Vol. 12. Chicago: University of Chicago Press.

Sherman, L. W. (1993) Defiance, deterrence, and irrelevance: a theory of the criminal sanction, *Journal of Research in Crime and Delinquency* 30: 445–473.

Sherman, L. W. (1999) The defiant imagination: Consilience and the science of sanctions. The 1999 Edwin H. Sutherland Award Address to the American Society of Criminology. Toronto, CA: November 18, 1999.

Sherman, L. W. (2003) Reason for emotion: Reinventing justice with theories, innovations and research. The 2002 American Society of Criminology Presidential Address. *Criminology* 41: 1–38.

Sinnott-Armstrong, W. (2008) *Moral Psychology, Volume 3. The Neuroscience of Morality: Emotion, Brain Disorders, and Development.* Cambridge, MA: MIT Press.

Smith, D. A. and Visher, C. (1981) Street-level justice: Situational determinants of police arrest decisions, *Social Problems* 29: 167–177.

Stanford Encyclopedia of Philosophy (2006) *William Whewell.* Downloaded August 6, 2009 from http://plato.stanford.edu/entries/whewell/

Stannard, D. (1993) *American Holocaust.* New York: Oxford University Press.

Strang, H. (1991) *Homicides in Australia, 1989–90.* Canberra, Australia: Australian Institute of Criminology.

Strang, H. (2002) *Repair or Revenge: Victims and Restorative Justice.* Oxford: Oxford University Press.

Sunstein, C. (2009) Some effects of moral indignation on law, *Vermont Law Review* 33: 404–433.

Sutherland, E. H. (1934) *Principles of Criminology.* Philadelphia: Lippincott.

Sykes, G. and Matza, D. (1957) Techniques of neutralization: A theory of delinquency, *American Sociological Review* 22: 664–670.

Tankebe, J. (2009) Self-help, policing, and procedural justice: Ghanaian vigilantism and the rule of law, *Law and Society Review* 43: 245–269.

Thurman, J. (2009) Wilder women: The mother and daughter behind the Little House stories. *The New Yorker,* August 10.

Tuskegee University Archives, as posted by the University of Missouri at Kansas City Law School website at http://www.law.umkc.edu/faculty/projects/ftrials/shipp/lynchingyear.html downloaded on 11 August, 2009.

Tyler, T. (1990) *Why People Obey the Law.* New Haven: Yale University Press.

Vaux, R. (1817) *Memoirs of the Life of Anthony Benezet.* Philadelphia: York.

Weisburd, D. (1989) *Jewish Settler Violence.* University Park, PA: Pennsylvania State University Press.

Westley, W. (1970) *Violence and the Police.* Cambridge, MA: MIT Press.

Whewell, W. (1840) *The Philosophy of the Inductive Sciences, Founded Upon Their History*, Vol. II. London: John W. Parker.

Whewell, W. (1847) *The Philosophy of the Inductive Sciences, Founded Upon Their History*, second edition, Vol. I. London.

Wikstrom, P.-O. (2006) Individuals, settings and acts of crime: Situational mechanisms and the explanation of crime. Pp. 61–107 in P.-O. Wikstrom and R. J. Sampson (eds), *The Explanation of Crime: Context Mechanisms and Development.* Cambridge: Cambridge University Press.

Wilson, J. Q. (1968) *Varieties of Police Behavior: The Management of Law and Order in Eight Communities.* Cambridge: Harvard University Press.

20

A Vision of Race, Crime, and Justice Through the Lens of Critical Race Theory

Lee E. Ross

INTRODUCTION

This chapter presents an overview of critical race theory and its application to select areas of race, crime, and justice. Critical race theory concerns the study and transformation of relationships among race, racism, and power. Unlike traditional civil rights, which embraces incrementalism and systematic progress, critical race theory questions the very foundations of the legal order. In examining the dynamics of race, crime, and justice, this chapter applies various themes and terminologies – such as interest convergence, legal indeterminacy, and first person narratives – to assess their potential to inform and facilitate an understanding of racial disparities in American criminal justice systems.

WHAT IS CRITICAL RACE THEORY?

Over the last three decades, the fields of legal studies, criminology, and education have witnessed a number of exciting theoretical developments. Few have been as promising and insightful as critical race theory (CRT). This theory concerns the study and transformation of relationships among race, racism, and power. Unlike traditional civil rights, which embraces incrementalism and systematic progress, critical race theory questions the very foundations of the legal order, including equality theory, legal reasoning, enlightenment rationalism, and neutral principles of constitutional law (Delgado and Stefani, 2001: 3). Over the course of its development, critical race theory has assumed many operational definitions. Matsuda (2002) characterizes it as:

> The work of progressive legal scholars of color who are attempting to develop a jurispru-
> dence that accounts for the role of racism in American law and that works toward the
> elimination of racism as part of a larger goal of eliminating all forms of subordination.
>
> (p. 331)

Today, hundreds of American legal academics consider themselves critical race theorists; they teach courses and write articles and books about race, civil rights, and constitutional law from this perspective. Interestingly, critical race theory, which began as a movement in law (as critical legal studies), has a prominent place in the field of education. For example, critical race theorists explore a variety of issues such as school discipline and hierarchy, controversies over curriculum and history, intelligence, and achievement testing. In the process, critical race theorists have influenced other disciplines as well. In the field of political science, for instance, researchers have pondered voting strategies.

Critics allege that the core claim of both critical race theory and feminist jurispru-dence is that law is merely a mask for white male power relations (see MacDonald, 1995). The law, critics further claim, is virtually indistinguishable from politics. Moreover, the purported objectivity and neutrality of legal reasoning is a sham (MacDonald, 1995). These ideals have emerged with feminist insights into the rela-tionships of power and the construction of social roles, a concern for addressing historic wrongs, and sympathetic understandings of notions of nationalism and group empowerment. Equally important, critical race theory contains an academic dimension as it attempts to both understand our social situation and to change it. It sets out not only to ascertain how society organizes itself along racial lines and hierarchies, but also to transform it for the better.

Conceived by critical legal studies, pioneers in the area of critical race theory included the likes of Derrick Bell, Alan Freeman, and Richard Delgado. Confronting the reality of a fading Civil Rights Movement, these men recognized that overt prac-tices of racism often times yielded to more subtle and covert forms of racism that rendered it far more difficult to discern. Imagine placing a white jellybean into a jar of other white jellybeans, shaking the jar up and finding it later on. The difficulty is that all the jellybeans, like racism, look ordinarily similar: virtually indistinguishable from one another. For critical race theorists, so too is racism. Its ordinariness and prevalence renders it harder to recognize – much less address. Consequently, formal rules that demand color-blind treatment will enable remedies to only the most flagrant forms of racism (i.e., the black jellybean).

The idea that racism and sexism are limited phenomena perpetuated by a few intentional bad actors is one of the most destructive myths of all. Discrimination, according to Hayman (1997), results simply from bureaucratic practices, from the unthinking repetition of the ordinary ways of operating in the world. The modern, righteously indignant and seemingly egalitarian calls for a color-blind society ignore the history and tradition of our treatment of race in America (Levitt, 1999). At the heart of the myth of merit is the [Achilles heel] of purposeful discrimination: if only we can eradicate intentional, malicious discrimination, the market, freed from discrimination, will guarantee equality of opportunity.

Among a myriad of themes commonly used by scholars to promote discussions of critical race theory, most begin with an exploration of racism itself. For critical race theorists, racism is ordinary, not aberrational – "normal science." Racism, forever alive and well, manifests itself though various disparities within nearly every sector of society, whether in the prison system, the banking and lending industry, the educational system, or within a healthcare industry where racial disparities in longevity, diabetes, and infant mortality rates are readily apparent.

Mortgage redlining practices that deny low-cost loans to anyone wanting to buy a house in the black part of town would be a prime example (Delgado and Stefancic, 2001). For the most part, critical race theory rejects the idea that extremist individuals perpetuate racism today and theorize instead that societal systems are to blame for the continuation of racism. For Valdes *et al.* (2002: 2), "critical race theory describes and critiques not a world of bad actors, wronged victims, and innocent bystanders, but a world in which all of us are more or less complicit in sociological webs of domination and subordination." Regarding the purpose of the law, Delgado theorizes that critical race theory exposes "traditional claims of legal neutrality, objectivity, color-blindness, and meritocracy" as camouflages for the self-interest of dominant groups in American society (cited from Ladson-Billings and Tate, 1995: 52). Overall, critical race theory acknowledges the inextricable racialized subordination based on gender, class, immigration status, surname, phenotype, accent and sexuality (Crenshaw, 1989; Valdes *et al.*, 2002).

While membership and identity in the CRT movement was minimal, the spirit of European philosophers, theorists, and American activists imparted both vision and inspiration. European influences included important figures like Antonio Gramsci and Jacques Derrida. The American tradition is exemplified by such figures as Sojourner Truth, Frederick Douglass, W. E. B. DuBois, César Chávez, Martin Luther King Jr., and the Black Panther and Chicano Movements of the sixties and early seventies. Critical race theory is also credited with various spin-off movements that include an emerging Asian American jurisprudence, a powerful Latino-critical (*LatCrit*) contingent, a spirited queer-crit interest group, and Native American scholars who address indigenous people's rights, sovereignty, and land claims.

IN THE BEGINNING

Organizationally, critical race theory came into being either at UC-Berkeley or at Harvard University. One version suggests that students at Harvard University were disgruntled that a prominent civil rights lawyer, Jack Greenberg, was hired to replace Derrick Bell, an African-American law professor who left to take a deans position elsewhere (see Delgado and Stetancic, 2005). Students, upset at these developments, boycotted the class taught by Greenberg and started their own alternative course which met on Saturday mornings. Various guest speakers were brought in, including Charles Lawrence, author of a famous article on unconscious racism, and Richard Delgado, who spoke about imperial racism. Student organizers of the Saturday series included Kimberly Crenshaw and Mara Matsuda, who went on to become law professors and major architects for critical race theory (Delgado and Stefancic, 2005: p. 4). At the same time, a similar movement took place on the west coast at

UC-Berkeley in the form of high profile speakers, student sit-ins, and rallies to hire more professors of color. In 1989, the first ever critical race theory workshop was convened in Madison, Wisconsin.

TYPES OF RACISM

Britannica Encyclopedia defines racism as "any action, practice, or belief that reflects the racial worldview-the ideology that humans are divided into separate and exclusive biological entities called "races," and that there is a causal link between inherited physical traits and traits of personality, intellect, morality, and other cultural behavioral features, that some "races" are innately superior to others. To the contrary, *Social Construction Thesis* holds that race and races are products of social thought and relations. Organizations and institutions that practice racism discriminate against, and marginalize a class of people who share a common racial designation. The term "racism" is usually applied to the dominant group in a society, because it is that group which has the means to oppress others, but readily applies to any individual or group(s), regardless of social status or dominance. Consequently, inequalities are a logical and predictable result of a racialized society where discussions of race and racism continue to be muted and marginalized (Ladson-Billings and Tate, 1995).

When we speak of racism, we think of Wellman's (1977) definition of "culturally sanctioned beliefs which, regardless of the intentions involved, defend advantages whites have because of the subordinated positions of racial minorities." We must therefore contend with the "problem facing White people [of coming] to grips with the demands made by Blacks and Whites while at the same time avoiding the possibility of institutional challenge and reorganization that might affect them" (Wellman, 1977: 42).

According to Nobel Laureate Toni Morrison, race has become metaphorical – a way of referring to and disguising forces, events, classes, and expressions of social decay and economic division far more threatening to the body politic than "biological race" (Morrison, 1993: 63). For Omi and Winant (1994), the paradigm of race has been conflated with notions of ethnicity, class, and nation. Moreover, theories of race – of it meaning, its transformations, and the significance of racial events – have never been a top priority in social science. In the U.S., although the "founding fathers" of American sociology were explicitly concerned with the state of domestic race relations, racial theory remained one of the least developed fields of sociological inquiry (p. 9).

Barbara Field (1990), a historian from Columbia University, argued in *Slavery, Race, and Ideology in the United States of America*, that 'racism' is a 'historical phenomenon', which does not explain racial ideology (p. 100). She suggests that investigators should consider the term to be an American rhetorical device with a historical explanation – but not as an explanation in itself. Much like the notion of reification, where concepts used to represent reality are regarded as real, using race as a word with real meaning is a common error.

There are two, closely related, forms of racism: individuals acting against other individuals, and acts by a total community against another community. These are called individual and institutional racism. Individual racism consists of both overt and covert acts by individuals, which can directly cause death, injury or the violent destruction of property. Institutional racism on the other hand is more covert and subtle, less identifiable in terms of specific individuals committing the acts, but no less destructive. It often originates in the operation of established and respected forces in the society, and thus frequently receives far less public condemnation than the first type. In furtherance of this discussion, the next section introduces readers to important themes related to critical race theory. Given the scope of the chapter, however, these themes are limited to those most relevant toward issues of race, crime, and justice.

LEGAL INDETERMINACY

Critical legal studies, a prelude to critical race theory, distinguishes itself from other theoretical perspectives with its ideal of legal indeterminacy – the idea that not every legal case has *one* correct outcome. A given body of legal doctrine is said to be "indeterminate" by demonstrating that every legal rule in that body of legal doctrine is opposed by a counter rule that can be used in a process of legal reasoning. According to Delgado and Stefancic (2001: 5), one can decide most legal cases either way by emphasizing one line of authority over another, or interpreting one fact differently from the way one's adversary does. In terms of legal theory, the following question sums up the indeterminacy debate quite nicely: Can the law constrain the results reached by adjudicators in legal disputes? This question has generated tremendous discussion among scholars. Some members of the critical legal studies movement – primarily legal academics in the United States – argued that the answer to this question is "no." In other words, disputes cannot be resolved with clear answers and, thus, there is at least some amount of uncertainty in legal reasoning and its application to disputes.

The indeterminacy thesis, in its strongest form, is the proposition that a judge can "square" any result in a particular case with the existing legal materials using legitimate legal arguments (see Solum, 1987). To paraphrase Solum (1987), the existing body of legal doctrines – statutes, administrative regulations, and court decisions – permits a judge to justify any desired result in any particular case. Put another way, the idea is that a competent adjudicator can square a decision in favor of either side in any given lawsuit with the existing body of legal rules. Hence, the expression, "square the deal." Closely related to this line of thought is the *theory of judicial shamanism*: a postmodern analytical approach to judicial reasoning. It broadens the constitutional atheism proclaimed by the Critical Legal Studies movement (CLS) with the suggestion that judicial reasoning is a contemporary form of shamanism.

CRIMINAL LAW AND LEGAL INDETERMINACY

Constant reminders of legal indeterminacy can be witnessed in an examination of criminal procedure throughout various aspects of American criminal justice systems.

In the 1985 Supreme Court case of *Tennessee v. Garner*, the Court held that the police might not invariably use deadly force on a fleeing suspect, even though they have probable cause to authorize an arrest (a "seizure" of the person under the Fourth Amendment). As life is a distinct fundamental right – quite apart from the liberty and privacy interests ordinarily associated with Fourth Amendment safeguards – the Court refused to authorize the use of deadly force in the absence of any threat to the police or the public. Civil libertarians embraced this decision, but with guarded optimism, given a lack of compelling reasons to have prevented the court from ruling otherwise. Law, after all – even in its finest hour – is a function of time, place, and circumstance.

Yet, the circumstances surrounding the *Garner* case were ripe for constitutional protections. Thus, the court ruled that whenever an officer restrains the freedom of a person to walk away, the officer has seized that person. When considering whether the seizure was constitutional, the specter of legal indeterminacy surfaces. To determine the constitutionality of a seizure [the court] must balance the nature and quality of the intrusion on the individual's Fourth Amendment interests against the importance of the governmental interests alleged to justify the intrusion. In other words, reasonableness depends on not only *when* a seizure is made, but also *how* it is carried out. In an earlier case, *Bell v. Wolfish* (1979), the court ruled that the test of reasonableness under the Fourth Amendment [was] *not capable of precise definition or mechanical application*. Even more uncertain (and indeterminate) is that the "reasonableness" of a particular use of force must be judged from the perspective of a reasonable officer on the scene, rather than with the 20/20 vision of academic or scholarly hindsight.

In contrast, one need only consider the current atmosphere of increased government surveillance under the guise and rubric of national security since the events of 9–11. Assume for the moment that Garner was a suspected terrorist in possession of an incendiary device. He refuses to halt when ordered by police and deadly force was used to make his arrest. We soon realize there is little to prevent a court from validating police use of deadly force on a 'fleeing terrorist.' Hence, the indeterminacy thesis serves as an unpleasant reminder of the precariousness of criminal law. In this example, some would argue that the climate and circumstance makes the use of deadly force perfectly reasonable. Nonetheless, this hypothetical illustrates that the court could have ruled either way. This is what breathes new life into the *theory of legal indeterminacy*.

Closely related to this concept is the notion of suspending the constitution when the rights of individuals potentially conflict with the interests of government. Under the United States Patriot Act, for instance, the government has the power to access one's medical records, tax records, information about books borrowed from libraries – all without probable cause. It also has the potential to allow the government to break into your home and conduct secret searches without telling you for weeks, months, or indefinitely. Axioms that have stood the test of time, such as "tough cases make bad law," suggest that the theory of legal indeterminacy is alive and well where contrary rulings, dripping with contempt for *stare decisis and precedent law*, can be expected. After all, the states' compelling interest is arguably greater than a citizen's civil right.

Giorgio Agamben (2005) underscores this point further in the book *State of Exception* where he described a situation in which a domestic or international crisis creates a pretext for the suspension of some aspect of the juridical order. A state of exception often implies a suspension of judicial oversight of civil liberties and the use of summary judgment against civilians by members of the military or executive. For some scholars, the state of exception is a legitimate part of positive law because it is based on necessity, a fundamental source of law. Similar to the individual's claim of self-defense in criminal law, the polity has a right to self-defense when its sovereignty is threatened. Consequently, when government exercises this right, it might involve a technical violation of existing statutes (*legge*) but it does so in the name of upholding the juridical order (*diritto*). Supposedly, the end justifies the means.

On the other hand, some regard the assumed legitimacy of dictatorial action (in times of crisis) a matter of interpretation. Carl Schmitt (2005), in *Political Theology and Dictatorship*, emphasizes that declaring a state of exception is the prerogative of the sovereign and therefore essentially extra-juridical. For Schmitt (2005), however, while the state of exception always involves the suspension of the law, it serves two different purposes: commissarial and sovereign. A "commissarial dictatorship" aims at restoring the existing constitution and a "sovereign dictatorship" constitutes a new juridical order. Thus, the state of exception is a violation of law that expresses the more fundamental logic of politics itself.

The principle of legal indeterminacy is also seen in the 1987 death penalty case of *McCleskey v. Kemp*. Here, the Supreme Court, by a 5–4 vote, rejected an equal protection and Eighth Amendment (cruel and unusual punishment) challenge to a Georgia death penalty statute that raised this issue. The challenge was based on a state-of-the-art statistical study showing that murderers of white people were 4.3 times more likely to get the death penalty than comparable murderers of blacks. Put simply, the study showed that Georgia's capital case prosecutors and juries valued white lives far more than black lives. However, Justice Lewis Powell, the author of *McCleskey* and the swing vote in the case, was unimpressed with these statistics. In his view, if Georgia's death penalty really was [racially] discriminatory, the statistical study would have shown that a disproportionate number of Georgia's death penalty defendants were black. Powell took considerable comfort in the fact that, instead, the only significant racial disparity in the Georgia system correlated not with the race of capital defendants, but rather with the race of their victims (Lazarus, 2001). Yet, it is clear that the philosophy of critical race theorists would suggest that the court could have ruled otherwise. Moreover, deficient legal reasoning in the absence of compelling arguments leaves the door open for reversal.

INTEREST CONVERGENCE

Interest convergence (or material determinism) adds a further dimension to critical race theory. Here, racism is endowed with the propensity to advance the interests of whites in both a material and psychic manner. Therefore, it is not surprising that large segments of society have little interest in eradicating it (see Delgado and Stefancic, 2001).

In a classic article, Derrick Bell (1980) argued that civil rights advances for blacks tended to coincide with changing economic conditions and self-interest of elite whites. Using the famous 1954 case of *Brown v. Board of Education of Topeka Kansas* as an example, he suggested that sympathy, mercy, and evolving standards of social decency did not fully explain the U.S. Supreme Court's sudden decision in favor of school integration. Rather, Bell thought that world and domestic considerations – not oral qualms over the plight of blacks – precipitated this path breaking decision (cited from Delgado and Stefani, 2001: 19). Given the climate at that time, Bell regarded the *Brown* decision as somewhat of a concession, where cooperation and national survival took precedence over racism. In describing conditions that led up to this decision, Bell asserts:

> During that period, as well, the United States was locked in a Cold War, a titanic struggle with the forces on international communism for the loyalties of the uncommitted Third World, much of which was black, brown, or Asian. It would ill serve the U.S. interests if the world press continued to carry stories of lynchings, racists sheriffs, or murders like that of Emmett Till. It was time for the United States to soften its stance toward domestic minorities. The interest of whites and blacks, for a brief moment, converged.
>
> (cited from Delgado and Stefancic, 2001: p. 19)

Subsequent research and the passage of time offered further testimony to the validity of his claims. For instance, despite the gallantry and performance of blacks during the Korean War, they eventually returned home to conditions of racial segregation and continued Jim Crow practices. In spite of noble attempts to eradicate segregated schools and to insure equal access to quality education, the *Brown* decision did not meet with the successes it had envisioned. Once handed down, the African-American community, along with forward-thinking white Americans, placed sufficient pressure on the legal and political system to bring an end to state-supported segregation in all public facilities within twenty years through the Civil Rights Movement, led by Dr. Martin Luther King, Jr. The nation paid a high price for its moral conversion, however, in the form of riots, assassinations, and additional government programs to enforce the Court's decision, such as court-ordered busing and affirmative action programs.

Today, students of color are more segregated than ever before in the educational system (see Orfield, 1988). Instead of providing for better educational opportunities, school desegregation has meant increased white flight along with a loss of African-American teaching and administrative positions (Ladson-Billings and Tate, 1995: 56). Over the last thirty years, for instance, various institutions of higher education have provided unpleasant reminders in their challenges to college admission policies based on race-based affirmative action as some view it as a form of reverse discrimination. Ironically, those advocating the elimination of race-based affirmative action policies argue that it would lead to legislation that fosters a color-blind society – the exact antithesis of what critical race theory espouses. Critical race theorists, after all, do not seek a color-blind society endowed with mythical notions of equality before the law. They recognized that legislation espousing a color-blind society carries with it a potential double-edged sword. Moreover, Crenshaw (1988: 1331) argued:

> The civil rights community ... must come to grips with the fact that antidiscrimination discourse is fundamentally ambiguous and can accommodate conservative as well as liberal views of race and equality ... [a]ntidiscrimination law presents an ongoing ideological struggle in which occasional winners harness the moral, coercive, consensual power of

law. Nonetheless, the victories it offers can be ephemeral and the risks of engagement substantial.

(cited from Ladson-Billings and Tate, 1995: 56)

Ladson-Billings (1998) builds an even stronger case for interest convergence by depicting what transpired in the state of Arizona over the Martin Luther King, Jr. Holiday commemoration. Originally, the state of Arizona insisted that the King Holiday was too costly and therefore failed to recognize it for state workers and agencies. When members of professional sports organizations (i.e., the National Basketball Association, and the National Football League) threatened to boycott sporting events held in Arizona, the state literally changed its position overnight. Fearing a loss of revenue that a boycott would produce, the states interests (in protecting the revenue) converged with that of the African American community to honor Dr. King.

INTEREST CONVERGENCE IN CRIMINAL JUSTICE SYSTEM

Perhaps similar claims can be made in the criminal justice arena when considering other landmark decisions, such as the U.S. Supreme Court decision in *Powell v. Alabama*, commonly referred to as the Scottsboro case. Here, nine black men (and boys) were accused of raping two white women on a freight train near Paint Rock, Alabama. They were arrested on March 25, 1931, tried without adequate counsel, and hastily convicted based on shallow evidence. All but one was sentenced to death. Ultimately, the Supreme Court, by a vote of 7–2, reversed the convictions because the state of Alabama failed to provide adequate assistance of counsel as required by the Sixth Amendment and the due process clause of the 14th Amendment.

This decision, and other less publicized ones spanning from 1910 to 1940 became the pillars of the judicial reforms, which would constitute the due process revolution in American law and criminal procedure (cited from Hawkins *et al.*, 2003: 437). While the court specified a clear mandate to provide attorneys to those accused of capital crimes (rape and murder at that time), this case too, provides a prime example of other constitutional gains that have gradually eroded through the passage of time. For instance, once counsel is appointed, are constitutional rights somehow violated in cases where counsel is proven incompetent or ineffective? Citing numerous examples of incompetent counsel in recent death penalty cases and inequities in the imposition of capital punishment in America, the American Civil Liberties Union (ACLU, 2003) has called upon the United States Congress to ensure effective legal representation for all defendants facing possible execution. Their request was made with knowledge of a Texas man convicted in a state court for the stabbing to death of his companion. He was given a new trial after a federal judge discovered that the defendant's lawyer had slept through the bulk of the original trial. The federal court judge is paraphrased as saying: sleeping counsel is equivalent to no counsel at all. Adding further context, a recent report on indigent defense by the Texas Defender Service found that judges often appointed defense attorneys – not based on their competence or experience – but rather, their reputation for rapidly moving cases through the system. The importance of this cannot be over-stated as the study concluded that death row prisoners "face a one-in-three chance of being executed without having the case properly investigated by a competent attorney or without having any claims of innocence or unfairness heard" (ACLU, 2003).

MIRANDA REVISITED

Other examples of an erosion of rights relate to one's Fifth Amendment rights while held incommunicado and interrogated by police. In *Miranda v. Arizona*, a 1966 ruling, the Court held that criminal suspects must be informed of their right to consult with an attorney and of their right against self-incrimination prior to questioning by police. Nearly 40 years later in 2003 the United States Supreme Court ruled 6–3 to eliminate the universality of having to read Miranda rights before interrogation. Consequently, police could aggressively question a person without first apprising them of their constitutional protections. This ruling resulted from a 1977 incident in which an officer, Oliverio Martinez, was shot five times by Oxnard, California police who allegedly violated his Fifth Amendment rights when questioning him. While awaiting emergency treatment for his injuries, Martinez was interrogated at length without being read his Miranda rights. In the hospital, officers continued to interrogate him. Martinez who was in pain, had stated that he did not want to answer, and had begged the officer to stop his questioning. Mel Lipman, president of the American Humanist Association, regards this is a serious problem. He adds: "if Miranda rights are not needed in questioning, it is possible that future witnesses will be committing a crime by simply pleading for their silence" (American Humanist Association, 2003). Some regard this decision as a significant infringement of Fifth Amendment protections, further eroding basic civil liberties, given its potential to promote hostile and coercive actions to obtain information.

ADDITIONAL THEMES

Differential racialization and first person narrative, alongside intersectionality and anti-essentialism provide additional insights into the nature and study of critical race theory. A brief mentioning of each is essential – but an in-depth exploration of each is beyond the scope of this chapter. Nonetheless, differential racialization suggests that the dominant society racializes different minority groups at different times in response to shifting needs such as the labor market. Throughout American history, labor market forces have dictated the need and status of Blacks, Mexicans, Asians and other persons of color. Closely related to this is that popular images and stereotypes of People of Color have also changed through time; sometimes depicted as happy-go-lucky, while at other times seen as menacing and brutish.

For more than 125 years, the U.S. Census Bureau has played a vital role in racial classification, often exceeding the black/white binary. When the question of race was first asked in 1890, there were almost 16 categories ranging from black to white. Ladson-Billings (2005: 116) speaks to this issue in the following manner:

> Asians were phenotypically determined to be White. In the Lemon Grove School District Incident, Mexican American parents won their suit against having their children sent

to a segregated school because they were categorized as White, and for a short period, the Cherokee Indians were considered White as they worked hard to assimilate in U.S. Society.

Perhaps more obvious are the events of 9–11 that have resulted in the differential racialization of Arabs and Moslems, regarded by some as more deserving of suspicion and government surveillance than others. Ironically, African-Americans appear to embrace the "focus on others" as a welcomed reprieve, given their historical (and continued) victimizations from racial profiling under the familiar adage of "diving while black." In economic terms, some groups (i.e., migrant workers and other laborers) are highly sought after, despite their perceived illegal immigrant status. In the twinkling of an eye, migrant workers are potentially racialized in response to shifting needs in the labor market. In some parts of the United States, migrant labor is valued and accepted, especially within cheap labor industries (i.e., farming, building, and house cleaning). As the political winds change, however, public perceptions tend to blow in a different direction. Clouded by suspicions of involvement in terrorist related activities or failure to provide adequate documentation, migrant workers are potentially transformed into "illegal immigrants." Similar practices are portrayed, for instance, in the continued reliance on Asian professionals to sustain some American economies, such as the computer industry. Most troubling, however, is the potential of racialization to "divide and conquer" the oppressed.

Contemporary examples of differential racialization resemble instances where white families adopt transracially. No longer a white family by virtue of their child(ren), they become racialized others. Other examples of racialization are alluded to by Ladson-Billings (1998: 11) in relation to the infamous O. J. Simpson trial:

> The criminal trial jury was repeatedly identified as the "Black" jury despite the presence of one White and one Latino juror. However, the majority White civil case jury was not given a racial designation. When whites are exempted from racial designations and become "families," "jurors," "students," teacher," etc. their ability to apply a CRT analytical rubric is limited.

INTERSECTIONALITY

Other important concepts of critical race theory include intersectionality and anti-essentialism, which suggest that no person has a single, easily stated, unitary identity. Rather, everyone has potentially conflicting, overlapping identities, loyalties, and allegiances, which makes claims of discrimination unusually difficult to sustain in a court of law. The complexity of this concept is portrayed through and examination of hate crime legislation which promotes stiffer punishments for crimes motivated by hate. According to the Dictionary of Sociology (1998), hate crimes – or bias motivated crimes – are defined as "crimes committed out of racial, religious, or sexual prejudice, which target minority groups, and which often violate anti-discrimination laws." Such crimes are usually crimes of violence motivated against (for example) women, Jews, Blacks, or gays. In Great Britain, however, the definition of a hate crime incident is exceedingly flexible and depends largely on the subjective perception of the victim. Hence, "anyone can be a victim of hate crime if they believe themselves to be so," even those historically regarded as proverbial offenders (Hall, 2005: 11).

In terms of critical race theory, hate crimes based on race are easily disguised in the midst of other relevant demographics, such as gender. Take for instance a Black lesbian who is physically attacked by a white male after voicing atheistic beliefs while drinking at a local bar. The question might become: what motivated the attack? Was it her race, gender, sexual orientation, her non-religious beliefs, or some combination of these? Was she a victim of a hate crime? Given the intersectionality and anti-essentialism of her identity (in general), the practicality of hate crime legislation, despite good intentions, is severely undermined. A CRT analysis, on the other hand, would explore the nature of the threat, including its meaning and intent. More potently, it requires an examination of the social context that lead to disparate treatment and outcomes.

FIRST PERSON NARRATIVE

Everyone loves a good story and the last theme of this chapter entails how stories (i.e., first person narratives) are utilized by unique People of Color. Critical race theory recognizes that the experiential knowledge of People of Color as legitimate, appropriate, and critical to understanding, analyzing and teaching about racial subordination (cited from Yosso, 2005). Drawing explicitly on the lived experiences of People of Color, Critical race theory includes various methods, such as storytelling, family histories, biographies, scenarios, parables, *cuentos, testiminios*, chronicles and narratives (Yosso, 2005: 74).

Delgado and Stefancic (2001) defined counter-story-telling as "a method of telling a story that aims to cast doubt on the validity of accepted premises as myths, especially ones held by the majority" (p. 144). Historically, story telling has been a kind of medicine to heal the wounds of pain caused by racial oppression. The story of one's condition leads to the realization of how one came to be oppressed and subjugated, thus allowing one to stop inflicting mental violence on oneself (Ladson-Billings, 1998: 14). This concept maintains that because of their different histories and experiences with oppression, Black, Indian, Asian, and Latino/a writers and thinkers may be able to communicate to their white counterparts matters that the whites are unlikely to know.

Well-told stories describing the reality of black and brown lives can help readers bridge the gap between their worlds and those of others. Engaging stories can foster an understanding of what life is like for others, and invite readers into a new and unfamiliar world. For instance, it is often pointed out that white-collar and corporate/industrial crime – perpetuated mostly by whites – causes more personal injury, death, and property loss than all street crime combined, even on a per capita basis (see Delgado and Stefani, 2001: 43). Historically, though, the bulk of criminal justice resources is targeted toward street crime and the processing of offenders stereotypically perceived as dangerous. That is a belief that often translates into policy. In this context, preconceptions and myths, for example about black criminality, shape mindset – the bundle of received wisdoms, stock stories, and suppositions that allocate suspicion, place the burden of proof on one party or the other, and tell us in cases of divided evidence what really happened. Critical race theorists use counter stories to challenge, displace, or mock these pernicious narratives and beliefs. The primary reason, then, that stories, or narratives, are deemed important among CRT scholars is they add necessary contextual contours to the seeming "objectivity" of positivist perspectives. It does so in a manner that reveals the contingency, cruelty, and self-serving notions of these presuppositions.

CRIMINAL JUSTICE THROUGH THE LENS OF CRITICAL RACE THEORY

Why is a CRT perspective important to incorporate into our understanding of criminal justice system practices? Given the current practices and conditions of justice systems world-wide, an application of CRT principles enable readers to examine social reality through a different lens when addressing perceived injustices. According to Yasso (2005: 75): looking through a CRT lens means analyzing deficit theorizing and data that they may be limited by its omission of the voices of People of Color. Such deficit informed research often 'sees' deprivation in Communities of Color. Indeed, one of the most prevalent forms of contemporary racism in U.S. school systems and other systems is deficit thinking. *Deficit thinking* refers to the notion that students (particularly those of low-income, racial/ethnic minority background) fail in school because such students and their families have internal defects (deficits) that thwart the learning process (Valencia, 1997). Examples of this include notions of educability; unmotivated; inadequate family support. Moreover, deficit thinking, an endogenous theory, "blames the victim" rather than examining how the schools are structured to prevent certain students from learning (see also Crenshaw, 1993).

Similar remnants of deficit thinking are evidenced in the criminal justice system by widely held perceptions and treatment of criminal offenders, many of whom are viewed as beyond rehabilitation and psychopathic. Traditionally, affective and inter-personal traits such as egocentricity, deceit, shallow affect, manipulativeness, selfishness, and lack of empathy, guilt or remorse, have played a central role in the conceptualization and diagnosis of psychopathy (see Widiger and Corbitt, 1996). Defined as a person with an antisocial personality disorder, psychopaths tend to manifest aggressive, perverted, criminal, or amoral behavior without empathy or remorse. Personality characteristics of psychopaths are highly correlated with the *DSM-IV-R* classifications of antisocial personality disorder (APD). The field of Criminology tends to treat APD as so synonymous, in fact, with criminal behavior that practically all convicted criminals (65–75%) have this deficit (see Hare, 1996; McCord, 1964).

In terms of critical race theory, the failure to differentiate between psychopathy and APD can have serious consequences for clinicians and for society. For example, most jurisdictions consider psychopathy as an aggravating rather than a mitigating factor in determining criminal responsibility. In some states, an offender convicted of first-degree murder and diagnosed as psychopathic is likely to receive the death penalty on the ground that psychopaths are cold-blooded, remorseless, untreatable and almost certain to re-offend (see Meloy, 1990). Given the existing racial disparities in arrests, prosecution, conviction, and sentencing rates, these classifications serve to perpetuate common stereotypes of what criminals look like and what the types of punishments they "deserve." Most damaging, however, is the potential of these diagnoses to exacerbate racial disparities in the imposition of the death sentences where racial disparities are already exceedingly pronounced.

Building on the work of radical criminologists, it is no surprise that critical race theorists believe the disproportionate criminalization of African-Americans and other Persons of Color is a product, in large part, of the way we define crime. Many lethal acts, such as marketing defective automobiles, alcohol, and pharmaceuticals or waging undeclared wars, are not considered crimes at all (Delgado and Stefancic, 2001: 113). By the same token, many things that young black men and Latino men are prone to do, such as congregating on street corners, cruising in low-riders (drop tops), or scrawling graffiti in public places, are energetically policed. Critical race theorists are concerned that racial profiling that targets certain minority youth because they are viewed as more likely involved in crime or perpetrators of crime. Both practices tend to penalize law-abiding people of color and alienate youths.

Along more radical lines, some critical race theorists urge jury nullification to combat the disproportionate incarceration of young black men (see Butler, 1995). In jury nullification, the jury – usually containing some black jurors – exercises its discretion to acquit black defendants if they thought the case was racially motivated (such as the perception that an arresting officer was racist), or if they thought it useless to send a *non-violent* offender to jail. The power of jurors to nullify verdicts derived from English Common law, which gave citizens the discretionary power to correct what they perceived as unjust laws and punishments. In a highly referenced American case one judge, well versed in critical race theory, applied a similar analysis in the case of a black defendant. Under a three-strikes-and-you are out type of law, the judge was required to sentence the man to a long term. On noticing that two of his previous offenses had been automobile-connected, the judge declined to do so. Reasoning that racial profiling by the police causes black motorists to be pulled over more frequently than whites, she concluded that the defendant's two prior convictions had likely been tainted by racism. Consequently, she sentenced him to the shorter term appropriate as a repeat offender (Delgado and Stefancic, 2001: 115).

In a similar context, Butler (1995) proposed that one way to remedy injustices in the criminal justice system is to apply principles of affirmative action to the criminal law. Similar to the concept of jury nullification, he advocated that only black juries deliberate on cases involving both black offenders and black victims. Likewise, only an all black jury should decide the fate of a black murderer facing a potential death sentence. There have been noted objections to this approach. Kennedy (1997: 299) for instance, characterizes Butler's approach as "profoundly misleading and that problems of the criminal justice system require judicious attention – not a campaign of defiant sabotage." According to Kennedy (1997), a campaign of jury nullification could actually backfire as there is nothing to prevent White jurors from doing the same thing in cases involving White-on-Black crime. Criticisms of this nature, regarding the utility of critical race theory, are but a microcosm of even broader concerns that are outlined below.

A CRITIQUE OF CRITICAL RACE THEORY

The themes of critical race theory have circulated for nearly 30 years, encompassing powerful notions, like the centrality and intersectionality of race and racism, the challenge to the dominant ideology, commitment to social justice, and the promotion of an interdisciplinary perspective. This section entails a critical review of the contemporary status of critical race theory and problems it has encountered along the way toward achieving acceptance before a skeptical and often times defensive audience. We begin with Solorzano and Villipando (1998), who expressed doubts that critical race theory had achieved its goals, especially in its ability to understand forms of subtle discrimination. They assert:

> indeed, we know very little about whom, where, and how these microaggressions are initiated and responded to. Without careful documentation and analysis, these racial and gender microaggressions can easily be ignored or downplayed.
>
> (1998: 132)

Just as other theories are inadequate toward explaining many disparities in the arena of race, crime, and justice, critical race theory also has its shortcomings, not the least of which is proving racism. Part of the problem is that evidence of racism in the criminal justice system is often measured by historical standards of positivism. Yet, positivistic approaches are woefully inadequate at discerning more subtle and hidden forms of racism. Critical race theory appears to use a different standard of measurement to capture the experiences and perceptions of oppressed people who are typical victims of social injustice.

Levitt (1999), in a classic essay, explores the increasing intolerance that critical theorists – particularly critical race theorists – face in response to their call for inclusion in society's collective decision-making. Typically, most of the opposition and critical reviews derive from conservatives. Take George Will (1996) for instance, who accuses critical race theorists of "playing the race card." Or Rosen (1996), in his assertion that some critical race scholars indulge in "a vulgar racial essentialism," and that [t]he rhetoric of the movement is already reverberating beyond the lecture hall and seminar room. In harsher terms, Judge Richard Posner of the United States Court of Appeals labels critical race theorists and postmodernists as the "lunatic core" of radical legal egalitarianism. Interestingly, Posner (1997) is less harsh on selected critical legal studies and radical feminist scholars, who simply "have plenty of goofy ideas and irresponsible dicta" (cited from Levitt, 1999). Compounding the case against critical race theorist are the likes of those who claim that critical race scholarship "fails the test for rational discourse."

Highly judgmental and less tolerant of critical race theory; Farber and Sherry (1997) refer to CRT scholars as "radical multiculturalists" whose arguments are "beyond all reason." Radical multiculturalism, Farber and Sherry diagnose, is "a paranoid mode of thought that sees behind every social institution nothing but the tracks of white supremacy and male oppression" (p. 132). This sentiment sufficiently describes the attitudes of many who reject CRT premises.

Regarded by some as radical scholarship, traditionalist fear that critical race theory tends to distort public discourse (Farber and Sherry, 1997). They characterize critical race theorists in the following manner:

> ... [T]heir disdain for standards, objectivity, and truths leads [the] radical scholars to indulge in a form of writing that is blatantly subjective. Instead of offering theoretical or doctrinal analysis, radical multiculturalists tell stories. These stories are intended to "explode the dominant myths or received knowledge, disrupt the established order, shatter complacency, and seduce the reader".
>
> (p. 24)

AN ASSAULT ON STORY-TELLING

Clearly, some themes of critical race theory are more scrutinized than others. "Story-telling" has become the poster child of illegitimacy and scrutiny, given its challenge to traditional notions of epistemology that looks at how one knows reality. For scientists, the way of knowing reality is via the scientific method. Traditionalists claim that story telling is inherently problematic because stories cannot be verified, are inevitably subjective, and may be atypical of real world experiences. Moreover, narrative methodology "reject[s] the linearity, abstraction, and scientific objectivity of rational argument" (Levitt, 1999). Therefore, for the traditionalists, storytelling is neither legal nor academic, and threatens the credibility of the scholarly enterprise. As stories are unrepresentative or atypical, they are of limited value. Levitt (1999), raises the following concerns:

> ... [R]ather than relying solely on legal or interdisciplinary authorities, empirical data, or rigorous analysis, legal scholars have begun to offer stories, often about their own real or imagined experiences. ... Often the story recounts how the author was mistreated because of race, gender, or sexual orientation.

Yet story telling is defended by many critical race theorists who regard it as exceedingly useful and undeniably powerful in its effect. Fearing that some are missing the point, Murray (1996) asserts: "at hand is an attempt to transform the meritocratic ideal by including what has been up to now excluded: the valuable, concrete, lived experiences of oppressed peoples." For Levitt (1999), the problem is not story telling, *per se*, but a lack of dialogue. She reminds readers that using narrative to move toward inquiry is not only an obligation owed by a storyteller; it is an obligation due by a reader. This obligation on readers includes distinguishing metaphorical stories from stories of actual experience, and asking different purpose and credibility questions with respect to made-up stories, once-upon-a time stories, parables, and accounts offered as factual renditions of events. Thus, critical race theory acknowledges an interactive relationship between the researcher and the participants (Guba and Lincoln, 1994).

SUMMARY AND CONCLUSION

This chapter attempted to spell out the potential of critical race theory as an analytic tool in criminology and criminal justice regarding issues of race, crime, and justice.

A critical race theoretical perspectives is regarded are more appropriate than competing perspectives, such as conflict theory, which maintains that the fundamental causes of crime are the social and economic forces operating within society. Moreover, the criminal justice system and criminal law are thought to be operating on behalf of rich and powerful social elites, with resulting policies aimed at controlling the poor. The inability of Conflict Theory to address more subtle and covert forms of racism, however, is a severe limitation on it usefulness.

Critical race theory, on the other hand, challenges us to view race and racism through the lens of People of Color while providing ways of systematizing the search for knowledge (Delgado and Stefancic, 2005). In the process, it helps avoid the search for easy answers, focuses attention on social construction and mindset, asks us to attend to the material factors underlying race and racism, and goes beyond the ordinariness of racist action and treatment (Delgado and Stefancic, 2005). In the now famous words of Justice Blackmun in his dissenting opinion in the *Bakke* case, "[I]n order to get beyond racism, we must first take account of race. There is no other way. And in order to treat some people equally, we must treat them differently." Race continues to play a significant role in explaining inequality, discrimination, and disparities in American justice systems. One way to understand and appreciate the dynamic intersection between issues of race, crime, and justice is through an examination and appreciation of critical race theory.

REFERENCES

Agamben, G. (2005). *State of Exception*. Chicago: University of Chicago Press.

American Civil Liberties Union (2003). Inadequate Representation. Retrieved on 10/16/2006, from http//www.aclu.org/capital/unequal/10390pub20031008.html

American Humanist Association (2003). Retrieved on 10/18/2006, from (http://www.americanhumanist.org/press/FifthAmendment053003.html).

Bell, D. (1980). *Brown* and the Interest Convergence Dilemma. In D. Bell (ed.), *Shades of Brown: New Perspectives on School Desegregation* (pp. 90–106). New York: Teachers College Press.

Butler, P. (1995). Racially based jury nullification: Black power in the criminal justice system," *Yale Law Journal*, 105: 677.

Crenshaw, K. (1993). Race, reform, and retrenchment: Transformation and legitimation in antidiscrimination law. *Harvard Law Review*, 101(7): 1331–1387.

Crenshaw, K. (1989). Demarginalizing the intersection between race and sex: A black feminist critique of antidiscrimination doctrine, Feminist theory and antiracist politics. *University of Chicago Law Forum*, pp. 139–167.

Crenshaw, K. (1993). Mapping the margins: Intersectionality, identity politics and the violence against women of color. *Standford Law Review*, 43: 1241–1299.

Delgado, R. and Stefancic, J. (2001). *Critical Race Theory: An Introduction*, New York: New York University Press.

Delgado, R. and Stefancic, J. (2005). The role of critical race theory in understanding race, crime, and justice issues. Paper presented at John Jay College of Criminal Justice, CUNY (December 13, 2005).

Dictionary of Sociology (1998). Originally published by Oxford University Press.

Farber, D. and Sherry, S. (1997). Beyond all reason: The radical assault on truth in American Law. New York: Oxford University Press.

Field, B. (1990). *Slavery, Race, and Ideology in the United States of America*. New York: Bantam Books.

Guba, G. and Lincoln, Y. S. (1994). Competing paradigms in qualitative research. In N. K. Denzin and Y. S. Lincoln (eds), Handbook of qualitative research (pp. 105–117). Thousand Oaks, CA: SAGE.

Hall, N. (2005). *Hate Crime*. Portland, Oregon: Wilan Publishing.

Hare, R. (1996). Psychopathy: A clinical construct whose time has come. *Criminal Justice and Behavior* 23: 25–54.

Hawkins, D. F., Myers, S. L. and Stone, R. N. (eds) (2003). *Crime Control and Social Justice: The Delicate Balance*. Westport, Connecticut: Greenwood Press.

Hayman, R. Jr. (1997). *The Smart Culture: Society, Intelligence, and Law*. New York: New York University Press.

Kennedy, R. (1997). *Race, Crime and the Law*. New York: Vintage Books.

Ladson-Billings, G. (1998). Just what is critical race theory and what is it doing in a *nice* field like education? *Qualitative Studies in Education*, 1(11): 7–24.

Ladson-Billings, G. (2005). The evolving role of critical race theory in educational scholarship. *Race, Ethnicity and Education*, 1(8): 115–119.

Ladson-Billings, G. and Tate, W. F. (1995). Towards a critical theory of education. *Teachers College Record*, 97(1): 47–68.

Lazarus, E. (2001). The coming era of federal executions? Legal Challenges we can expect if more federal defendants share McVeigh's fate. Retrieved on 2/16/2007, from http://writ.news.findlaw.com/lazarus/20010123.html

Levitt, N. (1999). Critical of race theory; Race, reason, merit, and civility. *Georgetown Law Journal*, 87(3): 795–822. Avialable at: http://workers.bepress.com/nancy-lerit/16

MacDonald, H. (1995). Law school humbug. *The City Journal*. Retrieved 11/21/2006, from http://www.city-journal.org/html/5_4_a2.html on 10/2006

Matsuda, M. J. (2002). I and Thou and We and the Way to Peace. *Issues in Legal Scholarship*, The origins and Fate of Antisubordination Theory: Article 6 http://www.bepress.com/ils/iss2/art6

McCord, W. J. (1964). *The Psychopath: An Essay on the Criminal Mind*. Princeton: Van Nostrand.

Meloy, J. R. (1990). *Symposium on the Psychopath and the Death Penalty*. American Academy of Psychiatry and the Law, 21st Annual Meeting. October 27, 1990; San Diego. Retrieved on 2/4/2007, from www.psychiatrictimes.com/p960239.html

Morrison, T. (1993). *Playing in the Dark*. Random House.

Murray, Y. M. (1996). Merit-teaching. *Hastings Constitutional Law Quarterly*, 1073(23): 1080–1081.

Omi, M. and Winant, H. (1994). *Racial Formation in the Unite States: 1960s to 1990s*. New York: Routledge Publishing.

Orfield, G. (1988). The growth and concentration of Hispanic enrollment and the future of American education. Presented at *National Council of La Raza Conference*, Albuquerque, NM.

Posner, R. (1997). The Skin Trade, *New Republic*, October 13, p. 40.

Rosen, J. (1996). The bloods and the crits: O. J. Simpson, critical race theory, the law, and the triumph of color in America, *New Republic*, December 9, p. 27.

Schmitt, C. (2005). *Political Theology* and *Dictatorship*. Chicago: University of Chicago Press. Retrieved on 10/18/2006, from http://muse.jhu.edu/journals/theory_and_ event/v009/9.2kohn.html

Solorzano, D. and Villalpando, O. (1998). The Chicano educational experience: A proposed framework for effective schools in Chicano students in an urban context, *Urban Education*, 36: 308–342.

Solum, L. (1987). On the indeterminacy crisis: Critiquing critical dogma, *The University of Chicago Law Review,* 54: 462.

Valdes, F., Culp, J. and Harris, A. P. (eds) (2002). *Crossroads, Directions, and a New Critical Race Theory*. Philadelphia: Temple University Press.

Valencia, R. R. (1997). *The Evolution of Deficit Thinking: Educational Thought and Practice*. Pennsylvania: Taylor & Francis Inc.

Wellman, D. (1977). *Portraits of White Racism*. Cambridge, England: Cambridge University Press.

Widiger, T. A. and Corbitt, E. (1996). Antisocial personality disorder. In T. A. Widiger, A. J. Frances, H. A. Pincus, M. B. First, R. R. Ross and W. W. Davis (eds). *(1996) DSM-IV Sourcebook* (Volume 2. pp. 703–716). Washington, D.C.: American Psychiatric Association.

Will, G. E. (1996). Playing the race card, *Portland Oregonian* (Nov. 29, at B8).

Yosso, T. J. (2005). Whose culture has capital? A critical race theory discussion of community cultural wealth. *Race, Ethnicity and Education*, 1(8): 69–91.

Cases cited

Bell v. Wolfish, 441 U.S. 520 (1979)

Brown v. Board of Education of Topeka, Kansas, 384 U.S. 483; (1954)

McCleskey v. Kemp, 481 U.S. 279 (1987)

Miranda v. Arizona, 384 U.S. 436; 86 S. Ct. 1602; 16 L. Ed. 2d 694; (1966)

Powell v. Alabama, 53 S. Ct. 55, 287 U.S. 45 S. Ct. (1932)

Regents of the University of California v. Bakke, 438 U.S. 265; 407 (1978)

Tennessee v. Edward Garner et al., 471 U.S. 1; 105 S. Ct. 1694; (1985)

21

A Green Criminology Perspective

Rob White

INTRODUCTION

There is a growing interest in environmental issues within criminology and in pursuing what can broadly be called green criminology. Green criminology, also sometimes known as 'environmental criminology' (but not to be confused with the urban study and crime mapping variation of the same name), refers to the study of environmental harm, environmental laws and environmental regulation by criminologists. There is also a growing network of environmental criminologists across the English-speaking world, as evidenced in recent book collections (Beirne and South, 2007; Clifford, 1998; Edwards *et al.*, 1996; South and Beirne, 2006) and special editions of journals such as *Social Justice, Theoretical Criminology* and *Current Issues in Criminal Justice* (South, 1998; White, 2005; Williams, 1996). Even those who purport to be 'against green criminology' (Halsey, 2004) can be considered part of the deliberations surrounding how criminologists approach the study of environmental issues.

This chapter provides an introduction and overview of the key theoretical developments within green or environmental criminology. The main focus of attention is on those debates and divisions that are central to the emergent literature on environmental crime. The chapter begins by describing three frameworks that tend to inform how green criminologists conceptualise the nature of the problem – what they see as most important for analysis and action, and which thus shape their conceptions of harm and criminality. This is followed by a description of environmental crimes that are identified within the green criminological literature. The final section outlines three divergent perspectives on how environmental harm might be responded to at a policy, strategic and action level.

THEORETICAL FRAMEWORKS

There is no green criminology *theory* as such. Rather, as observed by South (1998), there is what can loosely be described as a green 'perspective'. Elements of this perspective generally include things such as a concern with specifically environmental issues, social justice, ecological consciousness, the destructive nature of global capitalism, the role of the nation-state (and regional and global regulatory bodies), and inequality and discrimination as these relate to class, gender, race and nonhuman animals. Corporate definitions of a green agenda are sometimes explicitly rejected (Lynch and Stretesky, 2003), insofar as corporations are generally seen to be integral to the problems of environmental harm. The green criminology perspective, therefore, tends to begin with a strong sensitivity toward crimes of the powerful, and to be infused with issues pertaining to power, justice, inequality and democracy.

Within the spectrum of ideas and activities associated with green criminology are several different kinds of analytical framework. Some of these pertain to eco-philosophy, that is, to ways in which the relationship between humans and nature can be conceptualised. Academic work in this area might include consideration of gendered views of the natural and social worlds (Lane, 1998; Plumwood, 2005), exploration of anthropocentric, biocentric and ecocentric perspectives (Halsey and White, 1998) through to postmodern versions of a constitutive green criminology (Halsey, 2004). Less abstractly, however, most environmental criminology can be distinguished on the basis of who precisely it is that is being victimised. As indicated in Table 21. 1, there are three broad theoretical tendencies that generally frame how specific writers view the nature of environmental issues, including harm and responses to harm.

Environmental justice

Analysis of environmental issues proceeds on the basis that someone or something is indeed being harmed. *Environmental justice* refers to the distribution of environments among peoples in terms of access to and use of specific natural resources in defined geographical areas, and the impacts of particular social practices and environmental hazards on specific populations (e.g., as defined on the basis of class, occupation, gender, age, ethnicity). In other words, the concern is with **human beings** at the centre of analysis. The focus of analysis therefore is on human health and well-being and how these are affected by particular types of production and consumption.

It is important to distinguish between environmental issues that affect everyone, and those that disproportionately affect specific individuals and groups (see Low and Gleeson, 1998; Williams, 1996). In some instances, there may be a basic 'equality of victims', in that some environmental problems threaten everyone in the same way, as in the case for example of ozone depletion, global warming, air pollution and acid rain (Beck, 1996). As extensive work on specific incidents and patterns of victimisation demonstrate, however, it is also the case that some people are more likely to be disadvantaged by environmental problems than others. For instance, studies have identified disparities involving many different types of environmental hazards that especially adversely affect people of colour, ethnic minority groups and indigenous

Table 21.1   Green theoretical frameworks

Environment Rights and Environmental Justice

Environmental rights as an extension of human or social rights so as to enhance the quality of human life.

Intergenerational Responsibility: equity and future generations
Environmental Justice: equity for present generations

Environmental Harm is constructed in relation to human-centred notions of value and use.

Ecological Citizenship and Ecological Justice

Ecological citizenship acknowledges that human beings are merely one component of complex ecosystems that should be preserved for their own sake via the notion of the rights of the environment.

Global Trans-boundary: issues of scale and interconnectedness
Ecological Justice: quality of biosphere and rights of non-human species

Environmental Harm is constructed in relation to notions of ecological harm and destructive techniques of human intervention.

Animal Rights and Species Justice

Nonhuman animals have rights based upon utilitarian notions (maximising pleasure and minimising pain), inherent value (right to respectful treatment) and an ethic of responsible caring.

Anti-speciesism: addressing the discriminatory treatments of animals as Other
Animal rights: dealing with issues of animal abuse and suffering, and the nurturing of respectful relationships

Environmental Harm is constructed in relation to the place of nonhuman animals within environments and their intrinsic right to not suffer abuse, whether this be one-on-one, institutionalised harm or harm arising from human actions the affect climates and environments on a global scale.

Source: extension of a model developed by White (2007).

people in places such as Canada, Australia and the USA (Brook, 2000; Bullard, 1994; Langton, 1998; Rush, 2002; Stretesky and Lynch, 1999). There are thus patterns of 'differential victimisation' that are evident with respect to the siting of toxic waste dumps, extreme air pollution, chemical accidents, access to safe clean drinking water and so on (see Chunn *et al.*, 2002; Williams, 1996). Another dimension of differential victimisation relates to the subjective disposition and consciousness of the people involved. The specific groups who experience environmental problems may not always describe or see the issues in strictly environmental terms. This may be related to lack of knowledge of the environmental harm, alternative explanations for the calamity (e.g., an act of God) and socio-economic pressures to 'accept' environmental risk (see Julian, 2004). The environmental justice discourse places *inequalities* in the distribution of environmental quality at the top of the environmental agenda (see Harvey 1996; Julian, 2004).

Ecological justice

On the other hand, *ecological justice* refers to the relationship of human beings generally to the rest of the natural world, and includes concerns relating to the health of the *bio-sphere*, and more specifically **plants** and **creatures** that also inhabit the biosphere (Cullinan, 2003; Smith, 1998). The main concern is with the quality of the planetary environment (that is frequently seen to possess its own intrinsic value) and the rights of other species (particularly animals) to life free from torture, abuse and destruction of habitat. Specific practices, and choices, in how humans interact with particular environments present immediate and potential risks to everything within them. Ecological notions of rights and justice see humans as but one component of complex ecosystems that should be preserved for their own sake, as supported by the notion of the rights of the environment. In this framework, all living things are bound together and environmental matters are intrinsically global and trans-boundary in nature (as witnessed, for example, by the spread of the bird flu virus worldwide or polluted river waters across national borders). Ecological justice demands that how humans interact with their environment be evaluated in relation to potential harms and risks to specific creatures and specific locales as well as the biosphere generally.

Within this broad approach there may be philosophical differences in terms of the value put on the interests of humans and on the environment. From a deep green or biocentric perspective, for example, AIDS or famine may simply be seen as nature's way of controlling population growth and thus as good for the planet as a whole (see White, 1994). From this vantage point, an act or omission is not criminal if it ultimately benefits the biosphere generally. This fundamentally misanthropic perspective frequently seeing humans as the problem, and therefore it is humans who need to be controlled or in some cases even eradicated. Related to this attitude, it is notable that members of the environmental justice movements are critical of mainstream environmental groups precisely because of their 'focus on the fate of "nature" rather than humans' (Harvey, 1996: 386). To put it differently, taking action on environmental issues involves choices and priorities. Many communities who suffer from the 'hard end' of environmental harm feel that their wellbeing ought to take priority over 'natural environments' or specific plants and animals as such.

The other major strand of ecological thinking provides a progressive contrast to the biocentric view. While an ecocentric or social ecology perspective likewise acknowledges human authorship of environmental degradation, it does so within the context of political economy and the different forms and types of social power. Criminality is related to exploitation of both environments and humans by those who control the means of production (Field, 1998). Environmental deviance is linked to particular social power contexts, which in the contemporary world are dominated by large corporations and upper-class stakeholders (Simon, 2000). The interplay between nature and humans is such that social justice is equally important and inextricably bound to issues of ecology. An ecocentric approach therefore recognises the central role of humans in acting upon the natural world, while simultaneously calling for accountability in how production and consumption processes relate to the ecospheric limits of the planet.

Animal rights

The third strand of green criminology is that represented by those who wish to include consideration of *animal rights* within the broad perspective (Beirne, 2007; Benton, 1998). In specific terms, concepts such as speciesism may be invoked. This refers to the practice of discriminating against **nonhuman animals** because they are perceived as inferior to the human species in much the same way that sexism and racism involve prejudice and discrimination against women and people of different colour (Munro, 2004). The animal-centred discourse of animal rights shares much in common with the environment-centred discourse of green criminology, but certain differences, as well as the commonalities, are also apparent (Beirne, 2007). For example, nonhuman animals are frequently considered in primarily instrumental terms (as pets, as food, as resources) in environmental criminology, or categorised in mainly anthropomorphic terms (such as 'wildlife', 'fisheries') that belie the ways in which humans create and classify animals as Other. From an animal rights theoretical framework, one key issue revolves around how rights are constructed: via utilitarian theory that emphasises the consequential goal of minimising suffering and pain; via rights theory that emphasises the right to respectful treatment; and via feminist theory that emphasises the ethic of responsible caring (Beirne, 2007). The other key issue is with practical and conceptual action that is needed to better define animal abuse, and how best to respond to this.

Tensions can exist between both animal rights and environmental justice views, and animal rights and ecological justice approaches. Where do we draw the line when it comes to the rights of (which) animals and the rights of humans (does the mosquito biting into my arm have a right to live)? Trees and rocks and streams are not sentient beings capable of suffering, so where do they fit into the ethical universe? Yet, very often conceptualisation of environmental harm encapsulates the concerns of all three strands – protection of biodiversity within our forests is not incompatible with sustaining localised environments, protecting endangered species and ensuring human happiness. Clearfelling of old growth forests, for example, can be highly problematic from the point of view of human enjoyment, nurturing of nonhuman animals, and conservation of complex eco-systems.

There are many concrete links between the health of natural environments, diverse human activity and the exploitation of animals. And, increasingly, the language of rights is being used to frame responses to harm and abuse that are evident across the three areas of concern. It will be interesting to see how the dialogue between these three theoretical frameworks will unfold in the coming years. These frameworks, of course, do have major consequences with regard to where individual scholars and researchers put their time and energy. The study of environmental crime, including animal cruelty, is greatly influenced by the perspective one has about the natural world generally, and thereby which issues ought to receive specific priority.

ENVIRONMENTAL CRIME

Environmental crime is now starting to appear as a distinct category of crime in criminology textbooks and other professional publications such as journals (see for example, Carrabine et al., 2004; Rosoff et al., 1998; White and Habibis, 2005). The categorisation of environmental harm is varied in that there are different ways in which environmental crimes have been conceptualised and sorted. From the point of view of environmental law, for example, environmental harm encapsulates a wide range of concerns, some of which are subject to criminal sanctions but many of which are not (Boyd, 2003). The kinds of issues canvassed under environmental law relate to laws and policies intended to protect water (e.g., pollution), air (e.g., ozone depletion), land (e.g., pesticide regulation) and biodiversity (e.g., endangered species). From the point of view of harm, writers have also incorporated under the

Table 21.2   Types of green crimes

Primary Green Crimes

Crimes of air pollution
  (e.g., burning of corporate waste)
Crimes of deforestation
  (e.g., destruction of rainforests)
Crimes of species decline and against animal rights
  (e.g., traffic in animals and animal parts)
Crimes of water pollution
  (e.g., lack of drinking water)

Secondary or Symbiotic Green Crimes

State violence against oppositional groups
  (e.g., French bombing of the *Rainbow Warrior*)
Hazardous waste and organised crime
  (e.g., toxic and general waste dumping both legal and illegal)

Source: Carrabine *et al.* (2004).

environmental harm umbrella concerns relating to employee health (e.g., exposure to radioactivity) and pathological indoor environments (e.g., the home, hospitals, workplaces) (Curson and Clark, 2004; Rosoff *et al.*, 1998). Criminologists and others are thus categorising environmental crimes in varying ways, and how they do so has implications for the study of environmental harm.

For instance, Carrabine *et al.* (2004) discuss environmental crimes in terms of primary and secondary crimes. Green crimes are broadly defined simply as crimes against the environment. Primary crimes are those crimes that result directly from the destruction and degradation of the earth's resources, through human actions. Secondary or symbiotic green crime is that crime arises out of the flouting of rules that seek to regulate environmental disasters.

The list of crimes associated with this typology is by no means exhaustive. For example, in recent years researchers have studied environmental harms associated with the following kinds of concern:

- Exploitation of bio-technology and the corporate colonisation of nature, particularly in regards to the development and marketing of genetically modified food (South, 2007; Walters, 2006).
- The transborder movement and dumping of waste products (Block, 2002; Pearce and Tombs, 1998; Rosoff *et al.*, 1998).
- The problem of illegal, unreported and unregulated fishing and how best to intervene in preventing over exploitation of ocean resources (Anderson and McCusker, 2005; Lugten, 2005; McMullan and Perrier, 2002).
- Under globalised systems of production, the generation of toxic waste in less developed countries by companies based in advanced industrialised nations (Low and Gleeson, 1998).
- The diminishment in the quality and quantity of drinking water worldwide and the influence of transnational corporations in controlling water resources (Whelan, 2005; White, 2003).
- Environmental degradation on indigenous people's lands perpetrated by governments and companies (Rush, 2002).
- Inequalities in the distribution of environmental risk, especially as this relates to poor and minority populations (Bullard, 1994; Stretesky and Lynch, 1999; Zilney *et al.*, 2006).

Table 21.3   Mapping of environmental harm

Focal Considerations:
[Identify issues pertaining to victims of harm]

Environmental Justice	Ecological Justice	Animal Rights
[human beings]	[bio-sphere]	[nonhuman animals]

Geographical Considerations:
[Identify issues pertaining to each geographical level]

International	National	Regional/State	Local

Locational Considerations:
[Identify issues pertaining to specific kinds of sites]

'Built' Environments	'Natural' Environments
[e.g., urban, rural, suburban]	[e.g., ocean, wilderness, desert]

Temporal Considerations:
[Identify issues pertaining to changes over time]

Environmental Effects	Environmental Impact	Social Impact
[short-term/long-term]	[manifest/latent]	[immediate/lasting]

Source: White (2005).

• The one-on-one and the systematic institutionalised abuse of animals, as well as how changing environments affect the lives and wellbeing of nonhuman animals (Beirne, 2004, 2007).
• The environmental and social damage caused by enforced pursuit of structural adjustment policies generated by the World Bank (Friedrichs and Friedrichs, 2002).

The range of substantive topic areas that green criminology is presently investigating is growing. So too, the complexities involved in studying environmental harm are likewise being acknowledged. For example, environmental harm can be analytically studied in regards to four types of perspective: focal considerations; geographical considerations; locational considerations; and temporal considerations.

Exploration of themes and issues within each of these areas can be used to explore the diversity of perspectives, approaches and concepts that are utilised in contemporary environmental criminology (see White, 2005).

Focal considerations

Focal considerations refer to concerns that centre on the key actors or players who are at the centre of investigation into environmental harm. In other words, the emphasis is on identifying issues pertaining to the victims of harm, including how to define whom or what is indeed an environmental 'victim' (Williams, 1996). Within criminology there are significant issues surrounding scale, activities and legalities as these pertain to environmental harm. A strict legalist approach tends to focus on the central place of criminal law in the definition of criminality (Situ and Emmons, 2000). However, other writers argue that, as with criminology in general, the concept of 'harm' ought to encapsulate those activities that may be legal and 'legitimate' but which nevertheless negatively impact on people, environments and nonhuman animals (Beirne, 2004; Lynch and Stretesky, 2003).

Geographical considerations

Students of environmental harm have to be cognisant of the varying issues that pertain to different geographical levels. Some issues are of a planetary scale (e.g., global warming), others regional (e.g., oceans and fisheries), some are national in geographical location (e.g., droughts in Australia), while others are local (e.g., specific oil spills). Similarly, laws tend to be formulated in particular geographically defined jurisdictions. With regard to nation-states such as Australia, relevant laws include international law, federal laws, state laws and local government by-laws.

Locational considerations

A distinction can be made between geographical area and 'place'. The latter refers to specific kinds of sites as described in the language of 'natural' and 'built' environment. There is considerable overlap, interconnection and interplay between these types of environments. Nevertheless, the distinction is useful, particularly when assessing which environmental issues appeal to which sections of the population and for what reasons (Tranter, 2004; White, 2005). The precise nature of an environmental issue is in itself linked to specific group interests and consciousness of harm. For example, environmental issues have been categorised according to three different types of harm (Crook and Pakulski, 1995; Curson and Clark, 2004; Tranter, 2004; White, 2005). *Brown* issues tend to be defined in terms of urban life and pollution; *green* issues mainly relate to wilderness areas and conservation matters; and *white* issues refer to science laboratories and the impact of new technologies. The mobilisation of opinion is crucial to determination of what is or is not considered a 'crime' (or 'harm'), and how the state will in the end respond to the phenomenon in question. The complex relationship between human and non-human 'rights' is thus played out in practice through the importance of 'place' in the lives of diverse communities.

Temporal considerations

Another key issue for consideration relates to issues pertaining to changes over time. To some extent, such considerations are ingrained in contemporary environmental impact assessment in the guise of the 'precautionary principle' (Deville and Harding, 1997; Harvey, 1998). That is, what we do with and in the environment has consequences, some of which we cannot foresee. Temporal considerations can be distinguished in terms of environmental effects, environmental impacts and social impacts. The short-term effects of environmental degradation include such things as the release of chlorofluorocarbons into the atmosphere, the long-term effect being the accumulation of greenhouse gases and ultimately climate warming. Environmental impacts begin with global warming as a manifest consequence of planetary change, and results in the latent consequences of changes in sea levels and changes in regional temperatures and precipitation (among other things). The social impacts of environmental change are both immediate, as in the case of respiratory problems or increased probability of disease outbreak, and long-term (e.g., lower quality of life, alteration of physiological functioning).

There are, then, a number of intersecting dimensions that need to be considered in any analysis of specific instances of environmental crime. These include consideration of who the victim is (human or non-human); where the harm is manifest (global through to local levels); the main site in which the harm is apparent (built or natural environment); and the time frame within which harm can be analysed (immediate and delayed consequences). We also have to be aware of the methodological difficulties and opportunities associated with investigation of environmental harm. For example, on the one hand, the mainstream press underreports the incidence and seriousness of environmental harm, particularly those linked to big business interests (Simon, 2000) and this can inhibit our knowledge of the harms. Corporate offenders also have the legal and political resources to shield their operations from outside scrutiny and to ward off prying eyes. On the other hand, criminologists are utilising alternative sources of information – such as evidence drawn from medical literature and from environmental protection agencies – rather than relying solely upon conventional criminal justice sources or information supplied by perpetrators (Lynch and Stretesky, 2006; Lynch *et al.*, 2002).

RESPONDING TO ENVIRONMENTAL HARM

Socio-legal approach

There are three main approaches to the analysis and study of environmental criminalisation and regulation. One is to chart existing environmental legislation and to provide a sustained socio-legal analysis of specific breaches of law, the role of law enforcement agencies, and the difficulties and opportunities of using criminal law against environmental offenders (del Frate and Norberry, 1993; Gunningham *et al.*, 1995; Heine *et al.*, 1997; Situ and Emmons, 2000). Recent work in this area has, for example, examined the role of police in environmental law enforcement, from a global to a local level (Tomkins, 2005), while other study has indicated the uses of

---

Table 21.4   Responding to environmental harm

Socio-Legal Approach

Emphasis on use of criminal law as presently constituted.
Attempts to improve quality of investigation, law enforcement, prosecution and conviction on
   illegal environmentally-related activity.

Regulatory Approach

Emphasis on social regulation, using many different means, as the key mechanism to prevent and
   curtail environmental harm.
Attempts to reform existing systems of production and consumption through adoption of
   constellation of measures, including enforced self-regulation and bringing
   non-government groups directly into the regulatory process.

Social Action Approach

Emphasis on need for fundamental social change, and to challenge the hegemony of transnational
   capital and dominant nation-states in setting the environmental agenda.
Attempts to engage in social transformation through emphasis on deliberative democracy and citizen
   participation, and support for the radical as well as other wings of the social movements.

---

satellite technologies in surveillance of potential land degradation practices (Bartel, 2005). There are many challenges to the enforcement of environmental laws, and new ways of doing things have had to be developed. For instance, investigation of toxic waste and pollution spills requires the sophisticated tools and scientific know-how associated with environmental forensics (Murphy and Morrison, 2007). In a similar vein, DNA testing is already being used in relation to logging, fishing and endangered species, that is, to track illegal possession and theft of animals and plants.

In practical terms, the socio-legal approach requires a close examination of environmental law enforcement in its own right as well as scrutiny of legal processes surrounding prosecution and sentencing. For example, one of the initial questions to be asked of environmental crime is who is actually going to do the policing (Tomkins, 2005)? Many jurisdictions have specialist agencies – such as environmental protection agencies – which are given the mandate to investigate and prosecute environmental crimes. The police generally play an auxiliary role in relation to the work of these agencies. In other countries, however, members of the police service are especially trained up to be environmental police. In Israel, for example, an environmental unit was established in 2003 within the police service. It is financed by the Ministry of the Environment and includes police officers who form the Green Police. Within a particular national context, there may be considerable diversity in environmental law enforcement agencies and personnel, and police will have quite different roles in environmental law enforcement depending upon the city or state within which they work (see Situ and Emmons, 2000; Tomkins, 2005).

Specific kinds of crime may involve different agencies, depending upon the jurisdiction. For example, the policing of abalone poaching in Australia is generally undertaken by civilian authorities (Tailby and Grant, 2002), as is lobster poaching in Canada (McMullan and Perrier, 2002). The transborder nature of illegal fishing operations – across state as well as international boundaries – means that often a local police service (such as Tasmanian Police) will necessarily have to work collaboratively with national agencies (such as the Australian Federal Police), which in turn, will have relationships with regional partner police services (such as Indonesia in the South East Asian context) and international organisations (such as Interpol). The powers and resources available to specific law enforcement officials will vary greatly from jurisdiction to jurisdiction, and from agency to agency, depending upon whether or not the police are directly involved, and whether or not agents have been granted specific powers of investigation, arrest, use of weapons and so on to enforce environmental laws. Criminal enforcement of environmental law is basically shaped by specific national context, and the legislative and organisational resources dedicated to policing local environmental harms as well as those involving transborder incidents (see Blindell, 2006; Faure and Heine, 2000).

Environmental law enforcement is a relatively new area of police work (Blindell, 2006; Tomkins, 2005) and is at a stage when perhaps more questions are being asked than answers can be provided. Certainly what would be useful is comparative assessment of local and nationally based 'good practice' in this area. So too, an assessment of how police work that 'gets a result' translates into prosecution processes and actual sentences for environmental offenders will provide insight into how the work of the courts impacts upon the morale and activities of those working in the field (McMullen and Perrier, 2002).

The main emphasis in the socio-legal approach is how to best utilise existing legal and enforcement mechanisms to protect environments and creatures within specific environments (e.g., illegal fishing). For those who view environmental harm in a wider lens than that provided by criminal law, this approach has clear limitations. In particular, the focus on criminal law, regardless of whether or not the analyst is critical or confirming, offers a rather narrow view of 'harm' that can obscure the ways in which the state facilitates destructive environmental practices and environmental victimisation. In other words, a strictly legal definition of harm belies the enormous harms that are legal and 'legitimate' but that nevertheless negatively impact on people, environments and animals (Lynch and Stretesky, 2003).

Regulatory approach

A second approach to environmental harm shifts the focus away from criminal sanctions as such and toward regulatory strategies that might be used to improve environmental performance. Here the main concern is with varying forms of 'responsive regulation' (Ayres and Braithwaite, 1992; Braithwaite, 1993) and 'smart regulation' (Gunningham and Grabosky, 1998). These approaches attempt to recast the state's role by using non-government, and especially private sector, participation and resources in fostering regulatory compliance in relation to the goal of 'sustainable development'. Increasingly important to these discussions is the perceived and potential role of third-party interests, in particular non-government environment organisations, in influencing policy and practice (Braithwaite and Drahos, 2000; Gunningham and Grabosky, 1998; O'Brien et al., 2000). The main concern of this kind of approach is with reform of existing methods of environmental protection. The overall agenda of writers in this genre has been summarised as follows: 'Generally speaking, environmental reformers are optimistic about the possibilities of addressing environmental harms without fundamentally changing the status quo. Either implicitly or tacitly, minimization ("risk management") rather than elimination of environmental depredation is conceived as the reformist object' (Chunn et al., 2002: 12).

Analysis of new regulatory regimes, however, offer equivocal results in terms of effectiveness. For example, analysis of Canadian environmental law and policies reveals a patchwork of legislative and regulatory measures that fundamentally fail to protect the environment (Boyd, 2003). At its broadest level, the ways in which regulation works or does not work is fundamentally shaped by systemic imperatives and philosophical vision. For instance, Boyd (2003) contrasts a model of regulation based upon an effort to mitigate the environmental impacts of an energy and resource intensive industrial economy, with that based upon ecological principles that are oriented to decreasing the consumption of energy and natural resources. However complex the laws and regulations in the first scenario, they cannot succeed in achieving sustainability because the system as a whole is inherently geared to growth in energy and resource consumption (see also White, 2002). In the latter case, the emphasis is on restructuring the economy to incorporate ecological limits, and thus to reduce environmental harm over time.

At a more mundane level, specific areas of regulation are now being subjected to empirical evaluation. For example, Stretesky (2006) points out that, while concepts such as corporate self-policing have been discussed at a theoretical level, very little grounded research has actually been undertaken. Yet, the shift from state command-and-control regimes to market-based regulation is a core concern of contemporary regulation theorists, especially in the area of environmental regulation (see Grabosky, 1994, 1995; Gunningham and Grabosky, 1998). In the study of self-policing in relation to the US Environmental Protection Agency, Stretesky (2006) found that there are a wide range of specific issues that require further examination, including how corporate culture impacts upon compliance with environmental regulatory efforts through to possible impacts of sanction severity on deterring potential offenders. A key point that is emphasised is that if the policy shift from direct regulation to market-based incentives is so important to policy makers then much more research about the dynamics and consequences of this shift is warranted.

Social action approach

In the third approach, writers tend to be more sceptical of the previous perspectives and developments, arguing that many key elements of such strategies dovetail with neo-liberal ideologies and practices (especially the trend towards deregulation of corporate activity) in ways that will not address systemic environmental degradation (Snider, 2000). Furthermore, from the point of view of the restructuring of class relationships on a global scale, reforms in environmental management and regulation are seen to be intrinsically linked to the efforts of transnational corporations to further their hegemonic control over the planet's natural resources (Goldman, 1998a,b; Pearce and Tombs, 1998; White, 2002). In this type of analysis, political struggle and the contest over class power are viewed as central to any discussion of environmental issues. Issues of gender, ethnicity and race are important to these discussions as well; sometimes being incorporated into a specifically eco-socialist understanding of capitalism and nature (Chunn *et al.*, 2002; O'Connor, 1994; Pepper, 1993), and sometimes being posed in terms of a postmodernist understanding of contemporary society (Lane, 1998).

Rather than focusing on the notions of effectiveness, efficiency and the idea of win-win regulatory strategies, this approach is concerned with social transformation (Chunn *et al.*, 2002). As such, the analysis proceeds from the view that critical analysis must be counter-hegemonic to dominant hierarchical power relationships, and that present institutional arrangements require sustained critique and systemic change. A social action approach therefore implies the necessity of breaking with the logic of the present system and indeed of breaking the law. Lane (1998) points out that if the law were to shift from being anthropocentric (human-centred) toward ecocentric (nature-centred), then nature would be seen to have value in its own right and rights: 'Not only would this criminalize previously acceptable behaviour, but also liberate behaviour that is currently seen as criminal' (Lane, 1998: 245). Thus, for example, the clearfelling of old growth forests (presently legal) would be criminalised because of its ecological damage, and the logging protestor would be free from prosecution in that they are protecting what ought to be protected by law. The transformation required for this to happen, however, demands forms of social action that will most probably cut across the legal/illegal divide. Given the powerful interests that support much environmentally harmful activity, social change will inevitably involve conflict.

By its very nature, the development of environmental criminology as a field of sustained research and scholarship will incorporate many different perspectives and strategic emphases. For some, the point of academic concern and practical application will be to reform aspects of the present system. Critical analysis, in this context, will consist of thinking of ways to improve existing methods of environmental regulation and perhaps to seek better ways to define and legally entrench the notion of environmental crime. For others, the issues raised above are inextricably linked to the project of social transformation. From this perspective, analysis ought to focus on the strategic location and activities of transnational capital, as supported by hegemonic nation-states on a world scale, and it ought to deal with systemic hierarchical inequalities. Such analysis opens the door to identifying the strategic sites for resistance, contestation and struggle on the part of those fighting for environmental justice, ecological justice and animal rights. In the end, it is clear that there are major political divisions within the broad spectrum of green criminological work (and indeed within green political movements), and these have major implications for whether action will be take in collaboration with capitalist institutions and state authorities, or whether it will be directed towards radically challenging these institutions and authorities.

A crucial aspect of environmental criminology is that is values highly the importance of deliberation and democratic participation. It is for this reason that writers also pay attention to practices that stifle dissent and prevent needed dialogue. Whether it be the employment of Strategic Lawsuits Against Public Participation [SLAPPS] (Beder, 1997), or litigation involving environmentalists against unionists (McCulloch, 2005), or incessant 'greenwashing' (Athanasiou, 1996; Hager and Burton, 1999), there are concerted attempts to shut down debate and to limit political agitation around environmental issues. For green criminology, the concern here is twofold: first, to investigate how the forces of the state (and capital) are mobilised against those who wish to preserve, protect and nurture; and second, to seriously contemplate how citizen participation can best contribute to enhanced problem-solving on environmental questions (Rippe and Schaber, 1999; Steele, 2001). Participatory and deliberative democracy are mechanisms for potential positive change. But they, too, require critical scrutiny as well as active promotion (Martin, 2004).

CONCLUSION

Defining environmental harm, establishing the contours of green criminology, making claims about which 'victims' to prioritise, and engaging in specific action to prevent harm and abuse, are each contentious areas and each is likely to be subject to ongoing debate within environmental criminology. Nevertheless, as this chapter has tried to demonstrate, the core elements of a green criminology do provide a nodal point around which a new field of theoretical endeavour can coalesce. Differences in particular emphasis do not undermine the shared vision of a planet in which humans, environments and animals are no longer exploited as they so frequently are at the present moment in history.

From the point of view of criminology as a field, environmental criminology constitutes a departure from both mainstream concerns, that tend to revolve around street crime and working class criminality, and from critical criminology that focuses on conventional crimes of the powerful through analysis of white-collar and corporate crime. Central to green criminology are concerns that dovetail with the progressive politics of socialist and feminist criminology (e.g., essentially anti-capitalist, in favour of ecological sustainability, emphasis on participatory democracy, dealing with issues of social justice and social inequality), while lending its particular emphasis on environmental degradation and animal abuse.

In its varying theoretical frameworks, green criminology is grappling with new concepts (e.g., intergenerational equity, precautionary principle), new issues (e.g., rights as applied to the environment, and to nonhuman animals), new trends (e.g., climate change and the social impacts associated with this – witness New Orleans) and profoundly disturbing events (e.g., toxic spillage in the Ivory Coast). Green criminology is a theoretical perspective that is inherently challenging – to criminology as a fairly conservative analytical and practical field of human endeavour, and to the powers that be, which would much prefer silence to dissent, obfuscation to transparency, and passivity to action. The promise of green criminology is a better understanding of environmental harm and the impetus to see, judge and act on matters that are radically altering the fundamental nature of our world.

REFERENCES

Anderson, K. and McCusker, R. (2005) *Crime in the Australian Fishing Industry: Key Issues.* Trends and Issues in Crime and Criminal Justice No. 297. Canberra: Australian Institute of Criminology.

Athanasiou, T. (1996) *Divided Planet: The Ecology of Rich and Poor.* Boston: Little, Brown and Company.

Ayres, I. and Braithwaite, J. (1992) *Responsive Regulation: Transcending the Deregulation Debate.* New York: Oxford University Press.

Bartel, R. (2005) When the heavenly gaze criminalises: Satellite surveillance, land clearance regulation and the human–nature relationship, *Current Issues in Criminal Justice*, 16(3): 322–339.

Beck, U. (1996) World risk society as cosmopolitan society? Ecological questions in a framework of manufactured uncertainties, *Theory, Culture, Society*, 13(4): 1–32.

Beder, S. (1997) *Global Spin: The Corporate Assault on Environmentalism.* Melbourne: Scribe Publications.

Beirne, P. (2004) From animal abuse to interhuman violence? A critical review of the progression thesis, *Society and Animals*, 12(1): 39–65.

Beirne, P. (2007) Animal rights, animal abuse and green criminology, in P. Beirne and N. South (eds), *Issues in Green Criminology: Confronting Harms Against Environments, Humanity and Other Animals.* Devon: Willan.

Beirne, P. and South, N. (eds) (2007) *Issues in Green Criminology: Confronting Harms Against Environments, Humanity and Other Animals.* Devon: Willan.

Benton, T. (1998) Rights and Justice on a Shared Planet: more rights or new relations?, *Theoretical Criminology*, 2(2): 149–175.

Blindell, J. (2006) 21st Century policing – The role of police in the detection, investigation and prosecution of environmental crime', *ACPR Issues* No.2. Adelaide: Australasian Centre for Policing Research.

Block, A. (2002) 'Environmental crime and pollution: Wasteful reflections, *Social Justice*, 29(1–2): 61–81.

Boyd, D. (2003) *Unnatural Law: Rethinking Canadian Environmental Law and Policy*. Vancouver: UBC Press.

Braithwaite, J. (1993) Responsive business regulatory institutions, in C. Coady and C. Sampford (eds), *Business Ethics and the Law*. Sydney: Federation Press.

Braithwaite, J. and Drahos, P. (2000) *Global business regulation*. Cambridge: Cambridge University Press.

Brook, D. (2000) Environmental genocide: Native Americans and toxic waste, *American Journal of Economics and Sociology*, 57(1): 105–113.

Bullard, R. (1994) *Unequal Protection: Environmental Justice and Communities of Color*. San Francisco: Sierra Club Books.

Carrabine, E., Iganski, P., Lee, M., Plummer, K. and South, N. (2004) *Criminology: A Sociological Introduction*. London: Routledge.

Chunn, D., Boyd, S. and Menzies, R. (2002) 'We all live in Bhopal': Criminology Discovers Environmental Crime', in S. Boyd, D. Chunn and R. Menzies (eds), *Toxic Criminology: Environment, Law and the State in Canada*. Halifax: Fernwood Publishing.

Clifford, M. (ed.) (1998) *Environmental Crime*. Baltimore, MD: Aspen.

Crook, S. and Pakulski, J. (1995) Shades of green: Public opinion on environmental issues in Australia, *Australian Journal of Political Science*, 30: 39–55.

Cullinan, C. (2003) *Wild Law: A Manifesto for Earth Justice*. London: Green Books in association with The Gaia Foundation.

Curson, P. and Clark, L. (2004) Pathological environments, in R. White (ed.), *Controversies in Environmental Sociology*. Melbourne: Cambridge University Press.

del Frate, A. and Norberry, J. (eds) (1993) *Environmental Crime: Sanctioning Strategies and Sustainable Development*. Rome: UNICRI /Sydney: Australian Institute of Criminology.

Deville, A. and Harding, R. (1997) *Applying the Precautionary Principle*. Sydney: The Federation Press.

Edwards, S., Edwards, T. and Fields, C. (eds), (1996) *Environmental Crime and Criminality*. New York: Garland.

Faure, M. and Heine, G. (2000) *Criminal Enforcement of Environmental Law in the European Union*. Copenhagen: Danish Environmental Protection Agency.

Field, R. (1998) Risk and justice: capitalist production and the environment, in D. Faber (ed.), The *Struggle for Ecological Democracy: Environmental Justice Movements in the US*. New York: Guilford Press.

Friedrichs, D. and Friedrichs, J. (2002) The World Bank and crimes of globalization: A case study, *Social Justice*, 29(1–2): 13–36.

Goldman, M. (1998a) Introduction: The political resurgence of the commons, in M. Goldman (ed.), *Privatizing Nature: Political Struggles for the Global Commons*. London: Pluto Press in association with Transnational Institute.

Goldman, M. (1998b) Inventing the commons: Theories and practices of the commons' professional, in M. Goldman (ed.), *Privatizing Nature: Political Struggles for the Global Commons*. London: Pluto Press in association with Transnational Institute.

Grabosky, P. (1994) Green markets: Environmental regulation by the private sector, *Law and Policy*, 16(4): 419–448.

Grabosky, P. (1995) Regulation by reward: On the use of incentives as regulatory instruments, *Law and Policy*, 17(3): 256–279.

Gunningham, N. and Grabosky, P. (1998) *Smart Regulation: Designing Environmental Policy*. Oxford: Clarendon Press.

Gunningham, N., Norberry, J. and McKillop, S. (eds) (1995) *Environmental Crime, Conference Proceedings*. Canberra: Australian Institute of Criminology.

Hager, N. and Burton, B. (1999) *Secrets and Lies: The Anatomy of an Anti-Environmental PR Campaign*. New Zealand: Craig Potton Publishing.

Halsey, M. (2004) Against 'Green' Criminology, *British Journal of Criminology*, 44(4): 833–853.

Halsey, M. and White, R. (1998) Crime, ecophilosophy and environmental harm, *Theoretical Criminology*, 2(3): 345–371.

Harvey, D. (1996) *Justice, Nature and the Geography of Difference*. Oxford: Blackwell.

Harvey, N. (1998) *Environmental Impact Assessment: Procedures, Practice, and Prospects in Australia*. Melbourne: Oxford University Press.

Heine, G., Prabhu, M. and del Frate, A. (eds) (1997) *Environmental Protection: Potentials and Limits of Criminal Justice*. Rome: UNICJRI.

Julian, R. (2004) Inequality, social differences and environmental resources, in R. White (ed.), *Controversies in Environmental Sociology*. Melbourne: Cambridge University Press.

Lane, P. (1998) Ecofeminism meets criminology, *Theoretical Criminology*, 2(2): 235–248.

Langton, M. (1998) *Burning questions: Emerging Environmental Issues for Indigenous Peoples in Northern Australia*. Darwin: Centre for Indigenous Natural and Cultural Resource Management.

Low, N. and Gleeson, B. (1998) *Justice, Society and Nature: An Exploration of Political Ecology*. London: Routledge.

Lugten, G. (2005) Big Fish To Fry – International Law and Deterrence of the Toothfish Pirates, *Current Issues in Criminal Justice*, 16(3): 307–321.

Lynch, M. and Stretesky, P. (2003) The meaning of green: Contrasting criminological perspectives, *Theoretical Criminology*, 7(2): 217–238.

Lynch, M. and Stretesky, P. (2006) Toxic crimes: Examining corporate victimization of the general public employing medical and epidemiological evidence, in N. South and P. Beirne (eds), *Green Criminology*. The International Library of Criminology, Criminal Justice and Penology, Second Series. Aldershot: Ashgate.

Lynch, M., Stretesky, P. and McGurrin, D. (2002) Toxic crimes and environmental justice: Examining the hidden dangers of hazardous waste, in G. Potter (ed.), *Controversies in White-Collar Crime*. Cincinnati: Anderson Publishing.

Martin, E. (2004) Sustainable development, postmodern capitalism, and environmental policy and management in Costa Rica, *Contemporary Justice Review*, 7(2): 153–169.

McCulloch, J. (2005) Loggerheads over old growth forests: Growing civil society against state crime and the timber wedge, *Current Issues in Criminal Justice*, 16(3): 351–367.

McMullan, J. and Perrier, D. (2002) Lobster poaching and the ironies of law enforcement, *Law and Society Review*, 36(4): 679–720.

Munro, L. (2004) Animals, 'nature' and human interests, in R. White (ed.), *Controversies in Environmental Sociology*. Melbourne: Cambridge University Press.

Murphy, B. and Morrison, R. (2007) *Introduction to Environmental Forensics*. Amsterdam: Elsevier.

O'Brien, R., Goetz, A., Scholte, J. and Williams, M. (2000) *Contesting Global Governance: Multilateral Economic Institutions and Global Social Movements*. Cambridge: Cambridge University Press.

O'Connor, J. (1994) Is sustainable capitalism possible?, in M. O'Connor (ed.), *Is Capitalism Sustainable?: Political Economy and the Politics of Ecology*. New York: The Guilford Press.

Pearce, F. and Tombs, S. (1998) *Toxic Capitalism: Corporate Crime and the Chemical Industry*. Aldershot: Dartmouth Publishing Company.

Pepper, D. (1993) *Eco-Socialism: From Deep Ecology to Social Justice*. New York: Routledge.

Plumwood, V. (2005) Gender, eco-feminism and the environment, in R. White (ed.), *Controversies in Environmental Sociology*. Melbourne: Cambridge University Press.

Rippe, K. and Schaber, P. (1999) Democracy and environmental decision-making, *Environmental Values*, 8(1): 75–88.

Rosoff, S., Pontell, H. and Tillman, R. (1998) *Profit Without Honor: White-Collar Crime and the Looting of America*. Upper Saddle River, USA: Prentice Hall.

Rush, S. (2002) Aboriginal resistance to the abuse of their national resources: The struggles for trees and water, in S. Boyd, D. Chunn and R. Menzies (eds), *Toxic Criminology: Environment, Law and the State in Canada*. Halifax: Fernwood Publishing.

Simon, D. (2000) Corporate environmental crimes and social inequality: New directions for environmental justice research, *American Behavioral Scientist*, 43(4): 633–645.

Situ, Y. and Emmons, D. (2000) *Environmental Crime: The Criminal Justice System's Role in Protecting the Environment*. Thousand Oaks: Sage.

Smith, M. (1998) *Ecologism: Towards Ecological Citizenship*. Minneapolis: University of Minnesota Press.

Snider, L. (2000) The sociology of corporate crime: An obituary (or: Whose knowledge claims have legs?). *Theoretical Criminology*, 4(2): 169–206.

South, N. (1998) A green field for criminology? A proposal for a perspective, *Theoretical Criminology*, 2(2): 211–233.

South, N. (2007) The 'corporate colonisation of nature': bio-prospecting, bio-piracy and the development of green criminology, in P. Beirne and N. South (eds), *Issues in Green Criminology: Confronting Harms Against Environments, Humanity and Other Animals*. Devon: Willan.

South, N. and Beirne, P. (2006) *Green Criminology*. The International Library of Criminology, Criminal Justice and Penology, Second Series. Aldershot: Ashgate.

Steele, J. (2001) Participation and deliberation in environmental law: Exploring a Problem-solving approach, *Oxford Journal of Legal Studies*, 21(3): 415–442.

Stretesky, P. (2006) Corporate self-policing and the environment, *Criminology*, 44(3): 671–708.

Stretesky, P. and Lynch, M. (1999) Corporate environmental violence and racism, *Crime, Law and Social Change*, 30: 163–184.

Tailby, R. and Gant, F. (2002) *The Illegal Market in Australian Abalone*, Trends and Issues in Crime and Criminal Justice No.225. Canberra: Australian Institute of Criminology.

Tomkins, K. (2005) Police, law enforcement and the environment, *Current Issues in Criminal Justice*, 16(3): 294–306.

Walters, R. (2004) Criminology and genetically modified food, *British Journal of Criminology*, 44(1): 151–167.

Walters, R. (2006) Crime, bio-agriculture and the exploitation of hunger, *British Journal of Criminology*, 46(1): 26–45.

Whelan, J. (2005) Neo-liberal water policy and socio-environmental harm, *Current Issues in Criminal Justice*, 16(3): 286–293.

White, R. (1994) Green politics and the question of population, *Journal of Australian Studies*, 40: 27–43.

White, R. (2002) Environmental harm and the political economy of consumption, *Social Justice*, 29(1–2): 82–102.

White, R. (2003) Environmental issues and the criminological imagination, *Theoretical Criminology*, 7(4): 483–506.

White, R. (2005) Environmental harm in global context: exploring the theoretical and empirical complexities, *Current Issues in Criminal Justice*, 16(3): 271–285.

White, R. (2007) Green criminology and the pursuit of social and ecological justice, in P. Beirne and N. South (eds), *Issues in Green Criminology: Confronting Harms Against Environments, Humanity and Other Animals*. Devon: Willan.

White, R. and Habibis, D. (2005) *Crime and Society*. Melbourne: Oxford University Press.

Williams, C. (1996) An environmental victimology, *Social Justice*, 23(4): 16–40.

Zilney, L., McGurrin, D. and Zahran, S. (2006) Environmental justice and the role of criminology: An analytical review of 33 years of environmental justice research, *Criminal Justice Review*, 31(1): 47–62.

22

Global Criminology

Katja Franko Aas

The topic of this chapter is global criminology, yet it begins with an image of what we tend to think of as the opposite of globalization, namely, localization.

> There are bars outside the windows but also inside the cells making it difficult for the detainees to open the windows themselves. Unlike in Britain, where the wardens are mostly employees of private security firms, in Köpernick they are police officers. Detainees have limited room to move and must ask the police for permission to open a window, smoke a cigarette, or fetch hot water for tea – and permission can be (and sometimes is) refused.
>
> There are no work or training possibilities in Köpernick and detainees are only allowed one hour's exercise in the yard. Visitors can be received but are separated from the detainees by Perspex, and from other visitors / detainees by a small partition ....
>
> (Welch and Schuster, 2005: 341–342)

The detention centre in Köpernick, Germany, is not a prison and is usually not thought of as one, yet the resemblance to prisons is unmistakable. The sovereign state's power to take away the freedom of its subjects is in this case wielded over populations who, paradoxically, are in search of its protection – asylum seekers and migrants. A recent map produced by the Migereurop network[1] shows the European territory covered with dots representing detention facilities for asylum seekers and irregular migrants and extending further to the neighbouring territories of North Africa and Eastern Europe.

The above example is a useful starting point for our discussions since it shows that globalization, far from being a progress of global mobility and de-territorialization, also represents immobility, re-territorialization and localization. The example indicates the complex and contradictory nature of global transformations, where global mobility and immobility are two complementary processes, and where the language of freedom and opportunity goes hand in hand with pervasive structural inequality. Globalization is 'paradoxical in the way it unifies and delineates, internationalizes and localizes' (Findlay, 1999: 3). Immobility can be seen as an 'underside' of globalization, and various immobilization strategies are becoming vital elements of social exclusion in the deeply stratified global order. The mark of the excluded in the era of time/space compression is, as Bauman points out (1998: 113), immobility. This is true not only for the detainees in Köpernick but also for the inmates of prisons and other correctional institutions, for the subjects of electronic and satellite monitoring (Nellis, 2009), and those immobilized by the current war on terror (Cole, 2003).

Criminology should be therefore well suited to examine globalization's darker sides and paradoxes. However, one of the difficulties we face in approaching the subject of 'global criminology' is that it could until recently hardly claim its existence (see for example Aas, 2007; Barak, 2007; Findlay, 2003, 2008; Sheptycki and Wardak, 2005). If the term *global criminology* is to denote a perception of the world as a shared analytical, social and ethical space, then this has been a somewhat neglected domain of criminological theory. Criminological knowledge has traditionally had a far greater affinity with the nation state (Christie, 1997; Foucault, 1980; Walters, 2003), thus neglecting a range of issues, such as colonialism, state crime, corporate crime and genocide, which fall outside the nation state's scope of interests (Agozino, 2003; Green and Ward, 2004; Morrison, 2006). Notwithstanding, there exists by now a wealth of criminological investigations of globalization and its impact on issues of crime and crime control – what might be termed 'criminology of globalization'. From transnational organized crime, transnational policing, human trafficking and penal policy transfers, to name just a few, global flows and mobilities are making a great impact on the criminological agenda. In what follows, I shall examine this burgeoning field of criminology of globalization, including its impact on our understanding of the role of the nation state. I will then suggest that, by acknowledging globalization's transformative potential, criminological theory is taking a first step towards developing a global criminology. By engaging systematically with questions of global interconnectedness criminology is forced to widen its analytical, epistemological, and methodological scope and thus open up to issues of global inequality, global processes of social control and exclusion, and the vast categories of 'global others', whose security impact is increasingly felt not only on the battlefields of the developing world, but also in the midst of the prosperous West.

GLOBALIZATION AND ITS DISCONTENTS

Globalization is a widely discussed topic and there are numerous definitions of the subject in the expanding globalization literature. Many have noted a discomfort with using the term, since the debates about globalization in the past decades have been highly polarized and divisive. Besides serving as a theoretical category of social science, globalization is used in various contexts as a 'political category of blame', 'cultural category of fear', and 'an economic category of opportunity and enterprise' (Ericson and Stehr, 2000: 30). Some therefore prefer not to use the term globalization at all, and talk of transnationalization in order to avoid over-generalisation and to 'suggest that transnational practices impact on human relationships in diverse ways in different places' (Sheptycki, 2005: 79). Unlike in other social sciences, globalization is a term which has been used somewhat cautiously by criminologists.[2] A common use of the term is to denote transnational penal policy transfers, for example, in the field of youth justice (Muncie, 2004) and the spread of zero tolerance policing (Jones and Newburn, 2007). However, several authors have warned that we cannot take for granted that these surface similarities in penal policy in fact imply deeper convergencies and may, eventually, lead to global penal convergence (Jones and Newburn, 2004, 2007; Loader and Sparks, 2002: 11; Melossi, 2004). The substance of zero tolerance policing is quite different in Oslo than it is in New York or in Mexico City, although the rhetoric may be similar. Similarly, risk-based forms of justice employ essentially different techniques in different Western jurisdictions (O'Malley, 2004). The exclusionary tone of the US actuarial justice should be distinguished from the more inclusive and welfare oriented tones of Australian and Scandinavian risk thinking. This distinctiveness of risk is easily overlooked in the predominantly general and abstract writing about risk society and actuarial justice.

As an acknowledgment of the need for nuance and contextualization, Roland Roberton's term (1995) *glocalization* has enjoyed a considerable academic popularity. The term denotes the reflexivity between the global and the local and between the universal and the particular. Global transformation thus involve not only 'top down' processes of neo-liberal hegemony and homogenization, but in equal measure also complex, 'bottom up', processes of transnational connectivity, cultural change and resistance (see, e.g., dela Porta *et al.*, 2007; Flynn and Brotherton, 2008). What may at first glance appear as globalization of penal policies needs to be contextualized and seen in specific local – or better 'glocal' – contexts. As Melossi (2004: 84) points out, '[p]unishment is deeply embedded in the national/cultural specificity of the environment which produces it', and penal policies change their character as they move to a new cultural setting. Although politicians, criminal justice policy makers, researchers and bureaucrats may borrow from the same international vocabulary of terms, discourses and expressions, this does not mean that these are in practice translated into similar actions. We need therefore to be aware of the cultural embeddedness of crime and punishment, and should not 'read the emerging – global – landscape too flatly' (Loader and Sparks, 2002: 100). Humans are active agents in adapting and, not least, resisting to global change.

However, I would like to suggest that the perception of globalization as a process of homogenization of penality is insufficient not only because it overstates the importance of similarity at the expanse of local variety, as suggested by the above discussion. More importantly, it offers a too narrow understanding of global transformations altogether. These are not only, perhaps not even primarily, a top-down process of homogenization, often more appropriately termed Americanization or Westernization. Rather, globalization's impact on contemporary penality is at once more complex, less predictable, and ultimately, more profound. Far from being a singular development leading to a homogenous world system, globalization is better understood as a multiple set of cross-border connections that sometimes reinforce one another, but are often also conflicting. It is not an either – or development, but has many modalities and can unravel in an uneven pace. For example, 'globalization's effect on criminology and policy is not necessarily related to its effect on crime' (Chan, 2005: 340). There is therefore a vital need to acknowledge the diversity of the global.

The perception of globalization as homogenization fails to distinguish between homogenization and interdependence (Chan, 2005). Through global interdependence worldwide social relations link distant localities in such a way that local happenings are shaped by events occurring many miles away and vice versa (Giddens, 1990). Globalization thus denotes 'the expanding scale, growing magnitude, speeding-up and deepening impact of interregional flows and patterns of social interaction' (Held and McGrew, 2003: 4). Security concerns today are increasingly played out under the sign of globalization. Due to the cross-border interconnectedness national and local policing and social control efforts often mark a search for local solutions to globally produced problems. Concerns about local disorder are progressively intertwined with global transformations, such as transnational migration, global business interests, de-industrialization, consumerism, etc. (Aas, 2007). Furthermore, discourses about crime and punishment, racial and religious hatred, as well as fear and solidarity, increasingly transcend national boundaries and gain transnational dimensions. Through the expanding global media and communication networks, a disappearance of a child in Portugal, or a murder in the Netherlands, can have an impact far beyond their immediate local and national surroundings, indicating the emergence of 'transnational public spheres' – discursive arenas that overflow the boundaries of nations and states (Fraser, 2005). In highly publicized murder cases, such as the James Bulger case, these communications may even form, as Valier (2004: 103) suggests, 'transnational vengeful networks'.

Academic discussions often pitch the above transformations as a national versus global contest. The global is seen as an emerging structure which is growing at the expense of the national and the local. However, as an analytical term, globalization is perhaps better suited as adjective qualifier, rather than a noun describing a finished process or even a social structure. Urry (2002: 59) suggests that we should envision the global as an unfinished process, 'which problematizes the fixed, given and static notions of social order'. Furthermore, as pointed out by Sassen (2007), the global and the national are not two distinct, binary opposite, master categories which are competing in a zero sum game. Global transformations undoubtedly change the dynamics between the national, local and the global, yet these transformations have not necessarily given primacy to one at the expense of the other. Globalization clearly brings the expansion of self-evidently global processes and institutions, however, the global can also be constituted inside the national and the local. 'Studying the global, then, entails a focus not only on that which is explicitly global in scale but also on locally scaled practices and conditions that are articulated with global dynamics' (ibid.: 18).

THE NEW INTERDEPENDENCE

Where then lies globalization's transformatory potential for criminological theory? While some authors doubt the novelty and the profound transformative impact of the present global transformations (Hirst and Thompson, 1996), others have pointed out their long historic antecedents. Capitalism has after all always functioned as a world economy. Giddens (1990) stresses the inherently globalising (stretching and disembedding) tendencies of modernity. The globalizing process can be seen as an essential part of the transition towards the late modernity (Appadurai, 1996; Findlay, 1999). A question for debate is though whether globalization can in fact be accounted for through the use of old terms such as modernity. Frequently, even those who recognize globalization as a profound contemporary transformation tend to assimilate it to modernity, thus 'reviving modernity's flagging hold on reality' and having inevitable and predictable consequences (Albrow, 1996: 86).

On the other hand, a considerable part of globalization theorizing has been marked precisely by its stress on novelty and difference. Fascinated by the intensity of the stretching of social relations – the famous time–space compression (Harvey, 1990) – and the variety of transnational flows, they argue that these developments cannot be accounted for through the use of old paradigms. The new terminology aims to dismantle the old stabilities and knowledges, and builds on the notions of networks, flows, scapes, displacement, disjuncture and dislocation (see, e.g., Appadurai, 1996; Castells, 1996; Urry, 2000). These perspectives challenged the view of societies as self-contained systems, stressing the porosity of borders and the hybridity of cultures and belongings. Now, it can no longer be taken for granted that each country embodies its own distinctive culture and that the terms 'society' and 'culture' can be simply appended to the names of nation states (Gupta and Ferguson, 2002: 66).

Globalization fundamentally destabilizes one of the cornerstones of modernity: the nation state – society nexus. The notion of strong nation-states and stable social entities is increasingly undermined by the flows of capital, people, information and cultural impulses. The various global flows, mobilities and 'scapes' challenge the idea that we are dealing with homogenous, territorially delineated units of research, if indeed, we ever have been. They challenge 'the assumptions about the nation-state as container of social processes' (Sassen, 2007: 4). Consequently, several scholars have urged for a transcendence of the analytical and conceptual framework which is principally based on nation states. This is well expressed in the critique of the so-called methodological nationalism within the social sciences. Methodological nationalism can be 'understood as the assumption that the nation/state/society is the natural social and political form of the modern world' (Wimmer and Schiller, 2002: 301). It equates social boundaries with state boundaries, and has a nation-state outlook on society, law, justice and history (Aas, 2007; Beck, 2003). This methodological framework structures the choice of research phenomena and statistical indicators. Today there are, for example, no official statistics on human rights abuses and political violence (Human Security Report, 2005: 19). The transcendence of the national methodological framework does not mean that global aspects are per definitional vital in explaining local and national phenomena. It does mean, however, that they should be looked for as a possibility.

Due to the growing global interconnectedness the nation state and national societies no longer represents an adequate frame of reference for analysing social phenomena, including crime control and security policies. This view has transpired into much of contemporary writing about transnational crime and policing (Andreas and Nadelmann, 2008; Edwards and Gill, 2003; Goldsmith and Sheptycki, 2007; Nordstrom, 2007; Sheptycki, 2002; Sigel *et al.*, 2003). In cases such as cybercrime (Jewkes, 2003; Wall, 2001; Yar, 2006) and environmental degradation (Beirne and South, 2007; Lynch and Stretsky, 2003; White, 2008), the challenges have become transnational rather than being simply inter-national, and demand a simultaneous view of global, national and local levels. Local harms are a product of a long chain of geographically often dispersed and un-bounded events and actions. For example, a case of internet child pornography can involve suspects from 77 countries downloading images shot in Eastern Europe, uploaded to the web in Britain and posted on a Russian website hosted by an Austrian company.[3] Moreover, the aftermath of 9/11 marks progressive 'globalization of (in)security,' supported by a field of 'professionals of unease management' and of transnationalization of (in)securization processes (Bigo, 2005).

The spatially distributed nature of contemporary threats is partly captured by Ulrich Beck's concept of the 'world risk society' (2002: 41):

> [W]orld risk society does not arise from the fact that everyday life has generally become more dangerous. It is not a matter of the *increase*, but rather of *de-bounding* of uncontrollable risks. The de-bounding is three-dimensional: spatial, temporal and social.

De-bounded risks are no longer linked to specific geographic locations and national boundaries; moreover, they can have unlimited temporal dimensions (think of the future dangers of nuclear waste and global warming), and it is difficult to delineate their social dimensions in terms of causes, affectedness and responsibility. The concept of the world risk society fundamentally challenges the long held distinction between 'inside' and 'outside', 'domestic' and 'foreign' relations (Beck, 2002). This shift of focus is particularly relevant when it comes to analysing the emerging new dynamics of crime, policing and security, where governance to an increasing extent takes place in de-bounded spaces. The globalizing world is marked by interconnectedness and interdependence which is ultimately also security interdependence.

The events of 9/11 represent according to several commentators a hallmark of a post-Cold War development where previous distinctions between 'internal' and 'external' security become obsolete (Beck, 2002; Bigo, 2000; Flyghed, 2005). Defying the state-like nature of enemies in the previous world orders, the threat of terrorism is today presented as always potentially hidden inside the state, like a 'fifth colon', as well as trying to enter from the outside. Parallel with the hybridity of internal and external notions of security, the boundaries between crime and warfare also become harder to discern. 'Conventional resolutions of global conflict such as war state-against-state have been replaced ... by crime as warfare, and warfare as crime control' (Findlay, 2003: 234). Ethnic, religious and other conflicts are increasingly intermingled with drug trafficking, people smuggling and other forms of organized crime (Hogg, 2002: 196). If before it was still possible to distinguish between crime and war, and military and police domains (although the lines never have been clear cut), today, this distinction is becoming difficult. We have been witnessing a trend 'toward 'criminal justice militarization', in which social relations are redefined through a convergence of militaristic, police, and penal contexts' (Brown, 2005: 985). The military has, as Bigo (2000: 83) argues, acquired a new set of jobs such as anti-guerrilla tactics, prevention of terrorism, drugs prohibition enforcement, and international peace-enforcement. Similarly, the establishment of the US Department of Homeland Security can be seen as a response to the conflation of internal and external forms of security, which seeks to enhance communication and information sharing between different security agencies, including the FBI and the CIA (Ericson, 2007: 54). 'The view is that borderless threats require borderless law enforcement across organizational entities nationally and internationally, and across categories of citizens and non-citizens' (ibid.).

Terrorism has been described as the dark side of globalization (Powell in Urry, 2002). As Calhoun *et al.* (2002: 18) point out, globalization 'helped to create the conditions for the September 11 attacks; it shaped how people saw them, and, in turn, it will itself be influenced for decades to come not just by the attacks but by responses to them'. The attacks, and the responses to them, are essentially marked by various forms of global connectivity and interdependence: from the global media and communication networks, the intensification of international police co-operation, global surveillance technologies, and the problematization of immigrant – native relations, discussed further below. However, others have pointed out that globalization's darker sides are far more complex and pervasive than the popular media focus on Osama bin Laden and his alleged network suggests. Rather than simply representing the 'dark side' of globalization, illicit flows and activities are seen by some as representing its real nature (Naim, 2006). Transnational criminal networks have given nourishment to some of the most talked about forms of contemporary 'folk devilry' (Sheptycki, 2000), and the wealth of capital hidden in the money laundering havens of the Caymen Islands, Bermuda, Jersey and alike reveals the difficulty of delineating between globalization's licit and illicit sides (Abraham and Schendel, 2005).

The hybridization of internal and external security is in many ways at odds with criminology's traditionally national focus (Aas, 2007). In the post-9/11 world, criminology can no longer operate within the boundaries of the nation state it has operated within in modernity. Morrison (2006) thus argues that before 9/11, criminology inhabited a 'civilized space', where violence was an extraordinary event and where war was banished outside the boundaries of the Western world. In that respect, the threat of terrorism can be seen as a form of risk produced by the reflexivity of modernity. 'Violence formerly directed outwards to the 'other' (ibid.: 30) now strikes back at the heart of First world societies, thus, inextricably connecting globalization to colonialism. Also the diverse immigrant communities make the postcolonial legacies felt in the midst of Western metropolises. Consequently, the traditional criminologcal focus on issues of internal security is no longer sustainable. Foreign policy is no longer properly 'foreign' as external conflicts often have an almost immediate impact on national and local security strategies, although this by itself is not a new phenomenon. Security of the global North is inevitably connected to the development and social justice issues in the global South, an aspect which tends to be downplayed and underestimated by the proponents of militarized solutions to these problems. For example, Afghanistan, one of the world's poorest countries, accounts for about 90 per cent of the world's heroin production, regardless of the Western military presence there (UNODOC, 2007). In the case of illegal narcotics, just as in the case of irregular migration and terrorism, it becomes obvious that security problems of the West are essentially questions of development for the developing world, although the security aspects of these activities for citizens of developing countries should by no means be underestimated (Human Security Report, 2005). Transnational policing today is intertwined with the politics of international state-crafting and shaped by the involvement of international organizations, donor states and agancies (Goldsmith and Sheptycki, 2007). The new hybridity of contemporary security therefore demands of criminology a renewed emphasis on inter-disciplinary dialogue and lesson-drawing from the related fields of international relations, global sociology, security and development studies.

BEYOND THE STATE

Globalization has been in much of criminological writing, somewhat nostalgically, blamed for the demise of the golden age of the welfare state and for creating societies which are insecure, anxious about crime, lack confidence in the state, and are more punitive by nature (Cavadino and Dignan, 2006; Garland, 2001; Pratt, 2007; Pratt *et al.*, 2005). By reducing globalization to its economic motor – neo-liberalism – the predominant tone of criminology of globalization has been one of criminology *against* globalization. The decline of modernity, and of the unifying force of the nation-state, has arguably had profound criminogenic effects (Barak, 2007). According to Friedman (2003: xii), the triumph of globalization marks the progressive social fragmentation, 'the emergence of new culturally based identities, social movements, and higher levels of social disorder that are the basis of new forms of violence'. The social wreckage of neo-liberalism deepened social marginalization of populations which have been rendered superfluous by the 'progress' of global modernity (Bauman, 2002, 2004). De-industralization took out the life-line which sustained ghettoized populations in previous epochs and gave them a minimum of decency and social cohesion (Bourgois, 2003; Wacquant, 2001). Neo-liberal societies have been more prone to social exclusion, 'governance through crime' and the use of imprisonment (Cavadino and Dignan, 2006; Simon, 2007; Young, 1999). Furthermore, by exacerbating the colonizing tendencies of modernity, global transformations have been worldwide detrimental to local sustainability and indigenous communities (Currie, 1998).

Globalization is frequently seen as a breeding ground for 'global anomie' by privileging the winning mentality and encouraging new needs and desires at the same time as it has failed to deliver its promises for the vast majority of the world's population (Passas, 2000). Neo-liberalism's victory has been therefore also a victory of a value system which puts a premium on consumption, individualism and a search for quick and easy ways towards success at the same time as the opportunities of reaping profits from illicit activities proliferated. Castells' (2000) classic description of the 'pillage of Russia' outlines a tragic triumph of turbo-capitalism, built on systematic illegality and damaging lack of state regulation. The weakening of state regulatory controls 'opened the way for a wild competition to grab state property by whatever means, often in association with criminal elements' (ibid.: 187).

The popular 'withering away of the state' thesis therefore seems to be supported by numerous criminological accounts. The independence of licit and illicit global flows from state control has resulted in fundamental weakening of the state. The problem of organized crime and its hidden financial empires mirrors more general concerns about un-governability of global corporations and financial institutions which are escaping the control of nation states. 'Commercial crime relationships in particular are set free to benefit from opportunities not dissimilar to those enjoyed by multinational enterprise beyond the jurisdiction of the individual state and the limitations of single markets' (Findlay, 1999: 1). As Sheptycki (2000: 5) observes, the 'enormous and perhaps even the incalculable wealth hidden in offshore banks is testimony to the de-centring of the state in the transnational age'. The problem indicates the fragility of the present world order and 'calls into question many received – criminological – wisdoms about the locus of effective, sovereign crime control'

(Loader and Sparks, 2002: 98). Particularly in the global South, illicit private authorities and transnational actors, or what Caroline Nordström (2000) terms 'shadow sovereigns', increasingly steal sovereignty from nation states and challenge the state-based conceptions of sovereignty (Bially Mattern, 2007). The metaphor of stolen sovereignty may also be extended to describe a trend towards privatization and the introduction of market solutions in the field of punishment and social control. Crime control has become an industry (Christie, 2000), and security is no longer the exclusive prerogative of the state and a public good, but also a commodity (Jones and Newburn, 1998; Loader and Walker, 2001). In addition to the hybridity of internal/external security, globalization's impact on criminology also represents the blurring boundaries between the public and the private (Johnson and Shearing, 2003; Wakefield, 2003; Zedner, 2007). These developments have brought into question the centrality of the nation state as the main provider of security and as the main agent of punishment and social control (Loader and Walker, 2001).

One of the most salient theoretical assaults on the primacy of the state came from the Foucaultian governmentality theorists (Garland, 2001; Rose, 1999). Taking up Foucault's (1980) encouragement to 'cut off the king's head' in political thinking and social sciences, this vibrant body of literature has aimed to think alternatively about the diverse ways in which neo-liberal societies govern the conduct of its citizens (see for example Rose, 1999). By focusing on 'technologies of government', and the new rationalities and models of the persons subjected to government, such approaches reframed the traditionally dominant role accorded to the state in studies of social control (Johnston and Shearing, 2003; Rose, 1999, among other). It was argued that rather than being directly involved in regulating social behaviour, neo-liberal societies are being 'governed at a distance' – indirectly drawing upon a series of regulatory techniques which are able to intervene upon persons, activities and events far removed in space and time (Rose, 1999). Unlike the old Keynesian state, this new regulatory state (Braithwaite, 2000) no longer directly orchestrates the activities of social control nor is it the only actor involved in regulating social life. If traditionally the issues of security and justice were the main prerogative of the state, the neo-liberal styles of governance, on the other hand, encourage individuals, institutions and local communities to take active responsibility for managing their crime problems, in line with other risks and uncertainties (Garland, 2001).

A wealth of criminological research has thus in the past decades outlined how state power and sovereignty had being relinquished in several ways: 'outwards' to the commercial sector and the private security industry; 'downwards' to citizens, private organizations and municipalities; and 'upwards' to the emerging new levels of international co-operation and global governance (Loader and Walker, 2001: 10). This 'de-nationalizing of sovereignty' (Sassen, 2007) has been widely theorized in the field of policing where concepts such as plural policing (Jones and Newburn, 2006) and nodal governance (Johnston and Shearing, 2003) denote the multiplication of policing capabilities. Moreover, policing activities increasingly move beyond the policing of territory and transcend national boundaries, partly in pursuit of the illicit flows they are trying to control, and partly developing their own, independent dynamics (Deflem, 2002; Goldsmith and Sheptycki, 2007; Sheptycki, 2000). Contemporary global anti-terrorism and anti-drug efforts in particular indicate a development of global governance and of 'pooling' of sovereignty, where the

transnational system develops its own bureaucracy existing 'above' that of the apparatuses of nation states (Mathiesen, 2003; Sheptycki, 2000: 216). This emerging
research field draws attention, on the one hand, to the regulatory challenges represented by the new global flows and spaces such as the internet, and on the other
hand, regulatory deficits that often exists between new forms of global governance
and democratic institutions (Loader and Walker, 2006).

The emerging sphere of global governance is based on a novel type of territorial-
ity, where security efforts and political processes are no longer directly territorially
anchored, and where the mode of governance can be best described as polycentric:
marked by plurality of actors, jurisdictions and rationalities. A frequently neglected,
yet vital aspect and generator of contemporary global governance, is transnationalization of law. For a long time, the powers of legal regulation and criminalization had
been primarily vested into the nation state as a prerequisite of its sovereignty. Now,
however, the power to form definitions of criminality is gradually moving to
transnational and international actors, which has among other been the case with
cybercrime, terrorism, human smuggling and trafficking. The transnationalization of
law has furthermore created new jurisdictions, such as the International Criminal
Court (the first global public court), the European Court of Human Rights and the
expanding system of international tribunals, where the state not only loses its powers
of criminalization but can itself become a criminalized party.

However, a question can be asked whether these developments in fact signify a
diminution of state authority and, more crucially, a reduction in the coercive capacities of states? Even though demising powers of the state is a common currency of
globalization debates, several criminological developments also run contrary to this
predicament. For example, in the past five years, prison populations have grown in
about two-thirds of countries worldwide. In numerous jurisdictions, they have doubled or tripled in the past two decades (Christie, 2000; Stern, 2006: 99). The state in
the new global order is not simply accepting its diminished role but is instead, with
a varying degree of success, attempting to reassert its authority, often by 'acting out'
on issues of crime (Garland, 2001) and by inventing new forms of punitiveness (Pratt
et al., 2005). It is becoming increasingly apparent that global transformations have
not only produced the neo-liberal state. A product of the emerging world risk society
is also the 'security state', which far from withering away, is marked by a remarkable
expansion and growth of state surveillance and control capabilities (Ericson, 2007;
Haggerty and Ericson, 2006; Mathiesen, 2003). The rationality of the evolving world
risk society therefore runs in several ways against the classic neo-liberal cannon of
minimal state intervention and expenditure. As Beck (2002: 47) reports:

> When asked whether the $40 billion that the US government requested from Congress for
> the war against terrorism didn't contradict the neoliberal creed to which the Bush adminis-
> tration subscribes, its spokesman replied laconically: 'Security comes first.'

Looking at the UK developments, Crawford (2006) points out that the British state
seems to be expanding its net and repertoire of social controls and sponsors social
engineering, similar to the projects that lay at the heart of the 'old style' welfare
state. Instead of 'hands off' government envisaged by the neo-liberal ideologists,
there is increasing evidence that 'hands on' governance still seems to hold much
purchase on contemporary strategies of social control (ibid.).

In summary, the discussion in this section revealed the many ideal-typical modalities of state sovereignty in the global order – the welfare, the neo-liberal, the regulatory, the 'weak' and the security state. Rather than seeing the nation state as demolished, these findings present it as reconfigured and clearly warrant a move beyond simplistic perceptions of the state as a victim of a 'hostile take-over' by private service providers, international actors, non-state agencies and local communities. It may in fact seem that even though the modern nation state may be losing some of its powers, it is essentially not losing its influence (Castells, 2004: 303). Although state sovereignty has been privatized and denationalized in numerous settings, one should also keep in mind the persistent centrality of the state as the agent of punishment and a regulator of social life. Much of the writing about the neo-liberal state has taken the dramatic US developments as its main point of departure; however, the broader applicability of this line of argument outside the Anglo-American world still demands thorough examination. Furthermore, as Sassen (2007: 34) points out, the challenges confronting states today are far more differentiated than notions of overall decline in significance of the state suggest. States, for example, actively participate in setting up new mechanisms by which globalization is furthered, the institutions of international criminal justice being one such example. The nation state is not necessarily antithetic to globalization, but may in fact play a vital role in it. For analytical purposes it is therefore inadequate to focus on the nation-state and the global system as two distinct entities. A more productive way of conceptualizing the phenomenon of the changing state sovereignty may be to look at the 'variety of negotiations between the global and the national' (ibid.: 22).

CRIME CONTROL AS GATE-KEEPING

The complex and contradictory fate of the national is furthermore evident in the emerging dynamics of contemporary social and cultural belonging, where cultural hybridization and homogenization seem to go hand in hand with the resurgence of the national as the locus of identity-making and belonging. Despite the salience of the space of flows, space and territory continue to matter, which is particularly evident in the debates surrounding international migration. Rather than creating a borderless world, globalization has gone hand in hand with intensification of border controls and progressive securitization of migration (Bigo and Guild, 2005; Bosworth, 2008; Brotherton and Kretsedemas, 2008; Huysmans, 2006; Weber and Bowling, 2008). The trend is also crucially transforming contemporary penal discourse since many aspects of international migration are being 'governed through crime' (Simon, 2007). Discourses about human trafficking, transnational organized crime and terrorism symbolically represents popular concerns about global movements of people, and the perceived dangers of the foreign 'contaminating' the local. Divisions between 'the West and the Rest' have gained a renewed urgency through the perceptions of the 'war on terror' as a clash of civilizations, and through the projections of the daily difficulties of integration as minor battles in this planetary struggle. The figure of what Melossi (2003) terms the 'deviant immigrant' seems to embody the dangers and insecurities resulting from the rapid pace of social change and the intensity of glocal transformations. The deviant immigrant discourse is strongly reminiscent of Garland's (2001) 'criminology of the other' and marks a reversal of the modernist criminological project, moving beyond correction and integration of offenders into society towards expanding social control (Aas, 2007; Hudson, 2003; Welch and Schuster, 2005). As Bourdieu and Wacquant (1999) observe, the opposition between 'natives' and 'immigrants' is gradually obscuring traditional class divisions within societies. The inequalities produced by the neo-liberal economic order are translated into political struggles about 'who has the right to claim all the advantages attached to membership in the national community' (ibid.: 188).

According to several recent theoretical persepctives, the volotile nature of native–immigrant relations is crucially transforming contemporary penality (Calavita, 2005; Melossi, 2003; Young, 1999) by progressively blending punitive and 'gate-keeping' aspects of punishment. The drawing of moral boundaries, a traditional concern of criminal law, is today performed not only through the discourse of punishment, but also through practices of banishment and expulsion (Aas, 2007). Punishment of immigrant crime (and the debates surrounding it) seems to perform a double task: on the one hand, the classical Durkheimian function of strengthening social bonds and social solidarity, and on the other hand, its task is to form a sort of 'purifying filter' protecting the local and the national from threatening foreign elements (ibid.). Panopticon, the paradigmatic model of modern punishment and social control, thus finds a competing concept in the ban-opticon (Bigo, 2005). While panopticon forcefully includes everyone in its machinery of normalization, the purpose of the ban-opticon is banishment and exclusion on the grounds of security. Punishment thus becomes a central vehicle through which Western societies discuss membership and a method for keeping people at the borderlands of citizenship.

The phenomenon has been, in the US context, described as 'crimmigration law' (Stumpf, 2006), denoting the progressive convergence and the blurring objectives between the crime control and the immigration system. While before these were two distinct systems, now, there is evidence of increasing reliance of law enforcement on immigration law, and vice versa. Crime is being controlled through the immigration process, and at the opposite end, there is increasing reliance of immigration on criminal law process. According to Cole (2004), in the aftermath of 9/11, immigration law became a centrepiece of US anti-terrorism measures. Immigration law was turned from 'an administrative mechanism for controlling entry and exit of foreign nationals into an excuse for holding suspicious persons without meeting the constitutional requirements that ordinarily apply to preventive detention' (ref.). The example reveals the ambiguous and problematic nature of immigration detention, where criminal punitiveness increasingly transpires into the immigration process (Bosworth, 2007; Weber, 2002; Welch and Schuster, 2005). Also expulsion and deportation can be used as a form of punishment which is added to, or exchanged with, ordinary criminal penalties (Albrecht, 2000: 147). We are therefore witnessing expanding patterns of criminalization of migration. In the EU context, foreign nationals and ethnic minority members constitute a growing proportion of the swelling prison populations and account for much of the European prison population surge since the 1990s (Albrecht, 2000; Melossi, 2003).[4] Also the development of the so-called 'Area of Freedom, Security and Justice', offers an example of the progressive intertwining of crime and migration control (Huysmans, 2006). The estimated

6 million irregular migrants or 'sans papiers' in Europe (GCIM, 2005) furthermore serve as a potent reminder of the size and the nature of the emerging marginalized populations of 'global others'.

TOWARDS GLOBAL CRIMINOLOGY?

Globalization presents a crucial analytical dilemma for criminology: the question of boundaries. This chapter has argued that global transformations demand of criminology an expansion of its theoretical and epistemological scope; a move beyond the geographical boundaries of the nation state. As Russel Hogg (2002: 209) observes: 'To whom are we obliged and what is the scope of the 'social contract' – the 'imagined community' – to which we belong in an increasingly global world?' What is to be the scope of our knowledge about crime, justice and social exclusion? In the concluding part of this chapter, it will be suggested that a move beyond the boundaries of the nation state presents itself not only as analytical but, increasingly, also as ethical imperative. Global transformations discussed in this chapter are remaking the traditional outsider labels and introducing novel categories of global others into the criminological vocabulary. Global criminology would therefore need to transcend its methodological nationalist focus and address the plight of these populations, who find themselves in a double bind – expelled for various reasons from their countries of origin and unwelcome in their countries of destination – thus ending up in various 'non-spaces', such as refugee camps and detention facilities (Pickering, 2005; Welch and Schuster, 2005).

The inadequacy of the traditional nation-state frame of understanding is for example revealed in the shifting terms of recent political and scholarly debates about security, which mark a shift of focus from state to human security (Human Security Report, 2005; Kaldor, 2007; Wood and Shearing, 2007). This shift is based on the acknowledgement that there are essential differences between the two: 'secure states do not automatically mean secure people' (Human Security Report, 2005). A question can be asked though about which notion of security is criminological theory drawing on – secure people or secure states? And if secure people, which people – citizens or aliens, the West or the 'Rest'? Global criminological perspectives would therefore need to address the implicit notions of 'us' and 'them' which have hitherto been mainly left unchallenged by criminological theory. Questions of citizenship and boundary drawing are therefore of crucial importance and have become a topic of several recent perspectives on social justice (Benhabib, 2004; Fraser, 2005). In the heyday of what has been termed as the Westphalian frame (i.e., the territorial nation-state) there was a sharp distinction between 'domestic' and 'international' space. Today, disputes about justice in many cases transcend the nation-state framework. 'No longer addressed exclusively to national states or debated exclusively by national publics, claimants no longer focus solely on relations among fellow citizens' (Fraser, 2005: 72). Justice today is increasingly 'abnormal' in a sense that it no longer addresses one's fellow citizens in a bounded community and that participants no longer share some common assumptions about justice. The global is gradually becoming the site of collective action for disempowered actors and not only for the international elites. According to Fraser (2005: 81), when the major sources of injustice belong to the space of flows, 'they cannot be made answerable to claims of justice that are framed in terms of the state-territorial principle'. This should apply to a variety of criminological issues such as migration, the global criminal economy, corruption, cybercrime, environmental crime, as well as the 'war on drugs', secret rendition flights and other methods used in the war on terror. In the post-Westphalian world view conflicts are no longer territorialized – now new units emerge, using the trans-national, regional and sub-national stage for making claims about justice.

Within this new framework it is no longer clear what the scope of justice is and who counts as the subject of justice (Fraser, 2005). If, in the post-war social democratic societies, the 'who of justice' was the citizenry of the territorial state; now, on the other hand, boundaries become of crucial importance as they define some as members and others as aliens (Benhabib, 2004). This boundary-drawing and frame-setting excludes some people as non-members which do not even have 'the right to have rights'. The nation-state frame of justice can be therefore a source of injustice in itself due to 'the injustice of mis-framing' (Fraser, 2005). Through the mis-framing some are excluded from making claims (for example, asylum seekers and 'enemy combatants'), while some actors are shielded from critique and from the reach of justice because they operate outside the national space (exemplified by tax havens and state crime).

A lesson for critical criminology may be that the continuing support for the Westphalian territorial imagination can become (and has been) in itself a major source of injustice. The tight political and scholarly grip of the territorial state has been, according to Morrison (2006), tantamount to 'criminological apartheid' by producing silence about atrocities happening outside the boundaries of Western criminology. Increasingly though, the transcendence of the national framework is broadening criminological horizons by incorporating previously neglected topics and phenomena, such as human rights and transitional justice (Parmentier and Weitekamp, 2007), state crime (Green and Ward, 2005) and ecological justice (White, 2008). Furthermore, a vital task for global criminology, if it is to be deserved of its name, would be to disturb the hegemony of Western thought within criminology, and to establish, as Cain (2000) suggests, some kind of 'interactive globalization'. This is inevitably a difficult, if not an impossible task. Criminologists have, as Cohen (1982: 85) remarked, 'either ignored the Third World completely or treated it in a most theoretically primitive fashion, while the general literature on development and colonialism is remarkably silent about crime'. Several observers have pointed out the centrality of colonialism for the emergence of western modernity and the criminological enterprise (Agozino, 2003; Anthony and Cunneen, 2008; Brown, 2002; Morrison, 2006). However, much of contemporary criminology is still theoretically and empirically underdeveloped when it comes to the Third world and colonial struggles, and post-colonial universities are mainly reduced to importing Western courses about policing and prison administration (Agozino, 2004). Post-colonial studies raise a similar critique of criminology as the above-mentioned challenge to methodological nationalism. However, while critics see methodological nationalism primarily as an unproductive epistemological approach, post-colonial studies point out that Ethnocentrism has been essential in the historic domination of the West over its colonies. Furthermore, a closer examination of its colonial undertones might shed light not only on criminology's colonial past, but also more importantly give a certain insight into the contemporary penal strategies of othering. The present day criminologies of the other are marked not only by the fear of crime but also bear traces of old colonial anxieties (Aas, 2007; Brown, 2002).

A vital question for critical criminology is therefore whether, in the face of global transformations, to defend the embattled territorial nation-state, or whether to transcend the nation-state order and, consequently, include in its repertoire of outsider also the 'global others'. The issue reveals the complex and contradictory nature of global transformatons for critical criminology and critical globalization theory. The defence of the embattled nation state is often proposed in order to reverse the effects of neo-liberalism and spread of power to potentially ungovernable and politically unaccountable transnational forces and actors. Nevertheless, a question can be asked whether we are to join the sceptical voices of globalization critics and try to reverse the time, or are we to seize the opportunities for new forms of political and social action provided by the emerging global forums? There exist salient arguments for the persistent importance of the state, which 'may play a positive role in producing the forms of trust and solidarity between strangers that are essential ingredients in secure democratic societies' (Loader and Walker, 2007: 25). At the same time there is a growing need for a vocabulary of social justice which address the 'security gap' between the global 'haves' and 'have nots' (Kaldor, 2007), and which would reconfigure security as a 'global public good' (Loader and Walker, 2007). Globalism is increasingly seen as offering possibilities for empowerment and development of 'globalization from below' (dela Porta *et al.*, 2007). The planetary awareness of the common fate of humanity is informing not only environmental debates, but also new forms of penal cosmopolitanism, based on the discourse of human rights and building notions of justice which are not based on citizenship. Ironically, also resistance to globalization is essentially dependant on various global interconnections and networks (dela Porta *et al.*, 2007). Global transformations therefore offer a complex picture and defy clear categorizations and old stabilities of knowledge and political action.

NOTES

1 http://www.migreurop.org/IMG/pdf/carte-en.pdf

2 For exception see, among other, Findlay, 1999; Loader and Sparks, 2002; Muncie, 2004; Baker and Roberts, 2005; Aas, 2007.

3 http://newsvote.bbc.co.uk/mpapps/pagetools/print/news.bbc.co.uk/2/hi/europe/6341737.stm

4 According to the data provided by the International Centre for Prison Studies, foreigners constitute approximately 32 per cent of the total of the German prison population, 21 per cent of the French, 17 per cent of the Norwegian, whereas numbers for a number of other European countries are considerably higher reaching as high as 42 per cent in Belgium and in Greece.

REFERENCES

Aas, K. F. (2007) *Globalization and Crime.* London: Sage Publications.

Abraham, I. and van Schendel, W. (eds) (2005) *Illicit Flows and Criminal Things: States, Borders, and the Other Side of Globalization.* Bloomington and Indianapolis: Indianan University Press.

Agozino, B. (2003) *Counter-Colonial Crimiology: A Critique of Imperialist Reason*. London: Pluto Press.

Appadurai, A. (1996) *Modernity at Large: Cultural Dimensions of Globalization*. Minneapolis: University of Minneapolis Press.

Albrecht, H.-J. (2000) Foreigners, migration, immigration and the development of criminal justice in Europe, in P. Green and A. Rutherford (eds), *Criminal Polocy in Transition*. Oxford, Portland: Hart Publishing.

Albrow, M. (1996) *The Global Age*. Cambridge: Polity Press.

Andreas, P. and Nadelmann, E. (2008) *Policing the Globe: Criminalization and Crime Control in International Relations*. Oxford University Press USA.

Anthony, T. and Cunneen, C. (2008) *The Critical Criminology Companion*. Federation Press.

Baker, E. and Roberts, J. V. (2005) Globalization and the new punitiveness, in Pratt *et al.* (eds), *The New Punitiveness: Trends, Theories, Perspectives*. Cullompton: Willan.

Barak, G. (2007) *Violence, Conflict and World Order: Critical Conversations on Statesanctioned Justice*. Plymouth, UK: Rowman & Littlefield.

Bauman, Z. (1998) *globalization: The Human Consequences*. Cambridge: Polity Press.

Bauman, Z. (2002) *Society under Siege*. Cambridge UK: Polity.

Bauman, Z. (2004) *Wasted Lives: Modernity and its Outcasts*. Cambridge UK: Polity.

Beck, U. (2002) The terrorist threat: World risk society revisited, *Theory, Culture and Society*, 19(4): 39–55.

Beck, U. (2003) The analysis of global inequality: From national to cosmopolitan perspective, in M. Kaldor *et al.* (eds), *Global Civil Society*. London: The Centre for the Study of Global Governance, Yearbook 2003.

Beirne, P. and South, N. (eds) (2007) *Issues in Green Criminology: Confronting Harms Against Environments, Humanity and Other Animals*. Cullompton: Willan.

Benhabib, S. (2004) *The Rights of Others: Aliens, Residents and Citizens*. Cambridge: Cambridge University Press.

Bially Matter, J. (2007) *Stealing sovereignty: Toward a theory of 'illicit' transnational political movements*, paper presented at the Norwegian Institute of International Affairs (19.10.2007).

Bigo, D. (2000) When two become one: internal and external securitisation in Europe, in M. Kelstrup and M. C. Williams (eds), *International Relations Theory and the Politics of European Integration*. London and New York: Routledge.

Bigo, D. (2005) Globalized in-security: The field of the professionals of the unease management and the ban-opticon, *Traces: a Multilingual Series of Cultural Theory*, 4: 34–87.

Bigo, D. and Guild, E. (2005) *Controlling Frontiers: free movement into and within Europe*. Aldershot: Ashgate.

Bosworth, M. (2007) Border Crossings: Immigration Detention and the Exclusive Society, in M. Lee (ed.), *Human Trafficking*. Cullompton: Willan Publishing. pp. 159–177.

Bosworth, M. (2008) Border Control and the Limits of the Sovereign State, *Socio Legal Studies*, 17(2): 199–215.

Bourdieu, P. and Wacquant, L. (1999) On the Cunning of Imperialist Reason, *Theory, Culture & Society*, 16(1): 41–58.

Bourgois, P. (2003) *In Search of Respect: Selling Crack in El Barrio*, 2nd edition. Cambridge: Cambridge University Press.

Braithwaite, J. (2000) The new regulatory state and the transformation of criminology, *British Journal of Criminology*, 40(2): 222–238.

Brotherton, D. C. and Kretsedemas, P. (2008) *Keeping Out the Other: A Critical Introduction to Immigration Enforcement Today*. New York: Columbia University Press.

Brown, M. (2002) The politics of penal excess and the echo of colonial penality, *Punishment & Society*, 4(4): 403–423.

Brown, M. (2005) 'Setting the conditions' for Abu Ghraib: the prison nation abroad, *American Quarterly*, Sept. 2005: 973–997.

Cain, M. (2000) Orientalism, occidentalism and the sociology of crime, *British Journal of Criminology*, 40: 239–260.

Calavita, K. (2005) *Immigrants at the Margins: Law, Race and Exclusion in the Southern Europe*. Cambridge: Cambridge University Press.

Calhoun, C., Price, P. and Timmer, A. (2002) Introduction, in C. Calhoun *et al.* (eds), *Understanding September 11*. New York: The New Press.

Castells, M. (1996) *The Rise of the Network Society*. Oxford: Blackwell Publishers.

Castells, M. (2000) *End of Millenium*, 2nd edition. Oxford: Blackwell Publishers.

Castells, M. (2004) *The Power of Identity*, 2nd edition. Oxford: Blackwell Publishers.

Cavadino, M. and Dignan, J. (2006) *Penal Systems: a Comparative Approach*. London: Sage.

Chan, J. (2005) Globalisation, reflexivity and the practice of criminology, in J. Sheptycki and A. Wardak (eds), *Transnational and Comparative Criminology*. London: Glasshouse Press.

Christie, N. (1997) Four blocks against insight: notes on the oversocialization of criminologists, *Theoretical Criminology*, 1(1): 13–23.

Christie, N. (2000) *Crime Control as Industry: Towards Gulags, Western Style*, 3rd edition. London: Routledge.

Cohen, S. (1982) Western crime control models in the Third World: benign or malignant?, *Research in Law, Deviance and Social Control*, 4: 85–119.

Cole, D. (2004) *Enemy Aliens: Double Standards and Constitutional Freedoms in the War on Terrorism*. New York and London: The New Press.

Crawford, A. (2006) Networked governance and the post-regulatory state?, *Theoretical Criminology*, 10(4): 449–479.

Currie, E. (1998) Crime and market Society: Lessons from the United States, in P. Walton and J. Young (eds), *The New Criminology Revisited*. Basingstoke: MacMillan Press.

Deflem, M. (2002) *Policing World Society: Historical Foundations of International Police Cooperation*. Oxford: Oxford University Press.

Dela Porta, D., Andretta, M., Mosca, L. and Reiter, H. (eds) (2007) *Globalization from Below: transnational activists and protest networks*. Minneapolis: University of Minnesota Press.

Edwards, A. and Gill, P. (2003) *Transnational Organised Crime: Perspectives on Global Security*. London: Routledge.

Ericson, R. and Stehr, N. (2000) The ungovernability of modern societies: States, democracies, markets, participation, and citizens, in Ericson, R. and Stehr, N. (eds), *Governing Modern Societies*. Toronto: University of Toronto Press.

Ericson, R. (2007) *Crime in an Insecure World*. Cambridge: Polity Press.

Findlay, M. (1999) *The Globalization of Crime*. Cambridge: Cambridge University Press.

Findlay, M. (2003) *The Globalization of Crime: Understanding Transnational Relationships in Context*. Cambridge: Cambridge University Press.

Findlay, M. (2008) *Governing Through Globalised Crime: Futures for International Criminal Justice*. Cullompton: Willan Pulishing.

Flyghed, J. (2005) Crime-conrol in the post-wall era: the menace of security, *Journal of Scandinavian Studies in Criminology and Crime Prevention*, 6: 165–182.

Flynn, M. and Brotherton, D. C. (2008) *Globalizing the Streets: Cross-Cultural Perspectives on Youth, Social Control, and Empowerment*. New York: Columbia University Press.

Foucault, M. (1980) *Power/Knowledge: Selected Interviews and Other Writings 1972–1977*, C. Gordon (ed.). New York: Pantheon Books.

Fraser, N. (2005) Reframing justice in a globalizing world, in *New Left Review*, Nov./Dec.: 69–88.

Fraser, N. (2005a) Transnationalizing the public sphere, available at: http://www.republicart.net/disc/publicum/fraser01_en.htm.

Friedman, J. (ed.) (2003) *Globalization, the State, and Violence*. Walnut Creek: Altamira Press.

Garland, D. (2001) *The Culture of Control: Crime and Social Order in Contemporary Society*. Oxford: Oxford University Press.

GCIM (2005) *Migration in an Interconnected World: New Directions for Action.* Report of the Global Commission on International Migration: www.gcim.org.

Giddens, A. (1990) *The Consequences of Modernity.* Cambridge: Polity Press.

Goldsmith, A. and Sheptycki, J. (2007) *Crafting Transnational Policing: Police Capacity-building and Global Policing Reform.* Onati: Hart Publishing.

Goldsmith, A. and Sheptycki, J. (2007) *Crafting Transnational Policing: Police Capacity-Building and Global Policing Reform.* Oxford and Portland, Oregon: Hart Publishing.

Green, P. and Ward, T. (2004) *State Crime: Governments, Violence and Corruption.* London: Pluto Press.

Gupta, A. and Ferguson, J. (2002) Beyond 'Culture': Space, identity and the politics of difference, in J. X. Inda and R. Rosaldo (eds), *The Anthropology of Globalization: A Reader.* Oxford: Blackwell.

Haggery, K. and Ericson, R. (2006) *The New Politics of Surveillance and Visibility.* Toronto: University of Toronto Press.

Harvey, D. (1990) *The Condition of Postmodernity: an Enquiry into the Origins of Cultural Change.* Oxford: Blackwell Publishers.

Held, D. and McGrew, A. (eds) (2003) *The Global Transformations Reader*, 2nd edition. Cambridge: Polity.

Hirst, P. and Thompson, G. (1996) *Globalization in Question.* London: Polity Press.

Hogg, R. (2002) Criminology beyond the nation state: global conflict, human rights and 'the new world disorder', in C. Karrington and R. Hogg (eds), *Critical Criminology: Issues, Debates, Challenges.* Cullompton: Willan.

Hudson, B. (2003) *Justice in the Risk society: Challenging and Re-affirming Justice in Late-Modernity*, London: Sage.

Human Security Report (2005) *War and Peace in the 21st Century*, The University of Bristish Columbia, Canada: Human Security Centre.

Huntington, S. P. (1996) *The Clash of Civilizations and the Remaking of World Order.* New York: Simon & Schuster.

Huysmans, J. (2006) *The Politics of Insecurity: Fear, Migration and Asylum in the EU.* London and New York: Routledge.

Jewkes, Y. (ed.) (2003) *Dot.Cons: Crime, Deviance and Identity on the Internet.* Cullompton: Willan Publishing.

Johnston, L. and Shearing, C. (2003) *Governing Security: Explorations in Policing and Justice.* New York: Routledge.

Jones, T. and Newburn, T. (1998) *Private Security and Public Policing.* Oxford: Clarendon Press.

Jones, T. and Newburn, T. (2004) The convergence of US and UK crime control policy: Exploring substance and process, in T. Newburn and R. Sparks (eds) *Criminal Justice and Political Cultures.* Cullompton: Willan Publishing.

Jones, T. and Newburn, T. (2006) *Plural Policing: a Comparative Perspective.* London: Routledge.

Jones, T. and Newburn, T. (2007) *Policy Transfer and Criminal Justice.* Maidenhead: Open University Press.

Kaldor, M. (2007) *Human Security: Reflections on Globalization and Intervention.* Cambridge: Polity Press.

Loader, I. and Walker, N. (2001) 'Policing as public good: Reconstructing the connections between policing and the state, *Theoretical Criminology* 5(1): 9–35.

Loader, I. and Sparks, R. (2002) Contemporary landscapes of crime, order and control, in M. Maguire *et al.* (eds), *The Oxford Handbook of Criminology.* Oxford: Oxford University Press.

Lynch, M. J. and Stretsky, P. B. (eds) (2003) Special issue of *Theoretical Criminology*, vol. 7(2).

Mathiesen, T. (2003) The rise of the surveillant state in times of globalisation, in C. Sumner (ed.) *The Blackwell Companion to Criminology.* Maiden, Oxford, Victoria and Berlin: Blackwell Publishing.

Melossi, D. (2003) 'In a peaceful life': Migration and the crime of modernity in Europe/Italy, *Punishment & Society,* 5(4): 371–397.

Melossi, D. (2004) The cultral embeddedness of social control, in T. Newburn, and R. Sparks (eds), *Criminal Justice and Political Cultures: National and International Dimensions of Crime Control.* Cullompton: Willan Publishing.

Morrison, W. (2006) *Criminology, Civilisation and the New World Order: Rethinking Criminology in a Global Context.* London: Glasshouse Press.

Muncie, J. (2004) Youth justice: Globalisation and multi-modal governance, in T. Newburn and R. Sparks (eds), *Criminal Justice and Political Cultures: National and International Dimensions of Crime Control.* Cullompton: Willan Publishing.

Naim, M. (2006) *Illicit: How Smugglers, Traffickers and Copycats are Hijacking the Global Economy.* New York: Anchor Books.

Nellis, M. (2009) 24/7/365: mobility, locatability and the satellite tracking of offenders, in K. F. Aas *et al.* (eds), *Technologies of Insecurity: The surveillance of everyday life'.* Abingdon: Routledge-Cavendish.

Nordstrom, C. (2000) Shadows and sovereigns, *Theory Culture Society* 17(4): 35–54.

Nordstrom, C. (2007) *Global Outlaws: Crime, Money, and Power in the Contemporary World.* Berkeley: University of California Press.

O'Malley, P. (2004) Globalising risk? Distinguishing styles of 'neoliberal' criminal justice in Australia and the USA, in T. Newburn and R. Sparks (eds), *Criminal Justice and Political Cultures: National and International Dimensions of Crime Control.* Cullompton: Willan Publishing.

Parmentier, S. and Weitekamp, E. (eds) (2007) *Crime and Human Rights.* Oxford: Elsevier Ltd.

Passas, N. (2000) Global anomie, dysnomie, and economic crime: hidden consequences of neoliberalism and globalization in Russia and around the world, *Social Justice,* 27(2): 16–43.

Pickering, S. (2005) *Refugees and State Crime.* Sydney: The Federation Press.

Pratt, J., Brown, D., Brown, M., Hallsworth, S. and Morrison, W. (eds) (2005) *The New Punitiveness: Trends, Theories, Perspectives.* Cullompton: Willan.

Pratt, J. (2007) *Penal Populism.* London: Routledge.

Robertson, R. (1995) Glocalization: time-space and homogeneity – heterogeneity?, in M. Featherstone, S. Lash and R. Robertson (eds), *Global Modernities.* London: Sage.

Rose, N. (1999) *Powers of Freedom: Refraiming Political Thought.* Cambridge: Cambridge University Press.

Said, E. (1978/1985) *Orientalism.* London: Penguin Books.

Sassen, S. (2007) *A Sociology of Globalization.* New York & London: W.W. Norton & Company.

Sheptycki, J. W. E. (ed.) (2000) *Issues in Transnational Policing.* London: Routledge.

Sheptycki, J. (2002) *In Search of Transnational Policing.* Aldershot: Ashgate.

Sheptycki, J. (2005) Relativism, transnationalisation and comparartive criminology, in J. Sheptycki and A. Wardak (eds), *Transnational and Comparative Criminology.* London: Glasshouse Press.

Sheptycki, J. and Wardak, A. (eds) (2005) *Transnational and Comparative Criminology.* London: Glasshouse Press.

Sigel, D. *et al.* (2003) *Global Organized Crime: Trends and Developments.* Dordrecht/Boston/London: Kluwer Academic Publishers.

Simon, J. (2007) *Governing Through Crime: How the War on Crime Transformed America and Created a Culture of Fear.* Oxford: Oxford University Press.

Stern, V. (2006) *Creating Criminals: Prisons and People in a Market Society.* London and New York: Zed Books.

Stumpf, J. P. (2006) The crimmigration crisis: Immigrants, crime, and sovereign power, *Bepress Legal Series,* paper 1635, available at: http://law.bepress.com/expresso/eps/1635/

UNODOC (2007) United Nations Office on Drugs and Crime, Annual report, available at: http://www.unodc.org/unodc/annual_report_2007.html

Urry, J. (2000) *Sociology Beyond Societies: Mobilities for the Twenty-first Century.* London: Routledge.

Urry, J. (2002) The global complexities of September 11th, in *Theory, Culture and Society*, 19(4): 57–69.

Valier, C. (2004) *Crime and Punishment in Contemporary Culture*. London and New York: Routledge.

Wacquant, L. (2001) Deadly symbiosis: When ghetto and prison meet and mesh, in *Punishment and Society*, 3(1 (2001)): 95–134.

Wall, D. (ed.) (2001) *Crime and the Internet: Cybercrimes and Cyberfears*. London: Routledge.

Walters, R. (2003) *Deviant Knowledge: Criminology, Politics and Policy*. Cullompton: Willan Publishing.

Weber, L. (2002) The detention of asylum seekers–20 reasons why criminologists should care, *Current Issues in Criminal Justice: Special Issue – Refugee Issues and Criminology*, 14(1): 9–30.

Weber, L. and Bowling, B. (2008) Valiant beggars and global vagabonds: Select, eject, immobilize, *Theoretical Criminology*, 12(3): 355–375.

Wood, J. and Shearing, C. (2007) *Imagining Security*. Cullompton: Willan Publishing.

Welch, M. and Schuster, L. (2005) Detention of asylum seekers in the US, UK, France, Germany and Italy, in *Criminal Justice*, 5(4): 331–355.

White, R. (2008) *Crimes Against Nature: Environmental Criminology and Ecological Justice*. Cullompton: Willan Publishing.

Wimmer, A. and Schiller, N. G. (2002) Methodological nationalism and beyond: nation-state building, migration and the social sciences, in *Global Networks,* 2(4): 301–334.

Yar, M. (2006) *Cybercrime and Society*. London: Sage.

Young, J. (1999) *The Exclusive Society*. London: Sage.

Zedner, L. (2003) Too much security?, *International Journal of the Sociology of Law*, 31: 155–184.

23

Penology

Michael Cavadino

Penology is the study of punishment, including the study of 'penality' – a useful if slightly annoying word which is used to encompass both concrete penal practices and also the *ideas* which people have about punishment. At least since the classic work of Durkheim (1960, 1973), penology has always importantly involved an attempt to understand and also to influence *changes* in the practices, cultures and ideologies that exist in the real world. In this chapter I sketch various developments in penology over the last few decades, all of which can be seen as ways of trying to understand, come to terms with, confront and engage with contemporary trends in punishment itself. Often – typically, indeed – these attempts have been part of a moral mission, as theorists hope, sometimes desperately, sometimes despairingly, that their work may play a part in reducing the human misery brought about by both crime and punishment. Thus, penology has both an analytical (or explanatory) aspect, seeking to provide a convincing account of why punishment changes as it does, and a normative or prescriptive side which seeks to shape those changes.

This vision of penology as an engagement with penal change is one theme of what follows. Another is the continuing relevance of the ideas, in ever-permutating combinations, of the three 'Founding Fathers' of sociology: Marx, Weber and Durkheim. To put it far too simply, the Marxist tradition emphasizes the role of economics and class conflict in explaining social and historical developments; Durkheimian analysis stresses the importance of culture and 'collective sentiments'; while the Weberian stream of sociology posits an interaction between economics and culture while injecting other key concepts such as legitimacy and the notion that as modern society develops it becomes increasingly 'rationalized' and bureaucratic. (For a slightly less simplistic account, see Cavadino and Dignan, 2007: ch. 3; and for one much less simplistic see Garland, 1990.)

Before we begin our examination of recent and current penology, we must first understand that at any one time there exists a variety of penologies. One kind of penology is merely technical, seeking to 'evaluate' penal measures in a purely instrumental way, to judge whether they are effective, efficient or cost-effective and see whether they can be improved in these terms. Another kind of penological work is primarily analytical, seeking to understand why punishment and penality are as they are and why they change as they do. Others are primarily normative, with the moral mission to influence punishment being paramount. Penologies with this normative dimension may be conservative, liberal/reformist or radical in their approaches and prescriptions. It would be easy to fill a whole book with these varied penologies (even if we excluded the purely technical ones as insufficiently theoretical for this particular handbook), so we have to be selective. This chapter contains a distinct bias, paying most attention to analytical theories pitched around the liberal-to-radical band of the spectrum. The rationale (or excuse) for this is that it is these theories which have developed in the most interesting manner over recent years and which have attracted the greatest academic interest. They also have the advantage of theorizing *about* the other kinds of penologies on offer, seeking to explain their nature, development and influence – all of which makes them particularly suitable for discussion in a theoretical handbook.

AMONG THE RUINS OF REHABILITATION

Let us begin with the *decline of the rehabilitative ideal* in the 1970s (Bottoms, 1980; Cavadino and Dignan, 2007: 41–43).[1] Prior to this, official and academic discourse about punishment in developed Western societies (if not the actual practice of punishment) had been dominated by the theory of criminological positivism, which prescribed that each individual offender should receive the reformative 'treatment' which that particular offender needed. David Garland (2001) is one important writer who refers to this as 'penal welfarism': the view that responses to crime should be oriented around the welfare of offenders, on the assumption that attending to their needs would assist their rehabilitation and thus benefit not only themselves but also society. The era of 'rehabilitative optimism', during which it was fondly believed that criminological science could effectively solve the problem of crime by treating the criminal, came to an end in much of the West[2] as positivism was successfully assailed by theoretical critiques, empirical research apparently showing its practical ineffectiveness, and even revolts by some American prisoners who perceived a certain injustice in the fact that they were being detained indefinitely until they were deemed to have been successfully 'treated' (Cavadino and Dignan, 2006: 52, 61n).

Much penological work of the time fell into two categories, mirroring a dichotomy in criminology generally between liberalism and radicalism. One strand was an establishment-minded liberal positivism which clung to the rehabilitative ideal. The second strand represented a radical rejection of both positivism and liberal reformism, with a generally Marxist tenor, comprising academics who identified with the 'New Left' of that era. Theoretically, the latter tended to be – whether they all recognized it or not – essentially 'left functionalists' whose Marxism was combined with the Durkheimian notion that social institutions perform the latent function of preserving existing (capitalist) society intact. Thus, for example, the Norwegian penologist Thomas Mathiesen (1974: 76–78; 1990; Cavadino and Dignan, 2007: 194–196) analysed the 'social functions of imprisonment' as including the 'expurgatory function' (removing into prison those who threaten to disrupt the processes of production) and the 'diverting function', distracting attention from those powerful members of society who are in reality the seriously dangerous and anti-social ones. The opposition of these radicals to the social and penal *status quo* was combined with a (slightly ambiguous and ambivalent) rejection of liberal and social democratic approaches to reforming both society and punishment, for they saw not only conservativism but reformism as ultimately serving the function of legitimizing and thereby reinforcing an unjust system. Reform of offenders, reform of the penal system[3] and reform of capitalist democracy were all regarded with scepticism. One major and still enduring sub-strand was *penal abolitionism* (Mathiesen, 1974; Sim, 1992, 1994), whose agenda was (and still is) the full-scale abolition of prisons as opposed to reforming them.

What took the place of the rehabilitative ideal? Before answering this, it is worth mentioning a significant but historically unsuccessful attempt to engineer a new hegemony in penology to replace positivism: the *Justice Model* (Bottomley, 1980; Cavadino and Dignan, 2007: 54–56; Hudson, 1987; von Hirsch, 1976). (This was and is a primarily *normative* penology: it seeks to prescribe how punishment should be rather than explain its reality.) The Justice Model was a liberal approach steadfastly opposed to key features of positivism such as indeterminate sentences and individualized sentencing aimed at reforming offenders. Committed to the twin principles of due process in procedure and proportionate 'just deserts' in punishment (with the severity of penalties calibrated to the degree of seriousness of the offence, but favouring an overall reduction in levels of punishment), the Justice Model had a wide appeal to left-of-centre academics. It had a major impact on both sides of the Atlantic and elsewhere, exerting noticeable influence on sentencing reforms in countries including Sweden and Finland, and forming the basis of the English Criminal Justice Act 1991 (Cavadino and Dignan, 2006: chs 4 and 10). But despite playing a significant role in the downfall of the rehabilitative ideal, it was fated to see its progress overtaken and eclipsed by more powerful forces in the shape of 'the New Punitiveness' and 'the New Penology' (see the next section).

A very different kind of penology – this time analytical rather than overtly prescriptive – was born with the publication of Michel Foucault's *Discipline and Punish* (1977; and see Cavadino and Dignan, 2007: 73–75; Garland, 1990: chs 6–8). Labelled (by others, though not by himself) as an exemplar of 'post-Marxism', 'postmodernism' and 'post-structuralism', Foucault's highly influential account of punishment portrayed it as enmeshed in practices of *power*. It is vital to grasp that for Foucault power is not a simple one-way exercise of direction and domination from the top down but a complex and multi-faceted, multi-directional, constantly shifting set of practices, intimately related to the *knowledge* of the different parties involved and to social *discourse*. In line with the theme of this chapter, Foucault's whole enterprise can be said to be an examination of the nature of historical change, including penal change. *Discipline and Punish* itself centred on the 'great transformation' in punishment between the late eighteenth and early nineteenth centuries in which the prison became central to penality. He explained this shift from 'corporal' to 'carceral' punishment as `the moment when it became understood that it was more efficient and profitable in terms of the economy of power to place people under surveillance than to subject them to some exemplary penalty' (Foucault, 1980: 38). He thus clearly retained a strong element of Marxian analysis along with a generally radical aura, but seemed to abandon the Marxist dogma that the economic 'base' of society ultimately determines history, paying much closer attention to ideologies which are embodied and conveyed in discourse and enmeshed in complex and shifting relations of 'power/knowledge'. As Garland (1990: ch. 8) adeptly demonstrated, Foucault also owes a large (and largely unacknowledged debt) to Weber, sharing with him an interest in the forces of discipline, bureaucracy and rationalization on the development of punishment as modern society has evolved.

Foucault's popularity with the radical wing of criminology was immense, casting a spell (or if you prefer, a pall) whose influence may have diminished, but still lingers noticeably. His concepts and terminology run through and permeate much subsequent penology. One notable application of his ideas was the 'dispersal of discipline' thesis developed by Stanley Cohen (1979, 1985; Cavadino and Dignan, 2007: 172–176). Cohen took Foucault's concept of *discipline* – whereby the emerging prison sought to control offenders and 'normalize' them into conformity – and suggested that modern society was moving from the *concentration* of this discipline within the prison to its *dispersal* throughout society by means of the 'community corrections' movement. For the decline of the rehabilitative ideal had not led to the demise of non-custodial methods of dealing with offenders; on the contrary, they continued to proliferate in the form of a widening variety of community programmes and orders, such as community service, training programmes and (later) curfews and electronic monitoring of offenders. These, said Cohen, *blurred* the distinction between the prison and society outside; *widened the net* of formal social control to capture more and more citizens within it; *thinned the mesh* of that net to exert tighter control, and served to *penetrate* into society's informal networks. Thomas Mathiesen (1983) took the idea further (and beyond the bounds of mere penology), pointing to developments such as CCTV cameras and other forms of surveillance and intelligence technology as leading to a society in which 'discipline' was exerted not only over deviant individuals but over whole groups and categories of people. A certain pessimism and penal dystopianism was in the air.

INTO THE CULTURE OF CONTROL

And perhaps quite rightly so. For by far the most noticeable development in penality since the demise of the rehabilitative ideal has been '*the New Punitiveness*' (Pratt *et al.*, 2005): a trend leading to a dramatic increase in the sheer amount and harshness of punishment in most countries in the world. As in so many other fields, the United States of America has been a world leader in this development: the US prison population and imprisonment rates are the highest in the world, and numbers of American prisoners have quintupled since the early 1970s. Within the same period the US has also reintroduced and massively expanded its use of capital punishment. Along with – and encouraging – this increased harshness in penal practice has come a harsher ideology about how offenders should be dealt with, commonly referred to in penology as *populist punitiveness* (a phrase coined by Bottoms, 1995). Public and media discussion about crime has increasingly taken the form of consistently urging tougher punishment as the appropriate response to crime. Policies with populist appeal and slogans such as 'three strikes and you're out' and 'zero tolerance' have been prominent. This development has its own penology to justify it – the 'right realist' movement in criminology, associated with figures such as the American writer James Q. Wilson (1975).

But alongside this escalating harshness there have been other developments in both punishment and penology as well. Perhaps the most salient is the *'New Penology'*, named and analysed by Feeley and Simon (1992). This is an approach to criminal justice which is 'managerial rather than transformative' (Feeley and Simon, 1992: 452): it is not concerned with reforming and treating the offender (or indeed – unlike the 'New Punitiveness' – with placing moral blame on criminals and making them suffer). Instead 'it is concerned with techniques to identify, classify, and manage groupings sorted by dangerousness' (ibid.). Such techniques include statistical methods of carrying out 'risk assessments' of offenders, and applying new tools of offender management (for example, electronic surveillance and monitoring) based on the outcome of such assessments. So at the same time that punishment has become harsher, more intense and intrusive, it has also tended to take on a more managerial aspect.

The New Penology and the New Punitiveness between them do not exhaust all the trends to be found in punishment since the decline of the rehabiitative ideal. There has also been a strong movement (and a burgeoning literature) aimed at promoting *restorative justice* – responding to crime by informal processes that seek to involve offenders, victims and others affected, with an emphasis on reparation (see generally Dignan, 2005). Remarkably, despite going against the tide of both the New Punitiveness (by seeking humanity rather than harshness in punishment) and the New Penology (by advocating a less formal, less bureaucratic and more personalized approach), restorative justice has since the early 1990s become 'one of the most rapidly proliferating criminal justice innovations' (Hudson, 2003a: 75), and it deserves much more space than we have been able to afford it here.

How was penology to comprehend what was happening to penality, with the combination of these very different trends within the same era? One popular suggestion has been the notion that all these developments can be seen as representing a transition from the 'modern' age of punishment into a coming era of *'postmodern'* penality (Feeley and Simon 1992; Pratt, 2000; Simon, 1993; Simon and Feeley 1995). The idea is that society in general is moving from 'modernity'[4] into 'postmodernity' and that punishment is naturally changing with it. Modernity in the penal realm is seen as being characterized by 'penal welfarism', and more specifically the project of diagnosing, treating and rehabilitating individual offenders – essentially the 'rehabiitative ideal' or 'individualized treatment model', which is now being abandoned. In its place comes the new emerging postmodern penology, whose features are said to include the New Punitiveness (with its rising levels of punishment), the New Penology (with its burgeoning technocratic managerialism), a shift towards managing and controlling aggregate categories of deviants and potential deviants rather than individuals (as described by Mathiesen, 1983), a retreat from notions of individual rights, and the adoption of a diverse range of penal techniques both novel (such as electronic tagging) and 'premodern' (including informal and restorative justice).

While all these trends can certainly be discerned, a number of writers (such as Garland, 1995, 2001; Cavadino and Dignan, 2006: 7–9) think that it adds little coherence to the picture simply to label them all 'postmodern'. Instead, such developments can perhaps be more comprehensibly conceptualized as facets of *a continuing process of modernization*. Rather than talk of a 'postmodern' era, such writers prefer to speak of the current age as one of 'late modernity' (cf. Giddens, 1991). This can be placed in the context of a Weberian sociology which investigates how power is legitimated – how those who wield power in society manage to represent that power as morally acceptable to those who are subject to it. Weber (1968) envisaged a rationalized 'legal authority' becoming the characteristic form of authority in more developed and complex societies, as opposed to the 'traditional' and 'charismatic' types of legitimation found more commonly in less modern times. The most appropriate administrative form for a system of legal authority (because it is the most efficient form) is *bureaucracy* (Weber, 1968: chs 3 and 11). The development of the managerialist and bureaucratic New Penology is very much in line with what Weberian theory would suggest in a society which is continuing to become more modern. The deployment of new technology (such as CCTV and electronic monitoring of offenders) and other new scientific techniques (such as new methods of assessing the risks that offenders pose) also fit in well with the view that what we are witnessing is a continuance of modernization rather than a step beyond modernity.

More complex, however, is the relationship of modernization to other phenomena such as the supposed decline of human rights discourse in the penal realm, the abandonment of penal welfarism and a concomitant resurgence of interest in 'premodern' modes of punishment including informal and restorative justice, and generally rising levels of punishment and punitiveness. Are these indeed signs of a rupturing departure from modernity? First, rights discourse. It is true that – associated with the unsympathetic attitude towards offenders manifested in the New Punitiveness – there has recently been more hostility to the notion of the rights of offenders. However, it is important to note that the decline in the recognition of rights is only partial and in some respects (and in some countries) the reverse has been happening. For example, the operation of the European Convention on Human Rights has contributed to a greater recognition of the formal legal rights of prisoners in many European countries.

What of the demise of penal welfarism and rehabilitation? At this point it is necessary to question the postmodern theorists' identification of individualized rehabilitation as the hallmark of penal modernism. Prior to the decline of the rehabilitative ideal, rehabilitation was indeed assumed by those of progressive inclinations to be *the* appropriate modern way – the humane, rational and effective response to crime. But from the 1970s onwards, proponents of the 'Justice Model' have argued – on the contrary, and reverting to early Enlightenment thinking on the subject – that the treatment model violated human rights. A (modernist) attachment to human rights would be better served by giving offenders their 'just deserts' in the form of punishment proportionate to the severity of the crime. Another liberal school of thought prefers restorative justice, whereby positive measures (such as reparation) are taken to repair the relationships between offenders, victims and their communities. Again, this is seen as a more humane, enlightened, rational and progressive response to crime, more in keeping with the legitimate rights of both offenders and victims. More appropriately modern, you could say, despite its deep historical roots.

So the decline of individualized rehabilitation in such countries as the United States and the United Kingdom – is not necessarily a sign of 'postmodernism'. It can instead be seen as *in part* a development within modern human rights discourse, replacing one interpretation of human rights with others. On the other hand, it can also be seen as partly resulting from the *rationalizing* tendency of an intensifying modernism. Rational research and auditing of penal techniques seemed to show that attempts to 'treat' offenders were in reality ineffective, inefficient and arbitrary – because it seemed that 'nothing worked' to reform criminals – while the attempt to do so by leaving them in the hands of supposed experts who had vast discretion over their treatment led to unacceptable disparity and waste of resources. Tellingly, since the 1990s there has been a revision of this conclusion. In the United Kingdom it has now become the received managerialist (and governmental) wisdom that some things *do* work to some extent to reduce reconviction rates for the right kind of offender, and there has been a revival of official interest in rehabilitation as one strand within a largely managerialist penal strategy. (Theorists of postmodernism might have difficulty explaining such an apparent lapse back into modernism.)

It must be accepted, however, that neither the Justice Model nor the restorative justice approach can be said to have replaced the rehabilitative ideal, except perhaps within the limited realm of liberal penological theory. In most respects the emphasis on rehabilitation has been largely supplanted on the one hand by the New Penology, and on the other by the New Punitiveness. The former, as we have seen, fits a modernizing narrative rather than one of postmodernization. But what of the latter?

The rise of the harsh 'New Punitiveness' since the early 1970s in many (but not all[5]) countries has also been put forward as representing the eclipse of modernism in favour of postmodernism and/or 'regression to a stone-age morality' – as Stuart Hall (1980: 3) once put it nicely, if without total historical accuracy. On the other hand, it too can be seen as another consequence of late modernity. In modern societies, traditional authority and traditional deference crumble and need to be replaced by new legitimations for authority which accord with the understandings of modern citizens. We have seen a general decline in public trust in and deference to their social 'betters', including politicians, judges and supposed experts in crime and punishment. One result has been a rise in 'the popularization of crime politics' (Simon and Feeley, 1995: 168), whereby politicians appeal over the heads of the experts and criminal justice practitioners to 'Ordinary Joe' voters at the level of common sense rather than knowledge imparted by experts. Since at present most people's common sense (falsely) tells them that a strategy of harsh punishments is likely to be effective in reducing crime rates – or at any rate this is what politicians believe most people think[6] – this is what politicians have been increasingly promising and delivering. The irrationalism of this development, with its appeals to emotion rather than intellect, pulls strongly against the general rationalizing tendency of modernity. But it is nevertheless also a product of the same modernization of society: both ultimately spring from the decline of traditional authority and the search for new methods of legitimating authority in a modern age.

Something similar can be said about the reintroduction of elements of informal and restorative justice into penality. Paradoxically, one possible consequence of late modernity's quest for greater efficiency may be to recognize the limitations that are inherent in the bureaucratizing process, which fails to satisfy the personal needs of people for less formal relationships and interactions. Moreover, the intransigent fact remains that any social system is always held in being to a much greater extent by informal than by formal processes of social control. This leads, for example, to official interest (albeit often intermittent and uncomprehending) in forms of informal and restorative justice, which may be granted a licensed rôle within or alongside the formal criminal justice system. Uneven and not entirely rational developments – but still perhaps recognizably belonging to a modern, still modernizing world.

The most noteworthy and ambitious attempt to date to forge an overarching theorization of the new penal times is David Garland's *The Culture of Control* (2001) (a work which, spanning matters other than punishment, is more than simply 'penology'). As we have seen, Garland rejects the 'postmodern penality' theory, preferring to talk of 'late modernity', and bases his analysis on a theoretical approach spelt out in his previous work (Garland, 1990) which seeks to combine the insights of the Marxist, Durkheimian and Weberian sociological traditions along with those of theorists including Foucault and Norbert Elias.

Garland sketches the replacement of 'penal welfarism' in the closing decades of the twentieth century with a new set of arrangements for crime control and a new set of cultural attitudes towards crime and how it should be handled. Concentrating on the USA and the United Kingdom, he points to a number of 'indices of change' in their culture since the 1970s, which include the decline of the rehabilitative ideal, the re-emergence of punitive sanctions including the 'reinvention of the prison', the expansion and commercialization of crime prevention, the 'return of the victim', new managerial styles of criminal justice and crime control, and the politicization of crime control associated with a populist punitiveness (Garland, 2001: ch. 1). (Most of this could be summed up as the 'New Punitiveness' combined with the 'New Penology' of Feeley and Simon.) Responses to crime have been split between the punitive and the pragmatic (or managerial). Parallel to this comes a dichotomized 'official criminology'. On the one hand we have a 'criminology of the self', by which Garland means theories such as the 'rational actor' approach which underlies much of the theory and practice of crime prevention: viewing potential criminal offenders as rational actors much like ourselves, who can be manipulated out of committing crime by removing or altering their opportunities for doing so. On the other hand, there is a 'criminology of the other', which views the criminal as 'the threatening outcast, the fearsome stranger' (p. 137) on whom we feel we can justly impose severe penalties.

Garland's explanation for these developments is rooted in two main factors: the social changes associated with late modernity, and the shift towards 'neo-liberal' (free market) politics in the late twentieth century (p. x). One particularly controversial element in his theory is the weight he gives to rising crime levels, which he describes as 'a massive and incontestable social fact' (p. 90) and a feature of late modern societies. In these 'high crime societies' the politically influential professional middle classes, who were previously largely isolated from the effects of crime in their everyday lives, now feel more threatened by crime. This combines with other psychological stresses brought about by the disruptive changes caused by the development of late modernity, giving rise to serious insecurities in the psyche of modern citizens (ch. 6). All of this encourages a new cultural formation he terms 'the crime complex', centred around the attempt to exercise control over the risks and insecurities posed by crime. He (again controversially: see Beckett, 2001: 922–923) places relatively little explanatory weight on the actions and rhetoric of politicians or the influence of the media in encouraging punitiveness, seeming to see punitive policies more as a Durkheimian expression of the emotional reactions of a populace stressed out by late modernity, with politicians and the media primarily reflecting their concerns. Not that Garland sees political changes as irrelevant: far from it. His other main explanatory factor (along with the move into late modernity) is the shift towards 'neo-liberal' politics in the late twentieth century, with their emphasis on free markets, deregulation, lower taxes and reductions in state spending on welfare. This attack on 'welfarism' in general also helped to destroy *penal* welfarism, as neo-liberal policies created an environment where the poor came to be seen not as victims of social injustice but as 'undeserving, deviant, dangerous, different' (p. 102) and their crimes were seen in a similar light.

Why the bifurcation between punitive and pragmatic approaches to crime? For Garland this is because the two approaches are largely pursued by different actors who may be responding to the same general situation but whose own location within that situation varies. The high crime rates of late modernity undermine the claim of the 'sovereign state' to be able to protect the populace from crime. The (pragmatic) response of administrators is to accept high crime rates as inevitable and manage them by resorting to the 'criminology of the self', for example employing managerial crime prevention and harm reduction approaches and placing responsibility on citizens rather than the state to guard themselves against crime. On the other hand, politicians in their search for electoral popularity have denied the conclusion that the state's power to control crime is limited, and have asserted that increased punitiveness is the answer, or have simply channelled public hatred of the criminal into more punitive policies. Government ministers, 'caught in a contradictory location between the administrative and political domains' (p. 112) – having to run for elected office but also having to run state departments with responsibility for criminal justice – are caught on the cusp between these two responses.

One paradoxical indicator of the potency and influence of Garland's work is the high degree of scrutiny and criticism it has received from other commentators (surely a serious compliment). One criticism is that he overstates 'the decline of the rehabilitative ideal', an ideal which was never as hegemonic as he claims and which never did the near-complete vanishing act that he implies (Zedner, 2002: 344–346). Another point of disagreement is Garland's emphasis on rising crime levels as contributing to the 'crime complex', with some critics doubting that there has been such a rise (Beckett, 2001: 914–918) or that high crime rates are indeed an inevitable effect of late modernity (Zedner, 2002: 350), while there is also a general lack of good evidence that crime rates are associated in any way with the degree of punitiveness in societies.[7] Again, is late modernity really such an anxious and insecure time compared with other epochs? And even if it is, why should its general everyday insecurities and anxieties about matters other than crime be turned into punitiveness as Garland claims (Beckett, 2001: 919–922; O'Donnell, 2005: 271–272)? Some feel that Garland underplays the role of politicians and the media in fomenting punitiveness, placing too much emphasis on the responses of ordinary people to their insecure and anxious late modern lives. Beckett (2001: 922) for example argues that 'although Garland is right to emphasize the importance of everyday experience and its emotional consequences, we need to analyze how such experiences are given meaning, paying particular attention to the role of political and cultural discourses in this process'. One recurring criticism of Garland is that he over-generalizes from the two countries with which he is most familiar and on which he concentrates: the United States and the United Kingdom. Although he acknowledges that there may be international variations, he does claim that other late modern societies are moving in similar directions. Critics have cast doubt on this, or at least argued that Garland's generalizing sweep is inadequate to deal with punishment in more than a limited range of countries. (We shall say more about penal variation between countries in the section on comparative penology which follows.)

Before we move away from the analysis of the late modern (or postmodern if you prefer) 'culture of control' we need to delineate two other related concepts: the 'risk society' and 'governing through crime'. First, the *risk society* (a notion popularized by Beck, 1992). Some of the developments in how society responds to crime and to criminals could be explained in changes in the way society deals with the possibility of adverse events (including of course crime) occurring. The 'risk society thesis' holds that contemporary societies have become centrally preoccupied with avoiding such unpleasantnesses. This is not only because changing times bring with them new kinds of risk, but also because 'the expectation of mastery of the social and natural environment which is the hallmark of modernism … demands that risks will be recognized and countered. Risk society theory explains how this expectation engenders expectations of safety and security that can never be satisfied' (Hudson, 2003b: 44). (Thus perhaps, to answer a question we posed earlier, it is not that life today is any more insecure than it often has been; rather, these days we foolishly assume we have a right to demand that the state keeps us secure from all danger.) This combines with the modern lack of deference to traditional authority to engender mistrust of the state and its experts who are supposed to keep us safe but so often fail to do so, again highlighting what Garland (1996) calls 'the limits of the sovereign state'.

Castel (1991) speaks of a move from 'dangerousness' to 'risk'. 'Dangerousness' is seen as a characteristic of individuals (such as 'dangerous offenders'); Castel argues that since the 1970s this notion has been supplanted by 'risk' which represents a combination of factors that make dangerous behaviour more or less likely and render it capable of being managed. The picture seen in the totality of penal developments is more complex, however. The general 'risk society' thesis (and in particular Castel's claim of a move 'from dangerousness to risk') seems to fit best with Feeley and Simon's managerial 'New Penology'. This does not however adequately encompass developments more associated with the 'New Punitiveness', which has included many developments aimed at preventing the occurrence of serious crimes by labelling particular individuals as dangerous and keeping them confined for long periods. Thus, Seddon (2008) found in the context of measures in the United Kingdom introduced to deal with the threat supposedly posed by persons with the controversial label of 'dangerous severe personality disorder' (DSPD) that while certain 'New Penology'-type actuarial risk assessment and risk management techniques were indeed in operation, the 'DSPD initiative' was largely driven by populist punitiveness and concerns and rhetoric centred around the notion that we need to be kept safe from a discrete number of dangerous, scary individuals. Again, both developments – the managerial and the punitive – need to be explained.

Jonathan Simon's *Governing Through Crime* (2007) makes a claim about crime similar to the one that 'risk society' theory makes about risk: that crime, the fear of crime and attempts to prevent and control crime have now become central to society and to its governance. (His book is specifically about American society, but is obviously capable of wider application. Like Garland, Simon deals with matters far wider than just punishment.) In an analysis which pays overt homage to both Garland and Foucault (see for example pp. 16–17, 23–25) Simon traces this development back to the collapse of Roosevelt's welfarist New Deal in the 1970s and the simultaneous discovery by politicians of the 'war on crime' as a tool for exercising power. The resulting creation of a 'culture of fear' undermines democracy: on the one hand political debate is by-passed by exploiting the public's fear of crime to make opposition to oppressive measures impossible, while the measures themselves (such as the 'Patriot Act' which followed the 9/11 terrorist attack in 2001) erode civil liberties and increase the power of the state. Nor is it simply a matter of formal state power: Simon sees families, schools, and the places where people live and work as increasingly also being 'governed through crime' (with attempts at crime prevention such as gated communities having their own anti-democratic and inegalitarian effects). What Simon does is to take an *analysis* similar to Garland's and hone it into a pointed *normative critique* of American policies on crime and their deleterious effects on governance generally.

No doubt the next few years will see appraisals and criticisms of Simon as they have of Garland. Possible criticisms may include that he overstates the extent to which crime and its fear dominates all of society and politics, and implicitly underestimates the possibilities of reviving a more rational discussion on crime and criminal justice in America (cf. Tonry, 2004). It might also be said that the concept of 'governing through crime' is insufficiently differentiated, and may have different dimensions – yet again, one perhaps related to the New Punitiveness and another to the New Penology. On the one hand, politicians seek to 'govern through crime' by exploiting fear to gain electoral advantage so that they can gain and retain the power of elected office – hence the New Punitiveness. Rather differently, the state and dominant groups within society may 'govern through crime' because crime prevention measures give them greater – managerial, rationalized – control over the general populace, in line with the Weberian, modernizing logic of the New Penology.

GOING GLOBAL? THE COMPARATIVE DIMENSION

We saw above that Garland's analysis of the 'culture of control', whatever its merits, has been criticized as over-generalizing from just two countries, the United States and the United Kingdom. Simon's 'governing through crime' theory is quite specifically about the United States. So what kind of different penology might we have if we raised our eyes and widened our geographical gaze?

The first point that emerges from even a cursory glance around the penal systems of the world is that there are massive differences, despite the fact that we are now supposed to be living in an increasingly 'globalized' world. Present day prison population rates vary widely, indeed wildly: in the mid-2000s they ranged from 738 per 100,000 population[8] in the United States through 148 in England and Wales down to 26 in Nepal (Walmsley, 2007). There are many other international differences: while many countries have abolished capital punishment, it remains an important feature of some countries' penality; and the decline in the belief in rehabilitation which is such a feature of theories such as Garland's has been by no means universal.[9] We do not (certainly not yet) have a 'globalized' penality (Cavadino and Dignan, 2006: ch. 2). Why do differences exist, and what can we learn from them?

A book with the fitting title *Contrasts in Tolerance* (Downes, 1988) was the first major work in comparative penology, primarily a bilateral comparison of two Western European countries, England (and Wales) and the Netherlands. The Netherlands at the time had a much lower imprisonment rate than England – indeed, the lowest of any medium- or large-sized country in Western Europe – and by comparing it with England, Downes set out to discover what factors were important in making the difference. Like his successors in the field of comparative penology to date, he did not quite get to the bottom of it. Despite carefully examining eight separate theories purporting to explain the Netherlands' (then) relative leniency he found them all wanting to some extent, although a few of them were plausible as partial explanations. Economic and resource constraints on the penal system did not seem to provide any kind of explanation; but Downes was persuaded by the evidence to afford greater weight to cultural factors, including the cultures of the political and judicial worlds. A general Dutch 'culture of tolerance' combined with a consensual 'politics of accommodation' to allow a relatively lenient sentencing culture among the judges to flourish and produce low levels of imprisonment.

More recently, Cavadino and Dignan's *Penal Systems: A Comparative Approach* (2006) compared twelve countries in Western Europe, North America, Africa, Asia and Australasia, and found evidence of a strong association between the penality of a country and its *political economy*. Using a modified version of the typology developed by Esping-Andersen (1990), they assigned the countries in their study to the following categories. *'Neo-liberal'* nations – exemplified most strongly by the United States, but in recent decades also including countries such as Britain, Australia and New Zealand – are marked by free-market capitalism, high levels of material inequality and a relatively undeveloped welfare state. The general culture of neo-liberalism is individualistic rather than communitarian or collectivistic. In *'conservative corporatist'* countries (such as Germany and other nations in continental Western Europe), important national interest groups (notably organizations representing employers and workers) are integrated with the national state and are expected to act in accordance with a consensual 'national interest'. In return, members of these groups enjoy welfare benefits that are more generous than those found in neo-liberal countries. The ideology and culture of conservative corporatism is a *communitarian* one which seeks to *include* and integrate all citizens within the nation. Conservative corporatist states produce significantly less inequality than does neo-liberalism, but they are not strongly egalitarian. The *'social democratic'* version of corporatism is exemplified by Sweden and the other Nordic countries. These countries share the consensual, communitarian approach of conservative corporatism, but their welfare systems are more generous and more egalitarian, being based on universal benefits. Cavadino and Dignan found that countries with 'neo-liberal' political economies tended to have the highest levels of punishment (as measured by indices such as imprisonment rates); 'conservative corporatist' nations had lower levels; while 'social democratic' countries were lower again.[10] It was also noticeable that countries whose political economies altered over time by *moving in the direction* of neo-liberalism tended simultaneously to become more punitive, and that the most neo-liberal countries (notably the US) also tended to be the most punitive.

The association of neo-liberalism with punitiveness is relevant to our assessment of theories such as Garland's 'culture of control' thesis and Simon's notion of 'governing through crime'. On the one hand, it supports Garland's argument that 'the free market, socially conservative policies that came to dominate the USA and the UK in the 1980s' (p. x) have been one potent factor in the rise of punitiveness (and Simon's similar emphasis on the eclipse of New Deal welfarism in the United States). On the other hand, however, it may support the view of critics that studies such as those of Garland and Simon, which concentrate on the crime and punishment scenes in the US and UK – both countries being in the neo-liberal camp – may be of limited scope, and should not be unthinkingly generalized and assumed to apply to countries which do not share the neo-liberal political economy and culture. (Unless of course the whole world does eventually go neo-liberal as the process of 'globalization' continues on its course.)

Comparative penology has not yet got to the bottom of exactly why there should be this link between political economy and punishment (for a general discussion see Cavadino and Dignan, forthcoming), although it does not seem to be a result of higher crime rates in more inegalitarian countries in turn producing higher punishment rates.[11] One possibility is that in these different kinds of political economy we find different *cultural attitudes* within the populace towards our deviant and marginalized fellow citizens. The *neo-liberal* society with its individualistic ethos tends to *exclude* both those who fail in the economic marketplace and those who fail to abide by the law – in the latter case by means of imprisonment, or even more radically by execution. Such exclusion is felt to be justified because both economic failure and crime are seen as the fault of the individual, not the responsibility of society. On the other hand, corporatist societies – and to an even greater extent, social democratic ones – have traditionally had a different culture and a different, more inclusive attitude towards the failing or deviant citizen. But it is unclear how well this explanation fits with empirical evidence about public attitudes to crime and punishment in different countries. Other possible explanations (or partial explanations) involve the cultural attitudes and electorally-motivated strategies of political actors (as opposed to the attitudes of the general public), or to the varying influence of the media in promoting punitive policies in different types of nation. Lacey (2008) suggests that the nature of political institutions and arrangements in different types of country could be crucial. She argues that punitive populism in the politics of law and order is much more likely to thrive in countries with the kind of political institutions which tend to be associated with the neo-liberal political economy. For example, neo-liberal countries usually have 'first past the post' electoral systems which encourage political parties to try to outbid each other with punitive policies assumed to have electoral appeal, while corporatist countries more often have proportional representation systems which foster coalition-building and consensual politics; such a politics is favourable to both a corporatist political economy and to a less populist and relatively lenient penality. Uncovering the relative merits of these rival explanations – and thereby exposing the social, economic and political roots of punitiveness – remains a major task for comparative penology.

CONCLUSION

We did say that this chapter would have to be selective. For example we have paid little attention to the still-vigorous school of abolitionist penology; neglected left-reformist penologists such as Tony Bottoms in the United Kingdom and Michael Tonry and Elliott Currie in the United States; and said shamefully little about restorative justice and its theorists. All this will doubtless be rectified one day when Sage publishes a handbook of theoretical *penology*.

We have seen, however, that recent penology has been dominated by attempts to explain and reconcile those far-from-identical twin trends, the New Punitiveness and the New Penology. Hopefully it has also been at least intermittently clear throughout this chapter, as promised, that penology continues to draw inspiration from the theoretical traditions founded by Marx, Weber and Durkheim. Perhaps even more interesting is the way in which a wide range of penologists have sought to integrate and synthesize the insights of these varying traditions; no longer do the different schools engage in doctrinaire three-sided trench warfare claiming that a monopoly of wisdom lies in one true tradition alone. For example, we have seen that Garland explicitly draws on the insights of Marx, Weber, Durkheim and Foucault in constructing his theories. His approach is not far removed from the 'radical pluralist' synthesizing theoretical framework espoused by Cavadino and Dignan (2006: 12–14; 2007: 30–32; 81–84; Cavadino, 1992), except that he is wary of anything resembling a 'general theory'.[12] Open-ended theorizing, open to illuminating ideas from all quarters, open-minded about what the future of punishment might hold[13] – much penology today at least has the virtue of being refreshingly undogmatic while still retaining a good measure of intellectual rigour. With luck this will stand penology in good stead as it faces up to the massive challenge of analysing, evaluating and trying to influence punishment as it continues to develop (as it surely will) in ways both encouraging and horrendous.

ACKNOWLEDGEMENTS

The author wishes to thank David Scott for his assistance with this chapter.

NOTES

1 Bottoms (1980) and Cavadino and Dignan (2007) refer more dramatically to the *'collapse'* of the rehabilitative ideal.

2 But by no means everywhere, as we shall see: see below, note 9.

3 See Mathiesen (1974: 25, 202–211), who from an abolitionist position argues for radicals to distinguish between 'positive reforms' which have the ultimate effect of strengthening repressive institutions and 'negative reforms' which undermine them.

4 'Modernity' is roughly defined by Giddens (1991: 1) as referring to 'modes of social life or organisation which emerged in Europe from about the seventeenth century onwards'.

5 For example, Finland significantly reduced its use of imprisonment between 1976 and 1999 (Cavadino and Dignan, 2006: ch. 10). There have also been reductions in prison populations in

some African and Eastern European countries, while various other countries have had relatively stable prison populations in recent years.

6 Although in fact there is evidence to the contrary, at least in some countries: see for example Cavadino and Dignan, 2006: 37 n. 9; 2007: 388; Roberts and Hough, 2005).

7 For example, in both the US and England crime rates have fallen considerably in recent decades (after 1980 in the US, and since the mid-1990s in England), yet at the same time punishment levels have *risen* significantly in both countries.

8 This is the commonest, albeit rather crude, method of comparing levels of punishment in different countries: dividing the number of prisoners by the population of the country as a whole. See Cavadino and Dignan (2006: 4–5) for a discussion of this measure and whether it is an appropriate one to use.

9 As a generalization, rehabilitative optimism can be said to have declined significantly or even collapsed in English-speaking countries such as the US, United Kingdom, Australia and New Zealand and also in Nordic countries, but to have survived in continental Western Europe. See further Cavadino and Dignan (2006).

10 Cavadino and Dignan also studied Japan, whose 'oriental corporatism' (intensely communitarian, highly hierarchical and authoritarian) produced the lowest imprisonment rates of all twelve countries.

11 To clarify: although there is good evidence that more unequal countries suffer from worse crime rates, there seems to be little association between high rates of *crime* and high levels of *punishment* (Cavadino and Dignan, forthcoming).

12 This wariness is a legacy of the 'postmodern' rejection of 'totalizing' modernist theories 'which viewed society as a closed, mechanical system, and left little room for agency, contingency and accident in the historical process' (Garland, 1990: 284). See further Cavadino (1992: 13–6).

13 One interesting, open and vital question for the future concerns what new directions penality may take following the 'credit crunch' of 2008 and whatever shifts in countries' political economies occur as a result.

REFERENCES

Beck, U. (1992) *The Risk Society: Towards a New Modernity*. London: Sage.

Beckett, K. (2001) Crime and control in the culture of late modernity, *Law and Society Review*, 35: 899–929.

Bottomley, A. K. (1980) The 'justice model' in America and Britain: Development and analysis, in Bottoms and Preston (1980), pp. 25–52.

Bottomley, K., Fowles, T. and Reiner, R. (eds) (1992) *Criminal Justice: Theory and Practice*. London: British Society of Criminology.

Bottoms, A. E. (1980) An Introduction to 'The Coming Crisis', in Bottoms and Preston (1980), pp. 1–24.

Bottoms, A. E. (1995) The philosophy and politics of punishment and sentencing, in C. Clarkson and R. Morgan (eds), *The Politics of Sentencing Reform*. Oxford: Clarendon Press, pp. 17–49.

Bottoms, A. E. and Preston, R. H. (eds) (1980) *The Coming Penal Crisis: A Criminological and Theological Exploration*. Edinburgh: Scottish Academic Press.

Castel, R. (1991) From dangerousness to risk, in G. Burchell, C. Gordon and P. Miller (eds), *The Foucault Effect: Studies in Governmentality*. Hemel Hempstead: Harvester Wheatsheaf, pp. 281–298.

Cavadino, M. (1992) Theorising the penal crisis, in Bottomley *et al.* (1992), pp. 1–22.

Cavadino, M. and Dignan, J. (2006) *Penal Systems: A Comparative Approach* (Sage Publications, 2006)

Cavadino, M. and Dignan, J. (forthcoming) Penal Comparisons: Puzzling relations, in A. Crawford, (ed.), *International and Comparative Criminal Justice and Urban Governance: Convergence and Divergence in Global, National and Local Settings*. Cambridge: Cambridge University Press.

Cavadino, M. and Dignan, J. (2007) *The Penal System: An Introduction* (4th edition). London: Sage Publications.

Cohen, S. (1979) The punitive city: notes on the dispersal of social control, *Contemporary Crises*, 3: 339–363.

Cohen, S. (1985) *Visions of Social Control*. Cambridge: Polity Press.

Dignan, J. (2005) *Understanding Victims and Restorative Justice*. Maidenhead: Open University Press.

Downes, D. (1988) *Contrasts in Tolerance: Post-War Penal Policy in the Netherlands and England and Wales*. Oxford: Oxford University Press.

Durkheim, E. (1960) *The Division of Labor in Society*. Glencoe: Free Press. (First published 1893).

Durkheim, E. (1973) Two laws of penal evolution, *Economy and Society*, 2: 285–308 (first published 1901).

Esping-Andersen, G. (1990) *The Three Worlds of Welfare Capitalism*. Cambridge: Polity Press.

Feeley, M. and Simon, J. (1992) The new penology, *Criminology*, 39: 449–474.

Foucault, M. (1977) *Discipline and Punish: The Birth of the Prison*. London: Allen Lane (first published in French in 1975).

Foucault, M. (1980) Prison talk, in C. Gordon (ed.), *Michel Foucault: Power/Knowledge, Selected Interviews and Other Writings 1972–1977*. Brighton: Harvester Press.

Garland, D. (1990) *Punishment and Modern Society: A Study in Social Theory*. Oxford: Clarendon Press.

Garland, D. (1995) Penal modernism and postmodernism, in T. Blomberg and S. Cohen (eds), *Punishment and Social Control: Essays in Honour of Sheldon Messinger*. New York: Aldine De Gruyter, pp. 181–209.

Garland, D. (1996) The limits of the sovereign state, *British Journal of Criminology*, 36: 445–471.

Garland, D. (2001) *The Culture of Control: Crime and Social Order in Contemporary Society*. Oxford: Oxford University Press.

Giddens, A. (1991) *The Consequences of Modernity*. Cambridge: Polity Press.

Hall, S. (1980) *Drifting into a Law and Order Society*. London: Cobden Trust.

Hudson, B. (1987) *Justice Through Punishment: A Critique of the 'Justice Model' of Corrections*. London: Macmillan Education.

Hudson, B. (2003a) *Understanding Justice: An Introduction to Ideas, Perspectives and Controversies in Modern Penal Theory*. Maidenhead: Open University Press.

Hudson, B. (2003b) *Justice in the Risk Society: Challenging and RE-Affirming Justice in Late Modernity*. London: Sage.

Lacey, N. (2008) *The Prisoners' Dilemma: Political Economy and Punishment in Contemporary Democracies*. Cambridge: Cambridge University Press.

Mathiesen, T. (1974) *The Politics of Abolition: Essays in Political Action Theory*. Oxford: Martin Robertson.

Mathiesen, T. (1983) The future of control systems – the case of Norway, in Garland, D. and Young, P. (eds), *The Power to Punish: Contemporary Penality and Social Analysis*. London: Heinemann, pp. 130–145.

Mathiesen, T. (1990) *Prison on Trial*. London: Sage.

O'Donnell, I. (2005) The Primacy of the Prison? in Kilcommins, S., O'Donnell, I., O'Sullivan, E. and Vaughan, B. (eds), *Crime, Punishment and the Search for Order in Ireland*. Dublin: Institute of Public Administration, pp. 232–287.

Pratt, J. (2000) The return of the wheelbarrow men: or, the arrival of postmodern penality, *British Journal of Criminology*, 40: 127–145.

Pratt, J., Brown, D., Hallsworth, S., Brown, M. and Morrison, W. (eds) (2005) *The New Punitiveness: Trends, Theories, Perspectives*. Cullompton: Willan.

Roberts, J. V. and Hough, M. (2005) *Understanding Public Attitudes to Criminal Justice*, Maidenhead: Open University Press.

Seddon, T. (2008) Dangerous liaisons: Personality disorder and the politics of risk, *Punishment and Society*, 10: 301–317.

Sim, J. (1992) When You Ain't Got Nothing You Got Nothing to Lose: The Peterhead Rebellion, the State and the Case for Prison Abolition', in Bottomley *et al.* (1992), pp. 273–300.

Sim, J. (1994) The abolitionist approach: A British perspective, in A. Duff, S. Marshall, R. E. Dobash, and R. P. Dobash (eds), *Penal Theory and Penal Practice: Tradition and Innovation in Criminal* Justice. Manchester: Manchester University Press, pp. 263–284.

Simon, J. (1993) *Poor Discipline: Parole and the Social Control of the Underclass, 1890–1990.* Chicago: University of Chicago Press.

Simon, J. (2007) *Governing Through Crime: How the War on Crime Transformed American Democracy and Created a Culture of Fear.* New York: Oxford University Press.

Simon, J. and Feeley, M. (1995) True crime: The new penology and public discourse on crime, in T. Blomberg and S. Cohen (eds), *Punishment and Social Control: Essays in Honour of Sheldon Messinger.* New York: Aldine De Gruyter, pp. 147–180.

Tonry, M. (2004) *Thinking About Crime: Sense and Sensibility in American Penal Culture.* Oxford: Oxford University Press.

von Hirsch, A. (1976) *Doing Justice: The Choice of Punishments* (Report of the Committee for the Study of Incarceration). New York: Hill and Wang.

Walmsley, R. (2007) *World Prison Population List* (7th edition). London: International Centre for Prison Studies, King's College London.

Weber, M. (1968) *Economy and Society.* New York: Bedminster Press.

Wilson, J. Q. (1975) *Thinking About Crime.* New York: Basic Books.

Zedner, L. (2002) Dangers of dystopias in penal theory, *Oxford Journal of Legal Studies*, 22: 341–366.

24

Approaches to Victims and Victimisation*

Paul Rock

INTRODUCTION

Most discussions of approaches to victimisation, sometimes lumped together and called victimology, begin with the declaration that they are too intellectually thin and underdeveloped to be called a theory,[1] and there is a temptation, to which I shall also succumb, to devote space to speculating on why that should be so. Theory, according to the *Oxford English Dictionary*, is 'A scheme or system of ideas or statements held as an explanation or account of a group of facts or phenomena; ... a statement of what are held to be the general laws, principles, or causes of something known or observed.' Social theory, adds Marshall (1994), 'embraces a set of interrelated definitions and relationships that organises our concepts of and understanding of the empirical world in a systematic way'. It would be difficult to argue that there is a fully coherent victimological theory in that sense, and, at the very outset, it should perhaps be observed that there is no good reason why so diverse and complex an entity as victims and victimisation should or could be covered by one consolidated set of consistent arguments. Helen Reeves, at one time chief executive officer of Victim Support, the largest voluntary organisation for victims in England and Wales, and as knowledgeable as anyone about the field, once remarked that to search for a single theory or description of victims and victimisation would be quite as quixotic as a search for a single theory or description of criminals and crime. But there is more that can be said about the theoretically-emaciated state of victimology, and, in saying it, one may begin to learn something interesting about the world of ideas centred on the victim.

THE NEGLECT OF THE VICTIM

It is commonplace to remark that, until very recently, victims were neglected in Anglo-American criminal law and procedure (Christie, 1977). Victim activists used to talk about the 'forgotten person' who appeared only as a witness, an applicant for compensation or as a complainant or alleged victim until the conclusion of a trial. The prime conflict at law did not touch significantly on the victim: it was deemed to be between two parties only, the prosecution and the defendant, and the individual victim merely provided evidence of an offence that, for all practical purposes, was committed not so much against him or her but against the collectivity in the form of the Crown, the State, commonwealth or community. Crime itself was conceived to be an offence against something larger than, and independent of, the interests and person of an individual (see Blackstone, 1769: 5–7), whilst private wrongs were a matter for tort and civil procedure, not the criminal trial (Elias, 1983: 2). Garland observed that 'individuals and victims featured hardly at all, other than as members of the public, whose complaints triggered state action. Their interests were subsumed under the general public interest' (Garland, 2000: 357).

Almost without exception, the foundational writings of criminology followed suit and made (and, in many cases, continue to make) no reference to victims. The crimes they described were curiously intransitive, as if they lacked a target, an object and an impact, and as if, by extension, their enactment as crimes was sometimes both mysterious and a little absurd (see Sutherland and Cressey, 1970). Kenneth Burke once said that a way of seeing is always a way of not seeing, and, focusing on crimes and criminals, many criminologists most emphatically did not see the victim. It is small wonder that if and when they became engaged in policy questions, their interest was chiefly in repealing criminal legislation, mitigating penalties, supporting the offender and reducing prison populations. Those who busied themselves with victims may also have subscribed to these goals – there is no incompatibility between them – but the conventional criminologists and penal reformers chose to look elsewhere. As a member of the John Howard Society of Canada, a penal reform and community service organisation, once said to me, 'prisoners are *our* victims.'

The explanation of that neglect is not mysterious. Criminology is a minor discipline with few practitioners and many gaps, and it is not remarkable that the victim should also have been overlooked for a while. After all, we know very little about crime and justice in Asia, Latin America and Saharan Africa; very little about rural crime and policing in Europe and North America; the crimes of the elderly (see Stephens, 1976) or of Roma; and trafficking in people, weapons, art and archaeological artefacts. In such an ill-mapped world, victims could be taken as little more than the population of just another tract of *terra incognita*. But other epistemological and methodological issues were in play.

Each of the major theoretical approaches seemed to have had good reasons to ignore victims and victimisation.

The more positivist criminologists looked for the origins and development of crime in the body and mind of the criminal, the principal causal factors being constitutional, genetic, psychiatric or psychological, and the victim appeared not at all because he or she lay outside the central field of inquiry. Functionalist writers were interested less in the surface appearances of crime and control – appearances, they held, that could be misconstrued by naïve common-sense reasoning. The proper business of science was to reveal the extraordinary and deep matters that are inaccessible to the lay man and woman (see Davis, 1971). If common-sense reasoning did pay attention to victims, if what was sometimes disparaged as saloon-bar criminology pointed at them, victims became all the more invalid, part of a naïve populist rhetoric that should be disregarded. The theorist's eye was turned elsewhere, towards what were represented as the deep structures of society where crime and control were instruments of the unseen hands that performed surprising and unrecognised services for the collectivity: prostitution buttressing marriage and the family; the stigma of illegitimacy buttressing primogeniture; organised crime introducing order into otherwise chaotic markets and ineffectual political regimes; deviance resolving problems of anomaly and ambiguity in classification schemes (Douglas, 1966); crime reinforcing social cohesion (Erikson, 1966); and, in a later, radical twist, offenders and prisoners deflecting popular discontents from structured inequalities on to mass-produced scapegoats (Foucault, 1979; Reiman, 2003) through a process, following Edward Said (1995), that criminologists have increasingly chosen to describe as 'othering' (Young, 2007). 'Othering' reduces devalued groups such as immigrants to outcast, reified creatures who share nothing in common with the common mass of the population and who may serve as scapegoats for collective ills. There was and is no place in such a scheme for the commonplace pathos and pains of individual victimisation in everyday life.

Symbolic interactionism or 'labelling theory', the approach ostensibly wedded to an empathetic description of how people jointly construct lines of action, should have accommodated the victim in its analyses of rule-breaking, but it failed to do so because it chose chiefly to hearken to what were called crimes without victims: the crimes that are 'created when we attempt to ban through criminal legislation the exchange between willing partners of strongly desired goods or services' (Schur, 1974: 6), and their repression was used to illustrate the folly and oppressiveness of many rules and much formal control (Schur, 1965). (Stan Cohen once remarked that, while lawyers tend to see laws and control as benign, sociologists almost invariably regard them as malign.) The interactionist's was a largely self-regarding focus that, for purposes of appreciation and easy access to research populations, allowed them to examine themselves and others in their own milieu, the sexual deviants, political radicals, nudists and drug-users who may have had no discernible individual victims. Indeed, Cohen and Taylor, two prominent labelling theorists, confessed they had been merely reporting themselves: they 'took notes about our own "normal" deviance; smoking dope with our students, organising anti-Vietnam war demonstrations, watching porno movies' (1976: 2). They had no notion of rule-breaking as harmful. Rather it was amusing, romantic and sometimes heroic. Lacking a clear vision of the victim, formal control could become little more than an aggravating factor that amplified and confirmed deviance (see Schur, 1973), generating so-called 'secondary deviation' (Lemert, 1951), and exerted, in many cases, to no good purpose other than to express the inflated moral indignation of the community and provide work for agencies of social control (Becker, 1963; Erikson, 1966; Sutherland and Cressey, 1970). In that formulation, in a relativised, negotiated and confused world, there was a 'vacillation between the image of the deviant as mismanaged victim and the deviant as cultural hero' (Cohen, 1979: 19). It 'is not easy', said Sagarin on one occasion, 'to divide the world into victims and offenders. The hunted fugitive is a victim, but so are people upon whom he preys; and, potentially, the hunters – the decision-making, overdog, and putatively oppressive police – may be victims as well' (1975: 133).

Radical criminologists preferred to talk of crime and formal control as the ephemera of a capitalist society in transition- criminality being the fruit of possessive individualism, class resentment or primitive rebellion (Hobsbawm, 1971) and law being part of bourgeois legality – that would not survive the coming of socialism. And, while capitalism lasted, it was argued by some, there were other, more pressing issues to consider: the problems of class conflict, racism, structured oppression and exploitation (Hillyard *et al.*, 2004). In the language of the time, criminology should 'constitute its own object' and occupy itself with a core critical agenda, not with the petty ideological distractions of volume crime that capitalism and its legislators placed in its path. Not untypical was Herman and Julia Schwendinger's introduction to what was then a new journal, *Crime and Social Justice* (1974: 1): radical criminology, they recalled, had emerged in the United States of the 1960s 'where political movements were scourging American institutions: when the endemic causes of gender, racial and class inequality were being laid bare; when crimes against humanity and violations of constitutional law were being exposed at the highest levels of government; and when popular rage over the carnage produced by the U.S. government in Southeast Asia, Latin America, and Africa had ruptured the political fabric of our country'.

Those themes were held to be the topics appropriate to a critical criminology, not, say, routine household theft, burglary and malicious damage (and see Schwendinger and Schwendinger, 1970). A terminology of moral crusade (Becker, 1963), mystification (Box, 1983), moral panic (Cohen, 2002) and moral censure (Sumner, 1990) was in its turn frequently deployed, sometimes carelessly, to dismiss popular fears about crime as ideologically manipulated, misdirected and irrational. Anxieties about everyday crime became tantamount to figments of false consciousness. If there were authentic victims to be acknowledged, they were the immiserated proletariat, the racial underclass, the poor and unheeded victims of corporate crime (Pearce, 1976), and the prisoners and criminals, who were the real casualties of class-based, racist societies and their repressive criminal justice systems (Crime and Justice Associates, 1982; Mathiesen, 1974). So it was that Dignan could complain of Quinney, one early radical, that he:

> drew attention to structural factors relating to the way society is organized, and also the role of the state itself and the legal system in the social construction of both victims and offenders ... such insights tend to see offenders as the principal victims of state oppression and to downplay or ignore altogether those who were in turn victimized by them.
>
> (2005: 33)

The personal victim of mundane crime could then be readily represented as a symptom of obfuscation,[2] demagoguery, penal populism, authoritarian populism, or some other term for the political malaise that was thought to distract what were sometimes called the subaltern classes. Some even took it that Marxism should not deign to busy itself with crime at all (Hirst, 1975).

There was, by extension, something of a distaste in criminology at large, and in radical criminology in particular, about any involvement with the victim, victimisation or policies for victims conventionally defined. To study victims was in effect to collude with the reactionary politics of the mob and the machinations of the powerful. Take an observation made by Garland, an astute, disinterested and far from polemical writer, a man who currently wields great influence in criminological theory: 'The dominant voice of crime policy is no longer the expert or even the practitioner but that of the long-suffering, ill-served people – especially of "the victim" and the fearful, anxious members of the public' (Garland, 2001: 13).[3] One wonders why the word 'victim' should have been conveyed in such a sceptical fashion, as if it were intended to suggest that the victim's status was merely alleged or *soi-disant*, and not really achieved in good faith at all.

And there was something else permeating that unease. Victims do have something of the uncomfortable 'other' about them. They have been described informally by David Downes as a hybrid of pariah and saint. They are necessarily somewhat disreputable, stigmatised figures, blighted by misfortune, (often misleadingly) portrayed as angry and vindictive (see Hough and Roberts, 1998), perhaps best avoided by lay person, practitioner and criminologist alike. To approach too close to victims, or to allow victims too great a role in criminal proceedings, is likely to reintroduce emotional, irrational and angry lay men and women into a system best left to the clinical management of the professional (see Rock, forthcoming).

Those fears are old and deeply entrenched. Over 150 years ago, the Attorney General of England and Wales, speaking before a committee entrusted with a major review of the system of prosecutions, said that the injured party was 'one who is smarting under a sense of injury, smarting with a sense of wrong, and desirous of bringing the vengeance of law on the person who has injured him.' (Select Committee on Public Prosecutors, 1855: 186). A 100 years later, the legal campaigner, C. H. Rolph, wrote:

> The law for centuries has required the citizen to smother his natural [sic] desire for revenge and leave it to the police and the courts to deal with the offender. The disabled man's injury is the State's injury. When he was coshed, the community was coshed. Vengeance is mind, saith the State; but it does not repay. ... Last November, the Home Secretary was presented with a petition, organized by a former Lord Mayor of Birmingham and signed by 87,000 people asking for heavier sentences on violent criminals, the revival of flogging and 'adequate compensation for victims – as far as possible at the expense of their attackers' (1958)

Another 50 years on, when professional associations were consulted in 2005 about the proposal that the families of homicide victims be allowed to deliver impact statements at trial, the General Council of the Bar replied:

> We also see a possibility of victims in high profile cases being pressurised by other parties with an axe to grind. That could be pressure to tell a more lurid story or it might be pressure to back off. Victims by definition will be emotionally vulnerable. A proportion come from disadvantaged sections of society and will be of modest intellectual and educational attainment.

And a journalist, Patience Wheatcroft, dismissed what was envisaged as mere pandering, and proceeded to claim in *The Times* (2 September 2005) that it was 'just another of those dangerous consequences of misguided populist moves from which this Government never seems to learn'.

The *New Shorter Oxford English Dictionary* defines *victim* as a sacrifice, 'A person killed or tortured by another; a person subjected to cruelty, oppression, or other harsh or unfair treatment or suffering death, injury, ruin, etc., as a result of impersonal agency. ... A person who is taken advantage of; a dupe.' It is a word that evokes images of submissiveness, pain, loss of control and defeat. Those bereaved by

murder and manslaughter have certainly told me of the primitive fear and embarrassment they believed they could excite, how people would not know what to say to
them, sometimes crossing the road in an attempt to avoid them lest their bad luck
become contagious (Rock, 1998a).

Victims are riddled with taboos. Their very existence is disturbing because it can
challenge the belief in a just world where people should not expect to incur harm
unless they have somehow earned their suffering through their own misdeed or fool-
ishness (see Lerner, 1980). To think otherwise would turn beliefs in any sort of
effective moral order quite upside down.

THE ORIGINS OF VICTIMOLOGY

There is a conventional account of the genesis and evolution of victimology (see
Maguire, 1991: 374) and, although there may be room for dispute about some of
its particulars, its very acceptance has become a shaping academic and ideological
influence that must be taken seriously. Victimology, we have been repeatedly
told, was founded more or less independently in the 1940s by – and the histories
vary somewhat – three or four men (see Sebba, 1982: 225): a Romanian lawyer,
Beniamin Mendelsohn;[4] a professor of law at the State University of Colorado,
Boulder, Hans von Hentig;[5] a Hungarian criminologist resident first in England
and then the United States, Stephen Schafer (see Doerner and Lab, 1995); and
a German–American psychiatrist and campaigner against the corrupting influence
of comic magazines, Fredric Wertham.[6] Criminology proper being barren, and
victims being tainted, victimology could not but appear with an odd genealogy, late
and from the side-lines, and it exhibited some peculiar traits. The website of
the World Society of Victimology (www.victimology.nl), one of its parent bodies,
candidly admitted:

> Not only has the 'science' of victimology suffered because of its inauspicious origins as the
> wayward sub-discipline of criminology, but its very subjects, 'victims' have been weighed
> down by negative imagery that connotes their status with that of the 'weak' underdog.
> Victimology ... does not carry the academic weight of theory and critique that is the domain
> of criminology.

It was inevitable that the first victimologists were unconventional scholars, lying
on the frontiers of the academic study of crime, psychology and the law, wedded to
doctrines that may now appear somewhat eccentric or *passé*, later to be described by
one unfriendly critic as 'the lunatic fringe of criminology' (Becker, 1981: 4). One
man claimed by some as the father of victimology, Hans von Hentig, declared, for
instance, that he was attached to the Italian school of criminal anthropology
(a school associated with the largely reviled figure of Cesare Lombroso[7]) and to
ideas of moral imbecility and constitutional immorality. And it was Beniamin
Mendelsohn, also claimed as the father of victimology, who first awarded the sub-
discipline a name and declared it his ambition to analyse the victim from the 'the
bio-psycho-social point of view' (1963: 239), a project that betrayed a certain gran-
diosity of purpose.

VICTIM-PRECIPITATION

The principal foundational idea that united those first scholars was victim-precipitation (Meier and Miethe, 1993: 464) and, for good or bad reasons, it came to dog the political and analytic standing of the sub-discipline thereafter. Victim-precipitation was propounded first by Mendelsohn, and it alludes to the criminally provocative, collusive or causal impact of the victim in a dyadic relation variously called the 'penal couple' (Mendelsohn, 1963: 241); the 'reciprocal action between perpetrator and victim' (von Hentig, 1940: 303); the 'duet theory of crime' (von Hentig, 1948: 397); a 'situated transaction' (Luckenbill, 1977); 'the functional responsibility for crime' (Schafer, 1968: 55), or, simply, 'the victim–offender relationship' (Wolfgang, 1957: 1).

At one pole, victim-precipitation portrays crime somewhat neutrally as an interactive process or evolving relation between victim and offender, in which each influences not only the conduct of the other but also the form and content of any crime that may ensue. Douglas and Waksler (1982: 249) argued perfectly reasonably that 'perpetrator and victim commonly appear to be involved in a social encounter where the acts of each affect those of the other'. And Reiss said much the same when he stressed 'the importance of theories about victimization focusing upon the behavior of all parties to crime events rather than resorting to separate theories about victimization and offending or about victims and offenders' (1981: 710). Little exception could be taken to those formulations.

Of course, not all crime is recognisably interactive – some burglaries are only tangentially so – but the attention of the early victimologists was fixed on the graver instances of law-breaking, on rape, assault and murder, and it is important to note that it was framed from the start in a very special way that has perhaps been too little appreciated.

Aspects of victims and victimisation become visible through the assumptions, ambitions, methods and questions that scholars apply to observe them. In this, victimology's first big idea, victimisation was seen through the eyes of Mendelsohn, a practising defence attorney, and his epiphany occurred during the course of a murder trial. Thoughts of victim-precipitation (and victimology) welled up in his groundwork for a defence case: 'It was while preparing for the trial of Stephan Codreanu arraigned in 1945 for a crime passionel', he recalled, 'that I began to elaborate the doctrine of Victimology. ... There can be no doubt that, had it not been for the perversity of his former wife, he would never have been guilty of two crimes. ...' (1963: 241). Responsibility for Codreanu's offence should, in effect, be assigned to his wife. The implications are startling.

There are perhaps three principal defences in any murder trial: the defendant was not there at the time of the alleged offence; someone else did it; or the victim provoked the offence or struck the first blow, thereby lessening the charge to one of manslaughter, on the one hand, or self-defence, on the other. Defence lawyers are not obliged to be disinterested and impartial. They are supposed to be fearless in the discharge of their obligations to promote their clients' interests. They must accept instructions. In murder cases fought in the adversarial system, not only is the victim silent but there is no one briefed formally to speak on his or her behalf. A defence, in other words, is a lop-sided and motivated construction, one of a pair of competing narratives, that is almost invariably balanced by an equal and opposite account. What Mendelsohn introduced into victimology from the beginning was but one side of such a pair, and it is not remarkable that victim-precipitation could occasionally take a peculiar and distorted form. Victims were to be represented just as their perpetrators would have wished, as people who were causally and, indeed, often culpably complicit in their own downfall. They provoked, conspired or were gulled into becoming a target. They effectively deserved their own fate.

So it was that Porterfield and Talbert could remark: 'It is amazing to note the large number of would-be murderers who become the victim' (1954: 48). So it was that von Hentig, having also taken up the baton of victim-precipitation, produced a curious taxonomy of murder victims which included the depressive, 'who lacks ordinary prudence and discretion'; the greedy of gain, 'who lack all normal inhibitions and well-founded suspicions'; the wanton type, where 'female foibles play a role'; and the tormentor-type, 'the most primitive way of solving a personal conflict [being] to annihilate physically the cause of the trouble' (1940: 304–306). 'Are we permitted', he continued, 'to say that in some cases criminality is a self-consuming process of anti-social elements in which criminals prey on criminaloids, killers on suicides or other killers, oversexed on oversexed, dishonest individuals on dishonest?' (1940: 309).

Despite its lack of narrative balance, victim-precipitation played an influential part for a while in the development of theories of criminal victimisation. It certainly inspired a pioneering study, *Patterns in Criminal Homicide*. Marvin Wolfgang, its author, acknowledged that 'von Hentig ... provided the most useful theoretical basis for analysis of the victim–offender relationship' (Wolfgang, 1957: 1), and then proceeded to employ police and other official records to examine patterns of victim involvement in killings in Philadelphia (Wolfgang, 1958). He was followed by Luckenbill (1977), Polk (1994) and others, all of whom leaned heavily on von Hentig, Wolfgang and the 'duet theory of crime'. Quite typical was Avison (1973: 58), who argued that:

> the role of the victim is not restricted to precipitation of the crime ... The victim can contribute in many different ways to the interaction preceding the aggressive behavior, and it may be more meaningful to consider such involvement on a continuum ... culminating in active participation by the victim.

FEMINISM AND VICTIMOLOGY

The second, double-edged strand of ideas injected into victimology was both internally contradictory and quite at odds with the theorising I have just described, and it only uncertainly belongs to the body of victimology proper at all. What was called second-wave feminism arose in the 1960s and 1970s to protest the injustices inflicted on women and girls; to locate those injustices in the structure and functioning of a patriarchal order; to disclose the everyday experiences of women as politically-freighted; and, in the conduct of research, to restore dignity and humanity to those who were studied by eschewing imbalances in power between the scholar and subject, levelling hierarchy, and letting women themselves speak as authorities about their own lives (Oakley, 1981).

Feminist criminology had a radical tinge, and it arose in large measure as a protest against the domain assumptions of radical criminology. Women, it was said, were raped, abused and assaulted, and their neglect by male criminologists constituted not only a political and sexist affront but an analytic and empirical gap. It was not good enough to dismiss crimes against women as epiphenomenal, an ideological mystification, or as a canker which would disappear when a 'fully socialist society' (see Taylor *et al.*, 1973) at last came into being. Wrongs were real and immediate, and they required exposure, analysis and redress. Smart, a *protégée* of Ian Taylor, the co-author of the polemical *The New Criminology*, wrote her own countering feminist manifesto, *Women, Crime and Criminology* (1977), in which she lambasted the way in which women as offenders and victims had been anathematised, and she proposed their reinstatement within an analytic framework emphasising the workings of patriarchal power and male myopia. Women, her successors came to argue, are kept firmly in their place by the exercise of male coercion (Brownmiller, 1977; Madriz, 1997: 352; Pagelow, 1981: 1476). They are encouraged through fear of male violence and male censure (Hollander, 2001: 85) to remain submissive and unambitious (Bourgois, 1996; Kurz, 1989: 490) within the private, domestic sphere. Daly (1994: 779) observed that, although 'feminist analyses of the causes of men's violence toward women were (and are) varied, the structural sources of men's power and entitlement over individual women was prominently featured'.

Women were, in short, represented as victims generically and individually under the workings of patriarchy (Wright, 1995: 111). And looming large, the first stirrings of the new victimology supplied an appropriate butt not only for contesting the meanings of victimisation, gender and power but also for establishing a countervailing feminist criminology. Like *The New Criminology* (Taylor *et al.*, 1973) before it, early feminist criminology was elaborated through what was called 'immanent critique', a series of running criticisms which amounted through accretion to the provision of an alternative theory, and one of its prime objects was the failing of criminology and victimology to comprehend female victimisation.

Matters came to a head when a student of Marvin Wolfgang, Menachem Amir, applied without significant modification his supervisor's formulae, methodology and even the style of his book title, not to cases of homicide, but to rape (Amir, 1971). Murder victims tend not to be available for observation and interview[8] but rape victims might well be so. Yet Amir followed Wolfgang and faithfully relied on official records, talking neither to rape complainants nor to any other participant, and hearing no insider's account of what might have happened (see Lotz, 1975: 381). Quoting von Hentig once more, he said: 'We are accustomed to believe that forcible rape is an act which falls upon the victim without her aid or cooperation, but there is often "some reciprocal action between perpetrator and victim" in such cases' (1967: 493). He then proceeded to produce an inventory of victim characteristics that could trigger a rape, and they included meeting an offender in a bar, picnic or party, possessing a 'bad' reputation and consuming alcohol. That was a cluster of allegations too far and it was timely, serving as a useful foil for the shaping of a new version of criminology. It became an iconic target for a number of feminists who renamed victim-precipitation 'victim-blaming' (Clark and Lewis, 1977). Lamb (1996: 78, 79) protested:

> At the root of all victim-blaming are the perpetrator's own attempts to present the victim as the cause of his violence or abuse. ... Perpetrators will ... claim that their victims are almost

directly responsible for their fates, that the little girl wanted to be fondled, that the raped woman was asking for it, and that the abused wife provoked her beating ...

The political and intellectual standing of victim-precipitation plummeted in some quarters and, with it, that of victimology itself. Said Meier and Miethe (1993: 463):

> The implication of blame in victim-precipitation analyses has inhibited full development of the concept. When Wolfgang's student Menachem Amir ... adopted the concept in a study of forcible rape that parallels Wolfgang's research on homicide, it caused a major political controversy.

Some, like Ezzat Fattah, may have protested about the manner in which that debate had unfolded, describing it as a series of 'unwarranted attacks and unfounded ideological criticism' (Fattah, 2000: 2) that revealed no flaws in the integrity of the idea of victim-precipitation itself, only in its execution (Fattah, 1979: 200), but damage had manifestly been done.

Once feminism had been established as a solid enterprise in the 1980s and 1990s, it became possible for women criminologists to move on, distance themselves critically from its early writings and embark on a flurry of revisions. They were to acknowledge that, in concentrating almost wholly on the woman as victim, there was an all too frequent collusion in the manufacture of an imagery that stressed defeat, passivity, submission and resignation. There had been an exclusive but indefensible preoccupation with the victimisation of women that obscured criminal acts committed against men, as if men were never victims and always perpetrators (Walklate, 2000: 189). There were abundant male victims of domestic violence (Mirrlees-Black, 1999; Grady, 2002: 77).[9] There were male victims of rape and violence (Stanko, 1990). There were female offenders (Carlen, 1985, 1988), including, exceptionally, violent (Shaw, 1995) and sexual offenders (Matravers, 2000). There were varieties of women differentiated by class and race, not just a solidary mass (Hooks, 1982). Gender was to become interpreted as a dialectical concept, taking its meaning from the paired contrasts of male and female, and portions of academic feminism began to progress towards a more balanced consideration of masculinity as a counterpoint to their work on femininity (see Newburn and Stanko, 1994). Criminology itself was recognised as intellectually diverse, subject to no one orthodoxy but fissured by the debates which ran through its parent disciplines of sociology, psychology, law, statistics and social anthropology. And it no longer became possible to speak of a unitary feminist criminology (or victimology) but of *feminisms* (Adamson *et al.*, 1988) and *criminologies* (see Gelsthorpe and Morris, 1990). One of the mothers of feminist criminology, Carol Smart, even came to question whether it was any longer politically or analytically defensible to consider women in a context of crime, victimisation and criminal justice at all (1989). Placing them in such a restricted setting dwarfed analysis and invited uncongenial associations.

Feminist criminology had been galvanised in part by a practical and political preoccupation with the victims of rape, incest and domestic violence, and by a methodology and epistemology that restored a voice to those whom it studied. There was to be a concomitant strain: those who had founded the early rape crisis centres and women's refuges in the 1970s elevated the authority of victims' experiences and of practical action, and, on occasion, they challenged the right of academic writers and clinicians to define what they were doing and who they were. They would prefer to subordinate the cold analysis of the monograph and textbook to the authenticity of fervent testimony, and their evidence lay in narratives of pain and transcendence relayed by the victims themselves (Eastel, 1994; Plummer, 1994). Muir, the president of an Australian victims' organisation, the National Association for Loss and Grief, said quite characteristically: 'The telling of individual stories about the human experience of being a victim of crime is an attempt to give voice to an experience which cannot adequately be described through the interpretation of crime statistics' (1998: 179). In common with other primary and secondary victims of traumatic crime (Caffell, 1994; Dardenne, 2005; Ivison, 1997; Spungen, 1983), theirs were stories of suffering and fortitude, and there was a discernible shift over time away from what was thought to be the quietism and defeat of the language of victimisation. Those who had been raped, assaulted or abused were to be called survivors, not victims, and they were described as the casualties of patriarchy, not of crime commonly conceived. In their methods of accounting, they drew away from the world of crime, criminal justice, criminology and victimology.

But they (and other activists)[10] were also frequently to be found in the same spaces – the conferences, workshops and seminars – as the academic writers with whom they were in uneasy relation and whose legitimacy they questioned. At the beginning, too, they were mistrustful of men (the Women's Aid Federation of England would not allow men into their buildings, although the 'independent' refuges did otherwise). To be sure, alignments were not always uniform (members of the Canadian and American women's movement were always more pragmatic than many of their English counterparts, for example (see Gottschalk, 2006)). Neither were they unchanging over time. But a series of political and existential tensions about definition, authority, hierarchy and ownership were planted in and around victimology by feminists and others and there they remain. Consider the following excerpt from an activist text which perfectly condenses that family of core themes, and hints at the contradictions, which I have described:

> SISTERHOOD IS POWERFUL! INTERNATIONAL SISTERHOOD IS EVEN MORE POWERFUL! This slogan captures well one of the assumptions of those who organized the International Tribunal. Our struggle must not only be conducted within nations, but across national boundaries. Nations are man-made. 'I belong to No-man's land' proclaimed one of the buttons sold at the Tribunal. Unlike a traditional Tribunal there was no panel of judges at the International Tribunal on Crimes Against Women. We were all our own judges. Moreover, the women present completely rejected patriarchal definitions of crime; all man-made forms of women's oppression were seen as crimes. Most of the crimes testified about are not recognized as such by patriarchal nations ... Personal testimony was emphasized because of the belief that it is through sharing our personal experiences of oppression that we become politicized and motivated to struggle against that oppression and the societal conditions producing it, rather than by engaging in abstract theoretical debates divorced from our personal experiences.
>
> (Russell and Van de Ven, 1976: xv)

Coming from within the radical fold, the feminist challenge had legitimacy and it made its mark on radical criminology. In tandem with the new instrument of crime surveys, which I shall touch on next, it obliged some radical criminologists to trim and admit that not all mundane crime could be lightly dismissed, and that the victimisation of women should certainly be taken seriously as a political and social problem. Jones, MacLean and Young certainly remarked how there had been 'a general tendency in radical thought to idealize [its] historical subject (in this case the working class) and to play down intra-group conflict, blemishes and social disorganisation.

But the power of the feminist case resulted in a sort of cognitive schizophrenia amongst radicals' (1986: 2–3). To be sure, shibboleths remained: it proved awkward politically for those recanting authors to probe too extensively into the background of the high numbers of black women victims they had unearthed in a local crime survey, because that would have dangerously exposed the part played by the black *offenders* who were presumably their partners, but a dent had been made, and it prepared the way for what was to be called 'left realism', the newly pragmatic socialist criminology which more readily accommodated the brute facts of crime and victimisation, and inserted victims into a new conceptual contrivance, a quadrilateral of forces, that was built on the offender, informal social control, the state and, importantly, the victim (Lea and Young, 1984).

CRIME SURVEYS

The third principal source and underpinning of victimology was empirical – but no empirical inquiry is ever free of theorising. Large household surveys of victims were conducted first in the United States, in 1973,[11] in the wake of the urban riots of the 1960s (Lipsky and Olson, 1977), and they were designed principally to assist the curtailing of violence by ascertaining the extent and character of criminal victimisation (President's Crime Commission, 1967). They were followed by similar surveys in Canada in 1981 (where they were at first opportunistically presented as an exploration of trends in violence succeeding the imminent abolition of capital punishment (Rock, 1986)), the United Kingdom in 1982 (where they were at first opportunistically presented within government as a purposive way of responding to the 1981 Brixton riots, and later as a mechanism to improve what was called 'the criminal justice data base' (Rock, 1990)), and elsewhere. There were eventually to be international crime surveys in 1989, 1992, 1996–1997 and 2000 (see http://www.icpsr. umich.edu/cocoon/ICPSR/SERIES/00175.xml) which compared victimisation rates across nations and over time (Van Dijk *et al.,* 1990) and local surveys which looked intensively at crime in small areas (Anderson *et al.*, 1991; Bottoms *et al.*, 1987; Jones *et al.*, 1986; Smith, 1982).

Crime surveys chart a population sample's experience of crime over a given period, usually of a year. They are flexible instruments, adaptable to different purposes and changing in significance. In the beginning, they were a means of securing a better measure of offending, and they concentrated on the victim chiefly as a source of data closest to the crime that could act as 'an important alternative to police records' (www.homeoffice.gov.uk/rds/bcs). The authors of the first British Crime Survey reported in 1983: 'It is one thing to identify the shortcomings of statistics or recorded offences as a measure of crime, quite another to provide an alternative. Only recently has a research technique been developed with this aim in mind – the sample survey of victimisation, or "crime survey"' (Hough and Mayhew, 1983: 1). The international crime surveys were similarly prompted by 'two main reasons ... The first was the inadequacy of offences recorded by the police for comparing crime in different countries. The second was the absence of any alternative standardised measures' (http://ruljis.leidenuniv.nl/group/jfcr/www/icvs/ introduction).

But it was inevitable that crime surveys also came to yield copious information about the impact, distribution (Clarke *et al.,* 1985; Home Office, 2004a, 2004b), incidence, trends, demographics and severity of crime; victims' experiences and perceptions of crime and the criminal justice system (Home Office, 2002); their fear of crime and incivilities (Block, 1993; Garofalo, 1979); and much else. They mapped crime on a scale and in ways hitherto conceived impossible, and unaffordable by the scholar, and victimology was flooded with new data. An analytic industry was established on their back, showing, for example, how crime was massively concentrated spatially (in what became known as 'hot spots' (Pease *et al.*, 2004; Sherman *et al.*, 1989), socially and temporally (Tseloni and Pease, 2003)). Victimisation was not distributed broadly and evenly across society, but in relatively dense pockets where groups and individuals (Pease and Farrell, 1993) could expect repeatedly to be subject to burglary, theft, robbery and assault (over two-fifths of reported crime was experienced by 4 per cent of victims in England and Wales in 1994 (National Board for Crime Prevention)).

The best predictor of who might be a victim of property crime is recent victimisation (Polvi, *et al.*, 1991). The best predictor of where a property crime might take place is a home recently burgled and the homes adjacent to it (Bowers *et al.*, 2004). Crime is so concentrated that offenders, victims and witnesses could not but be recruited from very much the same populations (so that, for instance, the young men who assault young men in city centres at night are most likely to have been observed by other young men, because it was they who are out and about at that time and in those places). Crime predominantly took place within, not across, social strata, members of the working class attacking other members of the working class, the young the young, males males, minority ethnic groups minority ethnic groups, and so on. At the very epicentre, where offending was most rife, such social areas could be chaotic and confused indeed. Consider the graphic observations of one 'hot spot', life in an apartment reported by Hazel Genn 'where fights, verbal abuse, sexual assault and property theft were commonplace, and where the use of violence in the resolution of conflict was virtually automatic' (1988: 99):

> Endless streams of neighbours coming in and out. Aggression is very noticeable. There are many mock fights both between women and between men and women. There is some pride displayed in the extent to which the women are knocked about by men. During the afternoon when Kath mentioned the new bruises on her arm, a neighbour took down her trousers to reveal a sizeable bruise on her thigh ... [The next day] the women become more and more agitated and restless. They kept joking about 'feeling like a good fight', and it is easy to see how fights occur. The women are bored and become angry with the children, so that by mid-afternoon everyone is dying for something to happen.
>
> (96–97)

Those new maps of crime were to supply the second dent to radical criminology: crime was evidently not centred on attempts by offenders to secure the equitable redistribution of property between the social classes. It did not serve, as the radicals used to say, to expropriate the expropriators or to exercise class justice, but, in David Downes' words, as a 'regressive tax on the poor'. Much property crime makes the poor even poorer, and much violence makes the lot of oppressed people even more oppressive. In the wake of the first British Crime Survey, the radical criminologists Lea and Young confessed somewhat ruefully that they had believed that 'property offences are directed solely against the bourgeoisie and that violence against the person is carried out by amateur Robin Hoods in the course of their righteous attempts to redistribute wealth. All of this is, alas, untrue' (1984: 262).

Smith and Gray (1985: 124) reported of a survey in London that 'to a considerable extent the police deal with a limited clientele of people who tend to be in trouble both as victims and as offenders ... people who tend to be repeatedly victims also have a much higher chance of being arrested.' It became increasingly difficult to conceive of victims and offenders as groups entirely apart, the one innocent and the other guilty, but as members of substantially overlapping groups, no longer always a confrontation between black and white, but of 'grey versus grey' (Antilla, 1964: 8). Elias (1983: 253) remarked that in certain volatile areas, 'it becomes almost a matter of chance as to who will be the victim and who will be the offender for any particular crime, almost a matter of who strikes first. Consequently, it is difficult to clearly attribute guilt'. The moral universe of victims became a little more insecure in the academy, even though broader political, lay and activist accounts remained substantially unaffected.

ROUTINE ACTIVITIES THEORY

If victim-precipitation is recognised conventionally as the first big idea in victimology, a second is effectively an extrusion of that idea, and that is routine activities theory (or what some call life-style theory; Walklate, 1989: 6) victimologically construed, and it flowed in part out of the crime survey. There is an obvious and strong affinity between hazard-based theories and crime surveys which 'reveal that some persons may be prone to victimisation' (Gottfredson and Hindelang, 1981: 123) and which present the 'tabulation of crime data in ways that would be indicative of risk' (Gottfredson, 1981: 714).

The theory is economy itself: it predicts that crime will occur where there is a convergence in space and time of what are named 'likely offenders, suitable targets and an absence of capable guardians', and that 'the spatio-temporal organisation of society affects patterns of crime ... Strong variations in specific predatory crime rates from hour to hour, day to day [affect reporting] ... and these variations appear to correspond to the various tempos of the related legitimate activities upon which they feed' (Cohen and Felson, 1979: 588, 592).

Convergence is likely to be enabled by the increased mobility and capacity to remove goods offered by motor vehicles; by the building of roads that encourage movement and the dispersal of populations (particularly in the United States, Canada and Australia); by shifting patterns of employment that may leave homes unattended in the daytime; by the demographics of divorce, late marriage, physical longevity and small families that lead to a proliferation of single-person households with their weak guardianship; by new forms of technology which may reduce the size and increase the portability of electrical and electronic goods, and much else. Ken Pease was wont to begin public lectures by reflecting on the lack of highwaymen on freeways and motorways: technology had moved on, he would say, and with it there were companion changes in patterns of targets, criminality and exposure to victimisation. In a more cynical guise, and reverting to a form of victim-blaming, those notions of weak guardianship and what was called situational crime prevention (see Newman *et al.*, 1997), were to be recast as 'responsibilisation' whereby victims were to be obliged or entrusted by new forms of governance no longer to rely largely on the State but to protect themselves (see O'Malley and Palmer, 1996).

STUDIES OF POLICIES AND POLICY-MAKING

The campaigns waged by activists, and the discovery of new information and of new ways of thinking about crime and crime prevention have had a political impact that converged with a new politics that has sought to improve the efficiency and legitimacy of the criminal justice system by awarding victims greater centrality. Criminologists, political scientists (see Gottschalk, 2006), lawyers and sociologists have dilated upon the victim as a figure hovering on the threshold of greater participation and influence – sometimes taken to be a baneful influence (see Ashworth, 2000) – in legislation and criminal procedure. My own work has concentrated on the emergence and evolution of a politics of victims in Canada (1986) and England and Wales (1990, 1998a, 2004); and my prime interest has been in how conceptions of, and policies towards, victims have always taken shape in a larger environment of preoccupations with issues that may have had only a tangential bearing on the express needs and desires of victims themselves. Victims in these states have rarely shared the lasting collective identity or weight required to make their own mark on policy-making. They have instead been the oblique and sometimes unintended beneficiaries of other, more pressing political projects dedicated, for example, to increasing the numbers of successful prosecutions. A survey of academic work and a map of practical policy implementation in this area in England and Wales have been recently supplied by Matthew Hall (2009), and he makes it clear that the criminal justice system is still an array of loosely-coupled institutions which only remotely resembles a system, and that images of, and policies towards, victims remain correspondingly fragmented.

MISCELLANEOUS VICTIMOLOGICAL IDEAS

Victim-precipitation, feminist criminology and routine activities theory are the main home-grown constituents of a full-blown victimology. But victims have also been studied by several sociologists, psychologists and criminologists who might never choose to call themselves victimologists, knowingly contribute to the body of victimological theory, or regularly subscribe to the journals or attend the conferences of victimology.

Their writings are necessarily piecemeal. There is, first, what might be identified as standard scholarly work which alighted on victims, discovering new facts and new patterns of association, but not fully warranting or claiming the title of victimology, unless victimology includes any piece of academic writing that refers at some point to the victim. Perhaps the most recent and interesting example is what is in effect a resuscitation or rediscovery of the 'duet theory' of crime by Randall Collins, a man who would not call himself a criminologist or victimologist at all, and who, despite teaching at the university where Marvin Wolfgang once taught, makes no mentions of von Hentig or Schafer or Wolfgang's work on homicide. Following Goffman, he has written persuasively and in detail about the choreographed interplay between aggressor and victim in violent transactions. He has analysed how victims can enter into what he calls interaction ritual chains of 'emotional entrainment' whereby they can become progressively dominated, steered and incapacitated by violent offenders.

Looking, say, at episodes of domestic violence or crowd disturbance, he narrates how, step by step, people may come collaboratively to assume the roles and identities of victim and offender (2008).

Take too segments of John Braithwaite's much-cited work. It alludes to the role that can be played by victims and their supporters in mobilising sentiments of shame and animating rituals of reintegration in confrontations or 'conferences' with offenders and their supporters, and it has reawakened an interest in the potentially rehabilitative role of the victim in areas of criminology, criminal justice policy and dispute resolution. But Braithwaite's victim is a relatively minor figure who hardly occupies centre stage and it would be difficult to claim that *Crime, Shame and Reintegration* (1989) is a piece of victimology. Perhaps a better candidate would be the evaluation of RISE, a restorative justice experiment conducted in Canberra by his colleague, Heather Strang (2002), which looked squarely at victims' responses, although it was instigated, she said, somewhat as an afterthought and late in the planning of the larger project.

Restorative justice, it should be remarked, is now championed by claims that it benefits the victims, that it reduces recidivism and reduces prison numbers (see http://www.rethinking.org.nz/images/PDF/070428A%20Outline%20of%20 Conference%20Report.pdf), and that all may gain (see Braithwaite, 2002). If they *can* be persuaded to participate, and that may not be an easy task, victims do tend to report that they welcome an opportunity to be heard and that they feel less fearful of offenders whom they may demonise less frequently (see Miers *et al.*, 2001; Sherman and Strang, 2007).

Another instance would be the influential study of Shapland and her colleagues of the passage of victims of violence through the criminal justice system (1985), in which they reported a decaying satisfaction with police responses, a hunger for information and control, an interest in monetary compensation that was far outweighed by a yearning for symbolic recognition and acknowledgement, and an experience of their vicissitudes in the criminal justice as, in effect, a form of 'secondary victimisation'. The reiterated complaint made by victims after cross-examination in court was that they were themselves made to feel on trial, as if they were the wrongdoer. After all, lawyers in the adversarial system do indeed tend to subject witnesses to identical techniques of questioning, irrespective of whether they testify on behalf of the prosecution or the defence, in the hope that they will expose (or be seen trying to expose) flaws of memory, inconsistencies of testimony, and defects of character (Rock, 1993).

Another instance would be Maguire and Bennett's study of burglary (1982), which was conceived initially as a study of crime and criminals, but whose chapters on victims and the impact of crime were to create more of a stir because it had hitherto been supposed that trauma and trauma-like reactions stemmed only from the graver forms of violent crime (Waller and Okihiro, 1978). Burglary, it appeared, can (but does not inevitably) generate many of the same experiences of invasion and defilement as crimes against the person. Significant numbers of victims were distressed, and distressed for long periods. Some, indeed, were so upset by the knowledge that an outsider had entered their home and rifled through their possessions that they never returned (Maguire, 1980). Crimes against property, it appeared, can be experienced as a form of pollution and may not actually be so very different in some of their consequences from other crime.

A final example would be Morgan and Zedner's work (1992) uncovering the extent of anguish suffered by child victims at first and second hand, victims who, as witnesses and household members, had often previously been overlooked unless it was as the direct and obvious target of abuse or violence. Children tend to be mute bystanders, all too readily overshadowed, but they could be as discomfited as any by mundane crime such as burglary. Morgan and Zedner's research was one of the first of a number of empirical studies that began to map formerly unexplored victim populations (for a more recent summary of work on child victimisation, see Finkelhor *et al.*, 2005). Running in tandem to their book, there was, for instance, research on racist (Bowling, 1998; Sampson and Phillips, 1992) and 'homophobic' crime, and crimes against the elderly and the disabled, and the population of known victims began to grow ever more crowded, possibly, indeed, overcrowded (see Sykes, 1992), as they became swollen with groups newly identified or clamouring for recognition. It became evident that fresh groups of victims were continually emerging or being invented (Pendergast, 1997); that generalisation was becoming more fraught; and that definitions and boundaries were unstable and eagerly disputed, with prizes to be won in the competitive world of 'identity politics' (Jacobs and Potter, 1998).

Clearly at stake are questions of recognition, compensation, exculpation and much else. It seemed that there were not only 'primary' victims, the immediate casualities of crime, but 'secondary' victims, who had a family connection with those casualties; and others more distant still.[12] Debates about eligibility could become quite heated. Were the police officers, court staff, jurors (Robertson *et al.*, 2009), medical and paramedical staff who responded to traumatic incidents to be called 'tertiary victims'? Were the families of those killed in homicides or in traffic 'accidents'? Who was to count as family? And what of the families of serious offenders, some of whom laid claim to the title of 'the other victims of crime'? (Rock, 1998b). Might not whole communities be victimised as a result of a serious crime such as mass or serial murder? (Newman, 2004). Most contentious of all was the proposal contained in the 2009 *Report of the Consultative Group on the Past* that the families of paramilitaries who had been killed in the Northern Ireland 'troubles' should be compensated uniformly and without judgement (see http://www.cgpni.org/fs/doc/Consultative%20Group%20on%20the%20Past%20Full%20Report.pdf).

Holstein and Miller reflected that:

> 'victim' is a categorisation device ... an interpretive framework ... that provides a set of instructions for understanding social relations ... As an act of interpretive reality construction, victimisation unobtrusively advises others in how they should understand persons, circumstances, and behaviors under consideration.
>
> (1990: 105, 107)

And those social relations and that framework are not fixed but emergent and contested, and they may well be anything but unobtrusive.

OPPORTUNISTIC WORK

There was to be yet one more tier of incidental work that was the outcome of encounters between victimology, criminology and sociology. Sprey (1979: 255) said of one collection of papers that it 'fails to suggest even a semblance of order or generality ... the overall picture ... remains confused ... the reader is confronted with a large number of rather loosely related papers in which, with very few exceptions, the focus simply has been shifted from the criminal to the victim.' And it is to that mode of theorising which I shall now finally turn.

Criminology has made occasional use of victims and victimology to develop points about questions lying more squarely in its heartland. It was in that sense that victims have been described instrumentally as failures of crime prevention (Block remarked, for example, that 'the study of victims of crime is most importantly the study of the failure of crime prevention by citizenry and by the police and secondarily the study of the active participation and precipitation of criminal events by their victims' (1981: 761)). They have been construed as checks on the adequacy of official, recorded crime statistics ('Citizens', it has been said, 'decide whether or not to invoke the law in the first instance ... The best available data for the systematic study of this most important juncture in the application of criminal law (and of the forces driving its application) are victimisation surveys' (Gottfredson and Hindelang, 1981: 118, 119)). They offer, by extension, opportunities to promote the better measurement of vulnerability to crime, propensities to report crime, and trends in crime data over time. Those are all interesting enough areas, but it is not clear that they should be classified under the heading of victimology.

A final variation on that theme has been the effective transposition of criminals and victims in the analysis of familiar criminological questions. There has, for instance, been a modest interest in the growth of victims' movements and campaigns but it has sometimes been lodged in a stock criminological frame (see Davies *et al.*, 2003: 4). Take Boutellier (2000), who represents the new focus simply as part of a demagogic politics of reaction in which victims are no more than a pretext for class oppression. His is standard radical criminology in a new guise. Take Elias' *The Politics of Victimisation* (1986), which again elaborated established radical arguments about the need to supplant ruling class-generated, state-based categories of crime and insert in their place a list of broad structural and human rights abuses, including inequality, alienation, competition, bureaucracy and violence, that victimise the powerless. The book is of interest, but it tends merely to offer the standard arguments of radical criminology in a new key.

CONCLUSION

Intellectual perspectives on victimisation have succeeded in introducing the victim into criminological analysis, filling a central void; they have promoted the idea that crime is processual, emergent and interactive, although that is an idea besmirched by the murky origins of victim-precipitation and only recently redeemed by Randall Collins' work; they have illuminated the negotiated and contested character of claims to victim status, showing, obliquely, that those claims are sometimes resisted; they make it clear that there is no straightforward or transparent connection between victimisation and the fear of crime, or between types of crime and their impact on different groups; they show how crime is massively concentrated in time, space and society; they have underscored how sharp moral, political and existential separations between victim and offender may not always be empirically defensible; they have exposed the hazards of generalising and imputing stereotypical traits to victims; and they have pointed to the manner in which exposure to the criminal justice system may exacerbate victimisation and encourage what some call 'secondary victimisation'. We have moved far away from simple stereotypes of vulnerability and victimisation, away from the little old lady who represented Christie's 'ideal victim' (1986), and towards a more nuanced appreciation of crime and its effects. We have also, in effect, come to appreciate more intelligently what theoretical perspectives on victimisation cannot and do not reveal, and that is helpful indeed. But beyond that it would be difficult not to conclude that victimology is simply another *rendez-vous* sub-discipline where different approaches meet around an empirical area and share as a common denominator the word 'victim' (Levine, 1978). Consider two self-critical observations made in the formative days of the sub-discipline. The first was framed as the conclusions of a conference, the International Study Institute on Victimology held in Bellagio in 1976 (604):

> so far it can only be stated that the universe of events that have some probability of being defined as victimizing, conceptually define the parameters of victimology. Beyond this admittedly circular definition, little consensus has emerged.

The other was culled from the prospectus for the World Society of Victimology, also drafted in the 1970s:

> From its beginning, victimology has been an international and an interdisciplinary subject. The need for information about the victim's contribution to the commission of crime, the offender–victim relationship, the victim's vulnerability and recidivism, the victim's role in the criminal justice system, the potential victim's fear of crime and attitudes towards legislation and law enforcement stimulated victimological research throughout the world.

If victimology is somewhat ragged and incoherent, if it has not succeeded in being unified theoretically, it can never the less lay claim to an important achievement, and that is that we are now obliged to look much more cautiously at our stock of academic, moral and political ideas about the world of crime, deviance and control. It has become a little more difficult to think merely in terms of discrete groups of good guys and bad guys, white hats and bad hats, virtuous citizens and predatory offenders.

ACKNOWLEDGEMENTS

I am grateful to Meredith Rossner and Heather Strang for reading and commenting an earlier draft of this chapter.

NOTES

*This is a modified version of a chapter which originally appeared as 'Theories of victimisation', in S. Walklate (ed.); *A Handbook of Victimology*, Willan, Devon, 2007.

1 There are exceptions. Robert Elias, for instance, claimed that victimology has sought to build a scientific discipline substantially defining and framing the aspect of society it wishes to study, by devising a set of specific question, and some general theories, and by developing scientific methodologies' (1986: 21). But the poverty of victimological theory is a reiterated complaint. Adler (1979: 266), reviewing a special issue of the journal *Victimology*, remarks: 'The lack of attention to theory building is a weakness both of this collection of articles and of the literature in this area as a whole.' Very similarly, Silverman (1988: 214) asserts: 'I find it difficult to take victimology seriously as a sub-discipline, since it offers no unique theory or methodology.' And Meisenhelder (1980: 586) says in yet another review of a victimological compendium, 'There is ... one serious defect – the essay fails to address the glaring need for serious theoretical work in the area of victimology ... papers are almost totally devoid of theoretical content.'

2 Consider the tone and burden of the following statement by Stuart Hall and his associates: mugging 'has – when accompanied by violence – sometimes resulted in serious physical and emotional consequences for its victims, many of whom are old or unable to cope with the shock of the encounter, and few of whom have very much of the world's wealth at their command. This is not a pretty social development to contemplate ... [But] [o]ur argument is simply not conducted within [an] individual frame of reference, or within the given, common-sense calculus of individual praise or blame. To blame the actions of individuals within a given historical structure, without taking that structure itself into account, is an easy and familiar way of exercising the moral conscience without bearing any of its costs. It is the last refuge of liberalism' (Hall *et al.*, 1978: 181–182, emphasis in original).

3 Elsewhere he states 'The interests and feelings of victims – actual victims, victims' families, potential victims, the projected figure of "the victim" are now routinely invoked in support of measures of punitive segregation' (Garland, 1996: 445).

4 Robert Elias (1986: 17) names Mendelsohn as the founder of victimology.

5 Sandra Walklate (1989) locates the beginnings of victimology in H. Von Hentig's *The Victim and His Criminal* (1948). For an early reference of Von Hentig to the importance of the victim, see Von Hentig (1940).

6 Lucia Zedner (2002: 420) claims that the progenitor of victimology was Wertham, who, she says, invented the word in 1949 in *The Show of Violence*.

7 Charles Goring (1919: 16), the man appointed eventually by the Prison Commissioners to assess Lombroso's anthropometric claims, concluded that Lombroso worked 'not by methods of disinterested investigation, but, rather, by a leap of the imagination, the notion thus reached then forming the basis upon which he conducted his researches, and constructed his theory – the whole fabric of the Lombrosian doctrine, judged by the standards of science, is fundamentally unsound.' Mannheim (1965: 215) said that Lombroso's 'style and his basic approach ... were often highly intuitive, not to say fanciful. While imagination and inspiration are truly indispensable elements of scientific research, the flashes of insight have to be rigidly controlled to guard against the dangers that unconscious bias may lead to imaginary discoveries not borne out by the facts.'

8 Those who may eventually be identified as victims of homicide do not necessarily die immediately. Under the so-called 'year and a day rule' rule, for instance, it was sufficient in England and Wales that a person died within a specified time to become eligible as a murder victim. Presumably, a number of such people could be amenable to interview.

9 Although it should be noted that the frequency and severity of their injuries seemed less than that of women.

10 For instance, the Australasian Society of Victimology was founded in 1988 by victims' organisations that were themselves largely the creation of people who had been traumatised by serious crimes such as murder (see Robinson, 2004: 64).

11 Although the British General Household Survey of 1972 (OPCS, 1972) did contain a question about experience of burglary.

12 For example, the Victims of Crime Review Report 3 disseminated by the Government of South Australia (Justice Strategy Unit, 2000) recommended that the definition of a victim contained in the Criminal Injuries Compensation Act 1978 should be repealed and replaced by three categories: primary, secondary and related.

PAUL ROCK

REFERENCES

Adamson, M., Briskin, L. and McPhail, M. (1988) *Feminist Organizing for Change*. Toronto: Oxford
University Press.
Adler, E. (1979) Review of victimology: Special issue on spouse abuse and domestic violence,
Contemporary Sociology, 8(2): 266–267.
Amir, M. (1967) Victim precipitated forcible rape, *Journal of Criminal Law, Criminology, and Police
Science*, 58(4): 493–502.
Amir, M. (1971) *Patterns in Forcible Rape*. Chicago: University of Chicago Press.
Anderson, S., Kinsey, R., Loader, I. and Smith, C. (1991) *'Cautionary Tales': A Study of Young People
in Edinburgh*. Edinburgh: Centre for Criminology.
Antilla, I. (1964) Victimology – A new territory in criminology, *Scandinavian Studies in Criminology*,
5: 7–10.
Ashworth, A. (2000) Victims' rights, defendants' rights and criminal procedure, in A. Crawford and
J. Goodey (eds), *Integrating a Victim Perspective Within Criminal Justice*. Aldershot: Ashgate Dartmouth.
Avison, N. (1973) Victims of homicide, in I. Drapkin and E. Viano (eds), *Victimology: A New Focus*,
Lexington, MA: Lexington Books.
Becker, C. (1981) Criminal Theories of Causation and Victims' Contributions to the Etiology of Crime,
PhD thesis, University of Cambridge.
Becker, H. (1963) *Outsiders*. New York: Free Press.
Blackstone, W. (1769) *Commentaries on the Laws of England*, Book 4. Oxford: Clarendon Press,
Block, R. (1981) Victim-offender dynamics in violent crime, *Journal of Criminal Law and Criminology*,
72(2): 743–761.
Block, R. (1993) A cross-national comparison of victims of crime: victim surveys of twelve countries,
International Review of Victimology, 2: 183–207.
Bottoms, A., Mawby, R. and Walker, M. (1987) A localised crime survey in contrasting areas of a city,
British Journal of Criminology, 27(2): 125–154.
Bourgois, P. (1996) In search of masculinity: Violence, respect and sexuality among Puerto Rican crack
dealers in East Harlem, *British Journal of Criminology*, 36: 412–427.
Boutellier, H. (2000) *Crime and Morality: The Significance of Criminal Justice in Post-Modern Culture*.
Dordrecht: Kluwer Academic.
Bowers, K., Johnson, S. and Pease, K. (2004) Prospective hot-spotting: The future of crime mapping?,
British Journal of Criminology, 44: 641–658.
Bowling, B. (1998) *Violent Racism: Victimisation, Policing, and Social Control*. Oxford: Clarendon Press.
Box, S. (1983) *Power, Crime, and Mystification*. London: Routledge.
Braithwaite, J. (1989) *Crime, Shame and Reintegration*. Cambridge: Cambridge University Press.
Braithwaite, J. (2002) *Restorative Justice and Responsive Regulation*. New York: Oxford University Press.
Brownmiller, S. (1977) *Against Our Will: Men, Women and Rape*. Harmondsworth: Penguin.
Caffell, C. (1994) *In Search of the Rainbow's End: A Father's Story*. London: Hodder and Stoughton.
Carlen, P. (ed.) (1985) *Criminal Women: Some Autobiographical Accounts*. Cambridge: Polity Press.
Carlen, P. (1988) *Women, Crime and Poverty*. Milton Keynes: Open University Press.
Christie, N. (1977) Conflicts as property, *British Journal of Criminology*, 17: 1–15.
Christie, N. (1986) The ideal victim, in E. Fattah (ed.) *From Crime Policy to Victim Policy*. Basingstoke:
Macmillan, pp. 17–30.
Clark, L. and Lewis, D. (1977) *Rape: The Price of Coercive Sexuality*. Toronto: Women's Press.
Clarke, R., Ekblom, P., Hough, M. and Mayhew, P. (1985) Elderly victims of crime and exposure to risk,
British Journal of Criminology, 24(1): 1–9.
Cohen, L. and Felson, M. (1979) Social change and crime rates trends: A routine activity approach,
American Sociological Review, 44: 588–608.
Cohen, S. (1979) Guilt, justice and tolerance, in D. Downes and P. Rock (eds), *Deviant Interpretations*.
Oxford: Martin Robertson.

Cohen, S. (2002) *Folk Devils and Moral Panics*, 3rd edn. New York: Routledge.

Cohen, S. and Taylor, L. (1976) *Escape Attempts: The Theory and Practice of Resistance to Everyday Life*. London: Allen Lane.

Collins, R. (2008) *Violence: A Micro-Sociological Theory*. Princeton: Princeton University Press.

Crime and Justice Associates (1982) *The Iron Fist and the Velvet Glove: An Analysis of the U.S. Police*. San Francisco: Synthesis Publications.

Daly, K. (1994) Men's violence, victim advocacy, and feminist redress: Comment, *Law and Society Review*, 28(4): 777–86.

Dardenne, S. (2005) *I Choose to Live*, London: Virago.

Davies, P., Francis, P. and Jupp, V. (2003) Understanding victimisation: Theory, research and policy, in P. Davies, P. Francis and V. Jupp (eds), *Victimisation: Theory, Research and Policy*. Basingstoke: Palgrave Macmillan.

Davis, M. (1971) That's interesting! towards a phenomenology of sociology and a sociology of phenomenology, *Philosophy of the Social Sciences*, 1: 309–344.

Dignan, J. (2005) *Understanding Victims and Restorative Justice*. Maidenhead: Open University Press.

Doerner, W. and Lab, S. (1995) *Victimology*. Cincinnati, OH: Anderson Publishing.

Douglas, J. and Waksler, F. (1982) *The Sociology of Deviance: An Introduction*. Boston: Little, Brown and Co.

Douglas, M. (1966) *Purity and Danger*. London: Routledge and Kegan Paul.

Eastel, P. (1994) *Voices of the Survivors*. Melbourne: Spinifex.

Elias, R. (1983) *Victims of the System*. New Brunswick, NJ: Transaction.

Elias, R. (1986) *The Politics of Victimisation*, New York: Oxford University Press.

Erikson, K. (1966) *Wayward Puritans*. New York: John Wiley.

Fattah, E. (1979) Some recent theoretical developments in victimology, *Victimology*, 4(2): 198–213.

Fattah, E. (2000) Victimology past, present and future, *Criminologie*, 33(1): 17–46.

Finkelhor, D., Ormrod, R., Turner, H. and Hamby, A. (2005) The victimisation of children and youth: A comprehensive national survey, *Child Maltreatment*, 10(1): 5–25.

Foucault, M. (1979) *Discipline and Punish*. Harmondsworth: Penguin.

Garland, D. (1996) The limits of the sovereign state: strategies of crime control in contemporary society, *British Journal of Criminology*, 36(4): 445–471.

Garland, D. (2000) The culture of high crime societies, *British Journal of Criminology*, 40(3): 347–375.

Garland, D. (2001) *The Culture of Control*. Oxford: Oxford University Press.

Garofalo, J. (1979) Victimisation and the fear of crime, Journal of *Research in Crime and Delinquency*: 80–104.

Gelsthorpe, L. and Morris, A. (eds) (1990) *Feminist Perspectives in Criminology*. Milton Keynes: Open University Press.

General Council of the Bar (2005) *Response by the General Council of the Bar to the Consultation Paper Hearing the Relatives of Murder and Manslaughter Victims'*, London.

Genn, H. (1988) Multiple victimisation, in M. Maguire and J. Pointing (eds), *Victims of Crime*. Milton Keynes: Open University Press.

Goring, C. (1919) *The English Convict*. London: HMSO.

Gottfredson, M. (1981) On the etiology of criminal victimisation, *Journal of Criminal Law and Criminology*, 72(2): 714–726.

Gottfredson, M. and Hindelang, M. (1981) Sociological aspects of criminal victimisation, *Annual Review of Sociology*, 7: 107–128.

Gottschalk, M. (2006) *The Prison and the Gallows*, Cambridge: Cambridge University Press

Grady, A. (2002) Female-on-male domestic abuse: Uncommon or ignored?, in C. Hoyle and R. Young (eds), *New Visions of Crime Victims*. Oxford: Hart Publishing.

Hall, M. (2009) *Victims of Crime: Policy and Practice in Criminal Justice*. Cullompton: Willan.

Hall, S., Critcher, C., Jefferson, T. and Clarke, J. (1978) *Policing the Crisis*. London: Macmillan.

Hillyard, P., Sim, J. and Tombs, S. (2004) Leaving a stain upon the silence: Contemporary criminology and the politics of dissent, *British Journal of Criminology*, 44: 369–390.

Hirst, P. (1975) Marx and Engels on law, crime and morality, in I. Taylor, P. Walton and J. Young (eds), *Critical Criminology*. London: Routledge and Kegan Paul.

Hobsbawm, E. (1971) *Primitive Rebels*. Manchester: Manchester University Press.

Hollander, J. (2001) Vulnerability and dangerousness: The construction of gender through conversation about violence, *Gender and Society*, 15(1): 83–109.

Holstein, J. and Miller, G. (1990) Rethinking victimisation: An interactional approach to victimology, *Symbolic Interaction*, 13(1): 103–122.

Home Office (2002) *Crime, Policing and Justice: The Experience of Older People: Findings from the British Crime Survey, Statistical Bulletin 8/02*. London: Home Office.

Home Office (2004a) *Violence at Work: Findings from the 2002/2003 British Crime Survey, Home Office Online Report 4/04*. London: Home Office.

Home Office (2004b) *Ethnicity, Victimisation and Worry about Crime: Findings from the 2001/02 and 2002/03 British Crime Surveys*, Home Office Research Findings 237. London: Home Office.

Hooks, B. (1982) *Ain't I a Woman: Black Women and Feminism*. London: Pluto Press.

Hough, M. and Mayhew, P. (1983) *The British Crime Survey: First Report*. London: HMSO.

Hough, M. and Roberts, J. (1998) *Attitudes to Punishment: Findings from the British Crime Survey*. London: Home Office.

International Study Institute on Victimology (1976) Conclusions and recommendations, in E. Viano (ed.), *Victims and Society*. Washington: Visage Press.

Ivison, I. (1997) *Fiona's Story*. London: Virago.

Jacobs, J. and Potter, K. (1998) *Hate Crimes: Criminal Law and Identity Politics*. New York: Oxford University Press.

Jones, T., MacLean, B. and Young, J. (1986) *The Islington Crime Survey: Victimisation and Policing in Inner-City London*. Aldershot: Gower.

Justice Strategy Unit (2000) *Review on Victims of Crime: Report 3*. Adelaide: Government of South Australia.

Kurz, D. (1989) Social science perspectives on wife abuse, *Gender and Society*, 3(4): 489–505.

Lamb, S. (1996) *The Trouble with Blaming*, Cambridge, MA: Harvard University Press.

Lea, J. and Young, J. (1984) *What is to be Done about Law and Order?* London: Penguin.

Lemert, E. (1951) *Social Pathology*. New York; McGraw-Hill.

Lerner, M. (1980) *The Belief in a Just World: A Fundamental Delusion*. London: Plenum Press.

Levine, K. (1978) Empiricism in victimological research, *Victimology*, 3: 1–2.

Lipsky, M. and Olson, D. (1977) *Commission Politics: The Processing of Racial Crisis in America*. New Brunswick, NJ: Transaction.

Lotz, R. (1975) Review of Menachem Amir. Patterns in forcible rape, in *Contemporary Sociology*, 4(4): 381–382.

Luckenbill, D. (1977) Criminal homicide as a situated transaction, Social Problems, 75(2): 176–186.

Madriz, E. (1997) Images of criminals and victims: A study on women's fear and social control, *Gender and Society*, 11(3): 342–356.

Maguire, M. (1980) The impact of burglary upon victims, *British Journal of Criminology*, 20: 261–275.

Maguire, M. (1991) The needs and rights of victims of crime, *Crime and Justice*, 14: 363–433.

Maguire, M. and Bennett, T. (1982) *Burglary in a Dwelling*. London: Heinemann.

Marshall, G. (1994) *Oxford Concise Dictionary of Sociology*. Oxford, Oxford University Press.

Mathiesen, T. (1974) *The Politics of Abolition*. London: Martin Robertson.

Matravers, A. (2000) Justifying the Unjustifiable: Stories of Women Sex Offenders, PhD thesis, University of Cambridge.

Matza, D. (1964) *Delinquency and Drift*. New York: John Wiley.

Matza, D. (1969) *Becoming Deviant*. Englewood Cliffs, NJ: Prentice Hall.

Meier, R. and Miethe, T. (1993) Understanding theories of criminal victimisation, *Crime and Justice*, 17: 459–499.

Meisenhelder, T. (1980) Review of W. Parsonage (ed.), Perspectives on victimology, *Social Forces*, 59(2) 586–587.

Mendelsohn, B. (1963) The origin of the doctrine of victimology, *Excerpta Criminologica*, 3: 239–245.

Miers, D. *et al.* (2001) *An Exploratory Study of Restorative Justice Schemes.* London: Home Office.

Mirrlees-Black, C. (1999) *Domestic Violence: Findings from a New British Crime Survey Self-Completion Questionnaire.* London: Home Office.

Morgan, J. and Zedner, L. (1992) *Child Victims: Crime, Impact, and Criminal Justice.* Oxford: Clarendon Press.

Muir, H. (1998) Voices of victims of crime – The wounded storytellers, in B. Giuliano (ed.), *Survival and Beyond.* Curtin, ACT: National Association for Loss and Grief.

National Board for Crime Prevention (1994) *Wise After the Event: Tackling Repeat Victimisation.* London: Home Office.

Newburn, T. and Stanko, E. (eds) (1994) *Just Boys Doing Business?:* Men, Masculinities and Crime. London: Routledge.

Newman, G., Clarke, R. and Shoham, S. (eds) (1997) *Rational Choice and Situational Crime Prevention.* Aldershot: Ashgate.

Newman, K. (2004) *Rampage: The Social Roots of School Shootings*, New York, N.Y.: Basic Books.

Oakley, A. (1981) Interviewing women: A contradiction in terms, in H. Roberts (ed.), *Doing Feminist Research.* London: Routledge and Kegan Paul.

O'Malley, P. and Palmer, D. (1996) Post-Keynesian policing, *Economy and Society*, 25(2): 137–155.

OPCS (1972) *General Household Survey.* London: Office of Population Censuses and Surveys.

Pagelow, M. (1981) Review of R. Dobash and R. Dobash, Violence against wives: a case against the patriarchy *American Journal of Sociology*, 86(6): 1475–1476.

Pearce, F. (1976) *Crimes of the Powerful: Marxism, Crime and Deviance.* London: Pluto Press.

Pease, K. and Farrell, G. (1993) *Once Bitten, Twice Shy: Repeat Victimisation and its Implications for Crime Prevention*, Home Office Crime Prevention Unit 46. London: Home Office.

Pease, K., Bowers, K. and Johnson, S. (2004) Prospective hot-spotting: The future of crime mapping?, *British Journal of Criminology*, 44(5): 641–658.

Pendergast, M. (1997) *Victims of Memory: Incest Accusations and Shattered Lives.* London: Harper Collins.

Plummer, K. (1994) *Telling Sexual Stories: Power, Change and Social Worlds.* London: Routledge.

Polk, K. (1994) *When Men Kill.* Cambridge: Cambridge University Press.

Polvi, N., Looman, T., Humphries, C. and Pease, K. (1991) The time course of repeat burglary victimisation, *British Journal of Criminology*, 31: 411–414.

Porterfield, A. and Talbert, R. (1954) *Mid-Century Crime in Our Culture.* Fort Worth, TX: Leo Potishman Foundation.

President's Crime Commission (1967) *The Challenge of Crime in a Free Society.* Washington, DC: US Government Printing Office.

Reiman, J. (2003) *The Rich get Richer and the Poor get Prison.* Boston, MA: Allyn and Bacon.

Reiss, A. (1981) Foreword: Towards a revitalisation of theory and research on victimisation by crime, *Journal of Criminal Law and Criminology*, 72(2): 704–713.

Robertson, N., Davies, G. and Nettleingham, A. (2009) Vicarious traumatisation as a consequence of jury service, *The Howard Journal*, 48: 1–12.

Robinson, J. (2004) *Crime: It Can Happen to You.* Kent Town, SA: Wakefield Press.

Rock, P. (1986) *A View from the Shadows: The Ministry of the Solicitor General of Canada and the Justice for Victims of Crime Initiative.* Oxford: Clarendon Press.

Rock, P. (1990) *Helping Victims of Crime: The Home Office and the Rise of Victim Support in England and Wales.* Oxford: Clarendon Press.

Rock, P. (1993) *The Social World of an English Crown Court.* Oxford: Clarendon Press.

Rock, P. (1998a) *After Homicide.* Oxford: Clarendon Press.

Rock, P. (1998b) Murderers, victims and survivors: The social construction of deviance, *British Journal of Criminology*, 38: 185–200.

Rock, P. (forthcoming) Hearing victims of crime: The delivery of impact statements as ritual behaviour in four London trials for murder and manslaughter, in A. Bottoms and J. Roberts (eds), *Victims in the Criminal Justice System*, Willan.

Rolph, C. (1958) Wild justice, *New Statesman*, 18 January.

Russell, D. and Van de Ven, N. (eds) (1976) *Crimes Against Women: Proceedings of the International Tribunal*. Millbrae, CA: Les Femmes.

Sagarin, E. (1975) *Deviants and Deviance*. New York: Praeger.

Said, E. (1995) *Orientalism*, Harmondsworth: Penguin.

Sampson, A. and Phillips, C. (1992) *Multiple Victimisation: Racial Attacks on an East London Estate*. London: Home Office Police Department.

Schafer, S. (1968) *The Victim and His Criminal: A Study in Functional Responsibility*. New York: Random House.

Schur, E. (1965) *Crimes without Victims*. Englewood Cliffs, NJ: PrenticeHall.

Schur, E. (1973) *Radical Nonintervention: Rethinking the Delinquency Problem*. Englewood Cliffs, NJ: PrenticeHall.

Schur, E. (1974) The case for abolition, in E. Schur and H. Bedau (eds), *Victimless Crimes*. Englewood Cliffs, NJ: PrenticeHall.

Schwendinger, H. and Schwendinger, J. (1970) Defenders of order or guardians of human rights?, *Issues in Criminology*, 5: 123–157.

Sebba, L. (1982) The victim's role in the penal process, *American Journal of Comparative Law*, 30(2): 217–240.

Select Committee on Public Prosecutors (1855) *Report*. London: House of Commons.

Shapland, J., Willmore, J. and Duff, P. (1985) *Victims in the Criminal Justice System*. Aldershot: Gower.

Shaw, M. (1995) Conceptualising violence by women, in R. Dobash, R. Dobash and L. Noaks (eds), *Gender and Crime*. Cardiff: University of Wales Press.

Sherman, L. and Strang, H. (2007) *Restorative Justice: The Evidence*, London: The Smith Institute.

Sherman, L., Gartin, P. and Buerger, M. (1989) Hot spots of predatory crime. *Criminology*, 27: 27–55.

Silverman, R. (1988) Review of R. Elias, The politics of victimisation: Victims, victimology, and human rights, *Contemporary Sociology*, 17: 2.

Smart, C. (1977) *Women, Crime and Criminology: A Feminist Critique*. London: Routledge and Kegan Paul.

Smart, C. (1989) *Feminism and the Power of Law*. London: Routledge.

Smith, D. and Gray, J. (1985) *Police and People in London: The PSI Report*, Vol. 1. Aldershot: Gower.

Smith, S. (1982) Victimisation in the inner city, *British Journal of Criminology*, 22(2): 386–402.

Sprey, J. (1979) Review of E. Viano (ed.): Victims and society, *Contemporary Sociology*, 8(2): 255.

Spungen, D. (1993) *And I Don't Want to Live this Life*. New York: Villard Books.

Stanko, E. (1990) *Everyday Violence: How Women and Men Experience Sexual and Physical Danger*. London: Pandora.

Stephens, J. (1976) *Loners, Losers, and Lovers: Elderly Tenants in a Slum Hotel*. Seattle, WA: University of Washington Press.

Strang, H. (2002) *Repair or Revenge: Victims and Restorative Justice*. Oxford: Clarendon Press.

Sumner, C. (ed.) (1990) *Censure, Politics and Criminal Justice*. Milton Keynes: Open University Press.

Sutherland, E. and Cressey, D. (1970) *Principles of Criminology*. Philadelphia, PA: J. B. Lippincott.

Sykes, C. (1992) *A Nation of Victims: The Decay of the American Character*. New York: St Martin's Press.

Taylor, I., Walton, P. and Young, J. (1973) *The New Criminology*. London: Routledge and Kegan Paul.

Tseloni, A. and Pease, K. (2003) Repeat personal victimisation, *British Journal of Criminology*. 43: 196–212.

Van Dijk, J., Mayhew, P. and Killias, M. (1990) *Experiences of Crime Across the World*. Deventer: Kluwer Law and Taxation Publishers.

Von Hentig, H. (1940) Remarks on the interaction of perpetrator and victim, *Journal of Criminal Law and Criminology*, 31: 303–309.

Von Hentig, H. (1948) *The Criminal and His Victim*. Hamden, CT: Archon Books.

Walklate, S. (1989) *Victimology: The Victim and the Criminal Justice Process*. London: Unwin Hyman.

Walklate, S. (2000) Researching victims, in R. King and E. Wincup (eds), *Doing Research on Crime and Justice*. Oxford: Oxford University Press.

Waller, I. and Okihiro, N. (1978) *Burglary: The Victim and the Public*. Toronto: University of Toronto Press.

Wertham, F. (1949) *The Show of Violence*. New York: Vintage.

Wolfgang, M. (1957) Victim-precipitated criminal homicide, *Journal of Criminal Law, Criminology and Police Science*, 48(1): 1–11.

Wolfgang, M. (1958) *Patterns in Criminal Homicide*. Philadelphia: University of Pennsylvania Press.

Wright, R. (1995) Women as victims and as resisters: Depictions of the oppression of women in criminology textbooks, *Teaching Sociology*, 23(2): 111–121.

Young, J. (2007) *The Vertigo of Late Modernity*, Thousand Oaks, California: Sage

Zedner, L. (2002) Victims, in M. Maguire, R. Morgan and R. Reiner (eds), *The Oxford Handbook of Criminology*, 3rd edn. Oxford: Oxford University Press.

FURTHER READING

Fattah, E. (1991) *Understanding Criminal Victimisation*. Scarborough, Ontario: Prentice Hall.

Hoyle, C. and Young, R. (eds) (2002) *New Visions of Crime Victims*. Oxford: Hart Publishing.

Zedner, L. (2002) Victims in M. Maguire, R. Morgan and R. Reiner (eds), *Oxford Handbook of Criminology*. Oxford: Oxford University Press.

25

News Media Criminology

Chris Greer

INTRODUCTION

The news media are a defining feature of the crime and justice landscape. Especially today in a globalised context of hyper-mediatisation and high crime consciousness, news media representations are key indicators of the nature and extent of crime, the appropriateness and efficacy of criminal justice, and the wider state of the nation. Yet serious attention to news media within criminology has historically been patchy and recently appears alarmingly to have dropped off the radar. This chapter discusses the major theoretical issues and debates that have shaped what might loosely be termed news media criminology in Britain. It identifies key interventions, situating them both theoretically and chronologically in order to document the development of the field. What becomes apparent is just how few of the definitive interventions have come from within criminology. From its origins in the 1960s, the *field* of news media criminology was characterised by prolific and engaged research and a voracious interdisciplinarity that cut across the emerging areas of critical criminology, sociology of mass communications, media studies and cultural studies. Today, only research on content abounds and, as criminology has made the transition from *field* to *discipline*, that original enthusiasm for interdisciplinarity has been replaced with disciplinisation and self-referentialism.

For the purposes of discussion, the theoretical history is divided into two broad categories corresponding with two broad time periods: Marxist and Post-Marxist. The period of Marxist interventions – roughly from the 1960s to the 1980s – has been characterised by theoretical homogeneity and fragmentation. There were debates and conflicts within Marxism, and a wider context of theoretical pluralism within criminology. But the overriding concern shared across studies on news media, crime and justice was the reproduction of 'dominant ideology' and, though it was not always articulated in these terms, the legitimation of the 'Authoritarian State'. The question was not *whether* Marxism, but *which* Marxism. The Post-Marxist period, in contrast, has been characterised by theoretical diversity and fragmentation. There were direct challenges to Marxist readings from within, and the expansion of traditional class-based notions of 'dominant ideology' to embrace gender and ethnicity.

But this period has also seen the emergence of new frameworks for understanding crime news that seek to move beyond the reproduction of 'dominant ideology' as the paradigmatic concern.

The first part of this chapter focuses on the Marxist and Post-Marxist theoretical perspectives that have shaped the field of news media criminology in Britain, bearing in mind that the most influential studies have not all been British. The second part explores some of the key theoretical concepts that have remained central to research on news media, crime and justice – newsworthiness, fear of crime and moral panic. The final part discusses current dilemmas in theory and research and suggests that new intellectual resources are needed to engage with the rapid, intersecting transformations in the crime, justice and media environments. In closing, I point to some areas that might benefit from further theoretical and empirical attention.

THEORETICAL PERSPECTIVES

Two theoretical paradigms shaped news media research in the twentieth century – the liberal pluralist paradigm and the control paradigm. Liberal pluralist approaches are underpinned by the ideals of classical liberal theory, and emphasize the principles of freedom, choice and democracy. From this perspective, news selection and production is shaped by public interests and consumer demand, the sovereignty of professional journalistic values, equal competition for media access by a diversity of news sources, and the collective values of a society built around more or less organic consensus. The role of the news media is to accurately inform audiences, protect democracy and serve the interests of the social majority. In contrast, control approaches are influenced by Marxist and critical theory, and stress the unequal distribution of economic and cultural power throughout society. Here, news selection and production is shaped by elite interests and the demands of capitalist enterprise, implicit and explicit constraints on media workers' professional autonomy, the dominance of a narrow range of powerful sources, and the normalisation of ruling class values throughout a society built around a manufactured consensus. From this perspective, the role of news media is to reproduce dominant ideology, legitimate the capitalist system, and thus serve the interests of the ruling elite. The liberal pluralist paradigm tends to be popular among media practitioners and those who command cultural, economic and political power. The control paradigm has been far more influential within the academy, and has predominated in research on news media, crime and justice.

Marxist interventions

Three institutional Centres drove the development of British news media research in the sixties and seventies: the Birmingham Centre for Contemporary Cultural Studies (CCCS) at Birmingham University, the Centre for Mass Communication Research (CMCR) at Leicester University and the Glasgow University Media Group (GUMG). None of these Centres were primarily criminological, yet their influence on theorising news media, crime and justice has been profound. The Centres were united in their rejection of the largely American tradition of liberal pluralism. Each advocated the multidisciplinary study of the communication process as a whole. And each sought to investigate media influence at the level of everyday social action rather than individual psychology. Ultimately, they were all concerned to understand the role of news media in the reproduction of 'dominant ideology'. Alongside their commonalities, however, there were important differences. Not least of these were the Centres' different foundational disciplines and, relatedly, their contrasting readings and applications of Marxism and critical theory. The CCCS synthesised cultural studies and structural Marxism. The GUMG established a critical media studies that retained the action-orientation of an instrumental Marxism. And the CMCR used the sociology of mass communications to develop a critical political economy. It is useful to briefly summarise some of the key differences between these readings of Marx, before considering how they shaped the work that each centre produced.

Situating Marx

Instrumental Marxists are concerned with how economic, political and cultural elites use their power in a market society to ensure that information flows and exchanges reinforce their own minority capitalist interests. This action-oriented reading of Marx requires on some level the acceptance of a unified elite with shared intent that is sufficiently coherent to manage the media in a uniform fashion. The media in this model are seen to work more or less directly in the service of the ruling class, and media content is shaped internally through newsroom hierarchies and journalistic self-censorship, and externally through direct pressures from, for example, advertising agencies, big business and government.

Structural Marxism detaches the workings of key structures and institutions – the state, the economy, the law, the education system, the media – from the conscious agency of the individuals within them. State institutions are seen to operate with relative autonomy, but nonetheless function together as part of a system that is structurally-oriented to maintaining the dominance of the capitalist order. Structural Marxist media analysts are interested in how systems and processes of signification and representation collectively reproduce dominant ideology at the levels of popular discourse, understanding and everyday rituals, thus ensuring its normalisation and acceptance throughout society. Both instrumental and structural Marxists adhere to the base-superstructure metaphor and tend to remain faithful, in the final instance, to the notion of economic determination. But whereas an instrumental Marxist position sees power acting in a conscious, top-down manner, relatively unchallenged, structural Marxists highlight the contested nature of ideology and the requirement for dominant interests to be constantly re-negotiated and legitimated through state apparatuses and practices. News production here is structurally-oriented, rather than individually directed, to reinforce the dominant ideology.

Finally, political economy theorists reject the action-oriented, interventionist approach adopted by instrumental Marxists, but are also critical of what is seen as structural Marxism's over-reliance on ideological factors. Political economists focus their analyses on the relations between the economic processes and structures of media production and the ideological content of media. Unlike structural Marxists, who view ideology as relatively autonomous and more than simply a reflection of the economic base, political economists see ideology, along with other cultural processes, as of secondary importance to and determined by the economic requirements of capitalist accumulation. And whereas structural Marxists see ideology as a site of ongoing struggle, political economists tend to view ideology as the means through which struggle is obliterated (Curran *et al.,* 1982). It is those who command the greatest resources who ultimately achieve greatest success in putting their point of view across in news media coverage. Resource-starved organisations find themselves marginalised, and frequently excluded from the communications process altogether.

Institutional readings

The central research interest of the CCCS was the relationship between popular culture and ideology and, in particular, the issue of meaning: how it is produced, ordered, negotiated – how it shapes and situates everyday existence at the level of cultural and social practices. Hall (1973) rejected the long-standing notion that meaning is an essential or fixed quality of media texts, insisting instead that they are 'polysemic' and can be read in multiple ways. How texts are 'encoded' by producers has no necessary connection with how they may subsequently be 'decoded' by consumers. Meaning was thus conceptualised as fluid, dynamic and subject to the influence of wider contextual factors like gender, race and class. Yet it can nonetheless be structured and ordered in particular ways through ideology. Thus a key concern was to understand how dominant ideology was reflected and reinforced in the mass media, and how it may variously be appropriated, resisted or subverted by everyday consumers. The CCCS's particular form of Marxism derived from a synthesis of Althusser's structuralism, Gramsci's writings on hegemony, and Barthes' semiotic work on texts. The resulting theoretical framework retained the core concerns of a structuralist approach, but sought to overcome what were seen as the restrictions of economic determination. Rather than being determined in any straightforward sense by the economic base-superstructure model, ideology was viewed as being implicitly embedded in all cultural structures and practices, including media production. This structural-culturalist approach to understanding news media and ideology was most influentially applied in Hall *et al.*'s (1978) *Policing the Crisis.*

Hall *et al.* (1978) explore the creation of a moral panic around 'mugging' during a period of economic recession, high unemployment and social unrest they identify with a 'crisis in hegemony'. Sensational media coverage of this 'new' crime wave simultaneously tapped into existing fears around law and order, race and social decline, and provided a folk devil – the young black street criminal – against whom all 'respectable' people could unite. The moral panic, and the wider sense of crisis it simultaneously invoked and represented, generated the right conditions for the state to reassert and relegitimate itself – policing the crisis, crucially with the consent of the people, by cracking down on the problem of crime. As Jefferson recalls (2008: 114), the authors were interested in understanding how the relatively autonomous institutions of the state – the police, the judiciary and the media (Althusser's (1971) ideological state apparatus) – contributed to the panic independently, whilst simultaneously functioning collectively to reproduce the ideas of the ruling class: the dominant ideology. They suggested that dominant ideology is continually reproduced in the media because news production is structurally oriented, in the name of journalistic 'objectivity' and 'impartiality', to appeal first to those accredited experts who represent and command institutional power. This places powerful groups in the position to establish 'an initial definition or *primary interpretation* of the topic in question' (Hall *et al.*, 1978: 58). Once the primary definition has been established it is extremely difficult to override, and future debate is contained within a forum of 'controlled discourse', governed by the primary definers:

> The media, then, do not simply 'create' the news; nor do they simply transmit the ideology of the 'ruling class' in a conspiratorial fashion. Indeed, we have suggested that, in a critical sense, the media are frequently not the 'primary definers' of news events at all; but their structured relationship to power has the effect of making them play a crucial but secondary role in *reproducing* the definitions of those who have privileged access, as of right, to the media as 'accredited sources'. From this point of view, in the moment of news production, the media stand in a position of structured subordination to the primary definers
>
> (Hall *et al.*, 1978: 59).

In this reading, powerful institutional sources are the primary definers, while the media are reduced to playing a secondary role. Journalists are largely stripped of agency and influence. Their autonomy is removed.

Like the CCCS, the GUMG were motivated to explore 'the vexed questions of cultural power and the consensual legitimation of beliefs' (1976: 14) and both Centres were united in their rejection of economic determinism. While the 'simple 'base/superstructure' view of broadcasting might account for a small proportion of output', they argued, 'it can in no way explain and analyse the inherent contradictions and varieties of permitted views and the surface openness that exists across the range of broadcasting output' (GUMG, 1980: 412). The GUMG's first major research project, *Bad News* (1976), combined quantitative and qualitative content analysis, supplemented with interviews and participant observation, to analyse television news coverage of industrial disputes (see also Eldridge, 2006). They found a clear absence of alternative views or comment to challenge the dominant ideological position, and explained what they call news 'bias' as follows (GUMG, 1976: 267–268):

> Our analysis goes beyond saying merely that the television news 'favour' certain individuals and institutions by giving them more time and status. Such criticisms are crude. The nature of our analysis is deeper than this: in the end it relates to the picture of society in general and industrial society in particular, that television news constructs. This at its most damaging … includes the laying of blame for society's industrial and economic problems at the door of the workforce. This is done in the face of contradictory evidence which, when it appears, is either ignored, smothered, or at worst, is treated as if it supports the inferential frameworks utilized by the producers of news.

From this perspective media personnel are empowered with an agency and intentionality they are denied in the work of the CCCS. The GUMG's follow-up study *More Bad News* (1980: 400) confirmed this view, finding that journalists 'actively embrace' the dominant ideological viewpoint 'in a way that would be hard to justify as impartial'. Their activities include 'not only the agenda-setting functions we have described, but also a systematic partiality in the reporting and interpretive use of government statistics' (1980: 401). Here, journalists are not secondary players, 'structurally subordinated' in a communication process shaped by the cultural and economic power of state institutions. They are primary definers and news is conceptualised as 'the manifestation of the collective cultural codes of those employed to do this selective and judgemental work for society' (1976: 14). Hall (1978) interpreted this action-oriented reading as a weakness, an instrumentalism betraying a 'simplistic notion of television "bias"… as though simply directed by the 'ruling class'. Conversely, the GUMG saw in the CCCS a structural determinism that blinded them to, or, still worse, rendered insignificant the agency of news personnel and the crucial intervening role of senior media managers on the basis of fractional class interests.

The Centres also differed in their approach to empirical research. Whereas the CCCS drew from Louis Althusser, a structural Marxist who retained a deep scepticism toward empirical analysis, the GUMG identified more readily with Ralph Miliband, an instrumental Marxist who vociferously defended it. For Althusser, power operates in a non-linear fashion and derives from a set of 'hidden relations' that defy direct empirical investigation. However, underpinning structures of power, ideology and meaning can be revealed through theoretical analysis. From this perspective, research should be theory-led. More mundanely, the CCCS was poorly funded and staffed largely by humanities graduates with limited formal training in conducting empirical research. For financial and intellectual reasons, then, their primary research site was the text, not the street. Of course, much empirical work was carried out at the CCCS, including classic ethnographies (Hebdidge, 1979; Willis, 1977) and the groundbreaking audience research by Morley and Brunsdon (Brunsdon and Morley, 1978; Morley, 1980). But throughout the 1970s it was inconsistent and sometimes marginalised in studies that prioritised theoretical sophistication. In *Resistance Through Rituals* (1976), for example, 'literary ethnography' takes the place of direct empirical observation (Blackman, 1998). And despite its detailed, if unsystematic, newspaper content analysis, the key focus of *Policing the Crisis*, as Bennett notes (1982: 302), is less on the relationship between ideology and 'reality', and more on the relationship between ideologies. In contrast, the GUMG developed what they describe as a 'positivist critique, though not in any arcane sense of limiting itself to checking and producing the facts'. The aim in *Bad News* (1976) was to analyse how 'viewers were given a misleading portrayal of industrial disputes in the UK when measured against the independent reality of events' (1980: xiii). For this group of just-as-poorly-funded but empirically trained sociologists, developing theory should not come at the expense of empirically testing it. This, for the GUMG, was a fundamental problem within the CCCS and cultural studies more generally. Privileging the symbolic over the material simultaneously privileges the abstract-theoretical over the substantive-empirical. Theory is enough: no further evidence is required (Philo, 1999; Philo and Miller, 2001).

The political economy approach of the Leicester CMCR was grounded in the sociology of mass communications, and empirically-oriented. The aim was to explore the relations between the economic structure and organisation of the cultural industries, their ideological content, and wider social, cultural and political life. With respect to media production, the CMCR sought to understand the role of mass communications in the maintenance and legitimation of structural inequalities in a class society. Whilst the CCCS and the GUMG were united in their rejection of economic determination, the CMCR placed economic forces at the heart of the media production process. For Murdock and Golding (1977: 37) these forces:

> ... work consistently to exclude those voices lacking economic power or resources ... the underlying logic of cost operates systematically, consolidating the position of groups already established in the main mass-media markets and excluding those groups who lack the capital base required for successful entry. Thus the voices which survive will largely

belong to those least likely to criticize the prevailing distribution of wealth and power. Conversely, those most likely to challenge these arrangements are unable to publicize their dissent or opposition because they cannot command resources needed for effective communication to a broad audience.

Members clearly acknowledged the relevance of other factors in the news production process, including the 'controls and constraints imposed by the state and the political sphere' and 'the inertia exerted by dominant cultural codes and traditions' (Golding and Murdock, 1979: 198). They also accepted the 'relative autonomy' of production personnel and the 'pertinent effects of professional ideologies and practices' (ibid.). But these factors were of secondary importance to the material and determining impact of economic forces. The Leicester CMCR's political economy approach thus represented a return to the base-superstructure metaphor. The role of media is that of 'legitimation through the production of false consciousness, in the interests of a class which owns and controls the media' (Bennett, 1982: 26). This macro-sociological account of control through concentration of ownership, monopolisation and diversification lay beyond the reach of a micro-oriented culturalist framework. As Golding and Murdock (2000: 72) put it, 'Cultural studies offers an analysis of the ways the cultural industries work that has little or nothing to say about how they actually operate as industries, and how their economic organisation impinges on the production and circulation of meaning. Nor does it examine the ways in which people's consumption choices are structured by their position in the wider economic formation. Exploring these dynamics is the primary task for a critical political economy of communications'.

In one of the CMCR's first major texts, Halloran *et al.* (1970) analysed press and television reporting of the 1968 Vietnam demonstrations in London's Grosvenor Square. Building on the work of Lang and Lang (1955) and Boorstin (1963), they developed the notion of 'inferential structures' – frameworks which guide journalists' construction of 'events as news' on the basis of values and definitions already legitimated in the public mind; that is, on the basis of the prevailing consensus.

> The media can create 'news' which is based not on the event itself but on those aspects of it to which they have assigned a particular prominence, i.e. the *'event as news'* … in other words, the event achieves reality by being reported, while in addition consequences may flow from the report which actually shape the original reality in accordance with the meaning given to it by the 'news'
>
> (Halloran *et al.*, 1970: 90).

By combining this framework with an analysis of 'news values' adapted from the work of Norwegian media researchers Galtung and Ruge (1965), Halloran *et al.* (1970: 315, emphasis in original) illustrate the media's role in 'defining the situation and in cultivating the assumption that *this is the way it is*'. They illustrate how the demonstrations were defined early on as likely to involve violence between the forces of law and order (the police) and the forces of anarchy (the demonstrators). Though the protests turned out to be largely peaceful, the event was still reported in line with the dominant inferential structure – the 'framework of violence' – and thus it was the issue of violence, minimal though it was, that provided 'the news'. The influence of the CMCR's work on 'inferential structures' is evident in Hall *et al.*'s (1978: 59) model of 'primary definition', and in the GUMG's analyses of television news 'bias' (GUMG, 1976, 1980). It also featured across a number of classic crime news analyses that emerged from the interdisciplinary environment of the time, most vividly encapsulated within the National Deviancy Conference.

The national deviancy conference and the violent society

As the Leicester and Birmingham Centres were developing their particular institutional research approaches in the late 1960s (the GUMG would not be established until 1974), a critical criminology was finding form in the National Deviancy Conference (NDC). The NDC was not contained within any one institution. Nevertheless, it constituted the institutionalisation of critical criminological theory and research. What is so striking about this period is that news media research commanded a significant presence within critical criminology; a presence that, for reasons outlined later in this chapter, is missing today. Though not a direct product of the NDC meetings, *The Manufacture of News: Deviance, Social Problems and the Mass Media* (1973) combined contributions by core NDC members with a series of previously published and original pieces by leading media researchers across a range of fields. Motivated by the belief that much mainstream media research was 'on the wrong lines', and deliberately stepping away from American mainstream concerns regarding the direct effects of media exposure, Cohen and Young (1973: 10) wanted to explore 'the conceptions of deviance and social problems revealed in the mass media and the implicit view of society behind such conceptions'. Hall and Murdock both provided chapters – Hall on the ideological role of news photographs, and the representation of violence (Hall, 1971, 1973), and Murdock (1973) on the reporting of political deviance. Other chapters analysed news values, representations of sexuality and race, and moral panics. The contributions encapsulated the Marxism and shared politics that defined news media criminology at that time, presenting work by the CCCS and CMCR side-by-side, and offered an clear, if critical, endorsement of control readings of news production.

The Marxist reading of news media, crime and justice was further reinforced by Chibnall (1977). Combining content analysis with interviews and observations, and drawing heavily from the work of the CCCS and the CMRC, Chibnall (1975: 115–116) established that law-and-order-news 'neutralizes deviant world views by either denying their status as beliefs which should be taken seriously by sensible people, or condemning them as manifestations of wickedness or corruption'. This elite-orientation is not, however, a 'product of editorial conspiracy, but a reflection of the social organization of reporting, and the professional imperatives and commercial interests which underlie it' (ibid.). The explanatory framework leans toward a structural rather than action-oriented understanding of news production. Regarding journalist-source power relations, Chibnall finds that 'the journalist is always in an inferior negotiating position – the journalist who cannot get information is out of a job, whereas the policeman who retains it is not' (Chibnall, 1977: 155). This notion of 'structured subordination' was simultaneously being developed in the CCCS mugging research and would find full articulation as the theory of 'primary definition' in *Policing the Crisis* (1978). Though the two studies emerged 'quite autonomously' (Chibnall, 1977: 76), they overlap significantly in their theoretical approach and substantive interest in how the press communicated public anxieties at a time of rapid social change and mobilised the blanket conceptualisations 'Violent Society' and 'Law and Order crisis' to capture the public imagination. The differences lie in their methodologies and overall aims. Chibnall (1977) used content analysis, interviews and observation to deconstruct crime news and identify its component parts, locating crime reporting within the wider context of press ideology and political economy. Hall *et al.* (1978) employed content analysis to investigate the creation of a moral panic around mugging as part of wider efforts to legitimate the shift toward an authoritarian state at a time of hegemonic crisis. Chibnall looks at the everyday, while Hall *et al.* focus on the exceptional; Chibnall theorises the ideological role of the news media, while Hall *et al.* explore the news media to formulate a theory of the Authoritarian state.

From authoritarian state to national security state

In a study that postdates the British Marxist work by a decade, and remains influential in British news media criminology and critical criminology today, Herman and Chomsky (1988: 298) developed their 'propaganda model', in which 'the raw material of news' passes through five filters, 'leaving only the cleansed residue fit to print'. The five filters are media ownership and profit orientation, the influence of advertising, the role of experts, 'flak' as a means of disciplining the media, and anti-communism as the 'national religion'. Through meticulous empirical research on the reporting of 'terrorism' and close consideration of the media's alleged collusion in the 'criminalisation' of non-friendly regimes, Herman and Chomsky demonstrate how economic, political, military and cultural elites effectively conspire to control the content and flow of media information. As in much British Marxist research, journalists are seen to have little influence or autonomy in the news production process. Power lies with the state and large corporations. Whilst journalists may feel they are acting objectively and writing in accordance with prevailing and accepted journalistic news values, in practice they are subordinated to reproduce the interests of an active ruling elite. Thus, Herman and Chomsky cast the news media as a key functionary of the 'National Security State', operating to 'manufacture consent' around elite ideas in the name of the 'national interest' and, in so doing, engendering acceptance of a social order that reflects the interests of a powerful few, rather than the wider majority.

The decline of marxism and the fracturing of critical criminology

Though different researchers got there by different theoretical and methodological means, and presented different levels of evidence to substantiate their respective claims, Marxist interventions shared an overriding concern with the power of ruling class interests to marginalize dissenting discourses and opinion and maintain the socio-cultural and economic *status quo*. By the late 1970s Marxism was losing influence within the social sciences, and the critical criminology that found collective expression in the NDC was fragmenting. When *Manufacturing Consent* (1988) was published in the US, itself running against the grain of more nuanced studies of news production, the Marxist turn in British social sciences had passed. With it, criminological interest in news media markedly declined. Critical Criminology split into four distinct domains – Critical Criminology, Left Realist Criminology, Governmental Criminology, and Critical Legal Studies (see McLaughlin, this volume).

For Critical Criminology the media's role in constructing the Authoritarian State and the Violent Society had been demonstrated: the media work had been done. For Left Realist Criminology, media research had been colonised by Critical Criminologists – an issue of moral panics, deviancy amplification and ideological mystification. Furthermore, in the victimisation survey Left Realists found a means to get *behind* media representations and ideological mystifications and to access the empirical *reality* of the crime problem: a problem, they insisted, was palpably not a media construction. For Governmental Criminology, Foucault provided news ways of exploring relations of power and knowledge at the level of micro-institutional discourses. Media discourses were of little interest in this context. And Critical Legal Studies focused on the operation of law, again with little space for media research. Within each of these new manifestations of critical criminology, news media work was no longer a priority. Within orthodox criminology the news media were then, as they are today, a curiosity to be engaged with between research projects and, even then, to be explored largely though positivistic, quantitative content analysis. Thus, as was the case before the NDC gave rise to a succession of groundbreaking, multi-disciplinary analyses, researching news media, crime and justice in the UK fell to those outside criminology. The studies that emerged in this post-Marxist climate, including those conducted by members of the three Centres, would foreground different elements of news selection and production, challenging the determinism that had characterised so much critical research and seeking a more holistic understanding of the mass communication process.

Post-Marxist interventions

Throughout the 1980s the theoretical homogeneity that characterised the period of predominantly Marxist research on news media, crime and justice gave way to a more pluralistic period of theoretical development. A growing body of media research came to challenge what was perceived as the over-determinism inherent within Marxist variants of the control paradigm, most explicit in instrumental readings of news production, but also evident in structuralist work. The underpinning idea that, in the last instance, the news media operate as a 'largely uncritical conduit for official views' (Schlesinger *et al.,* 1983: 166), was identified as a particular point of contention. The conception of dominant ideology was also diversified in this period to explore ideological legitimation of inequalities not only in terms of class, but also in terms of gender, race and other social divisions. And new theoretical frameworks emerged that focused on aspects of the social formation other than class.

Over three books that remain widely cited in British research today, Ericson, Baranek and Chan (1987; 1989; 1991) produced a highly sophisticated and detailed analysis of journalistic practices, source activities, and the role of news as an agency of social control across Canadian television, press and radio. Through a combination of content analysis, interviews and ethnographic observation they explore how journalists and sources engage in 'legitimation work' in the representation of crime and justice, and how news contributes to the formation of a stable 'symbolic canopy', based on but not restricted to dominant ideology, that helps to reinforce the 'consensual paradigm' for society as a whole (Ericson *et al.,* 1987: 27–43). Ericson *et al.* are avowedly anti-instrumentalist in their approach. And whilst they draw much from the structural Marxist work of Hall *et al.* (1978) and Chibnall (1977), the political economy work of the CMCR, and the methods of the GUMG, they remain critical of the determinism inherent within the control paradigm. Research has consistently reaffirmed the asymmetrical relations between journalists and powerful sources, they argue, because it has been 'grounded in the perspective of journalists' (ibid.: 125) and thus overlooks the important levels of 'convergence' between media and source organisations. Consideration of source perspectives reveals that the police, for example, are constrained by news discourses just as journalists are constrained by police discourses: 'police-reporter transactions entail controls from both sides, and interdependency' (Ericson *et al.*, 1989: 125). In Canada, just as in Britain, 'the police are the primary definers of crime and its control to the public' (1989: 123). But while the police 'controlled the primary definitions of the subject of address (crime, criminality and its control by the police), they sensed a loss of control over the specific terms of the communication process (Ericson *et al.*, 1989: 123). The news media 'provide a somewhat open terrain for struggles for justice, even though particular issues and institutional sources predominate. The documented variation by medium and market shows pluralism in meanings and values' (Ericson *et al.*, 1991: i).

   This challenge to the control paradigm was also reflected in British news media research. In a number of large-scale studies on the press and television coverage of terrorism, industrial conflict and crime, Schlesinger, Tumber, Murdock and Elliott, in various combinations, argued that privileging journalist perspectives overlooks the complexities of source-media management strategies, inter-source competition and journalist-source power relations. In relation to representations of terrorism, for example, Schlesinger *et al.* (1983: 32) find that, though official perspectives pre-dominate, media images 'were a good deal more diverse and complex than simpler assumptions about television's relation to the state and to dominant ideology pre-dict'. In direct reference to the structural-culturalist work of Hall *et al.* (1978), Schlesinger *et al.* (1991: 399) argue that ' "Primary definition", which ought to be an empirically ascertainable outcome, is taken instead to be an *a priori* effect of the privileged access of the powerful'. Combining content analysis and interviews with journalists and sources, these authors confirm that definitional advantage is structur-ally determined to a degree, but it can seldom be guaranteed (see also Schlesinger and Tumber, 1994). Access to the media is not, as Hall *et al.* (1978: 59) would have it, simply granted 'as of right'. It needs to be won through a variety of carefully managed media methods and practices that can be subject to frequent disruption. Off the record disclosures and internal leaks cannot be totally managed. By definition these interventions may stray from the official line and diminish considerably the extent to which powerful institutions can maintain a coherent organisational voice, still less ensure definitional control in the news media. Nor does the theory of pri-mary definition account for the actions taken by non-official sources to enter into and sometimes successfully reframe the terms of a given debate. Furthermore, the notion of journalistic 'structured subordination' fails to account for occasions on which media actively challenge powerful institutions on issues of policy or practice, or investigative exposés force undesired or unintended official responses (Miller, 1998, 1993; Greer and McLaughlin, 2010). Schlesinger and colleagues (1983, 1989, 1991, 1994) insist that flows of information between journalists and sources are more complex than Marxist readings suggested, and that the reproduction of elite ideas in news content, though structurally advantaged, is by no means guaranteed. The dominance of any ideological position should be considered an 'achievement rather than a wholly structurally determined outcome' (Schlesinger, 1989: 79).

These arguments against the control paradigm could only be mounted from within that paradigmatic framework. The dominant ideology thesis had, in effect, established the 'inferential structure' or 'primary definition' within which further discussion or debate took place. The fundamental problematic remained the reproduction of dominant ideology as defined through class. With the development of critical feminist research on crime reporting the control paradigm underwent some conceptual reconfiguration. Here, dominant ideology is no less important, but it is framed primarily in terms of gender, and relates to the tendency of news reports to reinforce gender stereotypes that maintain unequal power relations, including economic inequality, in a patriarchal society. Though critical feminist research on crime news has been plentiful (Cameron and Fraser, 1987; Meyers, 1997; Soothill and Walby, 1991), only a few studies have engaged in depth with production processes (see, for example, Chancer, 2003; Kitzinger and Skidmore, 1995). One important example, influential in the British context, is Benedict's (1992) radical feminist analysis of the reporting of five high profile sex crime cases in the US. Benedict worked as a journalist and a rape counsellor before entering academia. This professional insight supplements content analysis, interviews with journalists and editors, and an academic feminist reading of power, gender, race and class to explore the structural and cultural arrangements that shape press reporting of sexual violence against women. The central theme is the prevailing tendency to polarise women in sex crime cases into either 'virgins' or 'whores' (ibid.: 26). It is suggested that the press' insensitive and sometimes cruel treatment of women in sex crime cases is seldom due to individual malice. Rather, it results from characteristics of society that are deeply embedded within the culture, namely the gender-biased nature of language and prevailing myths about women, sex and rape. These myths, or dominant ideological meanings, guide how news is both produced and processed, but do so implicitly in a way that can influence even the most well meaning commentators. Thus, 'a myth-saturated woman will be just as insensitive to rape cases as a myth-saturated man, especially given the conditions and habits of newsroom behaviour' (1992: 6). This is structural-culturalism read through gender. Of course, much critical feminist research retains a clear Marxist sensibility, and class, if not *the* defining factor, remains a core concern. In the period of post-Marxist news media criminology, other frameworks emerged to further challenge class as the defining problematic.

For 'risk society' theorists, the transition from modernity to late-modernity has been characterised by a shift away from the focus on economic inequality and toward the nature, patterning and control of 'risk' (Beck, 1992). Whereas modernity was characterised by the positive problem of acquiring 'goods' (income, education, housing and health), the 'risk society' is characterised by the negative problem of avoiding 'bads' (global warming, AIDS, pollution … and crime). In the unequal society, the distribution of 'goods' could be broadly understood in terms of class. In the unsafe or 'risk' society, 'bads' are global and affect everyone more or less equally, regardless of class position. Collectivism is replaced by individualism. The state and its agencies are problems rather than solutions. Remedies to problems are not to be found in social policy, but in changing the behaviour of the people responsible (Reiner *et al.,* 2001). In the shift from the class society to the risk society, the control paradigm's focus on dominant ideology loses purchase. It is the 'risk society' that provides the conceptual framework for Reiner, Livingstone and Allen's (2000, 2001) research on media representations of crime and justice in the post-War era. They find that over time news reports of criminal offending include less acknowledgement of possible structural causation and more condemnation of what is presented as individual evil. Portrayals of criminal justice remain broadly supportive, but are increasingly complex and critical, focusing more, for example, on police ineffectiveness, systemic corruption, and conflict between official institutions. And, in the most significant change, crime victims shift from being incidental characters to becoming the central focus for highly emotionalised news stories built around their experiences of suffering (Reiner *et al.,* 2000: 187). The study does not engage with the news production process (though it does engage with audiences), and thus does not address changing journalist-source relations. But the risk society is a useful theoretical framework within which to explore media representations of crime and justice, and the changing political and cultural sensibilities that shape the late modern condition. Given the extent to which the thesis has been embraced by criminologists, it is surprising that it has not featured in more criminological analyses of the news.

THEORETICAL CONCEPTS

Theoretical perspectives rise and fall, and drift in and out of academic favour. Theoretical concepts have an enduring and defining significance: they can be radically theorised and theorised in radically different ways, but they exist independently of the various theoretical positions within which they may be situated. As such, theoretical concepts are more than just research sites; they have an existence and life of their own. Three concepts that continue to shape the research agenda in news media criminology are newsworthiness, fear of crime and moral panics.

Crime newsworthiness

Journalists' decisions regarding newsworthiness – which events to select for inclusion as news, and how to present those events once selected – are informed by their sense of 'news values'. The first academic exploration of news values was presented by Norwegian media researchers Galtung and Ruge (1965). Their analysis resulted in the identification of twelve news values that, they suggested, work collectively to inform the selection and production of events as news. This theoretical framework has been adopted and adapted by myriad researchers since, and features prominently in many of the studies discussed above. Remarkably, Galtung and Ruge's (1965) original insights were based on content analysis and, as they put it, 'a simplified psychology of perception and some additional assumptions' (1965: 64). No journalists or sources were interviewed or observed. 'The proper thing to do', they conceded, 'in order to test their validity would be to observe journalists at work … and we have no such data. For want of this the [news values] should be anchored in general reasoning and social science findings' (1965: 66). Forty years later, after much empirical testing, it is striking how well their framework still stands up to scrutiny.

There are of course variations in emphasis and articulation across studies, and some more substantive differences, but the different accounts of newsworthiness are most notable for their similarities. A consideration of news values helps us understand the nature of media content. Crime and justice events that are technologically accessible, easy to visualize, meet the required threshold for news visibility and fit within the routines and cycles of news production are more likely to be covered than abstract issues and debates that develop over longer periods. This event-orientation promotes a corresponding focus on individuals (as victims, offenders, justice officials). Individualization and personalization promote the simplification of news stories and serve to reinforce the common association between criminality and individual pathology rather than wider social, structural and political factors. Interpersonal crimes of sex and violence can be more easily presented as dramatic and titillating than non-violent crimes – for example, most property offences – particularly when they have high levels of proximity (spatial nearness and cultural meaningfulness) to the consumer. Crimes are more newsworthy if they are particularly audacious, violent or novel, involve famous or notable people, or take place in famous or notable places. Crimes are also more likely to be reported if they feature 'ideal victims', for example young children or older people, and there is a risk of further attacks.

Most sociological accounts have explored newsworthiness from the perspective of journalists, prioritizing *their* consideration of the pragmatics of news production, *their* assumptions about audience interests, and *their* assessment of the likely relevance and impact of the story on those audiences. The focus is on the background factors – organizational, ideological, cultural, economic – that shape the selection and production of crime as news, prior to its dissemination to audiences. However, Katz (1987) points out that 'whatever the influences on new organizations that affect their selection and rejection of particular stories, daily newsreaders have an independent fascination with the stories that are published' (Katz, 1987: 48). Katz thus theorises newsworthiness from the perspective of the consumer, and is interested in understanding the symbolic relevance and psycho-social utility of crime news. The principal focus here, then, is on the foreground factors – existential, moral, emotional – that make crime news 'required reading' for people on a daily basis. Whilst 'novelty' had been identified as a key determinant of crime newsworthiness across most research studies, Katz offers a different interpretation. His analyses suggests that the most newsworthy crimes seldom appear to be particularly unexpected or novel. Political scandals and stories of high level corruption confirm for many what they knew all along, yet such stories invariably attract considerable media attention. Banks are routine targets for robberies, yet they continue to generate substantial media interest when they are hit. If the key to understanding crime newsworthiness is not its unexpectedness, Katz argues (1987: 63), a more fruitful approach may be to consider crime's 'symbolic value in articulating the normatively expected'. From this perspective, crime is not newsworthy because it appeals to readers' base or morbid interests, or because it shocks them in the short term, or frightens them in the long term. Rather, crime is newsworthy because its reporting presents readers with the opportunity to engage in a daily ritual moral workout, allowing them to question and confirm (or otherwise) their own moral fortitude. In essence, crime news 'speaks dramatically to issues that are of direct relevance to readers' existential challenges, whether or not readers are preoccupied with the possible personal misfortune of becoming victims to crime' (Katz, 1987: 68).

FEAR OF CRIME

There has been much debate around an adequate definition of fear that might be applied to explorations of news media – or other factors – and fear of crime (Hope and Sparks, 2000). Some commentators have queried the apparent academic preoccupation with endowing the concept of 'fear' with essentialist qualities that, for the purposes of longitudinal and comparative research, persist across time and place (Bourke, 2005). Others have questioned the tendency to characterise fear of crime as an unqualified social ill, and asked if some level of 'functional fear' – as opposed to 'dysfunctional worry' – might in fact be 'a motivating force that encourages vigilance and stimulates precautionary activity' (Jackson and Gray, 2010). Particularly within the context of high crime societies, purportedly characterised by 'existential anxiety' and 'ontological insecurity' and giving rise to 'criminologies of everyday life' (Giddens, 1991; Bauman, 1997; Garland, 2001), 'fear' can become a catchall phrase used to describe any range of emotional responses. It can be intimately connected, for example, with anger, distrust, shame, jealousy and rage, as well as vigilance, consideration and caution, and cannot be easily isolated for empirical analysis. What is most important, argues Bourke (2005), is the social and cultural context in which the term is used, when it is used, and by whom.

The most widely cited body of literature on media and fear of crime also clearly demonstrates some of the main conceptual and methodological problems within this field of research. Gerbner et al.'s 'cultivation research' has over several decades explored the correlation between viewing television violence and beliefs regarding politics, public safety and social order (Gerbner and Gross, 1976; Gerbner et al., 1994). The central finding is that 'heavy' television viewers cultivate a world-view which more closely resembles the 'television message' than 'light' television viewers. Because television overstates both the seriousness and risk of criminal victimization, portraying the world as 'mean and scary', heavy viewing is said to cultivate higher fear of crime. Fearful citizens tend to be depoliticised, more dependent on established authority, more punitive, and more likely to acquiesce to authoritarian measures of control. The now well rehearsed problems with the cultivation project include: its simplification and de-contextualising of the categories 'media', 'violence' and 'fear'; its attempts to quantify the creative and highly variable processes of interpretation and influence; and its search for a straightforward causal connection between media and fear of crime (Sparks, 1992; Ditton et al., 2004). Yet the central claim underpinning cultivation research – that particular forms of distorted and distorting media communication can generate widespread anxiety, punitive sentiments, and the tacit acceptance of authoritarian governance – finds much wider support. This position is explicit in Hall et al.'s (1978) Policing the Crisis, where it is read through a Gramscian reading of the state's repressive response to a 'crisis in hegemony'. It is central to recent and widespread claims that the state is harnessing a culture of fear in a post-9/11 risk society in order to legitimate tough anti-terror legislation or, more generally, to govern through crime (Simon, 2006; Mythen and Walklate, 2006; Furedi, 2005). Analysts of 'penal populism', now an organising concept within criminology, have been at pains to understand the roles of mass media and fear of crime, both individually and in terms of their interconnections, in the apparent rise of punitive sentiment and the collapse of faith in the ability of authorities to deliver public protection (Bottoms, 1995; Roberts *et al.*, 2003; Pratt, 2007). Yet empirically substantiating the intuitive connection between these variables remains elusive.

The more revealing research has moved beyond the search for simplistic causal connections, and sought to develop a contextually aware understanding of media and fear of crime. Kitzinger and Skidmore's (1995: 12) study on news coverage of child sex abuse uses mixed-methods to explore news content, production and, crucially, consumption and influence. Both members of the Glasgow University Media Group, Kitzinger and Skidmore were instrumental in developing the GUMG's particular brand of audience research. Here, focus groups are run to assess 'the potential and limits of people's ability to deconstruct and 'resist' media accounts' (1995: 1). The group discussions raised the useful distinction between intellectual and emotional knowledge. While most participants 'knew' abuse happened more often in domestic or institutional settings, 'their fear often focused on external sites such as woodland or wasteland' (ibid.: 9). And though many 'knew' that abuse is most often committed by someone the child knows, 'their fear focused on strangers' (ibid.: 9). In fact, they argue, 'audience understandings of how they might detect child abuse, the sources of danger and their ideas about intervention were often in conflict with the information which children's charities and social work agencies are trying to promote' (ibid.: 8). This contextual understanding of media and fear of crime has been probed further by Ditton *et al.* (2004), whose combination of quantitative questionnaires and qualitative interviews revealed that it is not the 'objectively determined randomness, localness or sensationalism that is important, but rather the interpretation of media content as relevant to and by the consumer' (Ditton *et al.*, 2004: 607).

Moral panics

The term 'moral panic' was first used by Young (1971) in his study of subcultures and drugtaking. Cohen (1972) developed and extended the concept in his analysis of the sensationalistic, heavy handed and ultimately 'disproportionate' reaction to the Mods and Rockers disturbances in an English seaside resort in 1964. Though the damage was in financial terms minor, Cohen traces the spiralling social reaction through initial intolerance, media stereotyping, moral outrage, increased surveillance, labelling and marginalisation, and deviancy amplification leading to further disturbances that seemed justify the initial concerns. The flamboyant misbehaviour of youth subcultures, independent and sexually and economically liberated, affronted the post-War values of hard work, sobriety and deferred gratification. At a time of rapid social change, they were a visible index of a world that was slipping away – 'folk devils' who provided a crystallising focus for social anxiety and 'respectable fears'. Reflecting the pluralistic theoretical interests of the NDC, Cohen built upon social constructionism, symbolic interactionism, deviancy amplification and labelling, but also incorporated the lesser known academic literature on 'disaster research' to describe the various phases of a moral panic – warning, impact, inventory, reaction – and chart its progression. In his analysis of the mass communication process, he drew in particular from the Leicester CMCR's work on 'inferential structures' (Halloran *et al.*, 1970). These theoretical resources were combined with in depth content analysis, questionnaires, interviews, and voluntary work in the local community to develop a fully sociological account of youth, culture, change and anxiety in post-War Britain.

Hall *et al.* (1978) politicised the concept of moral panic. In their analysis of a 'mugging' moral panic as an ideological intervention to address an escalating crisis in state hegemony (see above), it was inevitable that the concept would be read through the CCCS's particular form of structural Marxism. Yet, *Policing the Crisis* draws also from an eclectic mix of influences, connecting 'new deviancy theory, news media studies and research on urban race relations with political economy, state theory and notions of ideological consent' (McLaughlin, 2008: 146). For some critical criminologists, it represents the high point of Marxist theorising about crime, law and order and the state (*Crime, Media, Culture*, Special Section, 4,1). Acknowledging the sophistication within the CCCS work, Cohen (2007) has nonetheless noted a wider tendency to over-politicise the concept at the expense of its sociological meaning and application. Hall (2007) has suggested in response that politicisation was a necessary developmental stage, and that the full explanatory potential of the moral panic concept was, in fact, only realised through its construction as ideology.

Goode and Ben Yehuda (1994) developed Cohen's discussion of moral panic by paying particular attention to the criteria that should be in place before it can be suggested that a 'moral panic' is occurring. They identify five key features of the phenomenon: (i) *concern* (a reported condition or event generates anxiety); (ii) *hostility* (the condition or event is condemned and, where there are clearly identifiable individuals who can be blamed, these are portrayed as 'folk devils'); (iii) *consensus* (the negative social reaction is widespread and collective); (iv) *disproportionality* (the extent of the problem and the threat is poses are exaggerated); (v) *volatility* (media attention and the associated panic emerge suddenly and with intensity, but can dissipate quickly too).

'Moral panic' is one of the most widely used terms in the sociological analysis of crime and justice, and has transcended academic discourses to become commonplace in political rhetoric and popular conversation (Altheide, 2009). Given its prolific usage, it is surprising that few commentators have subjected the concept to sustained and rigorous critical investigation. With the split in the criminological left in the late-1970s, the concept was dismissed by Left Realists as 'left idealism', and accused of obfuscating the painful 'realities' of criminal victimisation by propagating the view that 'the crime problem' is socially constructed (Young, 1979). In exploring the anatomy of the concept, critics have queried the notions of 'disproportionality' and 'volatility'. The first, since this assumes a superior knowledge of the objective reality of the issue against which the reaction is measured, and a corresponding assumption of what a 'proportionate' reaction would look like (Waddington, 1986). The second, because in a contemporary multi-media world characterised by ontological insecurity and state of a permanent free-floating anxieties, the notion of discreet, self-contained, volatile moral panics may need some rethinking (McRobbie and Thornton, 1995). Cohen has responded to all of these criticisms (Cohen, 2002). But such critical interventions, both from within and outside of criminology, have barely interrupted the general tendency to arbitrarily apply the concept to explain everything from global warning to 'Swine Flu'. The broadly uncritical application of the moral panic concept has led Garland (2008) to reassert two elements of the original analysis, which are absent from many contemporary studies: (i) the *moral dimension* of the social reaction – most issues can be moralised, but many are not in and of themselves 'moral', and cannot automatically be analysed as such; and (ii) the idea that the deviant conduct in question is somehow *symptomatic* of a wider problem – a threat to established values, or a particular way of life.

THEORETICAL DILEMMAS

In order to make sense of contemporary news media representations of crime and justice, it is necessary to take account of dramatic changes in both the crime and justice and media arenas, and to engage in depth with the increasingly interactive relationship between them. Within criminology there is now a substantial literature detailing transformations across the crime and justice landscape. Different scholars foreground different elements and explain them in different ways, but the common-alities across accounts are significant, and include: the ascendancy of neo-conservative, populist criminologies, the politicisation of law and order and the rise of 'governing through crime', the emergence of victim-centred justice, the re-emotionalisation of crime and justice, net-widening and 'defining down' of deviance and, underpinning all of this, the hypermediatisation of crime, control and social order (Ericson, 2006; Garland, 2001; Reiner, 2007; Simon, 2006; Young, 2007).

This process of hypermediatisation has taken place across a rapidly changing media environment. There are more news platforms, sites and formats than ever before, and the sheer amount of available information is unprecedented. Within an intensely competitive market, news becomes increasingly commodified and journal-ists increasingly adversarial, while sources of all kinds become more professional and adept at dealing with the media. Faced with greater choice in a diversified and highly interactive environment, media-savvy news audiences fragment. This 24–7 global news mediasphere is light-years from the altogether more homogenous condi-tions explored in Marxist and Post-Marxist analyses of reporting crime. As the media environment has changed, so has the terrain upon which struggles over media power and influence are played out. As McNair puts it (2006: 49):

> News … is not manufactured (neither, therefore, is consent), nor is it 'constructed'. Nor does it just happen. It *emerges* from the interacting elements of the communication environment which prevails in a given media space. These spaces contain many social actors striving to manufacture and shape the news, but none has any guarantee of success … [J]ust as no amount of meteorological data-gathering can make the weather entirely predictable, so no social actor, be he president, prime minister or pope, can predict with any certainty what tomorrow's news will contain.

In the UK, an already fragmented government struggles to control the crime news agenda in a climate where the putative 'facts' of the crime problem – as derived from official statistics, victim surveys, performance indicators – are spun into a web of conflicting narratives, used simultaneously by competing interests as evidence of success and failure, or dismissed altogether as fabrication and 'moral panic'. Hyper-adversarial press reporters go on the attack (Barnett, 2002; Fallows, 1996), subjecting official institutions and their senior managers – the police, the courts, the prison service, government offices – to a constant barrage of criticism for failing to deliver in the democratically mandated task of 'public protection'. Media campaigns are launched in the name of high profile crime victims, whose increasingly vociferous and empowered representatives now routinely employ professional PR advisers to make their cases more 'media-friendly', and therefore more suitable to widespread public articulation and dissemination. Media audiences, tired of the 'permanent crisis in criminal justice', are actively encouraged to participate in the news production process. The rise of the 'citizen journalist', capable not only of emailing, texting or phoning in their views and concerns, but also of providing news organisations with live footage of events as they happen, presents an additional challenge to official institutional attempts to manage the news process (Gillmor, 2004). Whilst citizens were once content to consume the news, today they are increasingly involved in producing it. The classic modernist frameworks for understanding crime and justice news still have much to offer. But they cannot embrace the complexity of contemporary flows of communication power and associated perceptions of public credibility in the 24-7 global news mediasphere.

Though transformations in the crime and justice and media landscapes have been well documented separately, their complex interaction has yet to be adequately explored. As this chapter has illustrated, many if not most of the defining studies on news media, crime and justice have come from outside criminology. The foundational Marxist studies from the Centres at Birmingham, Leicester and Glasgow, the interdisciplinary works emerging from the NDC, and the diverse Post-Marxist interventions were mostly situated within sociological media studies and cultural studies. Likewise many of the most significant developments or critical commentaries on core theoretical concepts – newsworthiness, fear of crime, moral panics. Yet whilst the sociology of media and communications and cultural studies have moved on, news media criminology all too frequently remains locked-in to a now outdated framework of understanding.

The interdisciplinary, engaged and sustained news media research that defined the Marxist and early Post-Marxist periods, has been replaced with a growing reliance on superficial content analysis. This is no doubt partly attributable to logistical convenience. The emergence of online searchable newspaper databases allow researchers to search, retrieve, collate and examine entire bodies of news coverage at the push of a button. The analysis of text-based documents can of course reveal much in terms of the meanings given to crime and criminal justice in news discourses. But online newspaper databases strip news content of its form, colour and style – erasing visual imagery and surrounding stories and context. News media analyses are thus increasingly based upon a 'news residue' – standardised, decontextualised words on a computer screen (Greer, 2009). The visual is perhaps 'the' defining characteristic of news media today. Since visual attractiveness has always been fundamental to television, studies on news broadcasting have naturally featured some discussion of visual as a defining characteristic (Chermak, 1995; Cottle, 2006;

Golding and Elliott, 1979; Schlesinger *et al.*, 1983). Yet whilst the image has always been fundamental to printed news, there has until recently been little engagement with the visual in criminological studies of the press (Hayward and Presdee, 2010; Greer, 2003; Jones and Wardle, 2008). In a increasingly visual context of hypermediatisation, attention to news images must surely be a priority. Furthmore, the rise in news media content analysis has been paralleled with a corresponding decline in research on the news production process. Criminologists are no longer engaging with journalists or sources. Finally, with the exception of research on fear of crime, news media criminology has tended more often to assume than evidence media influence. This was a fundamental dilemma that the GUMG sought to address in their research, but news media criminology has been slow to capitalise on the availability of methodological approaches which can start to make meaningful sense of the influence on consumers of media images of crime and justice. Even Cultural Criminology, which is highly sensitised to issues of media and mediatisation, has thus far had little to say on the news media (Greer, 2009).

Criminology does not currently have the intellectual resources to apprehend the massive transformations across the news media environment in recent decades, the visually spectacular presentation of crime news as a hypercommodified product, or the increasingly interactive manner in which it is created and consumed. What is needed is the systematic testing of new theoretical ideas and empirical questions: how chaotic is the global news mediasphere; how much influence can powerful source organisations retain in this climate; is it possible to manage, if not control, the news process? who are the primary definers in the global news mediasphere? Answering these questions requires the development of new theoretical and methodological tools that permit the sustained and in depth engagement with the contemporary media environment. The acquisition and application of such tools in turn requires a renewed focus on interdisciplinarity.

REFERENCES

Altheide, D. (2009) Moral Panic: From Social Concept to Public Discourse, in *Crime, Media, Culture: An International Journal* 5(1): 79–99.

Althusser, L. (1971) Ideology and the State, in *Lenin and Philosophy and Other Essays*. London: New Left Books.

Bauman, Z. (1997) *Postmodernity and its Discontents*. Cambridge: Polity.

Beck, U. (1992) *The Risk Society: Towards a New Modernity*. London: Sage.

Becker, H. (1963) *Outsiders – Studies in the Sociology of Deviance*. New York: Free Press of Glencoe.

Becker, H. (1967) Whose side are we on, in J. D. Douglas (ed.) (1970) *The Relevance of Sociology*, New York, Appleton-Century Crofts.

Benedict, H. (1992) *Virgin or Vamp: How the Press Covers Sex Crimes*. Oxford: Oxford University Press.

Bennett, T. (1982) Media, reality, signification, in M. Gurevitch, T. Bennett, J. Curran and J. Woollacott (eds), *Culture, Society and the Media*. London: Methuen.

Barnett, S. (2002) Will a crisis in journalism provoke a crisis in democracy, *Political Quarterly*, 73(4): 400–408.

Blackman, S. (1998) The school: 'poxy cupid'. An ethnographic and feminist account of a resistant female youth culture: the new wave girls, in T. Skelton and G. Valentine (eds), *Cool Places: Geographies of Youth Cultures*. London: Routledge.

Boorstin, D. (1963) *The Image*. Harmondsworth: Penguin Books.

Bottoms, A. E. (1995) The Philosophy and Politics of Punishment and Sentencing, in C. Clarkson and R. Morgan (eds) *The Politics of Sentencing Reform*. Oxford: Clarendon.

Bourke, J. (2005) *Fear: A Cultural History*. London: Virago.

Brundson, C. and Morley, D. (1978) *Everyday TV: Nationwide*. London: British Film Institute.

Cameron, D. and Frazer, E. (1987) *The Lust to Kill: A Feminist Investigation of Sexual Murder*. Cambridge: Polity Press.

Chancer, L. (2003) *High Profile Crimes: When Legal Cases Become Social Causes*. Chicago: University of Chicago Press.

Chermak, S. (1995) *Victims in the News: Crime and the American News Media*. Boulder, CO: Westview Press.

Chibnall, S. (1977) *Law and Order News: An Analysis of Crime Reporting in the British Press*. London: Tavistock.

Cohen, S. (1972/2002) *Folk Devils and Moral Panics: The Creation of the Mods and Rockers*. London: MacGibbon and Kee (third edition, Routledge, 2002).

Cottle, S. (2006) *Mediatized Conflict: Developments in Media and Conflict Studies*. Buckingham: Open University Press

Cohen, S. (2007) *Moral Panics Then and Now*, Panel discussion at the British Academy, 9th March, 2007 (available at http://www.britac.ac.uk/perspectives/0703moralpanics.cfm).

Cohen, S. and Young, J. (eds) (1973) *The Manufacture of News: Social Problems, Deviance and Mass Media*, London: Constable (revised edition 1981).

Cumberbatch, G. (1989) Violence in the media: the research evidence, in G. Cumberbatch and D. Howitt (eds), *A Measure of Uncertainty: the Effects of the Mass Media*. London: John Libbey.

Curran, J., Gurevitch, M. and Woollacott, J. (1982) The study of the media: Theoretical approaches, in M. Gurevitch, T. Bennett, J. Curran and J. Woollacott (eds), *Culture, Society and the Media*. London: Methuen.

Davies, P., Francis, P. and Greer, C. (eds) (2007) *Victims, Crime and Society*. London: Sage.

Ditton, J., Chadee, D., Farrall, S., Gilchrist, E. and Bannister, J. (2004) From imitation to intimidation: a note on the curious and changing relationship between the media, crime and fear of crime, *British Journal of Criminology*, 44(4): 595–610.

Eldridge, J. (2006) The work of the glasgow Media Group: An insider's story, in D. Berry and J. Theobold (eds), *Radical Mass Media Critcism: A Cultural Geneology*. London: Black Rose Books.

Ericson, E. (2006) *Crime in an Insecure World*. Cambridge: Polity Press.

Ericson, R., Baranek, P. and Chan, J. (1987) *Visualising Deviance: A Study of News Organisation*. Milton Keynes: Open University Press.

Ericson, R., Baranek, P. and Chan, J. (1989) *Negotiating Control: A Study of News Sources*. Milton Keynes: Open University Press.

Ericson, R., Baranek, P. and Chan, J. (1991) *Representing Order: Crime, Law and Justice in the News Media*. Milton Keynes: Open University Press.

Fallows, J. (1996) *Breaking the News: How the Media Undermine American Democracy*, New York: Pantheon Books.

Furedi, F. (2005) *Politics of Fear*. London: Continuum.

Galtung, J. and Ruge, M. (1965) The structure of foreign news: The presentation of the Congo, Cuba and Cyprus crises in four Norwegian newspapers, *Journal of Peace Research*, 2(1): 64–91.

Garland, D. (2001) *The Culture of Control: Crime and Social Order in Contemporary Society*, Oxford: Oxford University Press.

Garland, D. (2008) On the concept of moral panic, in *Crime, Media, Culture: An International Journal*, 4(1): 9–30.

Gerbner, G. and Gross, L. (1976) Living with television: the violence profile, in *Journal of Communication*, 26(1): 173–199.

Gerbner, G., Gross, L., Morgan, M. and Signorielli, N. (1994) Growing up with television; The cultivation perspective, in J. Bryant and D. Zillman (eds), *Media Effects*. Hillsdale, NJ: Lawrence Erlbaum.

Giddens, A. (1991) *Modernity and Self-Identity*. Cambridge: Polity.

Gillmor, D. (2004) *We the Media: Grassroots Journalism by the People, for the People*. Sebastopol, CA: O'Reilly Media.

Glasgow University Media Group (1976) *Bad News*. London: Routledge.

Glasgow University Media Group (1980) *More Bad News*. London: Routledge.

Golding, P. and Elliott, P. (1979) *Making the News*. London: Longman.

Golding, P. and Murdock, G. (1979) Ideology and Media: the Question of Determination, in M. Barret, A. Kuhn, J. Wolff and P. Corrigan (eds), *Ideology and Cultural Production*, London: St Martin's Press.

Golding, P. and Murdock, G. (2000) Culture, communications, and political economy, in J. Curran and M. Gurevitch (eds), *Mass Media and Society*, third edition. London: Edward Arnold.

Goode, E. and Ben-Yehuda, N. (1994) *Moral Panics: The Social Construction of Deviance*. Oxford: Blackwell.

Green, D. (2008) *When Children Kill Children: Penal Populism and Political Culture*. Oxford: Oxford University Press.

Greer, C. (ed.) (2009) *Crime and Media: A Reader*. London: Routledge.

Greer, C. (2003) *Sex Crime and the Media: Sex Offending and the Press in a Divided Society,* Cullompton: Willan.

Greer, C. and McLaughlin, E. (2009) A Crisis in Confidence: The News Media Humiliation of Sir Ian Blair, paper given at British Society of Criminology Seminar Series, London School of Economics (November 2009), and All Souls Criminology Seminar Series, University of Oxford (January 2010).

Gunter, B. (1987) *Television and the Fear of Crime*. London: John Libbey.

Hale, C. (1996) Fear of crime: A review of the literature, *International Review of Victimology*, 4: 79–150.

Hall, S. (1971) A world at one with itself, reproduced in S. Cohen and J. Young (eds) (1973) *The Manufacture of News: Social Problems, Deviance and the Mass* Media. London: Constable.

Hall, S. (1973) The determination of news photographs, in S. Cohen and J. Young (eds), *The Manufacture of News: Social Problems, Deviance and the Mass* Media. London: Constable.

Hall, S. (1977–78) Debate, *Screen*. London, winter 113.

Hall, S. (1980) Introduction to media studies at the centre, in S. Hall, D. Hobson, A. Lowe and P. Willis (eds), *Culture, Language, Media*. London: Routledge.

Hall, S. (1982) The rediscovery of ideology, in M. Gurevitch, T. Bennett, J. Curran and J. Woollacott (eds), *Culture, Society and the Media*. London: Methuen.

Hall, S. (2007) *Moral Panics Then and Now*, panel discussion at the British Academy, 9th March 2007 (available at http://www.britac.ac.uk/perspectives/0703moralpanics.cfm).

Hall, S., Critcher, C., Jefferson, T., Clarke, J. and Roberts, B. (1978) *Policing the Crisis: Mugging, the State and Law and Order*. London: Macmillan.

Hall, S. and Jefferson, T. (1976) *Resistance Through Rituals: Youth Subcultures in Post-War Britain.* London: Routledge.

Halloran, J., Elliott, P. and Murdock, G. (1970) *Demonstrations and Communication. A Case Study.* Harmondsworth: Penguin.

Hamm, M. (2007) High crimes and misdemeanors: George Bush and the Sins of Abu Ghraib, in *Crime, Media, Culture: An International Journal*, 3(3): 259–284.

Hayward, K. and Presdee, M. (eds) (2010) *Framing Crime: Cultural Criminology and the Image*. London: Routledge.

Hebdige, D. (1979) *Subculture: The Meaning of Style*. London: Routledge.

Herman, E. and Chomsky, N. (1988) *Manufacturing Consent: The Political Economy of the Mass Media*. New York: Pantheon.

Hope, T. and Sparks, R. (eds) (2000) *Crime, Risk and Insecurity: Law and Order in Everyday Life and Political Discourse*. London: Routledge.

Jackson, J. and Gray, E. (2010) Functional Fear and Public Insecurities About Crime, *British Journal of Criminology*, 50(1): 1–22.

Jefferson, T. (2008) Policing the crisis revisited: The state, masculinity, fear of crime and racism, in *Crime, Media, Culture: An International Journal*, 4(1): 113–121.

Jewkes, Y. (2004) *Media and Crime*. London: Sage.

Jones, P. and Wardle, C. (2008) No emotion, no sympathy: The visual construction of Maxine Carr. *Crime Media Culture: An International Journal*, 4(1): 53–71.

Katz, J. (1987) What makes crime news, in *Media, Culture and Society*, 9: 47–76.

Kitzinger, J. and Skidmore, P. (1995) Child sexual abuse and the media, *Summary Report to ESRC*. Award no. R000233675. Report available from Glasgow Media Group.

Lang, K. and Lang, G. (1955) The inferential structure of political communications: a study in unwitting bias, *Public Opinion Quarterly*, 19: 168–183.

McLaughlin, E. (2008) Hitting the panic buttom: policing/'mugging'/media/crisis, in *Crime, Media, Culture: An International Journal*, 4(1):145–154.

McNair, B. (2006a) *Cultural Chaos: Journalism, News and Power in a Globalised World*. London: Routledge.

McNair, B. (2006b) The culture of chaos, in *The Guardian,* May 1st 2006: 1.

McRobbie, A. and Thornton, S. (1995) Rethinking 'moral panic' for multi-mediated social worlds, in *British Journal of Sociology*, 46(4): 559–574.

Meyers, M. (1997) *News Coverage of Violence Against Women: Engendering Blame*, Thousand Oaks, London: Sage.

Miller, D. (1993) Official sources and 'primary definition' The case of Northern Ireland, *Media, Culture and Society*, 15: 385–406.

Miller, D. (1998) Public relations and journalism: Promotional strategies and media power, in A. Briggs and P. Cobley (eds), *The Media: An Introduction*. London: Longman.

Morley, D. (1980) *The 'Nationwide' Audience: Structure and Decoding*. London: British Film Institute.

Murdock, G. (1973) Political deviance: The press presentation of militant mass demonstration, in S. Cohen and J. Young (eds), *The Manufacture of News: Social Problems, Deviance and the Mass Media*. London: Constable.

Murdock, G. (1982) Large corporations and the control of the communications industries, in M. Gurevitch, T. Bennett, J. Curran and J. Woollacott (eds), *Culture, Society and the Media*. London: Methuen.

Murdock, G. and Golding, P. (1974) Communication: the continuing crisis, *New Society*, 25th April 1974: 179–181.

Murdock, G. and Golding, P. (1977) Capitalism, communication and class relations, in J. Curran and M. Gurevitch (eds), *Mass Communication and Society*. London: Arnold.

Mythen, G. and Walklate, S. (2006) Communicating the terrorist risk: Harnessing a culture of fear, in *Crime, Media, Culture: An International Journal*, 2(2): 123–142.

Pratt, J. (2007) *Penal Populism*, London: Routledge.

Philo, G. (1999) Good news: the Glasgow University Media Group, *Variant*, 2(7): 2–4.

Philo, G. and Miller, D. (2001) Media/cultural studies and social sciences, in G. Philo and D. Miller (eds), *Market Killing: What the Free Market Does and What Social Scientists Can Do About It*. London: Longman.

Reiner, R. (2007) *Law and Order: An Honest Citizen's Guide to Crime and Control*. Cambridge: Polity.

Reiner, R., Livingstone, S. and Allen, J. (2000) Casino culture: media and crime in a winner-loser society in K. Stenson and D. Cowell (eds), *Crime, Risk and Justice*. Cullompton: Willan.

Reiner, R., Livingstone, S. and Allen, J. (2001) No more happy endings? The media and popular concern about crime since the Second World War, in T. Hope and R. Sparks (eds), *Crime, Risk and Insecurity*. London: Routledge.

Roberts, J. *et al*. (2003) *Penal Populism and Public Opinion: Lessons from Five Countries*. New York: Oxford University Press, Inc.

Sacco, V. (1982) The effects of mass media on perceptions of crime: A reanalysis of the Issues, in *Pacific Sociological Review*, 25(4): 475–493.

Schlesinger, P. (1989) Rethinking the sociology of journalism: Source strategies and the limits of media-centrism', in M. Ferguson (ed.), *Public Communication: The New Imperatives.* London: Sage.

Schlesinger, P. and Tumber, H. (1994) *Reporting Crime: The media politics of criminal justice.* Oxford: Clarendon Press.

Schlesinger, P., Murdock, G. and Elliott, P. (1983) *Televising 'Terrorism': Political Violence in Popular Culture.* London: Commedia.

Schlesinger, P., Tumber, H. and Murdock, G. (1991) The media politics of crime and criminal justice, *British Journal of Sociology*, 42(3): 397–420.

Simon, J. (2006) *Governing Through Crime: How the War on Crime Transformed American Democracy and Created a Culture of Fear.* Oxford: Oxford University Press.

Soothill, K. and Walby, S. (1991) *Sex Crime in the News.* London: Routledge.

Sparks, R. (1992) *Television and the Drama of Crime: Moral Tales and the Place of Crime in Public Life.* Buckingham: Open University Press.

Waddington, P. A. J. (1986) Mugging as a Moral Panic: A Question of Proportion, *British Journal of Sociology*, 37(2): 245–59.

Wilkins, L. (1964) Information and the definition of deviance, reproduced in S. Cohen and J. Young (eds) (1973) *The Manufacture of News: Social Problems, Deviance and Mass Media.* Constable: London.

Willis, P. (1977) *Learning to Labour: How Working-class Kids get Working-class Jobs.* Farnborough: Saxon House.

Young, J. (1971) The role of the police in the as amplifiers of deviancy, negotiators of reality, and translators of fantasy: Some consequences of our present system of drug control as seen in Notting Hill, in S. Cohen and J. Young (eds), *Images of Deviance.* Harmondsworth: Penguin.

Young, J. (1979) Left idealism, reformism and beyond: from the new criminology to marxism, B. Fine, R. Kinsey, J. Lea, S. Picciotto and J. Young (eds), *Capitalism and the Rule of Law: from Deviancy to Marxism.* London: Hutchinson.

Young, J. (2002) Critical criminology in the twenty-first century: Critique, irony and the always unfinished, in K. Harrington and R. Hogg (eds), *Critical Criminology: Issues, Debates, Challenges.* Cullompton: Willan.

Young, J. (2007) *Vertigo of Late Modernity.* London: Sage.

Index